PUBLIC ADMINISTRATION

CLASSIC READINGS

Seventh Edition

Jay M. Shafritz
Professor Emeritus
University of Pittsburgh

Albert C. Hyde
Advisory Consultant
Formerly-Senior Consultant with The Brookings Institution

WADSWORTH
CENGAGE Learning™

Australia • Brazil • Japan • Korea • Mexico • Singapore • Spain • United Kingdom • United States

WADSWORTH
CENGAGE Learning™

***Public Administration: Classic Readings*, Seventh Edition**
Jay M. Shafritz, Albert C. Hyde

Publisher: Suzanne Jeans
Executive Editor: Carolyn Merrill
Development Editor: Thomas Finn
Assistant Editor: Laura Ross
Editorial Assistant: Nina Wasserman
Media Editor: Laura Hildebrand
Marketing Manager: Lydia LeStar
Marketing Coordinator: Josh Hendrick
Senior Marketing Communications Manager: Heather Baxley
Associate Content Project Manager: Sara Abbott
Art Director: Linda Helcher
Print Buyer: Fola Orekoya
Rights Acquisition Specialist, Image: Amanda Groszko
Senior Rights Acquisition Specialist, Text: Katie Huha
Production Service/Compositor: Integra Software Services Pvt. Ltd.
Cover Image: Vlad Siaber/ © Shutterstock

International Edition:

ISBN-13: 978-1-111-34276-0

ISBN-10: 1-111-34276-8

Cengage Learning International Offices

Asia
www.cengageasia.com
tel: (65) 6410 1200

Australia/New Zealand
www.cengage.com.au
tel: (61) 3 9685 4111

Brazil
www.cengage.com.br
tel: (55) 11 3665 9900

India
www.cengage.co.in
tel: (91) 11 4364 1111

Latin America
www.cengage.com.mx
tel: (52) 55 1500 6000

UK/Europe/Middle East/Africa
www.cengage.co.uk
tel: (44) 0 1264 332 424

Represented in Canada by Nelson Education, Ltd.
www.nelson.com
tel: (416) 752 9100 / (800) 668 0671

Cengage Learning is a leading provider of customized learning solutions with office locations around the globe, including Singapore, the United Kingdom, Australia, Mexico, Brazil, and Japan. Locate your local office at: **www.cengage.com/global**

For product information: **www.cengage.com/international**
Visit your local office: **www.cengage.com/global**
Visit our corporate website: **www.cengage.com**

Printed in Canada
1 2 3 4 5 6 7 15 14 13 12 11

CHRONOLOGICAL CONTENTS

TOPICAL CONTENTS

Public Management

Public Policy and Analysis

Program Evaluation

Intergovernmental Relations

Public Service Ethics

PREFACE

Be assured—the editors are not so bold as to assert that these are *the* classics of public administration. The field is so diverse that there can be no such list. However, we do contend that it is possible to make a list of many of the discipline's most significant writers and provide representative samples of their work. That is what we have attempted here. It is readily admitted that writers of equal stature have not found their way into this collection and that equally important works of some of the authors included here are missing. Considerations of space and balance necessarily prevailed.

The primary characteristic of a classic in any field is its enduring value. We have classic automobiles, classic works of literature, and classic techniques for dealing with legal, medical, or military problems, and so on. Classics emerge and endure through the years because of their continuing ability to be useful. *The Three Musketeers* is as good an adventure story today as it was in 1844 when Alexandre Dumas wrote it. But how many other nineteenth-century novels can you name? Few have general utility for a twenty-first-century audience. It has been no different with the professional literature of public administration. Much has been written, but what is still worth reading today or will be tomorrow? The intent of this collection is to make readily available some of the most worthwhile material from the past that will be equally valuable for tomorrow.

We had three criteria for including a selection. First, the selection had to be relevant to a main theme of public administration. It had to be a basic statement that was consistently echoed or attacked in subsequent years. It also had to be important—of continuing relevance. This leads to our second criterion—significance. The selection had to be generally recognized as a significant contribution to the realm and discipline of public administration. An unrecognized classic seems to us to be a contradiction. As a general rule, we asked ourselves, "Should the student of public administration be expected to be able to identify this author and his or her basic themes?" If the answer was yes, then it was so because such a contribution has long been recognized by the discipline as an important theme by a significant writer. Whereas the editors can and expect to be criticized for excluding this or that particular article or writer, it would be difficult to honestly criticize us for our inclusions. The writers chosen are among the most widely quoted and reprinted practitioners and academics in public administration. The basic idea of this book was simply to bring them together. The final criterion for inclusion was readability. We sought selections that would be read and appreciated by people with or without a substantial background in public administration.

The selections are arranged in chronological order starting with Woodrow Wilson in 1887. We hope that when presented in this order, the collection will give the reader a sense of the continuity of the discipline's thinking and show how the various writers and themes literally build on each other. This also facilitates introducing the writers' themes as representative of a particular era. Obviously, many authors can span (and have spanned) the decades with their contributions to the literature of the discipline. Nevertheless, the selections reprinted here should be viewed and discussed in their historical context. Although many of the selections might seem quite old to a student readership, do not for a moment think that they are dated. They are considered classics in the first place because of their continuing value to each new generation.

We are pleased that this text is so widely used in schools of, and courses on, public administration. We naturally hesitate to change a product that has proved so useful to our peers. But with each edition, we have done updates to include other important themes, which must be done within the same space constraints. This edition is no different. To make room, we have deleted three selections (but they are discussed in the introductory sections) and slimmed down some of our introductions to enable us to add six new selections. Three of those new selections are aimed at deepening the topical section dealing with intergovernmental relations and governance.

A new section for the twenty-first century has been added, even if it may be too soon to tell whether developments in public administration since 2000 fully merit the label of "new thinking." What is very apparent is that the pace and scale of political, economic, social, and technological change in the environment since 2000 does represent a new era. Consequently it needs to be discussed as such. The global economy demands a global perspective on the purpose and design of public administration—whether it is the United States, the European Union, Russia, China, Brazil, India, South Africa, wherever. We fully expect that much will be different within our field as American public administration meets global governance issues. Future editions will surely reflect this inevitable movement.

In past editions, we have thanked many of our colleagues and friends for their help in the preparation of the current and earlier editions. The list has grown longer with each edition. We thought for this edition we would simply acknowledge the obvious—that a work like *Classics of Public Administration* is the result of an ongoing conversation with old and new colleagues and increasingly old and new students. It has been our great fortune to have colleagues and friends who have both supported the book and taken the time to educate us about what they feel is truly classic about our field.

Two special notes of appreciation are warranted. Professor Eric Zeemering at San Francisco State University's Public Administration Department was instrumental in getting us current on the course and direction of intergovernmental relations. His advice on how to shape our expanded section in this edition is greatly appreciated. Finally Professor Katherine Naff, also at San Francisco State, and Professor David Rosenbloom of The American University remain our oldest and more frequent advisors on classics. With each edition, we hope we are getting a little closer to their standard for what classics should be.

We are also pleased to acknowledge the helpful insights of many past users and instructors who prepared detailed assessments for this and earlier editions, including, most recently, Pat Kircher, California Baptist University; John Kiefer, University of New Orleans; Lawson Veasey, Jacksonville State University; and David Connelly, Utah Valley University. Finally, we thank the publishing team at Wadsworth, including Matt DiGangi, Sara Abbott, Katie Huha, and Suzanne Jeans.

Jay M. Shafritz
Professor Emeritus
The University of Pittsburgh

Albert C. Hyde
Advisory Consultant
Formerly Senior Consultant with The Brookings Institution

PUBLIC ADMINISTRATION

Part One

EARLY VOICES AND THE FIRST QUARTER CENTURY

1880S TO 1920S

Writings on public administration go back to ancient civilization.[1] The ancient Egyptians and Babylonians left considerable advice on the techniques of management and administration. So did the civilizations of China, Greece, and Rome. Modern management techniques can be traced from Alexander the Great's use of staff[2] to the assembly-line methods of the arsenal of Venice;[3] from the theorizing of Niccolo Machiavelli on the nature of leadership[4] to Adam Smith's advocacy of the division of labor;[5] and from Robert Owen's assertion that "vital machines" (employees) should be given as much attention as "inanimate machines"[6] to Charles Babbage's contention that there existed "basic principles of management."[7]

The history of the world can be viewed as the rise and fall of public administrative institutions. Those ancient empires that rose and prevailed were those with better administrative institutions than their competitors. Brave soldiers have been plentiful in every society but they were ultimately wasted if not backed up by administrators who can feed and pay them. Marcus Tullius Cicero, the ancient Roman orator, is usually credited with first saying that "the sinews of war are infinite money."

Rome, like Egypt, Persia, and other empires before it, conquered much of the ancient world (well, at least that centered around the Mediterranean) because it had an organizational doctrine that made its soldiers far more effective than competing forces—and because its legions were backed up by a sophisticated administrative system of supply based on regular if not equitable taxes. The Roman Empire only fell when its legions degenerated into corps of mercenaries and when its supply and tax bases were corrupted. Napoleon was wrong. Armies do not "march on their stomachs," as he said; they march on the proverbial backs of the tax collectors and on the roads built by administrators. Regular pay allows for discipline. Strict discipline is what makes a mob an army. And a disciplined military, obedient to the leaders of the state, is a precondition for civilization. This is the classic chicken and egg problem. Which comes first—effective public administration or an effective military? The rise and fall of ancient Rome proved that you could not have one without the other.

Early bureaucrats in ancient Rome and modern Europe literally wore uniforms that paralleled military dress. After all, the household servants of rulers traditionally wore livery. It indicated that the wearer was not free but the servant of another. Government administrators are still considered servants in this sense; they are public servants because they, too, have accepted obligations that mean they are not completely free. Indeed, until early in the twentieth century many otherwise civilian public officials in Europe—most notably diplomats—had prescribed uniforms.

Both victorious soldiers and successful managers tend to be inordinately admired and disproportionately rewarded as risk takers. True, the specific risks and rewards are different; but the phenomenon is the same. They both may have to put their careers, and sometimes significant parts of their anatomy as well, "on the line" to obtain a goal for their state or organization. Notice again the military language for "the line" originally referred to the line of battle where they faced the enemy. This is why line officers today are still those who perform the services for which the organization exists. This is the direct link between the Roman centurion and the fire chief, hospital director, or school principal. Life on the line is still a daily struggle.

It is possible to find most of the modern concepts of management and leadership stated by one or another of the writers of the classical, medieval, and pre-modern world. However, our concern is not with this prehistory of modern management but with the academic discipline and occupational specialty that is U.S. public administration.

CIVIL SERVICE REFORM AND MERIT IN GOVERNMENT

"Any city in the present state of municipal advancement and progress which has no provision for civil service is as much behind the times as a city without electric lights, telephones or street cars."

—Board of Freeholders, City of Kansas City

The American City (1911)

American public administration did not invent the concept of a creating a public service that would be based on merit. Would-be reformers of American government in the late nineteenth century not only borrowed from the European experience but also were fond of noting that possessing such systems was an essential step in "enlightenment" for the United States if it was to develop as a civilized nation. The first real steps toward creating a modern state of public administration in the United States were taken following the Civil War and at the heart was the struggle to limit the spoils system of rewarding political party members with government job appointments as opposed to establishing a civil service system where appointments and tenure were based on merit.[8]

While federal civil service reform is generally dated from the post–Civil War period, the political roots of the reform effort go back much earlier—to the beginning of the republic. Thomas Jefferson was the first president to face the problem of a philosophically hostile bureaucracy. While sorely pressed by his supporters to remove Federalist officeholders and replace them with Republican partisans, Jefferson was determined not to remove officials for political reasons alone. He maintained in a letter in 1801 to William Findley that "Malconduct is a just ground of removal, mere difference of political opinion is not." With occasional defections from this principle, even by Jefferson himself, this policy was the norm rather than the exception down through the administration of Andrew Jackson. President Jackson's rhetoric on the nature of public service was far more influential than his administrative example. In claiming that all men, especially the newly enfranchised who did so much to elect him, should have an equal opportunity for public office, Jackson played to his plebeian constituency and put the patrician civil service on notice that they had no natural monopoly on public office. The spoils system, used only modestly by Jackson, flourished under his successors. The doctrine of rotation of office progressively prevailed over the earlier notion of stability in office.

Depending on your point of view, the advent of modern merit systems is either an economic, political, or moral development. Economic historians would maintain that the demands of industrial expansion—a dependable postal service, a viable transportation network, and so on—necessitated a government service based on merit. Political analysts could argue rather persuasively that it was the demands of an expanded suffrage and democratic rhetoric that sought to replace favoritism with merit. Economic and political considerations are so intertwined that it is impossible to say which factor is the true origin of the merit system. The moral impetus behind reform is even more difficult to define. As moral impulses tend to hide economic and political motives, the weight of moral concern undiluted by other considerations is impossible to measure. Nevertheless, the cosmetic effect of moral overtones was of significant aid to the civil service reform movement, because it accentuated the social legitimacy of the reform proposals.

With the ever-present impetus of achieving maximum public services for minimum tax dollars, business interests were quite comfortable in supporting civil service reform, one of a variety of strategies they used to have power pass from the politicos to themselves. The political parties of the time were almost totally dependent for financing on assessments made on the wages of their members in public office. With the decline of patronage, the parties had to seek new funding sources, and American business was more than willing to assume this new financial burden—and its concomitant influence.

Civil service reform was both an ideal—an integral symbol of a larger national effort to establish a new form of more responsive government; and an institutional effort—a series of internal reforms intent on creating new bureaucratic authority structures. Historians have sought to capture how the "Progressive Era" reflected the interplay between reform movements at the federal level and state and local governments in the context of political and social changes occurring after the Civil War.[9] Civil service reform was integral to that vision for change and viewed as embracing, in the words of one of the early reform champions, Dorman Eaton, "certain great principles which embody a theory of political morality, of official obligation, of equal rights, and common justice in government."[10]

Dorman B. Eaton had been appointed chair of the first Civil Service Commission established by President Grant in 1871. When the commission concluded unsuccessfully in 1875, Eaton went to England at the request of President Rutherford Hayes to undertake a study of the British civil service system. His report—published as a book in 1880 with the title *Civil Service in Great Britain: A History of Abuses and Reforms and their Bearing upon American Politics*—obviously advocated the adoption of the merit system in America. His book enumerated the principles the civil service system would entail, as the listing of brief excerpts illustrate:

1. "Public office creates a relation of trust and duty of a kind which requires all authority and influence pertaining to it to be exercised with the same absolute conformity to moral standards, to the spirit of the constitution and the laws, and to the common interest of the people....
2. In filling offices, it is the right of the people to have the worthiest citizens in the public service for the general welfare,....
3. The personal merits of the candidate—are in themselves the highest claim upon an office....
4. Party government and the salutary activity of parties are not superseded, but they are made purer and more efficient, by the merit system of office which brings larger capacity and higher character to their support"....[11]

When President Garfield was assassinated in 1881 by an insane and disappointed office-seeker, the movement for civil service reform would finally produce legislative results. Eaton would be prominent in providing the language for the Pendleton Act of 1883, which created a federal civil service system based on merit. Under the act, a civil service commission was established and a class of civil service was created where employees would be hired through open competitive examinations and promoted and retained based on merit. Thus, at the federal level, progress toward implementing reform was generally measured in terms of the percentage of government employees who were in the classified service. While the Pendleton Act did not make civil service mandatory for all federal agencies, coverage under civil service would grow from 10 percent in the 1880s to nearly 70 percent between the world wars.[12]

However, the relatively rapid categorization of federal positions under civil service was not all that it seemed to be. Frederick Mosher noted in his examination of the public service that the ranks of the civil service were largely concentrated in entry-level employees. Indeed, the requirement that entrance to federal service "be permitted only at the lowest grade" was specifically removed by the Congress creating "an open civil service with no prohibition of what we now call lateral entry."[13] Within two decades of its existence, the Civil Service Commission would be bemoaning the lack of upward mobility and promotions for the talented workers they felt had been selected for employment under civil service, a situation Mosher notes that would not be remedied until the 1940s. Thus it was relatively easy for a federal agency to accept civil service as the new norm because it applied to entry-level hires and did not preclude an agency from appointing—via lateral entry—higher-level employees of their own choosing.

Civil service reform was also an important issue for state and local governments. While only three states (Massachusetts in 1883, New York in 1884, and Ohio in 1902) passed legislation that required civil service for municipalities, adoption of civil service reform was widespread. But a distinction about the means of adoption should be made especially where it concerns the importance of requiring civil service procedures by law. Some assessments of the adoption of civil service reform during the first quarter of the twentieth century conclude that the Pendleton Act was a weak statute in that it did not require federal agencies to classify their positions under civil service and did not mention state and local governments. Another interpretation of the fact that only three states enacted statewide legislation on civil service reform would be that it reaffirms the "relative autonomy" that most cities enjoyed from higher governmental authority, be it federal or state.[14]

Still, over 200 cities adopted civil service reform by the 1930s, the majority from states that did not have a mandatory state statute. The National Civil Service Reform League, which regularly reported on which states and municipalities had adopted the "competitive system," noted in their 1911 report six variations for adoption of civil service from charter provisions to popular votes establishing local commissions.[15]

Thinking back on the premises of civil service reform and the promise of the merit system could not be more instructive, especially now, when some states and local governments have moved away from civil service. In 1996, the State of Georgia passed legislation terminating civil service coverage for new state employees. Other states, notably Florida, South Carolina, Arkansas, Missouri, and North Dakota, have followed suit.[16] In a 2006 survey of state reform efforts, 28 of the 50 states were identified as having expanded the numbers of "at-will employees" or public sector workers who are not under the protection of civil service guidelines.[17] Public administration has always been in a debate about how to make the public workforce more responsive and productive—only this time it is the bureaucracy and over-protectionism of the civil service that is the target of reform.

CALLING FOR A NEW DISCIPLINE ON RUNNING A GOVERNMENT

While Alexander Hamilton,[18] Thomas Jefferson,[19] Andrew Jackson,[20] and other notables of the first century of the republic have dealt with the problem of running the administrative affairs of the state, it was not until 1887 that we find a serious claim made that public administration should be a self-conscious, professional field. This came from Woodrow Wilson's famous 1887 essay, "The Study of Administration." Although it attracted slight notice at the time, it has become customary to trace the origins of the academic discipline of public administration to that essay.

While Woodrow Wilson (1856–1924) would later be president, first of the American Political Science Association, then of Princeton University, and later of the United States, in the mid-1880s he was a struggling young instructor at Bryn Mawr College for Women. During this time he worked on several textbooks now long forgotten; wrote fiction under a pen name (but it was all rejected); and wrote a political essay that remains his most enduring contribution as a political scientist. On November 11, 1886, Wilson wrote to the editor of the *Political Science Quarterly* to whom he had submitted his article.[21] Wilson asserted that he had very modest aims for his work, which he thought of as "a semi-popular introduction to administrative studies." He even said that he thought his work might be "too slight." Ironically, one hundred years later, the American Society for Public Administration would launch a Centennial's Agenda Project to identify the critical issues for the field and cite the publication of Wilson's essay as "generally regarded as the beginning of public administration as a specific field of study."[22]

In "The Study of Administration," Wilson attempted to refocus political science's study of governments. Rather than be concerned with the great maxims of lasting political truth, he argued that political science should concentrate on how governments are administered. This was necessary because, in his words, "It is getting harder to run a constitution than to frame one."

Wilson wanted the study of public administration to focus not only on personnel problems, as many other reformers of the time had advocated, but also on organization and management in general. The reform movement of the time, which had already secured the passage of the first lasting federal civil service reform legislation, the Pendleton Act of 1883, had a reform agenda that both started and ended with merit appointments. Wilson sought to move the concerns of public administration a step further by investigating the "organization" and "methods of our government offices" with a view toward determining "first, what government can properly and successfully do, and secondly, how it can do these proper things with the utmost possible efficiency and at the least possible cost either of money or energy." Wilson was concerned with organizational efficiency and economy—that is, productivity in its most simplistic formulation.

By authoring this essay, Wilson is also credited with positing the existence of a major distinction between politics and administration. This was a common and necessary political tactic of the reform movement because arguments that public appointments should be based on fitness and merit, rather than partisanship, necessarily had to assert that "politics" were out of place in public service. In establishing what became known as the politics-administration dichotomy, Wilson was really referring to "partisan" politics. While his subtlety was lost on many, Wilson's main themes—that public administration should be premised on a science of management and separate from traditional politics—fell on fertile intellectual ground. The ideas of this then-obscure professor eventually became the dogma of the discipline and remained so until after World War II. While the politics-administration dichotomy would be later discredited, his ideas are still highly influential and essential to an understanding of the evolution of public administration.[23]

THE CASE FOR A POLITICS-ADMINISTRATION DICHOTOMY

A more carefully argued examination of the politics-administration dichotomy was offered by Frank J. Goodnow (1859–1939) in his book, *Politics and Administration,* published in 1900. Goodnow, one of the founders and first president (in 1903) of the American Political Science Association, was one of the most significant voices and writers of the progressive reform movement.[24] To Goodnow, modern administration presented a number of dilemmas involving political and administrative functions that had now supplanted the traditional concern with the separation of powers among the various branches of government. Politics and administration could be distinguished, he argued, as "the expression of the will of the state and the execution of that will."

Reprinted here is Goodnow's original analysis of the distinction between politics and administration. Note how even Goodnow had to admit that when the function of political decision making and administration was legally separated, there developed a "tendency for the necessary control to develop extra-legally through the political party system." The articulation of the politics-administration dichotomy also reflected the next phase in the emergence of American public administration. Whereas the first phase before World War I focused primarily on the evils of patronage and spoils systems and eliminating corruption in municipal government, the second phase would emphasize the growth of public spending and the ascendance of the "new management" in government. City managers, executive budget systems, and centralized and accountability-driven administrative systems were all key reform themes.[25]

SELF-GOVERNMENT AND THE PROBLEM OF MUNICIPAL ADMINISTRATION

As public administration struggled to establish its identity, it was aided greatly by the progressive reform movement that sought to raise the standards of honesty in government and to enlarge the level of public services provided to citizens, especially in American cities. While the term has its origins in religious concepts that argued for the infinite improvability of the human condition, rather than ordained class distinctions, by the end of the nineteenth century it had come to mean a responsibility of classes for one another and a willingness to use all government and social institutions to give that responsibility legal effect.

To a large extent the movement was a reaction to Social Darwinism, Charles Darwin's concept of biological evolution applied to the development of human social organization and economic policy. The major influence on American Social Darwinism was the Englishman, Herbert Spencer, who spent much of his career on the application of concepts such as "natural selection" and "survival of the fittest" to his ideas of social science. American Social Darwinists, generally speaking, occupied a wide range of theories, from an absolute rejection of the idea of government intervention in social development (meaning let the poor fend for themselves) to elaborate methods of developmental influence that could affect the various races into which they believed all humans, even Europeans, were divided (meaning let's educate the poor only well enough so that they can be servants and factory workers). The progressive movement was to a large extent an antidote to, and the repudiation of, this doctrine of Social Darwinism.

In the United States, the progressive movement was most associated with the search for greater democratic participation by the individual in government, and the application of science and specialized knowledge and skills to the improvement of life. Politically, the movement reached its national climax in 1911, with the creation of the Progressive Party as a break between the Republican Party professionals, who backed the incumbent, William Howard Taft, and the Republican opponents of political machine politics and party regularity, who nominated former Republican president, Theodore Roosevelt. The split in the Republican Party caused the Democratic candidate, Woodrow Wilson, to be elected in 1912. Wilson in fact represented many of the programs the progressives had supported (banking reforms, antitrust laws, and business regulation), but he did not support many of the progressive interests in national social policy.

The progressives got their name from their belief in the doctrine of progress—that governing institutions could be improved by bringing science to bear on public problems. It was a disparate movement, with each reform group targeting a level of government, a particular policy, and so on. Common beliefs included that good government was possible and that the cure of the evils of democracy is more democracy (per a quote from H. L. Menchen from his book in 1926, *Notes on Democracy*). At the national level, they achieved civil service reform and introduced the direct primary, the initiative, the referendum, and the recall. At the local level, they spawned the commission and council-manager forms of government. It was the progressive influence that initially forged the fledgling discipline of public administration.

As public administration struggled to establish its identity, it was aided greatly by the progressive reform movement that sought to raise the standards of honesty in government and to increase the level of public services provided to citizens, especially in American cities. This effort was further fueled by reform-oriented journalists—the "muckrakers" who publicized both the corruption found among city political machines and the deplorably inadequate living standards and levels of poverty of the working classes, especially among immigrants.[26]

While the progressive movement sought to offer solutions to many vexing social problems, these problems were often first identified and dug up by the muckrakers. This was President Theodore Roosevelt's term, taken from John Bunyan's *Pilgrim's Progress* (1678), for a journalist who wrote exposés of business and government corruption. Some of the most famous muckrakers were Lincoln Steffens who, in *The Shame of the Cities* (1904), found many big cities "corrupt and contented"; Ida M. Tarbell who exposed the monopolistic practices of John D. Rockefeller and forced the breakup of Standard Oil; and Upton Sinclair whose exposure of the poisonous practices of the meatpacking industry in *The Jungle* (1906) led to the passage of the Pure Food and Drug Act of 1906. Today, anyone who writes an exposé of governmental corruption or incompetence might be called a muckraker, although they prefer to be called investigative journalists.

The effort to control corruption would be realized with the passage of civil service reform legislation and the creation of stronger city charters and city management systems. Efforts to assist the poor and needy would take much greater effort and in fact would follow a different track entirely. Indeed, it was the settlement movement, based on an English model where social-minded upper-class groups would establish "settlement houses" for the poor and live with them in a group setting. The first settlement houses were tried in New York City in the mid-1880s, but the best-known model opened its doors in 1889 in Chicago at Hull House. The founder was a remarkable 29-year-old woman, Jane Addams[27] (1860–1935), who would lead this movement and provide a unique American definition to the idea of providing a social setting for immigrants to escape the poverty cycle and succeed by their own efforts.

Hull House would be credited with an impressive list of first accomplishments, from establishing the first public playgrounds, public kitchens, and citizenship preparation and special education classes in Chicago to helping bring about the first juvenile courts and public employment bureaus. Addams herself would be a national figure who helped shape the American social work movement. She would be awarded the Nobel Peace prize in 1931. Out of all her work about political and social reform—for she saw them as inexorably intertwined—a 1904 address is included that was published in the *American Journal of Sociology* in 1905, "Problems of Municipal Administration." Unlike Woodrow Wilson's plea for searching for new ways to run government because of the complexities of the time, Addams was highly critical of the founders, those men of the eighteenth century who had no real idea of (or empathy for) "the difficulties and blunders which a self-governing people was sure to encounter." In her address she lays out a different vision of self-governance and what the roles of government, its administrators, and its citizens should be.[28]

THE IMPACT OF SCIENTIFIC MANAGEMENT

At about the same time Woodrow Wilson was calling for a science of management, Frederick W. Taylor (1856–1915) was independently conducting some of his first experiments in a Philadelphia steel plant. Taylor, generally considered the "father of scientific management," pioneered the development of time and motion studies. Today, scientific management is frequently referred to as pseudo-scientific management because of its conceptualization of people as merely extensions of machines—as human interchangeable parts of a large impersonal production machine. Premised on the notion that there was "one best way" of accomplishing any given task, scientific management sought to increase output by discovering the fastest, most efficient, and least fatiguing production methods. The job of the scientific manager, once the one best way was found, was to impose this procedure on the entire workforce. Classical organization theory would evolve from this notion. If there was one best way to accomplish any given production task, then correspondingly, there must also be one best way to accomplish a task of social organization. Such principles of social organization were assumed to exist and to be waiting to be discovered by diligent scientific observation and analysis.

Strangely enough, while Taylor's 1911 book *Principles of Scientific Management*[29] is the work for which he is best known, the credit for coining the term *scientific management* belongs not to Taylor but to an associate of his, Louis D. Brandeis (1856–1941). Brandeis, who would later be a Supreme Court justice, needed a catchy phrase to describe the new-style management techniques of Taylor and his disciples when he was to present arguments that railroad rate increases should be denied before the Interstate Commerce Commission. Brandeis and his associates dramatically argued that the railroads could save "a million dollars a day" by applying scientific management methods. The highly publicized hearings beginning in 1910 caused a considerable sensation and vastly expanded Taylor's reputation. Ironically, Taylor was initially opposed to the phrase, thinking that it sounded too academic. But he quickly learned to embrace it. So did the rest of the country. In the first half of the twentieth century, scientific management was gospel and Frederick W. Taylor was its prophet.[30] Taylor's greatest public-sector popularity came in 1912 after he presented his ideas to a Special Committee of the House of Representatives to Investigate the Taylor and Other Systems of Shop Management. A portion of that testimony is reprinted here.

Taylor's comprehensive statement of scientific management principles was focused on what he called the duties of management. These duties included:

1. Replacing traditional rule-of-thumb methods of work accomplishment with systematic, more scientific methods of measuring and managing individual work elements
2. Studying scientifically the selection and sequential development of workers to ensure optimal placement of workers into work roles
3. Obtaining the cooperation of workers to ensure full application of scientific principles
4. Establishing logical divisions within work roles and responsibilities between workers and management

What seems so obvious today was revolutionary in 1912. Taylor himself even insisted in his *Principles of Scientific Management* that "scientific management does not necessary involve any great invention, nor the discovery of new or startling facts." Nevertheless, it did "involve a certain combination of elements which have not existed in the past, namely, old knowledge so collected, analyzed, grouped and classified into laws and rules that it constitutes a science."

BUDGETING REFORM AS A CORNERSTONE OF PUBLIC ADMINISTRATION

Perhaps the other most significant early scholar of public administration along with Frank Goodnow (remember that Woodrow Wilson abandoned scholarship for politics) was William F. Willoughby (1867–1960). He was a member of the Taft Commission of 1912, which issued the first call for a national executive budgeting system, and later director of the Institute for Governmental Research, which would become part of the Brookings Institution. He also had a key role in writing the Budget and Accounting Act of 1921, which would finally accomplish the objectives of the Taft Commission by establishing an executive budget system at the national level along with the Budget Office and the General Accounting Office.

Willoughby wrote widely on the myriad issues of public administration. He believed that public administration had universal aspects that were applicable to all branches of government.[31] His early public administration text[32] was the first of a trilogy covering all three branches of government.[33] But it is his early work on budgetary reform that is of special interest. Writing in 1918, he outlined developments that were leading to the creation of modern budget systems in state governments. In an excerpt from *The Movement for Budgetary Reform in the States,*[34] Willoughby argues that budget reform would involve three major threads: (1) how budgets would advance and provide for popular control, (2) how budgets would enhance legislative and executive cooperation, and (3) how budgets would ensure administrative and management efficiency. Rather prophetic when you consider such public financial headlines on taxpayer's revolts from "Proposition 13" movements to grassroots tea party protests, and other forms of expenditure and revenue limitation laws (thread 1: popular control); continued infighting and increasing gridlock between the executive and legislative branches over budgetary control, deficits, and balanced budgets (thread 2: executive-legislative cooperation); and the effectiveness or lack of it in overburdened budgeting systems in maintaining managerial practices (thread 3: management effectiveness).

These early voices—Wilson, Goodnow, Taylor, and Willoughby—all had profound influences on the development of public administration. To begin with, they identified many of the critical themes that would be permanent parts of the field of study that is modern public administration. But to an even greater extent, they were prophetic voices, writing at a time when government employment and expenditures were still at very modest levels. At the turn of the century in 1900, federal, state, and local governments included slightly more than a million employees combined. Total government outlays were less than $1.5 billion or just over 3 percent of U.S. gross domestic product. By the 1920s, government employment would triple and expenditures would be at just less than $90 billion or about 12 percent of GDP.[35] Modern public administration would be founded on a scope that was without precedent in the United States' brief experience. In short, public administration was to be a field of study, not about a function or an enterprise, but rather about an entire major sector of what would grow to be the largest and most influential economy in the twentieth century.

PUBLIC ADMINISTRATION AND THE NEW ROLE OF GOVERNMENT

The aftermath of World War I marked the beginning of this change process for public administration. At the conclusion of all previous wars, the U.S. government had quickly returned to basic minimal levels. However, this time the scope and influence of government in U.S. life would not diminish. The United States was changing from a rural agricultural society to an urban industrial nation. This required a considerable response from public administration because so many new functions and programs would be established. The number of paved highways would increase tenfold in the 1920s. Cities would install traffic management systems, and states would impose driving tests. As the population became increasingly urban, vastly expanded programs would be needed in public parks and recreation, public works, public health, and public safety. Public administration as an activity was booming throughout the 1920s. The federal government's response to the Great Depression of the 1930s would make public administration all the more pervasive as part of American life.[36]

Public administration theorists, such as Dwight Waldo,[37] Vincent Ostrom,[38] Nicholas Henry,[39] and Howard McCurdy,[40] have described the pattern of development within public administration within public administration after the First World War as a period of orthodoxy. The tenets of this orthodox ideology held that "true democracy and true efficiency are synonymous, or at least reconcilable,"[41] that the work of government could be neatly divided into decision making and execution, and that administration was a science with discoverable principles. The initial imprint of the scientific management movement, the progressive reform political movement, and the politics-administration dichotomy became central focuses for public administration as both a profession and a field of study.

A critical linkage for the study of administration was its concern, indeed almost obsession, with organization and control. By definition, control was to be built into organizational structure and design to assure both accountability and efficiency. In fact, early management theorists assumed that organization and control were virtually synonymous. Remember that traditional administrative notions were based on historical models provided by the military and the Roman Catholic Church, which viewed organizational conflict as deviancy to be severely punished. When government units were small, less significant, and relatively provincial, the management of their organizations was less consequential. However, as the size, scope, and level of effort increased, pressures for better organization and control mounted. Under the influence of the scientific management movement, public administration became increasingly concerned with understanding bureaucratic forms of organization. The division of labor; span of control; organizational hierarchy and chain of command; reporting systems; departmentalization; and the development of standard operating rules, policies, and procedures became critical concerns to scholars and practitioners in the field.

Bureaucracy emerged as a dominant feature of the contemporary world. Virtually everywhere one looked in both developed and developing nations, economic, social, and political life were extensively and ever-increasingly influenced by bureaucratic organizations. Bureaucracy, while often used as a general invective to refer to any organization that is perceived to be inefficient, is more properly used to refer to a specific set of structural arrangements. It may also be used to refer to specific kinds of behavior patterns that are not restricted to formal bureaucracies. It is widely assumed that the structural characteristics of organizations correctly defined as "bureaucratic" influence the behavior of individuals—whether clients or bureaucrats—who interact with them.

THE THEORY OF BUREAUCRACY

Contemporary thinking along these lines begins with the work of the brilliant German sociologist Max Weber (1864–1920). His analysis of bureaucracy, first published in 1922 after his death, is still the main point of departure for all further analyses on the subject. Drawing on studies of ancient bureaucracies in Egypt, Rome, China, and the Byzantine Empire, as well as on the more modern ones emerging in Europe during the eighteenth and nineteenth centuries, Weber used an "ideal-type" approach to extrapolate from the real world the central core of features characteristic of the most fully developed bureaucratic form of organization. Weber's "Bureaucracy," reprinted here, is neither a description of reality nor a statement of normative preference. It is merely an identification of the major variables or features that characterize bureaucracies. The fact that such features might not be fully present in a given organization does not necessarily imply that the organization is nonbureaucratic. It may be an immature rather than a fully developed bureaucracy.

Weber's work on bureaucracy was not translated into English and made generally available until 1946. Still, his influence was phenomenal. Usually credited with being the "father" of modern sociology, Weber's work emphasized a new methodological rigor that could advance the study of organizations. Weber himself played a crucial role in helping to write a constitution for the Weimar Republic in Germany just before his death in 1920. The experience of the ill-fated Weimar Republic, certainly not attributable in any way to Weber, added perhaps another point of support to Woodrow Wilson's contention that it is harder to run a constitution than to frame one. Yet the clarity and descriptive quality of Weber's analysis of bureaucratic organizations provided both orthodox theorists and critics with a reference point from which to debate both the good and bad effects of bureaucratic structures.

A FIRST TEXTBOOK FOR PUBLIC ADMINISTRATION

While Woodrow Wilson provided the rationale for public administration to be an academic discipline and professional specialty, it remained for Leonard D. White (1891–1958) to most clearly articulate its preliminary objectives. A U.S. Civil Service commissioner from 1934 to 1937, White spent most of his career at the University of Chicago.[42] In the preface to his pioneering 1926 book *Introduction to the Study of Public Administration,* the first text in the field, he noted four critical assumptions that formed the basis for the study of public administration: (1) administration is a unitary process that can be studied uniformly, at the federal, state, and local levels; (2) the basis for study is management, not law; (3) administration is still an art, but the ideal of transformance to a science is both feasible and worthwhile; and (4) the recognition that administration "has become, and will continue to be the heart of the problem of modern government."[43] Reprinted here is the preface and first chapter from White's 1926 book, which, through four decades and four editions, became one of the most influential of public administration texts.[44]

White's text was remarkable for its restraint in not taking a prescriptive cookbook approach to public administration. He recognized that public administration was above all a field of study that had to stay close to reality—the reality of its largely untrained practitioner base that still professed great belief in the art of administration. Even more interesting, his work avoided the potential pitfall of the politics-administration dichotomy. Defining public administration as emphasizing the managerial phase, he left unanswered "the question [of] to what extent the administration itself participates in formulating the purposes of the state"[45] and avoided any controversy as to the precise nature of administrative action.

CRITICAL THINKING ABOUT INDIVIDUALS AND BEHAVIOR

The emphasis in White's introductory textbook in public administration was decidedly macro—an economic term often used to describe how overall government systems and their parts interact. In these early days, there was also great concern about micro issues: how individuals within organizations operated and how decisions were made. Mary Parker Follett (1868–1933)[46] made significant contributions in public administration's quest to understand how organizations worked. Indeed, one might say that she was a major voice for what today would be called participatory management. She wrote about the advantages of exercising "power with" as opposed to "power over." Her "law of the situation" was contingency management in its humble origins. Reprinted here is her discussion, "The Giving of Orders," which draws attention to the problems caused when superior-subordinate roles inhibit the productivity of the organization.

Follett was one of the first to focus on the theory of individuals within organizations. By the late 1920s research was under way at the Hawthorne experiments (to be discussed in more depth in the next section) by Elton Mayo (1880–1949)[47] and his associates from the Harvard Business School. This major examination of traditional scientific management principles sought to confirm the relationship between conditions and management interventions in work environment and productivity but ended up launching the human relations approach.[48] The Hawthorne experiments would confirm Follett's suggestions that workers were more responsive to peer pressure than to management controls and that factories, indeed all work settings, are above all social situations.

Notes

1. For histories of ancient public administration, see William C. Beyer, "The Civil Service of the Ancient World," *Public Administration Review* 19 (spring 1959); Michael T. Dalby and Michael S. Werthman, eds., *Bureaucracy in Historical Perspective* (Glenview, Ill.: Scott, Foresman, 1972); E. N. Gladden, *A History of Public Administration: Volume 1. From the Earliest Times to the Eleventh Century* (London: Frank Cass, 1972).
2. William W. Tam, *Alexander the Great* (Boston: Beacon Press, 1956); Donald W. Engels, *Alexander the Great and the Logistics of the Macedonian Army* (Berkeley: University of California Press, 1978).
3. Frederic Chapin Lane, *Venetian Ships and Shipbuilders of the Renaissance* (Baltimore: The Johns Hopkins Press, 1934).
4. See Machiavelli, *The Discourses* (1513) and *The Prince* (1532). For a modern appreciation, see Anthony Jay, *Management and Machiavelli: An Inquiry into the Politics of Corporate Life* (New York: Holt, Rinehart and Winston, 1967).
5. See Smith's *The Wealth of Nations* (1776), Chapter 1.
6. Robert Owen (1771–1858) was a Welsh industrialist, social reformer, and utopian socialist who was one of the first writers to consider the importance of the human factor in industry. His model factory communities, New Lanark in Scotland and New Harmony in Indiana, were among the first to take a modern approach to personnel management. For biographies, see J. F. C. Harrison, *Quest for the New Moral World: Robert Owen and the Owenites in Britain and America* (New York: Scribner's, 1960); Sidney Pollard, ed., *Robert Owen, Prophet of the Poor* (Lewisburg, Pa.: Bucknell University Press, 1971).
7. Charles Babbage (1792–1871) is the English inventor best known as the "father" of the modern computer; but he also built upon the assembly line concepts of Adam Smith and anticipated the scientific management techniques of Frederick W. Taylor. See his *On the Economy of Machinery and Manufactures* (London: Charles Knight, 1832).
8. The two most definitive histories of the first era of civil service reform remain Paul Van Riper's *History of the United States Civil Service* (Evanston, Ill: Row, Peterson, 1958) and J. Shafritz's *Public Personnel Management: The Heritage of Civil Service Reform* (New York: Praeger 1975).
9. Two especially insightful histories are William E. Nelson, *The Roots of American Bureaucracy 1830–1900* (Harvard University Press, 1982) and Ari Hoogenboom, *Outlawing the Spoils: A History of the Civil Service Reform Movement 1865–1883* (Urbana, Ill.: University of Illinois Press, 1961).
10. Dorman Eaton, *Civil Service in Great Britain: A History of Abuses and Reforms and Their Bearing upon American Politics* (New York: Harper & Brothers, 1880).
11. Eaton pp. 3–4.
12. See Chapters 1 and 2, *Personnel Management in Government, 5th, edition* by J. Shafritz et al. (New York: Marcel Dekker, 2001) for an overview of the progression of civil service coverage in both the federal and state and local sectors.
13. Frederick C. Mosher, *Democracy and the Public Service* (New York: Oxford University Press, 1968), p. 69.
14. This particular assessment, in addition to being a superb methodological illustration of neo-institutionalism, has an excellent summary history of early civil service adoption efforts: Pamela S. Tolbert and Lynne G. Zucker, "Institutional Sources of Change in the Formal Structure of Organizations: The Diffusion of Civil Service Reform 1880–1935," *Administrative Science Quarterly* 28, no. 1 (March 1983): 22–39.

15. This early accounting is according to Albert De Roode, "Civil Service Reform in Municipalities," *The American City* Vol. IV Jan 1911 pp. 20–25.
16. Perhaps the most comprehensive assessment of the state civil service trends over the last decade is *Civil Service Reform in the States* edited by J. Edward Kellough and Lloyd Nigro (State University of New York Press, 2006) with chapters devoted to eight different state reform experiences by different authors.
17. These trends were reported in a recent symposium in *Review of Public Personnel Administration*, June 2006: "Civil Service Reform Today," edited by James S. Bowman and Jonathan P. West.
18. See Lynton K. Caldwell, "Alexander Hamilton: Advocate of Executive Leadership," *Public Administration Review* 4, no. 2 (1944); Lynton K. Caldwell, *The Administrative Theories of Hamilton and Jefferson* (Chicago: University of Chicago Press, 1944); Leonard D. White, *The Federalists: A Study in Administrative History* (New York: Macmillan, 1948).
19. See Lynton K. Caldwell, "Thomas Jefferson and Public Administration," *Public Administration Review* 3, no. 3 (1943); Leonard D. White, *The Jeffersonians: A Study in Administrative History, 1801–1829* (New York: Macmillan, 1951).
20. See Albert Somit, "Andrew Jackson as Administrator," *Public Administration Review* 8 (summer 1948); Leonard D. White, *The Jacksonians: A Study in Administrative History, 1829–1861* (New York: Macmillan, 1954).
21. Wilson's letter was reprinted in *Political Science Quarterly* (December 1941).
22. James Carroll and Alfred Zuck, *"The Study of Administration" Revisited: Report on the Centennial Agendas Project* (Washington, D.C.: American Society for Public Administration, 1985).
23. For accounts of the influence of Wilson's essay, see Louis Brownlow, "Woodrow Wilson and Public Administration," *Public Administration Review* 16 (spring 1956); Richard J. Stillman, "Woodrow Wilson and the Study of Administration: A New Look at an Old Essay," *American Political Science Review* 67 (June 1973); Jack Rabin and James S. Bowman, eds., *Politics and Administration: Woodrow Wilson and American Public Administration* (New York: Marcel Dekker, 1984). However, revisionist scholars have contended that Wilson's influence was far more a post–World War II than a contemporary phenomenon. Paul Van Riper notes that none of the early public administration scholars cited Wilson's essay. In "The American Administrative State: Wilson and the Founders—An Unorthodox View," *Public Administration Review 43* (November–December 1983), Van Riper writes: "In reality, any connection between Wilson's essay and the later development of the discipline is pure fantasy! An examination of major political and social science works of the period between 1890 and World War I shows no citation whatever of the essay." Then how did Wilson's essay become so influential? According to Daniel W. Martin, "The Fading Legacy of Woodrow Wilson," *Public Administration Review* 48 (March–April 1988): "My simple answer, although too simple an answer, is the glowing reprint of Wilson's article in the December 1941 *Political Science Quarterly.* It was a masterwork of public relations, complete with a photo static copy of Wilson's tentative letter of submission." Thereafter, Wilson's essay, cited only modestly in the interwar period, grew to its current influence.
24. For appreciations, see Charles G. Haines and Marshall E. Dimock eds., *Essays on the Law and Practice of Governmental Administration: A Volume in Honor of Frank J. Goodnow* (Baltimore: The Johns Hopkins Press, 1935); Lurton W. Blassingame, "Frank J. Goodnow: Progressive Urban Reformer," *North Dakota Quarterly* (Summer 1972).
25. Leonard White comments extensively on the new management in his monograph on social trends in the United States as part of a series commissioned by the President's Research Committee on Social Trends, charted by President Hoover in 1929. See *Trends in Public Administration* (New York: McGraw-Hill, 1933).
26. There are any number of excellent historical and social works science on the progressive reform era in the late nineteenth century in the United States, but Martin J. Schiesl's work, *The Politics of Efficiency* (Berkeley, CA: University of California Press, 1977), provides a superb contextual assessment of municipal reform from an administrative perspective.
27. Jane Addams's works are extensive—she was a prolific writer and lecturer. Her autobiographical account, *Twenty Years at Hull House*—perhaps her best-known book—is still in print today. Most

scholars would chose her 1902 work, *Democracy and Social Ethics* (most recently reprinted by the University of Illinois Press, Urbana in 2002), as her first major work—the book that pushed her into national prominence. For the reader who wants a broad selection of the range of Addams's works there is *The Jane Addams Reader* edited by Jean Bethke Ekstain (New York: Basic Books, 2002).

28. For an interesting comparative examination of the settlement movement exemplified by Jane Addams and of the Municipal Research Movement led by the New York Bureau of Municipal Research and other champions of the city manager movement such as Henry Bruere, see Camilla Stivers, *Bureau Men, Settlement Women: Constructing Public Administration in the Progressive Era* (Lawrence Kan.: University Press of Kansas, 2000).
29. Frederick W. Taylor, *Principles of Scientific Management* (New York: Harper and Bros., 1911). Taylor's other major book is *Shop Management* (New York: Harper and Bros., 1903).
30. For biographies, see Frank Barkley Copley, *Frederick W. Taylor: Father of Scientific Management* (New York: Harper and Bros., 1923); Subhir Kakar, *Frederick Taylor: A Study in Personality and Innovation* (Cambridge, Mass.: MIT Press, 1970).
31. Marshall Dimock, "W. F. Willoughby and the Administrative Universal," *Public Administrative Review* 35 (September–October 1975).
32. William F. Willoughby, *Principles of Public Administration* (Baltimore: The Johns Hopkins Press, 1927).
33. The other two were *Principles of Judicial Administration* (Washington, D.C.: Brookings Institution, 1929) and *Principles of Legislative Organization and Administration* (Washington, D.C.: Brookings Institution, 1936).
34. William F. Willoughby, *The Movement for Budgetary Reform in the States* (New York: D. Appleton and Company for the Institute for Government Research, 1918), pp. 1–8.
35. Solomon Fabricant, *The Trend of Government Activity in the United States Since 1900* (New York: National Bureau of Economic Research, 1952), pp. 11–24.
36. For explanations of the growth of government during the 1920s, see Geoffrey Perret, *America in the Twenties: A History* (New York: Simon and Schuster, 1982), pp. 251–252, 426, 429, 431, 463, 490.
37. Dwight Waldo, *The Administrative State: A Study of the Political Theory of American Public Administration* (New York: Ronald Press, 1948), pp. 206–207.
38. Vincent Ostrom, *The Intellectual Crisis in American Public Administration*, rev. ed. (Tuscaloosa: University of Alabama Press, 1974), p. 36.
39. Nicholas Henry, *Public Administration and Public Affairs* (Englewood Cliffs, NJ: Prentice-Hall, 1975), pp. 8–9.
40. Howard E. McCurdy, *Public Administration: A Bibliographic Guide to the Literature* (New York: Marcel Dekker, 1986), p. 22.
41. Waldo, *The Administrative State*, p. 206.
42. For appreciations of White's varied intellectual contributions to public administration, see John M. Gaus, "Leonard Dupree White 1891–1958," *Public Administration Review* 18 (Summer 1958); Herbert J. Storing, "Leonard D. White and the Study of Public Administration," *Public Administration Review* 25 (March 1965).
43. Leonard D. White, *Introduction to the Study of Public Administration* (New York: Macmillan, 1926), p. viii.
44. The fourth, and last, edition would be published in 1955.
45. White, p. 2.
46. For her collected papers, see Henry C. Metcalf and Lyndall Urwick, eds., *Dynamic Administration: The Collected Papers of Mary Parker Follett* (New York: Harper and Bros., 1942); for an appreciation of her contributions, see Elliot M. Fox, "Mary Parker Follett: The Enduring Contribution," *Public Administration Review* 28 (December 1968).
47. For a biography, see Lyndall F. Urwick, *The Life and Work of Elton Mayo* (London: Urwick, Orr and Partners, 1960).
48. The definitive account of the studies themselves is to be found in F. J. Roethlisberger and William J. Dickson, *Management and the Worker* (Cambridge, Mass.: Harvard University Press, 1939).

1

The Study of Administration

Woodrow Wilson

I suppose that no practical science is ever studied where there is no need to know it. The very fact, therefore, that the eminently practical science of administration is finding its way into college courses in this country would prove that this country needs to know more about administration, were such proof of this fact required to make out a case. It need not be said, however, that we do not look into college programmers for proof of this fact. It is a thing almost taken for granted among us, that the present movement called civil service reform must, after the accomplishment of its first purpose, expand into efforts to improve, not the *personnel* only, but also the organization and methods of our government offices: because it is plain that their organization and methods need improvement only less than their *personnel.* It is the object of administrative study to discover, first, what government can properly and successfully do, and, secondly, how it can do these proper things with the utmost possible efficiency and at the least possible cost either of money or of energy. On both these points there is obviously much need of light among us; and only careful study can supply that light.

Before entering on that study, however, it is needful:

I. To take some account of what others have done in the same line; that is to say, of the history of the study.
II. To ascertain just what is its subject matter.
III. To determine just what are the best methods by which to develop it, and the most clarifying political conceptions to carry with us into it.

Unless we know and settle these things, we shall set out without chart or compass.

Source: Political Science Quarterly 2 (June 1887).

I

The science of administration is the latest fruit of that study of the science of politics which was begun some twenty-two hundred years ago. It is a birth of our own century, almost of our own generation.

Why was it so late in coming? Why did it wait till this too busy century of ours to demand attention for itself? Administration is the most obvious part of government; it is government in action; it is the executive, the operative, the most visible side of government, and is of course as old as government itself. It is government in action, and one might very naturally expect to find that government in action had arrested the attention and provoked the scrutiny of writers of politics very early in the history of systematic thought.

But such was not the case. No one wrote systematically of administration as a branch of the science of government until the present century had passed its first youth and had begun to put forth its characteristic flower of systematic knowledge. Up to our own day all the political writers whom we now read had thought, argued, dogmatized only about the *constitution* of government; about the nature of the state, the essence and seat of sovereignty, popular power and kingly prerogative; about the greatest meanings lying at the heart of government, and the high ends set before the purpose of government by man's nature and man's aims. The central field of controversy was that great field of theory in which monarchy rode tilt against democracy, in which oligarchy would have built for itself strongholds of privilege, and in which tyranny sought opportunity to make good its claim to receive submission from all competitors. Amidst this high warfare of principles, administration could command no pause for its own consideration. The question was always: Who shall make law, and what shall that law be? The other question, how law should be administered with enlightenment, with equity, with speed, and without friction, was put aside as "practical detail" which clerks could arrange after doctors had agreed upon principles.

That political philosophy took this direction was of course no accident, no chance preference or perverse whim of political philosophers. The philosophy of any time is, as Hegel says, "nothing but the spirit of that time expressed in abstract thought"; and political philosophy, like philosophy of every other kind, has only held up the mirror to contemporary affairs. The trouble in early times was almost altogether about the constitution of government; and consequently that was what engrossed men's thoughts. There was little or no trouble about administration—at least little that was heeded by administrators. The functions of government were simple, because life itself was simple. Government went about imperatively and compelled men, without thought of consulting their wishes. There was no complex system of public revenues and public debts to puzzle financiers; there were, consequently, no financiers to be puzzled. No one who possessed power was long at a loss how to use it. The great and only question was: Who shall possess it? Populations were of manageable numbers; property was of simple sorts. There were plenty of farms, but no stocks and bonds: more cattle than vested interests.

I have said that all this was true of "early times"; but it was substantially true also of comparatively late times. One does not have to look back of the last century for the beginnings of the present complexities of trade and perplexities of commercial speculation, nor for the portentous birth of national debts. Good Queen Bess, doubtless, thought that the monopolies of the sixteenth century were hard enough to handle without burning her hands; but they are not remembered in the presence of the giant monopolies of the nineteenth century. When Blackstone lamented that corporations had no bodies to be kicked and no souls to be damned, he was anticipating the proper time for such regrets by full a century. The perennial discords between master and workmen which now so often disturb industrial society began before the Black Death and the Statute of Laborers; but never before our own day did they assume such ominous proportions as they wear now. In brief, if difficulties of governmental action are to be seen gathering in other centuries, they are to be seen culminating in our own.

This is the reason why administrative tasks have nowadays to be so studiously and systematically adjusted to carefully tested standards of policy, the reason why we are having now what we never had before, a science of administration. The weightier debates of constitutional principle are even yet by no means concluded; but they are no longer of more immediate practical moment than questions of administration. It is getting to be harder to *run* a constitution than to frame one.

Here is Mr. Bagehot's graphic, whimsical way of depicting the difference between the old and the new in administration:

> In early times, when a despot wishes to govern a distant province, he sends down a satrap on a grand horse, and other people on little horses; and very little is heard of the satrap again unless he send back some of the little people to tell what he has been doing. No great labour of superintendence is possible. Common rumour and casual report are the sources of intelligence. If it seems certain that the province is in a bad state, satrap No. 1 is recalled, and satrap No. 2 sends out in his stead. In civilized countries the process is different. You erect a bureau in the province you want to govern; you make it write letters and copy letters; it sends home eight reports *per diem* to the head bureau in St. Petersburg. Nobody does a sum in the province without some one doing the same sum in the capital, to "check" him, and see that he does it correctly. The consequence of this is, to throw on the heads of departments an amount of reading and labour which can only be accomplished by the greatest natural aptitude, the most efficient training, the most firm and regular industry.[1]

There is scarcely a single duty of government which was once simple which is not now complex; government once had but a few masters; it now has scores of masters. Majorities formerly only underwent government; they now conduct government. Where government once might follow the whims of a court, it must now follow the views of a nation.

And those views are steadily widening to new conceptions of state duty; so that at the same time that the functions of government are every day becoming more complex and difficult, they are also vastly multiplying in number. Administration is everywhere putting its hands to new undertakings. The utility, cheapness, and success of the government's postal service, for instance, point towards the early establishment of governmental control of the telegraph system. Or, even if our government is not to follow the lead of the governments of Europe in buying or building both telegraph and railroad lines, no one can doubt that in some way it must make itself master of masterful corporations. The creation of national commissioners of railroads, in addition to the older state commissions, involves a very important and delicate extension of administrative functions. Whatever hold of authority state or federal governments are to take upon corporations, there must follow cares and responsibilities which will require not a little wisdom, knowledge, and experience. Such things must be studied in order to be well done. And these, as I have said, are only a few of the doors which are being opened to offices of government. The idea of the state and the consequent ideal of its duty are undergoing noteworthy change; and "the idea of the state is the conscience of administration." Seeing every day new things which the state ought to do, the next thing is to see clearly how it ought to do them.

This is why there should be a science of administration which shall seek to straighten the paths of government, to make its business less unbusinesslike, to strengthen and purify its organization, and to crown its dutifulness. This is one reason why there is such a science.

But where has this science grown up? Surely not on this side of the sea. Not much impartial scientific method is to be discerned in our administrative practices. The poisonous atmosphere of city government, the crooked secrets of state administration, the confusion, sinecurism, and corruption ever and again discovered in the bureaux at Washington forbid us to believe that any clear conceptions are as yet very widely current in the United States. No; American writers have hitherto taken no very important part in the advancement of this science. It has found its doctors in Europe. It is not of our making; it is a foreign science, speaking very little of the language of English or American principle. It employs only foreign tongues; it utters none but what are to our minds alien ideas. Its aims, its examples, its conditions, are almost exclusively grounded in the histories of foreign races, in the precedents of foreign systems, in the lessons of foreign revolutions. It has been developed by French and German professors, and is consequently in all parts adapted to the needs of a compact state, and made to fit highly centralized forms of government; whereas, to answer our purposes, it must be adapted, not to a simple and compact, but to a complex and multiform state, and made to fit highly decentralized forms of government. If we would employ it, we must Americanize it, and that not formally, in language merely, but radically, in thought, principle, and aim as well. It must learn our constitutions by heart; must get the bureaucratic fever out of its veins; must inhale much free American air.

If an explanation be sought why a science manifestly so susceptible of being made useful to all governments alike should have received attention first in Europe, where government has long been a monopoly, rather than in England or the United States, where government has long been a common franchise, the reason will doubtless be found to be twofold: first, that in Europe, just because government was independent of popular assent, there was more governing to be done; and, second, that the desire to keep government a monopoly made the monopolists interested in discovering the least irritating means of governing. They were, besides, few enough to adopt means promptly.

It will be instructive to look into this matter a little more closely. In speaking of European governments I do not, of course, include England. She has not refused to change with the times. She has simply tempered the severity of the transition from a polity of aristocratic privilege to a system of democratic power by slow measures of constitutional reform which, without preventing revolution, has confined it to paths of peace. But the countries of the continent for a long time desperately struggled against all change, and would have diverted revolution by softening the asperities of absolute government. They sought so to perfect their machinery as to destroy all wearing friction, so to sweeten their methods with consideration for the interests of the governed as to placate all hindering hatred, and so assiduously and opportunely to offer their aid to all classes of undertakings as to render themselves indispensable to the industrious. They did at last give the people constitutions and the franchise; but even after that they obtained leave to continue despotic by becoming paternal. They made themselves too efficient to be dispensed with, too smoothly operative to be noticed, too enlightened to be inconsiderately questioned, too benevolent to be suspected, too powerful to be coped with. All this has required study; and they have closely studied it.

On this side of the sea we, the while, had known no great difficulties of government. With a new country, in which there was room and remunerative employment for everybody, with liberal principles of government and unlimited skill in practical politics, we were long exempted from the need of being anxiously careful about plans and methods of administration. We have naturally been slow to see the use or significance of those many volumes of learned research and painstaking examination into the ways and means of conducting government which the presses of Europe have been sending to our libraries. Like a lusty child, government with us has expanded in nature and grown great in statute, but has also become awkward in movement. The vigor and increase of its life has been altogether out of proportion to its skill in living. It has gained strength, but it has not acquired deportment. Great, therefore, as has been our advantage over the countries of Europe in point of ease and health of constitutional development, now that the time for more careful administrative adjustments and larger administrative knowledge has come to us, we are at a signal disadvantage as compared with the transatlantic nations; and this for reasons which I shall try to make clear.

Judging by the constitutional histories of the chief nations of the modern world, there may be said to be three periods of growth through which government has passed in all the most highly developed of existing systems, and through which it promises to pass in all the rest. The first of these periods is that of absolute rulers, and of an administrative system adapted to absolute rule; the second is that in which constitutions are framed to do away with absolute rulers and substitute popular control, and in which administration is neglected for these higher concerns; and the third is that in which the sovereign people undertake to develop administration under this new constitution which has brought them into power.

Those governments are now in the lead in administrative practice which had rulers still absolute but also enlightened when those modern days of political illumination came in which it was made evident to all but the blind that governors are properly only the servants of the governed. In such governments administration has been organized to subserve the general weal with the simplicity and effectiveness vouchsafed only to the undertakings of a single will.

Such was the case in Prussia, for instance, where administration has been most studied and most nearly perfected. Frederick the Great, stern and masterful as was his rule, still sincerely professed to regard himself as only the chief servant of the state, to consider his great office a public trust; and it was he who, building upon the foundations laid by his father, began to organize the public service of Prussia as in very earnest a service of the public. His no less absolute successor, Frederic William III . . . in his turn, advanced the work still further, planning many of the broader structural features which give firmness and form to Prussian administration today. Almost the whole of the admirable system has been developed by kingly initiative.

Of similar origin was the practice, if not the plan, of modern French administration, with its symmetrical divisions of territory and its orderly gradations of office. The days of the Revolution—of the Constituent Assembly—were days of constitution-*writing*, but they can hardly be called days of constitution-*making*. The Revolution heralded a period of constitutional development—the entrance of France upon the second of those periods which I have enumerated—but it did not itself inaugurate such a period. It interrupted and unsettled absolutism, but did not destroy it. Napoleon succeeded the monarchs of France, to exercise a power as unrestricted as they had ever possessed.

The recasting of French administration by Napoleon is, therefore, my second example of the perfecting of civil machinery by the single will of an absolute ruler before the dawn of a constitutional era. No corporate, popular will could ever have effected arrangements such as those which Napoleon commanded. Arrangements so simple at the expense of local prejudice, so logical in their influence to popular choice, might be decreed by a Constitutional Assembly, but could be established only by the unlimited authority of a despot. The system of the year VIII was ruthlessly thorough and heartlessly perfect. It was, besides, in large part, a return to the despotism that had been overthrown.

Among those nations, on the other hand, which entered upon a season of constitution-making and popular reform before administration had received the impress of liberal principle, administrative improvement has been tardy and half-done. Once a nation has embarked in the business of manufacturing constitutions, it finds it exceedingly difficult to close out that business and open for the public a bureau of skilled, economical administration. There seems to be no end to the tinkering of constitutions. Your ordinary constitution will last you hardly ten years without repairs or additions; and the time for administrative detail comes late.

Here, of course, our examples are England and our own country. In the days of the Angevin kings, before constitutional life had taken root in the Great Charter, legal and administrative reforms began to proceed with sense and vigor under the impulse of Henry II's shrewd, busy, pushing, indomitable spirit and purpose; and kingly initiative seemed destined in England, as elsewhere, to shape governmental growth at its will. But impulsive, errant Richard and weak, despicable John were not the men to carry out such schemes as their father's. Administrative development gave place in their reigns to constitutional struggles; and Parliament became king before any English monarch had had the practical genius or the enlightened conscience to devise just and lasting forms for the civil service of the state.

The English race, consequently, has long and successfully studied the art of curbing executive power to the constant neglect of the art of perfecting executive methods. It has exercised itself much more in controlling than in energizing government. It has been more concerned to render government just and moderate than to make it facile, well-ordered, and effective. English and American political history has been a history, not of administrative development, but of legislative oversight—not of progress in governmental organization, but of advance in law-making and political criticism. Consequently, we have reached a time when administrative study and creation are imperatively necessary to the well-being of our governments saddled with the habits of a long period of constitution-making. That period has practically closed, so far as the establishment of essential principles is concerned, but we cannot shake off its atmosphere. We go on criticizing when we ought to be creating. We have reached the third of the periods I have mentioned—the period, namely, when the people have to develop administration in accordance with the constitutions they won for themselves in a previous period of struggle with absolute power; but we are not prepared for the tasks of the new period.

Such an explanation seems to afford the only escape from blank astonishment at the fact that, in spite of our vast advantages in point of political liberty, and above all in point of practical political skill and sagacity, so many nations are ahead of us in administrative organization and administrative skill. Why, for instance, have we but just begun purifying a civil service which was rotten full fifty years ago? To say that slavery diverted us is but to repeat what I have said—that flaws in our constitution delayed us.

Of course all reasonable preference would declare for this English and American course of politics rather than for that of any European country. We should not like to have had Prussia's history for the sake of having Prussia's administrative skill; and Prussia's particular system of administration would quite suffocate us. It is better to be untrained and free than to be servile and systematic. Still there is no denying that it would be better yet to be both free in spirit and proficient in practice. It is this even more reasonable preference which impels us to discover what there may be to hinder or delay us in naturalizing this much-to-be-desired science of administration.

What, then, is there to prevent?

Well, principally, popular sovereignty. It is harder for democracy to organize administration than for monarchy. The very completeness of our most cherished political successes in the past embarrasses us. We have enthroned public opinion; and it is forbidden us to hope during its reign for any quick schooling of the sovereign in executive expertness or in the conditions of perfect functional balance in government. The very fact that we have realized popular rule in its fullness has made the task of *organizing* that rule just so much the more difficult. In order to make any advance at all we must instruct and persuade a multitudinous monarch called public opinion—a much less feasible undertaking than to influence a single monarch called a king. An individual sovereign will adopt a simple plan and carry it out directly: he will have but one opinion, and he will embody that one opinion in one command. But this other sovereign, the people, will have a score of differing opinions. They can agree upon nothing simple: advance must be made through compromise, by a compounding of differences, by a trimming of plans and a suppression of too straightforward principles. There will be a succession of resolves running through a course of years, a dropping fire of commands running through a whole gamut of modifications.

In government, as in virtue, the hardest of hard things is to make progress. Formerly the reason for this was that the single person who was sovereign was generally either selfish, ignorant, timid or a fool—albeit there was now and again one who was wise. Nowadays the reason is that the many, the people, who are sovereign have no single ear which one can approach, and are selfish, ignorant, timid, stubborn, or foolish with the selfishnesses, the ignorances, the stubbornnesses, the timidities, or the follies of several thousand persons—albeit there are hundreds who are wise. Once the advantage of the reformer was that the sovereign's mind had a definite locality, that it was contained in one man's head, and that consequently it could be gotten at; though it was his disadvantage that that mind learned only reluctantly or only in small quantities, or was under the influence of some one who let it learn only the wrong things. Now, on the contrary, the reformer is bewildered by the fact that the sovereign's mind has no definite locality, but is contained in a voting majority of several million heads; and embarrassed by the fact that the mind of this sovereign also is under the influence of favorites, who are none the less favorites in a good old-fashioned sense of the word because they are not persons but preconceived opinions; *i.e.*, prejudices which are not to be reasoned with because they are not the children of reason.

Wherever regard for public opinion is a first principle of government, practical reform must be slow and all reform must be full of compromises. For wherever public opinion exists it must rule. This is now an axiom half the world over, and will presently come to be believed even in Russia. Whoever would effect a change in a modern constitutional government must first educate his fellow-citizens to want *some* change. That done, he must persuade them to want the particular change he wants. He must first make public opinion willing to listen and then see to it that it listen to the right things. He must stir it up to search for an opinion, and then manage to put the right opinion in its way.

The first step is not less difficult than the second. With opinions, possession is more than nine points of the law. It is next to impossible to dislodge them. Institutions which one generation regards as only a makeshift approximation to the realization of a principle, the next generation honors as the nearest possible approximation to that principle, and the next worships as the principle itself. It take scarcely three generations for the apotheosis. The grandson accepts his grandfather's hesitating experiment as an integral part of the fixed constitution of nature.

Even if we had clear insight into all the political past, and could form out of perfectly instructed heads a few steady, infallible, placidly wise maxims of government into which all sound political doctrine would be ultimately resolvable, *would the country act on them?* That is the question. The bulk of mankind is rigidly unphilosophical, and nowadays the bulk of mankind votes. A truth must become not only plain but also commonplace before it will be seen by the people who go to their work very early in the morning; and not to act upon it must involve great and pinching inconveniences before these same people will make up their minds to act upon it.

And where is this unphilosophical bulk of mankind more multifarious in its composition than in the United States? To know the public mind of this country, one must know the mind, not of Americans of the older stocks only, but also of Irishmen, of Germans, of negroes. In order to get a footing for new doctrine, one must influence minds cast in every mould of race, minds inheriting every bias of environment, warped by the histories of a score of different nations, warmed or chilled, closed or expanded by almost every climate of the globe.

So much, then, for the history of the study of administration, and the peculiarly difficult conditions under which, entering upon it when we do, we must undertake it. What, now, is the subject-matter of this study, and what are its characteristic objects?

II

The field of administration is a field of business. It is removed from the hurry and strife of politics; it at most points stands apart even from the debatable ground of constitutional study. It is a part of political life only as the methods of the counting-house are a part of the life of society; only as machinery is part of the manufactured product. But it is, at the same time, raised very far above the dull level of mere technical detail by the fact that through its greater principles it is directly connected with the lasting maxims of political wisdom, the permanent truths of political progress.

The object of administrative study is to rescue executive methods from the confusion and costliness of empirical experiment and set them upon foundations laid deep in stable principle.

It is for this reason that we must regard civil-service reform in its present stages as but a prelude to a fuller administrative reform. We are now rectifying methods of appointment; we must go on to adjust executive functions more fitly and to prescribe better methods of executive organization and action. Civil-service reform is thus but a moral preparation for what is to follow. It is clearing the moral atmosphere of official life by establishing the sanctity of public office as a public trust, and, by making the service unpartisan, it is opening the way for making it businesslike. By sweetening its motives it is rendering it capable of improving its methods of work.

Let me expand a little what I have said of the province of administration. Most important to be observed is the truth already so much and so fortunately insisted upon by our civil-service reformers; namely, that administration lies outside the proper sphere of *politics*. Administrative questions are not political questions. Although politics sets the tasks for administration, it should not be suffered to manipulate its offices.

This is distinction of high authority; eminent German writers insist upon it as of course. Biuntschli, for instance, bids us separate administration alike from politics and from law.[2] Politics, he says, is state activity "in things great and universal," while "administration, on the other hand," is "the activity of the state in individual and small things. Politics is thus the special province of the statesman, administration of the technical official." "Policy does nothing without the aid of administration"; but administration is not therefore politics. But we do not require German authority for this position; this discrimination between administration and politics is now, happily, too obvious to need further discussion.

There is another distinction which must be worked into all our conclusions, which, though but another side of that between administration and politics, is not quite so easy to keep sight of: I mean the distinction between *constitutional* and administrative questions, between those governmental adjustments which are essential to constitutional principle and those which are merely instrumental to the possibly changing purposes of a wisely adapting convenience.

One cannot easily make clear to every one just where administration resides in the various departments of any practicable government without entering upon particulars so numerous as to confuse and distinctions so minute as to distract. No lines of demarcation, setting apart administrative from non-administrative functions, can be run between this and that department of government without being run up hill and down dale, over dizzy heights of distinction and through dense jungles of statutory enactment, hither and thither around "ifs" and "buts," "whens" and "howevers" until they become altogether lost to the common eye not accustomed to this sort of surveying, and consequently not acquainted with the use of the theodolite of logical discernment. A great deal of administration goes about *incognito* to most of the world, being confounded now with political "management," and again with constitutional principle.

Perhaps this ease of confusion may explain such utterances as that of Niebuhr's: "Liberty," he says, "depends incomparably more upon administration than upon constitution." [Barthold Georg Niebuhr (1776–1831) was a German historian.] At first sight this appears to be largely true. Apparently facility in the actual exercise of liberty does depend more upon administrative arrangements than upon constitutional guarantees; although constitutional guarantees alone secure the existence of liberty. But—upon second thought—is even so much as this true? Liberty no more consists in easy functional movement than intelligence consists in the ease and vigor with which the limbs of a strong man move. The principles that rule within the man, or the constitution, are the vital springs of liberty or servitude. Because dependence and subjection are without chains, are lightened by every easy-working device of considerate, paternal government, they are not thereby transformed into liberty. Liberty cannot live apart from constitutional principle; and no administration, however perfect and liberal its methods, can give men more than a poor counterfeit of liberty if it rest upon illiberal principles of government.

A clear view of the difference between the province of constitutional law and the province of administrative function ought to leave no room for misconception; and it is possible to name some roughly definite criteria upon which such a view can be built. Public administration is detailed and systematic execution of public law. Every particular application of general law is an act of administration. The assessment and raising of taxes, for instance, the hanging of a criminal, the transportation and delivery of the mails, the equipment and recruiting of the army, and navy, etc., are all obviously acts of administration; but the general laws which direct these things to be done are as obviously outside of and above administration. The broad plans of governmental action are not administrative; the detailed execution of such plans is administrative. Constitutions, therefore, properly concern themselves only with those instrumentalities of government which are to control general law. Our federal constitution observes this principle in saying nothing of even the greatest of the purely executive offices, and speaking only of that President of the Union who was to share the legislative and policy-making functions of government, only of those judges of highest jurisdiction who were to interpret and guard its principles, and not of those who were merely to give utterance to them.

This is not quite the distinction between Will and answering Deed, because the administrator should have and does have a will of his own in the choice of means for accomplishing his work. He is not and ought not to be a mere passive instrument. The distinction is between general plans and special means.

There is, indeed, one point at which administrative studies trench on constitutional ground—or at least upon what seems constitutional ground. The study of administration, philosophically viewed, is closely connected with the study of the proper distribution of constitutional authority. To be efficient it must discover the simplest arrangements by which responsibility can be unmistakably fixed upon officials; the best way of dividing authority without hampering it, and responsibility without obscuring it. And this question of the distribution of authority, when taken into the sphere of the higher, the originating functions of government, is obviously a central constitutional question. If administrative study can discover the best principles upon which to base such distribution, it will have done constitutional study, an invaluable service. Montesquieu did not, I am convinced, say the last word on this head.

To discover the best principle for the distribution of authority is of greater importance, possibly, under a democratic system, where officials serve many masters, than under others where they serve but a few. All sovereigns are suspicious of their servants, and the sovereign people is no exception to the rule; but how is its suspicion to be allayed by *knowledge?* If that suspicion could be clarified into wise vigilance, it would be altogether salutary; if that vigilance could be aided by the unmistakable placing of responsibility, it would be altogether beneficent. Suspicion in itself is never healthful either in the private or in the public mind. *Trust is strength* in all relations of life; and, as it is the office of the constitutional reformer to create conditions of trustfulness, so it is the office of the administrative organizer to fit administration with conditions of clear-cut responsibility which shall insure trustworthiness.

And let me say that large powers and unhampered discretion seem to me the indispensable conditions of responsibility. Public attention must be easily directed, in each case of good or bad administration, to just the man deserving of praise or blame. There is no danger in power, if only it be not irresponsible. If it be divided, dealt out in shares to many, it is obscured; and if it be obscured, it is made irresponsible. But if it be centred in heads of the service and in heads of branches of the service, it is easily watched and brought to book. If to keep his office a man must achieve open and honest success, and if at the same time he feels himself intrusted with large freedom of discretion, the greater his power, the less likely is he to abuse it, the more is he nerved and sobered and elevated by it. The less his power, the more safely obscure and unnoticed does he feel his position to be, and the more readily does he relapse into remissness.

Just here we manifestly emerge upon the field of that still larger question—the proper relations between public opinion and administration.

To whom is official trustworthiness to be disclosed, and by whom is it to be rewarded? Is the official to look to the public for his need of praise and his push of promotion, or only to his superior in office? Are the people to be called in to settle administrative discipline as they are called in to settle constitutional principles? These questions evidently find their root in what is undoubtedly the fundamental problem of this whole study. That problem is: What part shall public opinion take in the conduct of administration?

The right answer seems to be that public opinion shall play the part of authoritative critic.

But the *method* by which its authority shall be made to tell? Our peculiar American difficulty in organizing administration is not the danger of losing liberty, but the danger of not being able or willing to separate its essentials from its accidents. Our success is made doubtful by that besetting error of ours, the error of trying to do too much by vote. Self government does not consist in having a hand in everything, any more than housekeeping consists necessarily in cooking dinner with one's own hands. The cook must be trusted with a large discretion as to the management of the fires and the ovens.

In those countries in which public opinion has yet to be instructed in its privileges, yet to be accustomed to having its own way, this question as to the province of public opinion is much more readily soluble than in this country, where public opinion is wide awake and quite intent upon having its own way anyhow. It is pathetic to see a whole book written by a German professor of political science for the purpose of saying to his countrymen, "Please try to have an opinion about national affairs"; but a public which is so modest may at least be expected to be very docile and acquiescent in learning what things it has *not* a right to think and speak about imperatively. It may be sluggish, but it will not be meddlesome. It will submit to be instructed before it tries to instruct. Its political education will come before its political activity. In trying to instruct our own public opinion, we are dealing with a pupil apt to think itself quite sufficiently instructed beforehand.

The problem is to make public opinion efficient without suffering it to be meddlesome. Directly exercised, in the oversight of the daily details and in the choice of the daily means of government, public criticism is of course a clumsy nuisance, a rustic handling delicate machinery. But as superintending the greater forces of formative policy alike in politics and administration, public criticism is altogether safe and beneficent, altogether indispensable. Let administrative study find the best means for giving public criticism this control and for shutting it out from all other interference.

But is the whole duty of administrative study done when it has taught the people what sort of administration to desire and demand, and how to get what they demand? Ought it not to go on to drill candidates for the public service?

There is an admirable movement towards universal political education now afoot in this country. The time will soon come when no college of respectability can afford to do without a well-filled chair of political science. But the education thus imparted will go but a certain length. It will multiply the number of intelligent critics of government, but it will create no competent body of administrators. It will prepare the way for the development of a surefooted understanding of the general principles of government, but it will not necessarily foster skill in conducting government. It is an education which will equip legislators, perhaps, but not executive officials. If we are to improve public opinion, which is the motive power of government, we must prepare better officials as the *apparatus* of government. If we are to put in new boilers and to mend the fires which drive our governmental machinery, we must not leave the old wheels and joints and valves and bands to creak and buzz and clatter on as best they may at the bidding of the new force. We must put in new running parts wherever there is the least lack of strength or adjustment. It will be necessary to organize democracy by sending up to the competitive examinations for the civil service men definitely prepared for standing liberal tests as to technical knowledge. A technically schooled civil service will presently have become indispensable.

I know that a corps of civil servants prepared by a special schooling and drilled, after ap-pointment, into a perfected organization, with appropriate hierarchy and characteristic discipline, seems to a great many very thoughtful persons to contain elements which might combine to make an offensive official class—a distinct, semi-corporate body with sympathies divorced from those of a progressive, freespirited people, and with hearts narrowed to the meanness of a bigoted officialism. Certainly such a class would be altogether hateful and harmful in the United States. Any measures calculated to produce it would for us be measures of reaction and of folly.

But to fear the creation of a domineering, illiberal officialism as a result of the studies I am here proposing is to miss altogether the principle upon which I wish most to insist. That principle is, that administration in the United States must be at all points sensitive to public opinion. A body of thoroughly trained officials serving during good behavior we must have in any case: that is a plain business necessity. But the apprehension that such a body will be anything un-American clears away the moment it is asked, What is to constitute good behavior? For that question obviously carries its own answer on its face. Steady, hearty allegiance to the policy of the government they serve will constitute good behavior. That *policy* will have no taint of officialism about it. It will not be the creation of permanent officials, but of statesmen whose responsibility to public opinion will be direct and inevitable. Bureaucracy can exist only where the whole service of the state is removed from the common political life of the people, its chiefs as well as its rank and file. Its motives, its objects, its policy, its standards, must be bureaucratic. It would be difficult to point out any examples of impudent exclusiveness and arbitrariness on the part of officials doing service under a chief of department who really served the people, as all our chiefs of departments must be made to do. It would be easy, on the other hand, to adduce other instances like that of the influence of Stein in Prussia, where the leadership of one statesman imbued with true public spirit transformed arrogant and perfunctory bureaux into public spirited instruments of just government.

The ideal for us is a civil service cultured and self-sufficient enough to act with sense and vigor, and yet so intimately connected with the popular thought, by means of elections and constant public counsel, as to find arbitrariness or class spirit quite out of the question.

III

Having thus viewed in some sort the subject-matter and the objects of this study of administration, what are we to conclude as to the methods best suited to it—the points of view most advantageous for it?

Government is so near us, so much a thing of our daily familiar handling, that we can with difficulty see the need of any philosophical study of it, or the exact point of such study, should it be undertaken. We have been on our feet too long to study now the art of walking. We are a practical people, made so apt, so adept in self-government by centuries of experimental drill that we are scarcely any longer capable of perceiving the awkwardness of the particular system we may be using, just because it is so easy for us to use any system. We do not study the art of governing: we govern. But mere unschooled genius for affairs will not save us from sad blunders in administration. Though democrats by long inheritance and repeated choice, we are still rather crude democrats. Old as democracy is, its organization on a basis of modern ideas and conditions is still an unaccomplished work. The democratic state has yet to be equipped for carrying those enormous burdens of administration which the needs of this industrial and trading age are so fast accumulating. Without comparative studies in government we cannot rid ourselves of the misconception that administration stands upon an essentially different basis in a democratic state from that on which it stands in a nondemocratic state.

After such study we could grant democracy the sufficient honor of ultimately determining by debate all essential questions affecting the public weal, of basing all structures of policy upon the major will; but we would have found but one rule of good administration for all governments alike. So far as administrative functions are concerned, all governments have a strong structural likeness; more than that, if they are to be uniformly useful and efficient, they *must* have a strong structural likeness. A free man has the same bodily organs, the same executive parts, as the slave, however different may be his motives, his services, his energies. Monarchies and democracies, radically different as they are in other respects, have in reality much the same business to look to.

It is abundantly safe nowadays to insist upon this actual likeness of all governments, because these are days when abuses of power are easily exposed and arrested, in countries like our own, by a bold, alert, inquisitive, detective public thought and a sturdy popular self dependence such as never existed before. We are slow to appreciate this; but it is easy to appreciate it. Try to imagine personal government in the United States. It is like trying to imagine a national worship of Zeus. Our imaginations are too modern for the feat.

But, besides being safe, it is necessary to see that for all governments alike the legitimate ends of administration are the same, in order not to be frightened at the idea of looking into foreign systems of administration for instruction and suggestion; in order to get rid of the apprehension that we might perchance blindly borrow something incompatible with our principles. That man is blindly astray who denounces attempts to transplant foreign systems into this country. It is impossible: they simply would not grow here. But why should we not use such parts of foreign contrivances as we want, if they be in any way serviceable? We are in no danger of using them in a foreign way. We borrowed rice, but we do not eat it with chopsticks. We borrowed our whole political language from England, but we leave the words "king" and "lords" out of it. What did we ever originate, except the action of the federal government upon individuals and some of the functions of the federal supreme court?

We can borrow the science of administration with safety and profit if only we read all fundamental differences of condition into its essential tenets. We have only to filter it through our constitutions, only to put it over a slow fire of criticism and distil away its foreign gases.

I know that there is a sneaking fear in some conscientiously patriotic minds that studies of European systems might signalize some foreign methods as better than some American methods; and the fear is easily to be understood. But it would scarcely be avowed in just any company.

It is the more necessary to insist upon thus putting away all prejudices against looking anywhere in the world but at home for suggestions in this study, because nowhere else in the whole field of politics, it would seem, can we make use of the historical, comparative method more safely than in this province of administration. Perhaps the more novel the forms we study the better. We shall the sooner learn the peculiarities of our own methods. We can never learn either our own weaknesses or our own virtues by comparing ourselves with ourselves. We are too used to the appearance and procedure of our own system to see its true significance. Perhaps even the English system is too much like our own to be used to the most profit in illustration. It is best on the whole to get entirely away from our own atmosphere and to be most careful in examining such systems as those of France and Germany. Seeing our own institutions through such *media,* we see ourselves as foreigners might see us were they to look at us without preconceptions. Of ourselves, so long as we know only ourselves, we know nothing.

Let it be noted that it is the distinction, already drawn, between administration and politics which makes the comparative method so safe in the field of administration. When we study the administrative systems of France and Germany, knowing that we are not in search of *political* principles, we need not care a peppercorn for the constitutional or political reasons which Frenchmen or Germans give for their practices when explaining them to us. If I see a murderous fellow sharpening a knife cleverly, I can borrow his way of sharpening the knife without borrowing his probable intention to commit murder with it; and so, if I see a monarchist dyed in the wool managing a public bureau well, I can learn his business methods without changing one of my republican spots. He may serve his king; I will continue to serve the people; but I should like to serve my sovereign as well as he serves his. By keeping this distinction in view—that is, by studying administration as a means of putting our own politics into convenient practice, as a means of making what is democratically politic towards all administratively possible towards each—we are on perfectly safe ground, and can learn without error what foreign systems have to teach us. We thus devise an adjusting weight for our comparative method of study. We can thus scrutinize the anatomy of foreign governments without fear of getting any of their diseases into our veins; dissect alien systems without apprehension of blood-poisoning.

Our own politics must be the touchstone for all theories. The principles on which to base a science of administration for America must be principles which have democratic policy very much at heart. And, to suit American habit, all general theories must, as theories, keep modestly in the background, not in open argument only, but even in our own minds—lest opinions satisfactory only to the standards of the library should be dogmatically used, as if they must be quite as satisfactory to the standards of practical politics as well. Doctrinaire devices must be postponed to tested practices. Arrangements not only sanctioned by conclusive experience elsewhere but also congenial to American habit must be preferred without hesitation to theoretical perfection. In a word, steady, practical statesmanship must come first, closest doctrine second. The cosmopolitan what-to-do must always be commanded by the American how-to-do-it.

Our duty is to supply the best possible life to a *federal* organization, to systems within systems; to make town, city, county, state, and federal governments live with a like strength and an equally assured healthfulness, keeping each unquestionably its own master and yet making all interdependent with mutual helpfulness. The task is great and important enough to attract the best minds.

This interlacing of local self-government with federal self-government is quite a modern conception. It is not like the arrangements of imperial federation in Germany. There local government is not yet, fully, local *self*-government. The bureaucrat is everywhere busy. His efficiency springs out of *esprit de corps,* out of care to make ingratiating obeisance to the authority of a superior, or, at best, out of the soil of a sensitive conscience. He serves, not the public, but an irresponsible minister. The question for us is, how shall our series of governments within governments be so administered that it shall always be to the interest of the public officer to serve, not his superior alone but the community also, with the best efforts of his talents and the soberest service of his conscience? How shall such service be made to his commonest interest by contributing abundantly to his sustenance, to his dearest interest by furthering his ambition, and to his highest interest by advancing his honor and establishing his character? And how shall this be done alike for the local part and for the national whole?

If we solve this problem we shall again pilot the world. There is a tendency—is there not?—a tendency as yet dim, but already steadily impulsive and clearly destined to prevail, towards, first the confederation of parts of empires like the British, and finally of great states themselves. Instead of centralization of power, there is to be wide union with tolerated divisions of prerogative. This is a tendency towards the American type—of governments joined with governments for the pursuit of common purposes, in honorary equality and honorable subordination. Like principles of civil liberty are everywhere fostering like methods of government; and if comparative studies of the ways and means of government should enable us to offer suggestions which will practicably combine openness and vigor in the ad-ministration of such governments with ready docility to all serious, well-sustained public criticism, they will have approved themselves worthy to be ranked among the highest and most fruitful of the great departments of political study. That they will issue in such suggestions I confidently hope.

Notes

1. *Essay on Sir William Pitt.*
2. *Politik, S. 467.*

2

Politics and Administration

Frank J. Goodnow

If we analyze the organization of any concrete government, we shall find that there are three kinds of authorities which are engaged in the execution of the state will. These are, in the first place, the authorities which apply the law in concrete cases where controversies arise owing to the failure of private individuals or public authorities to observe the rights of others. Such authorities are known as judicial authorities. They are, in the second place, the authorities which have the general supervision of the execution of the state will, and which are commonly referred to as executive authorities. They are, finally, the authorities which are attending to the scientific, technical, and, so to speak, commercial activities of the government, and which are in all countries, where such activities have attained prominence, known as administrative authorities.

As government becomes more complex these three authorities, all of which are engaged in the execution of the will of the state, tend to become more and more differentiated. The first to become so differentiated are the judicial authorities. Not only is this differentiation of the judicial authorities first in point of time, it is also the clearest. Indeed, it is so clear in some instances as to lead many students, as has been pointed out, to mark off the activity of the judicial authorities as a separate power or function of government.

Enough has been said, it is believed, to show that there are two distinct functions of government, and that their differentiation results in a differentiation, though less complete, of the organs of government provided by the formal governmental system. These two functions of government may for purposes of convenience be designated respectively as Politics and Administration. Politics has to do with policies or expressions of the state will. Administration has to do with the execution of these policies.

It is of course true that the meaning which is here given to the word "politics" is not the meaning which has been attributed to that word by most political writers. At the same time it is submitted that the sense in which politics is here used is the sense in which it is used by most people in ordinary affairs. Thus the Century Dictionary defines "politics":

> In the narrower and more usual sense, the act or vocation of guiding or influencing the policy of a government through the organization of a party among its citizens—including, therefore, not only the ethics of government, but more especially, and often to the exclusion of ethical principles, the art of influencing public opinion, attracting and marshalling voters, and obtaining and distributing public patronage, so far as the possession of offices may depend upon the political opinions or political services of individuals.

An explanation of the word "administration" is not perhaps so necessary, since in scientific parlance it has not as yet acquired so fixed a meaning as has "politics." Block, in his *Dictionnaire de l'administration française*, defines "administration" as: "L'ensemble des services publiques destinés à concourir à l'exécution de la pensée du gouvernement et à l'application des lois d'intérêt general." The Century Dictionary speaks of it as: "The duty or duties of the administrator; specifically, the executive functions of government, consisting in the exercise of all the powers and duties of government, both general and local, which are neither legislative nor judicial."

These definitions, it will be noticed, both lay stress upon the fact that politics has to do with the guiding or influencing of governmental policy, while administration has to do with the execution of that policy. It is these two functions which it is here desired to differentiate, and for

---

Source: Frank J. Goodnow, Politics and Administration: A Study in Government (New York: Russell & Russell, 1900), pp. 17–26.

which the words "politics" and "administration" have been chosen.

The use of the word "administration" in this connection is unfortunately somewhat misleading, for the word when accompanied by the definite article is also used to indicate a series of governmental authorities. "The administration" means popularly the most important executive or administrative authorities. "Administration," therefore, when used as indicative of function, is apt to promote the idea that this function of government is to be found exclusively in the work of what are commonly referred to as executive or administrative authorities. These in their turn are apt to be regarded as confined to the discharge of the function of administration. Such, however, is rarely the case in any political system, and is particularly not the case in the American governmental system. The American legislature discharges very frequently the function of administration through its power of passing special acts. The American executive has an important influence on the discharge of the function of politics through the exercise of its veto power.

Further, in the United States, the words "administration" and "administrative," as indicative of governmental function, are commonly used by the courts in a very loose way. The attempt was made at the time of the formation of our governmental system, as has been pointed out, to incorporate into it the principle of the separation of powers. What had been a somewhat nebulous theory of political science thus became a rigid legal doctrine. What had been a somewhat attractive political theory in its nebulous form became at once an unworkable and unapplicable rule of law.

To avoid the inconvenience resulting from the attempt made to apply it logically to our governmental system, the judges of the United States have been accustomed to call "administrative" any power which was not in their eyes exclusively and unqualifiedly legislative, executive, or judicial, and to permit such a power to be exercised by any authority.[1]

While this habit on the part of the judges makes the selection of the word "administration" somewhat unfortunate; at the same time it is indicative of the fact to which attention has been more than once directed, that although the differentiation of two functions of government is clear, the assignment of such functions to separate authorities is impossible.

Finally, the different position assigned in different states to the organ to which most of the work of executing the will of the state has been intrusted, has resulted in quite different conceptions in different states of what has been usually called administration. For administration has been conceived of as the function of the executing, that is, the executive, authority. Recently, however, writers on administration have seen that, from the point of view both of theoretical speculation and of practical expediency, administration should not be regarded as merely a function of the executive authority, that is, the authority in the government which by the positive law is the executing authority. It has been seen that administration is, on the contrary, the function of executing the will of the state. It may be in some respects greater, and in others less in extent than the function of the executing authority as determined by the positive law.

There are, then, in all governmental systems two primary or ultimate functions of government, viz. the expression of the will of the state and the execution of that will. There are also in all states separate organs, each of which is mainly busied with the discharge of one of these functions. These functions are, respectively, Politics and Administration.

The Function of Politics

The function of politics, it has been shown, consists in the expression of the will of the state. Its discharge may not, however, be intrusted exclusively to any authority or any set of authorities in the government. Nor on the other hand may any authority or set of authorities be confined exclusively to its discharge. The principle of the separation of powers in its extreme form cannot, therefore, be made the basis of any concrete political organization. For this principle demands that there shall be separate authorities of the government, each of which shall be confined to the discharge of one of the functions of government which are differentiated. Actual political necessity however requires that there shall be harmony between the expression and execution of the state will.

Lack of harmony between the law and its execution results in political paralysis. A rule of conduct, *i.e.*, an expression of the state will, practically amounts to nothing if it is not executed. It is a mere *brutum fulmen*. On the other hand the execution of a rule of conduct which is not the expression of the state will is really an exercise by the executing authority of the right to express the state will.

Now in order that this harmony between the expression and the execution of the state will may be obtained, the independence either of the body which expresses the state will or of the body which executes it must be sacrificed. Either the executing authority must be subordinated to the expressing authority, or the expressing authority must be subjected to the control of the executing authority. Only in this way will there be harmony in the government. Only in this way can the expression of the real state will become an actual rule of conduct generally observed.

Finally, popular government requires that it is the executing authority which shall be subordinated to the expressing authority, since the latter in the nature of things can be made much more representative of the people than can the executing authority.

In other words, practical political necessity makes impossible the consideration of the function of politics apart from that of administration. Politics must have a certain control over administration, using the words in the broad senses heretofore attributed to them. That some such relation must exist between the two ultimate functions of government is seen when we examine the political development of any state.

If, in the hope of preventing politics from influencing administration in its details, the attempt is made to provide for the legal separation of the bodies in the government mainly charged with these two functions respectively, the tendency is for the necessary control to develop extra-legally. This is the case in the American political system.

The American political system is largely based on the fundamental principle of the separation of governmental powers. It has been impossible for the necessary control of politics over administration to develop within the formal governmental system on account of the independent position assigned by the constitutional law to executive and administrative officers. The control has therefore developed in the party system. The American political party busies itself as much with the election of administrative and executive officers as it does with the election of bodies recognized as distinctly political in character, as having to do with the expression of the state will. The party system thus secures that harmony between the functions of politics and administration which must exist if government is to be carried on successfully.[2]

On the other hand, if no attempt is made in the governmental system to provide for the separation of politics and administration, and if the governmental institutions are not put into comparatively unyielding and inflexible form through the adoption of a written constitution, the control and superintendence of the function of administration tends to be assumed by the governmental body which discharges the political function.

Notes

1. Bondy, "Separation of Government Powers," *Columbia College Series in History, Economics and Public Law* 5: 202 *et seq.*
2. Mr. H. J. Ford in his book entitled *The Rise and Growth of American Politics,* a most valuable and interesting work, is the first writer to call attention to the fact that this most important duty has been assumed by the political party in the American system of government.

3

Scientific Management

Frederick W. Taylor

What I want to try to prove to you and make clear to you is that the principles of scientific management when properly applied, and when a sufficient amount of time has been given to make them really effective, must in all cases produce far larger and better results, both for the employer and the employees, than can possibly be obtained under even this very rare type of management which I have been outlining, namely, the management of "initiative and incentive," in which those on the management's side deliberately give a very large incentive to their workmen, and in return the workmen respond by working to the very best of their ability at all times in the interest of their employers.

I want to show you that scientific management is even far better than this rare type of management.

The first great advantage which scientific management has over the management of initiative and incentive is that under scientific management the initiative of the workmen—that is, their hard work, their good will, their ingenuity—is obtained practically with absolute regularity, while under even the best of the older type of management this initiative is only obtained spasmodically and somewhat irregularly. This obtaining, however, of the initiative of the workmen is the lesser of the two great causes which make scientific management better for both sides than the older type of management. By far the greater gain under scientific management comes from the new, the very great, and the extraordinary burdens and duties which are voluntarily assumed by those on the management's side.

These new burdens and new duties are so unusual and so great that they are to the men used to managing under the old school almost inconceivable. These duties and burdens voluntarily assumed under scientific management, by those on the management's side, have been divided and classified into four different groups and these four types of new duties assumed by the management have (rightly or wrongly) been called the "principles of scientific management."

The first of these four groups of duties taken over by the management is the deliberate gathering in on the part of those on the management's side of all of the great mass of traditional knowledge, which in the past has been in the heads of the workmen, and in the physical skill and knack of the workman, which he has acquired through years of experience. The duty of gathering in of all this great mass of traditional knowledge and then recording it, tabulating it, and, in many cases, finally reducing it to laws, rules, and even to mathematical formulae, is voluntarily assumed by the scientific managers. And later, when these laws, rules, and formulae are applied to the everyday work of all the workmen of the establishment, through the intimate and hearty cooperation of those on the management's side, they invariably result, first, in producing a very much larger output per man, as well as an output of a better and higher quality; and, second, in enabling the company to pay much higher wages to their workmen; and, third, in giving to the company a larger profit. The first of these principles, then, may be called the development of a science to replace the old rule-of-thumb knowledge of the workmen; that is, the knowledge which the workmen had, and which was, in many cases, quite as exact as that which is finally obtained by the management, but which the workmen nevertheless in nine hundred and ninety-nine cases out of a thousand kept in their heads, and of which there was no permanent or complete record.

A very serious objection has been made to the use of the word "science" in this connection. I am much amused to find that this objection comes chiefly from the professors of this

Source: Excerpt from: Testimony before the U.S. House of Representatives, January 25, 1912.

country. They resent the use of the word science for anything quite so trivial as the ordinary, every-day affairs of life. I think the proper answer to this criticism is to quote the definition recently given by a professor who is, perhaps, as generally recognized as a thorough scientist as any man in the country—President McLaurin, of the Institute of Technology, of Boston. He recently defined the word science as "classified or organized knowledge of any kind." And surely the gathering in of knowledge which, as previously stated, has existed, but which was in an unclassified condition in the minds of workmen, and then the reducing of this knowledge to laws and rules and formulae, certainly represents the organization and classification of knowledge, even though it may not meet with the approval of some people to have it called science.

The second group of duties which are voluntarily assumed by those on the management's side, under scientific management, is the scientific selection and then the progressive development of the workmen. It becomes the duty of those on the management's side to deliberately study the character, the nature, and the performance of each workman with a view to finding out his limitations on the one hand, but even more important, his possibilities for development on the other hand; and then, as deliberately and as systematically to train and help and teach this workman, giving him, wherever it is possible, those opportunities for advancement which will finally enable him to do the highest and most interesting and most profitable class of work for which his natural abilities fit him, and which are open to him in the particular company in which he is employed. This scientific selection of the workman and his development is not a single act; it goes on from year to year and is the subject of continual study on the part of the management.

The third of the principles of scientific management is the bringing of the science and the scientifically selected and trained workmen together. I say "bringing together" advisedly, because you may develop all the science that you please, and you may scientifically select and train workmen just as much as you please, but unless some man or some men bring the science and the workmen together all your labor will be lost. We are all of us so constituted that about three-fourths of the time we will work according to whatever method suits us best; that is, we will practice the science or we will not practice it; we will do our work in accordance with the laws of the science or in our own old way, just as we see fit unless some one is there to see that we do it in accordance with the principles of the science. Therefore I use advisedly the words "bringing the science and the workman together." It is unfortunate, however, that this word "bringing" has rather a disagreeable sound, a rather forceful sound; and, in a way, when it is first heard it puts one out of touch with what we have come to look upon as the modern tendency. The time for using the word "bringing" with a sense of forcing, in relation to most matters, has gone by; but I think that I may soften this word down in its use in this particular case by saying that nine-tenths of the trouble with those of us who have been engaged in helping people to change from the older type of management to the new management—that is, to scientific management-that nine-tenths of our trouble has been to "bring" those on the management's side to do their fair share of the work and only one-tenth of our trouble has come on the workman's side. Invariably we find very great opposition on the part of those on the management's side to do their new duties and comparatively little opposition on the part of the workmen to cooperate in doing their new duties. So that the word "bringing" applies much more forcefully to those on the management's side than to those on the workman's side.

The fourth of the principles of scientific management is perhaps the most difficult of all of the four principles of scientific management for the average man to understand. It consists of an almost equal division of the actual work of the establishment between the workmen, on the one hand, and the management, on the other hand. That is, the work which under the old type of management practically all was done by the workman, under the new is divided into two great divisions, and one of these divisions is deliberately handed over to those on the management's side. This new division of work, this new share of the work assumed by those on the management's side, is so great that you will, I think, be able to understand it better in a numerical way when I tell you that in a machine shop, which, for instance, is doing an intricate business—I do not refer to a manufacturing company, but, rather, to an engineering company; that is, a machine shop which builds a variety of machines and is not engaged in manufacturing them, but, rather, in constructing them—will have one man on the management's side to every three workmen; that is, this immense share of the work—one third—has been deliberately taken out of the workman's hands and handed over to those on the management's side. And it is due to this actual sharing of the work between the two sides more than to any other one element that there has never (until this last summer) been a single strike under scientific management. In a machine shop, again, under this new type of management there is hardly a single act or piece of work done by any workman in the shop which is not preceded and followed by some act on the part of one of the men in the management. All day long every workman's acts are dovetailed in between corresponding acts of the management. First, the workman does something, and then a man on the management's side does something; then the man on the management's side does something, and then the workman does something; and under this intimate, close, personal cooperation between the two sides it becomes practically impossible to have a serious quarrel.

Of course I do not wish to be understood that there are never any quarrels under scientific management. There are some, but they are the very great exception, not the rule. And it is perfectly evident that while the workmen are learning to work under this new system, and while the management is learning to work under this new system, while they are both learning, each side to cooperate in this intimate way with the other, there is plenty of chance for disagreement and for quarrels and misunderstandings, but after both sides realize that it is utterly impossible to turn out the work of the establishment at the proper rate of speed and have it correct without this intimate, personal cooperation, when both sides realize that it is utterly impossible for either one to be successful without the intimate, brotherly cooperation of the other, the friction, the disagreements, and quarrels are reduced to a minimum. So, I think that scientific management can be justly and truthfully characterized as management in which harmony is the rule rather than discord.

There is one illustration of the application of the principles of scientific management with which all of us are familiar and with which most of us have been familiar since we were small boys, and I think this instance represents one of the best illustrations of the application of the principles of scientific management. I refer to the management of a first-class American baseball team. In such a team you will find almost all of the elements of scientific management.

You will see that the science of doing every little act that is done by every player on the baseball field has been developed. Every single element of the game of baseball has been the subject of the most intimate, the closest study of many men, and, finally, the best way of doing each act that takes place on the baseball field has been fairly well agreed upon and established as a standard throughout the country. The players have not only been told the best way of making each important motion or play, but they have been taught, coached, and trained to it through months of drilling. And I think that every man who has watched first-class play, or who knows anything of the management of the modern baseball team, realizes fully the utter impossibility of winning with the best team of individual players that was ever gotten together unless every man on the team obeys the signals or orders of the coach and obeys them at once when the coach gives those orders; that is, without the intimate cooperation between all members of the team and the management, which is characteristic of scientific management.

4

The Movement for Budgetary Reform in the States

William F. Willoughby

Introduction: Origin of Movement

Of few movements for political reform is it feasible to determine precisely the causes to which it owes its rise or to fix exactly the date of its origin. If one seeks for an explanation of the modern movement, now under full way, for the adoption by the several governing bodies of the United States of a budget as the central and controlling feature of their systems of financial administration, it must be found in a number of more or less distinct movements which have each found in this device an important means for achieving or promoting the object sought.

The Budget as an Instrument of Democracy Among these first place must be given to that effort continuously being put forth to devise means by which popular government, in the sense that the affairs of government shall be conducted in conformity with the popular will, may become a reality in fact as in name. It is hardly necessary to point out that the popular will cannot be intelligently formulated nor expressed unless the public has adequate means for knowing currently how governmental affairs have been conducted in the past, what are present conditions and what program for work in the future are under consideration. Of all means devised for meeting this requirement no single one approaches in completeness and effectiveness a budget if properly prepared. It at once serves to make known past operations, present conditions and future proposals, definitely locates responsibility and furnishes the means for control. Professor A. R. Hatton is thus justified when he says:

> Above and beyond its relation to economy and efficiency in public affairs it (the budget) may be made one of the most potent instruments of democracy. Given at least manhood suffrage, any government so organized as to produce and carry out a scientific budget system will be susceptible of extensive and intelligent popular control. On the contrary, those governments whatever their other virtues, which fail to provide adequate budget methods will neither reach the maximum of efficiency nor prove to be altogether responsible to the people.
>
> A new spirit in American politics is manifesting itself in the powerful movement for the reform of governmental organization and procedure in the interest of popular control and efficiency. There are naturally many features in the program for the accomplishment of this twofold object. No single change would add so largely to both democracy and efficiency as the introduction of proper budget methods.[1]

The Budget as an Instrument for Correlating Legislative and Executive Action Closely associated with this demand that more effective means be provided by which the popular will and the principle of popular control may be made effective is the feeling that the present working conditions of our legislative bodies and particularly their relations to the executive branch of government are far from satisfactory. The conviction has been growing that a mistake has been made in seeking to make of our legislatures boards of directors to concern themselves with the details of the activities, organization and methods of business of administrative services; that the true function of the legislature should be that of acting as an organ of public opinion in the larger sense and as the medium through which those concerned with the actual administration

---

Source: William F. Willoughby, The Movement for Budgetary Reform in the States (New York: D. Appleton and Company for the Institute for Government Research, 1918), pp. 1–8.

of affairs should be supervised, controlled, and held to a rigid accountability for the manner in which they discharge their duties.

This has led inevitably to the position that upon the executive should be placed the responsibility for the formulation of work programs and the decision, in the first instance at least, of the means to be employed in the putting of these programs into execution. This would appear to carry with it a great strengthening of the executive at the expense of the legislative branch of government. So it does in one sense. It is a canon of administrative science, however, that when discretionary powers and authority are increased a corresponding increase should be made in the means of controlling and supervising the manner in which these augmented powers are exercised. If legislatures are to surrender to the executive increased powers in respect to the conduct of administrative affairs, they must strengthen the means by which they may assure themselves that these powers are properly exercised. There are two methods by which superior direction, supervision and control may be exerted, by specification in advance, or, by the establishment of a proper accounting and reporting system, by establishing means through which full information may be currently available regarding the manner in which delegated authority is being exercised. Legislatures are being asked to give up the first method of control. If they do so, it is imperative that the conditions stated in the second alternative should be met.

It is at this point that the demand for the adoption of a budget finds its place as an integral part of the movement for the improvement of the working relations between the two branches of government. In the budget is to be found far the most effective means that has yet been devised whereby larger responsibility for the formulation and execution of financial and work programs may be conferred upon the executive and yet the latter be held to a more rigid accountability for the manner in which this responsibility is discharged. In a very true sense, therefore, the movement for the adoption of budgetary systems by our governing bodies is an integral and essential part of the whole greater movement for the accomplishment of governmental reforms generally.

The Budget as an Instrument for Securing Administrative Efficiency and Economy Still another movement which has logically resulted in the demand for budgetary reforms is that for placing the purely technical methods of governmental organization and administration upon a more efficient and economical basis. The question has been raised as to whether there are any inherent reasons why government officers should not be held to the same standards of efficiency and honesty as are demanded in the business world. The demand that they should be has become more insistent as the tasks imposed upon governments have become more numerous and complex and, in many cases, more nearly similar to the character of the tasks which private corporations are called upon to perform. In the business world it is recognized that no undertaking of magnitude, certainly none performed under a corporate form of organization, can be efficiently administered which does not have a system of accounts and reports that will permit the directing body, the board of directors, and the stockholders, to secure a clear picture of past operations, present conditions and future programs of activities. In all proposals looking to the reform of methods of business of governmental bodies, chief attention has consequently been placed upon the demand for the improvement of the methods by which their financial affairs are conducted. It is inconsistent to the last degree that governments should insist that corporations controlled by them should have systems of accounting and reporting corresponding to the most approved principles of modern accountancy while not providing for equally efficient systems for the management of their own financial affairs. The demand for improved methods of public administration has thus inevitably centered primarily upon the demand for improved methods of financial administration and, in order that this may be secured, upon the specific demand for the adoption of a budgetary system as the central feature of such an improved system.

Use of Budget First Demanded as a Feature of Municipal Reform Turning now to a history of the movement itself, the point of departure must be found in the great movement which has been so much in evidence during the present generation, for the improvement of methods of municipal administration. After repeated disappointments persons interested in municipal reform came to an appreciation that permanent reform was not to be accomplished by the putting in the field of citizens' tickets and the ousting of officials who subordinated the public good to private gain. More and more it was borne in upon them that if lasting improvements were to be effected, the system of municipal government itself and methods of administration had to be changed, that there must be established principles of administration and means of direction, supervision and control that would automatically, as it were, result in better administration or at least make it possible for all interested parties to determine, without the necessity for special investigations, whether affairs were being efficiently and economically administered or the reverse. It was found, in a word, that the problem had to be attacked from the technical as well as the moral standpoint.

This change in the method of approach found expression not only in the altered character of the work attempted by such organizations as the National Municipal League, but in the appreciation that a thorough study of the technical problems of municipal administration with a view to the formulation of concrete measures of reform could only be successfully undertaken by a permanent organization specially established and with a technically competent staff to undertake this work. Appreciation of this led to the creation by public spirited individuals of the large number of bureaus of municipal research which have contributed so powerfully during recent years to the improvement of methods of municipal administration in the United States. This is not the place to attempt any general characterization of the work of these bodies. It is only necessary for us to say that these bureaus have almost without exception concentrated a large part of their attention upon problems of financial administration and that all, likewise without exception, have bent their energies towards the securing by the cities with whose operations they concerned themselves of a budgetary system. This action was in large measure predicated upon the proposition that a municipality partakes in large measure of the characteristics of an ordinary business corporation and should be operated as such. This has meant that there should be employed by it the methods and agencies which have been found indispensable to the efficient operation of large business corporations. This view accepted, the demand at once arose that the expenditures of the city should be brought into direct relation to its possible or actual revenues and be based upon estimates and recommendations emanating from the spending departments. The advantage was at once seen of having the estimates and recommendations thus made by the several administrative services submitted to some central executive organ vested with authority to revise and reduce them when necessary and to bring them into due relation and proportion to one another. This was seen to be essential since spending departments are concerned primarily each in its own activities and are, therefore, interested in getting the largest possible allotment of funds from the general treasury. If the latter is to be protected and the relative as well as the absolute utility of different classes of work is to be determined, some organ must exist within the administration which is not itself a spending department but has the special function of balancing demands of spending departments and of protecting the general treasury from the demands being made upon it beyond its resources.

This fundamental feature was appreciated by municipal reformers prior to the establishment of bureaus of municipal research. Thus the National Municipal League as early as 1899 included in its draft of a model municipal corporation act a section providing that:

> It shall be the duty of the Mayor from time to time to make such recommendations to the Council as he may deem to be for the welfare of the city and on the _____ day of _____ in each year to submit to the Council the annual budget of current expenses of the city, any item in which may be reduced or omitted by the Council; but the Council shall not increase any item in nor the total of said budget.

The course of budgetary reform in municipalities was also materially promoted by the Bureau of the Census through the continuous pressure which it exerted upon municipalities to improve their methods of accounting and reporting and especially through the standard classification of municipal expenditures which it worked out in connection with experts representing the accounting profession and the National Municipal League. In later years the development of the commission and city manager types of municipal government, and the policy adopted by a number of the leading cities in their recent charter revisions to provide for boards of estimates among whose functions the most important duty was that of passing upon and revising estimates as originally framed by the spending departments, have likewise contributed powerfully to the promotion of budgetary reform. These all represent the definite adoption of the most fundamental principle of a budget that there should be a central budget framing organ to stand between the estimating departments and the fund-granting authority. In few, if any, cases, however, has the principle been adopted of vesting final authority in respect to the framing of a budget in the chief executive officer.

After all is said, however, to the bureaus of municipal research and allied organizations established by boards of trade and other citizen agencies belongs the chief credit for the persistent demand that a budget be made the foundation stone of the system of financial administration of all municipalities. Not only have they urged this without ceasing but they have done a large amount of work in the way of working out and installing systems of financial administration in various cities resting on this basis.

Movement for Budgetary Reform Carried Over to the States It was inevitable that the movement for budgetary reform in municipalities, once fairly under way, should be carried over to efforts looking to the improvement of state governments. Every reason dictating the necessity for this reform in the case of municipalities existed with increased force in the case of these governments. Here the conditions to be met, however, were much more difficult than those obtaining in the case of municipal governments. Broadly speaking, the administrative branch of municipal governments corresponds to the integrated type of organization, with the mayor at the head as administrator in chief. It has been pointed out in our consideration of the nature and functions of a budget[2] how essential is this form of organization to the proper operation of a budgetary system. It is unfortunate, both from the standpoint of budgetary reform and that of good administration generally, that this condition obtains in but few, if any, of the states. As is well known, in most if not all of the states the administrative branch consists of a large number of practically independent services. Only in small degree has the governor any positive powers of direction or any adequate power to control. The line of authority runs direct in each case to the legislature; and the authority of this body is often limited by the fact that the heads of these services owe their election to office, not to it, but to the people. It results from this that in the case of most, if not all, of the states the problem of the introduction of a thoroughly efficient budgetary system involves that of fundamentally recasting their systems of government.

Notes

1. Foreword to "Public Budgets," *Annals of the American Academy of Political and Social Science* (November 1915).
2. William F. Willoughby, *The Problem of a National Budget* (New York: D. Appleton, 1918), pp. 1–29.

5

Bureaucracy

Max Weber

1. Characteristics of Bureaucracy

Modern officialdom functions in the following specific manner:

I. *There is the principle of fixed and official jurisdictional areas, which are generally ordered by rules, that is, by laws or administrative regulations.* [Italics added]
   1. The regular activities required for the purposes of the bureaucratically governed structure are distributed in a fixed way as official duties.
   2. The authority to give the commands required for the discharge of these duties is distributed in a stable way and is strictly delimited by rules concerning the coercive means, physical, sacerdotal, or otherwise, which may be placed at the disposal of officials.
   3. Methodical provision is made for the regular and continuous fulfillment of these duties and for the execution of the corresponding rights; only persons who have the generally regulated qualifications to serve are employed.

   In public and lawful government these three elements constitute "bureaucratic authority." In private economic domination, they constitute bureaucratic "management." Bureaucracy, thus understood, is fully developed in political and ecclesiastical communities only in the modern state, and, in the private economy, only in the most advanced institutions of capitalism. Permanent and public office authority, with fixed jurisdiction, is not the historical rule but rather the exception. This is so even in large political structures such as those of the ancient Orient, the Germanic and Mongolian empires of conquest, or of many feudal structures of state. In all these cases, the ruler executes the most important measures through personal trustees, table-companions, or court-servants. Their commissions and authority are not precisely delimited and are temporarily called into being for each case.

II. *The principles of office hierarchy and of levels of graded authority mean a firmly ordered system of super- and subordination in which there is a supervision of the lower offices by the higher ones.* Such a system offers the governed the possibility of appealing the decision of a lower office to its higher authority, in a definitely regulated manner. With the full development of the bureaucratic type, the office hierarchy is monocratically organized. The principle of hierarchical office authority is found in all bureaucratic structures: in state and ecclesiastical structures as well as in large party organizations and private enterprises. It does not matter for the character of bureaucracy whether its authority is called "private" or "public." When the principle of jurisdictional "competency" is fully carried through, hierarchical subordination—at least in public office—does not mean that the "higher" authority is simply authorized to take over the business of the "lower." Indeed, the opposite is the rule. Once established and having fulfilled its task, an office tends to continue in existence and be held by another incumbent.

III. *The management of the modern office is based upon written documents ("the files"), which are preserved in their original or draught form.* There is, therefore, a staff of subaltern officials and scribes of all sorts. The body of officials actively engaged in a "public" office, along with the respective apparatus of material implements and the files, make up a "bureau." In private enterprise, "the bureau" is often called "the office."

In principle, the modern organization of the civil service separates the bureau from the private domicile of the official, and, in general, bureaucracy segregates official activity as something distinct from the sphere of private life. Public monies and equipment are divorced from the private property of the official. This condition is everywhere the product of a long development. Nowadays, it is found in public as well as in private enterprises; in the latter, the principle extends even to the leading entrepreneur. In principle, the executive office is separated from the household, business from private correspondence, and business assets from private fortunes. The more consistently the modern type of business management has been carried through the more are these separations the case. The beginnings of this process are to be found as early as the Middle Ages.

It is the peculiarity of the modern entrepreneur that he conducts himself as the "first official" of his enterprise, in the very same way in which the ruler of a specifically modern bureaucratic state spoke of himself as "the first servant" of the state. The idea that the bureau activities of the state are intrinsically different in character from the management of private economic offices is a continental European notion and, by way of contrast, is totally foreign to the American way.

IV. *Office management, at least all specialized office management—and such management is distinctly modern—usually presupposes thorough and expert training.* This increasingly holds for the modern executive and employee of private enterprises, in the same manner as it holds for the state official.

V. *When the office is fully developed, official activity demands the full working capacity of the official, irrespective of the fact that his obligatory time in the bureau may be firmly delimited.* In the normal case, this is only the product of a long development, in the public as well as in the private office. Formerly, in all cases, the normal state of affairs was reversed: official business was discharged as a secondary activity.

VI. *The management of the office follows general rules, which are more or less stable, more or less exhaustive, and which can be learned.* Knowledge of these rules represents a special technical learning which the officials possess. It involves jurisprudence, or administrative or business management.

The reduction of modern office management to rules is deeply embedded in its very nature. The theory of modern public administration, for instance, assumes that the authority to order certain matters by decree—which has been legally granted to public authorities—does not entitle the bureau to regulate the matter by commands given for each case, but only to regulate the matter abstractly. This stands in extreme contrast to the regulation of all relationships through individual privileges and bestowals of favor, which is absolutely dominant in patrimonialism, at least in so far as such relationships are not fixed by sacred tradition.

2. The Position of the Official

All this results in the following for the internal and external position of the official:

I. *Office holding is a "vocation."* This is shown, first, in the requirement of a firmly prescribed course of training, which demands the entire capacity for work for a long period of time, and in the generally prescribed and special examinations which are prerequisites of employment. Furthermore, the position of the official is in the nature of a duty. This determines the internal structure of his relations, in the following manner: Legally and actually, office holding is not considered a source to be exploited for rents or emoluments, as was normally the case during the Middle Ages and frequently up to the threshold of recent times. Nor is office holding considered a usual exchange of services for equivalents, as is the case with free labor contracts. Entrance into an office, including one in the private economy, is considered an acceptance of a specific obligation of faithful management in return for a secure existence. It is decisive for the specific nature of modern loyalty to an office that, in the pure type, it does not establish a relationship to a *person*, like the vassal's or disciple's faith in feudal or in patrimonial relations of authority. Modern loyalty is devoted to impersonal and functional purposes. Behind the functional purposes, of course, "ideas of culture-values" usually stand. These are *ersatz* for the earthly or supra-mundane personal master: ideas such as "state," "church," "community," "party," or "enterprise" are thought of as being realized in a community; they provide an ideological halo for the master.

The political official—at least in the fully developed modern state—is not considered the personal servant of a ruler. Today, the bishop, the priest, and the preacher are in fact no longer, as in early Christian times, holders of purely personal charisma. The supra-mundane and sacred values which they offer are given to everybody who seems to be worthy of them and who asks for them. In former times, such leaders acted upon the personal command of their master; in principle, they were responsible only to him. Nowadays, in spite of the partial survival of the old theory, such religious leaders are officials in the service of a functional purpose, which in the present-day "church" has become routinized and, in turn, ideologically hallowed.

II. *The personal position of the official is patterned in the following way:*

1. Whether he is in a private office or a public bureau, the modern official always strives and usually enjoys a distinct *social esteem* as compared with the governed. His social position is guaranteed by the prescriptive rules of rank order and, for the political official, by special definitions of the criminal code against "insults of officials" and "contempt" of state and church authorities.

The actual social position of the official is normally highest where, as in old civilized countries, the following conditions prevail: a strong demand for administration by trained experts; a strong and stable social differentiation, where the official predominantly derives from socially and economically privileged strata because of the social distribution of power; or where the costliness of the required training and status conventions are binding upon him. The possession of educational certificates—to be discussed elsewhere—are usually linked with qualification for office. Naturally, such certificates or patents enhance the "status element" in the social position of the official. For the rest this status factor in individual cases is explicitly and impassively acknowledged; for example, in the prescription that the acceptance or rejection of an aspirant to an official career depends upon the consent ("election") of the members of the official body. This is the case in the German army with the office corps. Similar phenomena, which promote this guild-like closure of officialdom, are typically found in patrimonial and, particularly, in prebendal officialdoms of the past. The desire to resurrect such phenomena in changed forms is by no means infrequent among modern bureaucrats. For instance, they have played a role among the demands of the quite proletarian and expert officials (the *tretyj* element) during the Russian revolution.

Usually the social esteem of the officials as such is especially low where the demand for expert administration and the dominance of status conventions are weak. This is especially the case in the United States; it is often the case in new settlements by virtue of their wide fields for profitmaking and the great instability of their social stratification.

2. The pure type of bureaucratic official is *appointed* by a superior authority. An official elected by the governed is not a purely bureaucratic figure. Of course, the formal existence of an election does not by itself mean that no appointment hides behind the election—in the state, especially, appointment by party chiefs. Whether or not this is the case does not depend upon legal statutes but upon the way in which the party mechanism functions. Once firmly organized, the parties can turn a formally free election into the mere acclamation of a candidate designated by the party chief. As a rule, however, a formally free election is turned into a fight, conducted according to definite rules, for votes in favor of one of two designated candidates.

In all circumstances, the designation of officials by means of an election among the governed modifies the strictness of hierarchical subordination. In principle, an official who is so elected has an autonomous position opposite the superordinate official. The elected official does not derive his position "from above" but "from below" or at least not from a superior authority of the official hierarchy but from powerful party men ("bosses"), who also determine his further career. The career of the elected official is not, or at least not primarily, dependent upon his chief in the administration. The official who is not elected but appointed by a chief normally functions more exactly, from a technical point of view, because, all other circumstances being equal, it is more likely that purely functional points of consideration and qualities will determine his selection and career. As laymen, the governed can become acquainted with the extent to which a candidate is expertly qualified for office only in terms of experience, and hence only after his service. Moreover, in every sort of selection of officials by election, parties quite naturally give decisive weight not to expert considerations but to the services a follower renders to the party boss. This holds for all kinds of procurement of officials by elections, for the designation of formally free, elected officials by party bosses when they determine the slate of candidates, or the free appointment by a chief who has himself been elected. The contrast, however, is relative: substantially similar conditions hold where legitimate monarchs and their subordinates appoint officials, except that the influence of the followings are then less controllable.

Where the demand for administration by trained experts is considerable, and the party followings have to recognize an intellectually developed, educated, and freely moving "public opinion," the use of unqualified officials falls back upon the party in power at the next election. Naturally, this is more likely to happen when the officials are appointed by the chief. The demand for a trained administration now exists in the United States, but in the large cities, where immigrant votes are "corralled?," there is, of course, no educated public opinion. Therefore, popular elections of the administrative chief and also of his subordinate officials usually endanger the expert qualification of the official as well as the precise functioning of the bureaucratic mechanism. It also weakens the dependence of the officials upon the hierarchy. This holds at least for the large administrative bodies that are difficult to supervise. The superior qualification and integrity of federal judges, appointed by the President, as over against elected judges in the United States is well known, although both types of officials have been selected primarily in terms of party considerations. The great changes in American metropolitan administrations demanded by reformers have proceeded essentially from elected mayors working with an apparatus of officials who were appointed by them. These reforms have thus come about in a "Caesarist" fashion. Viewed technically, as an organized form of authority, the efficiency of "Caesarism," which often grows out of democracy, rests in general upon the position of the "Caesar" as a free trustee of the masses (of the army or of the citizenry), who is unfettered by tradition. The "Caesar" is thus the unrestrained master of a body of highly qualified military officers and officials whom he selects freely and personally without regard to tradition or to any other considerations. This "rule of the personal genius," however, stands in contradiction to the formally "democratic" principle of a universally elected officialdom.

3. Normally, the position of the official is held for life, at least in public bureaucracies; and this is increasingly the case for all similar structures. As a factual rule, *tenure for life* is presupposed, even where the giving of notice or periodic reappointment occurs. In contrast to the worker in a private enterprise, the official normally holds tenure. Legal or actual life-tenure, however, is not recognized as the official's right to the possession of office, as was the case with many structures of authority in the past. Where legal guarantees against arbitrary dismissal or transfer are developed, they merely serve to guarantee a strictly objective discharge of specific office duties free from all personal considerations. In Germany, this is the case for all juridical and, increasingly, for all administrative officials.

   Within the bureaucracy, therefore, the measure of "independence," legally guaranteed by tenure, is not always a source of increased status for the official whose position is thus secured. Indeed, often the reverse holds, especially in old cultures and communities that are highly differentiated. In such communities, the stricter the subordination under the arbitrary rule of the master, the more it guarantees the maintenance of the conventional seigneurial style of living for the official. Because of the very absence of these legal guarantees of tenure, the conventional esteem for the official may rise in the same way as, during the Middle Ages, the esteem of the nobility of office rose at the expense of esteem for the freemen, and as the king's judge surpassed that of the people's judge. In Germany, the military officer or the administrative official can be removed from office at any time, or at least far more readily than the "independent judge," who never pays with loss of his office for even the grossest offense against the "code of honor" or against social conventions of the salon. For this very reason, if other things are equal, in the eyes of the master stratum the judge is considered less qualified for social intercourse than are officers and administrative officials, whose greater dependence on the master is a greater guarantee of their conformity with status conventions. Of course, the average official strives for a civil-service law, which would materially secure his old age and provide increased guarantees against his arbitrary removal from office. This striving, however, has its limits. A very strong development of the "right to the office" naturally makes it more difficult to staff them with regard to technical efficiency, for such a development decreases the career-opportunities of ambitious candidates for office. This makes for the fact that officials, on the whole, do not feel their dependency upon those at the top. This lack of a feeling of dependency, however, rests primarily upon the inclination to depend upon one's equals rather than upon the socially inferior and governed strata. The present conservative movement among the Badenia clergy, occasioned by the anxiety of a presumably threatening separation of church and state, has been expressly determined by the desire not to be turned "from a master into a servant of the parish."

4. The official receives the regular *pecuniary* compensation of a normally fixed *salary* and the old age security provided by a pension. The salary is not measured like a wage in terms of work done, but according to "status," that is, according to the kind of function (the "rank") and, in addition, possibly, according to the length of service. The relatively great security of the official's income, as well as the rewards of social esteem, make the office a sought-after position, especially in countries which no longer provide opportunities for colonial profits. In such countries, this situation permits relatively low salaries for officials.
5. The official is set for a "*career*" within the hierarchical order of the public service. He moves from the lower, less important, and lower paid to the higher positions. The average official naturally desires a mechanical fixing of the conditions of promotion: if not of the offices, at least of the salary levels. He wants these conditions fixed in terms of "seniority," or possibly according to grades achieved in a developed system of expert examinations. Here and there, such examinations actually form character *indelebilis* of the official and have lifelong effects on his career. To this is joined the desire to qualify the right to office and increasing tendency toward status group closure and economic security. All of this makes for a tendency to consider the offices as "prebends" of those who are qualified by educational certificates. The necessity of taking general personal and intellectual qualifications into consideration, irrespective of the often subaltern character of the educational certificate, has led to a condition in which the highest political offices, especially the positions of "ministers," are principally filled without reference to such certificates.

6

Introduction to the Study of Public Administration

Leonard D. White

Preface

Curiously enough, commentators on American political institutions have never produced a systematic analysis of our administrative system except from the point of view of the lawyer. Until the last few years even the text books have obstinately closed their eyes to this enormous terrain, studded with governmental problems of first magnitude and fascinating interest; and even today they dismiss the subject with a casual chapter. But certainly no one pretends that administration can still be put aside "as a practical detail which clerks could arrange after doctors had agreed upon principles."

The fact is that the last two decades have produced a voluminous literature dealing with the business side of government. The present volume represents an attempt to bring together the salient facts of American experience and observation and to deal with them analytically and critically. To accomplish this within the limits of a single volume is no easy task, implying as it does a constant danger of falling prey either to the Scylla of indiscriminate detail or the Charybdis of unsupported generalization. The total lack of any charted passage through these unexplored waters adds much to the hazards of the venture.

The book rests upon at least four assumptions. It assumes that administration is a — single process, substantially uniform in its essential characteristics wherever observed, and therefore avoids the study of municipal administration, state administration, or federal administration as such. It assumes that the study of administration should start from the base of management rather than the foundation of law, and is therefore more absorbed in the affairs of the American Management Association than in the decisions of the courts. It assumes that administration is still primarily an art but attaches importance to the significant tendency to transform it into a science. It assumes that administration has become, and will continue to be, the heart of the problem of modern government.

Chapter One Administration and the Modern State

Management has gradually become a profession. Its task has increased in difficulty, responsibility, and complexity, until today it touches all the sciences, from chemistry and mechanics to psychology and medicine. It calls to its service, therefore, men and women with tact and ideals, with the highest scientific qualifications and with a strong capacity for organization and leadership. It is employing lawyers and doctors, accountants and artists, and by directing their professions, is forming a supreme profession of its own, with all the implications consequent upon such a line of progress of standards, qualifications, apprenticeship, and technique.

Oliver Sheldon
Philosophy of Management

1. **The Scope and Nature of Public Administration** There is an essential unity in the process of administration, whether it be observed in city, state, or federal governments, that precludes a "stratified" classification of the subject. To treat it in terms of

Source: Reprinted with the permission of Scribner, an imprint of Simon & Schuster Adult Publishing Group, from INTRODUCTION TO THE STUDY OF PUBLIC ADMINISTRATION by Leonard D. White.

municipal administration, state administration, or national administration is to imply a distinction that in reality does not exist. The fundamental problems such as the development of personal initiative, the assurance of individual competence and integrity, responsibility, coordination, fiscal supervision, leadership, morale are in fact the same; and most of the subjects of administration defy the political boundaries of local and state government. Health administration, the licensing of medical practitioners, the control of trade, the reclamation of waste lands have little in fact actual relation to cities or counties or states as such. Nor do the respective phases of city, state, or federal government present any significant variation in the technique of their administration. At the outset, therefore, it seems important to insist that the administrative process is a unit, and to conceive it not as municipal administration, or state administration, or federal administration, but as a process common to all levels of government.

Public administration is the management of men and materials in the accomplishment of the purposes of the state. This definition emphasizes the managerial phase of administration and minimizes its legalistic and formal aspect. It relates the conduct of government business to the conduct of the affairs of any other social organization, commercial, philanthropic, religious, or educational, in all of which good management is recognized as an element essential to success. It leaves open the question to what extent the administration itself participates in formulating the purposes of the state, and avoids any controversy as to the precise nature of administrative action.[1]

The objective of public administration is the most efficient utilization of the resources at the disposal of officials and employees. These resources include not only current appropriations and material equipment in the form of public buildings, machinery, highways and canals, but also the human resources bound up in the hundreds of thousands of men and women who work for the state. In every direction good administration seeks the elimination of waste, the conservation of material and energy, and the most rapid and complete achievement of public purposes consistent with economy and the welfare of the workers.

The actual functioning of this branch of government may perhaps be made more realistic by an account of what takes place in a great department in the course of a day. For purposes of illustration a health department in a large city will suffice. Business commences at nine o'clock, when most of the employees are presumably at their desks. As they enter the office, they sign a time sheet or punch a time clock, dispose of their outer garments in lockers, exchange comment with their neighbors and settle down for the day's work. A steady stream of business develops; telephone calls from citizens, from field inspectors, and from special detail; [customer] window calls on a great variety of topics large and small; telegraphic reports from a neighboring city in which an epidemic is threatening; conferences within the bureaus; conferences between bureaus; messengers hurrying back and forth; policemen from local health stations bringing in samples for analysis, and anxious citizens seeking the results of samples brought in yesterday; a deputation from the undertakers protesting against the condition of the hospital morgues; an alderman seeking appointment for a local supporter; a score of prostitutes waiting in the anteroom for examination before appearing in the courtroom; a salesman protesting against the award of a contract for laboratory supplies; a handful of loiterers whispering in casual groups in the corridors, all seeming to the uninitiated observer the height of confusion and disorder. Further observation, however, dispels the first impression; the various kinds of work are segregated and assigned to specially trained men and women; certain types of inquiry or complaint are handled by a standardized method; forms are made out and sent on the proper route for final disposition; some business is transacted by a clerk, other business is referred to the assistant bureau chief, so that by a process of selection routine work is disposed of by the lower ranks of the service, while matters of importance are brought to the attention of the higher officials. Thus proceeds in an orderly fashion all the complicated business of the office; some spend the day making out forms, others filing correspondence, some answering telephone complaints and directing inspectors, others dictating correspondence, making bacteriological analyses, inspecting ventilation systems, granting licenses, making blue prints, while at the head of the service, the commissioner of public health maintains the necessary connections of the department with the city council and the mayor, with the party organization, with the finance committee, with the public, and with the health authorities of the state and the United States, not neglecting meanwhile to assure himself of the proper operation of the many phases of the work of the department itself.

All of this is a far cry from the Egyptian scribe who laboriously copied accounts on his roll of papyrus, but the natural history of administration connects its ancient and modern forms in an unbroken sequence of development. The process of specialization has indeed wrought a prodigious transformation in methods, but the essential administrative duties connected with military affairs, with finance, with the "king's" household are still performed with the same objectives as in ages past. What differentiates the modern public official from the scribe of antiquity is the marvelous material equipment with which he works, and the contribution which science has made, and continues to make, to his profession.

Public administration is, then, the execution of the public business; the goal of administrative activity the most expeditious, economical, and complete achievement of public programs. This obviously is not the sole objective of the state as an organized unit; the protection of private rights, the development of civic capacity and sense of civic responsibility, the due recognition of the manifold phases of public opinion, the maintenance of order, the provision of a national minimum of welfare, all bespeak the constant solicitude of the state. Administration must be correlated with other branches of government, as well as adjusted to the immense amount of private effort which in America far more than elsewhere supplements public enterprise. The following chapter deals with these adjustments, but here it is desirable to differentiate the adjacent fields of administration and administrative law.

It is said that "administrative law is that part of the public law which fixes the organization and determines the competence of the administrative authorities, and indicates to the individual remedies for the violation of his rights."[2] This definition rightly indicates that the subject matter belongs to the field of law, and points to its major objective, the protection of private rights. The objective of public administration is the efficient conduct of public business.

These two goals are not only different, but may at times conflict. Administration is of course bound by the rules of administrative law, as well as by the prescriptions of constitutional law; but within the boundaries thus set, it seeks the most effective accomplishment of public purposes. The whole matter is tersely set forth by Professor Freund.[3]

> The thought of those interested in public administration seems at the present time to be mainly concerned with problems of efficiency. This is easy to understand. With the rapid expansion of governmental control over all kinds of important interests we have, on the whole, held fast to the self-governmental theory of administrative organization which is not productive of the highest degree of expert knowledge and skill.
>
> Yet increased administrative powers call for increased safeguards against their abuses, and as long as there is the possibility of official error, partiality or excess of zeal, the protection of private right is as important an object as the effectuation of some governmental policy.

Students of government are familiar with the traditional division of governmental activities into the legislative, executive, and judicial.[4] It is important to understand that the work of the administration involves all three types of activity, although a strict application of the theory of separation of power would seem to confine it to "executive" business. After pointing out that the administrative commission exercises an authority which is in part executive, in part legislative, and in part judicial, Croly asserts "it is simply a means of consolidating the divided activities of government for certain practical social purposes," and proceeds to give a reasoned defense of this fusion of powers.[5] Administration more and more tends in fact to reach into the established fields of legislation and adjudication, raising important problems which will be the subject of study in later chapters.

Students of public affairs are gradually discerning, in fact, that administration has become the heart of the modern problem of government. In an earlier and simpler age, legislative bodies had the time to deal with the major issues, the character of which was suited to the deliberations of the lay mind; they were primarily problems involving judgments on important questions of political ethics, such as the enfranchisement of citizens by abolishing property qualifications, the disposition of the public land, the disestablishment of the Anglican Church, or the liberalization of a monarchist state. The problems which crowd upon legislative bodies today are often entangled with, or become exclusively technical questions which the layman can handle only by utilizing the services of the expert. The control of local government, the regulation of utilities, the enforcement of the prohibition amendment, the appropriation for a navy, the organization of a health department, the maintenance of a national service of agricultural research are all matters which can be put upon the statute book only with the assistance of men who know the operating details in each case. So we discover in the administrative service one official who knows all that can be known about the control of water-borne diseases, another who has at his fingertips the substance of all available information on wheat rust, and another who cannot be "stumped" on appropriations for the national park service. These men are not merely useful to legislators overwhelmed by the increasing flood of bills; they are simply indispensable. They are the government. One may indeed suggest that the traditional assignment of the legislature as the pivotal agency in the governmental triumvirate is destined at no distant date to be replaced by a more realistic analysis which will establish government as the task of administration, operating within such areas as may be circumscribed by legislatures and courts.

2. The Emergence of Administration It is from Great Britain of course that the United States derived its administrative institutions. Our local governments were patterned after the English model in the seventeenth century. Decentralized, self-governmental, dominated by the "squirearchy," they proved to be readily adaptable to the economic and social conditions of the New World. Even today the main lines of our administrative structure are profoundly influenced by their English origin; nowhere in the American commonwealths can be found the prototype of the continental intendant or his successor, the prefect.

But the modern social and economic environment in which administration operates, and the insistent demand for a greater and greater degree of state intervention are destined to force the issue whether a modern industrial, interventionist state can possibly operate on the restricted base of voluntary and substantially amateur effort which characterizes our administrative inheritance. The problems with which officials must grapple are now so varied in scope, so technical in character, so insistent for solution that it hardly seems possible that the state can hold its own except by adopting at least some of the essentials of bureaucratic administration. Is it not now imperative for democratic states to derive the advantage of a civil service characterized by permanence of tenure, special training for official position, professional interest on the part of the public official, undivided loyalty to the interests of the state? No one will understand that this suggestion is in favor of autocratic as contrasted with democratic institutions. But democracies can fruitfully borrow from more highly organized administrative systems those elements which can be properly adapted to their fundamental political institutions in order to make more effective the achievement of their own purposes and programs.

The fact is that the role of administration in the modern state is profoundly affected by the general political and cultural environment of the age. The *laissez faire* school of social philosophy, demanding the restriction of state activities to the bare minimum of external protection and police, created a situation in which administration was restricted in scope and feeble in operation. Officialdom was thought a necessary evil, bureaucracy an ever-present danger. On the continent irresponsible governments, able within large limits to defy the wishes of the people, and themselves often without programs of social betterment, contributed powerfully to the philosophic argument in favor of nonintervention by the state.

The industrial revolution and its many social, economic, and political implications are fundamentally responsible for the new social philosophy and the new concept of public administration. *Laissez faire* has been abandoned by philosophers and statesmen alike, and a new era of collective activity has been ushered in by the twentieth century. The expansion of industry on a national and international scale, the growth of transportation by railroad, motor truck and airplane, the transformation of communication by modern postal systems, the press, the telegraph, telephone, wireless and radio, the enormously increasing mobility of persons and ideas, the urbanization of industrial states and the crystallization of powerful social classes and economic interests have not only increased the area and intensity of administrative activity, but also have added new types of problems and magnified the importance and the difficulty of the old.

The industrial revolution has necessitated, in short, a degree of social cooperation in which *laissez faire* has become impossible; and gradually the new environment is building up in men's minds a conception of the role of the state which approximates the function assigned to it by the conditions of modern life. These new ideas involve the acceptance of the state as a great agency of social cooperation, as well as an agency of social regulation. The state becomes therefore an important means by which the program of social amelioration is effected. "The power of the civil service is increasing," writes an English scholar, "for the state has given up its old role of acting, in Lassalle's phrase, as night-watchman, as a mere dispenser of justice in the strictest sense of the word. Today it acts on the theory that the good of the individual and of society may be discovered by the processes of social reason and action, and be implemented through statutes."[6]

The enlarging positive program of the state does not imply by any means a corresponding diminution of its repressive and regulative activities. The struggle of classes over the distribution of the social surplus has led to the intervention of the state on behalf of the economically weak (children, women, laboring classes) by insistence on minimum wage, limited hours of labor, and healthful working conditions; the persistence of various groups of "reformers" has brought about prohibitions and regulations of diverse kinds (sale of cigarettes, narcotics, alcohol, censorship of motion pictures); the need for guaranteeing so far as possible the integrity of the processes of self-government has led to the regulation of elections and political parties, and the elaboration of such repressive legislation as corrupt practice acts.

In every direction, therefore, the task of the modern state is enlarging. In every direction likewise the range of public administration is being extended, for every phase of the new program of the state is reflected in additional administrative activity.

For these reasons it is not surprising that in the last two decades increasing attention has been given to the business side of government. The remarkable thing is that for over a hundred years of our national existence, the only phase of administration to emerge in the arena of national issues was the spoils system. In a brilliant essay Wilson explained the American failure to grasp the importance of sound administration. Writing in the *Political Science Quarterly*, he pointed out:

> No one wrote systematically of administration as a branch of the science of government until the present century had passed its first youth and had begun to put forth its characteristic flower of systematic knowledge. Up to our own day all the political writers whom we now read had thought, argued, dogmatized, only about the *constitution* of governments; about the nature of the state, the essence and seat of sovereignty, popular power and kingly prerogative. . . . The central field of controversy was that great field of theory in which monarchy rode tilt against democracy, in which oligarchy would have built for itself

> strongholds of privilege, and in which tyranny sought opportunity to make good its claim to receive submission from all competitors. The question, how law should be administered with enlightenment, with equity, with speed, and without friction, was put aside as a practical detail which clerks could arrange after doctors had agreed upon principles.

Unfortunately the future President of Princeton University and the United States never carried his penetrating researches beyond this preliminary study.

The interest of the twentieth century in public administration is due to a variety of causes. Of these the rapidly increasing cost of government, "the unprecedented cataclysm of public expenditure," is one of the most important.[7] The statement is made that the total revenues raised for municipal, county, state, and national purposes increased from $2,131,402,000 in 1912 to $6,346,332,000 in 1922, an increase of 198 percent; and the per capita revenues in 1912 increased from $21.96 to $58.37 in 1922.[8] The total net expenditures of the federal government reached their peak in the fiscal year 1920, at $5,687,712,849, since when there has been a progressive decline to an annual expenditure of about $3,000,000,000. The expenditures of the state governments, however, show a rapid increase since the war. In 1913 they were $3.95 per capita, and in 1922, $11.82.[9] Municipal expenditures show a per capita increase for all general departments from $17.34 in 1912 to $33.15 in 1922.[10] Dr. Mitchell and his associates estimate an increase in national income, 1913 to 1919, from 33.3 billions to 66.0 billions of dollars, or approximately two hundred per cent. This indicates that national income is not burdened by governmental expenditure to any substantially greater degree in recent years than before the war, but the outcry against high taxes is none the less real.[11] The wide publicity given to the rising tide of expenditure, the heavy burden of taxation, and the dramatic efforts of the national administration in favor of economy, have all emphasized the demand for greater efficiency. The pressure for more effective use of public resources is unremitting, and so long as existing high levels of taxation remain, every avenue will need to be explored in order to secure maximum results for every expenditure.

The World War brought into vivid contrast the administrative methods of democratic and autocratic governments, and gave rise to sharp criticisms of the time-honored plan of "muddling through." At an early date the war was declared to be one between democracy and autocracy, but at a later date there was general agreement that democracy had been forced to adopt the administrative methods of autocracy to gain its end.[12] The various administrative methods employed in the belligerent countries to control the food supply, however, furnish interesting illustrations of the democratic and autocratic approach to specific problems.

On a less dramatic scale, international competition in trade and industry continues to sharpen the demand for efficiency in government. The United States Chamber of Commerce has taken an active interest in greater efficiency "because as business men they already believed in efficiency and economy and wanted to see it applied to the municipal, state, and national governments; because they realized that efficient and economical government was a prime requisite for prosperity and business success; and because as good citizens, they desired to see an honest, sound and intelligent administration." In 1912 at the first annual meeting of the Chamber of Commerce there was discussion of budget reform for the federal government, followed by a referendum which almost unanimously adopted a specific proposal. Year after year the Chamber of Commerce has pressed the matter upon the attention of Congress.

This organization has also urged federal grants for the assistance of vocational schools, a federal department of public works, a general reorganization of the administrative system, improved methods of personnel management, and a permanent planning department in the post office. The New York Chamber of Commerce has also taken an active part in proposing better administration, both state and federal. The reorganization of the consular and diplomatic services achieved by the Rogers Act was urged by business interests. Secretary Hoover's recent revelations of monopolies in rubber, coffee, sisal, and other commodities controlled by foreign governments point to a new phase of international commercial competition which may have important reactions on the problems of our administrative organization. The fact of the matter is that American business has reached the point where it cannot continue to reap profits merely by enlarging its productivity to catch up with a home market protected by a high tariff wall. It is now a competitor in the world market, and is faced with the necessity of maintaining profits largely by reductions in the cost of production through better management and more effective use of resources. That is, it has been forced to consider on a large scale the reduction of expenses, and the most efficient utilization of its equipment. In this it has preceded government.

The insistence of powerful social groups upon the practical realization of their legislative programs is a constant spur to improved administrative methods. The enforcement of the eighteenth amendment is a significant illustration of the point. The advocates of stringent enforcement legislation failed to insist upon the selection of prohibition officials by merit. The lax and feeble enforcement of the Volstead Act quickly caused the Anti-Saloon League to demand better execution of the law; the issue shifted from policy to administration. This illustrates a universal transfer of interest, for when once a policy has received legislative sanction, the chief problem becomes one of administration. Similarly the agencies interested in limitation of the hours of labor, minimum wage, tax reform, and other issues become powerful exponents of sound administrative methods.

The scientific management movement has had a very important share in stimulating improvement in the methods of carrying on public business.[13] Commencing with the pioneer work of Frederick W. Taylor, the movement has developed constantly widening interests, and has eventually built up the outlines of a whole philosophy of social betterment on the basis of scientific control of the productive process.

The enormous improvements which have been made by scientific management in some industries have raised the question whether or not equally striking improvements are feasible in government. Whatever answer be given to this question, there can be no doubt that the achievements of scientific management have aroused a vast amount of dissatisfaction with the antiquated methods which have characterized many public offices. More and more clearly it is being understood that the promise of American life will never be realized until American administration has been lifted out of the ruts in which it has been left by a century of neglect.

NOTES

1. One of the earliest definitions by an American author is found in the following lines written by Woodrow Wilson: "The field of administration is the field of business. . . . The object of administrative study is to rescue executive methods from the confusion and costliness of empirical experiment and set them upon foundation laid deep in stable principle. . . . Public administration is the detailed and systematic execution of public law. Every particular application of general law is an act of administration" ("The Study of Administration," *Political Science Quarterly* 2 [June 1887]: pp. 210, 212).

   Goodnow defined the field in these terms: "Such then is what is meant in these pages by the function of administration—the execution, in nonjudicial matters, of the law or will of the state as expressed by the competent authority" (*Principles of Administrative Law of the United States,* [1905] p. 14). Goodnow's writings, however, do not make a clear distinction between administration and administrative law. This distinction is only now emerging in fact. It is recognized by the French phrases, *droit administratif* and *doctrine administrative,* by the German words *Verwaltungsrecht* and *Verwaltungskunde,* or *Verwaltungspolitik.* Note also the words "*les sciences administratives.*" See below for the author's differentiation.

2. Frank J. Goodnow, *Comparative Administrative Law* 1 (1893), pp. 8–9. The contrast is well brought forth by comparing two articles dealing with the two fields, respectively: J. D. Barnett, "Public Agencies and Private

Agencies," *Am. Pol. Sci. Rev.* 18 (1924): 34–48; and J. C. Logan, "Cooperation of Public and Private Welfare Agencies," *Annals* 105 (1923): 88–92.

3. *Proceedings, Am. Pol. Sci. Assoc.* 6 (1909): 58.
4. A careful definition of terms is to be found from the pen of the editor in the *Illinois Law Review* 15: 108–118. He writes: "Legislation is the declaration, independently of their application, of new rules of compulsory conduct, by an organ of the state, whose powers are specialized to exclude other functions except as incidental. Adjudication is the determination of a specific controversy, by the application of a rule of compulsory conduct, by an organ of the state, whose powers are specialized to exclude other functions except as incidental. The executive function is the factual and ultimate realization of a rule of compulsory conduct through an organ of the state, whose powers are specialized to exclude other functions except as incidental. Administrative power is a fourth term; its functions in pure theory must always be one of the three kinds of powers enumerated, but in practice may be and usually are a combination of two or more of these powers. Clear examples of this combination of powers are the Interstate Commerce Commission, the Federal Trade Board, and the numerous state public utility commissions."
5. Herbert A. Croly, *Progressive Democracy* (1914), ch. 17.
6. Herman Finer, "The Civil Service in the Modern State," *Am. Pol. Sci. Rev.* 19 (1925): 277–289.
7. *See* Henry J. Ford, *Cost of Our National Government* (1910); Edward B. Rosa, "Expenditures and Revenues of the Federal Government," *Annals* 95 (1921): 1; Herbert D. Brown, "The Historical Development of National Expenditures," *Proceedings of the Academy of Political Science* 9 (1921): 336–346.
8. "The Trend in Public Expenditures," *Annals* 113, pt. 1 (1924).
9. Austin F. MacDonald, "The Trend in Recent State Expenditures," *Annals* 113 (1924): 8–15; cf. Minnesota Tax Commission, "Cost of Government in Minnesota," *Biennial Report* (1918). "The economic fact which is going to force good municipal government—even scientific management in city affairs—is the growing cost of the undertaking. It is only because we do not have the figures which represent the difficulty of the task ahead of us that we are not appalled by it." Morris L. Cooke, "Scientific Management of the Public Business," *Am. Pol. Sci. Rev.* 9 (1915): 488–495; cf. "The Cost of Government, City of Detroit," *Public Business* 80: 97 (published by the Detroit Bureau of Governmental Research).
10. Lane W. Lancaster, "The Trend in City Expenditures," *Annals* 113 (1924): 15–22.
11. National Bureau of Economic Research, *Income in the United States* 1 (1921): 13.
12. Cf. Charles G. Fenwick, "Democracy and Efficient Government—Lessons of the War," *Am. Pol. Sci. Rev.* 14 (1920): 565–586.
13. See Frank B. Copley, *Frederic W. Taylor, the Father of Scientific Management* (1923); Horace B. Drury, *Scientific Management, A History and Criticism* (1915); Edward E. Hunt, *Scientific Management since Taylor* (1924); General William Crozier, "Scientific Management in Government Establishments," *Bulletin of the Taylor Society* 1 (1915); C. B. Thompson, "Literature of Scientific Management," *Quarterly Journal of Economics* 28 (1913–1914): 506–557; Henry H. Farquhar, "Positive Contributions of Scientific Management," *Ibid.* 33 (1918–1919): 466–503 and "Critical Analysis of Scientific Management," *Bulletin of the Taylor Society* 9 (1924): 16–30; Frederick A. Cleveland, "The Application of Scientific Management to the Activities of the State," *Tuck School Conference on Scientific Management* (1912): 313–335; Morris L. Cooke, "The Influence of Scientific Management upon Government," *Bulletin of the Taylor Society* 9 (1924): 31–38.

   Note also William H. Leffingwell, *Office Management* (1915); Richard H. Lansburgh, *Industrial Management* (1923).

   For a very significant change in the attitude of organized labor toward management read "Labor's Ideals Concerning Management," by President William A. Green of the American Federation of Labor, *Bulletin of the Taylor Society* 10 (1925): 241–253.

7

The Giving of Orders

Mary Parker Follett

To some men the matter of giving orders seems a very simple affair; they expect to issue their own orders and have them obeyed without question. Yet, on the other hand, the shrewd common sense of many a business executive has shown him that the issuing of orders is surrounded by many difficulties; that to demand an unquestioning obedience to orders not approved, not perhaps even understood, is bad business policy. Moreover, psychology, as well as our own observation, shows us not only that you cannot get people to do things most satisfactorily by ordering them or exhorting them; but also that even reasoning with them, even convincing them intellectually, may not be enough. Even the "consent of the governed" will not do all the work it is supposed to do, an important consideration for those who are advocating employee representation. For all our past life, our early training, our later experience, all our emotions, beliefs, prejudices, every desire that we have, have formed certain habits of mind that the psychologists call habit-patterns, action-patterns, motor-sets.

Therefore it will do little good merely to get intellectual agreement; unless you change the habit-patterns of people, you have not really changed your people. Business administration, industrial organization, should build up certain habit-patterns, that is, certain mental attitudes. For instance, the farmer has a general disposition to "go it alone," and this is being changed by the activities of the co-operatives, that is, note, *by the farmer's own activities.* So the workman has often a general disposition of antagonism to his employers which cannot be changed by argument or exhortation, but only through certain activities which will create a different disposition. One of my trade union friends told me that he remembered when he was a quite small boy hearing his father, who worked in a shoe-shop, railing daily against his boss. So he grew up believing that it was inherent in the nature of things that the workman should be against his employer. I know many working men who have a prejudice against getting college men into factories. You could all give me examples of attitudes among your employees which you would like to change. We want, for instance, to create an attitude of respect for expert opinion.

If we analyse this matter a little further we shall see that we have to do three things. I am now going to use psychological language: (1) build up certain attitudes; (2) provide for the release of these attitudes; (3) augment the released response as it is being carried out. What does this mean in the language of business? A psychologist has given us the example of the salesman. The salesman first creates in you the attitude that you want his article; then, at just the "psychological" moment, he produces his contract blank which you may sign and thus release that attitude; then if, as you are preparing to sign, some one comes in and tells you how pleased he has been with his purchase of this article, that augments the response which is being released.

If we apply this to the subject of orders and obedience, we see that people can obey an order only if previous habit-patterns are appealed to or new ones created. When the employer is considering an order, he should also be thinking of the way to form the habits which will ensure its being carried out. We should first lead the salesman selling shoes or the bank clerk cashing cheques to see the desirability of a different method. Then the rules of the store or bank should be so changed as to make it possible for salesman or cashier to adopt the new method. In the third place they could be made more ready to follow the new method by convincing in advance some one individual who will set an example to the others. You can usually convince one or two or three ahead of the

Source: From Scientific Foundations of Business Administration, by H. C. Metcalf (ed.). Copyright © 1926 The Williams & Wilkins Co. Reprinted by permission.

rank and file. This last step you all know from your experience to be good tactics; it is what the psychologists call intensifying the attitude to be released. But we find that the released attitude is not by one release fixed as a habit; it takes a good many responses to do that.

This is an important consideration for us, for from one point of view business success depends largely on this—namely, whether our business is so organized and administered that it tends to form certain habits, certain mental attitudes. It has been hard for many old-fashioned employers to understand that *orders will not take the place of training.* I want to italicize that. Many a time an employer has been angry because, as he expressed it, a workman "wouldn't" do so and so, when the truth of the matter was that the workman couldn't, actually couldn't, do as ordered because he could not go contrary to life-long habits. This whole subject might be taken up under the heading of education, for there we could give many instances of the attempt to make arbitrary authority take the place of training. In history, the aftermath of all revolutions shows us the results of the lack of training.

In this matter of prepared-in-advance behaviour patterns—that is, in preparing the way for the reception of orders, psychology makes a contribution when it points out that the same words often rouse in us a quite different response when heard in certain places and on certain occasions. A boy may respond differently to the same suggestion when made by his teacher and when made by his schoolmate. Moreover, he may respond differently to the same suggestion made by the teacher in the schoolroom and made by the teacher when they are taking a walk together. Applying this to the giving of orders, we see that the place in which orders are given, the circumstances under which they are given, may make all the difference in the world as to the response which we get. Hand them down a long way from President or Works Manager and the effect is weakened. One might say that the strength of favourable response to an order is in inverse ratio to the distance the order travels. Production efficiency is always in danger of being affected whenever the long-distance order is substituted for the face-to-face suggestion. There is, however, another reason for that which I shall consider in a moment.

All that we said . . . of integration and circular behaviour applies directly to the anticipation of response in giving orders. We spoke then of what the psychologists call linear and circular behaviour. Linear behaviour would be, to quote from Dr. Cabot's review of my book, *Creative Experience,* when an order is accepted as passively as the woodshed accepts the wood. In circular behaviour you get a "comeback." But we all know that we get the comeback every day of our life, and we must certainly allow for it, or for what is more elegantly called circular behaviour, in the giving of orders. . . . I should say that the giving of orders and the receiving of orders ought to be a matter of integration through circular behaviour, and that we should seek methods to bring this about.

Psychology has another important contribution to make on this subject of issuing orders or giving directions: before the integration can be made between order-giver and order-receiver, there is often an integration to be made within one or both of the individuals concerned. There are often two dissociated paths in the individual; if you are clever enough to recognize these, you can sometimes forestall a Freudian conflict, make the integration appear before there is an acute stage.

To explain what I mean, let me run over briefly a social worker's case. The girl's parents had been divorced and the girl placed with a jolly, easy-going, slack and untidy family, consisting of the father and mother and eleven children, sons and daughters. Gracie was very happy here, but when the social worker in charge of the case found that the living conditions involved a good deal of promiscuity, she thought the girl should be placed elsewhere. She therefore took her to call on an aunt who had a home with some refinement of living, where they had "high tastes," as one of the family said. This aunt wished to have Gracie live with her, and Gracie decided that she would like to do so. The social worker, however, in order to test her, said, "But I thought you were so happy where you are." "Can't I be happy and high, too?" the girl replied. There were two wishes here, you see. The social worker by removing the girl to the aunt may have forestalled a Freudian conflict, the dissociated paths may have been united. I do not know the outcome of this story, but it indicates a method of dealing with our co-directors—make them "happy and high, too."

Business administration has often to consider how to deal with the dissociated paths in individuals or groups, but the methods of doing this successfully have been developed much further in some departments than in others. We have as yet hardly recognized this as part of the technique of dealing with employees, yet the clever salesman knows that it is the chief part of his job. The prospective buyer wants the article and does not want it. The able salesman does not suppress the arguments in the mind of the purchaser against buying, for then the purchaser might be sorry afterwards for his purchase, and that would not be good salesmanship. Unless he can unite, integrate, in the purchaser's mind, the reasons for buying and the reasons for not buying, his future sales will be imperilled, he will not be the highest grade salesman.

Please note that this goes beyond what the psychologist whom I quoted at the beginning of this section told us. He said, "The salesman must create in you the attitude that you want his article." Yes, but only if he creates this attitude by integration, not by suppression.

Apply all this to orders. An order often leaves the individual to whom it is given with two dissociated paths; an order should seek to unite, to integrate, dissociated paths. Court decisions often settle arbitrarily which of two ways is to be followed without showing a possible integration of the two, that is, the individual is often left with an internal conflict on his hands. This is what both courts and business administration should try to prevent, the internal conflicts of individuals or groups.

In discussing the preparation for giving orders, I have not spoken at all of the appeal to certain instincts made so important by many writers. Some writers, for instance, emphasize the instinct of self-assertion; this would be violated by too rigid orders or too clumsily exercised authority. Other writers, of equal standing, tell us that there is an instinct of submission to authority. I cannot discuss this for we should first have to define instincts, too long an undertaking for us now. Moreover, the exaggerated interest in instincts of recent years, an interest which in many cases has received rather crude expression, is now subsiding. Or, rather, it is being replaced by the more fruitful interest in habits.

There is much more that we could learn from psychology about the forming of habits and the preparation for giving orders than I can even hint at now. But there is one point, already spoken of by implication, that I wish to consider more explicitly—namely, the manner of giving orders. Probably more industrial trouble has been caused by the manner in which orders are given than in any other way. In the *Report on Strikes and Lockouts,* a British Government publication, the cause of a number of strikes is given as "alleged harassing conduct of the foreman," "alleged tyrannical conduct of an underforeman," "alleged overbearing conduct of officials." The explicit statement, however, of the tyranny of superior officers as the direct cause of strikes is I should say, unusual, yet resentment smoulders and breaks out in other issues. And the demand for better treatment is often explicit enough. We find it made by the metal and woodworking trades in an aircraft factory, who declared that any treatment of men without regard to their feelings of self-respect would be answered by a stoppage of work. We find it put in certain agreements with employers that "the men must be treated with proper respect, and threats and abusive language must not be used."

What happens to man, *in* a man, when an order is given in a disagreeable manner by foreman, head of department, his immediate superior in store, bank or factory? The man addressed feels that his self-respect is attacked, that one of his most inner sanctuaries is invaded. He loses his temper or becomes sullen or is on the defensive; he begins thinking of his "rights"—a fatal attitude for any of us. In the language we have been using, the wrong behaviour pattern is aroused, the wrong motorset; that is, he is now "set" to act in a way which is not going to benefit the enterprise in which he is engaged.

There is a more subtle psychological point here, too; the more you are "bossed" the more your activity of thought will take place within the bossing-pattern, and your part in that pattern seems usually to be opposition to the bossing.

This complaint of the abusive language and the tyrannical treatment of the one just above the worker is an old story to us all, but there is an opposite extreme which is far too little considered. The immediate superior officer is often so close to the worker that he does not exercise the proper duties of his position. Far from taking on himself an aggressive authority, he has often evaded one of the chief problems of his job: how to do what is implied in the fact that he has been put in a position over others. The head of the woman's cloak department in a store will call out, "Say, Sadie, you're 36, aren't you? There's a woman down in the Back Bay kicking about something she says you promised yesterday." "Well, I like that," says Sadie, "Some of those Back Bay women would kick in Heaven." And that perhaps is about all that happens. Of course, the Back Bay lady has to be appeased, but there is often no study of what has taken place for the benefit of the store. I do not mean that a lack of connection between such incidents and the improvement of store technique is universal, but it certainly exists far too often and is one of the problems of those officials who are just above the heads of departments. Naturally, a woman does not want to get on bad terms with her fellow employees with whom she talks and works all day long. Consider the chief operator of the telephone exchanges, remembering that the chief operator is a member of the union, and that the manager is not.

Now what is our problem here? How can we avoid the two extremes: too great bossism in giving orders, and practically no orders given? I am going to ask how *you* are avoiding these extremes. My solution is to depersonalize the giving of orders, to unite all concerned in a study of the situation and obey that. Until we do this I do not think we shall have the most successful business administration. This is what does take place, what has to take place, when there is a question between two men in positions of equal authority. The head of the sales department does not give orders to the head of the production department, or vice versa. Each studies the market and the final decision is made as the market demands. This is, ideally, what should take place between foremen and rank and file, between any head and his subordinates. One *person* should not give orders to another *person*, but both should agree to take their orders from the situation. If orders are simply part of the situation, the question of someone giving and someone receiving does not come up. Both accept the orders given by the situation. Employers accept the orders given by the situation; employees accept the orders given by the situation. This gives, does it not, a slightly different aspect to the whole of business administration through the entire plant?

We have here, I think, one of the largest contributions of scientific management: it tends to depersonalize orders. From one point of view, one might call the essence of scientific management the attempt to find the law of the situation. With scientific management the managers are as much under orders as the workers, for both obey the law of the situation. Our job is not how to get people to obey orders, but how to devise methods by which we can best *discover* the order integral to a particular situation. When that is found, the employee can issue it to the employer, as well as employer to employee. This often happens easily and naturally. My cook or my stenographer points out the law of the situation, and I, if I recognize it as such, accept it, even though it may reverse some "order" I have given.

If those in supervisory positions should depersonalize orders, then there would be no overbearing authority on the one hand, nor on the other that dangerous *laissez-aller* which comes from the fear of exercising authority. Of course we should exercise authority, but always the authority of the situation. I do not say that we have found the way to a frictionless existence, far from it, but we now understand the place which we mean to give to friction. We intend to set it to work for us as the engineer does when he puts the belt over the pulley. There will be just as much, probably more, room for disagreement in the method I am advocating. The situation will often be seen differently, often be interpreted differently. But we shall know what to do with it, we shall have found a method of dealing with it.

I call it depersonalizing because there is not time to go any further into the matter. I think it really is a matter of *repersonalizing*. We, persons, have relations with each other, but we should find them in and through the whole situation. We cannot have any sound relations with each other as long as we take them out of that setting which gives them their meaning and value. This divorcing of persons and the situation does a great deal of harm. I have just said that scientific management depersonalizes; the deeper philosophy of scientific management shows us personal relations within the whole setting of that thing of which they are a part.

There is much psychology, modern psychology particularly, which tends to divorce person and situation. What I am referring to is the present zest for "personality studies." When some difficulty arises, we often hear the psychologist whose specialty is personality studies say, "Study the psychology of that man." And this is very good advice, but only if at the same time we study the entire situation. To leave out the whole situation, however, is so common a blunder in the studies of these psychologists that it constitutes a serious weakness in their work. And as those of you who are personnel directors have more to do, I suppose, with those psychologists who have taken personality for their specialty than with any others, I wish you would watch and see how often you find that this limitation detracts from the value of their conclusions.

I said above that we should substitute for the long-distance order the face-to-face suggestion. I think we can now see a more cogent reason for this than the one then given. It is not the face-to-face suggestion that we want so much as the joint study of the problem, and such joint study can be made best by the employee and his immediate superior or employee and special expert on that question.

I began this talk by emphasizing the advisability of preparing in advance the attitude necessary for the carrying out of orders, as in the previous paper we considered preparing the attitude for integration; but we have now, in our consideration of the joint study of situations, in our emphasis on obeying the law of the situation, perhaps got a little beyond that, or rather we have now to consider in what sense we wish to take the psychologist's doctrine of prepared-in-advance attitudes. By itself this would not take us far, for everyone is studying psychology nowadays, and our employees are going to be just as active in preparing us as we in preparing them! Indeed, a girl working in a factory said to me, "We had a course in psychology last winter, and I see now that you have to be pretty careful how you put things to the managers if you want them to consider favourably what you're asking for." If this prepared-in-advance idea were all that the psychologists think it, it would have to be printed privately as secret doctrine. But the truth is that the best preparation for integration in the matter of orders or in anything else, is a joint study of the situation. We should not try to create the attitude we *want*, although that is the usual phrase, but the attitude required for cooperative study and decision. This holds good even for the salesman. We said above that when the salesman is told that he should create in the prospective buyer the attitude that he wants the article, he ought also to be told that he should do this by integration rather than by suppression. We have now a hint of *how* he is to attain this integration.

I have spoken of the importance of changing some of the language of business personnel relations. We considered whether the words "grievances," "complaints," or Ford's "trouble specialists" did not arouse the wrong behaviour patterns. I think "order" certainly does. If that word is not to mean any longer external authority, arbitrary authority, but the law of the situation, then we need a new word for it. It is often the order that people resent as much as the thing ordered. People do not like to be ordered even to take a holiday. I have often seen instances of this. The wish to govern one's own life is, of course, one of the most fundamental feelings in every human being. To call this "the instinct of self-assertion," "the instinct of initiative," does not express it wholly. I think it is told in the life of some famous American that when he was a boy and his mother said, "Go get a pail of water," he always replied, "I won't," before taking up the pail and fetching the water. This is significant; he resented the command, the command of a person; but he went and got the water, not, I believe, because he had to, but because he recognized the demand of the situation. *That,* he knew he had to obey; *that,* he was willing to obey. And this kind of obedience is not opposed to the wish to govern one's self, but each is involved in the other; both are part of the same fundamental urge at the root of one's being. We have here something far more profound than "the egoistic impulse" or "the instinct of self-assertion." We have the very essence of the human being.

This subject of orders has led us into the heart of the whole question of authority and consent. When we conceive of authority and consent as parts of an inclusive situation, does that not throw a flood of light on this question? The point of view here presented gets rid of several dilemmas which have seemed to puzzle people in dealing with consent. The feeling of being "under" someone, of "subordination," of "servility," of being "at the will of another," comes out again and again in the shop stewards' movement and in the testimony before the Coal Commission. One man said before the Coal Commission, "It is all right to work *with* anyone; what is disagreeable is to feel too distinctly that you are working *under* anyone." *With* is a pretty good preposition, not because it connotes democracy, but because it connotes functional unity, a much more profound conception than that of democracy as usually held. The study of the situation involves the *with* preposition. Then Sadie is not left alone by the head of the cloak department, nor does she have to obey her. The head of the department says, "Let's see how such cases had better be handled, then we'll abide by that." Sadie is not under the head of the department, but both are *under* the situation.

Twice I have had a servant applying for a place ask me if she would be treated as a menial. When the first woman asked me that, I had no idea what she meant, I thought perhaps she did not want to do the roughest work, but later I came to the conclusion that to be treated as a menial meant to be obliged to be under someone, to follow orders without using one's own judgment. If we believe that what heightens self-respect increases efficiency, we shall be on our guard here.

Very closely connected with this is the matter of pride in one's work. If an order goes against what the craftsman or the clerk thinks is the way of doing his work which will bring the best results, he is justified in not wishing to obey that order. Could not that difficulty be met by a joint study of the situation? It is said that it is characteristic of the British workman to feel, "I know my job and won't be told how." The peculiarities of the British workman might be met by a joint study of the situation, it being understood that he probably has more to contribute to that study than anyone else. . . .

There is another dilemma which has to be met by everyone who is in what is called a position of authority: how can you expect people merely to obey orders and at the same time to take that degree of responsibility which they should take? Indeed, in my experience, the people who enjoy following orders blindly, without any thought on their own part, are those who like thus to get rid of responsibility. But the taking of responsibility, each according to his capacity, each according to his function in the whole . . . , this taking of responsibility is usually the most vital matter in the life of every human being, just as the allotting of responsibility is the most important part of business administration.

A young trade unionist said to me, "How much dignity can I have as a mere employee?" He can have all the dignity in the world if he is allowed to make his fullest contribution to the plant *and to assume definitely the responsibility therefor.*

I think one of the gravest problems before us is how to make the reconciliation between receiving orders and taking responsibility. And I think the reconciliation can be made through our conception of the law of the situation. . . .

We have considered the subject of symbols. It is often very apparent that an order is a symbol. The referee in the game stands watch in hand, and says, "Go." It is an order, but order only as symbol. I may say to an employee, "Do so and so," but I should say it only because we have both agreed, openly or tacitly, that that which I am ordering done is the best thing to be done. The order is then a symbol. And if it is a philosophical and psychological truth that we owe obedience only to a functional unity to which we are contributing, we should remember that a more accurate way of stating that would be to say that our obligation is to a unifying, to a process.

This brings us now to one of our most serious problems in this matter of orders. It is important, but we can touch on it only briefly; it is what we spoke of . . . as the evolving situation. I am trying to show here that the order must be integral to the situation and must be recognized as such. But we saw that the situation was always developing. If the situation is never stationary, then the order should never be stationary, so to speak; how to prevent it from being so is our problem. The situation is changing while orders are being carried out. . . . How is the order to keep up with the situation? External orders never can, only those drawn fresh from the situation.

Moreover, if taking a *responsible* attitude toward experience involves recognizing the evolving situation, a *conscious* attitude toward experience means that we note the change which the developing situation makes in ourselves; the situation does not change without changing us.

To summarize, . . . integration being the basic law of life, orders should be the composite conclusion of those who give and those who receive them; more than this, that they should be the integration of the people concerned and the situation; even more than this, that they should be the integration involved in the evolving situation. If you accept my three fundamental statements on this subject: (1) that the order should be the law of the situation; (2) that the situation is always evolving; (3) that orders should involve circular not linear behaviour—then we see that our old conception of orders has somewhat changed, and that there should therefore follow definite changes in business practice.

There is a problem so closely connected with the giving of orders that I want to put it before you for future discussion. After we have decided on our orders, we have to consider how much and what kind of supervision is necessary or advisable in order that they shall be carried out. We all know that many workers object to being watched. What does that mean, how far is it justifiable? How can the objectionable element be avoided and at the same time necessary supervision given? I do not think that this matter has been studied sufficiently. When I asked a very intelligent girl what she thought would be the result of profit sharing and employee representation in the factory where she worked, she replied joyfully, "We shan't need foremen any more." While her entire ignoring of the fact that the foreman has other duties than keeping workers on their jobs was amusing, one wants to go beyond one's amusement and find out what this objection to being watched really means.

In a case in Scotland arising under the Minimum Wage Act, the overman was called in to testify whether or not a certain workman did his work properly. The examination was as follows:

Magistrate: "But isn't it your duty under the Mines Act to visit each working place twice a day?"
Overman: "Yes."
Magistrate: "Don't you do it?"
Overman: "Yes."
Magistrate: "Then why didn't you ever see him work?
Overman: "They always stop work when they see an overman coming and sit down and wait till he's gone—even take out their pipes, if it's a mine free from gas. They won't let anyone watch them."

An equally extreme standard was enforced for a part of the war period at a Clyde engineering works. The chairman of shop stewards was told one morning that there was a grievance at the smithy. He found one of the blacksmiths in a rage because the managing director in his ordinary morning's walk through the works had stopped for five minutes or so and watched this man's fire. After a shop meeting the chairman took up a deputation to the director and secured the promise that this should not happen again. At the next works meeting the chairman reported the incident to the body of workers, with the result that a similar demand was made throughout the works and practically acceded to, so that the director hardly dared to stop at all in his morning's walk.

I have seen similar instances cited. Many workmen feel that being watched is unbearable. What can we do about it? How can we get proper supervision without this watching which a worker resents? Supervision is necessary; supervision is resented—how are we going to make the integration there? Some say, "Let the workers elect the supervisors." I do not believe in that.

There are three other points closely connected with the subject of this paper which I should like merely to point out. First, when and how do you point out mistakes, misconduct? One principle can surely guide us here: don't blame for the sake of blaming, make what you have to say accomplish something; say it in that form, at that time, under those circumstances, which will make it a real education to your subordinate. Secondly, since it is recognized that the one who gives the orders is not as a rule a very popular person, the management sometimes tries to offset this by allowing the person who has this onus upon him to give any pleasant news to the workers, to have the credit of any innovation which the workers very much desire. One manager told me that he always tried to do this. I suppose that this is good behaviouristic psychology, and yet I am not sure that it is a method I wholly like. It is quite different, however, in the case of a mistaken order having been given; then I think the one who made the mistake should certainly be the one to rectify it, not as a matter of strategy, but because it is better for him too. It is better for all of us not only to acknowledge our mistakes, but to do something about them. If a foreman discharges someone and it is decided to reinstate the man, it is obviously not only good tactics but a square deal to the foreman to allow him to do the reinstating.

There is, of course, a great deal more to this matter of giving orders than we have been able to touch on; far from exhausting the subject, I feel that I have only given hints. I have been told that the artillery men suffered more mentally in the war than others, and the reason assigned for this was that their work was directed from a distance. The combination of numbers by which they focused their fire was telephoned to them. The result was also at a distance. Their activity was not closely enough connected with the actual situation at either end.

Part Two

THE NEW DEAL TO MID-CENTURY

1930S TO 1950S

In the three decades that span the period between the world wars and the full emergence of the cold war, governments in the United States changed dramatically. At the federal level, the New Deal's efforts to cope with a worldwide depression significantly and rapidly altered the traditional roles of government. Reforms in state government and city management were equally significant. Reactive roles gave way to proactive roles. Government organization would be dominated by new themes: centralization, management planning, efficiency measurement, and new forms of social programs.

Still, there was uncertainty, both to the future of government and the focus of the field of public administration. In 1939, Leonard D. White published a revised edition of his pioneering textbook. His opening statement provides a fitting assessment of the state of public administration of this period of immense transformation:

> The ensuing decades which have passed since the first edition of this book [have] shaken the economic and political foundations of the contemporary world. The effect of the repeated crises of these years upon public administration has been great, exactly how great we cannot yet be sure. As a nation we are, however, slowly accepting the fact that the loose-jointed, easy-going, somewhat irresponsible system of administration which we carried over from our rural agricultural background is no longer adequate for present and future needs. The council-manager form of municipal government, the reconstruction of state governments and their administrative disciplining by federal authorities and the pending reform of the federal structure itself are unmistakable signs of adoption to new necessities.[1]

INITIAL EFFORTS TO CREATE A SCIENCE OF ADMINISTRATION

By the 1930s, management in both the public and private sectors in the United States was being established as an identifiable discipline. The influence of scientific management, or "Taylorism," was pervasive. Methodologies used to divine the one best way to accomplish physical tasks were increasingly applied to the problem of social organization. Luther Gulick's (1892–1993)[2] "Notes on the Theory of Organization" is generally acknowledged to be the definitive statement on the "principles" approach to managing organizations. In 1937, he and Lyndall Urwick (1891–1983) edited a collection, *Papers on the Science of Administration*. Overall, the Papers were a statement of the state of the art of organization theory. It was here that Gulick introduced his famous mnemonic, POSDCORB, which stands for the seven major functions of management: planning, organizing, staffing, directing, coordinating, reporting, and budgeting.

Gulick helped shape a critical distinction in orthodox public administration: the study of management and administration was to be focused on the role of upper-level management. Its organizational outlook took the point of view of the top. But this narrow focus was to be increasingly challenged. Even as Gulick wrote, his scientific approach to management was being confronted by the more humanistic focus that would ultimately supplant it. Although this was not immediately apparent, the theoreticians of the human relations and behavioral science approaches to management were very much contemporaries of Gulick; they were simply prophets before their time.

UNDERSTANDING ORGANIZATIONS AND HUMAN BEHAVIOR

Chester Barnard (1886–1961) followed Mary Parker Follett's major themes with a far more comprehensive theory in *The Functions of the Executive.*[3] Barnard, a Bell System executive who was closely associated with the Harvard Business School, and those faculty who were involved with the Hawthorne studies,[4] saw organizations as cooperative systems where the function of the executive was to maintain the dynamic equilibrium between the needs of the organization and the needs of its employees. In order to do this, management had to be aware of the interdependent nature of the formal and informal organizations. Barnard's chapter on the significance and role of informal organizations, "Informal Organizations and Their Relations to Formal Organizations," reprinted here, provided the theoretical foundations for a whole generation of empirical research.

Accompanying the growing repudiation of scientific management as the sole body of administrative wisdom was a challenge to Weber's "ideal" bureaucracy. Even before it was widely available in an English translation, Weber's work sired a lively debate about its underlying premises. In a 1940 issue of the journal *Social Forces*, Robert K. Merton (1910–2003), one of the most influential of modern sociologists, published an article, "Bureaucratic Structure, and Personality," which proclaimed that the "ideal-type" bureaucracy espoused by Weber had inhibiting dysfunctional characteristics that prevented it from being optimally efficient. This is a theme that has been echoed equally by subsequent empirical studies and the polemics of politicians. In the 1950s, Merton slightly revised the article for inclusion in his collection of essays, *Social Theory and Social Structure*, which is the version reprinted here, but the article is appropriately placed in 1940 for chronology.

As organizations grew from small offices and shops into large corporations and government agencies, the disciplined hierarchies and unambiguous functional assignments of bureaucracy evolved as the ideal structural form. It allowed for pervasive control from the top of an organizational pyramid. But tight control is a good news/bad news story. The good news is that it is possible to centrally monitor and regulate the behavior of the employees. The bad news is that there are high costs involved with excessive control and the line between tight control and excessive control is a thin one. Employees in organizational straitjackets are unlikely to exercise initiative. Like automatons—human robots—they perform their prescribed duties until appropriate bureaucratic authority tells them otherwise. A properly designed bureaucratic organization can be impressively efficient even though none of its individual bureaucrats are in any way exceptional individuals. This is why Herman Wouk, in his 1951 novel *The Caine Mutiny*, called the U.S. Navy "a machine invented by geniuses, to be run by idiots." These machines, whether governmental or industrial, can be extraordinarily impressive in performance even when run by mediocre people. Thus the French novelist Honoré de Balzac called bureaucracy "the giant power wielded by pygmies." In this sense bureaucracy, far from being incompetent, is a bastion of super-competence—its overall performance far exceeding the quality that could otherwise be expected from its miscellaneous human parts.

Unfortunately, bureaucracies often have within them the seeds of their own incompetence, like a bad genetic inheritance. Robert K. Merton has argued that bureaucracies have inherent dysfunctional and pathological elements that make them inefficient in operations. Merton found that bureaucracies have a "trained incapacity." This refers to a "state of affairs in which one's abilities function as inadequacies or blind spots. Actions based upon training and skills which have been successfully applied in the past may result in inappropriate responses under changed conditions." According to Merton, bureaucracy exerts constant pressures on people to be methodical and disciplined, to conform to patterns of obligations. These pressures eventually cause people to adhere to rules as an end rather than a means—as a matter of blind conformance.

The Hawthorne experiments of the 1930s had provided the first major empirical challenge to the scientific management notion that the worker was primarily an economic animal who would work solely for money. The Hawthorne experiments were undertaken at the Hawthorne Works of the

Western Electric Company near Chicago. This study, one of the most famous management experiments ever reported, was conducted by Elton Mayo and his associates from the Harvard Business School. The decade-long series of experiments started out as traditional scientific management examinations of the relationship between work environment and productivity. But the experimenters, because they were initially unable to explain the results of their findings, literally stumbled on a finding that today seems so obvious—that factories and other work situations are first of all social situations. The workers, as Mary Parker Follett had suggested a decade earlier, were more responsive to peer pressure than to management controls. The Hawthorne studies are generally considered to be the genesis of the human relations school of management thought, providing the first major empirical challenge to the scientific management notion that the worker was primarily an economic animal who would work solely for money.

It is important to note that the Mayo team began its work trying to fit into the mold of classical organization theory thinking. The team phrased its questions in the language and concepts industry was accustomed to using in order to see and explain certain problems, among them productivity in relationship to such factors as the amount of light, the rate of flow of materials, and alternative wage payment plans. The Mayo team succeeded in making significant breakthroughs in understanding only after it redefined the Hawthorne problems as social psychological problems—problems conceptualized in such terms as interpersonal relations in groups, group norms, control over one's own environment, and personal recognition. It was only after the Mayo team achieved this breakthrough that it became the "grandfather"—the direct precursor—of the field of organizational behavior and human resource theory. The Hawthorne experiments were the emotional and intellectual wellspring of modern theories of motivation. They showed that complex, interactional variables make the difference in motivating people—things like attention paid to workers as individuals, workers' control over their own work, differences between individuals' needs, management's willingness to listen, group norms, and direct feedback.

A particularly notable discovery that came out of the Hawthorne experiments was the Hawthorne effect—the discovery that production increases were due to the known presence of benign observers. The researchers' concern for and attention to the workers led the workers, who naturally wanted to be reciprocally nice, to increase production. This "effect" caused great confusion at first because the changing physical conditions (lighting, rest breaks, etc.) seemed to make no difference. Output just kept going up. Once they realized that the workers' perception of participation was the causal "variable," the effects of the "effect" were understood.

Psychologist Abraham H. Maslow (1908–1970),[5] took the basic Hawthorne finding that workers are as much social as economic creatures a step further when he first proposed his famous "needs hierarchy" in his 1943 *Psychological Review* article, "A Theory of Human Motivation," which is reprinted here.

Maslow asserted that humans had five sets of goals or basic needs arranged in a hierarchy of prepotency: physiological needs (food, water, shelter, and so on), safety needs, love or affiliation needs, esteem needs, and the final need for self-actualization—when an individual theoretically reaches self-fulfillment and becomes all that he or she is capable of becoming.[6] Once the lower needs are satisfied, they cease to be motivators of behavior. Conversely, higher needs cannot motivate until lower needs are satisfied. Maslow's psychological analysis of motivation proved to be the foundation for much subsequent research in organizational behavior. Others, such as Frederick Herzberg[7] and Chris Argyris,[8] would take Maslow's concepts and develop them into more comprehensive theories of motivation and organizational behavior. Still, Maslow's work, much as Weber's analysis of bureaucratic structure, would be a critical point of reference.

By the end of the period, the study of individual behavior within organizations underwent a rebirth. Few authors did more to popularize what was often referred to as the new "industrial humanism" than Douglas M. McGregor (1906–1964). His abstraction of the contending traditional and humanistic managerial philosophies evolved into his now famous Theory X and Theory Y sets of assumptions. Like Herbert Simon before him, McGregor pointed out the absurdity of maintaining universal principles of organizational arrangements. While such laws, principles, or proverbs may be appropriate in a highly disciplined hierarchical organization, such as an army, they may become ineffective and even dysfunctional when applied to modern organizations—especially governmental organizations, where a lack of hierarchical discipline is frequently considered to be a valuable check against autocratic tendencies. McGregor's 1957 article, "The Human Side of Enterprise," reprinted here, presented the main themes of his more famous 1960 book with the same title.[9]

McGregor hypothesized that a manager's assumptions about human behavior predetermined his administrative style. Because of the dominance of traditional theory in managerial thought, many managers had long accepted and acted on a set of assumptions that are at best true of only a minority of the population. McGregor labeled as Theory X the following assumptions:

1. The average human being has an inherent dislike of work.
2. Most people must be coerced or threatened with punishment to get them to put forth adequate effort.
3. People prefer to be directed and wish to avoid responsibility.

Theory X sounds very much like a traditional military organization, which, indeed, is where it comes from. While McGregor's portrait of the modern industrial citizen can be criticized for implying greater pessimism concerning human nature on the part of managers than is perhaps warranted, Theory X is all the more valuable as a memorable theoretical construct because it serves as such a polar opposite of Theory Y, which assumes the following:

1. The expenditure of physical and mental effort in work is as natural as play or rest.
2. A person will exercise self-direction and self-control in the service of objectives to which he is committed.
3. Avoidance of responsibility, lack of ambition, and emphasis on security are generally consequences of experience, not inherent human characteristics.
4. The capacity to exercise a relatively high degree of imagination, ingenuity, and creativity in the solution of organizational problems is widely, not narrowly, distributed in the population.

Although the real battle between the human relations approach and traditional mechanistic scientific management on the appropriateness of organizational structure would not be joined until the post–World War II period, there was great activity on the organizational front, especially reorganization. Reorganization would be a recurring theme in the practice and literature of public administration. In later years, scholars such as Harold Seidman,[10] Frederick C. Mosher,[11] and Peter L. Szanton[12] would produce significant works arguing the merits, objectives, and results of numerous reorganization efforts in government. But the first great example of reorganization was the effort recommended by the President's Committee on Administrative Management in 1936–1937.

THE GROWTH OF GOVERNMENT AND THE REFORM MOVEMENT

Commissions started with the conquest of England in 1066. William the Conqueror appointed commissioners to make an inventory of the assets of his new kingdom. This report, known as the Doomsday Book (because its findings were as beyond appeal as a doomsday judgment), is the predecessor of today's royal or presidential commissions and committees. Ever since, prime ministers and presidents have used these devices to investigate a matter of public concern and to issue recommendations for improvement. There is great public satisfaction to be had in the bringing together of a group of responsible, respected, supposedly objective but knowledgeable citizens to examine and report on a national problem or major disaster.

Such commissions have proven to be handy devices for modern presidents who, when faced with an intractable problem, such as crime, pornography, or urban riots, can, at slight expense, appoint a commission as a gesture to indicate his awareness of constituent distress. Whether that gesture has meaning or sincerity beyond itself is inconsequential for its immediate effect. Often, by the time a commission makes its report, six months to a year later, attention will have been diverted to other issues, and the recommendations can be safely pigeonholed or curtailed.

Major reform commission in the 1980s—President Reagan's Grace Commission—and later in the 1990s under President Clinton's reinventing government movement would once again make reorganization a fashionable theme in the practice and literature of American public administration. However, the primary example of government reorganization, the one that to this day is still the most significant, is the restructuring of the executive branch recommended by the President's Committee on Administrative Management in 1936–1937.[13] The committee was popularly known as the Brownlow Committee after its chairman, Louis Brownlow (1879–1963),[14] a major figure in the development of city management as a profession. The other members of the committee were Charles Merriam (1874–1953) of the University of Chicago and Luther Gulick of Columbia University and the Institute of Public Administration in New York City.

Government had grown rapidly during the New Deal period. Because there was little time, or, it was largely believed, inclination for planning, there existed many poorly conceived and poorly implemented organizational designs that were neither economical nor effective. These poor designs were often a reflection of the considerable political conflict between the executive and legislative branches. Both the presidency under Roosevelt and the Congress had deliberately contributed to this problem by establishing programs in new organizations or agencies with regard only to political objectives—as opposed to taking managerial considerations into account. This persistent struggle over organizational control would be addressed by the Brownlow Committee, which would provide the first formal assessment of government organization from a managerial perspective.

When it submitted its report to the president in January 1937, the proposals of the committee were simple enough. Essentially they combined to say that "the president needs help"; that he needs people around him with a "passion for anonymity." This particular passion seems to have faded in recent years along with the public's belief that a modern president writes his own speeches. Overall, the committee recommended a major reorganization of the executive branch. Most of the Brownlow Committee's introduction to its report and its section on "The White House Staff" are reprinted here.

The president agreed, and appropriate legislation was submitted to Congress in 1938. But Congress, in the wake of the president's efforts to "pack" the Supreme Court and fearful of too much power in the presidency, killed the bill. The president resubmitted a considerably modified reorganization bill the following year, and Congress passed the Reorganization Act of 1939. This law created the Executive Office of the President, brought into it the Bureau of the Budget (later to become the Office of Management and Budget in 1970 as a result of another reorganization effort) from the Department of the Treasury, and authorized the president to prepare future reorganization plans subject to a congressional veto.[15]

The Brownlow report, the Executive Office of the President, and many of the other recommendations of the Brownlow Committee that would eventually become law[16] have been sanctified by time. Yet the Brownlow Committee's major proposals aroused considerable controversy at the time. Modern scholars now recognize that there were different schools of thought regarding the development of public administration. The executive administration school, espoused by Frank J. Goodnow, viewed the roles and functions of government almost exclusively as opportunities for executive actions. In contrast, the legislative administrative school, as espoused by William F. Willoughby, viewed the relationship and especially the accountability of administration to the legislative branch as a central focus. This latter school believed that a considerable distinction existed between what was meant by "executive" and "administrative" and that the Constitution gave administrative power mainly to the Congress.

While the Congress was considering the Brownlow Committee's various proposals, the forces opposed to an increase in the administrative powers of the president at the expense of the Congress marshaled their arguments. One of the most eloquent was Lewis Meriam's[17] general analysis of the problem of reorganization, *Reorganization of the National Government: What Does It Involve?*

published in 1939 through the Brookings Institution. Just as the committee's report argued for increased presidential power, Meriam was cautioned against it. Forty years later, the only surviving member of the Brownlow Committee would concede a point to Meriam. In considering Nixon's abuses of the enhanced powers of the presidency that Luther Gulick helped to create, Gulick wrote that "we all assumed in the 1930s that all management, especially public management, flowed in a broad, strong stream of value-filled ethical performance. Were we blind or only naive until Nixon came along? Or were we so eager to take politics out of administration that we threw the baby out with the bathwater?"[18]

EARLY DEBATES ABOUT ACCOUNTABILITY, ETHICS, AND ADMINISTRATIVE RESPONSIBILITY

It is possible to get the impression that during this formative period of public administration most of the focus was on internal issues: management practices and problems, organizational behavior and structures, and budgeting and personnel issues. However, also ongoing was a profound discussion, indeed a debate, over external issues—specifically the concept of administrative responsibility. Basically the issue involved was how we could ensure that governmental administration, in pursuit of being responsive to interest groups, executive and legislative forces, and constituencies, would act legally and responsibly. The resulting debate among early scholars in public administration here was a forerunner to a more robust movement for ensuring ethical behavior within government.

A major perspective on this problem of administrative responsibility and accountability came from E. Pendleton Herring's (1903–2004)[19] 1936 book *Public Administration and the Public Interest.* Herring recognized the problems posed by the dramatic increase in the scope of government and the influence of administrative discretion. He accepted that laws passed by legislatures, institutions designed for compromise, were necessarily the products of legislative compromise and thus often so vague that they were in need of further definition. The bureaucrat, by default, had the job of providing definition to the general principles embodied in a statute by issuing supplemental rules and regulations, or as he argued: "Upon the shoulders of the bureaucrat has been placed in large part the burden of reconciling group differences and making effective and workable the economic and social compromises arrived at through the legislative process."[20] In effect, it became the job of the bureaucrat to ethically define the public interest.

Herring's discussion of the public interest and the critical roles played by bureaucrats and interest groups in public policy formulation correctly anticipated many of the critical issues still being grappled with in schools of public policy and administration today. Herring was a significant voice in what political science calls group theory, a school of thought that views government as representing various group interests and negotiating policy outcomes among them. According to Herring, the most basic task of a bureaucrat was to establish working relationships with the various special interests so that their concerns could be more efficiently brokered. While Herring looked on this process as highly desirable, a quarter century later Theodore J. Lowi would provide a devastating critique of why bureaucracy's penchant for establishing such harmonious working relationships was paralyzing modern government.

The larger issue of how to hold bureaucracy accountable—in other words administrative responsibility—was hotly discussed in the early 1940s by Carl Friedrich (1901–1984) and Herman Finer (1898–1969), two prominent political scientists. A lively debate ensued between the two. Friedrich argued that administrative responsibility is best assured internally, through professionalism or professional standards or codes. Internal checks and balances were necessary because the modern bureaucrat's policy expertise and specialized abilities were so extensive (necessarily so because of the increasing complexities of modern policies). Consequently, there was little real possibility for adequate review by an outside political or legislative source.[21] Finer argued, on the other hand, that administrative responsibility could only be maintained externally through legislative or popular controls. External checks and balances were the only way to ensure subordination of bureaucrats because internal power of control would, ultimately, lead to corruption. In Finer's view, some form of electoral or legislative review was the only possible way to avoid abuses of bureaucratic power.[22]

All of this work would be revisited in the 1960s and 1970s. The Civil Rights movement of the 1960s and the Vietnam War, and later most directly the Watergate scandal, would sorely test public confidence in government, elected officials, and government bureaucrats. Not only would the legitimacy of their behaviors (their rules and procedures) be questioned but also the correctness of the end purposes.

QUESTIONS ABOUT MANAGING RESOURCES IN GOVERNMENT

The 1930s saw the advent of increasingly larger government domestic programs and concomitant expenditures as part of Franklin Roosevelt's New Deal efforts to counter the national depression. Consequently, budgeting became of increasing importance. However, budgetary theory—that is, how to rationally allocate government resources—was woefully inadequate. The emphasis was on process and line-item budgeting, which stressed accountability and control. Performance budgeting, which stressed work measurement, much as scientific management, was increasingly advanced and used as an appropriate management-oriented budgetary process. Nevertheless, there remained little integration of the budgetary process with rational policy making and decision making. In 1940, V. O. Key, Jr. (1908–1963), the political scientist who was to play a leading role in the development of the behavioral approach to the study of U.S. politics,[23] wrote an article (reprinted here) bemoaning "The Lack of a Budgetary Theory." Greatly concerned about the overemphasis on mechanics, he posed what was soon acknowledged as the central question of budgeting: "On what basis shall it be decided to allocate X dollars to activity A instead of activity B?" Key then went on to elaborate on what he felt were the major areas of inquiry that should be researched to develop a budgeting theory. This, along with continuing pressure for even greater increases in the size of government programs, would set the stage for the major advances to come in this critical subfield of public administration.

Reflecting concerns about how government could best allocate resources in this new era of big government, the field of budgeting underwent a stage of consolidation and development of new techniques. Performance budgeting, which was in its prime, after being officially sanctioned by the Hoover Commission of 1949, stressed using the budget process as a tool for work measurement and efficiency analysis. Budgeting began to seriously address V. O. Key's concern for the need for budget theory.

One early response came from Verne B. Lewis, a federal budget officer[24] who in a 1952 Public Administration Review article presented a theory of alternative budgeting. Lewis's analysis began with his recognition of V. O. Key's budget questions from the previous decade as essentially making a case for an economic theory of budgeting. He advocated budget submissions prepared in a manner that would facilitate comparison and demonstrate a range of choices for service and funding levels and at the same time have the final choice provide realistic contracts, that is, specific, realistic expectations for the individual program managers. The implied rationale for this process almost seems a restating of Key's classic budgeting equation: For X level of funding, Y level of service can be provided; for X + I funding, Y + Z services, and so on.

Alternative budgeting, Lewis's preferred solution, was a means to overcome traditional budgetary review techniques that focus on item-by-item control. Rather, the focus would be on scaling levels of program services and goals to varying levels of funding. Lewis, a realist, saw clearly the influence of other factors such as "pride and prejudice, provincialism, and politics" in budgetary decisions.[25] His hope was for the advent of budgeting systems that could overcome these non-economic and non-rational factors.

REJECTING THE POLITICS-ADMINISTRATION DICHOTOMY

By the end of World War II, U.S. public administration had fully developed into a modern bureaucratic state. But the principles of administration as espoused by scientific management proved to be increasingly inadequate when gauged against the size and complexity of modern governments. In the postwar period, which is used broadly here to cover most of the 1940s and all of the 1950s, new challenges to the traditional themes of administration prevailed. Most prominent were the familiar issues of the nature and effects of bureaucratic organizations and the political dimensions of the new administrative state.

While the New Deal and World War II, as true wars against depression and oppression, were economic and military operations, they were also immense managerial undertakings. The experience of those years called into question much of what was then the conventional wisdom of public administration. The politics-administration dichotomy of the reform movement lost its viability amid the New Deal and the war effort. It was simply not possible to take purportedly value-free processes of business and apply them to government. Government, in spite of the best efforts of many reformers, was not a business and was not value free.[26]

The attack on the politics-administration dichotomy came from many quarters at once. David E. Lilienthal, in "Planning and Planners," a chapter from his 1944 book *TVA: Democracy on the March*,[27] wrote of his experiences with the Tennessee Valley Authority.[28] He found the planning process of government to be a blatantly political enterprise—one that was, not incidentally, both healthy and beneficial for a democratic society. Lilienthal's examination of planning and its effects at the TVA contains another critical dimension that would not take root until the 1970s. In voicing great concern about the responsibility of executing the actual plans, he was addressing the problem of implementation. His questions would later help form the crux of our concerns in public policy today: How does planning join the designer and implementer inside the organization? And how does planning ensure the participation of, and not the coercion of, the outside public to accept the plan?

Paul Appleby (1891–1963), a prominent New Deal administrator and dean of the Maxwell School at Syracuse University,[29] wrote perhaps the most skillful polemic of the era, which asserted that this theoretical insistence on apolitical governmental processes went against the grain of the U.S. experience. Appleby in *Big Democracy*[30] compared government to business. In his chapter "Government Is Different," reprinted here, he emphatically shattered public administration's self-imposed demarcation between politics and administration. He held that it was a myth that politics was separate and could somehow be taken out of administration.

Political involvement was good—not evil as many of the progressive reformers had claimed—because political involvement in administration acted as a check on the arbitrary exercise of bureaucratic power. It seems fair to say that Appleby's work was the obituary for the politics-administration dichotomy. In the future, those who would describe the political ramifications and issues of administration would not begin by contesting the politics-administration dichotomy as incorrect or irrelevant. Rather, they would begin from the premise, so succinctly put by Appleby, that "government is different because government is politics."

It would be inappropriate to conclude that the rejection of the politics–administration dichotomy came primarily from the experiences of a now much larger central government. In making the case that public administration should pay more attention to the relationships among governments as a core focus of the discipline, G. Homer Durham in a symposium article in the *Annals* in 1940, dismissed the separation of politics and administrations as defying "realistic analysis." For the "perplexed citizenry" to make sense of the administrative mechanisms and arrangements used by cooperating agencies making public policy or delivering public services, they must be viewed within a single context—administrative politics, if you will.[31] W. Brooke Graves in the same special issue made an even broader case demanding that problems of intergovernmental and interjurisdictional relations in the United States require more basic research about the forms, structures, funding mechanisms, and processes that have resulted from the increase in public services and the public demand for responsible administration.[32] These demands would result in a new emphasis in public administration, the emergence of intergovernmental relations as a major subfield within the discipline.

CREATING THEORIES OF DECISION MAKING AND PUBLIC ADMINISTRATION

Perhaps the most significant landmark in the public administration world of the 1940s was Herbert Simon's (1916–2001) book, *Administrative Behavior*, which urged that a true scientific method be used in the study of administrative phenomena, that the perspective of logical positivism be used in dealing with questions of policy making, and that decision making is the true heart of administration. It was here that Simon refuted the principles approach to public administration that then dominated administrative thinking. In "The Proverbs of Administration," his 1946 *Public Administration Review* article that was later incorporated into his book and that is reprinted here, Simon examined Gulick and Urwick's POSDCORB and its associated components and found them to be inconsistent, conflicting, and inapplicable to many of the administrative situations facing public administrators. Overall, Simon concluded that the so-called principles of administration were really "proverbs of administration."

The last section of Simon's article contains a brief discussion of the limitations on decision making, using the context of rationality. Simon posits a number of questions about how organizations make administrative decisions. His subsequent book presents the beginning of his concept of "bounded rationality" and goes on to build on the theoretical foundations of Chester I. Barnard to advocate a systems approach for examining the various facets of administrative behavior.[33] This initial work and his subsequent research on models and systems of decision making would, more than three decades later, make Simon the first non-economist to win the Nobel Prize in economics.

With the demise of the politics-administration dichotomy, the neat subdivision of what was political science and what was public administration was destroyed. Robert A. Dahl, one of the most significant of the behaviorists in political science,[34] analyzed the state of the art of the discipline of public administration in his 1947 *Public Administration Review* article, "The Science of Public Administration." He prescribed some sources of action for a discipline that had to rapidly emerge on its own terms. But more significantly, Dahl was serving notice to public administration theorists that to be accepted as political science (which was the field of study of most public administration academics), the accepted doctrine that administration is politics would have to move beyond mere revelation. A science of public administration should be created, he argued, that "states ends honestly" and

1. Recognizes the complexities of human behavior
2. Deals with the problems of normative values in administrative situations
3. Takes into account the relationship between public administration and its social setting

Dahl expanded this last point saying that "as long as the study of public administration is not comparative, claims for a science of public administration sound rather hollow." Over the next two decades comparative public administration would emerge as a major subset of the field,[35] but even today the subject is not taught in many public administration programs. Dahl also anticipated some of the difficulties in store for public administration if it wished to stay a branch of political science. Only much later, in the 1970s, would public administration begin to emerge out of both political science and business administration and become a field of study in its own right.

The initial critiques of the principles of administration and the politics-administration dichotomy received support from another very influential source, Dwight Waldo's (1913–2001) *The Administrative State*, first published in 1948. This was originally his doctoral dissertation at Yale. Waldo's influence on public administration would be immense as a writer (he was the field's foremost chronicler and pulse-taker) and as the editor of *Public Administration Review* from 1966 to 1977. In the 1960s, Waldo would gather public administration's younger academics at the Minnowbrook Conference in an attempt to define the problems facing the new public administration. He also sought to define public administration in terms of culture.[36] Only in the 1980s would this concern of organizational definition come into its own. But Waldo's overall perspective held that public administration was a subset of political science that the longstanding art of public administration would have to be fused with the newly emerging science of public administration.

Waldo's conclusion to *The Administrative State*, reprinted here, shows the wellsprings of his concerns in the postwar period as public administration struggled to find a place for itself. Above all, Waldo was a populist who was continually concerned about the values of democracy and the philosophy of public administration. Even in this brief excerpt he was already asking questions that we would not really start to face until the 1980s. For example, "Is training in the mechanics of administration and codes of professional ethics enough?" Some writers see *The Administrative State* as just another voice rejecting POSDCORB and other orthodox public-administration ideologies of the 1930s. It is really much more. It remains the seminal work of an individual who always posed great questions—the answers to which often provided the best indication of how much progress was being made in the field.

Philip Selznick (b. 1919), a sociologist, looked at the processes that Lilienthal and his associates used to gain local support for TVA programs and made famous a new buzzword, *cooptation*, which described the efforts of an organization to bring and subsume new elements into its policy-making process in order to prevent such elements from being a threat to the organization or its mission. Reprinted here is that portion of Selznick's 1949 book, *TVA and the Grass Roots*,[37] that contains his analysis of the process, results, and implications of using "The Cooptative Mechanism." It was the first major sociological treatment of the "powers" of administrative organizations and their impacts on democratic society and public participation in the policy-making process.

Selznick argued that in bureaucratic organizations, cooptation would reflect "a state of tension between formal authority and social power." A decade later in his *Leadership in Administration*,[38] he would examine more comprehensively the various facets of the use of bureaucratic power by administrative organizations and the process of selecting and fulfilling policy goals. Selznick anticipated many of the 1980s notions of "transformational leadership"[39] when he asserted that the function of an institutional leader is to help shape the environment in which the institution operates and to define new institutional directions through recruitment, training, and bargaining.

THE STATE OF PUBLIC ADMINISTRATION AT MID-CENTURY

The first Hoover Commission, 1947–1949, chaired by former President Herbert Hoover (1874–1964), was another milestone in public administration, since, as the first major national inquiry after World War II, it initiated a chain reaction of imitators in other Western democracies. The commission's specific task in relation to the machinery of government was supposed to be to reduce the number of government agencies created during World War II, but it did not do this. Instead, it focused on strengthening the executive branch of government and providing for a reorganization of executive branch agencies to provide a coherent purpose for each department. Instead of calling for a reduction of government agencies, the commission made a vigorous call for increased managerial capacity in the Executive Office of the President through:

1. Unified discretion over presidential organization and staff
2. A strengthened Bureau of the Budget
3. An office of personnel located in the Executive Office of the President
4. The creation of a staff secretary to provide liaison between the president and his subordinates

In addition, the commission recommended that executive branch agencies be reorganized to permit a coherent purpose for each department and better control by the president. Seventy-two percent of its recommendations (196 out of 273) were adopted, including passage of the Reorganization Act of 1949 and the establishment of the Department of Health, Education, and Welfare in 1953.

A second Hoover Commission (1953–1955), also chaired by former President Herbert Hoover, was reconvened, retaining many of the same commission members and staff. This commission had three ostensible purposes: (1) the promoting of economy, efficiency, and improved service in the transaction of the public business; (2) the defining and limiting of executive functions; and (3) the curtailment and abolition of government functions and activities competitive with private enterprise. A major recommendation was the elimination of nonessential government services and activities competitive with private enterprise, based on the assumptions that the federal government had grown beyond appropriate limits and that such growth should be reversed.

In contrast to the earlier commission, the second commission's recommendations accomplished little. In a mere 18 volumes, the former president and his 11 commissioners sought to deliver on these purposes. But the U.S. Congress was not so inclined, and this commission's recommendations went essentially nowhere. However, and more interesting for its historical import than what it accomplished at the time, the second Hoover Commission rigorously argued that a whole host of government activities should be turned over to the private sector. But there was no political will to do so in the mid-1950s.

At mid-century, public administration faced an American society in which the role of government had vastly changed. The impacts of three great events—World War I, the Depression and New Deal, and World War II—had radically altered the size, scope, and reach of government. The public sector was bigger, public sector organizations were larger and more sophisticated, and the trust and expectations of the American public in government to solve societal problems had been significantly raised. Dwight Waldo, in an edited volume of collected essays on public administration published in 1953, commented: "The welfare, happiness, and very lives of all of us . . . rest in significant measure upon the performance of the administrative mechanisms that surround and support us. . . . Willy-nilly, administration is everyone's concern. If we wish to survive, we had better be intelligent about it."[40]

Charles E. Lindblom's (b. 1917) 1959 *Public Administration Review* article, "The Science of 'Muddling Through,'" took a hard look at the rational models of the decisional processes of government. Lindblom rejected the notion that most decisions are made by rational total-information processes. Instead he saw such decisions—indeed, the whole policy-making process—as being dependent on small incremental decisions that tended to be made in response to short-term political conditions. Lindblom's thesis essentially held that decision making was controlled infinitely more by events and circumstances than by the will of those in policy-making positions. His analysis encouraged considerable work in that area of the discipline that sits most on the boundary between political science and public administration–public policy.[41] His article would also have a huge impact on budgeting theory, shaping the debate to such an extent that the dominant theory of budgeting for the next quarter century would be incremental budgeting.[42]

Lindblom's work marked both the closing of the postwar period and the full arrival of big government. Indeed, a major reason that politics, policy, and decision making were so important was the rather daunting size of government effort itself. By the end of the 1950s, there were more than 2.4 million federal civilian employees, 1.5 million state government employees, and 4.8 million local government employees. Government outlays or expenditures at the federal level had now reached $92 billion (the first $100 billion budget would occur in 1962). U.S. government spending (federal, state, and local) went from approximately 11 percent of GDP in 1929, the year of the great stock market crash, to nearly 50 percent toward the end of World War II, but it settled back to an average of 25 percent in the 1950s. Government was on a new plateau, and public administration would be operating at a new level for the foreseeable future.

Notes

1. Leonard D. White, *Introduction to the Study of Public Administration*, rev. ed. (New York: Macmillan, 1939), p. xiv.
2. Sometimes called the "Dean of American Public Administration," Gulick was the Eaton Professor of Municipal Science and Administration at Columbia University from 1931 to 1942; a close adviser to President Franklin D. Roosevelt from even before he became governor of New York; and a founder of the Institute of Public Administration, the American Society for Public Administration, and the National Academy of Public Administration. For an appreciation of his career, see Stephen K. Blumberg, "Seven Decades of Public Administration: A Tribute to Luther Gulick," *Public Administration Review* 41 (March–April 1981).
3. Chester I. Barnard, *The Functions of the Executive* (Cambridge, Mass.: Harvard University Press, 1938). Barnard's only other book was *Organization and Management: Selected Papers* (Cambridge, Mass.: Harvard University Press, 1948).
4. For biographical information, see William B. Wolf, *The Basic Barnard: An Introduction to Chester I. Barnard and His Theories of Organization and Management* (Ithaca, N.Y.: New York State School of Industrial and Labor Relations, Cornell University, 1974).
5. For an intellectual biography, see Frank G. Goble, *The Third Force: The Psychology of Abraham Maslow* (New York: Grossman Publishers, 1970). Maslow would later provide a more expansive analysis of his "needs hierarchy" in his text *Motivation and Personality*, 2d ed. (New York: Harper and Row, 1970).
6. The importance of the concept of self-actualization was established long before Maslow gave it voice. The nineteenth-century poet Robert Browning described its essence when he wrote that "a man's reach should exceed his grasp, or what's a heaven for?"
7. See the "motivation-hygiene" theory in Frederick Herzberg, Bernard Mausner, and Barbara Snyderman, *The Motivation to Work* (New York: Wiley, 1959).
8 See the "personality versus organization" hypothesis in Chris Argyris, *Personality and Organization* (New York: Harper and Row, 1957).
9. Douglas M. McGregor, *The Human Side of Enterprise* (New York: McGraw-Hill, 1960). For an evaluation of McGregor's impact and contributions by a colleague of his at MIT's Sloan School of Management, see Warren G. Bennis, "Chairman Mac in Perspective," *Harvard Business Review* (September–October 1972).
10. Harold Seidman, *Politics, Position, and Power: The Dynamics of Federal Organizations*, 3d ed. (New York: Oxford University Press, 1980).
11. Frederick C. Mosher, *Government Reorganization: Cases and Commentary* (Indianapolis, Ind.: Bobbs-Merrill, 1967).
12. Peter L. Szanton, ed., *Federal Reorganization:* "What Have We Learned?" (Chatham, N.J.: Chatham House, 1981). For a more recent assessment, Peri Arnold's *Making the Managerial Presidency: Comprehensive Reorganization Planning 1905–1996* (Lawrence, Kan.: University Press of Kansas, 1998) is invaluable.
13. For histories of the Brownlow Committee and executive reorganization in the New Deal, see Barry Karl, *Executive Reorganization and Reform in the New Deal* (Cambridge, Mass.: Harvard University Press, 1963); Richard Polenberg, *Reorganizing Roosevelt's Government: The Controversy over Executive Reorganization 1936–1939* (Cambridge, Mass.: Harvard University Press, 1966).
14. For Brownlow's autobiography, see *A Passion for Politics: The Autobiography of Louis Brownlow, First Half* (Chicago: University of Chicago Press, 1955); *A Passion for Anonymity: The Autobiography of Louis Brownlow, Second Half* (Chicago: University of Chicago Press, 1958). For a more objective appreciation, see Barry D. Karl, "Louis Brownlow," *Public Administration Review* 39 (November–December 1979).

15. In the 1983 case of *Immigration and Naturalization Service v. Chadha,* the U.S. Supreme Court questioned the constitutionality of congressional vetoes.
16. For example, the committee recommended "the reorganization of the Civil Service Commission as a central personnel agency." This would not happen until the Civil Service Reform Act of 1978.
17. Meriam, a Brookings Institution staff member, was the liaison between the Brownlow Committee and Brookings, which at the time was working for a congressional committee that was largely opposed to the Brownlow Committee's call for enhanced executive powers. For a biographical portrait, see Donald T. Critchlow, "Lewis Meriam, Expertise, and Indian Reform," *The Historian* 43, no. 4 (May 1981).
18. Blumberg, Stephen K. "Seven Decades of Public Administration: A Tribute to Luther Gulick," *Public Administration Review* 41 (March–April 1981), p. 247.
19. Herring, a Harvard professor who would later spend 20 years as president of the Social Science Research Council (1948–1968), also wrote a pioneering study on the role of pressure groups, *Group Representation before Congress* (New York: Russell and Russell, 1929), and one of the first studies on the relationship between a manager's background and behavior in office, *Federal Commissioners: A Study of Their Careers and Qualifications* (Cambridge, Mass.: Harvard University Press, 1936).
20. E. P. Herring, *Public Administration and the Public Interest* (New York: McGraw-Hill Book Company, 1936), p. 7.
21. Carl J. Friedrich, "The Nature of Administrative Responsibility," in *Public Policy,* ed. Carl J. Friedrich (Cambridge, Mass.: Harvard University Press, 1940).
22. Herman Finer, "Administrative Responsibility in Democratic Government," *Public Administration Review* 1 (autumn 1941).
23. Key's major works included *Politics, Parties, and Pressure Groups,* 5th ed. (New York: Crowell, 1964); *Southern Politics in State and Nation* (New York: Alfred A. Knopf, 1949); *American State Politics: An Introduction* (New York: Alfred A. Knopf, 1956); *Public Opinion and American Democracy* (New York: Alfred A. Knopf, 1961).
24. Lewis, after more than a decade with the Atomic Energy Commission, was the Director of Budget and Finance for the Department of State from 1961 to 1971.
25. Verne B. Lewis, "Toward a Theory of Budgeting," Public Administration Review (1952).
26. The most comprehensive analysis of the values of public administration from this period is in Dwight Waldo's *The Administrative State: A Study of the Political Theory of American Public Administration* (New York: Ronald Press, 1948), which attacked the "gospel of efficiency" that so dominated administrative thinking prior to World War II.
27. David E. Lilienthal, *TVA: Democracy on the March* (New York: Harper and Row, 1944).
28. Lilienthal was chairman of the TVA and later of the Atomic Energy Commission. He kept and later published comprehensive diaries of his experiences. See *The Journals of David E. Lilienthal,* 6 vols. (New York: Harper and Row, 1964–1976).
29. For a review of Appleby's work and influence, see Roscoe C. Martin, ed., *Public Administration and Democracy: Essays in Honor of Paul H. Appleby* (Syracuse, N.Y.: Syracuse University Press, 1965).
30. Paul H. Appleby, *Big Democracy* (New York: Knopf, 1945).
31. G. Homer Durham "Politics and Administration in Intergovernmental Relations," *Annals of the American Academy of Political and Social Science* 207 (January 1940): pp. 1–6.
32. W. Brooke Graves, "Readjusting Governmental Areas and Functions," *Annals of the American Academy of Political and Social Science* 207 (January 1940): pp. 203–209.
33. Because truly rational research on any problem can never be completed, humans put "bounds" on their rationality and make decisions not on the basis of optimal information but on the basis of satisfactory information. Thus, humans tend to make their decisions by "satisficing"—choosing a course of action that meets one's minimum standards for satisfaction. Simon, with James March, expands on these notions in *Organizations* (New York: Wiley, 1958).

34. Dahl was a prime exponent of pluralism and interest group participation in the political process. His major works include, with Charles E. Lindblom, *Politics, Economics and Welfare* (New York: Harper and Row, 1953); *A Preface to Democratic Theory* (Chicago: University of Chicago Press, 1956); *Who Governs? Democracy and Power in an American City* (New Haven, Conn.: Yale University Press, 1961); *Modern Political Analysis*, 3d ed. (Englewood Cliffs, N.J.: Prentice-Hall, 1976).
35. The major text in comparative public administration is Ferrel Heady, *Public Administration: A Comparative Perspective*, 6th ed. (New York: CRC Press, 2001).
36. The first chapter from his *The Study of Public Administration* (New York: Random House, 1955) is an extended analysis on the definition of public administration. It was reprinted in earlier editions of *Classics of Public Administration*.
37. Philip Selznick, *TVA and the Grass Roots* (Berkeley and Los Angeles: University of California Press, 1949).
38. Philip Selznick, *Leadership in Administration* (New York: Row, Peterson, 1957).
39. See, for example, Warren G. Bennis, "Transformative Power and *Leadership," in Leadership and Organizational Culture*, ed. T. J. Sergiovanni and J. E. Corbally (Urbana, Ill.: University of Illinois Press, 1984); Noel M. Tichy and David O. Ulrich, "The Leadership Challenge: A Call for the Transformational Leader," *Sloan Management Review* 26 (fall 1984).
40. Dwight Waldo, ed. "The Role of Administration in Modern Society," in *Ideas and Issues in Public Administration* (New York: McGraw-Hill, 1953), p. 2.
41. Lindblom's article created a new subfield in public administration "muddle analysis." See Yehezkel Dror, "Muddling Through: Science or Inertia?" *Public Administration Review* 24 (September 1964); John J. Bailey and Robert J. O'Connor, "Operational Incrementalism: Measuring the Muddles," *Public Administration Review* 35 (January–February 1975); Anthony J. Balzer, "Reflections on Muddling Through," *Public Administration Review* 39 (November–December 1979); Bruce Adams, 'The Limitations of Muddling Through: Does Anyone in Washington Really Think Anymore?" *Public Administration Review* 39 (November–December 1979); Charles E. Lindblom, "Still Muddling, Not Yet Through," *Public Administration Review* 39 (November–December 1979).
42. Of course, budgeting theory in the next decade, the 1960s, would be shaped first by Aaron Wildavsky—especially with his *The Politics of the Budgetary Process* (New York: Little, Brown, 1964)—and then by Alan Schick in a series of articles written for *Public Administration Review*. See especially the Budgeting Symposiums of 1966 and 1969.

Notes on the Theory of Organization

Luther Gulick

Every large-scale or complicated enterprise requires many men to carry it forward. Wherever many men are thus working together the best results are secured when there is a division of work among these men. The theory of organization, therefore, has to do with the structure of co-ordination imposed upon the workdivision units of an enterprise. Hence it is not possible to determine how an activity is to be organized without, at the same time, considering how the work in question is to be divided. Work division is the foundation of organization; indeed, the reason for organization.

1. The Division of Work

It is appropriate at the outset of this discussion to consider the reasons for and the effect of the division of work. It is sufficient for our purpose to note the following factors.

Why Divide Work? Because men differ in nature, capacity and skill, and gain greatly in dexterity by specialization; because the same man cannot be at two places at the same time; because the range of knowledge and skill is so great that a man cannot within his life-span know more than a small fraction of it. In other words, it is a question of human nature, time, and space.

In a shoe factory it would be possible to have 1,000 men each assigned to making complete pairs of shoes. Each man would cut his leather, stamp in the eyelets, sew up the tops, sew on the bottoms, nail on the heels, put in the laces, and pack each pair in a box. It might take two days to do the job. One thousand men would make 500 pairs of shoes a day. It would also be possible to divide the work among these same men, using the identical hand methods, in an entirely different way. One group of men would be assigned to cut the leather, another to putting in the eyelets, another to stitching up the tops, another to sewing on the soles, another to nailing on the heels, another to inserting the laces and packing the pairs of shoes. We know from common sense and experience that there are two great gains in this latter process: first, it makes possible the better utilization of the varying skills and aptitudes of the different workmen, and encourages the development of specialization; and second, it eliminates the time that is lost when a workman turns from a knife, to a punch, to a needle and awl, to a hammer, and moves from table to bench, to anvil, to stool. Without any pressure on the workers, they could probably turn out twice as many shoes in a single day. There would be additional economies, because inserting laces and packing could be assigned to unskilled and low-paid workers. Moreover, in the cutting of the leather there would be less spoilage because the less skillful pattern cutters would all be eliminated and assigned to other work. It would also be possible to cut a dozen shoe tops at the same time from the same pattern with little additional effort. All of these advances would follow, without the introduction of new labor saving machinery.

The introduction of machinery accentuates the division of work. Even such a simple thing as a saw, a typewriter, or a transit requires increased specialization, and serves to divide workers into those who can and those who cannot use the particular instrument effectively. Division of work on the basis of the tools and machines used in work rests no doubt in part on aptitude, but primarily upon the development and maintenance of skill through continued manipulation.

Specialized skills are developed not alone in connection with machines and tools. They

Source: From L. Gulick and L. Urwick, eds., Papers on the Science of Administration (New York: Institute of Public Administration, 1937), pp. 3-13. Reprinted by permission of Blackwell Publishing.

evolve naturally from the materials handled, like wood, or cattle, or paint, or cement. They arise similarly in activities which center in a complicated series of interrelated concepts, principles, and techniques. These are most clearly recognized in the professions, particularly those based on the application of scientific knowledge, as in engineering, medicine, and chemistry. They are none the less equally present in law, ministry, teaching, accountancy, navigation, aviation, and other fields.

The nature of these subdivisions is essentially pragmatic, in spite of the fact that there is an element of logic underlying them. They are therefore subject to a gradual evolution with the advance of science, the invention of new machines, the progress of technology and the change of the social system. In the last analysis, however, they appear to be based upon differences in individual human beings. But it is not to be concluded that the apparent stability of "human nature," whatever that may be, limits the probable development of specialization. The situation is quite the reverse. As each field of knowledge and work is advanced, constituting a continually larger and more complicated nexus of related principles, practices and skills, any individual will be less and less able to encompass it and maintain intimate knowledge and facility over the entire area, and there will thus arise a more minute specialization because knowledge and skill advance while man stands still. Division of work and integrated organization are the bootstraps by which mankind lifts itself in the process of civilization.

The Limits of Division There are three clear limitations beyond which the division of work cannot to advantage go. The first is practical and arises from the volume of work involved in man-hours. Nothing is gained by subdividing work if that further subdivision results in setting up a task which requires less than the full time of one man. This is too obvious to need demonstration. The only exception arises where space interferes, and in such cases the part-time expert must fill in his spare time at other tasks, so that as a matter of fact a new combination is introduced.

The second limitation arises from technology and custom at a given time and place. In some areas nothing would be gained by separating undertaking from the custody and cleaning of churches, because by custom the sexton is the undertaker; in building construction it is extraordinarily difficult to redivide certain aspects of electrical and plumbing work and to combine them in a more effective way, because of the jurisdictional conflicts of craft unions; and it is clearly impracticable to establish a division of cost accounting in a field in which no technique of costing has yet been developed.

This second limitation is obviously elastic. It may be changed by invention and by education. If this were not the fact, we should face a static division of labor. It should be noted, however, that a marked change has two dangers. It greatly restricts the labor market from which workers may be drawn and greatly lessens the opportunities open to those who are trained for the particular specialization.

The third limitation is that the subdivision of work must not pass beyond physical division into organic division. It might seem far more efficient to have the front half of the cow in the pasture grazing and the rear half in the barn being milked all of the time, but this organic division would fail. Similarly there is no gain from splitting a single movement or gesture like licking an envelope, or tearing apart a series of intimately and intricately related activities.

It may be said that there is in this an element of reasoning in a circle; that the test here applied as to whether an activity is organic or not is whether it is divisible or not—which is what we set out to define. This charge is true. It must be a pragmatic test. Does the division work out? Is something vital destroyed and lost? Does it bleed?

The Whole and the Parts It is axiomatic that the whole is equal to the sum of its parts. But in dividing up any "whole," one must be certain that every part, including unseen elements and relationships, is accounted for. The marble sand to which the Venus de Milo may be reduced by a vandal does not equal the statue, though every last grain be preserved; nor is a thrush just so much feathers, bones, flesh and blood; nor a typewriter merely so much steel, glass, paint and rubber. Similarly a piece of work to be done cannot be subdivided into the obvious component parts without great danger that the central design, the operating relationship, the imprisoned idea, will be lost.

A simple illustration will make this clear. One man can build a house. He can lay the foundation, cut the beams and boards, make the window frames and doors, lay the floors, raise the roof, plaster the walls, fit in the heating and water systems, install the electric wiring, hang the paper, and paint the structure. But if he did, most of the work would be done by hands unskilled in the work; much material would be spoiled, and the work would require many months of his time. On the other hand, the whole job of building the house might be divided among a group of men. One man could do the foundation, build the chimney, and plaster the walls; another could erect the frame, cut the timbers and the boards, raise the roof, and do all the carpentry; another all the plumbing; another all the paper hanging and painting; another all the electric wiring. But this would not make a house unless someone—an architect—made a plan for the house, so that each skilled worker could know what to do and when to do it.

When one man builds a house alone he plans as he works; he decides what to do first and what next, that is, he "co-ordinates the work." When many men work together to build a house this part of the work, the co-ordinating, must not be lost sight of.

In the "division of the work" among the various skilled specialists, a specialist in planning and co-ordination must be sought as well. Otherwise, a great deal of time may be lost, workers may get in each other's way, material may not be on hand when needed, things may be done in the wrong order, and there may even be a difference of opinion as to where the various doors and windows are to go. It is self-evident that the more the work is subdivided, the greater is the danger of confusion, and the greater is the need of overall supervision and coordination. Co-ordination is not something that develops by accident. It must be won by intelligent, vigorous, persistent and organized effort.

2. The Co-ordination of Work

If subdivision of work is inescapable, coordination becomes mandatory. There is, however, no one way to co-ordination. Experience shows that it may be achieved in two primary ways. These are:

1. By organization, that is, by interrelating the subdivisions of work by allotting them to men who are placed in a structure of authority, so that the work may be co-ordinated by orders of superiors to subordinates, reaching from the top to the bottom of the entire enterprise.
2. By the dominance of an idea, that is, the development of intelligent singleness of purpose in the minds and wills of those who are working together as a group, so that each worker will of his own accord fit his task into the whole with skill and enthusiasm.

These two principles of co-ordination are not mutually exclusive, in fact, no enterprise is really effective without the extensive utilization of both.

Size and time are the great limiting factors in the development of co-ordination. In a small project, the problem is not difficult; the structure of authority is simple, and the central purpose is real to every worker. In a large complicated enterprise, the organization becomes involved, the lines of authority tangled, and there is danger that the workers will forget that there is any central purpose, and so devote their best energies only to their own individual advancement and advantage.

The interrelated elements of time and habit are extraordinarily important in co-ordination. Man is a creature of habit. When an enterprise is built up gradually from small beginnings the staff can be "broken in" step by step. And when difficulties develop, they can be ironed out, and the new method followed from that point on as a matter of habit, with the knowledge that that particular difficulty will not develop again. Routines may even be mastered by drill as they are in the army. When, however, a large new enterprise must be set up or altered overnight, then the real difficulties of co-ordination make their appearance. The factor of habit, which is thus an important foundation of co-ordination when time is available, becomes a serious handicap when time is not available, that is, when change rules. The question of co-ordination therefore must be approached with different emphasis in small and in large enterprises; in simple and in complex situations; in stable and in new or changing organizations.

Co-ordination through Organization Organization as a way of co-ordination requires the establishment of a system of authority whereby the central purpose or objective of an enterprise is translated into reality through the combined efforts of many specialists, each working in his own field at a particular time and place.

It is clear from long experience in human affairs that such a structure of authority requires not only many men at work in many places at selected times, but also a single directing executive authority.[1] The problem of organization thus becomes the problem of building up between the executive at the center and the subdivisions of work on the periphery an effective network of communication and control.

The following outline may serve further to define the problem:

I. First Step: Define the job to be done, such as the furnishing of pure water to all of the people and industries within a given area at the lowest possible cost;
II. Second Step: Provide a director to see that the objective is realized;
III. Third Step: Determine the nature and number of individualized and specialized work units into which the job will have to be divided. As has been seen above, this subdivision depends partly upon the size of the job (no ultimate subdivision can generally be so small as to require less than the full time of one worker) and upon the status of technological and social development at a given time;
IV. Fourth Step: Establish and perfect the structure of authority between the director and the ultimate work subdivisions.

It is this fourth step which is the central concern of the theory of organization. It is the function of this organization (IV) to enable the director (II) to co-ordinate and energize all of the subdivisions of work (III) so that the major objective (I) may be achieved efficiently.

The Span of Control In this undertaking we are confronted at the start by the inexorable limits of human nature. Just as the hand of man can span only a limited number of notes on the piano, so the mind and will of man can span but a limited number of immediate managerial contacts. . . . The limit of control is partly a matter of the limits of knowledge, but even more is it a matter of the limits of time andof energy. As a result the executive of any enterprise can personally direct only a few persons. He must depend upon these to direct others, and upon them in turn to direct still others, until the last man in the organization is reached.

This condition placed upon all human organization by the limits of the span of control obviously differs in different kinds of work and in organizations of different sizes. Where the work is of a routine, repetitive, measurable and homogeneous character, one man can perhaps direct several score workers. This is particularly true when the workers are all in a single room. Where the work is diversified, qualitative, and particularly when the workers are scattered, one man can supervise only a few. This diversification, dispersion, and non-measurability is of course most evident at the very top of any organization. It follows that the limitations imposed by the span of control are most evident at the top of an organization, directly under the executive himself.

But when we seek to determine how many immediate subordinates the director of an enterprise can effectively supervise, we enter a realm of experience which has not been brought under sufficient scientific study to furnish a final answer. Sir Ian Hamilton says, "The nearer we approach the supreme head of the whole organization, the more we ought to work towards groups of three; the closer we get to the foot of the whole organization (the Infantry of the Line), the more we work towards groups of six."[2]

The British Machinery of Government Committee of 1918 arrived at the conclusion that "The Cabinet should be small in number—preferably ten or, at most, twelve."[3]

Henri Fayol said "[In France] a minister has twenty assistants, where the Administrative Theory says that a manager at the head of a big undertaking should not have more than five or six."[4]

Graham Wallas expressed the opinion that the Cabinet should not be increased "beyond the number of ten or twelve at which organized oral discussion is most efficient."[5]

Léon Blum recommended for France a Prime Minister with a technical cabine modelled after the British War Cabinet, which was composed of five members.[6]

It is not difficult to understand why there is this divergence of statement among authorities who are agreed on the fundamentals. It arises in part from the differences in the capacities and work habits of individual executives observed, and in part from the non-comparable character of the work covered. It would seem that insufficient attention has been devoted to three factors, first, the element of diversification of function; second, the element of time; and third, the element of space. A chief of public works can deal effectively with more direct subordinates than can the general of the army, because all of his immediate subordinates in the department of public works will be in the general field of engineering, while in the army there will be many different elements, such as communications, chemistry, aviation, ordnance, motorized service, engineering, supply, transportation, etc., each with its own technology. The element of time is also of great significance as has been indicated above. In a stable organization the chief executive can deal with more immediate subordinates than in a new or changing organization. Similarly, space influences the span of control. An organization located in one building can be supervised through more immediate subordinates than can the same organization if scattered in several cities. When scattered there is not only need for more supervision, and therefore more supervisory personnel, but also for a fewer number of contacts with the chief executive because of the increased difficulty faced by the chief executive in learning sufficient details about a far-flung organization to do an intelligent job. The failure to attach sufficient importance to these variables has served to limit the scientific validity of the statements which have been made that one man can supervise but three, or five, or eight, or twelve immediate subordinates.

These considerations do not, however, dispose of the problem. They indicate rather the need for further research. But without further research we may conclude that the chief executive of an organization can deal with only a few immediate subordinates; that this number is determined not only by the nature of the work, but also by the nature of the executive; and that the number of immediate subordinates in a large, diversified and dispersed organization must be even less than in a homogeneous and unified organization to achieve the same measure of co-ordination.

One Master From the earliest times it has been recognized that nothing but confusion arises under multiple command. "A man cannot serve two masters" was adduced as a theological argument because it was already accepted as a principle of human relation in everyday life. In administration this is known as the principle of "unity of command."[7] The principle may be stated as follows: A workman subject to orders from several superiors will be confused, inefficient, and irresponsible; a workman subject to orders from but one superior may be methodical, efficient, and responsible. Unity of command thus refers to those who are commanded, not to those who issue the commands.[8]

The significance of this principle in the process of co-ordination and organization must not be lost sight of. In building a structure of co-ordination, it is often tempting to set up more than one boss for a man who is doing work which has more than one relationship. Even as great a philosopher of management as Taylor fell into this error in setting up separate foremen to deal with machinery, with materials, with speed, etc., each with the power of giving orders directly to the individual workman.[9] The rigid adherence to the principle of unity of command may have its absurdities; these are, however, unimportant in comparison with the certainty of confusion, inefficiency and irresponsibility which arise from the violation of the principle.

Technical Efficiency There are many aspects of the problem of securing technical efficiency. Most of these do not concern us here directly. They have been treated extensively by such authorities as Taylor, Dennison, and Kimball, and their implications for general organization by Fayol, Urwick, Mooney, and Reiley. There is, however, one efficiency concept which concerns us deeply in approaching the theory of organization. It is the principle of homogeneity.

It has been observed by authorities in many fields that the efficiency of a group working together is directly related to the homogeneity of the work they are performing, of the processes they are utilizing, and of the purposes which actuate them. From top to bottom, the group must be unified. It must work together.

It follows from this (1) that any organizational structure which brings together in a single unit work divisions which are nonhomogeneous in work, in technology, or in purpose will encounter the danger of friction and inefficiency; and (2) that a unit based on a given specialization cannot be given technical direction by a layman.

In the realm of government it is not difficult to find many illustrations of the unsatisfactory results of non-homogeneous administrative combinations. It is generally agreed that agricultural development and education cannot be administered by the same men who enforce pest and disease control, because the success of the former rests upon friendly co-operation and trust of the farmers, while the latter engenders resentment and suspicion. Similarly, activities like drug control established in protection of the consumer do not find appropriate homes in departments dominated by the interests of the producer. In the larger cities and in states it has been found that hospitals cannot be so well administered by the health department directly as they can be when set up independently in a separate department, or at least in a bureau with extensive autonomy, and it is generally agreed that public welfare administration and police administration require separation, as do public health administration and welfare administration, though both of these combinations may be found in successful operation under special conditions. No one would think of combining water supply and public education, or tax administration and public recreation. In every one of these cases, it will be seen that there is some element either of work to be done, or of the technology used, or of the end sought which is non-homogeneous.

Another phase of the combination of incompatible functions in the same office may be found in the common American practice of appointing unqualified laymen and politicians to technical positions or to give technical direction to highly specialized services. As Dr. Frank J. Goodnow pointed out a generation ago, we are faced here by two heterogeneous functions, "politics" and "administration," the combination of which cannot be undertaken within the structure of the without producing inefficiency.

Caveamus Expertum At this point a word of caution is necessary. The application of the principle of homogeneity has its pitfalls. Every highly trained technician, particularly in the learned professions, has a profound sense of omniscience and a great desire for complete independence in the service of society. When employed by government he knows exactly what the people need better than they do themselves, and he knows how to render this service. He tends to be utterly oblivious of all other needs, because, after all, is not his particular technology the road to salvation? Any restraint applied to him is "limitation of freedom," and any criticism "springs from ignorance and jealousy." Every budget increase he secures is "in the public interest," while every increase secured elsewhere is "a sheer waste." His efforts and maneuvers to expand are "public education" and "civic organization," while similar efforts by others are "propaganda" and "politics."

Another trait of the expert is his tendency to assume knowledge and authority in fields in which he has no competence. In this particular, educators, lawyers, priests, admirals, doctors, scientists, engineers, accountants, merchants and bankers are all the same—having achieved technical competence or "success" in one field, they come to think this competence is a general quality detachable from the field and inherent in themselves. They step without embarrassment into other areas. They do not remember that the robes of authority of one kingdom confer no sovereignty in another; but that there they are merely a masquerade.

The expert knows his "stuff." Society needs him, and must have him more and more as man's technical knowledge becomes more and more extensive. But history shows us that the common man is a better judge of his own needs in the long run than any cult of experts. Kings and ruling classes, priests and prophets, soldiers and lawyers, when permitted to rule rather than serve mankind, have in the end done more to check the advance of human welfare than they have to advance it. The true place of the expert is, as it is said so well, "on tap, not on top." The essential validity of democracy rests upon this philosophy, for democracy is a way of government in which the common man is the final judge of what is good for him.

Efficiency is one of the things that is good for him because it makes life richer and safer. That efficiency is to be secured more and more through the use of technical specialists. These specialists have no right to ask for, and must not be given freedom from supervisory control, but in establishing that control, a government which ignores the conditions of efficiency cannot expect to achieve efficiency.

3. Organizational Patterns

Organization Up or Down? One of the great sources of confusion in the discussion of the theory of organization is that some authorities work and think primarily from the top down, while others work and think from the bottom up. This is perfectly natural because some authorities are interested primarily in the executive and in the problems of central management, while others are interested primarily in individual services and activities. Those who work from the top down regard the organization as a system of subdividing the enterprise under the chief executive, while those who work from the bottom up, look upon organization as a system of combining the individual units of work into aggregates which are in turn subordinated to the chief executive. It may be argued that either approach leads to a consideration of the entire problem, so that it is of no great significance which way the organization is viewed. Certainly it makes this very important practical difference: those who work from the top down must guard themselves from the danger of sacrificing the effectiveness of the individual services in their zeal to achieve a model structure at the top, while those who start from the bottom, must guard themselves from the danger of thwarting co-ordination in their eagerness to develop effective individual services.

In any practical situation the problem of organization must be approached from both top and bottom. This is particularly true in the reorganization of a going concern. May it not be that this practical necessity is likewise the sound process theoretically? In that case one would develop the plan of an organization or reorganization both from the top downward and from the bottom upward, and would reconcile the two at the center. In planning the first subdivisions under the chief executive, the principle of the limitation of the span of control must apply; in building up the first aggregates of specialized functions, the principle of homogeneity must apply. If any enterprise has such an array of functions that the first subdivisions from the top down do not readily meet the first aggregations from the bottom up, then additional divisions and additional aggregates must be introduced, but at each further step there must be a less and less rigorous adherence to the two conflicting principles until their juncture is effected.

An interesting illustration of this problem was encountered in the plans for the reorganization of the City of New York. The Charter Commission of 1934 approached the problem with the determination to cut down the number of departments and separate activities from some 60 to a manageable number. It was equally convinced after conferences with officials from the various city departments that the number could not be brought below 25 without bringing together as "departments" activities which had nothing in common or were in actual conflict. This was still too many for effective supervision by the chief executive. As a solution it was suggested by the author that the charter provide for the subdividing of the executive by the appointment of three or four assistant mayors to whom the mayor might assign parts of his task of broad supervision and co-ordination. Under the plan the assistant mayors would bring all novel and important matters to the mayor for decision, and through continual intimate relationship know the temper of his mind on all matters, and thus be able to relieve him of great masses of detail without in any way injecting themselves into the determination of policy. Under such a plan one assistant mayor might be assigned to give general direction to agencies as diverse as police, parks, hospitals, and docks without violating the principle of homogeneity any more than is the case by bringing these activities under the mayor himself, which is after all a paramount necessity under a democratically controlled government. This is not a violation of the principle of homogeneity *provided* the assistant mayors keep out of the technology of the services and devote themselves to the broad aspects of administration and co-ordination, as would the mayor himself. The assistants were conceived of as parts of the mayoralty, not as parts of the service departments. That is, they represented not the apex of a structure built from the bottom up, but rather the base of a structure extended from the top down, the object of which was to multiply by four the points of effective contact between the executive and the service departments.[10]

Organizing the Executive The effect of the suggestion presented above is to organize and institutionalize the executive function as such so that it may be more adequate in a complicated situation. This is in reality not a new idea. We do not, for example, expect the chief executive to write his own letters. We give him a private secretary, who is part of his office and assists him to do this part of his job. This secretary is not a part of any department; he is a subdivision of the executive himself. In just this way, though on a different plane, other phases of the job of the chief executive may be organized.

Before doing this, however, it is necessary to have a clear picture of the job itself. This brings us directly to the question, "What is the work of the chief executive? What does he do?"

The answer is POSDCORB.

POSDCORB is, of course, a made-up word designed to call attention to the various functional elements of the work of a chief executive because "administration" and "management" have lost all specific content.[11] POSDCORB is made up of the initials and stands for the following activities:

Planning, that is working out in broad outline the things that need to be done and the methods for doing them to accomplish the purpose set for the enterprise;

Organizing, that is the establishment of the formal structure of authority through which work subdivisions are arranged, defined and co-ordinated for the defined objective;

Staffing, that is the whole personnel function of bringing in and training the staff and maintaining favorable conditions of work;

Directing, that is the continuous task of making decisions and embodying them in specific and general orders and instructions and serving as the leader of the enterprise;

Co-ordinating, that is the all important duty of interrelating the various parts of the work;

Reporting, that is keeping those to whom the executive is responsible informed as to what is going on, which thus includes keeping himself and his subordinates informed through records, research and inspection;

Budgeting, with all that goes with budgeting in the form of fiscal planning, accounting and control.

This statement of the work of a chief executive is adapted from the functional analysis elaborated by Henri Fayol in his "Industrial and General Administration." It is believed that those who know administration intimately will find in this analysis a valid and helpful pattern, into which can be fitted each of the major activities and duties of any chief executive.

If these seven elements may be accepted as the major duties of the chief executive, it follows that they *may* be separately organized as subdivisions of the executive. The need for such subdivision depends entirely on the size and complexity of the enterprise. In the largest enterprises, particularly where the chief executive is as a matter of fact unable to do the work that is thrown upon him, it may be presumed that one or more parts of POSDCORB should be suborganized.

Notes

1. [That is,] when *organization is the basis of co-ordination.* Wherever the central executive authority is composed of several who exercise their functions jointly by majority vote, as on a board, this is from the standpoint of organization still a "single authority"; where the central executive is in reality composed of several men acting freely and independently, then organization cannot be said to be the basis of co-ordination; it is rather the dominance of an idea and falls under the second principle stated above.
2. Sir Ian Hamilton, *The Soul and Body of an Army* (London; Arnold, 1921), p. 230.
3. Great Britain. Ministry of Reconstruction. *Report of the Machinery of Government Committee.* (London; H. M. Stationery Office, 1918), p. 5.
4. Henri Fayol, "The Administrative Theory in the State" (address before the Second International Congress of Administrative Science at Brussels, September 13, 1923 ...).
5. Graham Wallas, *The Great Society* (London: Macmillan, 1919), p. 264.
6. Léon Blum, *La reforme gouvernementale* (Paris, Grasset: 1918; reprint, 1936), p. 59.
7. Henri Fayol, *Industrial and General Administration,* trans. J. A. Coubrough (Geneva: International Management Association, 1930).
8. Fayol terms the latter "unity of direction."
9. Frederick Winslow Taylor, *Shop Management* (New York: Harper and Row, 1911), p. 99.
10. This recommendation was also presented to the Thatcher Charter Commission of 1935, to which the author was a consultant. A first step in this direction was taken in Sec. 9, Chap. I of the new charter which provides for a deputy mayor, and for such other assistance as may be provided by ordinance.
11. See Minutes of the *Princeton Conference on Training for the Public Service,* 1935, p. 35. See also criticism of this analysis in Lewis Meriam, *Public Service and Special Training* (University of Chicago Press, 1936), pp. 1, 2, 10, and 15, where this functional analysis is misinterpreted as a statement of qualifications for appointment.

9

Informal Organizations and Their Relation to Formal Organizations

Chester I. Barnard

I. What Informal Organizations Are

It is a matter of general observation and experience that persons are frequently in contact and interact with each other when their relationships are not a part of or governed by any formal organization. The magnitude of the numbers involved varies from two persons to that of a large mob or crowd. The characteristic of these contacts or interactions is that they occur and continue or are repeated without any specific conscious *joint* purpose. The contact may be accidental, or incidental to organized activities, or arise from some personal desire or gregarious instinct, it may be friendly or hostile. But whatever the origins, the fact of such contacts, interactions, or groupings changes the experience, knowledge, attitudes, and emotions of the individuals affected. Sometimes we are aware of the fact that our emotions are affected, for example, by being in a crowd, more often we observe the effects of such relationships in others; still more frequently we are not aware of any permanent effects either in ourselves or in others by direct observation. But we nevertheless currently show that we infer such effects by using the phrase "mob psychology," by recognizing imitation and emulation, by understanding that there are certain attitudes commonly held, and very often by our use of the phrases "consensus of opinion" and "public opinion." The persistence of such effects is embodied in "states of mind" and habits of action which indicate the capacities of memory, experience, and social conditioning. As a result of these capacities some of the effects of contacts of persons with limited numbers of persons can spread through very large numbers in a sort of endless chain of interaction over wide territories and through long periods of time.

By informal organization I mean the aggregate of the personal contacts and interactions and the associated groupings of people that I have just described. Though common or joint purposes are excluded by definition, common or joint results of important character nevertheless come from such organization.

Now it is evident from this description that informal organization is indefinite and rather structureless, and has no definite subdivision. It may be regarded as a shapeless mass of quite varied densities, the variations in density being a result of external factors affecting the closeness of people geographically or of formal purposes which bring them specially into contact for conscious joint accomplishments. These areas of special density I call informal organizations, as distinguished from societal or general organization in its informal aspects. Thus there is an informal organization of a community, of a state. For our purposes, it is important that there are informal organizations related to formal organizations everywhere.

II. Consequences of Informal Organizations

Informal organization, although comprising the processes of society which are unconscious as contrasted with those of formal organization which are conscious, has two important classes of effects: (*a*) it establishes certain attitudes, understandings, customs, habits, institutions; and (*b*) it creates the condition under which formal organization may arise.

Source: Reprinted by permission of the publishers from The Functions of the Executive by Chester I. Barnard, Introduction by Kenneth R. Andrews, Cambridge, Mass.: Harvard University Press.

(*a*) The most general direct effects of informal organization are customs, mores, folklore, institutions, social norms and ideals—a field of importance in general sociology and especially in social psychology and in social anthropology. No discussion of these effects is necessary here, except on two points. The first is that as a result, as I think, of the inadequate attention to formal organization there is much confusion between formal institutions, resulting directly from formal organizational processes, and informal institutions resulting from informal organization; for example, a practice established by legal enactment, and a custom, the latter usually prevailing in the event of conflict. Not only locally, in restricted collectivities, but in broad areas and large collectivities, there is a divergence, and a corrective interaction, between institutions informally developed and those elaborated through formal organization practices. The first correspond to the unconscious or non-intellectual actions and habits of individuals, the second to their reasoned and calculated actions and policies. The actions of formal organizations are relatively quite logical.

(*b*) Informal association is rather obviously a condition which necessarily precedes formal organization. The possibility of accepting a common purpose, of communicating, and of attaining a state of mind under which there is willingness to cooperate, requires prior contact and preliminary interaction. This is especially clear in those cases where the origin of formal organization is spontaneous. The informal relationship in such cases may be exceedingly brief, and of course conditioned by previous experience and knowledge of both informal and formal organization.

The important consideration for our purposes, however, is that informal organization compels a certain amount of formal organization, and probably cannot persist or become extensive without the emergence of formal organization. This partly results from the recognition of similarity of needs and interests which continuation of contact implies. When these needs and interests are material and not social, either combination and cooperation—at least to the extent of the development of a distributive purpose—or conflict of interest, antagonism, hostility, and disorganization ensue.

Even when the needs and interests are not material but are social—that is, there is a gregarious need of interaction for its own sake—it likewise requires a considerable concentration upon definite purposes or ends of action to maintain the association. This is especially true if instead of gregarious impulses one goes back to a *need of action* as a primary propensity or instinct. It is an observable fact that men are universally active, and that they seek objects of activity. Correlative with this is the observation that enduring social contact, even when the object is exclusively social, seems generally impossible without activity. It will be generally noted that a purely passive or bovine kind of association among men is of short duration. They seem impelled to *do something.* It is frequently the case that the existence of organizations depends upon satisfactions in mere association, and that this is the uniform and only motive of all participants. In these cases, nevertheless, we can, I think, always observe a purpose, or concrete object of action, which may be of minor importance or even trivial. In these cases it may make no difference in a direct and substantial sense whether the objective is accomplished or not. For example, the discussion of some subject (or subjects) is essential to conversation which is socially desirable, yet the participants may be and frequently are rather indifferent to the subject itself. But the personal associations which give the satisfactions depends upon discussing *something.* This is easily observed in ordinary social affairs.

Thus a concrete object of action is necessary to social satisfactions. The simplest form of doing something together is, of course, conversation, but is evident that any particular form of activity for one reason or another is exhausted usually in a short time and that alternative methods of activity are on the whole not easy to devise either by individuals or groups. Hence, the great importance of established patterns of activity. Where circumstances develop so that a variety of outlets for activity involving associations are not readily available—as is often the case, for example, with unemployed persons—the situation is one in which the individual is placed in a sort of social vacuum, producing a feeling and also objective behavior of being "lost." I have seen this a number of times. Where the situation affects a number of persons simultaneously they are likely to do any sort of mad thing. The necessity for action where a group of persons is involved seems to be almost overwhelming. I think this necessity underlies such proverbs as "Idle hands make mischief," and I have no doubt that it may be the basis for a great deal of practice within armies.

The opposite extreme to lack of concrete objectives of action is a condition of social complexity such that action may take a great many different forms involving the possibilities of association with many different groups. In such situations the individual may be unable to decide which activity he wishes to indulge in, or what groups he wishes to be associated with. This may induce a sort of paralysis of action through inability to make choice[s], or it may be brought about by conflict of obligations. The resulting condition was described by the French sociologist Durkheim as "anomie." This I take to be a state of individual paralysis of social action due to the absence of effective norms of conduct.

The activities of individuals necessarily take place within local immediate groups. The relation of a man to a large organization, or to his nation, or to his church, is necessarily through those with whom he is in *immediate* contact. Social activities cannot be action at a distance. This seems not to have been sufficiently noted. It explains, or justifies, a statement made to me that comradeship is much more powerful than patriotism, etc., in the behavior of soldiers. The essential need of the individual is association, and that requires local activity or immediate interaction between individuals. Without it the man is lost. The willingness of men to endure onerous routine and dangerous tasks which they could avoid is explained by this necessity for action at all costs in order to maintain the sense of social integration, whether the latter arises from "instinct," or from social conditioning, or from physiological necessity, or all three. Whether this necessity for action in a social setting arises exclusively from biological factors, or is partly inherent in gregarious association, need not be considered.

Finally, purposive cooperation is the chief outlet for the logical or scientific faculties of men, and is the principal source of them as well. Rational action is chiefly a purposive cooperative action, and the personal capacity of rational action is largely derived from it.

For these reasons, either small enduring informal organizations or large collectivities seem always to possess a considerable number of formal organizations. These are the definite structural material of a society. They are the poles around which personal associations are given sufficient consistency to retain continuity. The alternative is disintegration into hostile groups, the hostility itself being a source of integrating purposes (defense and offense) of the groups which are differentiated by hostility. Thus as formal organization becomes extended in scope it permits and requires an expansion of societal cohesiveness. This is most obviously the case when formal organization complexes of government expand—government itself is insufficient, except where economic and religious functions are included in it. Where with the expansion of formal government complexes there is correlative expansion of religious, military, economic, and other formal organizations, the structure of a large-scale society is present. When these formal complexes fail or contract, social disintegration sets in. There appear to be no societies which in fact are not completely structured by formal organizations—beginning with families and ending in great complexes of states and religions.

This is not to deny, but to reaffirm, that the attitudes, institutions, customs, of informal society effect and are partly expressed through formal organization. They are interdependent aspects of the same phenomena—a society is structured by formal organizations, formal organizations are vitalized and conditioned by informal organization. What is asserted is that there cannot be one without the other. If one fails the other disintegrates. Nor is this to say that when disintegrated the separated or conflicting societies (except isolated societies) have no affect upon each other. Quite the contrary; but the effect is not cooperative but polemic; and even so requires formal organization within the conflicting societies. Complete absence of formal organization would then be a state of nearly complete individualism and disorder.

III. The Creation of Informal by Formal Organizations

Formal organizations arise out of and are necessary to informal organization; but when formal organizations come into operation, they create and require informal organizations.

It seems not easily to be recognized without long and close observation that an important and often indispensable part of a formal system of cooperation is informal. In fact, more often than not those with ample experience (officials and executives of all sorts of formal organizations) will deny or neglect the existence of informal organizations within their "own" formal organizations. Whether this is due to excessive concentration on the problems of formal organization, or to reluctance to acknowledge the existence of what is difficult to define or describe, or what lacks in concreteness, it is unnecessary to consider. But it is undeniable that major executives and even entire executive organizations are often completely unaware of wide-spread influences, attitudes, and agitations within their organizations. This is true not only of business organizations but also of political organizations, governments, armies, churches, and universities.

Yet one will hear repeatedly that "you can't understand an organization or how it works from its organization chart, its charter, rules and regulations, nor from looking at or even watching its personnel." "Learning the organization ropes" in most organizations is chiefly learning who's who, what's what, why's why, of its informal society. One could not determine very closely how the government of the United States works from reading its Constitution, its court decisions, its statutes, or its administrative regulations. Although ordinarily used in a derogatory sense, the phrase "invisible government" expresses a recognition of informal organization.

Informal organizations as associated with formal organization, though often understood intuitively by managers, politicians, and other organization authorities, have only been definitely studied, so far as I know, at the production level of industrial organizations. In fact, informal organization is so much a part of our matter-of-course intimate experience of everyday association, either in connection with formal organizations or not, that we are unaware of it, seeing only a part of the specific interactions involved. Yet it is evident that association of persons in connection with a formal or specific activity inevitably involves interactions that are incidental to it.

IV. The Functions of Informal in Formal Organizations

One of the indispensable functions of informal organizations in formal organizations—that of communication—has already been indicated. Another function is that of the maintenance of cohesiveness in formal organizations through regulating the willingness to serve and the stability of objective authority. A third function is the maintenance of the feeling of personal integrity, of self-respect, of independent choice. Since the interactions of informal organization are not consciously dominated by a given impersonal objective or by authority as the organization expression, the interactions are apparently characterized by choice, and furnish the opportunities often for reinforcement of personal attitudes. Though often this function is deemed destructive of formal organization, it is to be regarded as a means of maintaining the personality of the individual against certain effects of formal organizations which tend to disintegrate the personality.

The purpose of this chapter has been to show (1) that those interactions between persons which are based on personal rather than on joint or common purposes, because of their repetitive character become systematic and organized through their effect upon habits of action and thought and through their promotion of uniform states of mind; (2) that although the number of persons with whom any individual may have interactive experience is limited, nevertheless the endless-chain relationship between persons in a society results in the development, in many respects, over wide areas and among many persons, of uniform states of mind which crystallize into what we call mores, customs, institutions; (3) that informal organization gives rise to formal organizations, and that formal organizations are necessary to any large informal or societal organization; (4) that formal organizations also make explicit many of the attitudes, states of mind, and institutions which develop directly through informal organizations, with tendencies to divergence, resulting in interdependence and mutual correction of these results in a general and only approximate way; (5) that formal organizations, once established, in their turn also create informal organizations; and (6) that informal organizations are necessary to the operation of formal organizations as a means of communication, of cohesion, and of protecting the integrity of the individual.

10

Bureaucratic Structure and Personality

Robert K. Merton

A formal, rationally organized social structure involves clearly defined patterns of activity in which, ideally, every series of actions is functionally related to the purposes of the organization.[1] In such an organization there is integrated a series of offices, of hierarchized statuses, in which inhere a number of obligations and privileges closely defined by limited and specific rules. Each of these offices contains an area of imputed competence and responsibility. Authority, the power of control which derives from an acknowledged status, inheres in the office and not in the particular person who performs the official role. Official action ordinarily occurs within the framework of preexisting rules of the organization. The system of prescribed relations between the various offices involves a considerable degree of formality and clearly defined social distance between the occupants of these positions. Formality is manifested by means of a more or less complicated social ritual which symbolizes and supports the pecking order of the various offices. Such formality, which is integrated with the distribution of authority within the system, serves to minimize friction by largely restricting (official) contact to modes which are previously defined by the rules of the organization. Ready calculability of others' behavior and a stable set of mutual expectations is thus built up. Moreover, formality facilitates the interaction of the occupants of offices despite their (possibly hostile) private attitudes toward one another. In this way, the subordinate is protected from the arbitrary action of his superior, since the actions of both are constrained by a mutually recognized set of rules. Specific procedural devices foster objectivity and restrain the "quick passage of impulse into action."[2]

The Structure of Bureaucracy

The ideal type of such formal organization is bureaucracy and, in many respects, the classical analysis of bureaucracy is that by Max Weber.[3] As Weber indicates, bureaucracy involves a clear-cut division of integrated activities which are regarded as duties inherent in the office. A system of differentiated controls and sanctions is stated in the regulations. The assignment of roles occurs on the basis of technical qualifications which are ascertained through formalized, impersonal procedures (e.g., examinations). Within the structure of hierarchically arranged authority, the activities of "trained and salaried experts" are governed by general, abstract, and clearly defined rules which preclude the necessity for the issuance of specific instructions for each specific case. The generality of the rules requires the constant use of *categorization*, whereby individual problems and cases are classified on the basis of designated criteria and are treated accordingly. The pure type of bureaucratic official is appointed, either by a superior or through the exercise of impersonal competition; he is not elected. A measure of flexibility in the bureaucracy is attained by electing higher functionaries who presumably express the will of the electorate (e.g., a body of citizens or a board of directors). The election of higher officials is designed to affect the purposes of the organization, but the technical procedures for attaining these ends are carried out by continuing bureaucratic personnel.[4]

Most bureaucratic offices involve the expectation of life-long tenure, in the absence of disturbing factors which may decrease the size of the organization. Bureaucracy maximizes vocational security.[5] The function of security of tenure, pensions, incremental salaries and

Source: Reprinted with permission from The Free Press, a division of Simon & Schuster Adult Publishing Group, from Social Theory and Social Structure by Robert K. Merton.

regularized procedures for promotion is to ensure the devoted performance of official duties, without regard for extraneous pressures.[6] The chief merit of bureaucracy is its technical efficiency, with a premium placed on precision, speed, expert control, continuity, discretion, and optimal returns on input. The structure is one which approaches the complete elimination of personalized relationships and nonrational considerations (hostility, anxiety, affectual involvements, etc.).

With increasing bureaucratization, it becomes plain to all who would see that man is to a very important degree controlled by his social relations to the instruments of production. This can no longer seem only a tenet of Marxism, but a stubborn fact to be acknowledged by all, quite apart from their ideological persuasion. Bureaucratization makes readily visible what was previously dim and obscure. More and more people discover that to work, they must be employed. For to work, one must have tools and equipment. And the tools and equipment are increasingly available only in bureaucracies, private or public. Consequently, one must be employed by the bureaucracies in order to have access to tools in order to work in order to live. It is in this sense that bureaucratization entails separation of individuals from the instruments of production, as in modern capitalistic enterprise or in state communistic enterprise (of the midcentury variety), just as in the post-feudal army, bureaucratization entailed complete separation from the instruments of destruction. Typically, the worker no longer owns his tools nor the soldier, his weapons. And in this special sense, more and more people become workers, either blue collar or white collar or stiff shirt. So develops, for example, the new type of scientific worker, as the scientist is "separated" from his technical equipment—after all, the physicist does not ordinarily own his cyclotron. To work at his research, he must be employed by a bureaucracy with laboratory resources.

Bureaucracy is administration which almost completely avoids public discussion of its techniques, although there may occur public discussion of its policies.[7] This secrecy is confined neither to public nor to private bureaucracies. It is held to be necessary to keep valuable information from private economic competitors or from foreign and potentially hostile political groups. And though it is not often so called, espionage among competitors is perhaps as common, if not as intricately organized, in systems of private economic enterprise as in systems of national states. Cost figures, lists of clients, new technical processes, plans for production—all these are typically regarded as essential secrets of private economic bureaucracies which might be revealed if the bases of all decisions and policies had to be publicly defended.

The Dysfunctions of Bureaucracy

In these bold outlines, the positive attainments and functions of bureaucratic organization are emphasized and the internal stresses and strains of such structures are almost wholly neglected. The community at large, however, evidently emphasizes the imperfections of bureaucracy, as is suggested by the fact that the "horrid hybrid," bureaucrat, has become an epithet, a *Schimpfwort*.

The transition to a study of the negative aspects of bureaucracy is afforded by the application of Veblen's concept of "trained incapacity," Dewey's notion of "occupational psychosis" or Warnotte's view of "professional deformation." Trained incapacity refers to that state of affairs in which one's abilities function as inadequacies or blind spots. Actions based upon training and skills which have been successfully applied in the past may result in inappropriate responses *under changed conditions.* An inadequate flexibility in the application of skills, will, in a changing milieu, result in more or less serious maladjustments.[8] Thus, to adopt a barnyard illustration used in this connection by Burke, chickens may be readily conditioned to interpret the sound of a bell as a signal for food. The same bell may now be used to summon the trained chickens to their doom as they are assembled to suffer decapitation. In general, one adopts measures in keeping with one's past training and, under new conditions which are not recognized as *significantly* different, the very soundness of this training may lead to the adoption of the wrong procedures. Again, in Burke's almost echolalic phrase, "people may be unfitted by being fit in an unfit fitness"; their training may become an incapacity.

Dewey's concept of occupational psychosis rests upon much the same observations. As a result of their day to day routines, people develop special preferences, antipathies, discriminations and emphases.[9] (The term psychosis is used by Dewey to denote a "pronounced character of the mind.") These psychoses develop through demands put upon the individual by the particular organization of his occupational role.

The concepts of both Veblen and Dewey refer to a fundamental ambivalence. Any action can be considered in terms of what it attains or what it fails to attain. "A way of seeing is also a way of not seeing—a focus upon object *A* involves a neglect of object *B*."[10] In his discussion, Weber is almost exclusively concerned with what the bureaucratic structure attains: precision, reliability, efficiency. This same structure may be examined from another perspective provided by the ambivalence. What are the limitations of the organizations designed to attain these goals?

For reasons which we have already noted, the bureaucratic structure exerts a constant pressure upon the official to be "methodical, prudent, disciplined." If the bureaucracy is to operate successfully, it must attain a high degree of reliability of behavior, an unusual degree of conformity with prescribed patterns of action. Hence, the fundamental importance of discipline which may be as highly developed in a religious or economic bureaucracy as in the army. Discipline can be effective only if the ideal patterns are buttressed by strong sentiments which entail devotion to one's duties, a keen sense of the limitation of one's authority and competence, and methodical performance of routine activities. The efficacy of social structure depends ultimately upon infusing group participants with appropriate attitudes and sentiments. As we shall see, there are definite arrangements in the bureaucracy for inculcating and reinforcing these sentiments.

At the moment, it suffices to observe that in order to ensure discipline (the necessary reliability of response), these sentiments are often more intense than is technically necessary. There is a margin of safety, so to speak, in the pressure exerted by these sentiments upon the bureaucrat to conform to his patterned obligations, in much the same sense that added allowances (precautionary overestimations) are made by the engineer in designing the supports for a bridge. But this very emphasis leads to a transference of the sentiments from the *aims* of the organization onto the particular details of behavior required by the rules. Adherence to the rules, originally conceived as a means, becomes transformed into an end-in-itself; there occurs the familiar process of *displacement of goals* whereby "an instrumental value becomes a terminal value."[11] Discipline, readily interpreted as conformance with regulations, whatever the situation, is seen not as a measure designed for specific purposes but becomes an immediate value in the life-organization of the bureaucrat. This emphasis, resulting from the displacement of the original goals, develops into rigidities and an inability to adjust readily. Formalism, even ritualism, ensues with an unchallenged insistence upon punctilious adherence to formalized procedures.[12] This may be exaggerated to the point where primary concern with conformity to the rules interferes with the achievement of the purposes of the organization, in which case we have the familiar phenomenon of the technicism or red tape of the official. An extreme product of this process of displacement of goals is the bureaucratic virtuoso, who never forgets a single rule binding his action and hence is unable to assist many of his clients.[13] A case in point, where strict recognition of the limits of authority and literal adherence to rules produced this result, is the pathetic plight of Bernt Balchen, Admiral Byrd's pilot in the flight over the South Pole.

> According to a ruling of the department of labor Bernt Balchen . . . cannot receive his citizenship papers. Balchen, a native of Norway, declared his intention in 1927. It is held that he has failed to meet the condition of five years' continuous residence in the United States. The Byrd antarctic voyage

took him out of the country, although he was on a ship carrying the American flag, was an invaluable member of the American expedition, and in a region to which there is an American claim because of the exploration and occupation of it by Americans, this region being Little America.

The bureau of naturalization explains that it cannot proceed on the assumption that Little America is American soil. That would be *trespass on international questions* where it has no sanction. So far as the bureau is concerned, Balchen was out of the country and *technically* has not complied with the law of naturalization.[14]

Structural Sources of Overconformity

Such inadequacies in orientation which involve trained incapacity clearly derive from structural sources. The process may be briefly recapitulated. (1) An effective bureaucracy demands reliability of response and strict devotion to regulations. (2) Such devotion to the rules leads to their transformation into absolutes; they are no longer conceived as relative to a set of purposes. (3) This interferes with ready adaptation under special conditions not clearly envisaged by those who drew up the general rules. (4) Thus, the very elements which conduce toward efficiency in general produce inefficiency in specific instances. Full realization of the inadequacy is seldom attained by members of the group who have not divorced themselves from the meanings which the rules have for them. These rules in time become symbolic in cast, rather than strictly utilitarian.

Thus far, we have treated the ingrained sentiments making for rigorous discipline simply as data, as given. However, definite features of the bureaucratic structure may be seen to conduce to these sentiments. The bureaucrat's official life is planned for him in terms of a graded career, through the organizational devices of promotion by seniority, pensions, incremental salaries, etc., all of which are designed to provide incentives for disciplined action and conformity to the official regulations.[15] The official is tacitly expected to and largely does adapt his thoughts, feelings and actions to the prospect of this career. But *these very devices* which increase the probability of conformance also lead to an over-concern with strict adherence to regulations which induces timidity, conservatism, and technicism. Displacement of sentiments from goals onto means is fostered by the tremendous symbolic significance of the means (rules).

Another feature of the bureaucratic structure tends to produce much the same result. Functionaries have the sense of a common destiny for all those who work together. They share the same interests, especially since there is relatively little competition in so far as promotion is in terms of seniority. In-group aggression is thus minimized and this arrangement is therefore conceived to be positively functional for the bureaucracy. However, the *esprit de corps* and informal social organization which typically develops in such situations often leads the personnel to defend their entrenched interests rather than to assist their clientele and elected higher officials. As President Lowell reports, if the bureaucrats believe that their status is not adequately recognized by an incoming elected official, detailed information will be withheld from him, leading him to errors for which he is held responsible. Or, if he seeks to dominate fully, and thus violates the sentiment of self-integrity of the bureaucrats, he may have documents brought to him in such numbers that he cannot manage to sign them all, let alone read them.[16] This illustrates the defensive informal organization which tends to arise whenever there is an apparent threat to the integrity of the group.[17]

It would be much too facile and partly erroneous to attribute such resistance by bureaucrats simply to vested interests. Vested interests oppose any new order which either eliminates or at least makes uncertain their differential advantage deriving from the current arrangements. This is undoubtedly involved in part in bureaucratic resistance to change but another process is perhaps more significant. As we have seen, bureaucratic officials affectively identify themselves with their way of life. They have a pride of craft which leads them to resist change in established routines; at least, those changes which are felt to be imposed by others. This nonlogical pride of craft is a familiar pattern found even, to judge from Sutherland's *Professional Thief*, among pickpockets who, despite the risk, delight in mastering the prestige-bearing feat of "beating a left breech" (picking the left front trousers pocket).

In a stimulating paper, Hughes has applied the concepts of "secular" and "sacred" to various types of division of labor; "the sacredness" of caste and *Stände* prerogatives contrasts sharply with the increasing secularism of occupational differentiation in our society.[18] However, as our discussion suggests, there may ensue, in particular vocations and in particular types of organization, the *process of sanctification* (viewed as the counterpart of the process of secularization). This is to say that through sentiment-formation, emotional dependence upon bureaucratic symbols and status, and affective involvement in spheres of competence and authority, there develop prerogatives involving attitudes of moral legitimacy which are established as values in their own right, and are no longer viewed as merely technical means for expediting administration. One may note a tendency for certain bureaucratic norms, originally introduced for technical reasons, to become rigidified and sacred, although, as Durkheim would say, they are *laïque en apparence.*[19] Durkheim has touched on this general process in his description of the attitudes and values which persist in the organic solidarity of a highly differentiated society.

Primary versus Secondary Relations

Another feature of the bureaucratic structure, the stress on depersonalization of relationships, also plays its part in the bureaucrat's trained incapacity. The personality pattern of the bureaucrat is nucleated about this norm of impersonality. Both this and the categorizing tendency, which develops from the dominant role of general, abstract rules, tend to produce conflict in the bureaucrat's contacts with the public or clientele. Since functionaries minimize personal relations and resort to categorization, the peculiarities of individual cases are often ignored. But the client who, quite understandably, is convinced of the special features of *his* own problem often objects to such categorical treatment. Stereotyped behavior is not adapted to the exigencies of individual problems. The impersonal treatment of affairs which are at times of great personal significance to the client gives rise to the charge of "arrogance" and "haughtiness" of the bureaucrat. Thus, at the Greenwich Employment Exchange, the unemployed worker who is securing his insurance payment resents what he deems to be "the impersonality and, at times, the apparent abruptness and even harshness of his treatment by the clerks. . . . Some men complain of the superior attitude which the clerks have."[20]

Still another source of conflict with the public derives from the bureaucratic structure. The bureaucrat, in part irrespective of his position with*in* the hierarchy, acts as a representative of the power and prestige of the entire structure. In his official role he is vested with definite authority. This often leads to an actually or apparently domineering attitude, which may only be exaggerated by a discrepancy between his position within the hierarchy and his position with reference to the public.[21] Protest and recourse to other officials on the part of the client are often ineffective or largely precluded by the previously mentioned *esprit de corps* which joins the officials into a more or less solidary ingroup. This source of conflict *may* be minimized in private enterprise since the client can register an effective protest by transferring his trade to another organization within the competitive system. But with the monopolistic nature of the public organization, no such alternative is possible. Moreover, in this case, tension is increased because of a discrepancy between ideology and fact: the governmental personnel are held to be "servants of the people," but in fact they are often superordinate, and release of tension can seldom be afforded by turning to other agencies for the necessary service.[22] This tension is in part attributable to the confusion of the status of bureaucrat and client; the client may consider himself socially superior to the official who is at the moment dominant.[23]

Thus, with respect to the relations between officials and clientele, one structural source of conflict is the pressure for formal and impersonal treatment when individual, personalized consideration is desired by the client. The conflict may be viewed, then, as deriving from the introduction of inappropriate attitudes and relationships. Conflict with*in* the bureaucratic structure arises from the converse situation, namely, when personalized relationships are substituted for the structurally required impersonal relationships. This type of conflict may be characterized as follows.

The bureaucracy, as we have seen, is organized as a secondary, formal group. The normal responses involved in this organized network of social expectations are supported by affective attitudes of members of the group. Since the group is oriented toward secondary norms of impersonality, any failure to conform to these norms will arouse antagonism from those who have identified themselves with the legitimacy of these rules. Hence, the substitution of personal for impersonal treatment within the structure is met with widespread disapproval and is characterized by such epithets as graft, favoritism, nepotism, apple-polishing, etc. These epithets are clearly manifestations of injured sentiments.[24] The function of such virtually automatic resentment can be clearly seen in terms of the requirements of bureaucratic structure.

Bureaucracy is a secondary group structure designed to carry on certain activities which cannot be satisfactorily performed on the basis of primary group criteria.[25] Hence behavior which runs counter to these formalized norms becomes the object of emotionalized disapproval. This constitutes a functionally significant defence set up against tendencies which jeopardize the performance of socially necessary activities. To be sure, these reactions are not rationally determined practices explicitly designed for the fulfillment of this function. Rather, viewed in terms of the individual's interpretation of the situation, such resentment is simply an immediate response opposing the "dishonesty" of those who violate the rules of the game. However, this subjective frame of reference notwithstanding, these reactions serve the latent function of maintaining the essential structural elements of bureaucracy by reaffirming the necessity for formalized, secondary relations and by helping to prevent the disintegration of the bureaucratic structure which would occur should these be supplanted by personalized relations. This type of conflict may be generically described as the intrusion of primary group attitudes when secondary group attitudes are institutionally demanded, just as the bureaucrat-client conflict often derives from interaction on impersonal terms when personal treatment is individually demanded.[26]

Problems for Research

The trend towards increasing bureaucratization in Western Society, which Weber had long since foreseen, is not the sole reason for sociologists to turn their attention to this field. Empirical studies of the interaction of bureaucracy and personality should especially increase our understanding of social structure. A large number of specific questions invite our attention. To what extent are particular personality types selected and modified by the various bureaucracies (private enterprise, public service, the quasi-legal political machine, religious orders)? Inasmuch as ascendancy and submission are held to be traits of personality, despite their variability in different stimulus-situations, do bureaucracies select personalities of particularly submissive or ascendant tendencies? And since various studies have shown that these traits can be modified, does participation in bureaucratic office tend to increase ascendant tendencies? Do various systems of recruitment (e.g., patronage, open competition involving specialized knowledge or general mental capacity, practical experience) select different personality types?[27] Does promotion through seniority lessen competitive anxieties and enhance administrative efficiency? A detailed examination of mechanisms for imbuing the bureaucratic codes with affect would be instructive both sociologically and Zpsychologically. Does the general anonymity of civil service decisions tend to restrict the area of prestige-symbols to a narrowly defined inner circle? Is there a tendency for differential association to be especially marked among bureaucrats?

The range of theoretically significant and practically important questions would seem to be limited only by the accessibility of the concrete data. Studies of religious, educational, military, economic, and political bureaucracies dealing with the interdependence of social organization and personality formation should constitute an avenue for fruitful research. On that avenue, the functional analysis of concrete structures may yet build a Solomon's House for sociologists.

NOTES

1. For a development of the concept of "rational organization," see Karl Mannheim, *Mensch und Gesellschaft im Zeitalter des Umbaus* (Leiden: A. W. Sijthoff, 1935), esp. p. 28 ff.
2. H. D. Lasswell, *Politics* (New York: McGraw-Hill, 1936), pp. 120–121.
3. Max Weber, *Wirtschaft und Gesellschaft,* pt. III, chap. 6 (Tübingen: J. C. B. Mohr, 1922), pp. 650–678. For a brief summary of Weber's discussion, see Talcott Parsons, *The Structure of Social Action,* esp. p. 506 ff. For a description, which is not a caricature, of the bureaucrat as a personality type, see C. Rabany, "Les types sociaux: le fonctionnaire," *Revue Générale d'Administration* 88 (1907): 5–28.
4. Karl Mannheim, *Ideology and Utopia* (New York: Harcourt Brace Jovanovich, 1936), pp. 18n., 105 ff. See also Ramsay Muir, *Peers and Bureaucrats* (London: Constable, 1910), pp. 12–13.
5. E. G. Cahen-Salvador suggests that the personnel of bureaucracies is largely constituted by those who value security above all else. See his "La situation matérielle et morale des fonctionnaires," *Revue Politique et Parlementaire* (1926): 319.
6. H. J. Laski, "Bureaucracy," *Encyclopedia of the Social Sciences.* This article is written primarily from the standpoint of the political scientist rather than that of the sociologist.
7. Weber, op. cit., p. 671.
8. For a stimulating discussion and application of these concepts, see Kenneth Burke, *Permanence and Change* (New York: New Republic, 1935), pp. 50 ff.; Daniel Warnotte, "Bureaucratie et fonctionnarisme," *Revue de l'Institut de Sociologie* 17 (1937): 245.
9. Burke, op. cit., pp. 58–59.
10. Ibid., p. 70.
11. This process has often been observed in various connections. Wundt's *heterogony of ends* is a case in point; Max Weber's *Paradoxie der Folgen* is another. See also MacIver's observations on the transformation of civilization into culture and Lasswell's remark that "the human animal distinguishes himself by his infinite capacity for making ends of his means." See Merton, "The Unanticipated Consequences of Purposive Social Action," *American Sociological Review* 1 (1936): 894–904. In terms of the psychological mechanisms involved, this process has been analyzed most fully by Gordon W. Allport, in his discussion of what he calls "the functional autonomy of motives." Allport amends the earlier formulations of Woodworth, Tolman, and William Stern, and arrives at a statement of the process from the standpoint of individual motivation. He does not consider those phases of the social structure which conduce toward the "transformation of motives." The formulation adopted in this paper is thus complementary to Allport's analysis; the one stressing the psychological mechanisms involved, the other considering the constraints of the social structure. The convergence of psychology and sociology toward this central concept suggests that it may well constitute one of the conceptual bridges between the two disciplines. See Gordon W. Allport, *Personality* (New York: Henry Holt and Co., 1937), chap. 7.
12. See E. C. Hughes, "Institutional Office and the Person," *American Journal of Sociology,* 43 (1937): 404–413; E. T. Hiller, "Social Structure in Relation to the Person," *Social Forces* 16 (1937).
13. Mannheim, *Ideology and Utopia,* p. 106.
14. Quoted from the *Chicago Tribune* (June 24, 1931, p. 10) by Thurman Arnold, *The Symbols of Government* (New Haven: Yale University Press, 1935), 201–202. (My italics.)
15. Mannheim, *Mensch und Gesellschaft,* pp. 32–33. Mannheim stresses the importance of the "Lebensplan" and the "Amtskarriere." See the comments by Hughes, op. cit., p. 413.

16. A. L. Lowell, *The Government of England* (New York, 1908), 1:189 ff.

17. For an instructive description of the development of such a defensive organization in a group of workers, see F. J. Roethlisberger and W. J. Dickson, *Management and the Worker* (Boston: Harvard School of Business Administration, 1934).

18. E. C. Hughes, "Personality Types and the Division of Labor," *American Journal of Sociology* 33 (1928): 754–768. Much the same distinction is drawn by Leopold von Wiese and Howard Becker, *Systematic Sociology* (New York: John Wiley and Sons, 1932), pp. 222–225 passim.

19. Hughes recognizes one phase of this process of sanctification when he writes that professional training "carries with it as a byproduct assimilation of the candidate to a set of professional attitudes and controls, *a professional conscience and solidarity. The profession claims and aims to become a moral unit.*" Hughes, op. cit., p. 762 (italics inserted). In this same connection, Sumner's concept of *pathos,* as the halo of sentiment which protects a social value from criticism, is particularly relevant, inasmuch as it affords a clue to the mechanism involved in the process of sanctification. See his *Folkways,* pp. 180–181.

20. " 'They treat you like a lump of dirt they do. I see a navy reach across the counter and shake one of them by the collar the other day. The rest of us felt like cheering. Of course he lost his benefit over it. . . . But the clerk deserved it for his sassy way' " (E. W. Bakke, *The Unemployed Man,* pp. 79–80). Note that the domineering attitude was *imputed* by the unemployed client who is in a state of tension due to his loss of status and self-esteem in a society where the ideology is still current that an "able man" can always find a job. That the imputation of arrogance stems largely from the client's state of mind is seen from Bakke's own observation that "the clerks were rushed, and had no time for pleasantries, but there was little sign of harshness or a superiority feeling in their treatment of the men." In so far as there is an objective basis for the imputation of arrogant behavior to bureaucrats, it may possibly be explained by the following juxtaposed statements. "Auch der moderne, sei es öffentliche, sei es private, Beamte erstrebt immer und geniesst meist den Beherrschten gegenüber eine spezifisch gehobene, 'ständische' soziale Schätzung" (Weber, op. cit., p. 652). "In persons in whom the craving for prestige is uppermost, hostility usually takes the form of a desire to humiliate others" (K. Horney, *The Neurotic Personality of Our Time,* pp. 178–179).

21. In this connection, note the relevance of Koffka's comments on certain features of the pecking-order of birds. "If one compares the behavior of the bird at the top of the pecking list, the despot, with that of one very far down, the second or third from the last, then one finds the latter much more cruel to the few others over whom he lords it than the former in his treatment of all members. As soon as one removes from the group all members above the penultimate, his behavior becomes milder and may even become very friendly.... It is not difficult to find analogies to this in human societies, and therefore one side of such behavior must be primarily the effects of the social groupings, and not of individual characteristics" (K. Koffka, *Principles of Gestalt Psychology* [New York: Harcourt Brace Jovanovich, 1935], pp. 668–669).

22. At this point the political machine often becomes functionally significant. As Steffens and others have shown, highly personalized relations and the abrogation of formal rules (red tape) by the machine often satisfy the needs of individual "clients" more fully than the formalized mechanism of governmental bureaucracy.

23. As one of the unemployed men remarked about the clerks at the Greenwich Employment Exchange: " 'And the bloody blokes wouldn't have their jobs if it wasn't for us men out of a job either. That's what gets me about their holding their noses up' " (Bakke, op. cit., p. 80). See also H. D. Lasswell and G. Almond, "Aggressive Behavior by Clients towards Public Relief Administrators," *Am. Pol. Sci. Rev.* 28 (1934): 643–655.

24. The diagnostic significance of such linguistic indices as epithets has scarcely been explored by the sociologist. Sumner properly observes that epithets produce "summary criticisms" and definitions of social situations. Dollard also notes that "epithets frequently define the central issues in a society," and Sapir has rightly emphasized the importance of context of situations in appraising the significance of epithets. Of equal relevance is Linton's observation that "in case histories the way in which the community felt about a particular episode is, if anything, more important to our study than the actual behavior. . . ." A sociological study of "vocabularies of encomium and opprobrium" should lead to valuable findings.
25. Cf. Ellsworth Faris, *The Nature of Human Nature* (New York: McGraw-Hill, 1937), p. 41 ff.
26. Community disapproval of many forms of behavior may be analyzed in terms of one or the other of these patterns of substitution of culturally inappropriate types of relationship. Thus, prostitution constitutes a type-case where coitus, a form of intimacy which is institutionally defined as symbolic of the most "sacred" primary group relationship, is placed within a contractual context, symbolized by the exchange of that most impersonal of all symbols, money. See Kingsley Davis, "The Sociology of Prostitution," *American Sociological Review* 2 (1937): 744–755.
27. Among recent studies of recruitment to bureaucracy are Reinhard Bendix, *Higher Civil Servants in American Society* (Boulder: University of Colorado Press, 1949); Dwaine Marwick, *Career Perspectives in a Bureaucratic Setting* (Ann Arbor: University of Michigan Press, 1954); R. K. Kelsall, *Higher Civil Servants in Britain* (London: Routledge and Kegan Paul, 1955); W. L. Warner and J. C. Abegglen, *Occupational Mobility in American Business and Industry* (Minneapolis: University of Minnesota Press, 1955).

11

The Lack of a Budgetary Theory

V. O. Key, Jr.

On the most significant aspect of public budgeting, i.e., the allocation of expenditures among different purposes so as to achieve the greatest return, American budgetary literature is singularly arid. Toilers in the budgetary field have busied themselves primarily with the organization and procedure for budget preparation, the forms for the submission of requests for funds, the form of the budget document itself, and like questions.[1] That these things have deserved the consideration given them cannot be denied when the unbelievable resistance to the adoption of the most rudimentary essentials of budgeting is recalled and their unsatisfactory condition in many jurisdictions even now is observed. Nevertheless, the absorption of energies in the establishment of the mechanical foundations for budgeting has diverted attention from the basic budgeting problem (on the expenditure side), namely: On what basis shall it be decided to allocate x dollars to activity A instead of activity B?

Writers on budgeting say little or nothing about the purely economic aspects of public expenditure. "Economics," says Professor Robbins, "is the science which studies human behavior as a relationship between ends and scarce means which have alternative uses."[2] Whether budgetary behavior is economic or political is open to fruitless debate; nevertheless, the point of view and the mode of thought of the economic theorist are relevant, both in the study of and action concerning public expenditure. The budget-maker never has enough revenue to meet the requests of all spending agencies, and he must decide (subject, of course, to subsequent legislative action) how scarce means shall be allocated to alternative uses. The completed budgetary document (although the budget-maker may be quite unaware of it) represents a judgment upon how scarce means should be allocated to bring the maximum return in social utility.[3]

In their discussions of the review of estimates, budget authorities rarely go beyond the question of how to judge the estimates for particular functions, i.e., ends; and the approach to the review of the estimate of the individual agency is generally directed toward the efficiency with which the particular end is to be achieved.[4] Even in this sort of review, budget-makers have developed few standards of evaluation, acting, rather, on the basis of their impressionistic judgment, of a rudimentary cost accounting, or perhaps, of the findings of administrative surveys. For decisions on the requests of individual agencies, the techniques have by no means reached perfection.[5] It is sometimes possible to compute with fair accuracy whether the increased efficiency from new public works, such as a particular highway project, will warrant the capital outlay. Or, given the desirability of a particular objective, it maybe feasible to evaluate fairly precisely alternative means for achieving that end. Whether a particular agency is utilizing, and plans to utilize, its resources with the maximum efficiency is of great importance, but this approach leaves untouched a more fundamental problem. If it is assumed that an agency is operating at maximum efficiency, the question remains whether the function is worth carrying out at all, or whether it should be carried out on a reduced or enlarged scale, with resulting transfers of funds to or from other activities of greater or less social utility.

Nor is there found in the works of the public finance experts much enlightenment on the question herein considered. They generally dispose of the subject of expenditures with a few perfunctory chapters and hurry on to the core of their interest—taxation and other sources of

---

Source: "The Lack of a Budgetary Theory" by V.O. Key From American Political Science Review 34 (December 1940).

revenue. On the expenditure side, they differentiate, not very plausibly, between productive and unproductive expenditure; they consider the classification of public expenditures; they demonstrate that public expenditures have been increasing; and they discuss the determination of the optimum aggregate of public expenditure; but they do not generally come to grips with the question of the allocation of public revenues among different objects of expenditure.[6] The issue is recognized, as when Pigou says: "As regards the distribution, as distinct from the aggregate cost, of optional government expenditure, it is clear that, just as an individual will get more satisfaction out of his income by maintaining a certain balance between different sorts of expenditure, so also will a community through its government. The principle of balance in both cases is provided by the postulate that resources should be so distributed among different uses that the marginal return of satisfaction is the same for all of them. . . . Expenditure should be distributed between battleships and poor relief in such wise that the last shilling devoted to each of them yields the same real return. We have here, so far as theory goes, a test by means of which the distribution of expenditure along different lines can be settled."[7] But Pigou dismisses the subject with a paragraph, and the discussion by others is not voluminous.[8]

The only American writer on public finance who has given extended attention to the problem of the distribution of expenditures is Mabel Walker. In her *Municipal Expenditures,* she reviews the theories of public expenditure and devises a method for ascertaining the tendencies in distribution of expenditures on the assumption that the way would be pointed to "a norm of expenditures consistent with the state of progress at present achieved by society." While her method would be inapplicable to the federal budget,[9] and would probably be of less relevance in the analysis of state than of municipal expenditures, her study deserves reflective perusal by municipal budget officers and by students of the problem.[10]

Literature skirting the edges of the problem is found in the writings of those economists who have concerned themselves with the economic problems of the socialist state. In recent years, a new critique of socialism has appeared.[11] This attack [is], in the words of one who attempts to refute it, ". . . more subtle and technical than the previous ones, based on the supposed inability of a socialist community to solve purely economic problems. . . . What is asserted is that, even with highly developed technique, adequate incentives to activity, and rational control of population, the economic directors of a socialist commonwealth would be unable to balance against each other the worthwhileness of different lines of production or the relative advantages of different ways of producing the same good." [12] Those who believe this problem not insoluble in a socialist economy set out to answer the question: "What is the proper method of determining just what commodities shall be produced from the economic resources at the disposal of a given community?"[13] One would anticipate from those seeking to answer this question some light on the problems of the budget-maker in a capitalist state. But they are concerned only with the pricing of state-produced goods for sale to individuals in a socialist economy. Professor Dickinson, for example, excludes from his discussion goods and services provided in a socialist economy "free of charge to all members of society, as the result of a decision, based on other grounds than market demands, made by some authoritative economic organ of the community."[14] That exclusion removes from consideration the point at issue. Nevertheless, the critics of socialist theory do at least raise essentially the same problem as that posed in the present discussion; and their comment is suggestive.

Various studies of the economics of public works touch the periphery of the problem concerning the allocation of public expenditures. The principal inquiries have been prosecuted under the auspices of the National Resources Planning Board and its predecessor organizations. These reports, however, are concerned in the main with the question of how much in the aggregate should be spent, and when, in order to function as the most effective absorber of the shocks incidental to cyclical fluctuations. Two studies, by Arthur D. Gayer and John M. Clark, deal with public works outlays as stabilizers of the economic order and with related matters.[15] These works suggest factors relevant in the determination of the total amount of the capital budget; but in them the problem of selection among alternative public works projects is not tackled. In another study, the latter issue is approached by Russell V. Black from a rich background of city planning experience, and he formulates a suggestive but tentative set of criteria for the selection and programming of public works projects.[16]

Planning agencies and professional planners have been more interested in the abstract problem of ascertaining the relative utility of public outlays than has any other group. The issue is stated theoretically in a recent report: "The problem is essentially one of the development of criteria for selecting the objects of public expenditure. As a larger and larger proportion of the national income is spent for public purposes, the sphere of the price system with its freedom of choice of objects of expenditure is more and more restricted. Concurrently, the necessity for developing methods by which public officials may select objects of expenditure which will bring the greatest utility or return and most accurately achieve social aspirations becomes more pressing. In a sense, this constitutes the central problem of the productive state. If planning is to be 'over-all' planning, it must devise techniques for the balancing of values within a framework that gives due regard both to the diverse interests of the present and to the interests of the future."[17] Planning agencies have not succeeded in formulating any convincing principles, either descriptive or normative, concerning the allocation of public funds, but they have, within limited spheres, created governmental machinery facilitating the consideration of related alternative expenditures. The most impressive example is the Water Resources Committee (of the National Resources Planning Board) and its subsidiary drainage-basin committees.[18] Through this machinery, it is possible to consider alternatives in objectives and sequences of expenditure—questions that would not arise concretely without such machinery. Perhaps the approach toward the practical working out of the issue lies in the canalizing of decisions through the governmental machinery so as to place alternatives in juxtaposition and compel consideration of relative values. This is the effect of many existing institutional arrangements; but the issue is rarely so stated, and the structure of government, particularly the federal-state division, frequently prevents the weighing of alternatives.

It may be argued that for the best performance of individual public functions a high degree of stability in the amount of funds available year after year is desirable, and that the notion that there is, or needs to be, mobility of resources as among functions is erroneous. Considerable weight is undoubtedly to be attached to this view. Yet over periods of a few years important shifts occur in relative financial emphasis on different functions of government. Even in minor adjustments, the small change up or down at the margin may be of considerable significance. Like an individual consumer, the state may have certain minimum expenditures generally agreed upon, but care in weighing the relative utility of alternative expenditures becomes more essential as the point of marginal utility is approached. Moreover, within the public economy, frictions (principally institutional in character) exist to obstruct and delay adjustments in the allocation of resources in keeping with changing wants probably to a greater extent than in the private economy.

Efforts to ascertain more precisely the relative "values" of public services may be thought fruitless because of the influence of pressure groups in the determination of the allocation of funds. Each spending agency has its clientele, which it marshals for battle before budgetary and appropriating agencies.[19] And there are those who might contend that the pattern of expenditures resultant from the interplay of these forces constitutes a maximization of return from public expenditure, since it presumably reflects the social consensus on the relative values of different services. If this be true, the more efficient utilization of resources would be promoted by the devising of means more accurately to measure the political strength of interests competing for appropriations. That the appropriation bill expresses a social consensus sounds akin to the mystic doctrine of the "general will." Constantly, choices have to be made between the demands of different groups; and it is probably true that factors other than estimates of the relative political strength of contending groups frequently enter into the decisions. The pressure theory suggests the potential development in budget bureaus and related agencies of a strong bureaucracy strategically situated, and with a vested interest in the general welfare, in contrast with the particularistic drives of the spending agencies.

It is not to be concluded that by excogitation a set of principles may be formulated on the basis of which the harassed budget official may devise an automatic technique for the allocation of financial resources. Yet the problem needs study in several directions. Further examination from the viewpoints of economic theory and political philosophy could produce valuable results. The doctrine of marginal utility, developed most finely in the analysis of the market economy, has a ring of unreality when applied to public expenditures. The most advantageous utilization of public funds[20] resolves itself into a matter of value preferences between ends lacking a common denominator. As such, the question is a problem in political philosophy; keen analyses in these terms would be of the utmost importance in creating an awareness of the problems of the budgetary implementation of programs of political action of whatever shade. The discussion also suggests the desirability of careful and comprehensive analyses of the budgetary process. In detail, what forces go into the making of state budgets? What factors govern decisions of budgetary officials? Precisely what is the role of the legislature? On the federal level, the field for inquiry is broader, including not only the central budgetary agency, but departmental budget offices as well. Studies of congressional appropriating processes are especially needed.[21] For the working budget official, the implications of the discussion rest primarily in a point of view in the consideration of estimates in terms of alternatives—decisions which are always made, but not always consciously. For the personnel policy of budget agencies, the question occurs whether almost sole reliance on persons trained primarily in accounting and fiscal procedure is wise. The thousands of little decisions made in budgetary agencies grow by accretion into formidable budgetary documents which from their sheer mass are apt often to overwhelm those with the power of final decision. We need to look carefully at the training and working assumptions of these officials, to the end that the budget may most truly reflect the public interest.[22]

Notes

1. See A. E. Buck, *Public Budgeting* (New York, 1929); J. Wilner Sundelson, *Budgetary Methods in National and State Governments,* New York State Tax Commission, Special Report No. 14 (1938); idem, "Budgetary Principles," *Political Science Quarterly* 50 (1935): 236–263.
2. Lionel Robbins, *An Essay on the Nature and Significance of Economic Science,* 2d ed. (London, 1935), p. 16.
3. If the old saying that the state fixes its expenditures and then raises sufficient revenues to meet them were literally true, the budget officer would not be faced by a problem of scarcity. However, there is almost invariably a problem of scarcity in the public economy—to which all budget officers, besieged by spending departments, will testify.
4. See Buck, op. cit., chap. 11.
5. The development of standards for the evaluation of the efficiency of performance of particular functions—entirely apart from the value of the functions—is as yet in a primitive state. Such standards, for budgetary purposes at least, require cost accounting, which implies a unit of measurement. A standard of comparison is also implied, such as the performance of the same agency during prior fiscal periods, or the performance of other agencies under like conditions. In the absence of even crude measurement devices, budgetary and appropriating authorities are frequently thrown back upon the alternative of passing on individual items—three clerks, two messengers, seven stenographers, etc.—a practice which often causes exasperation among operating officials. Although our knowledge of budgetary behavior is slight, the surmise is probably correct that questions of the efficiency of

operation in achieving a particular end are generally hopelessly intermingled with the determination of the relative value of different ends. Operating officials often shy away from experimentation with devices of measurement, but it may be suggested that measures of the efficiency of performance should tend to divert the attention of budgetary and appropriating officials from concern with internal details to the pivotal question of the relative value of services.

6. See, for example, H. L. Lutz, *Public Finance.*
7. *A Study in Public Finance* (London, 1928), p. 50. See also E. R. A. Seligman, "The Social Theory of Fiscal Science," *Political Science Quarterly* 41 (1926): 193–218, 354–383; Gerhard Colm, "Theory of Public Expenditures," *Annals of the American Academy of Political and Social Science* 183 (1930): 1–11.
8. For a review of the literature, see Mabel L. Walker, *Municipal Expenditures* (Baltimore, 1930), chap. 3.
9. In this connection, see C. H. Wooddy, *The Growth of the Federal Government, 1915–1932* (New York, 1934).
10. In the field of state finance, a valuable study has been made by I. M. Labovitz in *Public Policy and State Finance in Illinois* (Social Science Research Committee, University of Chicago, publication pending).
11. See F. A. von Hayek, ed., *Collectivist Economic Planning* (London, 1935).
12. H. D. Dickinson, "Price Formation in a Socialist Community," *Economic Journal* 43: 237–250. See also, E. F. M. Durbin, "Economic Calculus in a Planned Economy," *Economic Journal* 46 (1936): 676–690; A. R. Sweezy, "The Economist in a Socialist Economy," in *Explorations in Economics; Notes and Essays Contributed in Honor of F. W. Taussig* (1936), pp. 422–433.
13. F. M. Taylor, "The Guidance of Production in a Socialist State," *American Economic Review* 19 (1929): 1–8.
14. Op. cit., p. 238. Of Soviet Russia, Brown and Hinrichs say: "In a planned economy, operating if necessary under pressure to accomplish a predetermined production, the decision with regard to major prices is essentially a political one" ("The Planned Economy of Soviet Russia," *Political Science Quarterly* 46 [1931]: 362–402).
15. J. M. Clark, *Economics of Planning Public Works* (Washington, D.C.: Government Printing Office, 1935); A. D. Gayer, *Public Works in Prosperity and Depression* (New York: National Bureau of Economic Research, 1935). See also the essay by Simeon E. Leland in National Resources Committee, *Public Works Planning* (Washington, D.C.: Government Printing Office, 1936).
16. *Criteria and Planning for Public Works* (Washington, D.C.: National Resources Board, 1934, mimeographed). See especially pp. 165–168.
17. National Resources Committee, *The Future of State Planning* (Washington, D.C.: Government Printing Office, 1938), p. 19. Mr. J. Reeve has called my attention to the fact that the problem of allocation of public expenditures has come to be more difficult also because of the increasingly large number of alternative purposes of expenditure.
18. For an approach to the work of the Water Committee in terms somewhat similar to those of this paper, see National Resources Committee, *Progress Report* (December 1938): 29–36. For an example of the work, see National Resources Committee, *Drainage Basin Problems and Programs, 1937 Revision* (Washington, D.C.: Government Printing Office, 1938).
19. E. B. Logan, "Group Pressures and State Finance," *Annals of the American Academy of Political and Social Science* 179 (1935): 131–135; Dayton David McKean, *Pressures on the Legislature of New Jersey* (New York, 1938), chap. 5.
20. This matter is really another facet of the problem of the determination of the "public interest" with which E. P. Herring grapples in *Public Administration and the Public Interest.*
21. For such studies, useful methodological ideas might be gleaned from Professor Schattschnider's *Politics, Pressures, and the Tariff.*
22. Helpful comments by I. M. Labovitz and Homer Jones on a preliminary draft of this paper are hereby acknowledged.

12

A Theory of Human Motivation

A. H. Maslow

I. Introduction

In a previous paper[1] various propositions were presented which would have to be included in any theory of human motivation that could lay claim to being definitive. These conclusions may be briefly summarized as follows:

1. The integrated wholeness of the organism must be one of the foundation stones of motivation theory.
2. The hunger drive (or any other physiological drive) was rejected as a centering point or model for a definitive theory of motivation. Any drive that is somatically based and localizable was shown to be atypical rather than typical in human motivation.
3. Such a theory should stress and center itself upon ultimate or basic goals rather than partial or superficial ones, upon ends rather than means to these ends. Such a stress would imply a more central place for unconscious than for conscious motivations.
4. There are usually available various cultural paths to the same goal. Therefore conscious, specific, local-cultural desires are not as fundamental in motivation theory as the more basic, unconscious goals.
5. Any motivated behavior, either preparatory or consummatory, must be understood to be a channel through which many basic needs may be simultaneously expressed or satisfied. Typically an act has *more* than one motivation.
6. Practically all organismic states are to be understood as motivated and as motivating.
7. Human needs arrange themselves in hierarchies of prepotency. That is to say, the appearance of one need usually rests on the prior satisfaction of another, more prepotent need. Man is a perpetually wanting animal. Also no need or drive can be treated as if it were isolated or discrete; every drive is related to the state of satisfaction or dissatisfaction of other drives.
8. *Lists* of drives will get us nowhere for various theoretical and practical reasons. Furthermore any classification of motivations must deal with the problem of levels of specificity or generalization of the motives to be classified.
9. Classifications of motivations must be based upon goals rather than upon instigating drives or motivated behavior.
10. Motivation theory should be human-centered rather than animal-centered.
11. The situation or the field in which the organism reacts must be taken into account, but the field alone can rarely serve as an exclusive explanation for behavior. Furthermore the field itself must be interpreted in terms of the organism. Field theory cannot be a substitute for motivation theory.
12. Not only the integration of the organism must be taken into account, but also the possibility of isolated, specific, partial or segmental reactions.
13. Motivations theory is not synonymous with behavior theory. The motivations are only one class of determinants of behavior. While behavior is almost always motivated, it is also almost always biologically, culturally, and situationally determined as well.

The present paper is an attempt to formulate a positive theory of motivation which will satisfy these theoretical demands and at the same time conform to the known facts, clinical and observational as well as experimental. It derives most directly, however, from clinical experience. This theory is, I think, in the functionalist tradition of James and Dewey, and is fused with the

Source: Psychological Review 50 (July 1943): 370–396.

holism of Wertheimer,[2] Goldstein,[3] and Gestalt Psychology and with the dynamicism of Freud[4] and Adler.[5] This fusion or synthesis may arbitrarily be called a "general-dynamic" theory.

It is far easier to perceive and to criticize the aspects in motivation theory than to remedy them. Mostly this is because of the very serious lack of sound data in this area. I conceive this lack of sound facts to be due primarily to the absence of a valid theory of motivation. The present theory then must be considered to be a suggested program or framework for future research and must stand or fall, not so much on facts available or evidence presented, as upon researches yet to be done, researches suggested perhaps, by the questions raised in this paper.

II. The Basic Needs

The "Physiological" Needs The needs that are usually taken as the starting point for motivation theory are the so-called physiological drives. Two recent lines of research make it necessary to revise our customary notions about these needs: first, the development of the concept of homeostasis, and second, the finding that appetites (preferential choices among foods) are a fairly efficient indication of actual needs or lacks in the body.

Homeostasis refers to the body's automatic efforts to maintain a constant, normal state of the blood stream. Cannon[6] has described this process for (1) the water content of the blood, (2) salt content, (3) sugar content, (4) protein content, (5) fat content, (6) calcium content, (7) oxygen content, (8) constant hydrogen-ion level (acid-base balance), and (9) constant temperature of the blood. Obviously this list can be extended to include other minerals, the hormones, vitamins, etc.

Young in a recent article[7] has summarized the work on appetite in its relation to body needs. If the body lacks some chemical, the individual will tend to develop a specific appetite or partial hunger for that food element.

Thus it seems impossible as well as useless to make any list of fundamental physiological needs for they can come to almost any number one might wish, depending on the degree of specificity of description. We can not identify all physiological needs as homeostatic. That sexual desire, sleepiness, sheer activity and maternal behavior in animals, are homeostatic, has not yet been demonstrated. Furthermore, this list would not include the various sensory pleasures (tastes, smells, tickling, stroking) which are probably physiological and which may become the goals of motivated behavior.

In a previous paper[8] it has been pointed out that these physiological drives or needs are to be considered unusual rather than typical because they are isolable, and because they are localizable somatically. That is to say, they are relatively independent of each other, of other motivations and of the organism as a whole, and secondly, in many cases, it is possible to demonstrate a localized, underlying somatic base for the drive. This is true less generally than has been thought (exceptions are fatigue, sleepiness, maternal responses) but it is still true in the classic instances of hunger, sex, and thirst.

It should be pointed out again that any of the physiological needs and the consummatory behavior involved with them serve as channels for all sorts of other needs as well. That is to say, the person who thinks he is hungry may actually be seeking more for comfort, or dependence, than for vitamins or proteins. Conversely, it is possible to satisfy the hunger need in part by other activities such as drinking water or smoking cigarettes. In other words, relatively isolable as these physiological needs are, they are not completely so.

Undoubtedly these physiological needs are the most prepotent of all needs. What this means specifically is, that in the human being who is missing everything in life in an extreme fashion, it is most likely that the major motivation would be the physiological needs rather than any others. A person who is lacking food, safety, love, and esteem would most probably hunger for food more strongly than for anything else.

If all the needs are unsatisfied, and the organism is then dominated by the physiological needs, all other needs may become simply nonexistent or be pushed into the background. It is then fair to characterize the whole organism by saying simply that it is hungry, for consciousness is almost completely preempted by hunger. All capacities are put into the service of hunger-satisfaction, and the organization of these capacities is almost entirely determined by the one purpose of satisfying hunger. The receptors and effectors, the intelligence, memory, habits, all may now be defined simply as hunger-gratifying tools. Capacities that are not useful for this purpose lie dormant, or are pushed into the background. The urge to write poetry, the desire to acquire an automobile, the interest in American history, the desire for a new pair of shoes are, in the extreme case, forgotten or become of secondary importance. For the man who is extremely and dangerously hungry, no other interests exist but food. He dreams food, he remembers food, he thinks about food, he emotes only about food, he perceives only food and he wants only food. The more subtle determinants that ordinarily fuse with the physiological drives in organizing even feeding, drinking or sexual behavior, may now be so completely overwhelmed as to allow us to speak at this time (but *only* at this time) of pure hunger drive and behavior, with the one unqualified aim of relief.

Another peculiar characteristic of the human organism when it is dominated by a certain need is that the whole philosophy of the future tends also to change. For our chronically and extremely hungry man, Utopia can be defined very simply as a place where there is plenty of food. He tends to think that, if only he is guaranteed food for the rest of his life, he will be perfectly happy and will never want anything more. Life itself tends to be defined in terms of eating. Anything else will be defined as unimportant. Freedom, love, community feeling, respect, philosophy, may all be waved aside as fripperies which are useless since they fail to fill the stomach. Such a man may fairly be said to live by bread alone.

It cannot possibly be denied that such things are true, but their *generality* can be denied. Emergency conditions are, almost by definition, rare in the normally functioning peaceful society. That this truism can be forgotten is due mainly to two reasons. First, rats have few motivations other than physiological ones, and since so much of the research upon motivation has been made with these animals, it is easy to carry the rat-picture over to the human being. Secondly, it is too often not realized that culture itself is an adaptive tool, one of whose main functions is to make the physiological emergencies come less and less often. In most of the known societies, chronic extreme hunger of the emergency type is rare, rather than common. In any case, this is still true in the United States. The average American citizen is experiencing appetite rather than hunger when he says "I am hungry." He is apt to experience sheer life-and-death hunger only by accident and then only a few times through his entire life.

Obviously a good way to obscure the "higher" motivations, and to get a lopsided view of human capacities and human nature, is to make the organism extremely and chronically hungry or thirsty. Anyone who attempts to make an emergency picture into a typical one, and who will measure all of man's goals and desires by his behavior during extreme physiological deprivation is certainly being blind to many things. It is quite true that man lives by bread alone—when there is no bread. But what happens to man's desires when there *is* plenty of bread and when his belly is chronically filled?

At once other (and "higher") needs emerge and these, rather than physiological hungers, dominate the organism. And when these in turn are satisfied, again new (and still "higher") needs emerge and so on. This is what we mean by saying that the basic human needs are organized into a hierarchy of relative prepotency.

One main implication of this phrasing is that gratification becomes as important a concept as deprivation in motivation theory, for it releases the organism from the domination of a relatively more physiological need, permitting thereby the emergence of other more social goals. The physiological needs, along with their partial goals, when chronically gratified cease to exist as active determinants or organizers of behavior. They now exist only in a potential fashion in the sense that they may emerge again to dominate the organism if they are thwarted. But a want that is satisfied is no longer a want. The organism is dominated and its behavior organized only by unsatisfied needs. If hunger is satisfied, it becomes unimportant in the current dynamics of the individual.

This statement is somewhat qualified by a hypothesis to be discussed more fully later, namely that it is precisely those individuals in whom a certain need has always been satisfied who are best equipped to tolerate deprivation of that need in the future, and that furthermore, those who have been deprived in the past will react differently to current satisfactions than the one who has never been deprived.

The Safety Needs If the physiological needs are relatively well gratified, there then emerges a new set of needs, which we may categorize roughly as the safety needs. All that has been said of the physiological needs is equally true, although in lesser degree, of these desires. The organism may equally well be wholly dominated by them. They may serve as the almost exclusive organizers of behavior, recruiting all the capacities of the organism in their service, and we may then fairly describe the whole organism as a safety seeking mechanism. Again we may say of the receptors, the effectors, of the intellect and the other capacities that they are primarily safety-seeking tools. Again, as in the hungry man, we find that the dominating goal is a strong determinant not only of his current world-outlook and philosophy but also of his philosophy of the future. Practically everything looks less important than safety (even sometimes the physiological needs which being satisfied, are now underestimated). A man, in this state, if it is extreme enough and chronic enough, may be characterized as living almost for safety alone.

Although in this paper we are interested primarily in the needs of the adult, we can approach an understanding of his safety needs perhaps more efficiently by observation of infants and children, in whom these needs are much more simple and obvious. One reason for the clearer appearance of the threat or danger reaction in infants is that they do not inhibit this reaction at all, whereas adults in our society have been taught to inhibit it at all costs. Thus even when adults do feel their safety to be threatened, we may not be able to see this on the surface. Infants will react in a total fashion and as if they were endangered, if they are disturbed or dropped suddenly, startled by loud noises, flashing light, or other unusual sensory stimulation, by rough handling, by general loss of support in the mother's arms, or by inadequate support.[9]

In infants we can also see a much more direct reaction to bodily illnesses of various kinds. Sometimes these illnesses seem to be immediately and *per se* threatening and seem to make the child feel unsafe. For instance, vomiting, colic or other sharp pains seem to make the child look at the whole world in a different way. At such a moment of pain, it may be postulated that, for the child, the appearance of the whole world suddenly changes from sunniness to darkness, so to speak, and becomes a place in which anything at all might happen, in which previously stable things have suddenly become unstable. Thus a child who because of some bad food is taken ill may, for a day or two, develop fear, nightmares, and a need for protection and reassurance never seen in him before his illness.

Another indication of the child's need for safety is his preference for some kind of undisrupted routine or rhythm. He seems to want a predictable, orderly world. For instance, injustice, unfairness, or inconsistency in the parents seems to make a child feel anxious and unsafe. This attitude may be not so much because of the injustice *per se* or any particular pains involved, but rather because this treatment threatens to make the world look unreliable, or unsafe, or unpredictable. Young children seem to thrive better under a system which has at least a skeletal outline of rigidity, in which there is a schedule of a kind, some sort of routine, something that can be counted upon, not only for the present but also far into the future. Perhaps one could express this more accurately by saying that the child needs an organized world rather than an unorganized or unstructured one.

The central role of the parents and the normal family setup are indisputable. Quarreling, physical assault, separation, divorce or death within the family may be particularly terrifying. Also parental outbursts or rage or threats of punishment directed to the child, calling him names, speaking to him harshly, shaking him, handling him roughly, or actual physical punishment sometimes elicit such total panic and terror in the child that we must assume more is involved than the physical pain alone. While it is true that in some children this terror may represent also a fear of loss of parental love, it can also occur in completely rejected children, who seem to cling to the hating parents more for sheer safety and protection than because of hope of love.

Confronting the average child with new, unfamiliar, strange, unmanageable stimuli or situations will too frequently elicit the danger or terror reaction, as for example, getting lost or even being separated from the parents for a short time, being confronted with new faces, new situations or new tasks, the sight of strange, unfamiliar or uncontrollable objects, illness or death. Particularly at such times, the child's frantic clinging to his parents is eloquent testimony to their role as protectors (quite apart from their roles as food-givers and love-givers).

From these and similar observations, we may generalize and say that the average child in our society generally prefers a safe, orderly, predictable, organized world, which he can count on, and in which unexpected, unmanageable or other dangerous things do not happen, and in which, in any case, he has all-powerful parents who protect and shield him from harm.

That these reactions may so easily be observed in children is in a way a proof of the fact that children in our society feel too unsafe (or, in a word, are badly brought up). Children who are reared in an unthreatening, loving family do *not* ordinarily react as we have described above.[10] In such children the danger reactions are apt to come mostly to objects or situations that adults too would consider dangerous.[11]

The healthy, normal, fortunate adult in our culture is largely satisfied in his safety needs. The peaceful, smoothly running "good" society ordinarily makes its members feel safe enough from wild animals, extremes of temperature, criminals, assault and murder, tyranny, etc. Therefore, in a very real sense, he no longer has any safety needs as active motivators. Just as a sated man no longer feels hungry, a safe man no longer feels endangered. If we wish to see these needs directly and clearly we must turn to neurotic or near-neurotic individuals, and to the economic and social underdogs. In between these extremes, we can perceive the expressions of safety needs only in such phenomena as, for instance, the common preference for a job with tenure and protection, the desire for a savings account, and for insurance of various kinds (medical, dental, unemployment, disability, old age).

Other broader aspects of the attempt to seek safety and stability in the world are seen in the very common preference for familiar rather than unfamiliar things, or for the known rather than the unknown. The tendency to have some religion or world-philosophy that organizes the universe and the men in it into some sort of satisfactorily coherent, meaningful whole is also in part motivated by safety-seeking. Here too we may list science and philosophy in general as partially motivated by the safety needs (we shall see later that there are also other motivations to scientific, philosophical or religious endeavor).

Otherwise the need for safety is seen as an active and dominant mobilizer of the organism's resources only in emergencies, *e.g.*, war, disease, natural catastrophes, crime waves, societal disorganization, neurosis, brain injury, chronically bad situation.

Some neurotic adults in our society are, in many ways, like the unsafe child in their desire for safety, although in the former it takes on a somewhat special appearance. Their reaction is often to unknown, psychological dangers in a world that is perceived to be hostile, overwhelming and threatening. Such a person behaves as if a great catastrophe were almost always impending, *i.e.*, he is usually responding as if to an emergency. His safety needs often find specific expression in search for a protector, or a stronger person on whom he may depend, or perhaps, a Fuehrer.

The neurotic individual may be described in a slightly different way with some usefulness as a grown-up person who retains his childish attitudes toward the world. That is to say, a neurotic adult may be said to behave "as if" he were actually afraid of a spanking, or of his mother's disapproval, or of being abandoned by his parents, or having his food taken away from him. It is as if his childish attitudes of fear and threat reaction to a dangerous world had gone underground, and untouched by the growing up and learning processes, were now ready to be called out by any stimulus that would make a child feel endangered and threatened.[12]

The neurosis in which the search for safety takes its clearest form is in the compulsive-obsessive neurosis. Compulsive obsessives try frantically to order and stabilize the world so that no unmanageable, unexpected or unfamiliar dangers will ever appear.[13] They hedge themselves about with all sorts of ceremonials, rules and formulas so that every possible contingency may be provided for and so that no new contingencies may appear. They are much like the brain-injured cases, described by Goldstein,[14] who manage to maintain their equilibrium by avoiding everything unfamiliar and strange and by ordering their restricted world in such a neat, disciplined, orderly fashion that everything in the world can be counted upon. They try to arrange the world so that anything unexpected (dangers) cannot possibly occur. If, through no fault of their own, something unexpected does occur, they go into a panic reaction as if this unexpected occurrence constituted a grave danger. What we can see only as a none-too-strong preference in the healthy person, *e.g.*, preference for the familiar, becomes a life-and-death necessity in abnormal cases.

The Love Needs If both the physiological and the safety needs are fairly well gratified, then there will emerge the love and affection and belongingness needs, and the whole cycle already described will repeat itself with this new center. Now the person will feel keenly, as never before, the absence of friends, or a sweetheart, or a wife, or children. He will hunger for affectionate relations with people in general, namely, for a place in his group, and he will strive with great intensity to achieve this goal. He will want to attain such a place more than anything else in the world and may even forget that once, when he was hungry, he sneered at love.

In our society the thwarting of these needs is the most commonly found core in cases of maladjustment and more severe psychopathology. Love and affection, as well as their possible expression in sexuality, are generally looked upon with ambivalence and are customarily hedged about with many restrictions and inhibitions. Practically all theorists of psychopathology have stressed thwarting of the love needs as basic in the picture of maladjustment. Many clinical studies have therefore been made of this need and we know more about it perhaps than any of the other needs except the physiological ones.[15]

One thing that must be stressed at this point is that love is not synonymous with sex. Sex may be studied as a purely physiological need. Ordinarily sexual behavior is multidetermined, that is to say, determined not only by sexual but also by other needs, chief among which are the love and affection needs. Also not to be overlooked is the fact that the love needs involve both giving *and* receiving love.[16]

The Esteem Needs All people in our society (with a few pathological exceptions) have a need or desire for a stable, firmly based (usually) high evaluation of themselves, for self-respect, or self-esteem, and for the esteem of others. By firmly based self-esteem, we mean that which is soundly based upon real capacity, achievement and respect from others. These needs may be classified into two subsidiary sets. These are, first, the desire for strength, for achievement, for adequacy, for confidence in the face of the world, and for independence and freedom.[17] Secondly, we have what we may call the desire for reputation or prestige (defining it as respect or esteem from other people), recognition, attention, importance or appreciation.[18] These needs have been relatively stressed by Alfred Adler and his followers, and have been relatively neglected by Freud and the psychoanalysts. More and more today however there is appearing widespread appreciation of their central importance.

Satisfaction of the self-esteem need leads to feelings of self-confidence, worth, strength, capability and adequacy of being useful and necessary in the world. But thwarting of these needs produces feelings of inferiority, of weakness and of helplessness. These feelings in turn give rise to either basic discouragement or else compensatory or neurotic trends. An appreciation of the necessity of basic self-confidence and an understanding of how helpless people are without it, can be easily gained from a study of severe traumatic neurosis.[19]

The Need for Self-Actualization Even if all these needs are satisfied, we may still often (if not always) expect that a new discontent and restlessness will soon develop, unless the individual is doing what he is fitted for. A musician must make music, an artist must paint, a poet must write, if he is to be ultimately happy. What a man *can* be, he *must* be. This need we may call self-actualization.

This term, first coined by Kurt Goldstein, is being used in this paper in a much more specific and limited fashion. It refers to the desire for self-fulfillment, namely, to the tendency for him to become actualized in what he is potentially. This tendency might be phrased as the desire to become more and more what one is, to become everything that one is capable of becoming.

The specific form that these needs will take will of course vary greatly from person to person. In one individual it may take the form of the desire to be an ideal mother, in another it may be expressed athletically, and in still another it may be expressed in painting pictures or in inventions. It is not necessarily a creative urge although in people who have any capacities for creation it will take this form.

The clear emergence of these needs rests upon prior satisfaction of the physiological, safety, love and esteem needs. We shall call people who are satisfied in these needs, basically satisfied people, and it is from these that we may expect the fullest (and healthiest) creativeness.[20] Since, in our society, basically satisfied people are the exception, we do not know much about self-actualization, either experimentally or clinically. It remains a challenging problem for research....

Notes

1. A. H. Maslow, "A Preface to Motivation Theory," *Psychosomatic Med.* 5 (1943): 85–92.
2. M. Wertheimer, unpublished lectures at the New School for Social Research.
3. K. Goldstein, *The Organism* (New York: American Book Co., 1939).
4. S. Freud, *New Introductory Lectures on Psychoanalysis* (New York: Norton, 1933).
5. A. Adler, *Social Interest* (London: Faber and Faber, 1938).
6. W. B. Cannon, *Wisdom of the Body* (New York: Norton, 1932).
7. P. T. Young, "The Experimental Analysis of Appetite," *Psychol. Bull.* 38 (1941): 129–164.
8. Maslow, op. cit.
9. As the child grows up, sheer knowledge and familiarity as well as better motor development make these "dangers" less and less dangerous and more and more manageable. Throughout life it may be said that one of the main conative functions of education is this neutralizing of apparent dangers through knowledge, *e.g.*, I am not afraid of thunder because I know something about it.
10. M. Shirley, "Children's Adjustments to a Strange Situation," *J. Abnorm. (Soc.) Psychol.* 37 (1942): 201–217.
11. A "test battery" for safety might be confronting the child with a small exploding firecracker, or with a bewhiskered face, having the mother leave the room, putting him upon a high ladder, a hypodermic injection, having a mouse crawl up to him, etc. Of course I cannot seriously recommend the deliberate use of such "tests" for they might very well harm the child being tested. But these and similar situations come up by the score in the child's ordinary day-to-day living and may be observed. There is no reason why these stimuli should not be used with, for example, young chimpanzees.
12. Not all neurotic individuals feel unsafe. Neurosis may have at its core a thwarting of the affection and esteem needs in a person who is generally safe.
13. A. H. Maslow and B. Mittelmann, *Principles of Abnormal Psychology* (New York: Harper and Row, 1941).
14. Goldstein, op. cit.
15. Maslow and Mittelmann, op. cit.
16. For further details, see A. H. Maslow, "The Dynamics of Psychological Security-Insecurity," *Character and Pers.* 10 (1942): 331–344; and J. Plant, *Personality and the Cultural Pattern* (New York: Commonwealth Fund, 1937), chap. 5.
17. Whether or not this particular desire is universal we do not know. The crucial question, especially important today, is "Will men who are enslaved and dominated inevitably feel dissatisfied and rebellious?" We may assume on the basis of commonly known clinical data that a man

who has known true freedom (not paid for by giving up safety and security but rather built on the basis of adequate safety and security) will not willingly or easily allow his freedom to be taken away from him. But we do not know that this is true for the person born into slavery. The events of the next decade should give us our answer. See discussion of this problem in E. Fromm, *Escape from Freedom* (New York: Farrar and Rinehart, 1941).

18. Perhaps the desire for prestige and respect from others is subsidiary to the desire for self-esteem or confidence in oneself. Observation of children seems to indicate that this is so, but clinical data give no clear support for such a conclusion.

19. A. Kardiner, *The Traumatic Neuroses of Our Time* (New York: Hoeber, 1941). For more extensive discussion of normal self-esteem, as well as for reports of various researchers, see A. H. Maslow, "Dominance, Personality and Social Behavior in Women," *J. Soc. Psychol.* 10 (1939): 3–39.

20. Clearly creative behavior, like painting, is like any other behavior in having multiple determinants. It may be seen in "innately creative" people whether they are satisfied or not, happy or unhappy, hungry or sated. Also it is clear that creative activity may be compensatory, ameliorative or purely economic. It is my impression (as yet unconfirmed) that it is possible to distinguish the artistic and intellectual products of basically satisfied people by inspection alone. In any case, here too we must distinguish, in a dynamic fashion, the overt behavior itself from its various motivations or purposes.

The Proverbs of Administration

Herbert A. Simon

A fact about proverbs that greatly enhances their quotability is that they almost always occur in mutually contradictory pairs. "Look before you leap!"—but "He who hesitates is lost."

This is both a convenience and a serious defect—depending on the use to which one wishes to put the proverbs in question. If it is a matter of rationalizing behavior that has already taken place or justifying action that has already been decided upon, proverbs are ideal. Since one is never at a loss to find one that will prove his point—or the precisely contradictory point, for that matter—they are a great help in persuasion, political debate, and all forms of rhetoric.

But when one seeks to use proverbs as the basis of a scientific theory, the situation is less happy. It is not that the propositions expressed by the proverbs are insufficient; it is rather that they prove too much. A scientific theory should tell what is true but also what is false. If Newton had announced to the world that particles of matter exert either an attraction or a repulsion on each other, he would not have added much to scientific knowledge. His contribution consisted in showing that an attraction was exercised and in announcing the precise law governing its operation.

Most of the propositions that make up the body of administrative theory today share, unfortunately, this defect of proverbs. For almost every principle one can find an equally plausible and acceptable contradictory principle. Although the two principles of the pair will lead to exactly opposite organizational recommendations, there is nothing in the theory to indicate which is the proper one to apply.[1]

Source: Reprinted with permission from Public Administration Review © 1946 by the American Society for Public Administration (ASPA), 1120 G Street, NW, Suite 700, Washington, D.C. 20005. *Reprinted by permission of Blackwell Publishing.*

It is the purpose of this paper to substantiate the sweeping criticism of administrative theory, and to present some suggestions—perhaps less concrete than they should be—as to how the existing dilemma can be solved.

Some Accepted Administrative Principles

Among the more common principles that occur in the literature of administration are these:

1. Administrative efficiency is increased by a specialization of the task among the group.
2. Administrative efficiency is increased by arranging the members of the group in a determinate hierarchy of authority.
3. Administrative efficiency is increased by limiting the span of control at any point in the hierarchy to a small number.
4. Administrative efficiency is increased by grouping the workers, for purposes of control, according to (*a*) purpose, (*b*) process, (*c*) clientele, (*d*) place. (This is really an elaboration of the first principle but deserves separate discussion.)

Since these principles appear relatively simple and clear, it would seem that their application to concrete problems of administrative organization would be unambiguous and that their validity would be easily submitted to empirical test. Such, however, seems not to be the case. To show why it is not, each of the four principles just listed will be considered in turn.

Specialization Administrative efficiency is supposed to increase with an increase in specialization. But is this intended to mean that *any* increase in specialization will increase efficiency? If so, which of the following alternatives is the correct application of the principle in a particular case?

1. A plan of nursing should be put into effect by which nurses will be assigned to districts and do all nursing within that district,

including school examinations, visits to homes of school children, and tuberculosis nursing.

2. A functional plan of nursing should be put into effect by which different nurses will be assigned to school examinations, visits to homes of school children, and tuberculosis nursing. The present method of generalized nursing by districts impedes the development of specialized skills in the three very diverse programs.

Both of these administrative arrangements satisfy the requirement of specialization—the first provides specialization by place; the second, specialization by function. The principles of specialization is of no help at all in choosing between the two alternatives.

It appears that the simplicity of the principle of specialization is a deceptive simplicity—a simplicity which conceals fundamental ambiguities. For "specialization" is not a condition of efficient administration; it is an inevitable characteristic of all group effort; however efficient or inefficient that effort may be. Specialization merely means that different persons are doing different things—and since it is physically impossible for two persons to be doing the same thing in the same place at the same time, two persons are always doing different things.

The real problem of administration, then, is not to "specialize," but to specialize in that particular manner and along those particular lines which will lead to administrative efficiency. But, in thus rephrasing this "principle" of administration, there has been brought clearly into the open its fundamental ambiguity: "Administrative efficiency is increased by a specialization of the task among the group in the direction which will lead to greater efficiency."

Further discussion of the choice between competing bases of specialization will be undertaken after two other principles of administration have been examined.

Unity of Command Administrative efficiency is supposed to be enhanced by arranging the members of the organization in a determinate hierarchy of *authority* in order to preserve "unity of command."

Analysis of this "principle" requires a clear understanding of what is meant by the term "*authority*." A subordinate may be said to accept authority whenever he permits his behavior to be guided by a decision reached by another, irrespective of his own judgment as to the merits of that decision.

In one sense the principle of unity of command, like the principle of specialization, cannot be violated; for it is physically impossible for a man to obey two contradictory commands—that is what is meant by "contradictory commands." Presumably, if unity of command is a principle of administration, it must assert something more than this physical impossibility. Perhaps it asserts this: that it is undesirable to place a member of an organization in a position where he receives orders from more than one superior. This is evidently the meaning that Gulick attaches to the principle when he says,

> The significance of this principle in the process of co-ordination and organization must not be lost sight of. In building a structure of co-ordination, it is often tempting to set up more than one boss for a man who is doing work which has more than one relationship. Even as great a philosopher of management as Taylor fell into this error in setting up separate foremen to deal with machinery, with materials, with speed, etc., each with the power of giving orders directly to the individual workman. The rigid adherence to the principle of unity of command may have its absurdities; these are, however, unimportant in comparison with the certainty of confusion, inefficiency and irresponsibility which arise from the violation of the principle.[2]

Certainly the principle of unity of command, thus interpreted, cannot be criticized for any lack of clarity or any ambiguity. The definition of authority given above should provide a clear test whether, in any concrete situation, the principle is observed. The real fault that must be found with this principle is that it is incompatible with the principle of specialization. One of the most important uses to which authority is put in an organization is to bring about specialization in the work of making decisions, so that each decision is made at a point in the organization where it can be made most expertly. As a result, the use of authority permits a greater degree of expertness to be achieved in decision making than would be possible if each operative employee had himself to make all the decisions upon which his activity is predicated. The individual fireman does not decide whether to use a two-inch hose or a fire extinguisher; that is decided for him by his officers, and the decision is communicated to him in the form of a command.

However, if unity of command, in Gulick's sense, is observed, the decisions of a person at any point in the administrative hierarchy are subject to influence through only one channel of authority; and if his decisions are of a kind that require expertise in more than one field of knowledge, then advisory and informational services must be relied upon to supply those premises which lie in a field not recognized by the mode of specialization in the organization. For example, if an accountant in a school department is subordinate to an educator, and if unity of command is observed, then the finance department cannot issue direct orders to him regarding the technical, accounting aspects of his work. Similarly, the director of motor vehicles in the public works department will be unable to issue direct orders on care of motor equipment to the fire-truck driver.[3]

Gulick, in the statement quoted above, clearly indicates the difficulties to be faced if unity of command is not observed. A certain amount of irresponsibility and confusion are almost certain to ensue. But perhaps this is not too great a price to pay for the increased expertise that can be applied to decisions. What is needed to decide the issue is a principle of administration that would enable one to weigh the relative advantages of the two courses of action. But neither the principle of unity of command nor the principle of specialization is helpful in adjudicating the controversy. They merely contradict each other without indicating any procedure for resolving the contradiction.

If this were merely an academic controversy—if it were generally agreed and had been generally demonstrated that unity of command must be preserved in all cases, even with a loss in expertise—one could assert that in case of conflict between the two principles, unity of command should prevail. But the issue is far from clear, and experts can be ranged on both sides of the controversy. On the side of unity of command there may be cited the dictums of Gulick and others.[4] On the side of specialization there are Taylor's theory of functional supervision, Macmahon and Millett's idea of "dual supervision," and the practice of technical supervision in military organization.[5]

It may be, as Gulick asserts, that the notion of Taylor and these others is an "error." If so, the evidence that it is an error has never been marshalled or published—apart from loose heuristic arguments like that quoted above. One is left with a choice between equally eminent theorists of administration and without any evidential basis for making that choice.

What evidence there is of actual administrative practice would seem to indicate that the need for specialization is to a very large degree given priority over the need for unity of command. As a matter of fact, it does not go too far to say that unity of command, in Gulick's sense, never has existed in any administrative organization. If a line officer accepts the regulations of an accounting department with regard to the procedure for making requisitions, can it be said that, in this sphere, he is not subject to the authority of the accounting department? In any actual administrative situation authority is zoned, and to maintain that this zoning does not contradict the principle of unity of command requires a very different definition of authority from that used here. This subjection of the line officer to the accounting department is no different, in principle, from Taylor's recommendation that in the matter of work programming a workman be subject to one foreman, in the matter of machine operation to another.

The principle of unity of command is perhaps more defensible if narrowed down to the following: In case two authoritative commands conflict, there should be a single determinate person whom the subordinate is expected to obey; and the sanctions of authority should be applied against the subordinate only to enforce his obedience to that one person.

If the principle of unity of command is more defensible when stated in this limited form, it also solves fewer problems. In the first place, it no longer requires, except for settling conflicts of authority, a single hierarchy of authority. Consequently, it leaves unsettled the very important question of how authority should be zoned in a particular organization (i.e., the modes of specialization) and through what channels it should be exercised. Finally, even this narrower concept of unity of command conflicts with the principle of specialization, for whenever disagreement does occur and the organization members revert to the formal lines of authority, then only those types of specialization which are represented in the hierarchy of authority can impress themselves on a decision. If the training officer of a city exercises only functional supervision over the police training officer, then in case of disagreement with the police chief, specialized knowledge of police problems will determine the outcome while specialized knowledge of training problems will be subordinated or ignored. That this actually occurs is shown by the frustration so commonly expressed by functional supervisors at their lack of authority to apply sanctions.

Span of Control Administrative efficiency is supposed to be enhanced by limiting the number of subordinates who report directly to any one administrator to a small number—say six. This notion that the "span of control" should be narrow is confidently asserted as a third incontrovertible principle of administration. The usual common-sense arguments for restricting the span of control are familiar and need not be repeated here. What is not so generally recognized is that a contradictory proverb of administration can be stated which, though it is not so familiar as the principle of span of control, can be supported by arguments of equal plausibility. The proverb in question is the following: Administrative efficiency is enhanced by keeping at a minimum the number of organizational levels through which a matter must pass before it is acted upon.

This latter proverb is one of the fundamental criteria that guide administrative analysis in procedures simplification work. Yet in many situations the results to which this principle leads are in direct contradiction to the requirements of the principle of span of control, the principle of unity of command, and the principle of specialization. The present discussion is concerned with the first of these conflicts. To illustrate the difficulty, two alternative proposals for the organization of a small health department will be presented—one based on the restriction of span of control, the other on the limitation of number of organization levels:

1. The present organization of the department places an administrative overload on the health officer by reason of the fact that all eleven employees of the department report directly to him and the further fact that some of the staff lack adequate technical training. Consequently, venereal disease clinic treatments and other details require an undue amount of the health officer's personal attention.

   It has previously been recommended that the proposed medical officer be placed in charge of the venereal disease and chest clinics and all child hygiene work. It is further recommended that one of the inspectors be designated chief inspector and placed in charge of all the department's inspectional activities and that one of the nurses be designated as head nurse. This will relieve the health commissioner of considerable detail and will leave him greater freedom to plan and supervise the health program as a whole, to conduct health education, and to coordinate the work of the department with that of other community agencies. If the department were thus organized, the effectiveness of all employees could be substantially increased.
2. The present organization of the department leads to inefficiency and excessive red tape by reason of the fact that an unnecessary supervisory level intervenes between the health officer and the operative employees, and that those four of the twelve employees who are best trained technically are engaged largely in "overhead" administrative duties. Consequently, unnecessary delays occur in securing the approval of

> the health officer on matters requiring his attention, and too many matters require review and review.
>
> The medical officer should be left in charge of the venereal disease and chest clinics and child hygiene work. It is recommended, however, that the position of chief inspector and head nurse be abolished and that the employees now filling these positions perform regular inspectional and nursing duties. The details of work scheduling now handled by these two employees can be taken care of more economically by the secretary to the health officer, and, since broader matters of policy have, in any event, always required the personal attention of the health officer, the abolition of these two positions will eliminate a wholly unnecessary step in review, will allow an expansion of inspectional and nursing services, and will permit at least a beginning to be made in the recommended program of health education. The number of persons reporting directly to the health officer will be increased to nine, but since there are few matters requiring the coordination of these employees, other than the work schedules and policy questions referred to above, this change will not materially increase his work load.

The dilemma is this: in a large organization with complex interrelations between members, a restricted span of control inevitably produces excessive red tape, for each contact between organization members must be carried upward until a common superior is found. If the organization is at all large, this will involve carrying all such matters upward through several levels of officials for decision and then downward again in the form of orders and instructions—a cumbersome and time-consuming process.

The alternative is to increase the number of persons who are under the command of each officer, so that the pyramid will come more rapidly to a peak, with fewer intervening levels. But this, too, leads to difficulty, for if an officer is required to supervise too many employees, his control over them is weakened.

If it is granted, then, that both the increase and the decrease in span of control has some undesirable consequences, what is the optimum point? Proponents of a restricted span of control have suggested three, five, even eleven, as suitable numbers, but nowhere have they explained the reasoning which led them to the particular number they selected. The principle as stated casts no light on this very crucial question. One is reminded of current arguments about the proper size of the national debt.

Organization by Purpose, Process, Clientele, Place Administrative efficiency is supposed to be increased by grouping workers according to (*a*) purpose, (*b*) process, (*c*) clientele, or (*d*) place. But from the discussion of specialization it is clear that this principle is internally inconsistent; for purpose, process, clientele, and place are competing bases of organization, and at any given point of division the advantages of three must be sacrificed to secure the advantages of the fourth. If the major departments of a city, for example, are organized on the basis of major purpose, then it follows that all the physicians, all the lawyers, all the engineers, all the statisticians will not be located in a single department exclusively composed of members of their profession but will be distributed among the various city departments needing their services. The advantages of organization by process will thereby be partly lost.

Some of these advantages can be regained by organizing on the basis of process *within* the major departments. Thus there may be an engineering bureau within the public works department, or the board of education may have a school health service as a major division of its work. Similarly, within smaller units there may be division by area or by clientele: e.g., fire department will have separate companies located throughout the city, while a welfare department may have intake and case work agencies in various locations. Again, however, these major types of specialization cannot be simultaneously achieved, for at any point in the organization it must be decided whether specialization at the next level will be accomplished by distinction of major purpose, major process, clientele, or area.

The conflict may be illustrated by showing how the principle of specialization according to purpose would lead to a different result from specialization according to clientele in the organization of a health department.

1. Public health administration consists of the following activities for the prevention of disease and the maintenance of healthful conditions: (1) vital statistics; (2) child hygiene—prenatal, maternity, postnatal, infant, preschool, and school health programs; (3) communicable disease control; (4) inspection of milk, foods, and drugs; (5) sanitary inspection; (6) laboratory service; (7) health education.

   One of the handicaps under which the health department labors is the fact that the department has no control over school health, that being an activity of the county board of education, and there is little or no coordination between that highly important part of the community health program and the balance of the program which is conducted by the city-county health unit. It is recommended that the city and county open negotiations with the board of education for the transfer of all school health work and the appropriation therefor to the joint health unit. . . .
2. To the modern school department is entrusted the care of children during almost the entire period that they are absent from the parental home. It has three principal responsibilities toward them: (1) to provide for their education in useful skills and knowledge and in character; (2) to provide them with wholesome play activities outside school hours, (3) to care for their health and to assure the attainment of minimum standards of nutrition.

   One of the handicaps under which the school board labors is the fact that, except for school lunches, the board has no control over child health and nutrition, and there is little or no coordination between that highly important part of the child development program and the balance of the program which is conducted by the board of education. It is recommended that the city and county open negotiations for the transfer of all health work for children of school age to the board of education.

Here again is posed the dilemma of choosing between alternative, equally plausible, administrative principles. But this is not the only difficulty in the present case, for a closer study of the situation shows there are fundamental ambiguities in the meanings of the key items— "purpose," "process," "clientele," and "place."

"Purpose" may be roughly defined as the objective or end for which an activity is carried on; "process" as a means for accomplishing a purpose. Processes, then, are carried on in order to achieve purposes. But purposes themselves may generally be arranged in some sort of hierarchy. A typist moves her fingers in order to type; types in order to reproduce a letter; reproduces a letter in order that an inquiry may be answered. Writing a letter is then the purpose for which the typing is performed; while writing a letter is also the process whereby the purpose of replying to an inquiry is achieved. It follows that the same activity may be described as purpose or as process.

This ambiguity is easily illustrated for the case of an administrative organization. A health department conceived as a unit whose task it is to care for the health of the community is a purpose organization; the same department conceived as a unit which makes use of the medical arts to carry on its work is a process organization. In the same way, an education department may be viewed as a purpose (to educate) organization, or a clientele (children) organization; the forest service as a purpose (forest conservation), process (forest management), clientele (lumbermen and cattlemen utilizing public forests), or area (publicly owned forest lands) organization. When concrete illustrations of this sort are selected, the lines of demarcation between these categories become very hazy and unclear indeed.

"Organization by major purpose," says Gulick, ". . . serves to bring together in a single large department all of those who are at work endeavoring to render a particular service."[6] But what is a particular service? Is fire protection a single purpose, or is it merely a part of the purpose of public safety?—or is it a combination of purposes including fire prevention and fire fighting? It must be concluded that there is no such thing as a purpose, or a unifunctional (single-purpose) organization. What is to be considered a single function depends entirely on language and techniques.[7] If the English language has a comprehensive term which covers both of two sub-purposes it is natural to think of the two together as a single purpose. If such a term is lacking, the two sub-purposes become purposes in their own right. On the other hand, a single activity may contribute to several objectives, but since they are technically (procedurally) inseparable, the activity is considered a single function or purpose.

The fact, mentioned previously, that purposes form a hierarchy, each sub-purpose contributing to some more final and comprehensive end, helps to make clear the relation between purpose and process. "Organization by major process," says Gulick, ". . . tends to bring together in a single department all of those who are at work making use of a given special skill or technology, or are members of a given profession."[8] Consider a simple skill of this kind—typing. Typing is a skill which brings about a means-end coordination of muscular movements, but at a very low level in the means-end hierarchy. The content of the typewritten letter is indifferent to the skill that produces it. The skill consists merely in the ability to hit the letter "*t*" quickly whenever the letter "*t*" is required by the content and to hit the letter "*a*" whenever the letter "*a*" is required by the content.

There is, then, no essential difference between a "purpose" and a "process," but only a distinction of degree. A "process" is an activity whose immediate purpose is at a low level in the hierarchy of means and ends, while a "purpose" is a collection of activities whose orienting value or aim is at a high level in the means-end hierarchy.

Next consider "clientele" and "place" as bases of organization. These categories are really not separate from purpose, but a part of it. A complete statement of the purpose of a fire department would have to include the area served by it: "to reduce fire losses on property in the city of X." Objectives of an administrative organization are phrased in terms of a service to be provided and an area for which it is provided. Usually, the term "*purpose*" is meant to refer only to the first element, but the second is just as legitimately an aspect of purpose. Area of service, of course, may be a specified clientele quite as well as a geographical area. In the case of an agency which works on "shifts," time will be a third dimension of purpose—to provide a given service in a given area (or to a given clientele) during a given time period.

With this clarification of terminology, the next task is to reconsider the problem of specializing the work of an organization. It is no longer legitimate to speak of a "purpose" organization, a "process" organization, a "clientele" organization, or an "area" organization. The same unit might fall into any one of these four categories, depending on the nature of the larger organizational unit of which it was a part. A unit providing public health and medical services for school-age children in Multnomah County might be considered (1) an "area" organization if it were part of a unit providing the same service for the state of Oregon; (2) a "clientele" organization if it were part of a unit providing similar services for children of all ages; (3) a "purpose" or a "process" organization (it would be impossible to say which) if it were part of an education department.

It is incorrect to say that Bureau A is a process bureau; the correct statement is that Bureau A is a process bureau *within* Department X.[9] This latter statement would mean that Bureau A incorporates all the processes of a certain kind in Department X, without reference to any special subpurposes, subareas, or subclientele of Department X. Now it is conceivable that a particular unit might incorporate all processes of a certain kind but that these processes might relate to only certain particular subpurposes of the department purpose. In this case, which corresponds to the health unit in an education department mentioned above, the unit would be specialized by both purpose and process. The health unit would be the only one in the education department using the medical art (process) and concerned with health (subpurpose).

Even when the problem is solved of proper usage for the terms "purpose," "process," "clientele," and "area," the principles of administration give no guide as to which of these four competing bases of specialization is applicable in any particular situation. The British

Machinery of Government Committee had no doubts about the matter. It considered purpose and clientele as the two possible bases of organization and put its faith entirely in the former. Others have had equal assurance in choosing between purpose and process. The reasoning which leads to these unequivocal conclusions leaves something to be desired. The Machinery of Government Committee gives this sole argument for its choice:

> Now the inevitable outcome of this method of organization [by clientele] is a tendency to Lilliputian administration. It is impossible that the specialized service which each Department has to render to the community can be of as high a standard when its work is at the same time limited to a particular class of persons and extended to every variety of provision for them, as when the Department concentrates itself on the provision of the particular service only by whomsoever required, and looks beyond the interest of comparatively small classes.[10]

The faults in this analysis are obvious. First, there is no attempt to determine how a service is to be recognized. Second, there is a bald assumption, absolutely without proof, that a child health unit, for example, in a department of child welfare could not offer services of "as high a standard" as the same unit if it were located in a department of health. Just how the shifting of the unit from one department to another would improve or damage the quality of its work is not explained. Third, no basis is set forth for adjudicating the competing claims of purpose and process—the two are merged in the ambiguous term "service." It is not necessary here to decide whether the committee was right or wrong in its recommendation; the important point is that the recommendation represented a choice, without any apparent logical or empirical grounds, between contradictory principles of administration.

Even more remarkable illustrations of illogic can be found in most discussions of purpose versus process. They would be too ridiculous to cite if they were not commonly used in serious political and administrative debate.

> For instance, where should agricultural education come: in the Ministry of Education, or of Agriculture? That depends on whether we want to see the best farming taught, though possibly by old methods, or a possibly out-of-date style of farming, taught in the most modern and compelling manner. The question answers itself.[11]

But does the question really answer itself? Suppose a bureau of agricultural education were set up, headed, for example, by a man who had extensive experience in agricultural research or as administrator of an agricultural school, and staffed by men of similarly appropriate background. What reason is there to believe that if attached to a Ministry of Education they would teach old-fashioned farming by new-fashioned methods, while if attached to a Ministry of Agriculture they would teach new-fashioned farming by old-fashioned methods? The administrative problem of such a bureau would be to teach new-fashioned farming by new-fashioned methods, and it is a little difficult to see how the departmental location of the unit would affect this result. "The question answers itself" only if one has a rather mystical faith in the potency of bureau—shuffling as a means for redirecting the activities of an agency.

These contradictions and competitions have received increasing attention from students of administration during the past few years. For example, Gulick, Wallace, and Benson have stated certain advantages and disadvantages of the several modes of specialization, and have considered the conditions under which one or the other mode might best be adopted.[12] All this analysis has been at a theoretical level—in the sense that data have not been employed to demonstrate the superior effectiveness claimed for the different modes. But though theoretical, the analysis has lacked a theory. Since no comprehensive framework has been constructed within which the discussion could take place, the analysis has tended either to the logical one-sidedness which characterizes the examples quoted above or to inconclusiveness.

The Impasse of Administrative Theory

The four "principles of administration" that were set forth at the beginning of this paper have now been subjected to critical analysis. None of the four survived in very good shape, for in each case there was found, instead of an unequivocal principle, a set of two or more mutually incompatible principles apparently equally applicable to the administrative situation.

Moreover, the reader will see that the very same objections can be urged against the customary discussions of "centralization" versus "decentralization," which usually conclude, in effect, that "on the one hand, centralization of decision-making functions is desirable; on the other hand, there are definite advantages in decentralization."

Can anything be salvaged which will be useful in the construction of an administrative theory? As a matter of fact, almost everything can be salvaged. The difficulty has arisen from treating as "principles of administration" what are really only criteria for describing and iagnosing administrative situations. Closet space is certainly an important item in the design of a successful house; yet a house designed entirely with a view to securing a maximum of closet space—all other considerations being forgotten—would be considered, to say the least, somewhat unbalanced. Similarly, unity of command, specialization by purpose, decentralization are all items to be considered in the design of an efficient administrative organization. No single one of these items is of sufficient importance to suffice as a guiding principle for the administrative analyst. In the design of administrative organization, as in their operation, overall efficiency must be the guiding criterion. Mutually incompatible advantages must be balanced against each other, just as an architect weighs the advantages of additional closet space against the advantages of a larger living room.

This position, if it is a valid one, constitutes an indictment of much current writing about administrative matters. As the examples cited in this chapter amply demonstrate, much administrative analysis proceeds by selecting a single criterion and applying it to an administrative situation to reach a recommendation; while the fact that equally valid, but contradictory, criteria exist which could be applied with equal reason, but with a different result, is conveniently ignored. A valid approach to the study of administration requires that *all* the relevant diagnostic criteria be identified; that each administrative situation be analyzed in terms of the entire set of criteria; and that research be instituted to determine how weights can be assigned to the several criteria when they are, as they usually will be, mutually incompatible.

An Approach to Administrative Theory

This program needs to be considered step by step. First, what is included in the description of administrative situations for purposes of such an analysis? Second, how can weights be assigned to the various criteria to give them their proper place in the total picture?

The Description of Administrative Situations Before a science can develop principles, it must possess concepts. Before a law of gravitation could be formulated, it was necessary to have the notions of "acceleration" and "weight." The first task of administrative theory is to develop a set of concepts that will permit the description in terms relevant to the theory, of administrative situations. These concepts, to be scientifically useful, must be operational; that is, their meanings must correspond to empirically observable facts or situations. The definition of "authority" given earlier in this paper is an example of an operational definition.

What is a scientifically relevant description of an organization? It is a description that, so far as possible, designates for each person in the organization what decisions that person makes and the influences to which he is subject in making each of these decisions. Current descriptions of administrative organizations fall far short of this standard. For the most part, they confine themselves to the allocation of *functions* and the formal structure of *authority.* They give little attention to the other types of organizational influence or to the system of communication.[13]

What does it mean, for example, to say: "The department is made up of three bureaus. The first has the function of ______, the second the function of ______, and the third the function of ______?" What can be learned from such a description about the workability of the organizational arrangement? Very little, indeed. For from the description there is obtained no idea of the degree to which decisions are centralized at the bureau level or at the departmental level. No notion is given as to the extent to which the (presumably unlimited) authority of the department over the bureau is actually exercised or by what mechanisms. There is no indication of the extent to which systems of communication assist the coordination of the three bureaus or, for that matter, to what extent coordination is required by the nature of their work. There is no description of the kinds of training the members of the bureau have undergone or of the extent to which this training permits decentralization at the bureau level. In sum, a description of administrative organizations in terms almost exclusively of functions and lines of authority is completely inadequate for purposes of administrative analysis.

Consider the term "centralization." How is it determined whether the operations of a particular organization are "centralized" or "decentralized"? Does the fact that field offices exist prove anything about decentralization? Might not the same decentralization take place in the bureaus of a centrally located office? A realistic analysis of centralization must include a study of the allocation of decisions in the organization and the methods of influence that are employed by the higher levels to affect the decisions at the lower levels. Such an analysis would reveal a much more complex picture of the decision-making process than any enumeration of the geographical locations of organizational units at the different levels.

Administrative description suffers currently from superficiality, oversimplification, lack of realism. It has confined itself too closely to the mechanism of authority and has failed to bring within its orbit the other, equally important, modes of influence on organizational behavior. It has refused to undertake the tiresome task of studying the actual allocation of decision-making functions. It has been satisfied to speak of "authority," "centralization," "span of control," "function," without seeking operational definitions of these terms. Until administrative description reaches a higher level of sophistication, there is little reason to hope that rapid progress will be made toward the identification and verification of valid administrative principles.

Does this mean that a purely formal description of an administrative organization is impossible—that a relevant description must include an account of the content of the organization's decisions? This is a question that is almost impossible to answer in the present state of knowledge of administrative theory. One thing seems certain: content plays a greater role in the application of administrative principles than is allowed for in the formal administrative theory of the present time. This is a fact that is beginning to be recognized in the literature of administration. If one examines the chain of publications extending from Mooney and Reilley, through Gulick and the President's Committee controversy, to Schuyler Wallace and Benson, he sees a steady shift of emphasis from the "principles of administration" themselves to a study of the *conditions* under which competing principles are respectively applicable. Recent publications seldom say that "organization should be by purpose," but rather that "under such and such conditions purpose organization is desirable." It is to these conditions which underlie the application of the proverbs of administration that administrative theory and analysis must turn in their search for really valid principles to replace the proverbs.

The Diagnosis of Administrative Situations Before any positive suggestions can be made, it is necessary to digress a bit and to consider more closely the exact nature of the proposition of administrative theory. The theory of administration is concerned with how an organization should be constructed and operated in order to accomplish its work efficiently. A fundamental principle of administration, which follows almost immediately from the rational character of "good" administration, is that among several alternatives involving the same expenditure that one should always be selected which leads to the greatest accomplishment of administrative objectives; and among several alternatives that lead to the same accomplishment that one should be selected which involves the least expenditure. Since this "principle of efficiency" is characteristic of any activity that attempts rationally to maximize the attainment of certain ends with the use of scarce means, it is as characteristic of economic theory as it is of administrative theory. The "administrative man" takes his place alongside the classical "economic man."[14]

Actually, the "principle" of efficiency should be considered a definition rather than a principle: it is a definition of what is meant by "good" or "correct" administrative behavior. It does not tell *how* accomplishments are to be maximized, but merely states that this maximization is the aim of administrative activity, and that administrative theory must disclose under what conditions the maximization takes place.

Now what are the factors that determine the level of efficiency which is achieved by an administrative organization? It is not possible to make an exhaustive list of these but the principal categories can be enumerated. Perhaps the simplest method of approach is to consider the single member of the administrative organization and ask what the limits are to the quantity and quality of his output. These limits include (*a*) limits on his ability to perform and (*b*) limits on his ability to make correct decisions. To the extent that these limits are removed, the administrative organization approaches its goal of high efficiency. Two persons, given the same skills, the same objectives and values, the same knowledge and information, can rationally decide only upon the same course of action. Hence, administrative theory must be interested in the factors that will determine with what skills, values, and knowledge the organization member undertakes his work. These are the "limits" to rationality with which the principles of administration must deal.

On one side, the individual is limited by those skills, habits, and reflexes which are no longer in the realm of the conscious. His performance, for example, may be limited by his manual dexterity or his reaction time or his strength. His decision-making processes may be limited by the speed of his mental processes, his skill in elementary arithmetic, and so forth. In this area, the principles of administration must be concerned with the physiology of the human body and with the laws of skill-training and of habit. This is the field that has been most successfully cultivated by the followers of Taylor and in which has been developed time-and-motion study....

On a second side, the individual is limited by his values and those conceptions of purpose which influence him in making his decisions. If his loyalty to the organization is high, his decisions may evidence sincere acceptance of the objectives set for the organization; if that loyalty is lacking, personal motives may interfere with his administrative efficiency. If his loyalties are attached to the bureau by which he is employed, he may sometimes make decisions that are inimical to the larger unit of which the bureau is a part. In this area the principles of administration must be concerned with the determinants of loyalty and morale, with leadership and initiative, and with the influences that determine where the individual's organizational loyalties will be attached.

On a third side, the individual is limited by the extent of his knowledge of things relevant to his job. This applies both to the basic knowledge required in decision making—a bridge designer must know the fundamentals of mechanics—and to the information that is required to make his decisions appropriate to the given situation. In this area, administrative theory is concerned with such fundamental questions as these: What are the limits on the mass of knowledge that human minds can accumulate and apply? How rapidly can knowledge be assimilated? How is specialization in the administrative organization to be related to the specializations of knowledge that are prevalent in the community's occupational structure? How is the system of communication to channel knowledge and information to the appropriate decision-points? What types of knowledge can, and what types cannot, be easily transmitted? How is the need for intercommunication of information affected by the modes of specialization in the organization? This is perhaps the *terra incognita* of administrative theory, and undoubtedly its careful exploration will cast great light on the proper application of the proverbs of administration.

Perhaps this triangle of limits does not completely bound the area of rationality, and other sides need to be added to the figure. In any case, this enumeration will serve to indicate the kinds of considerations that must go into the construction of valid and non-contradictory principles of administration.

An important fact to be kept in mind is that the limits of rationality are variable limits. Most important of all, consciousness of the limits may in itself alter them. Suppose it were discovered in a particular organization, for example, that organizational loyalties attached to small units had frequently led to a harmful degree of intraorganizational competition. Then, a program which trained members of the organization to be conscious of their loyalties, and to subordinate loyalties to the smaller group to those of the large, might lead to a very considerable alteration of the limits in that organization.[15]

A related point is that the term "rational behavior," as employed here, refers to rationality when that behavior is evaluated in terms of the objectives of the larger organization; for, as just pointed out, the difference in direction of the individual's aims from those of the larger organization is just one of those elements of nonrationality with which the theory must deal.

A final observation is that, since administrative theory is concerned with the nonrational limits of the rational, it follows that the larger the area in which rationality has been achieved the less important is the exact form of the administrative organization. For example, the function of plan preparation, or design, if it results in a written plan that can be communicated interpersonally without difficulty, can be located almost anywhere in the organization without affecting results. All that is needed is a procedure whereby the plan can be given authoritative status, and this can be provided in a number of ways. A discussion, then, of the proper location for a planning or designing unit is apt to be highly inconclusive and is apt to hinge on the personalities in the organization and their relative enthusiasm, or lack of it, toward the planning function rather than upon any abstract principles of good administration.[16]

On the other hand, when factors of communication or faiths or loyalty are crucial to the making of a decision, the location of the decision in the organization is of great importance. The method of allocating decisions in the army, for instance, automatically provides (at least in the period prior to the actual battle) that each decision will be made where the knowledge is available for coordinating it with other decisions.

Assigning Weights to the Criteria A first step, then, in the overhauling of the proverbs of administration is to develop a vocabulary, along the lines just suggested, for the description of administrative organization. A second step, which has also been outlined, is to study the limits of rationality in order to develop a complete and comprehensive enumeration of the criteria that must be weighed in evaluating an administrative organization. The current proverbs represent only a fragmentary and unsystematized portion of these criteria.

When these two tasks have been carried out, it remains to assign weights to the criteria. Since the criteria, or "proverbs," are often mutually competitive or contradictory, it is not sufficient merely to identify them. Merely to know, for example, that a specified change in organization will reduce the span of control is not enough to justify the change. This gain must be balanced against the possible resulting loss of contact between the higher and lower ranks of the hierarchy.

Hence, administrative theory must also be concerned with the question of the weights that are to be applied to these criteria—to the problems of their relative importance in any concrete situation. This question is not one that can be solved in a vacuum. Armchair philosophizing about administration—of which the present paper is an example—has gone about as far as it can profitably go in this particular direction. What is needed now is empirical research and experimentation to determine the relative desirability of alternative administrative arrangements.

The methodological framework for this research is already at hand in the principle of efficiency. If an administrative organization whose activities are susceptible to objective evaluation be subjected to study, then the actual change in accomplishment that results from modifying administrative arrangements in these organizations can be observed and analyzed.

There are two indispensable conditions to successful research along these lines. First, it is necessary that the objectives of the administrative organization under study be defined in concrete terms so that results, expressed in terms of these objectives, can be accurately measured. Second, it is necessary that sufficient experimental control be exercised to make possible the isolation of the particular effect under study from other disturbing factors that might be operating on the organization at the same time.

These two conditions have seldom been even partially fulfilled in so-called "administrative experiments." The mere fact that a legislature passes a law creating an administrative agency, that the agency operates for five years, that the agency is finally abolished, and that a historical study is then made of the agency's operations is not sufficient to make of that agency's history an "administrative experiment." Modern American legislation is full of such "experiments" which furnish orators in neighboring states with abundant ammunition when similar issues arise in their bailiwicks, but which provide the scientific investigator with little or nothing in the way of objective evidence, one way or the other.

In the literature of administration, there are only a handful of research studies that satisfy these fundamental conditions of methodology—and these are, for the most part, on the periphery of the problem of organization. There are, first of all, the studies of the Taylor group which sought to determine the technological conditions of efficiency. Perhaps none of these is a better example of the painstaking methods of science than Taylor's own studies of the cutting of metals.[17]

Studies dealing with the human and social aspects of administration are even rarer than the technological studies. Among the more important are the whole series of studies on fatigue, starting in Great Britain during World War I and culminating in the Westinghouse experiments.[18]

In the field of public administration, almost the sole example of such experimentation is the series of studies that have been conducted in the public welfare field to determine the proper case loads for social workers.[19]

Because, apart from these scattered examples, studies of administrative agencies have been carried out without benefit of control or of objective measurement of results, they have had to depend for their recommendations and conclusions upon *a priori* reasoning proceeding from "principles of administration." The reasons have already been stated why the "principles" derived in this way cannot be more than "proverbs."

Perhaps the program outlined here will appear an ambitious or even a quixotic one. There should certainly be no illusions, in undertaking it, as to the length and deviousness of the path. It is hard to see, however, what alternative remains open. Certainly neither the practitioner of administration nor the theoretician can be satisfied with the poor analytic tools that the proverbs provide him. Nor is there any reason to believe that a less drastic reconversion than that outlined here will rebuild those tools to usefulness.

It may be objected that administration cannot aspire to be a "science"; that by the nature of its subject it cannot be more than an "art." Whether true or false, this objection is irrelevant to the present discussion. The question of how "exact" the principles of administration can be made is one that only experience can answer. But as to whether they should be logical or illogical there can be no debate. Even an "art" cannot be founded on proverbs.

Notes

1. Lest it be thought that this deficiency is peculiar to the science—or "art"—of administration, it should be pointed out that the same trouble is shared by most Freudian psychological theories, as well as by some sociological theories.
2. Luther Gulick, "Notes on the Theory of Organization," in *Papers on the Science of Administration,* ed. Luther Gulick and L. Urwick (Institute of Public Administration, Columbia University, 1937), p. 9.
3. This point is discussed in Herbert A. Simon, "Decision-Making and Administrative Organization," *Pub. Adm. Rev.* 4 (winter 1944): 20–21.
4. Gulick, op. cit., p. 9; L. D. White, *Introduction to the Study of Public Administration* (Macmillan Co., 1939), p. 45.

5. Frederick W. Taylor, *Shop Management* (Harper and Bros., 1911), p. 99; Macmahon, Millett, and Ogden, *The Administration of Federal Work Relief* (Public Administration Service, 1941), pp. 265–268; and L. Urwick, who describes British army practice in "Organization as a Technical Problem," in *Papers on the Science of Administration,* ed. Luther Gulick and L. Urwick (Institute of Public Administration, Columbia University, 1937), pp. 67–69.
6. Gulick, op. cit., p. 21.
7. If this is correct, then any attempt to prove that certain activities belong in a single department because they relate to a single purpose is doomed to fail. See, for example, John M. Gaus and Leon Wolcott, *Public Administration and the U.S. Department of Agriculture* (Public Administration Service, 1940).
8. Gulick, op. cit., p. 23.
9. This distinction is implicit in most of Gulick's analysis of specialization. However, since he cites as examples single departments within a city, and since he usually speaks of "grouping activities" rather than "dividing work," the relative character of these categories is not always apparent in this discussion (Gulick, op. cit., pp. 15–30).
10. *Report of the Machinery of Government Committee* (H. M. Stationery Office, 1918).
11. Sir Charles Harris, "Decentralization," *Journal of Public Administration* 3 (April 1925): 117–233.
12. Gulick, op. cit., pp. 21–30; Schuyler Wallace, *Federal Departmentalization* (Columbia University Press, 1941); George C. S. Benson, "International Administrative Organization," *Pub. Adm. Rev.* 1 (autumn 1941): 473–486.
13. The monograph by Macmahon, Millett, and Ogden, op. cit., perhaps approaches nearer than any other published administrative study to the sophistication required in administrative description. See, for example, the discussion on pp. 233–236 of headquarters-field relationships.
14. For an elaboration of the principle of efficiency and its place in administrative theory see Clarence E. Ridley and Herbert A. Simon, *Measuring Municipal Activities* (International City Managers' Association, 2d ed., 1943), particularly chap. 1 and the preface to the second edition.
15. For an example of the use of such training, see Herbert A. Simon and William Divine, "Controlling Human Factors in an Administrative Experiment," *Pub. Adm. Rev.* 1 (autumn 1941): 487–492.
16. See, for instance, Robert A. Walker, *The Planning Function in Urban Government* (University of Chicago Press, 1941), pp. 166–175. Walker makes out a strong case for attaching the planning agency to the chief executive. But he rests his entire case on the rather slender reed that "as long as the planning agency is outside the governmental structure . . . planning will tend to encounter resistance from public officials as an invasion of their responsibility and jurisdiction." This "resistance" is precisely the type of nonrational loyalty which has been referred to previously, and which is certainly a variable.
17. F. W. Taylor, *On the Art of Cutting Metals* (American Society of Mechanical Engineers, 1907).
18. Great Britain, Ministry of Munitions, Health of Munitions Workers Committee, *Final Report* (H. M. Stationery Office, 1918); F. J. Roethlisberger and William J. Dickson, *Management and the Worker* (Harvard University Press, 1939).
19. Ellery F. Reed, *An Experiment in Reducing the Cost of Relief* (American Public Welfare Administration, 1937); Rebecca Staman, "What Is the Most Economical Case Load in Public Relief Administration?" *Social Work Technique* 4 (May–June, 1938): 117–121; Chicago Relief Administration, *Adequate Staff Brings Economy* (American Public Welfare Association, 1939); Constance Hastings and Saya S. Schwartz, *Size of Visitor's Caseload as a Factor in Efficient Administration of Public Assistance* (Philadelphia County Board of Assistance, 1939); Simon et al., *Determining Work Loads for Professional Staff in a Public Welfare Agency* (Bureau of Public Administration, University of California, 1941).

The Administrative State: Conclusion

Dwight Waldo

Students of administration, writes J. M. Gaus, have become "more uncertain in recent years as to the ends, aims and methods which they should advocate." It is difficult to view in their entirety and in perspective the writings on public administration that now pour from the presses. But this is hardly necessary to confirm the truth of Gaus's statement.

The situation at present is this: there is a large core of "orthodox" public administration ideology, but also a considerable measure of doubt and even iconoclasm; an increasing disposition to engage in empirical or functional studies in which theoretical postulates are obscure and perhaps denied, but also a number of foci of theoretical activity of great potential importance; and a number of theoretical problems that should be recognized, clearly stated, and competently treated. The field at present shows much evidence of vigor and growth, and considerable progress in criticism, synthesis, and creative thought can confidently be predicted.[1]

At the heart of "orthodox" ideology is the postulate that true democracy and true efficiency are synonymous, or at least reconcilable. Clustered about this postulate are a number of formulae for effecting this reconciliation. Another important doctrine is the politics administration formula; the notion that the work of government is divisible into two parts, decision and execution, and that execution (administration) is or can be made a science. "Science," to the orthodox, connotes fact-finding, rejection of theory, and perhaps Pragmatism. The notion that there are "principles," scientifically and ethically valid, that can be uncovered by scientific study, is also still an orthodox tenet. And students of administration remain generally of the opinion that the values and practices of American business can be accepted for governmental administration with only slight reservations.

There is an area of explicit doubt and skepticism about all of these tenets except the first: that true democracy and true efficiency are reconcilable. This is so fundamental that, by definition, it could hardly be denied by an American writer on public administration. But critical thinking has taken place even here, in the form of a broadening or rejection of the original *definitions* of democracy and efficiency. Concerning "politics-administration," doubt has arisen about both the possibility and the desirability of making a sharp separation of power or division of function between the deciding and the executing agencies of government. Thinking about the nature and imperatives of "science" and "principles" becomes increasingly more critical, more subtle. And there are those who would remodel extensively the historical structure—organization and procedures—of American business, as well as that of governmental administration, in the name of Democracy, or for the sake of giving the Expert his proper role.

One of the most obvious features of recent writing on public administration is its large volume and wide scope, together with an increasing tendency to specialized, factual or "empirical" studies. This increasing specialization is perhaps normal and desirable, representing healthy progress in the discipline. Much of the specialization, however, is in the functional aspects of administration, rather than in its institutional aspects. This fact, together with the sheer volume and increasing diversity of institutional study, poses in a very acute form the problem whether there is a study of administration "as such"; at least whether there is a "function of administration," as such, in which training or specialization is possible.

Source: From The Administrative State: A Study of the Political Theory of American Public Administration, 2nd ed., by Dwight Waldo (New York: Holmes and Meier, 1948, 1984), pp. 199–204.

In view of recent tendencies it is pertinent to ask of those who are digging ever deeper into the "stuff" of administration, whose object is to present a section of unvarnished administrative truth or criticism of naive "principles," this question: Have you not gone too far in rejecting principles and embracing an uncritical empiricism? In some sectors the pertinent question is whether sophistication has become cynicism, whether in rejecting nineteenth-century concepts of "principles" the purpose or theory that must enlighten and inform any significant inquiry has not also been denied. Without faith or purpose, individuals or societies stagnate.[2]

The future of administrative theory is dependent, of course, upon what happens in the world at large, and particularly what happens in and to these United States. Whether the One World for which we poured out our treasure of life and goods becomes Two Worlds and then, one day, No World—this is the First Fact. If new forms and methods of international—or "world"—cooperation do develop, administrative thinking will be turned in new directions (although to date the considerable amount of "international" writings on administration is generally characterized by a pedestrian, earthbound quality).[3] Upon the success of our business civilization in meeting the extraordinary economic and social stresses of postwar readjustment depends the course of much future thinking. In one way or another the development and use of atomic energy will have effects reaching to the very foundations of administrative thought. But before its implications can even be projected in imagination it is necessary for the thinking organism to recover from the shock of so fundamental and spectacular a fact. Administrative thought will affect, as well as reflect, the future events. But it will not be one of the Prime Forces, at least in the near future. The number of its devotees and the range of its influence are too limited. It is only now freeing itself from a strait jacket of its own devising—the instrumentalist philosophy of the politics-administration formula—that has limited its breadth and scope.

Whatever the far-reaching implications of world cooperation and atomic energy may be, the Second Great War's aftermath of chaos and ill-will seems likely to have more important effects upon administrative thinking in the short run. Two observations as to these effects may be hazarded. The first is that, since crises usually result in centralization and integration of authority, we may expect a strengthening of the currents of centralization and integration[4]—at least in comparison to what might have been the case had the end of the war brought with it "peace" and "normalcy." The second is in some sense the converse of the first: the success of the movement to decentralize and "democratize" administration depends upon the subsidence of threats to the security of America. Whatever force there is in the socialist belief that "you can't build socialism in one country" applies similarly to democracy.

In addition to economic, political, and social events that will influence the future of administrative thought, there are a number of movements and personalities that at present are impinging on administrative thinking and may give it content and direction in the future. . . .

Perhaps most important of the theoretical movements now influencing American administrative study is scientific management. At the level of technique or procedure, borrowing from and liaison with scientific management will undoubtedly continue. Although some doctrines, such as "pure theory of organization," have already affected public administration, how influential other theoretical aspects of scientific management will be remains to be seen. In its "democratic" or "anarchistic" doctrines, conceivably, there is enough force to reconstruct present patterns of administrative thought, at least if conditions become favorable. M. L. Cooke,[5] Ordway Tead,[6] Henri Fayol,[7] Oliver Sheldon,[8] Lyndall Urwick,[9] and Elton Mayo[10] may be mentioned as among the more prominent of those associated with the scientific management movement whose writings may possibly affect the future of public administration—as they have already in some degree. Several of these persons have been influenced by the philosophy of Mary Parker Follett. This is not the place to embark upon a discussion of her theories, but an understanding of some present tendencies must depend upon a reading of her works, as well as those of the more reflective scientific managers.

It is possible—though it appears at present unlikely—that Pragmatic philosophy may play a larger role in the future than in the past. In recent essays by Horace S. Fries,[11] for example, an attempt is made to demonstrate that Pragmatism (of the Dewey variety) is not only the philosophy of science, but the proper vehicle for expanding "democracy" in both scientific management and public administration.

The probability that the recent influx of foreign, especially continental, students of administration will exert a measurable influence over theoretical development has been touched upon above. Of the simple *fact* of influence there can be no doubt, but it is yet too early to state with any certainty what will be its force.

The problem of the place of the expert in a democratic society, particularly the expert in "things-in-general," cannot be regarded as having been satisfactorily treated,[12] and will probably continue to engage the attention of administrative writers. The problem is perhaps too broad to be solved by a few thinkers in a short period of time. The answer should evolve out of experience and the gradual reconstruction of our theory by thinkers in many fields.

Closely related is the problem of providing adequate preparation and a "philosophy" for our administrators. Are training in the mechanics of administration and codes of professional ethics enough? Or should our new Guardian Class be given an education commensurate with their announced responsibilities and perhaps be imbued with a political philosophy? The present gap between the content of our administrative curricula and what we announce to be the responsibilities of our Administrators is appalling.[13] Presuming that we are in the midst of some sort of "managerial revolution,"[14] can we say that either the problem of our philosophy *about* managers or the proper philosophy *for* managers has been satisfactorily treated?

The problem of the philosophy that our Administrators entertain is intimately related, in turn, to that of the adequacy of "theory of organization." The question is this: Are students of administration trying to solve the problems of human cooperation on too low a plane? Have they, by the double process of regarding more and more formal data over a wider and wider field of human organization, lost insight, penetration? Is formal analysis of organizations without regard to the purposes that inspire them but a tedious elaboration of the insignificant?

The main tenets of the public administration movement emerged in the decades preceding 1914; they crystallized into a general political theory in the Progressive years. This "orthodox" point of view is by no means an unchallenged faith; but generally, it is still gospel in our schools, at least in undergraduate courses. Perhaps the tenets of orthodoxy still represent the "truth" for our time and our needs. Assuredly, their air of certainty and stability appeals to the emotions in these days of crisis and confusion. But the apparent likelihood of a disintegration of the old outlook and the synthesis of a new must be recognized. In any event, if abandonment of the politics administration formula is taken seriously, if the demands of present world civilization upon public administration are met, administrative thought must establish a working relationship with every major province in the realm of human learning.

NOTES

1. There have been many evidences of a thirst for philosophy in recent years, and not a few invitations to students of political theory to join in broadening public administration. But any fruitful cross-fertilization will take considerable time and awaits development of a "philosophy for the philosophers." For the "political theorists" have also become objective, scientific; they are now in the position of the art-museum curator of cartoon humor, who "knows all about art, but doesn't know what he likes." Students of administration have generally been unread in the history of political thought, but they have had no doubts about "what they like." Students of theory can offer "sophistication" to students of administration, but they have a long way to go before they can offer much positive assistance with fundamental problems, such as the relationship of administration to democracy, or to science. Cf. Donald Morrison, "Public Administration and the Art of Governance," *Pub. Adm. Rev.* 5 (winter 1945):

83–87, 85, on the divorce of "theory" from "administration"—with mutual stultification.

2. "Perhaps our sorest lack is doctrine in the theological sense to govern the flow of cooperative energies in a free commonwealth" (F. Morstein Marx, "The Lawyer's Role in Public Administration," *Yale Law Journal* 5 [April 1946]: 498–526, 503).
3. The barrier between politics and administration, though being destroyed in the domestic field, is almost completely intact in our thinking about international matters. Urgently needed is some hard, creative thinking in the area lying between advanced administrative thought and advanced thinking on the future of world politics, represented—in my opinion—by E. H. Carr's *Nationalism—And After* (New York: 1945).
4. See, however, J. M. Gaus, "A Job Analysis of Political Science," *Am. Pol. Sci. Rev.* 40 (April 1946): 217–230, 224–225, on possible "decentralizing" effects of atomic-bomb rivalry. "I found myself . . . turning again to materials on regional centers, on the future role of state governments, on state capitals as contrasted with regional centers, on the experience of Great Britain during the war with regional commissioners, and a plexus of problems in political geography, comparative government, and administration."
5. I refer particularly to his more recent essays. See especially, "Notes on Governmental and Industrial Administration in a Democracy," *Soc. Adv. Man. Jour.* 3 (July–September 1938): 139–143.
6. Various of his books, but especially, *New Adventures in Democracy* (New York, 1939), and *Democratic Administrations* (New York, 1945). Cf. "What Is a Democratic Approach to Economic Problems?" *Annals* 165 (January 1933): 101–108; "Is Industrial Self-Government Possible?" *Advanced Management* 5 (January–March 1940): 21–25.
7. *Industrial and General Administration* (London, 1930), trans. J. A. Coubrough.
8. *The Philosophy of Management* (London, 1924). This is widely cited, but it does not appear that all the juice is yet squeezed from it.
9. Urwick's writings are very stimulating, deserve close attention. Cf. *Management of Tomorrow* (London, 1933); "A Republic of Administration," *Jour. Pub. Adm.* 13 (July 1935): 263–271; "Executive Decentralization with Functional Coordination," *Jour. Pub. Adm.* 13 (October 1935): 344–358; "Bureaucracy and Democracy," *Jour. Pub. Adm.* 14 (April 1936): 134–142; "An Industrial Esperanto," *Bull. Taylor Soc.* 14 (July 1929): 150–153; "The Problem of Organization: A Study of the Work of Mary Parker Follett," *Bull. Taylor Soc. and Soc. Indust. Engineers* 1 (July 1935): 163–169.
10. Particularly, *The Human Problem of an Industrial Civilization* (New York, 1933).
11. "Some Democratic Implications of Science in Scientific Management," *Advanced Management* (October 1940): 147–152; "Liberty and Science," *Pub. Adm. Rev.* 3 (summer 1943): 268–273. Fries's essays are profound statements of a legitimate viewpoint. But this viewpoint is to me as unsatisfying as the Hindu cosmology—and for the same reason.
12. In an introduction to Scudder Klyce's *Universe* (Winchester, Mass., 1921), M. L. Cooke expresses the opinion that Klyce's work provides a philosophical justification for the exercise of power by technical experts. I cannot comment on this, as I am unable to understand Klyce's strange work.
13. Speaking in 1945 to the Washington Chapter of the American Society for Public Administration, Herbert Emmerick listed as first among the administrative lessons of the war the failure of our administrative curricula to produce adequate line administrators, as distinguished from persons trained to do housekeeping and staffwork. To the same effect see M. E. Dimock, "Administrative Efficiency within a Democratic Polity," in *New Horizons in Public Administration* (Tuscaloosa, AL: University of Alabama Press, 1945), a symposium, 21–43, 41–42.
14. James Burnham's *The Managerial Revolution* (New York, 1941) is perhaps a significant book. It is not, however, within the scope of this essay. In terms of Burnham's treatment, the literature with which this study is concerned would be the ideological trappings of the new ruling group.

The fundamental defect of Burnham's book, the reviewers have emphasized, is that, despite the fact that the argument is set forth as a refutation of orthodox socialism, it is essentially Marxian. Burnham, that is to say, has a Marxian past, and the characteristic vices of that habit of mind are carried over—the neat black and white categorizing, the itch for simplicity, the presumption of omniscience, the proclamation of inevitability. Burnham simply puts new wine in the old Marxian bottles. (In his more recent *The Struggle for the World* [New York: 1947], in fact, he performs the feat of turning the Marxian approach against the Marxists.) For an essentially Marxian refutation of Burnham's "Marxism" see J. Donald Kingsley and David W. Petegorsky, "The Technicians and the New Society," chap. 14 in *Strategy for Democracy* (New York, 1942). This is an interesting essay discussing the general failure of left-wing movements of all kinds to recognize the need for "management" to achieve their objectives and the means by which a bureaucracy can be made to serve the ends of a "democratic collectivist state."

15

The Cooptative Mechanism

Philip Selznick

To risk a definition: *cooptation is the process of absorbing new elements into the leadership or policy determining structure of an organization as a means of averting threats to its stability or existence.* With the help of this concept we are enabled more closely and more rigorously to specify the relation between TVA and some important local institutions and thus uncover an important aspect of the real meaning and significance of the Authority's grassroots policy. At the same time, it is clear that the idea of cooptation plunges us into the field of bureaucratic behavior as that is related to such democratic ideals as "local participation."

Cooptation tells us something about the process by which an institutional environment impinges itself upon an organization and effects changes in its leadership, structure, or policy. Cooptation may be formal or informal, depending upon the specific problem to be solved.

Formal Cooptation

When there is a need for the organization to publicly absorb new elements, we shall speak of formal cooptation. This involves the establishment of openly avowed and formally ordered relationships. Appointments to official posts are made, contracts are signed, new organizations are established—all signifying participation in the process of decision and administration. There are two general conditions which lead an organization to resort to formal cooptation, though they are closely related:

1. When the legitimacy of the authority of a governing group or agency is called into question. Every group or organization which attempts to exercise control must also attempt to win the consent of the governed. Coercion may be utilized at strategic points, but it is not effective as an enduring instrument. One means of winning consent is to coopt into the leadership or organization elements which in some way reflect the sentiment or possess the confidence of the relevant public or mass and which will lend respectability or legitimacy to the organs of control and thus reestablish the stability of formal authority. This device is widely used, and in many different contexts. It is met in colonial countries, where the organs of alien control reaffirm their legitimacy by coopting native leaders into the colonial administration. We find it in the phenomenon of "crisis-patriotism" wherein normally disfranchised groups are temporarily given representation in the councils of government in order to win their solidarity in a time of national stress. Cooptation has been considered by the United States Army in its study of proposals to give enlisted personnel representation in the courts-martial machinery—a clearly adaptive response to stresses made explicit during World War II. The "unity" parties of totalitarian states are another form of cooptation; company unions or some employee representation plans in industry are still another. In each of these examples, the response of formal authority (private or public, in a large organization or a small one) is an attempt to correct a state of imbalance by formal measures. It will be noted, moreover, that what is shared is the responsibility for power rather than power itself.
2. When the need to invite participation is essentially administrative, that is, when the requirements of ordering the activities of a large organization or state make it advisable to establish the forms of self-government. The problem here is not one of decentralizing

Source: From TVA and the Grass Roots by Philip Selznick, pp. 13–16, 219–226.

> decision but rather of establishing orderly and reliable mechanisms for reaching a client public or citizenry. This is the "constructive" function of trade unions in great industries where the unions become effective instruments for the elimination of absenteeism or the attainment of other efficiency objectives. This is the function of self-government committees in housing projects or concentration camps, as they become reliable channels for the transmission of managerial directives. Usually, such devices also function to share responsibility and thus to bolster the legitimacy of established authority. Thus any given act of formal cooptation will tend to fulfill both the political function of defending legitimacy and the administrative function of establishing reliable channels for communication and direction.

In general, the use of formal cooptation by a leadership does not envision the transfer of actual power. The forms of participation are emphasized but action is channeled so as to fulfill the administrative functions while preserving the locus of significant decision in the hands of the initiating group. The concept of formal cooptation will be utilized primarily in the analysis of TVA's relation to the voluntary associations established to gain local participation in the administration of the Authority's programs.

Informal Cooptation

Cooptation may be, however, a response to the pressure of specific centers of power within the community. This is not primarily a matter of the sense of legitimacy or of a general and diffuse lack of confidence. Legitimacy and confidence may be well established with relation to the general public, yet organized forces which are able to threaten the formal authority may effectively shape its structure and policy. The organization faced with its institutional environment, or the leadership faced with its ranks, must take into account these outside elements. They may be brought into the leadership or policy-determining structure, may be given a place as a recognition of and concession to the resources they can independently command. The representation of interests through administrative constituencies is a typical example of this process. Or, within an organization, individuals upon whom the group is dependent for funds or other resources may insist upon and receive a share in the determination of policy. This type of cooptation is typically expressed in informal terms, for the problem is not one of responding to a state of imbalance with respect to the "people as a whole" but rather one of meeting the pressure of specific individuals or interest groups which are in a position to enforce demands. The latter are interested in the substance of power and not necessarily in its forms. Moreover, an open acknowledgment of capitulation to specific interests may itself undermine the sense of legitimacy of the formal authority within the community. Consequently, there is a positive pressure to refrain from explicit recognition of the relationship established. This concept will be utilized in analyzing the underlying meaning of certain formal methods of cooperation initiated in line with the TVA's grass-roots policy.

Cooptation reflects a state of tension between formal authority and social power. This authority is always embodied in a particular structure and leadership, but social power itself has to do with subjective and objective factors which control the loyalties and potential manipulability of the community. Where the formal authority or leadership reflects real social power, its stability is assured. On the other hand, when it becomes divorced from the sources of social power its continued existence is threatened. This threat may arise from the sheer alienation of sentiment or because other leaderships control the sources of social power. Where a leadership has been accustomed to the assumption that its constituents respond to it as individuals, there may be a rude awakening when organization of those constituents creates nucleuses of strength which are able to effectively demand a sharing of power.

The significance of cooptation for organizational analysis is not simply that there is a change in or a broadening of leadership, and *that this is an adaptive response, but also that this change is consequential for the character and role of the organization or governing body.* Cooptation results in some constriction of the field of choice available to the organization or leadership in question. The character of the coopted elements will necessarily shape the modes of action available to the group which has won adaptation at the price of commitment to outside elements. In other words, if it is true that the TVA has, whether as a defensive or as an idealistic measure, absorbed local elements into its policy-determining structure, we should expect to find that this process has had an effect upon the evolving character of the Authority itself. From the viewpoint of the initiators of the project, and of its public supporters, the force and direction of this effect may be completely unanticipated.

The important consideration is that the TVA's choice of methods could not be expected to be free of the normal dilemmas of action. If the sentiment of the people (its organized expression) is conservative, democratic forms may require a blunting of social purpose. A perception of the details of this tendency is all important for the attempt to bind together planning and democracy. Planning is always positive—for the fulfillment of some program—but democracy may negate its execution. This dilemma requires an understanding of the possible unanticipated consequences which may ensue when positive social policy is coupled with a commitment to democratic procedure. . . . [*Editors note—Text continues at page 219 here.*]

The use of voluntary associations is not new, and is far from unique or peculiar to the program or administration of the Tennessee Valley Authority.[1] Indeed, it is useful to think of the cooptation of citizens into an administrative apparatus as a general response made by governments to what has been called "the fundamental democratization" of society.[2] The rise of the mass man,[3] or at least the increasing need for governments to take into account and attempt to manipulate the sentiments of the common man, has resulted in the development of new methods of control. These new methods center about attempts to organize the mass, to change an undifferentiated and unreliable citizenry into a structured, readily accessible public. Accessibility for administrative purposes seems to lead rather easily to control for the same or broader purposes. Consequently, there seems to be a continuum between the voluntary associations set up by the democratic (mass) state—such as committees of farmers to boost or control agricultural production—and the citizens' associations of the totalitarian (mass) state. Indeed, the devices of corporatism emerge as relatively effective responses to the need to deal with the mass, and in time of war the administrative techniques of avowedly democratic countries and avowedly totalitarian countries tend to converge.

Democracy in administration rests upon the idea of broadening participation. Let the citizen take a hand in the working of his government, give him a chance to help administer the programs of the positive state. At its extreme, this concept of democracy comes to be applied to such structures as conscript armies, which are thought to be democratic if they include all classes of the population on an equal basis. If analysis and appraisal is to be significant, however, it is necessary to inquire into the concrete meaning of such an unanalyzed abstraction as "participation." In doing so, we shall have to distinguish between substantive participation, involving an actual role in the determination of policy, and mere administrative involvement. In the conscript army, we have a broadening involvement of citizens, with a concomitant abdication of power. The same may be said of the Japanese *tomari gumi*, neighborhood associations which helped to administer rationing and other wartime programs. Such organizations, which have had their counterparts in many parts of the world, involve the local citizens, but primarily for the convenience of the administration. It is easy enough for administrative imperatives which call for decentralization to be given a halo; that becomes especially useful in countries which prize the symbols of democracy. But a critical analysis cannot overlook that pattern which simply transforms an unorganized citizenry into a reliable instrument for the achievement of administrative goals, and calls it "democracy."[4]

The tendency for participation to become equivalent to involvement has a strong rationale. In many cases, perhaps in most, the initiation of local citizens' associations comes from the top, and is tied to the pressing problem of administering a program. The need for uniformity in structure; for a channel through which directives, information, and reports will be readily disseminated; for the stimulation of a normally apathetic clientele; and for the swift dispatch of accumulated tasks—these and other imperatives are met with reasonable adequacy when involvement alone has been achieved. Some additional impetus, not provided for in the usual responsibilities of the administrative agency, is normally required if the process is to be pushed beyond the level of involvement. Indeed, it is doubtful that much can be achieved beyond that level. Such associations, voluntary or compulsory,[5] are commonly established *ad hoc*, sponsored by some particular agency.[6] That agency is charged with a set of program responsibilities. These cannot be readily changed, nor can they be effectively delegated. As an administrative organization, the agency cannot abandon the necessity for unity of command and continuity of policy—not only over time but down the hierarchy as well. What, therefore, can be the role of the coopted local association or committee? It cannot become an effective part of the major policy determining structure of the agency.[7] In practice only a limited sphere of decision is permitted, involving some adaptation of general directives to local conditions, and within that circumscribed sphere the responsible (usually paid) officials of the agency will play an effective part.

With these general considerations in mind, it may be well to mention at least one phase of the historical context within which the TVA's use of voluntary associations has developed. Especially in the field of agricultural administration, the TVA's methods have paralleled an emerging trend in the administration of the federal government. This is not often recognized within the Authority, but there can be little doubt that the United States Department of Agriculture has gone much further in developing both the theory and the practice of citizen participation than has the TVA. The emergence of this trend accompanied the construction of a vast apparatus to administer an action program reaching virtually every farmer in the nation.

One formulation of the idea of "agricultural democracy" was undertaken in 1940 by M. L. Wilson, Director of Extension Work of the Department of Agriculture.[8] Wilson noted the movement toward a greater group interest on the part of farmers, and the pressure for equality through government intervention, culminating in the enactment of the Agricultural Adjustment Act of 1933 and subsequent New Deal agricultural legislation. The administration of the new government programs was based on the ideal of cooperation and voluntary participation, leading to a set of procedures which, in Wilson's view, can be thought of as the general principles of agricultural democracy:

1. Decentralized administration in varying degrees through community, county, and state farmer committees, elected by cooperating farmers or appointed by the Secretary of Agriculture.
2. The use of referendums in determining certain administrative policies, especially those having to do with quotas, penalties, and marketing agreements.
3. The use of group discussion and other adult education techniques as a means of promoting understanding of the problems and procedures involved in administration of the various programs and referendums.
4. Cooperative planning in program formulation and localization of programs.[9]

This program emphasizes the importance of participation within the democratic pattern of culture. Moreover, in theory, participation includes both policy forming and administrative functions.

The technique of coopting local citizens through voluntary associations and as individuals into the administration of various agricultural programs was widely developed during the nineteen-thirties. In 1940, it was reported that over 890,000 citizens were helping to plan and operate nine rural action programs:[10] community, county, and state committees of the Agricultural Adjustment Administration, operating through over 3,000 county agricultural associations; land-use planning committees organized through the Bureau of Agricultural Economics; farmer associations aiding in the administration of Farm Credit Administration loans; rehabilitation and tenant-purchase committees organized by the Farm Security Administration; local district advisory boards for the Grazing Service; cooperatives dealing with the Rural Electrification Administration; governing boards of conservation districts serviced by the Soil Conservation Service; these together form an administrative pattern of which the TVA ventures along this line were only a part. . . .

The trend toward cooptation of farmers in the administration of a national agricultural program reached a high point with the organization of the county land-use planning program in 1938. The idea of democratic planning with farmer participation was given considerable attention, and an attempt was made to construct a hierarchy of representative committees which would embody the democratic ideal.[11] At the same time, the achievement of a primary administrative objective was envisioned. The land-use planning organization program received its impetus from a conference of representatives of the Department of Agriculture and the Association of Land-Grant Colleges and Universities held at Mt. Weather, Virginia, in July, 1938. The Mt. Weather Agreement[12] recommended a system of coordinated land-use planning to overcome the confusion created by the existence of a large number of points of contact between governmental agencies and local farmers. By providing that local officials of the national agricultural agencies would be represented on the farmer committees, it was felt that a single point of contact would be established. It is possible that the land-use planning system would have been established without this impetus from a pressing administrative imperative, but it is clear that the latter was the occasion for the new organization. The problems of the officialdom were primary, and logically so, for their responsibilities had to do with the efficient execution of statutory programs—not the creation of new culture patterns. The latter might, time and resources permitting, have become an effective collateral objective, but it would be idle to suppose that the requirements of administration would not assume priority within the system.

The cooptative construction of systems of voluntary associations fulfills important administrative needs. These are general, and include:

1. The achievement of ready accessibility, which requires the establishment of routine and reliable channels through which information, aid, and requests may be brought to segments of the population. The committee device permits the assembling of leading elements on a regular basis, so that top levels of administration may have reason to anticipate that quota assignments will be fulfilled; and the local organization provides an administrative focus in terms of which the various line divisions may be coordinated in the field.
2. As the program increases in intensity it becomes necessary for the lower end of administration to be some sort of group rather than the individual citizen. A group-oriented local official may reach a far larger number of people by working through community and county organizations than by attempting to approach his constituency as individuals. Thus the voluntary association permits the official to make use of untapped administrative resources.
3. Administration may be decentralized so that the execution of a broad policy is adapted to local conditions by utilizing the special knowledge of local citizens; it is not normally anticipated, however, that the policy itself will be placed in jeopardy.
4. The sharing of responsibility, so that local citizens, through the voluntary associations or committees, may become identified with and committed to the program—and, ideally, to the apparatus—of the operating agency.

These needs define the relevance of the voluntary association device to the organizational problems of those who make use of it. It is only as fulfilling such needs as these that the continuity—in both structure and function—of this type of cooptation under democratic and totalitarian sponsorship can be understood.

From the above it is not surprising that criticisms of the county planning program have stressed deviations from the democratic ideal, particularly in lack of representativeness and the tendency for established organizations such as the Farm Bureau to take control of the local committees.[13] Insofar, however, as this represents criticism of a program developing toward complete fulfillment of the ideal, it is not basic. More significant for this analysis are such criticisms as the following:

> . . . it is the central thesis of this paper that county planning did not succeed because no desire to solve community and county problems was created in the population of the area in which the county planning program was to function. . . . Most administrators of county planning conceive of rural planning as another administrative problem, as a procedure.[14]

The normal pattern—perhaps inevitable because of the rapid creation of a nationally ramified system of committees—established an organization set down from above, oriented toward the administration of the national program. As a consequence, the problems of the local official qua official assumed priority. "One needed only to talk with representatives of the several agencies engaged in trying to 'enforce' the county planning system to recognize how ubiquitous this condition [of apathy] was."[15] To the extent that the problems of the officialdom are sufficiently pressing to stamp the character of the organization, it may be expected that involvement rather than meaningful participation will prevail. This same point is made in another way by John D. Lewis, in tracing one of the bases for the lack of complete representativeness.

> The pressure to "get things done" has tended to encourage appointment rather than election. The Division in Washington naturally expects its field agents to report results that will justify the high hope with which the program was launched, and the state office in turn pushes the county agents for progress reports with which to appease Washington administrators. Democratic procedure is notoriously slow procedure. Consequently the first thought of an overworked county agent, unless he is genuinely impressed by the importance of finding a truly democratic committee, will be to find a group of industrious and cooperative farmers who can be depended upon to work together harmoniously. With the best of intentions and with no thought of deliberately stacking the committee, he may set up a committee of "outstanding leaders" who have a sincere desire to act in the interest of the whole county, but who have only a second-hand knowledge and indirect concern about the problems of less successful farmers in the county.[16]

In effect, those responsible for organizing the system of committees or associations are under pressure to shape their actions according to exigencies of the moment, and those exigencies have to do primarily with the needs of administration. As the needs of administration become dominant, the tendency for democratic participation to be reduced to mere involvement may be expected to increase. At the extreme, the democratic element drops out and the cooptive character of the organizational devices employed becomes identified with their entire meaning.[17]

Notes

1. Perhaps as testimony to the effectiveness with which the grass-roots doctrine is circulated within the TVA, there appears to have developed a feeling that the Authority has somehow originated a unique administrative device, binding the agency to its client public in some special way. This is partly referrable to enthusiasm, partly to the prevalent idea that other federal agencies, lacking the halo of regional decentralization, are unlikely to be really interested in democratic administration. It is hardly necessary to enter that controversy here, or to lay undue emphasis upon it. Yet although the grass-roots method is considered one of the major collateral objectives of the Authority, relatively little attention has been paid to the mechanics of its implementation and certainly the experience of other organizations facing the same problems and using voluntary associations has not been seriously studied inside the Authority.
2. Karl Mannheim, *Man and Society in an Age of Reconstruction* (New York: Harcourt, Brace, 1941), p. 44 ff.
3. See Jose Ortega y Gasset, *The Revolt of the Masses* (New York: Norton, 1932).

4. This is no necessary reflection on the integrity or the intentions of the responsible leadership. It is normal for programs infused with a moral content to be reduced to those elements of the program which are relevant to action. Thus the moral ideal of socialism has been reduced rather easily to concrete objectives, such as nationalization of industry. Administrative objectives, such as the establishment of a ramified system of citizens' committees, are similar.
5. This distinction tends to melt away as the program administered comes closer to becoming an exclusive means of distributing the necessities of life, or if inducements are such as to eliminate any practical alternatives to participation.
6. This may be the effective situation, even where there is not legal sponsorship. Thus, the local soil conservation districts are creatures of the state legislatures, but serviced by the Department of Agriculture's Soil Conservation Service. It is probably not inappropriately that they have been known in some areas as "SCS" districts.
7. This might happen if the local groups formed an independent central organization, but that is not envisioned by the administrative agency, unless it already has control of a preexisting central organization, as when a national government utilizes a preexisting party structure to aid in the administration of its program.
8. "A Theory of Agricultural Democracy" (an address before the American Political Science Association, Chicago, December 28, 1940), published as Extension Service Circular 355, March 1941 (mim.). See also M. L. Wilson, *Democracy Has Roots* (New York: Carrick Evans, 1939), chap. 7; Howard R. Tolley, *The Farmer Citizen at War* (New York: Macmillan Co., 1943), pt. 5.
9. Wilson, "A Theory of Agricultural Democracy," p. 5. It is interesting to note that Mr. Wilson, Director of Extension Work, considered the AAA program to have represented the practical beginning of agricultural democracy. The TVA agriculturists, loyal essentially to the local extension service organizations, would not have made such a statement.
10. Carleton R. Ball, "Citizens Help Plan and Operate Action Programs," *Land Policy Review* (March–April 1940): 19.
11. See "The Land Use Planning Organization," County Planning Series No. 3, Bureau of Agricultural Economics, May 1940; *Land Use Planning Under Way*, prepared by the BAE in cooperation with the Extension Service, FSA, SCA, AAA, and Forest Service, USDA Washington, July 1940; John M. Gaus and Leon O. Wolcott, *Public Administration and the U.S. Department of Agriculture* (Chicago: Public Administration Service, 1940), p. 151 ff.
12. Reprinted as an appendix to Gaus and Wolcott, op. cit. Russell Lord (*The Agrarian Revival*, p. 193) notes extension service references to this agreement as "The Truce of Mt. Weather." Truce indeed, for by the middle of 1942 the Congress had scuttled the program, with the support of the American Farm Bureau Federation. See Charles M. Hardin, "The Bureau of Agricultural Economics Under Fire: A Study in Valuation Conflicts," *Journal of Farm Economics* 28 (August 1946).
13. See John D. Lewis, "Democratic Planning in Agriculture," *Am. Pol. Sci. Rev.* 35 (April and June 1941); Neal C. Gross, "A Post Mortem on County Planning," *Journal of Farm Economics* 25 (August 1943); Bryce Ryan, "Democratic Telesis and County Agricultural Planning," *Journal of Farm Economics* 22 (November 1940).
14. Gross, op. cit., p. 647.
15. Ibid, p. 653. Mr. Gross also points out that the units of planning tended to follow the convenience of the administrators, rather than local interest patterns.
16. Lewis, op. cit., p. 247.
17. Unless "democracy" is reinterpreted, so that it reaches a higher level with the subordination of the mass to the organization. The above account, one sided in its emphasis, in no way deprecates the democratic aims of the initiators of the planning program. We are concerned here only with the explication of underlying trends to which the concept of cooptation lends significance.

16

The Human Side of Enterprise

Douglas Murray McGregor

It has become trite to say that industry has the fundamental know-how to utilize physical science and technology for the material benefit of mankind, and that we must now learn how to utilize the social sciences to make our human organizations truly effective.

To a degree, the social sciences today are in a position like that of the physical sciences with respect to atomic energy in the thirties. We know that past conceptions of the nature of man are inadequate and, in many ways, incorrect. We are becoming quite certain that, under proper conditions, unimagined resources of creative human energy could become available within the organizational setting.

We cannot tell industrial management how to apply this new knowledge in simple, economic ways. We know it will require years of exploration, much costly development research, and a substantial amount of creative imagination on the part of management to discover how to apply this growing knowledge to the organization of human effort in industry.

Management's Task: The Conventional View

The conventional conception of management's task in harnessing human energy to organizational requirements can be stated broadly in terms of three propositions. In order to avoid the complications introduced by a label, let us call this set of propositions "Theory X":

1. Management is responsible for organizing the elements of productive enterprise—money, materials, equipment, people—in the interest of economic ends.
2. With respect to people, this is a process of directing their efforts, motivating them, controlling their actions, modifying their behavior to fit the needs of the organization.
3. Without this active intervention by management, people would be passive—even resistant—to organizational needs. They must therefore be persuaded, rewarded, punished, controlled—their activities must be directed. This is management's task. We often sum it up by saying that management consists of getting things done through other people.

Behind this conventional theory there are several additional beliefs—less explicit, but widespread:

4. The average man is by nature indolent—he works as little as possible.
5. He lacks ambition, dislikes responsibility, prefers to be led.
6. He is inherently self-centered, indifferent to organizational needs.
7. He is by nature resistant to change.
8. He is gullible, not very bright, the ready dupe of the charlatan and the demagogue.

The human side of economic enterprise today is fashioned from propositions and beliefs such as these. Conventional organization structures and managerial policies, practices, and programs reflect these assumptions.

In accomplishing its task—with these assumptions as guides—management has conceived of a range of possibilities.

At one extreme, management can be "hard" or "strong." The methods for directing behavior involve coercion and threat (usually disguised), close supervision, tight controls over behavior. At the other extreme, management can be "soft" or "weak." The methods for directing behavior involve being permissive, satisfying people's demands, achieving harmony. Then they will be tractable, accept direction.

This range has been fairly completely explored during the past half century, and management

Source: Reprinted by permission of the publisher from Management Review, November 1957.

has learned some things from the exploration. There are difficulties in the "hard" approach. Force breeds counter-forces: Restriction of output, antagonism, militant unionism, subtle but effective sabotage of management objectives. This "hard" approach is especially difficult during times of full employment.

There are also difficulties in the "soft" approach. It leads frequently to the abdication of management—to harmony, perhaps, but to indifferent performance. People take advantage of the soft approach. They continually expect more, but they give less and less.

Currently, the popular theme is "firm but fair." This is an attempt to gain the advantages of both the hard and the soft approaches. It is reminiscent of Teddy Roosevelt's "speak softly and carry a big stick."

Is the Conventional View Correct?

The findings which are beginning to emerge from the social sciences challenge this whole set of beliefs about man and human nature and about the task of management. The evidence is far from conclusive, certainly, but it is suggestive. It comes from the laboratory, the clinic, the schoolroom, the home, and even to a limited extent from industry itself.

The social scientist does not deny that human behavior in industrial organization today is approximately what management perceives it to be. He had, in fact, observed it and studied it fairly extensively. But he is pretty sure that this behavior is *not* a consequence of man's inherent nature. It is a consequence rather of the nature of industrial organizations, of management philosophy, policy, and practice. The conventional approach of Theory X is based on mistaken notions of what is cause and what is effect.

Perhaps the best way to indicate why the conventional approach of management is inadequate is to consider the subject of motivation.

Physiological Needs

Man is a wanting animal—as soon as one of his needs is satisfied, another appears in its place. This process is unending. It continues from birth to death.

Man's needs are organized in a series of levels—a hierarchy of importance. At the lowest level, but pre-eminent in importance when they are thwarted, are his *physiological needs.* Man lives for bread alone, when there is no bread. Unless the circumstances are unusual, his needs for love, for status, for recognition are inoperative when his stomach has been empty for a while. But when he eats regularly and adequately, hunger ceases to be an important motivation. The same is true of the other physiological needs of man—for rest, exercise, shelter, protection from the elements.

A satisfied need is not a motivator of behavior! This is a fact of profound significance that is regularly ignored in the conventional approach to the management of people. Consider your own need for air. Except as you are deprived of it, it has no appreciable motivating effect upon your behavior.

Safety Needs

When the physiological needs are reasonably satisfied, needs at the next higher level begin to dominate man's behavior—to motivate him. These are called *safety needs.* They are needs for protection against danger, threat, deprivation. Some people mistakenly refer to these as needs for security. However, unless man is in a dependent relationship where he fears arbitrary deprivation, he does not demand security. The need is for the "fairest possible break." When he is confident of this, he is more than willing to take risks. But when he feels threatened or dependent, his greatest need is for guarantees, for protection, for security.

The fact needs little emphasis that, since every industrial employee is in a dependent relationship, safety needs may assume considerable importance. Arbitrary management actions, behavior which arouses uncertainty with respect to continued employment or which reflects favoritism or discrimination, unpredictable administration of policy—these can be powerful motivators of the safety needs in the employment relationship *at every level,* from worker to vice president.

Social Needs

When man's physiological needs are satisfied and he is no longer fearful about his physical welfare, his *social needs* become important motivators of his behavior—needs for belonging, for association, for acceptance by his fellows, for giving and receiving friendship and love.

Management knows today of the existence of these needs, but it often assumes quite wrongly that they represent a threat to the organization. Many studies have demonstrated that the tightly knit, cohesive work group may, under proper conditions, be far more effective than an equal number of separate individuals in achieving organizational goals.

Yet management, fearing group hostility to its own objectives, often goes to considerable lengths to control and direct human efforts in ways that are inimical to the natural "groupiness" of human beings. When man's social needs—and perhaps his safety needs, too—are thus thwarted, he behaves in ways which tend to defeat organizational objectives. He becomes resistant, antagonistic, uncooperative. But this behavior is a consequence, not a cause.

Ego Needs

Above the social needs—in the sense that they do not become motivators until lower needs are reasonably satisfied—are the needs of greatest significance to management and to man himself. They are the *egoistic needs,* and they are of two kinds:

1. Those needs that relate to one's self esteem —needs for self-confidence, for independence, for achievement, for competence, for knowledge.
2. Those needs that relate to one's reputation — needs for status, for recognition, for appreciation, for the deserved respect of one's fellows.

Unlike the lower needs, these are rarely satisfied; man seeks indefinitely for more satisfaction of these needs once they have become important to him, but they do not appear in any significant way until physiological, safety, and social needs are all reasonably satisfied.

The typical industrial organization offers few opportunities for the satisfaction of these egoistic needs to people at lower levels in the hierarchy. The conventional methods of organizing work, particularly in mass-production industries, give little heed to these aspects of human motivation. If the practices of scientific management were deliberately calculated to thwart these needs, they could hardly accomplish this purpose better than they do.

Self-Fulfillment Needs

Finally—a capstone, as it were, on the hierarchy of man's needs—there are what we may call the *needs for self-fulfillment.* These are the needs for realizing one's own potentialities, for continued self-development, for being creative in the broadest sense of that term.

It is clear that the conditions of modern life give only limited opportunity for these relatively weak needs to obtain expression. The deprivation most people experience with respect to other lower-level needs diverts their energies into the struggle to satisfy *those* needs, and the needs for self-fulfillment remain dormant.

Management and Motivation

We recognize readily enough that a man suffering from a severe dietary deficiency is sick. The deprivation of physiological needs has behavioral consequences. The same is true—although less well recognized—of deprivation of higher-level needs. The man whose needs for safety, association, independence, or status are thwarted is sick just as surely as the man who has rickets. And his sickness will have behavioral consequences. We will be mistaken if we attribute his resultant passivity, his hostility, his refusal to accept responsibility to his inherent "human nature." These forms of behavior are *symptoms* of illness—of deprivation of his social and egoistic needs.

The man whose lower-level needs are satisfied is not motivated to satisfy those needs any longer. For practical purposes they exist no longer. Management often asks, "Why aren't people more productive? We pay good wages, provide good working conditions, have excellent fringe benefits and steady employment. Yet people do not seem to be willing to put forth more than minimum effort."

The fact that management has provided for these physiological and safety needs has shifted the motivational emphasis to the social and perhaps to the egoistic needs. Unless there are opportunities *at work* to satisfy these higher level needs, people will be deprived; and their behavior will reflect this deprivation. Under such conditions, if management continues to focus its attention on physiological needs, its efforts are bound to be ineffective.

People *will* make insistent demands for more money under these conditions. It becomes more important than ever to buy the material goods and services which can provide limited satisfaction of the thwarted needs. Although money has only limited value in satisfying many higher-level needs, it can become the focus of interest if it is the *only* means available.

The Carrot-and-Stick Approach

The carrot-and-stick theory of motivation (like Newtonian physical theory) works reasonably well under certain circumstances. The *means* for satisfying man's physiological and (within limits) his safety needs can be provided or withheld by management. Employment itself is such a means, and so are wages, working conditions, and benefits. By these means the individual can be controlled so long as he is struggling for subsistence.

But the carrot-and-stick theory does not work at all once man has reached an adequate subsistence level and is motivated primarily by higher needs. Management cannot provide a man with self-respect, or with the respect of his fellows, or with the satisfaction of needs for self-fulfillment. It can create such conditions that he is encouraged and enabled to seek such satisfactions for *himself*, or it can thwart him by failing to create those conditions.

But this creation of conditions is not "control." It is not a good device for directing behavior. And so management finds itself in an odd position. The high standard of living created by our modern technological know-how provides quite adequately for the satisfaction of physiological and safety needs. The only significant exception is where management practices have not created confidence in a "fair break"—and thus where safety needs are thwarted. But by making possible the satisfaction of low-level needs, management has deprived itself of the ability to use as motivators the devices on which conventional theory has taught it to rely—rewards, promises, incentives, or threats and other coercive devices.

The philosophy of management by direction and control—regardless of whether it is hard or soft—is inadequate to motivate because the human needs on which this approach relies are today unimportant motivators of behavior. Direction and control are essentially useless in motivating people whose important needs are social and egoistic. Both the hard and the soft approach fail today because they are simply irrelevant to the situation.

People, deprived of opportunities to satisfy at work the needs which are now important to them, behave exactly as we might predict—with indolence, passivity, resistance to change, lack of responsibility, willingness to follow the demagogue, unreasonable demands for economic benefits. It would seem that we are caught in a web of our own weaving.

A New Theory of Management

For these and many other reasons, we require a different theory of the task of managing people based on more adequate assumptions about human nature and human motivation. I am going to be so bold as to suggest the broad dimensions of such a theory. Call it "Theory Y," if you will.

1. Management is responsible for organizing the elements of productive enterprise—money, materials, equipment, people—in the interest of economic ends.
2. People are *not* by nature passive or resistant to organizational needs. They have become so as a result of experience in organizations.
3. The motivation, the potential for development, the capacity for assuming

responsibility, the readiness to direct behavior toward organizational goals are all present in people. Management does not put them there. It is a responsibility of management to make it possible for people to recognize and develop these human characteristics for themselves.

4. The essential task of management is to arrange organizational conditions and methods of operation so that people can achieve their own goals *best* by directing *their own* efforts toward organizational objectives.

This is a process primarily of creating opportunities, releasing potential, removing obstacles, encouraging growth, providing guidance. It is what Peter Drucker has called "management by objectives" in contrast to "management by control." It does *not* involve the abdication of management, the absence of leadership, the lowering of standards, or the other characteristics usually associated with the "soft" approach under Theory X.

Some Difficulties

It is no more possible to create an organization today which will be a full, effective application of this theory than it was to build an atomic power plant in 1945. There are many formidable obstacles to overcome.

The conditions imposed by conventional organization theory and by the approach of scientific management for the past half century have tied men to limited jobs which do not utilize their capabilities, have discouraged the acceptance of responsibility, have encouraged passivity, have eliminated meaning from work. Man's habits, attitudes, expectations—his whole conception of membership in an industrial organization—have been conditioned by his experience under these circumstances.

People today are accustomed to being directed, manipulated, controlled in industrial organizations and to finding satisfaction for their social, egoistic, and self-fulfillment needs away from the job. This is true of much of management as well as of workers. Genuine "industrial citizenship"—to borrow again a term from Drucker—is a remote and unrealistic idea, the meaning of which has not even been considered by most members of industrial organizations.

Another way of saying this is that Theory X places exclusive reliance upon external control of human behavior, while Theory Y relies heavily on self-control and self-direction. It is worth noting that this difference is the difference between treating people as children and treating them as mature adults. After generations of the former, we cannot expect to shift to the latter overnight.

Steps in the Right Direction

Before we are overwhelmed by the obstacles, let us remember that the application of theory is always slow. Progress is usually achieved in small steps. Some innovative ideas which are entirely consistent with Theory Y are today being applied with some success.

Decentralization and Delegation These are ways of freeing people from the too close control of conventional organization, giving them a degree of freedom to direct their own activities, to assume responsibility, and, importantly, to satisfy their egoistic needs. In this connection, the flat organization of Sears Roebuck & Co. provides an interesting example. It forces "management by objectives," since it enlarges the number of people reporting to a manager until he cannot direct and control them in the conventional manner.

Job Enlargement This concept, pioneered by IBM and Detroit Edison, is quite consistent with Theory Y. It encourages the acceptance of responsibility at the bottom of the organization; it provides opportunities for satisfying social and egoistic needs. In fact, the reorganization of work at the factory level offers one of the more challenging opportunities for innovation consistent with Theory Y.

Participation and Consultative Management Under proper conditions, participation and consultative management provide encouragement to people to direct their creative energies toward organizational objectives, give them some voice in decisions that affect them, provide significant opportunities for the satisfaction of social and egoistic needs. The Scanlon Plan is the outstanding embodiment of these ideas in practice.

Performance Appraisal Even a cursory examination of conventional programs of performance appraisal within the ranks of management will reveal how completely consistent they are with Theory X. In fact, most such programs tend to treat the individual as though he were a product under inspection on the assembly line.

A few companies—among them General Mills, Inc., Ansul Chemical, and General Electric Company—have been experimenting with approaches which involve the individual in setting "targets" or objectives *for himself* and in a *self*-evaluation of performance semiannually or annually. Of course, the superior plays an important leadership role in this process—one, in fact, which demands substantially more competence than the conventional approach. The role is, however, considerably more congenial to many managers than the role of "judge" or "inspector" which is usually forced upon them. Above all, the individual is encouraged to take a greater responsibility for planning and appraising his own contribution to organizational objectives; and the accompanying effects on egoistic and self-fulfillment needs are substantial.

Applying the Ideas

The not infrequent failure of such ideas as these to work as well as expected is often attributable to the fact that a management has "bought the idea" but applied it within the framework of Theory X and its assumptions.

Delegation is not an effective way of exercising management by control. Participation becomes a farce when it is applied as a sales gimmick or a device for kidding people into thinking they are important. Only the management that has confidence in human capacities and is itself directed toward organizational objectives rather than toward the preservation of personal power can grasp the implications of this emerging theory. Such management will find and apply successfully other innovative ideas as we move slowly toward the full implementation of a theory like Y.

The Human Side of Enterprise

It is quite possible for us to realize substantial improvements in the effectiveness of industrial organizations during the next decade or two. The social sciences can contribute much to such developments; we are only beginning to grasp the indications of the growing body of knowledge in these fields. But if this conviction is to become a reality instead of a pious hope, we will need to view the process much as we view the process of releasing the energy of the atom for constructive human ends—as a slow, costly, sometimes discouraging approach toward a goal which would seem to many to be quite unrealistic.

The ingenuity and the perseverance of industrial management in the pursuit of economic ends have changed many scientific and technological dreams into commonplace realities. It is now becoming clear that the application of these same talents to the human side of enterprise will not only enhance substantially these materialistic achievements, but will bring us one step closer to "the good society."

17

The Science of "Muddling Through"

Charles E. Lindblom

Suppose an administrator is given responsibility for formulating policy with respect to inflation. He might start by trying to list all related values in order of importance, e.g., full employment, reasonable business profit, protection of small savings, prevention of a stock market crash. Then all possible policy outcomes could be rated as more or less efficient in attaining a maximum of these values. This would of course require a prodigious inquiry into values held by members of society and an equally prodigious set of calculations on how much of each value is equal to how much of each other value. He could then proceed to outline all possible policy alternatives. In a third step, he would undertake systematic comparison of his multitude of alternatives to determine which attains the greatest amount of values.

In comparing policies, he would take advantage of any theory available that generalized about classes of policies. In considering inflation, for example, he would compare all policies in the light of the theory of prices. Since no alternatives are beyond his investigation, he would consider strict central control and the abolition of all prices and markets on the one hand and elimination of all public controls with reliance completely on the free market on the other, both in the light of whatever theoretical generalizations he could find on such hypothetical economies.

Finally, he would try to make the choice that would in fact maximize his values.

An alternative line of attack would be to set as his principal objective, either explicitly or without conscious thought, the relatively simple goal of keeping prices level. This objective might be compromised or complicated by only a few other goals, such as full employment. He would in fact disregard most other social values as beyond his present interest, and he would for the moment not even attempt to rank the few values that he regarded as immediately relevant. Were he pressed, he would quickly admit that he was ignoring many related values and many possible important consequences of his policies.

As a second step, he would outline those relatively few policy alternatives that occurred to him. He would then compare them. In comparing his limited number of alternatives, most of them familiar from past controversies, he would not ordinarily find a body of theory precise enough to carry him through a comparison of their respective consequences. Instead he would rely heavily on the record of past experience with small policy steps to predict the consequences of similar steps extended into the future.

Moreover, he would find that the policy alternatives combined objectives or values in different ways. For example, one policy might offer price level stability at the cost of some risk of unemployment; another might offer less price stability but also less risk of un-employment. Hence, the next step in his approach—the final selection—would combine into one the choice among values and the choice among instruments for reaching values. It would not, as in the first method of policy-making, approximate a more mechanical process of choosing the means that best satisfied goals that were previously clarified and ranked. Because practitioners of the second approach expect to achieve their goals only partially, they would expect to repeat endlessly the sequence just described, as conditions and aspirations changed and as accuracy of prediction improved.

By Root or by Branch

For complex problems, the first of these two approaches is of course impossible. Although such an approach can be described, it cannot

Source: Reprinted with permission from Public Administration Review.

be practiced except for relatively simple problems and even then only in a somewhat modified form. It assumes intellectual capacities and sources of information that men simply do not possess, and it is even more absurd as an approach to policy when the time and money that can be allocated to a policy problem are limited, as is always the case. Of particular importance to public administrators is the fact that public agencies are in effect usually instructed not to practice the first method. That is the say, their prescribed functions and constraints—the politically or legally possible—restrict their attention to relatively few values and relatively few alternative policies among the countless alternatives that might be imagined. It is the second method that is practiced.

Curiously, however, the literatures of decision-making, policy formulation, planning, and public administration formalize the first approach rather than the second, leaving public administrators who handle complex decisions in the position of practicing what few preach. For emphasis I run some risk of overstatement. True enough, the literature is well aware of limits on man's capacities and of the inevitability that policies will be approached in some such style as the second. But attempts to formalize rational policy formulation—to lay out explicitly the necessary steps in the process—usually describe the first approach and not the second.[1]

The common tendency to describe policy formulation even for complex problems as though it followed the first approach has been strengthened by the attention given to, and successes enjoyed by, operations research, statistical decision theory, and systems analysis. The hallmarks of these procedures, typical of the first approach, are clarity of objective, explicitness of evaluation, a high degree of comprehensiveness of overview, and, wherever possible, quantification of values for mathematical analysis. But these advanced procedures remain largely the appropriate techniques of relatively small-scale problem solving where the total number of variables to be considered is small and value problems restricted. Charles Hitch, head of the Economics Division of RAND Corporation, one of the leading centers for application of these techniques, has written:

> I would make the empirical generalization from my experience at RAND and elsewhere that operations research is the art of sub-optimizing, i.e., of solving some lower level problems, and that difficulties increase and our special competence diminishes by an order of magnitude with every level of decision making we attempt to ascend. The sort of simple explicit model which operations researchers are so proficient in using can certainly reflect most of the significant factors influencing traffic control on the George Washington Bridge, but the proportion of the relevant reality which we can represent by any such model or models in studying, say, a major foreign-policy decision, appears to be almost trivial.[2]

Accordingly, I propose in this paper to clarify and formalize the second method, much neglected in the literature. This might be described as the method of *successive limited comparisons*. I will contrast it with the first approach, which might be called the rational comprehensive method.[3] More impressionistically and briefly—and therefore generally used in this article—they could be characterized as the branch method and root method, the former continually building out from the current situation, step-by-step and by small degrees; the latter starting from fundamentals anew each time, building on the past only as experience is embodied in a theory, and always prepared to start completely from the ground up.

Let us put the characteristics of the two methods side by side in simplest terms. (See Figure 1.)

Assuming that the root method is familiar and understandable, we proceed directly to clarification of its alternative by contrast. In explaining the second, we shall be describing how most administrators do in fact approach complex questions, for the root method, the "best" way as a blueprint or model, is in fact not workable for complex policy questions, and administrators are forced to use the method of successive limited comparisons.

FIGURE 1

RATIONAL-COMPREHENSIVE (ROOT)	SUCCESSIVE LIMITED COMPARISONS (BRANCH)
1a. Clarification of values or objectives distinct from and usually prerequisite to empirical analysis of alternative policies.	1b. Selection of value goals and empirical analysis of the needed action are not distinct from one another but are closely intertwined.
2a. Policy-formulation is therefore approached through means-end analysis: First the ends are isolated, then the means to achieve them are sought.	2b. Since means and ends are not distinct, means-end analysis is often inappropriate or limited.
3a. The test of a "good" policy is that it can be shown to be the most appropriate means to desired ends.	3b. The test of a "good" policy is typically that various analysts find themselves directly agreeing on a policy (without their agreeing that it is the most appropriate means to an agreed objective).
4a. Analysis is comprehensive; every important relevant factor is taken into account.	4b. Analysis is drastically limited: i) Important possible outcomes are neglected. ii) Important alternative potential policies are neglected. iii) Important affected values are neglected.
5a. Theory is often heavily relied upon.	5b. A succession of comparisons greatly reduces or eliminates reliance on theory.

Intertwining Evaluation and Empirical Analysis (1b)

The quickest way to understand how values are handled in the method of successive limited comparisons is to see how the root method often breaks down in *its* handling of values or objectives. The idea that values should be clarified, and in advance of the examination of alternative policies, is appealing. But what happens when we attempt it for complex social problems? The first difficulty is that on many critical values or objectives, citizens disagree, congressmen disagree, and public administrators disagree. Even where a fairly specific objective is prescribed for the administrator, there remains considerable room for disagreement on sub-objectives. Consider, for example, the conflict with respect to locating public housing, described in Meyerson and Banfield's study of the Chicago Housing Authority[4]—disagreement which occurred despite the clear objective of providing a certain number of public housing units in the city. Similarly conflicting are objectives in highway location, traffic control, minimum wage administration, development of tourist facilities in national parks, or insect control.

Administrators cannot escape these conflicts by ascertaining the majority's preference, for preferences have not been registered on most issues; indeed, there often *are* no preferences in the absence of public discussion sufficient to bring an issue to the attention of the electorate. Furthermore, there is a question of whether intensity of feeling should be considered as well as the number of persons preferring each alternative. By the impossibility of doing otherwise, administrators often are reduced to deciding policy without clarifying objectives first.

Even when an administrator resolves to follow his own values as a criterion for decisions, he often will not know how to rank them when they conflict with one another, as they usually do. Suppose, for example, that an administrator must relocate tenants living in tenements scheduled for destruction. One objective is to empty the buildings fairly promptly, another is to find suitable accommodation for persons displaced, another is to avoid friction with residents in other areas in which a large influx would be unwelcome, another is to deal with all concerned through persuasion if possible, and so on.

How does one state even to himself the relative importance of these partially conflicting values? A simple ranking of them is not enough; one needs ideally to know how much of one value is worth sacrificing for some of another value. The answer is that typically the administrator chooses—and must choose—directly among policies in which these values are combined in different ways. He cannot first clarify his values and then choose among policies.

A more subtle third point underlies both the first two. Social objectives do not always have the same relative values. One objective may be highly prized in one circumstance, another in another circumstance. If, for example, an administrator values highly both the dispatch with which his agency can carry through its projects *and* good public relations, it matters little which of the two possibly conflicting values he favors in some abstract or general sense. Policy questions arise in forms which put to administrators such a question as: Given the degree to which we are or are not already achieving the values of dispatch and the values of good public relations, is it worth sacrificing a little speed for a happier clientele, or is it better to risk offending the clientele so that we can get on with our work? The answer to such a question varies with circumstances.

The value problem is, as the example shows, always a problem of adjustments at a margin. But there is no practicable way to state marginal objectives or values except in terms of particular policies. That one value is preferred to another in one decision situation does not mean that it will be preferred in another decision situation in which it can be had only at great sacrifice of another value. Attempts to rank or order values in general and abstract terms so that they do not shift from decision to decision end up by ignoring the relevant marginal preferences. The significance of this third point thus goes very far. Even if all administrators had at hand an agreed set of values, objectives, and constraints, and an agreed ranking of these values, objectives, and constraints, their marginal values in actual choice situations would be impossible to formulate.

Unable consequently to formulate the relevant values first and then choose among policies to achieve them, administrators must choose directly among alternative policies that offer different marginal combinations of values. Somewhat paradoxically, the only practicable way to disclose one's relevant marginal values even to oneself is to describe the policy one chooses to achieve them. Except roughly and vaguely, I know of no way to describe—or even to understand—what my relative evaluations are for, say, freedom and security, speed and accuracy in governmental decisions, or low taxes and better schools than to describe my preferences among specific policy choices that might be made between the alternatives in each of the pairs.

In summary, two aspects of the process by which values are actually handled can be distinguished. The first is clear: evaluation and empirical analysis are intertwined; that is, one chooses among values and among policies at one and the same time. Put a little more elaborately, one simultaneously chooses a policy to attain certain objectives and chooses the objectives themselves. The second aspect is related but distinct: the administrator focuses his attention on marginal or incremental values. Whether he is aware of it or not, he does not find general formulations of objectives very helpful and in fact makes specific marginal or incremental comparisons. Two policies, X and Y, confront him. Both promise the same degree of attainment of objectives *a*, *b*, *c*, *d*, and *e*. But X promises him somewhat more of *f* than does Y, while Y promises him somewhat more of *g* than does X. In choosing between them, he is in fact offered the alternative of a marginal or incremental amount of *f* at the expense of a marginal or incremental amount of *g*. The only values that are relevant to his choice are these increments by which the two policies differ; and, when he finally chooses between the two marginal values, he does so by making a choice between policies.[5]

As to whether the attempt to clarify objectives in advance of policy selection is more or less rational than the close intertwining of marginal evaluation and empirical analysis, the principal difference established is that for complex problems the first is impossible and irrelevant, and the second is both possible and relevant. The second is possible because the administrator need not try to analyze any values except the values by which alternative policies differ and need not be concerned with them except as they differ marginally. His need for information on values or objectives is drastically reduced as compared with the root method; and his capacity for grasping, comprehending, and relating values to one another is not strained beyond the breaking point.

Relations between Means and Ends (2b)

Decision-making is ordinarily formalized as a means-ends relationship: means are conceived to be evaluated and chosen in the light of ends finally selected independently of and prior to the choice of means. This is the means-ends relationship of the root method. But it follows from all that has just been said that such a means-ends relationship is possible only to the extent that values are agreed upon, are reconcilable, and are stable at the margin. Typically, therefore, such a means-ends relationship is absent from the branch method, where means and ends are simultaneously chosen.

Yet any departure from the means-ends relationship of the root method will strike some readers as inconceivable. For it will appear to them that only in such a relationship is it possible to determine whether one policy choice is better or worse than another. How can an administrator know whether he has made a wise or foolish decision if he is without prior values or objectives by which to judge his decisions? The answer to this question calls up the third distinctive difference between root and branch methods: how to decide the best policy.

The Test of "Good" Policy (3b)

In the root method, a decision is "correct," "good," or "rational" if it can be shown to attain some specified objective, where the objective can be specified without simply describing the decision itself. Where objectives are defined only through the marginal or incremental approach to values described above, it is still sometimes possible to test whether a policy does in fact attain the desired objectives; but a precise statement of the objectives takes the form of a description of the policy chosen or some alternative to it. To show that a policy is mistaken one cannot offer an abstract argument that important objectives are not achieved; one must instead argue that another policy is more to be preferred.

So far, the departure from customary ways of looking at problem-solving is not troublesome, for many administrators will be quick to agree that the most effective discussion of the correctness of policy does take the form of comparison with other policies that might have been chosen. But what of the situation in which administrators cannot agree on values or objectives, either abstractly or in marginal terms? What then is the test of "good" policy? For the root method, there is no test. Agreement on objectives failing, there is no standard of "correctness." For the method of successive limited comparisons, the test is agreement on policy itself, which remains possible even when agreement on values is not.

It has been suggested that continuing agreement in Congress on the desirability of extending old age insurance stems from liberal desires to strengthen the welfare programs of the federal government and from conservative desires to reduce union demands for private pension plans. If so, this is an excellent demonstration of the ease with which individuals of different ideologies often can agree on concrete policy. Labor mediators report a similar phenomenon: the contestants cannot agree on criteria for settling their disputes but can agree on specific proposals. Similarly, when one administrator's objective turns out to be another's means, they often can agree on policy.

Agreement on policy thus becomes the only practicable test of the policy's correctness. And for one administrator to seek to win the other over to agreement on ends as well would accomplish nothing and create quite unnecessary controversy.

If agreement directly on policy as a test for "best" policy seems a poor substitute for testing the policy against its objectives, it ought to be remembered that objectives themselves have no ultimate validity other than they are agreed upon. Hence agreement is the test of "best" policy in both methods. But where the root method requires agreement on what elements in the decision constitute objectives and on which of these objectives should be sought, the branch method falls back on agreement wherever it can be found.

In an important sense, therefore, it is not irrational for an administrator to defend a policy as good without being able to specify what it is good for.

Noncomprehensive Analysis (4b)

Ideally, rational-comprehensive analysis leaves out nothing important. But it is impossible to take everything important into consideration unless "important" is so narrowly defined that analysis is in fact quite limited. Limits on human intellectual capacities and on available information set definite limits to man's capacity to be comprehensive. In actual fact, therefore, no one can practice the rational comprehensive method for really complex problems, and every administrator faced with a sufficiently complex problem must find ways drastically to simplify.

An administrator assisting in the formulation of agricultural economic policy cannot in the first place be competent on all possible policies. He cannot even comprehend one policy entirely. In planning a soil bank program, he cannot successfully anticipate the impact of higher or lower farm income on, say, urbanization—the possible consequent loosening of family ties, possible consequent eventual need for revisions in social security and further implications for tax problems arising out of new federal responsibilities for social security and municipal responsibilities for urban services. Nor, to follow another line of repercussions, can he work through the soil bank program's effects on prices for agricultural products in foreign markets and consequent implications for foreign relations, including those arising out of economic rivalry between the United States and the U.S.S.R.

In the method of successive, limited comparisons, simplification is systematically achieved in two principal ways. First, it is achieved through limitation of policy comparisons to those policies that differ in relatively small degree from policies presently in effect. Such a limitation immediately reduces the number of alternatives to be investigated and also drastically simplifies the character of the investigation of each. For it is not necessary to undertake fundamental inquiry into an alternative and its consequences; it is necessary only to study those respects in which the proposed alternative and its consequences differ from the status quo. The empirical comparison of marginal differences among alternative policies that differ only marginally is, of course, a counterpart to the incremental or marginal comparison of values discussed above.[6]

Relevance as Well as Realism It is a matter of common observation that in Western democracies public administrators and policy analysts in general do largely limit their analyses to incremental or marginal differences in policies that are chosen to differ only incrementally. They do not do so, however, solely because they desperately need some way to simplify their problems; they also do so in order to be relevant. Democracies change their policies almost entirely through incremental adjustments. Policy does not move in leaps and bounds.

The incremental character of political change in the United States has often been remarked. The two major political parties agree on fundamentals; they offer alternative policies to the voters only on relatively small points of difference. Both parties favor full employment, but they define it somewhat differently; both favor the development of water power resources, but in slightly different ways; and both favor unemployment compensation, but not the same level of benefits. Similarly, shifts of policy within a party take place largely through a series of relatively small changes, as can be seen in their only gradual acceptance of the idea of governmental responsibility for support of the unemployed, a change in party positions beginning in the early 1930s and culminating in a sense in the Employment Act of 1946.

Party behavior is in turn rooted in public attitudes, and political theorists cannot conceive of democracy's surviving in the United States in the absence of fundamental agreement on potentially disruptive issues, with consequent limitation of policy debates to relatively small differences in policy.

Since the policies ignored by the administrator are politically impossible and so irrelevant, the simplification of analysis achieved by concentrating on policies that differ only incrementally is not a capricious kind of simplification. In addition, it can be argued that, given the limits on knowledge within which policymakers are confined, simplifying by limiting the focus to small variations from present policy makes the most of available knowledge. Because policies being considered are like present and past policies, the administrator can obtain information and claim some insight. Nonincremental policy proposals are therefore typically not only politically irrelevant but also unpredictable in their consequences.

The second method of simplification of analysis is the practice of ignoring important possible consequences of possible policies, as well as the values attached to the neglected consequences. If this appears to disclose a shocking shortcoming of successive limited comparisons, it can be replied that, even if the exclusions are random, policies may nevertheless be more intelligently formulated than through futile attempts to achieve a comprehensiveness beyond human capacity. Actually, however, the exclusions, seeming arbitrary or random from one point of view, need be neither.

Achieving a Degree of Comprehensiveness Suppose that each value neglected by one policy-making agency were a major concern of at least one other agency. In that case, a helpful division of labor would be achieved, and no agency need find its task beyond its capacities. The shortcomings of such a system would be that one agency might destroy a value either before another agency could be activated to safeguard it or in spite of another agency's efforts. But the possibility that important values may be lost is present in any form of organization, even where agencies attempt to comprehend in planning more than is humanly possible.

The virtue of such a hypothetical division of labor is that every important interest or value has its watchdog. And these watchdogs can protect the interests in their jurisdiction in two quite different ways: first, by redressing damages done by other agencies; and, second, by anticipating and heading off injury before it occurs.

In a society like that of the United States in which individuals are free to combine to pursue almost any possible common interest they might have and in which government agencies are sensitive to the pressures of these groups, the system described is approximated. Almost every interest has its watchdog. Without claiming that every interest has a sufficiently powerful watchdog, it can be argued that our system often can assure a more comprehensive regard for the values of the whole society than any attempt at intellectual comprehensiveness.

In the United States, for example, no part of government attempts a comprehensive overview of policy on income distribution. A policy nevertheless evolves, and one responding to a wide variety of interests. A process of mutual adjustment among farm groups, labor unions, municipalities and school boards, tax authorities, and government agencies with responsibilities in the fields of housing, health, highways, national parks, fire, and police accomplishes a distribution of income in which particular income problems neglected at one point in the decision processes become central at another point.

Mutual adjustment is more pervasive than the explicit forms it takes in negotiation between groups; it persists through the mutual impacts of groups upon each other even where they are not in communication. For all the imperfections and latent dangers in this ubiquitous process of mutual adjustment, it will often accomplish an adaptation of policies to a wider range of interests than could be done by one group centrally.

Note, too, how the incremental pattern of policy-making fits with the multiple pressure pattern. For when decisions are only incremental—closely related to known policies, it is easier for one group to anticipate the kind of moves another might make and easier too for it to make correction for injury already accomplished.[7]

Even partisanship and narrowness, to use pejorative terms, will sometimes be assets to rational decision-making, for they can doubly insure that what one agency neglects, another will not; they specialize personnel to distinct points of view. The claim is valid that effective rational coordination of the federal administration, if possible to achieve at all, would require an agreed set of values[8]—if "rational" is defined as the practice of the root method of decision-making. But a high degree of administrative coordination occurs as each agency adjusts its policies to the concerns of the other agencies in the process of fragmented decision-making I have just described.

For all the apparent shortcomings of the incremental approach to policy alternatives with its arbitrary exclusion coupled with fragmentation, when compared to the root method, the branch method often looks far superior. In the root method, the inevitable exclusion of factors is accidental, unsystematic, and not defensible by any argument so far developed, while in the branch method the exclusions are deliberate, systematic, and defensible. Ideally, of course, the root method does not exclude; in practice it must.

Nor does the branch method necessarily neglect long-run considerations and objectives. It is clear that important values must be omitted in considering policy, and sometimes the only way long-run objectives can be given adequate attention is through the neglect of short-run considerations. But the values omitted can be either long-run or short-run.

Succession of Comparison (5b)

The final distinctive element in the branch method is that the comparisons, together with the policy choice, proceed in a chronological series. Policy is not made once and for all; it is made and re-made endlessly. Policy-making is a process of successive approximation to some desired objectives in which what is desired itself continues to change under reconsideration.

Making policy is at best a very rough process. Neither social scientists, nor politicians, nor public administrators yet know enough about the social world to avoid repeated error in predicting the consequences of policy moves. A wise policy-maker consequently expects that his policies will achieve only part of what he hopes and at the same time will produce unanticipated consequences he would have preferred to avoid. If he proceeds through a *succession* of incremental changes, he avoids serious lasting mistakes in several ways.

In the first place, past sequences of policy steps have given him knowledge about the probable consequences of further similar steps. Second, he need not attempt big jumps toward his goals that would require predictions beyond his or anyone else's knowledge, because he never expects his policy to be a final resolution of a problem. His decision is only one step, one that if successful can quickly be followed by another. Third, he is in effect able to test his previous predictions as he moves on to each further step. Lastly, he often can remedy a past error fairly quickly—more quickly than if policy proceeded through more distinct steps widely spaced in time.

Compare this comparative analysis of incremental changes with the aspiration to employ theory in the root method. Man cannot think without classifying, without subsuming one experience under a more general category of experiences. The attempt to push categorization as far as possible and to find general propositions which can be applied to specific situations is what I refer to with the word "theory." Where root analysis often leans heavily on theory in this sense, the branch method does not.

The assumption of root analysts is that theory is the most systematic and economical way to bring relevant knowledge to bear on a specific problem. Granting the assumption, an unhappy fact is that we do not have adequate theory to apply to problems in any policy area, although theory is more adequate in some areas—monetary policy for example—than in others. Comparative analysis, as in the branch method, is sometimes a systematic alternative to theory.

Suppose an administrator must choose among a small group of policies that differ only incrementally from each other and from present policy. He might aspire to "understand" each of the alternatives—for example, to know all the consequences of each aspect of each policy. If so, he would indeed require theory. In fact, however, he would usually decide that, *for policy-making purposes,* he need know, as explained above, only the consequences of each of those aspects of the policies in which they differed from one another. For this much more modest aspiration, he requires no theory (although it might be helpful, if available), for he can proceed to isolate probable differences by examining the differences in consequences associated with past differences in policies, a feasible program because he can take his observations from a long sequence of incremental changes.

For example, without a more comprehensive social theory about juvenile delinquency than scholars have yet produced, one cannot possibly understand the ways in which a variety of public policies—say on education, housing, recreation, employment, race relations, and policing—might encourage or discourage delinquency. And one needs such an understanding if he undertakes the comprehensive overview of the problem prescribed in the models of the root method. If, however, one merely wants to mobilize knowledge sufficient to assist in a choice among a small group of similar policies—alternative policies on juvenile court procedures, for example—he can do so by comparative analysis of the results of similar past policy moves.

Theorists and Practitioners

This difference explains—in some cases at least—why the administrator often feels that the outside expert or academic problem-solver is sometimes not helpful and why they in turn often urge more theory on him. And it explains why an administrator often feels more confident when "flying by the seat of his pants" than when following the advice of theorists. Theorists often ask the administrator to go the long way round to the solution of his problems, in effect ask him to follow the best canons of the scientific method, when the administrator knows that the best available theory will work less well than the more modest incremental comparisons. Theorists do not realize that the administrator is often in fact practicing a systematic method. It would be foolish to push this explanation too far, for sometimes practical decision-makers are pursuing neither a theoretical approach nor successive comparisons, nor any other systematic method.

It may be worth emphasizing that theory is sometimes of extremely limited helpfulness in policy-making for at least two rather different reasons. It is greedy for facts; it can be constructed only through a great collection of observations. And it is typically insufficiently precise for application to a policy process that moves through small changes. In contrast, the comparative method both economizes on the need for facts and directs the analyst's attention to just those facts that are relevant to the fine choices faced by the decision-maker.

With respect to precision of theory, economic theory serves as an example. It predicts that an economy without money or prices would in certain specified ways misallocate resources, but this finding pertains to an alternative far removed from the kind of policies on which administrators need help. On the other hand, it is not precise enough to predict the consequences of policies restricting business mergers, and this is the kind of issue on which the administrators need help. Only in relatively restricted areas does economic theory achieve sufficient precision to go far in resolving policy questions; its helpfulness in policy-making is always so limited that it requires supplementation through comparative analysis.

Successive Comparison as a System

Successive limited comparisons is, then, indeed a method or system; it is not a failure of method for which administrators ought to apologize. Nonetheless, its imperfections, which have not been explored in this paper, are many. For example, the method is without a built-in safeguard for all relevant values, and it also may lead the decision maker to overlook excellent policies for no other reason than that they are not suggested by the chain of successive policy steps leading up to the present. Hence, it ought to be said that under this method, as well as under some of the most sophisticated variants of the root method—operations research, for example—policies will continue to be as foolish as they are wise.

Why then bother to describe the method in all the above detail? Because it is in fact a common method of policy formulation, and is, for complex problems, the principal reliance of administrators as well as of other policy analysts.[9] And because it will be superior to any other decision-making method available for complex problems in many circumstances, certainly superior to a futile attempt at superhuman comprehensiveness. The reaction of the public administrator to the exposition of method doubtless will be less a discovery of a new method than a better acquaintance with an old. But by becoming more conscious of their practice of this method, administrators might practice it with more skill and know when to extend or constrict its use. (That they sometimes practice it effectively and sometimes not may explain the extremes of opinion on "muddling through," which is both praised as a highly sophisticated form of problem-solving and denounced as no method at all. For I suspect that in so far as there is a system in what is known as "muddling through," this method is it.)

One of the noteworthy incidental consequences of clarification of the method is the light it throws on the suspicion an administrator sometimes entertains that a consultant or adviser is not speaking relevantly and responsibly when in fact by all ordinary objective evidence he is. The trouble lies in the fact that most of us approach policy problems within a framework given by our view of a chain of successive policy choices made up to the present. One's thinking about appropriate policies with respect, say, to urban traffic control is greatly influenced by one's knowledge of the incremental steps taken up to the present. An administrator enjoys an intimate knowledge of his past sequences that "outsiders" do not share, and his thinking and that of the "outsider" will consequently be different in ways that may puzzle both. Both may appear to be talking intelligently, yet each may find the other unsatisfactory. The relevance of the policy chain of succession is even more clear when an American tries to discuss, say, antitrust policy with a Swiss, for the chains of policy in the two countries are strikingly different and the two individuals consequently have organized their knowledge in quite different ways.

If this phenomenon is a barrier to communication, an understanding of it promises an enrichment of intellectual interaction in policy formulation. Once the source of difference is understood, it will sometimes be stimulating for an administrator to seek out a policy analyst whose recent experience is with a policy chain different from his own.

This raises again a question only briefly discussed above on the merits of likemindedness among government administrators. While much of organization theory argues the virtues of common values and agreed organizational objectives, for complex problems in which the root method is inapplicable, agencies will want among their own personnel two types of diversification: administrators whose thinking is organized by reference to policy chains other than those familiar to most members of the organization and, even more commonly, administrators whose professional or personal values or interests create diversity of view (perhaps coming from different specialties, social classes, geographical areas) so that, even within a single agency, decision-making can be fragmented and parts of the agency can serve as watchdogs for other parts.

Notes

1. James G. March and Herbert A. Simon similarly characterize the literature they also take some important steps, as have Simon's recent articles, to describe a less heroic model of policy-making. See *Organizations* (John Wiley and Sons, 1958), p. 137.
2. Charles Hitch, "Operations Research and National Planning—A Dissent," *Operations Research* 5 (October 1957): 718. Hitch's dissent is from particular points made in the article to which his paper is a reply: his claim that operations research is for low-level problems is widely accepted.

   For examples of the kind of problems to which operations research is applied, see C. W. Churchman, R. L. Ackoff, and E. L. Arnoff, *Introduction to Operations Research* (John

Wiley and Sons, 1957); and J. F. McCloskey and J. M. Coppinger, eds., *Operations Research for Management*, vol. 2 (Johns Hopkins Press, 1956).

3. I am assuming that administrators often make policy and advise in the making of policy and am treating decision-making and policy-making as synonymous for purposes of this paper.
4. Martin Meyerson and Edward C. Banfield, *Politics, Planning, and the Public Interest* (Free Press, 1955).
5. The line of argument is, of course, an extension of the theory of market choice, especially the theory of consumer choice, to public policy choices.
6. A more precise definition of incremental policies and a discussion of whether a change that appears "small" to one observer might be seen differently by another is to be found in my "Policy Analysis," *American Economic Review* 48 (June 1958): 298.
7. The link between the practice of the method of successive limited comparisons and mutual adjustment of interests in a highly fragmented decision-making process add a new facet to pluralist theories of government and administration.
8. Herbert Simon, Donald W. Smithburg, and Victor A. Thompson, *Public Administration* (Alfred A. Knopf, 1950), p. 434.
9. Elsewhere I have explored this same method of policy formulation as practiced by academic analysts of policy ("Policy Analysis," *American Economic Review* 48 [June 1958]: 298). Although it has been here presented as a method for public administrators, it is no less necessary to analysts more removed from immediate policy questions, despite their tendencies to describe their own analytical efforts as though they were the rational-comprehensive method with an especially heavy use of theory. Similarly, this same method is inevitably resorted to in personal problem-solving, where means and ends are sometimes impossible to separate, where aspirations or objectives undergo constant development, and where drastic simplification of the complexity of the real world is urgent if problems are to be solved in the time that can be given to them. To an economist accustomed to dealing with the marginal or incremental concept in market processes, the central idea in the method is that both evaluation and empirical analysis are incremental. Accordingly I have referred to the method elsewhere as "the incremental method."

Part Three

FROM JFK TO CIVIL SERVICE REFORM

THE 1960S AND 1970S

The 1960s and 1970s bore witness to dynamic change in the United States—politically, economically, and socially. This 20-year period began with a true sense of national optimism that the United States was ready to move forward as a dominant political and economic world leader. Behind this national optimism was great confidence in government institutions led by technological innovation and administrative capabilities. Indeed, some international observers would comment that there was a sense that the United States felt it owned the future. While much would remain unfulfilled at the end, these two decades showcased both the potential and the pitfalls of public administration in the modern era.

It began with John F. Kennedy's inauguration and fittingly his inaugural address when he told the nation "... ask not what your country can do for you but what you can do for your country." Perhaps no other single decade promised more for public administration in the United States than the 1960s. Dominated by the systems approach, modern public administration was confident, both of its mandate for change and of its capacity and expertise to foster change. Dwight Waldo, writing in retrospect about this decade, recognized it as the apex of the "scientific-technical era."[1] In 1961, Kennedy set a national objective to land U.S. astronauts on the moon by the end of the decade. The National Aeronautics and Space Administration (NASA) would achieve this feat of engineering and public administration in 1969.

An even more significant set of goals was embodied in the Great Society programs of the Johnson administration, which were to bring an unprecedented degree of social intervention and change. The range of social programs initiated was rivaled only by the New Deal. Similar confidence was exuded in the economic arena where a major tax cut revived a faltering and slow economy and heralded the triumph of Keynesian economics whereby government could "manage" the nation's economy through the use of various fiscal and monetary techniques.[2] Intergovernmental revenue transfer programs that would subsequently alter the scale of governmental budgeting at federal, state, and local levels were considered.[3] There were seemingly few obstacles that could not be overcome by the modern administrative state. It required only good policy analysis and planning, appropriately developed management systems, and the new professional-technical expertise of the art, science, and practice of public administration.

NEW PERSPECTIVES ON ORGANIZATIONS AND BUREAUCRACY

By the 1960s, the social sciences were strongly influenced by the systems approach to analyzing social phenomena. Chester I. Barnard's theories about organizations being cooperative systems had been consistently validated. Daniel Katz (1903–1998) and Robert L. Kahn (b. 1918) in their 1966 book, *The Social Psychology of Organizations*, sought to apply existing knowledge on social systems in general to organizations in particular. Reprinted here is a chapter from their book, "Organizations and the System Concept," which provides a systems framework for understanding how organizations operate. Katz and Kahn provide succinct definitions of the characteristics of open systems of organizations that reflected, in their view, the general state of modern organizational environments.

Closed systems, or traditional fixed bureaucratic structures, were fine if the environment was stable and controllable. They saw accurately that organizational environments were increasingly dynamic and unstable, and that environments could differ dramatically for various organizations. Katz and Kahn concluded that the traditional closed-system view of organizations led to a failure to fully appreciate the interdependence and interactions between organizations and their environments. Their work applying systems theory to organizational theory would mark the beginning of the realization that the old debate between human relations and scientific management—the debate between open and closed models of organizations—was over. Future efforts would be directed primarily toward understanding the interactions of the organizations and their environments as open dynamic systems.

Anthony Downs's (b. 1930)[4] Rand Corporation study, *Inside Bureaucracy*, was published in 1967. His work was an exhaustive analysis of U.S. bureaucracy, which, while derivative of the systems approach, sought to develop concepts and propositions that would aid in predicting the behavior of bureaus and bureaucrats. It was here that Downs sought to expand on Weber's "ideal type" by suggesting that two new elements be added to Weber's definition. First, the organization must be large; "any organization in which the highest ranking members know less than half of the other members can be considered large." Second, most of the organization's output cannot be "directly or indirectly evaluated in any markets external to the organization by means of voluntary quid pro quo transactions."

Downs's chapter, "Life Cycles of Bureaus," reprinted here, recognized stages of bureaucratic growth and stagnation as well as associated repercussions on administrative performance. Downs was bold, considering the times, in articulating his case of organizational behavior in pursuit of survival. After all, bureaucracies had been accused of being autocratic, inhumane, and insensitive to both their constituents and their own organizational members. Now Downs was examining them for behavior designed to ensure their own preservation. His last section examined the concept of death in bureaucracy and suggested that greater attention be given to understanding the policy and administrative implications for this stage of bureaucratic development.[5] Still, it is his concept of life cycle that has had a significant influence on subsequent organization theorists. Not only would organizational environments differ but organizational responses would be predicated upon their own stages of development at different times in their life cycles.

Ironically, just when society seemed to be coming to terms with bureaucratic institutions, Warren Bennis (b. 1925) was sounding their death knell. Bennis indicted present organizational formats as inadequate for a future that would demand rapid organizational and technological changes, participatory management, and the growth of a more professionalized workforce. He predicted in his 1967 *Personnel Administration* article, "Organizations of the Future," that organization would have to be, of necessity, more responsive and flexible to these needs and, in consequence, decidedly less bureaucratic, less structured, and less rigid.[6]

Bennis was one of the first to put together the concept that organizations in the future would rely on totally different ideas of the nature of human behavior and worth, power, and organizational form.[7] His article provided a summary of the lessons of behavioral science and open-systems theory and then constructed a number of predictions about the effects of these new organizational templates on society. His case was largely an external one; that is, the first consideration must be the interactions and impacts of organizations on society. Inherent in his work was a concern for "democratic organizational leadership," a theme to which he returned in the 1980s with his development of the idea of "transformational leadership."[8]

BUDGETING AND SYSTEMS THEORIES FOR GOVERNMENT GROWTH AND DECLINE

Budgeting during the 1960s would be dominated by the systems approach, in the form of PPBS (planning programming budgeting systems). First installed in the Department of Defense during the Kennedy administration, it seemed to represent the height of rationality for the budget process. Allen

Schick (b. 1934), in his 1966 *Public Administration Review* article, "The Road to PPB: The Stages of Budget Reform," reprinted here, chronicled the development of budgetary theory from the concerns for accountability and control, which were the hallmark of the line-item budget, to performance budgeting with its emphasis on managerial efficiency, to PPBS, which stressed objectives, planning, and program effectiveness.

In 1965, Lyndon Johnson mandated the use of PPBS for all federal agencies. The application of PPBS—which required among other things that agencies detail program objectives and indicators for evaluation, make five-year expenditure forecasts, and generate numerous special cost-benefit analyses and zero-based reviews of program activities—marked perhaps the zenith of the management systems approach to public administration. PPBS, initially developed by David Novick[9] and others at the Rand Corporation, had achieved remarkable success in the Department of Defense. (Indeed, it remains, albeit in modified form, in use there today.)

But PPBS's effectiveness was considerably lower in the domestic agencies. Numerous state governments also adopted the PPBS approach to budgeting as the systems approach to budgeting swept over public administration's most critical subfield. Allen Schick's article, exploring both the concepts and rationale embodied in PPBS and how budgetary reform had developed historically, remains one of the landmark essays in public budgeting. Schick, for many years with the Congressional Research Service staff and later at the University of Maryland and the Brookings Institution, would continue to write significant works on budgeting and become the generally recognized informal leader of the management systems approach to public budgeting.[10]

PPBS and budgeting systems theory was never without its critics. In 1964, Aaron Wildavsky (1930–1993) published *The Politics of the Budgetary Process*,[11] the immensely well-received critique of how budgeting was, in reality, an incremental process sharply influenced by political considerations. In 1969, he wrote a devastating critique of PPBS in his *Public Administration Review* article, "Rescuing Policy Analysis from PPBS," reprinted here. Aside from stating flatly that he thought PPBS was unworkable, Wildavsky demonstrated how the planning and analytical functions of PPBS were contradictory to the essential nature of budgeting. What was once mandatory for all federal agencies and widely adopted by state and local jurisdictions was, by the end of the decade, officially unadopted by the federal government and widely considered to be unusable in its original format. Nevertheless, the influence of PPBS as a major budgeting process remains. Indeed, many budget theorists would argue that the passage of the Government Performance Results Act in 1993 and the concurrent adoption by a majority of state governments of similarly focused performance-results budgeting approaches is PPBS "déjà vu."[12]

Wildavsky, who would later help establish and then become the first dean of the University of California at Berkeley's Graduate School of Public Policy,[13] was greatly influenced by Charles Lindblom, under whom he studied while a doctoral student at Yale. Incremental approaches to budgeting, or what would later be called "traditional budgeting," was the counter school of thought to the management systems emphasis. The principle contention was that budgets were inherently political and that studying budgeting and budgets was useful because it explained how and what choices (political compromises) had been made. Wildavsky even rebutted V. O. Key's classic question: "On what basis shall it be decided to allocate X dollars to activity A instead of activity B?" as unanswerable and irrelevant. What mattered was that the process of budgeting should facilitate decision making and assist in obtaining consensus about policy goals and program objectives.[14]

The debate over the politics of PPBS produced another interesting debate—what should be the goal of public organizations? Budget reform from the beginning has emphasized the pursuit of economy and efficiency, which often translated into eliminating waste and redundancy. Martin Landau wrote a provocative article in *Public Administration Review* in 1969 (reprinted here) arguing of all things that public organizations might find that redundancy is something to be valued, not avoided. Using examples from the domains of information management, organizational theory, and risk management, he made a very persuasive case that redundancy was a key element in public administration's need for reliability and adaptability.

In the 1960s, this argument went unheeded, in part because budgets were expanding and public agencies seemingly had the resources to build in "parallel" circuits to have the best of both worlds. In the next period, Public Administration would debate the merits of the Grace Commission's War on Waste and the National Performance Review's Reinvention Campaign. Both reform efforts advocated changing government to make it work better but cost less by eliminating or at least reducing redundancy. In today's management debate over whether efficiency or reliability is the true goal of public sector organizations, Landau's article is truly a classic worth rediscovering.

While government spending continued to rise, budgeting systems were hard pressed to cope with the twin pressures of high inflation and unemployment. President Nixon terminated PPBS in the federal domestic agencies and began to challenge what he called unrestrained congressional spending. He impounded congressionally approved funding for domestic programs that were over what was recommended in the executive budget. Domestic program recipients took the Nixon administration to court. However by the time cases were resolved (in favor of the program recipients), the funding had lapsed and Nixon was gone from office. President Ford replaced the disgraced Nixon and worked a temporary compromise with Congress to cover funding levels up to a point. But the controversy between Congress and the presidency over who would control the federal budget would escalate into open warfare in the 1980s.

The debate over who should set budget levels led in part to the next stage of budget reform, which was embodied in the form of zero-based budgeting (ZBB).[15] Peter A. Pyhrr first developed it for Texas Instruments and then for the state of Georgia while Jimmy Carter was governor. In 1976, presidential candidate Carter made the installation of zero-based budgeting a campaign promise, and in 1977, as president, he ordered its adoption by the federal government. The initial reaction to ZBB paralleled the reaction to PPBS in the 1960s, but the downfall of ZBB was even more rapid.

In large part, ZBB failed because the conditions that prevailed for most of the previous budgeting-system reforms had changed. In an era of acute resource scarcity, ZBB had little utility because there was little real chance that funding could be provided for any levels of program growth. Even Wildavsky and Schick agreed on the failure of this budgeting system—Schick even proclaimed it "decremental budgeting."[16] Other critics were even less kind—either assaulting it as a "fraud" or decrying it as a non-system of budgeting. ZBB's fate in the federal government was tied to the Carter presidency. After the inauguration of President Reagan in 1981, it was quietly rescinded. Initially, numerous state and local governments used ZBB techniques or some adaptation of ZBB, but over time it passed from an important stage of public budgeting development to what many might now unkindly call a management fad.

What was happening at the federal level was mirrored at the state and local level. Only here, the political pressure was more direct. As the late 1960s and early 1970s proceeded, high rates of inflation pushed individuals into higher and higher tax brackets even though their real income levels did not change. Property values escalated even more. With higher values came increased assessments and higher property taxes. U.S. politics changed in response. There began a withering of public support for continued government growth and public programs. California, with passage of Proposition 13, provided the first major example of how vulnerable public budgets could be to voter-compelled expenditure and revenue-limitation initiatives.[17] Reflecting on this new political-economic environment, Charles B. Levine (1939–1988) described how organizations had to adapt and alter budget strategies. His 1978 *Public Administration Review* article, "Organizational Decline and Cutback Management," reprinted here, recognized that over a half century of "positive budgeting" was over: a new period of "negative budgeting" was now reality.[18]

Levine laid out the management "rules" for cutback management. Briefly, public-sector managers would respond to revenue shortfalls based on the degree of political uncertainty (that is, the probability of the cuts being restored) and the magnitude of the budget shortfall. Responses could range from simply "stretching the budget to get through the fiscal year," "rationing demands" by limiting services or charging fees, and "selective withdrawal" by redrawing geographic divisions of the organization or terminating specific programs, to "retrenchment" by permanently altering the structure, programs, and staffing of the organization.

Cutback management was not intended to be a budget system; it was a process. Its objective was to fuse political-economic realities with management strategies that would reestablish in the public's mind the value of public sector programs and services. In its most basic sense, this was a return to V. O. Key's questions and the debate between Wildavsky and Schick about the basis of value in resource allocation decisions. In positive budgeting and strong growth environments, the public needed little reassurance of the value of public spending. In negative budgeting and weak or slow growth environments, the nexus between tax payments for public revenues and budget benefits for public expenditures had to be reestablished.

REDISCOVERING FEDERALISM—UNCOVERING IGR

While the mandates and indeed much of the energy for social change in the 1960s certainly emanated from the federal government, implementation of actual program results usually had to come about at the state and local government levels. Public administration, as it wrestled with social intervention, rediscovered, so to speak, its other half in a renewed interest in the U.S. "federal" system of government. The rise in federal spending sparked in the 1950s would soon spread to state and local governments, in the form of intergovernmental grants. In 1954, there were 38 federal aid programs to state and local governments; by the end of the 1970s, there were almost 500. By 1978, the Urban Institute reported that federal aid accounted for over 25 percent of state and local expenditures.[19]

Intergovernmental relations is federalism in action. It is the complex network of day-to-day interrelationships among the governments within a federal system. It is the political, fiscal, programmatic, and administrative processes by which higher units of government share revenues and other resources with lower units of government, generally accompanied by special conditions that the lower units must satisfy as prerequisites to receiving the assistance. In essence, intergovernmental relations are the sets of policies and mechanisms by which the interplay between different levels of government serving a common geographical area is managed. Such relations reflect the basic constitutional framework that links the levels of government, as well as dynamic contemporary factors including relative power, financial strengths, ethnic divisions, geographical factors, and so on.

But there was more to intergovernmental relations than simply handing out money. The Johnson administration's approach to intergovernmental relations was called "creative federalism," which implied that there would be joint planning and decision making among all levels of government (as well as the private sector) in the management of intergovernmental programs. Many new programs of this period had an urban-metropolitan focus, and much attention was given to antipoverty issues. Creative federalism sought to foster the development of a singular Great Society by integrating the poor into mainstream America. Its expansive efforts were marked by the rapid development of categorical grant programs to state and local governments and direct federal grants to cities, frequently bypassing state governments entirely. Great Society programs such as Head Start and the War on Poverty were all based on the concept of federal grants shaping activities and directions at the state and local levels. However, the idea that all wisdom rested in Washington was not always well received in state capitals or city halls.

Morton Grodzins (1917–1964) of the University of Chicago had long noted that people who have not worked in or studied public administration are often unaware of the complicated nature of intergovernmental relations. It is not simply a question of dividing the work between the levels: of assigning local issues to local government and national issues to federal government. The majority of issues have national, regional, and local implications. Grodzins used this concept of "marble-cake" federalism to describe the cooperative relationships among the varying levels of government that resulted in an intermingling of activities. This was in contrast to the more traditional view of "layer-cake" federalism that held that the three levels of government were totally separate.

In the first chapter of his book *The American System: A New View of Government in the United States,*[20] Grodzins observed that with tens of thousands of tax-levying governmental units, nearly half of which were school districts, the process of "federal governance" was immensely complex. He saw little correspondence between areas of governance and problems of government. "Government by chaos and cooperation," as he termed it, required a special understanding to perform adequate policy and program analysis. Remarkably, his overall assessment was quite positive: Shared functions could and did work, and intergovernmental grant and transfer programs could be designed and implemented effectively.

But many in public administration felt that a larger framework was needed to assess developments involving intergovernmental relations.[21] Some felt the emphasis needed to be on the relationships among units of government, not just the governments. This called for seeing intergovernmental relations as more than a complex system of fiscal and administrative processes by which higher units of government share revenues and other resources with lower units, generally accompanied by special conditions that the lower units must satisfy as prerequisites to receiving the assistance.

While acknowledging the pioneering work of others, Deil S. Wright (1930–2009) was one of the most significant voices in the analysis of intergovernmental trends. His highly influential text, *Understanding Intergovernmental Relations*, was essentially the standard work in the field for three decades.[22] Not only did he evaluate the effectiveness of the intergovernmental system from a political and economic perspective but he also examined the potential of "devolution," which was at the center of much of political debate of the period (and still today). Devolution here means transferring down to the states responsibility to carry out many initially federal financed and mandated social and regulatory programs in exchange for specific block grants of federal aid.

In Wright's historical analysis, first developed in a 1974 issue of *The Annals* (reprinted here) and included in his textbook, he saw five phases of development culminating in a "competitive phase" starting around 1965. Later he would amend this in his textbook as culminating in a "calculative" period in intergovernmental relations for the 1980s.[23] Calculative refers to the phase of intergovernmental relations concerned with strategies designed to cope with severe fiscal constraints, loss of public confidence, and declining federal support.

Wright was a major chronicler of the policy and management issues and challenges confronting the federal and state and local systems in the United States. Intergovernmental relations had to be taken more seriously if the nation was to avoid creating distrust and tension among the governments. As policies, programs, and budgeting became more intertwined, IGR had to evolve a true management capability—one Wright concluded of mastering "the successful management of complexity." This would, he argued, provide true context for public managers and elected politicians to see their roles and responsibilities in achieving joint success and not just blaming others for failures.

THE ADVANCE OF POLICY ANALYSIS AND PROGRAM EVALUATION

If journalism represents the first rough draft of history, it is also the first policy analysis that most people will hear or read on a new issue. The powers that be make policy, but it is then reported and explained to the public by the journalistic media. All the major news organizations, both print and TV, have reporters that specialize in various policy areas. Thus there are White House, congressional, Supreme Court, education, medical, consumer, and financial correspondents, among others. These analysts are almost always the first to tackle new policy issues. Scholarly analysis is usually years behind—unless, of course, it is done by the relatively small group of academics who also write for journalistic sources. The op-ed pages are full of college professors and think-tank denizens telling the public what the implications are of any new policy. All this—from the current buzz at work to the weekly news magazines—is informal policy analysis. These "quick and dirty" critiques of current issues are both ubiquitous and essential to a flourishing democracy. While they may be made with style, wit, and true depth of feeling, they tend to lack the methodological rigor of a formal policy analysis.

Formal policy analysis uses a set of techniques that seeks to answer the question of what the probable effects of a policy will be before they actually occur. A policy analysis undertaken on a program that is already in effect is more properly called a program evaluation. Nevertheless, policy analysis is used by many to refer to both before- and after-the-fact analyses of public policies. All policy analysis involves the application of systematic research techniques (drawn largely from the social sciences and based on measurements of program effectiveness, quality, cost, and impact) to the formulation, execution, and evaluation of public policy to create a more rational or optimal administrative system. To the extent that we make judgments on governmental policies from affirmative action to zoning variances, we all do policy analysis. Any judgment on a policy issue also requires an analysis, however superficial. Policy analysis can be viewed as a continuum from crude judgments made in a snap to the most sophisticated analysis using complicated methodologies.

Accompanying the systems approach that dominated so much of public administration in the 1960s was the advance of policy analysis. A direct and practical consideration of policy analysis in public administration was provided by Yehezkel Dror (b. 1928) in his 1967 *Public Administration Review* article, "Policy Analysts: A New Professional Role in Government Service." Dror's article, which is reprinted here, was one of the first to identify and define this old function but new occupational specialty. Policy analysis would encompass both the policy formulation process (that is, understanding the politics and participation aspects) and policy content (that is, consideration of alternative policy outcomes by analyzing costs, benefits, distribution of benefits, and so on). Economic analysis played a pivotal role in the policy analyst's trade, but Dror recognized the limitations of what he termed a "one-sided invasion of public decision making by economics." Dror, a major critic of the incremental approach to policy-making, was one of the first to call for constructing a policy sciences approach that would balance economic and political roles in policy analysis.[24]

By the beginning of the 1970s, it was generally conceded that many of the Great Society programs initiated during the Johnson administration were not working nearly as well as it was originally hoped. As these and other social programs came under increasing criticism, the field of program evaluation gained increasing prominence. The first stirrings were in 1967 when Edward Suchman of Columbia University published the first major work on evaluation theory, *Evaluation Research.*[25] Suchman's work argued that evaluation was essentially a field of study. Evaluative research and practice can and should be studied in a general context outside of evaluation applications in the various fields of specialization; in other words, evaluation was generic. The early 1970s produced several significant works on the various facets of evaluation. Carol H. Weiss's *Evaluation Research: Methods for Assessing Program Effectiveness*[26] was perhaps the best introduction to program evaluation theory, while Joseph Wholey and other scholars at the Urban Institute[27] were writing pioneering studies in applying program evaluation methods and applications.

But perhaps the most interesting and representative work written about evaluation during this period was that of Alice Rivlin (b. 1931). Of course, students of government will recognize this early evaluation theorist and economist who would in 1974 become the first director of the Congressional Budget Office and in the 1990s become the Clinton administration's director of the Office of Management and Budget. Rivlin delivered a series of lectures about evaluation and its potential impact on public decision making that were published by the Brookings Institution under the title of *Systematic Thinking for Social Action*[28] in 1971. The last chapter is reprinted here. Rivlin sets out to conclude her work by examining issues of "accountability," but she switches gears to assess three different models for improving government effectiveness: decentralization, community control (what one would today call devolution), and the market model (vouchers and customer choice). These three "models" would of course form the crux of the economic and political debate about what government should do, how it should do it, and, as Rivlin concluded in 1971, ensuring that "to do better, we must have a way of distinguishing better from worse."

The General Accounting Office (GAO, later renamed the Government Accountability Office), under the leadership of Elmer Staats, also helped elevate the general quality and value of program evaluation by setting evaluation standards and working actively to professionalize program evaluation as part of the expanded scope of audit.[29] Many state governments would initiate legislative evaluation commissions based on the GAO idea. Some would go even further. In 1976, Colorado would be the first state to enact a sunset law in which certain agencies and programs are given fixed termination dates and a comprehensive evaluation is conducted before program or agency reenactment. By the mid-1970s, evaluation was a vital and integral part of public administration.

Policy analysis also responded to the problems of failure in the 1960s. Jeffrey Pressman (1943–1977) and Aaron Wildavsky wrote their highly regarded case study of federal programs in the city of Oakland in which they made popular the term implementation as a new focus for public administration. The title of their work tells part of the story in itself: *Implementation: How Great Expectations in Washington Are Dashed in Oakland, or, Why It's Amazing That Federal Programs Work at All, This Being a Saga of the Economic Development Administration as Told by Two Sympathetic Observers Who Seek to Build Morals on a Foundation of Ruined Hopes.* Besides having what is generally regarded as the longest title in public administration literature, they related in their landmark book (the preface of which is reprinted here) what seems almost simplistic—that policy planning and analysis were not taking into account the difficulties of execution or "implementation." Their purpose in this work was to consider how a closer nexus between policy and implementation could be achieved. A direct result of their book would be a spate of works[30] reconsidering how policy analysis should accomplish this objective—an objective, it is fair to say, that has yet to be implemented.

Pressman and Wildavsky define implementation as "a process of interaction between the setting of goals and actions geared to achieving them" as well as "an ability to forge subsequent links in the causal chain so as to obtain the desired results." This definition usefully calls attention to the interaction between setting goals and carrying them out. This helps clarify that implementation is political in a very fundamental sense in that the activities that go on under its banner shape who gets what, when, and how from government. Like lawmakers, administrators and those with whom they interact during the implementation process exert power over program objectives and influence program inputs and outcomes. Implementation involves administrators, interest groups, and other actors with diverse values, mobilizing power resources, forming coalitions, consciously plotting strategies, and generally engaging in strategic behavior designed to ensure that their point of view prevails. The terrain may be different from that found in Congress or other legislatures, but the basic staples of the political process are very much present.

The goal of program implementation is necessarily the creation of the myriad details of everyday administrative life. It is the total process of translating a legal mandate, whether an executive order or an enacted statute, into appropriate program directives and structures that provide services or create goods. Implementation, the doing part of public administration, is an inherently political process. Architects often say that "God is in the details." So is implementation. Its essence is in the details. A law is passed, but the process of putting it into effect requires countless small decisions that necessarily alter it.

PUBLIC ADMINISTRATION IN A QUANDARY

What began in the 1960s as a period of great expansion and great change at all levels of government for public administration in government as well as in the academic world would not last. The decade ended on a questionable note because of a number of factors: the Vietnam War, the newfound militancy of public employees and students, the emergence of more sophisticated client groups, and the yet-to-be implemented commitment to equal employment opportunity and the concept of a representative bureaucracy. Perhaps the best analysis of the effects of these issues on public administration was provided by Dwight Waldo when he examined the implications of these trends in the 1968 *Public Administration Review* article, "Public Administration in a Time of Revolution."[31]

But the end of the 1960s was characterized by more than social unrest and public discontent over Vietnam. One of the major rallying cries of the political activists of the 1960s was "power to the people," which in administrative terms is a call for decentralization of public services, the ultimate decentralization being, of course, anarchy. Herbert Kaufman (b. 1922)[32] assessed its intertwined implications in his 1969 *Public Administration Review* article, "Administration Decentralization and Political Power." Central to his concerns about decentralization were the issues of leadership, bureaucratic representativeness, and the idea of neutral competence.[33]

Kaufman correctly saw that a modern, highly complex society needed new modes of representation to involve the public and ensure responsive administration. Kaufman accepted the notion that administrative decentralization could provide for greater local influence in public policy making. But it could also generate a number of other problems and conflicts, including possible interference with the pursuit of national mandates for economic and social equity, competition between local governments and programs, and decreased economies of scale leading to inefficiencies in government operations.

Another critical voice excerpted from the tremendous period of change that was the 1960s is that of Theodore J. Lowi (b. 1931).[34] His book *The End of Liberalism: Ideology, Policy, and the Crisis of Public Authority*[35] provided an expansive critique of the modern democratic government and a condemnation of the paralyzing effects of interest group pluralism. Lowi asserted that public authority was parceled out to private interest groups and resulted in a weak, decentralized government incapable of long-range planning. These powerful interest groups operated to promote private goals; they did not compete to promote the public interest. Government then became not an institution capable of making hard choices among conflicting values, but a holding company for interests. The various interests were promoted by alliances of interest groups, relevant government agencies, and the appropriate legislative committees. Lowi denied the very virtues that E. Pendleton Herring and other group theorists saw in their promotion of interest-group pluralism. Overall, Lowi presented a scathing indictment of the administrative process in which agencies charged with regulation were seen as basically protectors of those being regulated.

Lowi's critical analysis, a chapter of which is reprinted here, was widely received as accurate and penetrating, but his remedy, a return to legal or constitutional democracy, what he called "juridical democracy," was seen as unworkable. Despite its apparent flaws, there seemed to be no immediately available alternative to interest group pluralism and its often paralyzing effects on modern government. Still, Lowi's work is a very fitting epitaph for the post–World War II era up to the 1960s.

In this near quarter century of expansion, promise, and great change, public administration encountered a whole new set of obstacles and limitations, both external and internal. Some of public administration's most cherished ideas would be shaken badly in the aftermath of the perceived failure of many of the Great Society programs, the debacle of Watergate and the first resignation of a president, the fall of Vietnam, and the mounting fiscal crises that ravaged many state and local governments. Now an agenda for self-examination and reform was being formed, one that would shape public administration in the decade that would follow.

By the early 1970s, serious questions were being raised concerning the state of the discipline and profession of public administration. Dwight Waldo, having noted that public administration was "in a time of revolution," called a conference of younger academics in public administration through the auspices of his position as editor-in-chief of *Public Administration Review* and with some funds from the Maxwell School of Syracuse University. Held in 1968 at Syracuse University's Minnowbrook conference site, the papers that came out of it were edited by Frank Marini, then managing editor of *Public Administration Review,* and published in 1971 under the title *Toward a New Public Administration: The Minnowbrook Perspective.*[36]

The goal of the meeting was to identify what was relevant about public administration and how the discipline had to change to meet the challenges of the 1970s. H. George Frederickson's (b. 1934) paper, "Toward a New Public Administration," which is reprinted here, called for social equity in the performance and delivery of public services.[37] In many ways, Frederickson's paper epitomized the "new public administration" movement that called for what Frederickson termed second generation behavioralism in which administration would be more responsive to the public, more prescriptive, more client-oriented, and more normative—yet still be more scientific. Overall, the new public administration called for a proactive administrator with a burning desire for social equity to replace the traditional impersonal, neutral, gun-for-hire bureaucrat. Such a call was heeded by few, but discussed by many.

THE AFTERMATH OF WATERGATE AND THE REDISCOVERY OF PUBLIC SERVICE ETHICS

In terms of political events in the 1970s, few things stand out more than Watergate. Watergate is the name of a hotel-office-apartment complex in Washington, D.C. When individuals associated with President Nixon's reelection campaign were caught breaking into the Democratic National Committee Headquarters (then located in the Watergate complex) in 1972, the resulting cover-up and national trauma were condensed into one word: Watergate.

The aftermath of Watergate brought a major review of what was called the "administrative presidency."[38] Much of the focus of public administration's development since the 1930s had been to concentrate power and control in the executive branch. Now that it had been accomplished, Watergate provided a dramatic lesson in what could happen if such centralized power was abused. In response to a request from the Senate Select Committee on Presidential Campaign Activities, a special panel of the National Academy of Public Administration chaired by Frederick C. Mosher examined the situation and produced a report *Watergate: Implications for Responsible Government*,[39] which provided a detailed indictment of the Nixon administration's abuses of executive and administrative authority and power.

The report's "Overview" and its epilogue on "Ethics and Public Office" are reprinted here. Educational institutions were urged to "focus more attention on public sector ethics." Although codes of ethics had been around for years, the panel concluded that more sophisticated and effective codes of conduct and standards were needed. In a sense, the real significance of the report was the infusion back into public administration of a concern for ethics and the encouragement of a new generation of literature on the subject. This literature was launched in large part with John Rohr's (b. 1934) 1978 textbook *Ethics for Bureaucrats*, which was aptly subtitled "An Essay on Law and Values." Rohr pointed out that a textbook on public sector ethics was not truly possible until the "field of inquiry is sufficiently developed to have an established literature capable of being ordered, summarized, and presented in a way that is meaningful to the initiated."[40]

Rohr's "essay" covered a number of fronts, examining especially how modern bureaucrats should reconcile their discretionary authority with the governing process of a democratic "regime." Administrators with integrity must understand that they have a special moral obligation to the people they serve. They take seriously what Rohr called the "regime values" of their jurisdiction. In constitutional systems these values are established by the constitution, whether written, as in the United States, or unwritten, as in the United Kingdom. To a person of honor, an oath to "defend the Constitution of the United States against all enemies, foreign and domestic" is a serious matter. Thus, according to Rohr, the Constitution "is the moral foundation of ethics for bureaucrats." Those senior administrators who gain reputations for being ethical and honorable abide by a new-fashioned *noblesse oblige*. Originally, the "nobility obliged" by leading in war and demonstrating their honor and valor by taking physical risks to prove their courage—to demonstrate on the field of honor (a battlefield) just how honorable they were.

Lacking traditional nobility, republican governments give leadership roles to senior bureaucrats and elected officials. Once in office, their fellow citizens rightly expect them to take moral and career risks, parallel to the traditional risks of combat, to protect their fellow citizens, to protect the regime, and to protect the Constitution. And they must be heroic enough to risk not only their lives but their livelihoods as well. Louis Brandeis, later to be an Associate Justice of the U.S. Supreme Court, argued in the 1910 Glavis-Ballinger case that public administrators "cannot be worthy of the respect and admiration of the people unless they add to the virtue of obedience some other virtues—virtues of manliness, of truth, of courage, of willingness to risk position, of the willingness to risk criticism, of the willingness to risk the misunderstanding that so often comes when people do the heroic thing." It is often said that managers are paid more than workers because they are paid to take risks, to make decisions that can cost them their jobs. Public managers live in an even riskier environment. Not only must they take normal management risks but also they must risk their careers, their reputation, sometimes even their lives, to protect the values of the regime. Reprinted here is the selection from the first edition of Rohr's book on the meaning and implication of regime values.

THE RECOGNITION OF REPRESENTATIVE BUREAUCRACY AND CIVIL SERVICE REFORM

In 1944, J. Donald Kingsley, coauthor of the first full-scale text on public personnel administration, *Public Personnel Administration*,[41] published his historical analysis, *Representative Bureaucracy: An Interpretation of the British Civil Service*.[42] In 1967, Samuel Krislov (b. 1929), a constitutional law scholar,[43] expanded on Kingsley's concept of a governing bureaucracy made up from representative elements of the population being ruled.[44] Krislov, in *The Negro in Federal Employment*, examined the advantages of "representation in the sense of personification" and thereby gave a name to the goal for the movement for the fullest expression of civil rights in government employment: representative bureaucracy.

In a subsequent work in 1974, also entitled *Representative Bureaucracy*[45] (and reprinted here in part), Krislov explored the issues of merit systems, personnel selection, and social equity. Krislov asked more directly: How could any bureaucracy have legitimacy and public credibility if it failed to represent all sectors of its society? So, thanks in large part to Krislov, the phrase "representative bureaucracy" grew to mean that all social groups have a right to participation in their governing institutions. Over time, the phrase has even developed a normative overlay that all social groups should occupy bureaucratic positions in direct proportion to their number in the general population. And in 1978, with the passage of the Civil Service Reform Act, this became an official policy of the federal government. The 1978 law "directed agencies to take steps to eliminate the under representation of women and people of color in all federal occupations and at all grade levels."[46] Representation was further embedded in the nine merit system principles of the law.

The passage of civil service reform legislation at the federal level was perhaps the public administration highlight of the Carter presidency. The Carter reforms were not all positive. Much was made of some dysfunctional processes of current civil service practices: inflated performance appraisals, overgraded classifications, and very low dismissal rates of poor performers. But public administration was able to rise above this and focus not just on modernization, but professionalism and the larger questions of how the public service should be managed and its role and responsibilities. The concerns of public personnel administration, having been relegated to an intellectual backwater since the initial success of the reform movement, began to experience a renewal in the 1960s. In 1968, Frederick C. Mosher (1913–1990) of the University of Virginia published his now classic *Democracy and the Public Service*,[47] an examination of the history and evolution of the American civil service and the major impact of ever-increasing professionalism on it. Mosher confirmed the variety of factors that contributed to the renewal: the explosive growth of public employee unions, the demand for equal employment opportunity, and the needs of managing and motivating a more sophisticated and professionally led workforce.

Drastic change would and did occur. By the end of the decade, the Civil Service Reform Act of 1978 would restructure the U.S. Civil Service Commission into three new entities: the Office of Personnel Management, the Merit Systems Protection Board, and the Federal Labor Relations Authority. At all levels of government, the ideal of a Civil Service Commission as both protector of the merit system and of the rights of individual employees would give way to personnel directors responsible only to the jurisdiction's chief executive. The interests of employees would henceforth be looked after by quasi-judicial merit-systems review boards or the unions themselves. Change was experienced by the public sector unions too. As increasing numbers of state and local governments adopted collective bargaining, employee relations took on a whole new perspective. Public-sector strikes, even when illegal, would occur, dramatically challenging the traditional ideals embodied in the concept of public service.

LOOKING TO A NEW ERA

To sum up, the dynamic changes of the 1960s and reaction of the 1970s masked other patterns in the development of U.S. public administration. On the surface, the increase in federal budgetary expenditures was extraordinary, increasing from $95 billion in 1960 to $590 billion in 1979 at the federal level. But when the expenditure figures are calculated as a percentage of the gross domestic product, the ratio is about the same (18 to 20 percent of GNP). Federal civilian employment increased from 2.4 million to 2.9 million over this 20-year period, but in relation to the population, federal employment in 1979 was basically at the 1950 level. On the other hand, state and local government employment over this same twenty-year period increased from 6 to over 13 million. According to Frederick C. Mosher, these seemingly contradictory trends were "a consequence of fundamental shifts in the purposes, phases, and methods of federal operations."[48]

Essentially, Mosher argued, the federal government changed its pattern of involvement over the past two decades, from overt to covert. While the federal government decreased the number and level of activities it performed directly, it had, through income supports, contracts and grants, regulations, and loans and loan guarantees, stimulated massive efforts by state and local governments, non-profit organizations, and even private business. The result was a federal administrative posture that increasingly relied on indirect administrative coordination and funds transfer. Mosher complained that this massive change was not reflected "in our research, our literature, our teaching." While the focus of public administration remained on the federal government, the action was inexorably shifting to other levels. This trend would only continue to increase under the Reagan presidency and usher in a new era of public administration in the 1980s and 1990s.

NOTES

1. Dwight Waldo, *The Administrative State: A Study of the Political Theory of American Public Administration,* 2d ed. (New York: Holmes and Meier, 1984), p. xiii.
2. John Maynard Keynes (1883–1946) was the English economist who wrote the twentieth century's most influential book on economics, *The General Theory of Employment, Interest, and Money* (London: Macmillan, 1936), which called for using a government's fiscal and monetary policies to positively affect a capitalistic economy.
3. Revenue sharing was first seriously recommended by Walter Heller when he served as chairman of President Kennedy's Council of Economic Advisors. It did not become a reality until the State and Local Fiscal Assistance Act of 1972.

4. Downs is the economist generally credited with establishing the intellectual framework for "public choice" economics in his *An Economic Theory of Democracy* (New York: Harper and Row, 1957).
5. In this period, a significant body of literature emerged on policy termination. See, for example, Robert P. Biller, "On Tolerating Policy and Organizational Termination: Some Design Considerations," *Policy Sciences* 16 (June 1976); Carol L. Ellis, "Program Termination: A Word to the Wise," *Public Administration Review* 43 (July–August 1983).
6. For expansions of these themes, see his *Changing Organizations* (New York: McGraw-Hill, 1966) and, with Philip E. Slater, *The Temporary Society* (New York: Harper and Row, 1968).
7. See his and Philip E. Slater's "Democracy Is Inevitable," *Harvard Business Review* (March–April 1964).
8. Warren Bennis, "Transformative Power and Leadership," in *Leadership and Organizational Culture*, ed. Thomas J. Sergiovanni and John E. Corbally (Urbana, Ill.: University of Illinois Press, 1984).
9. David Novick, "The Origins and History of Program Budgeting," *California Management Review* 11, no. 1 (1968).
10. See for example Schick's *The Federal Budget*, revised edition (Washington, DC: The Brookings Institution, 2000). For a more critical perspective on the current shortfall of performance-based budgeting systems and performance measurement under the Government Performance Results Act, the article "Getting Performance Measures to Measure Up" in *Quicker, Better, Cheaper* edited by Dall W. Forsythe (Albany, New York: Rockefeller Institute Press, 2001) is instructive.
11. Aaron Wildavsky, *The Politics of the Budgetary Process*, 4th ed. (Boston: Little, Brown, 1964, 1984). This book would be completely redone in the late 1980s, given a new title, *The New Politics of the Budgetary Process*, and published in two editions before Wildavsky's death in 1993. The book is now in its fifth edition (with Naomi Caiden) published by Longman in 2003.
12. There are any number of excellent works introducing performance-based budgeting. Philip Joyce's "Using Performance Measures for Federal Budgeting: Proposals and Prospects," *Public Budgeting & Finance* (Winter 1993) is a good introductory article written when the Government Performance Results Act was passed. Katherine G. Willoughby and Julia Meyers are the leading experts on performance-based budgeting trends among the states (*Public Budgeting & Finance*, Spring 2000). Harry Hatry of the Urban Institute, along with Joseph Wholey, is probably the leading expert in this arena. See *Performance Measurement* (Washington, DC: The Urban Institute, 1999) and *Comparative Performance Measurement* (Washington, DC: The Urban Institute, 2001).
13. For Wildavsky's advice on how to create and manage a graduate school of public policy, see the appendix, "Principles for a Graduate School of Public Policy," to his *Speaking Truth to Power: The Art and Craft of Policy Analysis* (Boston: Little, Brown, 1979).
14. Wildavsky first addressed Key's question in a 1961 *Public Administration* article, "Political Implications of Budget Reform." Thirty years later, *Public Administration Review* asked him to write his own retrospective on this seminal article. See November–December 1992, pp. 594–599 for his reflections.
15. The best introduction to zero-based budgeting is still Graeme Taylor's article from *The Bureaucrat*: "Introduction to Zero-Base Budgeting" (Spring 1977).
16. For Schick's "obituary" of ZBB, see his article "The Road from ZBB," *Public Administration Review* 38 (March–April 1978).
17. See Jerry McCaffery and John H. Bowman, "Participatory Democracy and Budgeting: The Effects of Proposition 13," *Public Administration Review* 38 (November–December 1978): 530–538. Proposition 13 was a revolt by the middle class over rising taxes, especially on real estate, which were increasing dramatically in a period of double-digit inflation. By 1980, the tax revolt movement forced 38 states to reduce or at least stabilize tax rates.
18. See also Levine's edited work, *Managing Fiscal Stress* (Chatham, N.J.: Chatham House, 1980).

19. A good period assessment of the intergovernmental budget issues at this time is John Shannon's and James Kee's "The Rise of Competitive Federalism" *Public Budgeting and Finance*, Winter 1989, pp. 5–20.
20. Morton Grodzin's *The American System: A New View of Government in the United States* (Chicago: Rand McNally, 1966). This book was essentially completed before the author's death and then edited and prepared for publication by Darnel J. Elazar of Temple University, a former student of Grodzin and now a major voice on federalism in his own right.
21. William Anderson (1988–1975) is also recognized as one of the "intellectual parents" of the IGR field; see his 1960 study *Intergovernmental Relations in Review* or his 1955 study *The Nation or the States: Rivals or Partners* (both University of Minnesota Press) and earlier work dating back to 1934 with Public Administration Service: *The Units of Government in the United States*.
22. Deil S. Wright, *Understanding Intergovernmental Relations*, 3d ed. (Pacific Grove, Calif.: Brooks/ Cole, 1988). The first edition was published in 1978.
23. In the 1980s, Wright would add a new "contractive" phase, pushed by decreases in federal support levels but increases in federal mandates. New stresses caused by court actions have placed state and local government policy and program actions under intense scrutiny and financial pressure. Later in the 1990s, mostly as a result of the Republican congressional victories in 1994, Wright saw a new phase that he titled "coercive-collage." Wright essentially predicted the possibility of an entirely new relationship between federal and state and local governments, one marked by sharp contrasts with little coherence.
24. See his "Prolegomena to the Policy Sciences," *Policy Sciences I* (September 1970); *Design for Policy Sciences* (New York: American Elsevier, 1971); *Ventures in Policy Sciences* (New York: American Elsevier, 1971).
25. Edward Suchman, *Evaluation Research* (New York: Russell Sage Foundation, 1967).
26. Carol Weiss, *Evaluation Research* (Englewood Cliffs, N.J.: Prentice-Hall, 1972).
27. Joseph S. Wholey, *Federal Evaluation Policy* (Washington D.C.: Urban Institute, 1970).
28. Alice Rivlin, *Systematic Thinking for Social Action* (Washington, D.C.: Brookings Institution, 1971).
29. For the GAO's definition of the expanded scope of audit (which includes program evaluation), see Comptroller General of the United States, *Standards for Audit of Governmental Organizations, Programs, Activities, and Functions* (Washington, D.C.: U.S. General Accounting Office, 1981).
30. Examples include Eugene Bardach, *The Implementation Game* (Cambridge, Mass.: MIT Press, 1977); Robert T. Nakamura and Frank Smallwood, *The Politics of Policy Implementation* (New York: St. Martin's Press, 1980); George C. Edwards III, *Implementing Public Policy* (Washington, D.C.: Congressional Quarterly Press, 1980); Walter Williams and others, *Studying Implementation: Methodological and Administration Issues* (Chatham, N.J.: Chatham House, 1982).
31. Waldo would also use it in the title of a book he later edited that dealt with these same themes: *Public Administration in a Time of Turbulence* (Scranton, Pa.: Chandler Publishing Co., 1971).
32. Kaufman, a former Yale professor and Brookings Institution scholar, is the author of many landmark works in public administration, including *The Forest Ranger: A Study in Administrative Behavior* (Baltimore: Johns Hopkins University Press, 1960); with Wallace S. Sayre, *Governing New York City* (New York: Norton, 1960); *Administrative Feedback: Monitoring Subordinates' Behavior* (Washington, D.C.: Brookings Institution, 1973); *Are Government Organizations Immortal?* (Washington, D.C.: Brookings Institution, 1976); *Red Tape: Its Origins, Uses, and Abuses* (Washington, D.C.: Brookings Institution, 1977); *The Administrative Behavior of Federal Bureau Chiefs* (Washington, D.C.: Brookings Institution, 1981).
33. The concept of "neutral competence" envisions a continuous, politically committed cadre of bureaucrats at the disposal of elected or appointed political executives. For discussions, see Herbert Kaufman,

"Emerging Conflicts in the Doctrines of Public Administration," *American Political Science Review*.50 (December 1956); Hugh Heclo, "OMB and the Presidency: The Problem of 'Neutral Competence,'" *The Public Interest* 38 (winter 1975).

34. Lowi, a political scientist at Cornell University, is also the author of *At the Pleasure of the Mayor: Patronage and Power in New York City, 1898–1958* (New York: Free Press, 1964) and *American Government: Power and Purpose*, 11th ed. (New York: Norton, 2009).
35. Theodore J. Lowi, *The End of Liberalism: Ideology, Policy, and the Crisis of Public Authority*, 2nd ed. (New York: Norton, 1969, 1979).
36. Frank Marini, ed., *Toward a New Public Administration: The Minnowbrook Perspective* (Scranton, Pa.: Chandler, 1971).
37. Frederickson continued to expand his thoughts on his new public administration. See his "The Lineage of the New PA," *Administration and Society* 8 (August 1977); *The New Public Administration* (Tuscaloosa, AL: University of Alabama Press, 1980).
38. This is Richard Nathan's descriptive term for how Richard Nixon sought to use administrative tactics—reorganization, decentralization, and impoundment—to assert presidential authority over the federal bureaucracy. See Nathan's *The Plot That Failed: Nixon and the Administrative Presidency* (New York: Wiley, 1975).
39. Frederick C. Mosher and others, *Watergate: Implications for Responsible Government* (New York: Basic Books, 1974). Frederick C. Mosher was the son of William E. Mosher (1877–1945), the first dean of the Maxwell School at Syracuse University, the first president of the American Society for Public Administration and coauthor, with J. Donald Kingsley, of the first major text on public personnel administration. Frederick C. Mosher has proven to be that rare person who enters the profession in which his father was a giant and becomes a person of equal, if not greater, influence in his own right. Other works by Frederick C. Mosher include *Governmental Reorganization: Cases and Commentary* (Indianapolis, Ind.: Bobbs-Merrill, 1967); *Programming Systems and Foreign Affairs Leadership* (New York: Oxford University Press, 1970); *American Public Administration: Past, Present, Future* (Tuscaloosa, AL: University of Alabama Press, 1975).
40. John A. Rohr, *Ethics for Bureaucrats: An Essay on Law and Values* (Marcel Dekker Press, first edition, 1979). A second edition, revised and expanded, was published in 1989. Completing the cycle, Rohr wrote *Public Service, Ethics, and Constitutional Practice* in 1998 (Lawrence KS: University of Kansas Press, 1998) and dedicated it to public servants.
41. William E. Mosher and J. Donald Kingsley, *Public Personnel Administration* (New York: Harper and Row, 1936).
42. Donald Kingsley, *Representative Bureaucracy: An Interpretation of the British Civil Service* (Yellow Springs, Ohio: Antioch Press, 1944).
43. For example, see his *The Supreme Court and Political Freedom* (New York: Free Press, 1968); *The Judicial Process and Constitutional Law* (Boston: Little, Brown, 1972).
44. Kingsley's analysis dealt extensively with the British civil service in India.
45. Samuel Krislov, *Representative Bureaucracy* (Minneapolis: University of Minnesota Press, 1967).
46. For a comprehensive modern assessment, see Katherine C. Naff, *To Look Like America* (Boulder, CO: Westview Press, 2002).
47. Frederick C. Mosher, *Democracy and the Public Service* (New York: Oxford University Press, 1968; 2d ed., 1982).
48. Frederick C. Mosher, "The Changing Responsibilities and Tactics of the Federal Government," *Public Administration Review* 40 (November–December 1980), p. 541.

18

Organizations and the System Concept

Daniel Katz and Robert L. Kahn

The aims of social science with respect to human organizations are like those of any other science with respect to the events and phenomena of its domain. The social scientist wishes to understand human organizations, to describe what is essential in their form, aspects, and functions. He wishes to explain their cycles of growth and decline, to predict their effects and effectiveness. Perhaps he wishes as well to test and apply such knowledge by introducing purposeful changes into organizations—by making them, for example, more benign, more responsive to human needs.

Such efforts are not solely the prerogative of social science, however; common sense approaches to understanding and altering organizations are ancient and perpetual. They tend, on the whole, to rely heavily on two assumptions: that the location and nature of an organization are given by its name; and that an organization is possessed of built-in goals—because such goals were implanted by its founders, decreed by its present leaders, or because they emerged mysteriously as the purposes of the organizational system itself. These assumptions scarcely provide an adequate basis for the study of organizations and at times can be misleading and even fallacious. We propose, however, to make use of the information to which they point.

The first problem in understanding an organization or a social system is its location and identification. How do we know that we are dealing with an organization? What are its boundaries? What behavior belongs to the organization and what behavior lies outside it? Who are the individuals whose actions are to be studied and what segments of their behavior are to be included?

The fact that popular names exist to label social organizations is both a help and a hindrance. These popular labels represent the socially accepted stereotypes about organizations and do not specify their role structure, their psychological nature, or their boundaries. On the other hand, these names help in locating the area of behavior in which we are interested. Moreover, the fact that people both within and without an organization accept stereotypes about its nature and functioning is one determinant of its character.

The second key characteristic of the common sense approach to understanding an organization is to regard it simply as the epitome of the purposes of its designer, its leaders, or its key members. The teleology of this approach is again both a help and a hindrance. Since human purpose is deliberately built into organizations and is specifically recorded in the social compact, the by-laws, or other formal protocol of the undertaking, it would be inefficient not to utilize these sources of information. In the early development of a group, many processes are generated which have little to do with its rational purpose, but over time there is a cumulative recognition of the devices for ordering group life and a deliberate use of these devices.

Apart from formal protocol, the primary mission of an organization as perceived by its leaders furnishes a highly informative set of clues for the researcher seeking to study organizational functioning. Nevertheless, the stated purposes of an organization as given by its by-laws or in the reports of its leaders can be misleading. Such statements of objectives may idealize, rationalize, distort, omit, or even conceal some essential aspects of the functioning of the organization. Nor is there always agreement about the mission of the organization among its leaders and members. The university president may describe the purpose of his institution as one of turning out national leaders; the academic dean sees it as imparting the cultural heritage of the past, the academic

---

Source: From *The Social Psychology of Organizations*, by D. Katz and R. L. Kahn, pp. 14–29.

vice president as enabling students to move toward self-actualization and development, the graduate dean as creating new knowledge, the dean of men as training youngsters in technical and professional skills which will enable them to earn their living, and the editor of the student newspaper as inculcating the conservative values which will preserve the status quo of an outmoded capitalistic society.

The fallacy here is one of equating the purposes or goals of organizations with the purposes and goals of individual members. The organization as a system has an output, a product or an outcome, but this is not necessarily identical with the individual purposes of group members. Though the founders of the organization and its key members do think in teleological terms about organization objectives, we should not accept such practical thinking, useful as it may be, in place of a theoretical set of constructs for purposes of scientific analysis. Social science, too frequently in the past, has been misled by such short-cuts and has equated popular phenomenology with scientific explanation.

In fact, the classic body of theory and thinking about organizations has assumed a teleology of this sort as the easiest way of identifying organizational structures and their functions. From this point of view an organization is a social device for efficiently accomplishing through group means some stated purpose; it is the equivalent of the blueprint for the design of the machine which is to be created for some practical objective. The essential difficulty with this purposive or design approach is that an organization characteristically includes more and less than is indicated by the design of its founder or the purpose of its leader. Some of the factors assumed in the design may be lacking or so distorted in operational practice as to be meaningless, while unforeseen embellishments dominate the orga-nizational structure. Moreover, it is not always possible to ferret out the designer of the organization or to discover the intricacies of the design which he carried in his head. The attempt by Merton to deal with the latent function of the organization in contrast with its manifest function is one way of dealing with this problem.[1] The study of unanticipated consequences as well as anticipated consequences of organizational functioning is a similar way of handling the matter. Again, however, we are back to the purposes of the creator or leader, dealing with unanticipated consequences on the assumption that we can discover the consequences anticipated by him and can lump all other outcomes together as a kind of error variance.

It would be much better theoretically, however, to start with concepts which do not call for identifying the purposes of the designers and then correcting for them when they do not seem to be fulfilled. The theoretical concepts should begin with the input, output, and functioning of the organization as a system and not with the rational purposes of its leaders. We may want to utilize such purposive notions to lead us to sources of data or as subjects of special study, but not as our basic theoretical constructs for understanding organizations.

Our theoretical model for the understanding of organizations is that of an energic input output system in which the energic return from the output reactivates the system. Social organizations are flagrantly open systems in that the input of energies and the conversion of output into further energic input consist of transactions between the organization and its environment.

All social systems, including organizations, consist of the patterned activities of a number of individuals. Moreover, these patterned activities are complementary or interdependent with respect to some common output or outcome; they are repeated, relatively enduring, and bounded in space and time. If the activity pattern occurs only once or at unpredictable intervals, we could not speak of an organization. The stability or recurrence of activities can be examined in relation to the *energic input* into the system, the *transformation, of energies within the system,* and the *resulting product or energic output.* In a factory the raw materials and the human labor are the energic input, the patterned activities of production the transformation of energy, and the finished product the output. To maintain this patterned activity requires a continued renewal of the inflow of energy. This is guaranteed in social systems by the energic return from the product or outcome. Thus the outcome of the cycle of activities furnishes new energy for the initiation of a renewed cycle. The company which produces automobiles sells them and by doing so obtains the means of securing new raw materials, compensating its labor force, and continuing the activity pattern.

In many organizations outcomes are converted into money and new energy is furnished through this mechanism. Money is a convenient way of handling energy units both on the output and input sides, and buying and selling represent one set of social rules for regulating the exchange of money. Indeed, these rules are so effective and so widespread that there is some danger of mistaking the business of buying and selling for the defining cycles of organization. It is a commonplace executive observation that businesses exist to make money, and the observation is usually allowed to go unchallenged. It is, however, a very limited statement about the purposes of business.

Some human organizations do not depend on the cycle of selling and buying to maintain themselves. Universities and public agencies depend rather on bequests and legislative appropriations, and in so-called voluntary organizations the output reenergizes the activity of organization members in a more direct fashion. Member activities and accomplishments are rewarding in themselves and tend therefore to be continued, without the mediation of the outside environment. A society of bird watchers can wander into the hills and engage in the rewarding activities of identifying birds for their mutual edification and enjoyment. Organizations thus differ on this important dimension of the source of energy renewal, with the great majority utilizing both intrinsic and extrinsic sources in varying degree. Most large-scale organizations are not as self-contained as small voluntary groups and are very dependent upon the social effects of their output for energy renewal.

Our two basic criteria for identifying social systems and determining their functions are (1) tracing the pattern of energy exchange or activity of people as it results in some output and (2) ascertaining how the output is translated into energy which reactivates the pattern. We shall refer to organizational functions or objectives not as the conscious purposes of group leaders or group members but as the outcomes which are the energic source for a maintenance of the same type of output.

This model of an energic input-output system is taken from the open system theory as promulgated by von Bertalanffy.[2] Theorists have pointed out the applicability of the system concepts of the natural sciences to the problems of social science. It is important, therefore, to examine in more detail the constructs of system theory and the characteristics of open systems.

System theory is basically concerned with problems of relationships, of structure, and of interdependence rather than with the constant attributes of objects. In general approach it resembles field theory except that its dynamics deal with temporal as well as spatial patterns. Older formulations of system constructs dealt with the closed systems of the physical sciences, in which relatively self-contained structures could be treated successfully as if they were independent of external forces. But living systems, whether biological organisms or social organizations, are acutely dependent upon their external environment and so must be conceived of as open systems.

Before the advent of open-system thinking, social scientists tended to take one of two approaches in dealing with social structures; they tended either (1) to regard them as closed systems to which the laws of physics applied or (2) to endow them with some vitalistic concept like entelechy. In the former case they ignored the environmental forces affecting the organization and in the latter case they fell back upon some magical purposiveness to account for organizational functioning. Biological theorists, however, have rescued us from this trap by pointing out that the concept of the open system means that we neither have to follow the laws of traditional physics, nor in deserting them do we have to abandon science. The laws of Newtonian physics are correct generalizations but they are limited to closed systems. They do not apply in the same fashion to open systems which maintain themselves through constant commerce with their environment, i.e., a continuous inflow and outflow of energy through permeable boundaries.

One example of the operation of closed versus open systems can be seen in the concept of entropy and the second law of thermodynamics. According to the second law of thermodynamics a system moves toward equilibrium; it tends to run down, that is, its differentiated structures tend to move toward dissolution as the elements composing them become arranged in random disorder. For example, suppose that a bar of iron has been heated by the application of a blowtorch on one side. The arrangement of all the fast (heated) molecules on one side and all the slow molecules on the other is an unstable state, and over time the distribution of molecules becomes in effect random, with the resultant cooling of one side and heating of the other, so that all surfaces of the iron approach the same temperature. A similar process of heat exchange will also be going on between the iron bar and its environment, so that the bar will gradually approach the temperature of the room in which it is located, and in so doing will elevate somewhat the previous temperature of the room. More technically, entropy increases toward a maximum and equilibrium occurs as the physical system attains the state of the most probable distribution of its elements. In social systems, however, structures tend to become more elaborated rather than less differentiated. The rich may grow richer and the poor may grow poorer. The open system does not run down, because it can import energy from the world around it. Thus the operation of entropy is counteracted by the importation of energy and the living system is characterized by negative rather than positive entropy.

Common Characteristics of Open Systems

Though the various types of open systems have common characteristics by virtue of being open systems, they differ in other characteristics. If this were not the case, we would be able to obtain all our basic knowledge about social organizations through the study of a single cell.

The following nine characteristics seem to define all open systems.

1. Importation of Energy Open systems import some form of energy from the external environment. The cell receives oxygen from the bloodstream; the body similarly takes in oxygen from the air and food from the external world. The personality is dependent upon the external world for stimulation. Studies of sensory deprivation show that when a person is placed in a darkened soundproof room, where he has a minimal amount of visual and auditory stimulation, he develops hallucinations and other signs of mental stress.[3] Deprivation of social stimulation also can lead to mental disorganization.[4] Köhler's studies of the figural after-effects of continued stimulation show the dependence of perception upon its energic support from the external world.[5] Animals deprived of visual experience from birth for a prolonged period never fully recover their visual capacities.[6] In other words, the functioning personality is heavily dependent upon the continuous inflow of stimulation from the external environment. Similarly, social organizations must also draw renewed supplies of energy from other institutions, or people, or the material environment. No social structure is self-sufficient or self-contained.

2. The Through-Put Open systems transform the energy available to them. The body converts starch and sugar into heat and action. The personality converts chemical and electrical forms of stimulation into sensory qualities, and information into thought patterns. The organization creates a new product, or processes materials, or trains people, or provides a service. These activities entail some reorganization of input. Some work gets done in the system.

3. The Output Open systems export some product into the environment, whether it be the invention of an inquiring mind or a bridge constructed by an engineering firm. Even the biological organism exports physiological products such as carbon dioxide from the lungs which helps to maintain plants in the immediate environment.

4. Systems as Cycles of Events The pattern of activities of the energy exchange has a cyclic character. The product exported into the environment furnishes the sources of energy for the repetition of the cycle of activities. The energy reinforcing the cycle of activities can derive from some exchange of the product in the external world or from the activity itself. In the former instance, the industrial concern utilizes raw materials and human labor to turn out a product which is marketed, and the monetary return is used to obtain more raw materials and labor to perpetuate the cycle of activities. In the latter instance, the voluntary organization can provide expressive satisfactions to its member so that the energy renewal comes directly from the organizational activity itself.

The problem of structure, or the relatedness of parts, can be observed directly in some physical arrangement of things where the larger unit is physically bounded and its subparts are also bounded within the larger structure. But how do we deal with social structures, where physical boundaries in this sense do not exist? It was the genius of F. H. Allport which contributed the answer, namely that the structure is to be found in an interrelated set of events which return upon themselves to complete and renew a cycle of activities.[7] It is events rather than things which are structured, so that social structure is a dynamic rather than a static concept. Activities are structured so that they comprise a unity in their completion or closure. A simple linear stimulus-response exchange between two people would not constitute social structue. To create structure, the responses of A would have to elicit B's reactions in such a manner that the responses of the latter would stimulate A to further responses. Of course the chain of events may involve many people, but their behavior can be characterized as showing structure only when there is some closure to the chain by a return to its point of origin with the probability that the chain of events will then be repeated. The repetition of the cycle does not have to involve the same set of phenotypical happenings. It may expand to include more sub-events of exactly the same kind or it may involve similar activities directed toward the same outcomes. In the individual organism the eye may move in such away as to have the point of light fall upon the center of the retina. As the point of light moves, the movements of the eye may also change but to complete the same cycle of activity, i.e. to focus upon the point of light.

A single cycle of events of a self-closing character gives us a simple form of structure. But such single cycles can also combine to give a larger structure of events or an event system. An event system may consist of a circle of smaller cycles or hoops, each one of which makes contact with several others. Cycles may also be tangential to one another from other types of subsystems. The basic method for the identification of social structures is to follow the energic chain of events from the input of energy through its transformation to the point of closure of the cycle.

5. Negative Entropy To survive, open systems must move to arrest the entropic process; they must acquire negative entropy. The entropic process is a universal law of nature in which all forms of organization move toward disorganization or death. Complex physical systems move toward simple random distribution of their elements and biological organisms also run down and perish. The open system, however, by importing more energy from its environment than it expends, can store energy and can acquire negative entropy. There is then a general trend in an open system to maximize its ratio of imported to expended energy, to survive and even during periods of crisis to live on borrowed time. Prisoners in concentration camps on a starvation diet will carefully conserve any form of energy expenditure to make the limited food intake go as far as possible.[8] Social organizations will seek to improve their survival position and to acquire in their reserves a comfortable margin of operation.

The entropic process asserts itself in all biological systems as well as in closed physical systems. The energy replenishment of the biological organism is not of a qualitative character which can maintain indefinitely the complex organizational structure of living tissue. Social systems, however, are not anchored in the same physical constancies as biological organisms and so are capable of almost indefinite arresting of the entropic process. Nevertheless the number of organizations which go out of existence every year is large.

6. Information Input, Negative Feedback, and the Coding Process The inputs into living systems consist not only of energic materials which become transformed or altered in the work that gets done. Inputs are also informative in character and furnish signals to the structure about the environment and about its own functioning in relation to the environment. Just as we recognize the distinction between cues and drives in individual psychology, so must we take account of information and energic input for all living systems.

The simplest type of information input found in all systems is negative feedback. Information feedback of a negative kind enables the system to correct its deviations from course. The working parts of the machine feed back information about the effects of their operation to some central mechanism or subsystem which acts on such information to keep the system on target. The thermostat which controls the temperature of the room is a simple example of a regulatory device which operates on the basis of negative feedback. The automated power plant would furnish more complex examples. Miller emphasizes the critical nature of negative feedback in his proposition: *"When a system's negative feedback discontinues, its steady state vanishes, and at the same time its boundary disappears and the system terminates."*[9] If there is no corrective device to get the system back on its course, it will expend too much energy or it will ingest too much energic input and no longer continue as a system.

The reception of inputs into a system is selective. Not all energic inputs are capable of being absorbed into every system. The digestive system of living creatures assimilates only those inputs to which it is adapted. Similarly, systems can react only to those information signals to which they are attuned. The general term for the selective mechanisms of a system by which incoming materials are rejected or accepted and translated for the structure is coding. Through the coding process the "blooming, buzzing confusion" of the world is simplified into a few meaningful and simplified categories for a given system. The nature of the functions performed by the system determines its coding mechanisms, which in turn perpetuate this type of functioning.

7. The Steady State and Dynamic Homeostasis The importation of energy to arrest entropy operates to maintain some constancy in energy exchange, so that open systems which survive are characterized by a steady state. A steady state is not motionless or a true equilibrium. There is a continuous inflow of energy from the external environment and a continuous export of the products of the system, but the character of the system, the ratio of the energy exchanges and the relations between parts, remains the same. The catabolic and anabolic processes of tissue breakdown and restoration within the body preserve a steady state so that the organism from time to time is not the identical organism it was but a highly similar organism. The steady state is seen in clear form in the homeostatic processes for the regulation of body temperature; external conditions of humidity and temperature may vary, but the temperature of the body remains the same. The endocrine glands are a regulatory mechanism for preserving an evenness of physiological functioning. The general principle here is that of Le Châtelier who maintains that any internal or external factor making for disruption of the system is countered by forces which restore the system as closely as possible to its previous state.[10] Krech and Crutchfield similarly hold, with respect to psychological organization, that cognitive structures will react to influences in such a way as to absorb them with minimal change to existing cognitive integration.[11] The homeostatic principle does not apply literally to the functioning of all complex living systems, in that in counteracting entropy they move toward growth and expansion. This apparent contradiction can be resolved, however, if we recognize the complexity of the subsystems and their interaction in anticipating changes necessary for the maintenance of an overall steady state. Stagner has pointed out that the initial disturbance of a given tissue constancy within the biological organism will result in mobilization of energy to restore the balance, but that recurrent upsets will lead to actions to anticipate the disturbance:

> We eat before we experience intense hunger pangs. . . . energy mobilization for forestalling tactics must be explained in terms of a *cortical tension* which reflects the visceral proprioceptive pattern of the original biological disequilibration. . . . *Dynamic homeostasis* involves the maintenance of tissue constancies by establishing a constant physical environment—by reducing the variability and disturbing effects of external stimulation. Thus the organism does not simply restore the prior equilibrium. A new, more complex and more comprehensive equilibrium is established.[12]

Though the tendency toward a steady state in its simplest form is homeostatic, as in the preservation of a constant body temperature, the basic principle is *the preservation of the character of the system.* The equilibrium which complex systems approach is often that of a quasistationary equilibrium, to use Lewin's concept.[13] An adjustment in one direction is countered by a movement in the opposite direction and both movements are approximate rather than precise in their compensatory nature. Thus a temporal chart of activity will show a series of ups and downs rather than a smooth curve.

In preserving the character of the system, moreover, the structure will tend to import more energy than is required for its output, as we have already noted in discussing negative entropy. To insure survival, systems will operate to acquire some margin of safety beyond the immediate level of existence. The body will store fat, the social organization will build up reserves, the society will increase its technological and cultural base. Miller has formulated the proposition that the rate of growth of a system—within certain ranges—is exponential if it exists in a medium which makes available unrestricted amounts of energy for input.[14]

In adapting to their environment, systems will attempt to cope with external forces by ingesting them or acquiring control over them. The physical boundedness of the single organism means that such attempts at control over the environment affect the behavioral system rather than the biological system of the individual. Social systems will move, however, towards incorporating within their boundaries the external resources essential to survival. Again the result is an expansion of the original system.

Thus, the steady state which at the simple level is one of homeostasis over time, at more complex levels becomes one of preserving the character of the system through growth and expansion. The basic type of system does not change directly as a consequence of expansion. The most common type of growth is a multiplication of the same type of cycles or subsystems—a change in quantity rather than in quality. Animals and plant species grow by multiplication. A social system adds more units of the same essential type as it already has. Haire has studied the ratio between the sizes of different subsystems in growing business organizations.[15] He found that though the number of people increased in both the production subsystem and the subsystem concerned with the external world, the ratio of the two groups remained constant. Qualitative change does occur, however, in two ways. In the first place, quantitative growth calls for supportive subsystems of a specialized character not necessary when the system was smaller. In the second place, there is a point where quantitative changes produce a qualitative difference in the functioning of a system. A small college which triples its size is no longer the same institution in terms of the relation between its administration and faculty, relations among the various academic departments, or the nature of its instruction.

In short, living systems exhibit a growth or expansion dynamic in which they maximize their basic character. They react to change or they anticipate change through growth which assimilates the new energic inputs to the nature of their structure. In terms of Lewin's quasi-stationary equilibrium the ups and downs of the adjustive process do not always result in a return to the old level. Under certain circumstances a solidification or freezing occurs during one of the adjustive cycles. A new base line level is thus established and successive movements fluctuate around this plateau which may be either above or below the previous plateau of operation.

8. Differentiation Open systems move in the direction of differentiation and elaboration. Diffuse global patterns are replaced by more specialized functions. The sense organs and the nervous system evolved as highly differentiated structures from the primitive nervous tissues. The growth of the personality proceeds from primitive, crude organizations of mental functions to hierarchically structured and well-differentiated systems of beliefs and feelings. Social organizations move toward the multiplication and elaboration of roles with greater specialization of function. In the United States today medical specialists now outnumber the general practitioners.

One type of differentiated growth in systems is what von Bertalanffy terms progressive mechanization. It finds expression in the way in which a system achieves a steady state. The early method is a process which involves an interaction of various dynamic forces, whereas the later development entails the use of a regulatory feedback mechanism. He writes:

> It can be shown that the *primary* regulations in organic systems, that is, those which are most fundamental and primitive in embryonic development as well as in evolution, are of such nature of dynamic interaction. . . . Superimposed are those regulations which we may call *secondary*, and which are controlled by fixed arrangements, especially of the feedback type. This state of affairs is a consequence of a general principle of organization which may be called progressive mechanization. At first, systems—biological, neurological, psychological or social—are governed by dynamic interaction of their components; later on, fixed arrangements and conditions of constraint are established which render the system and its parts more efficient, but also gradually diminish and eventually abolish its equipotentiality.[16]

9. Equifinality Open systems are further characterized by the principle of equifinality, a principle suggested by von Bertalanffy in 1940.17 According to this principle, a system can reach the same final state from differing initial conditions and by a variety of paths. The well-known biological experiments on the sea urchin show that a normal creature of that species can develop from a complete ovum, from each half of a divided ovum, or from the fusion product of two whole ova. As open systems move toward regulatory mechanisms to control their operations, the amount of equifinality may be reduced.

Some Consequences of Viewing Organizations as Open Systems

In the following chapter we shall inquire into the specific implications of considering organizations as open systems and into the ways in which social organizations differ from other types of living systems. At this point, however, we should call attention to some of the misconceptions which arise both in theory and practice when social organizations are regarded as closed rather than open systems.

The major misconception is the failure to recognize fully that the organization is continually dependent upon inputs from the environment and that the inflow of materials and human energy is not a constant. The fact that organizations have built-in protective devices to maintain stability and that they are notoriously difficult to change in the direction of some reformer's desires should not obscure the realities of the dynamic interrelationships of any social structure with its social and natural environment. The very efforts of the organization to maintain a constant external environment produce changes in organizational structure. The reaction to changed inputs to mute their possible revolutionary implications also results in changes.

The typical models in organizational theorizing concentrate upon principles of internal functioning as if these problems were independent of changes in the environment and as if they did not affect the maintenance inputs of motivation and morale. Moves toward tighter integration and coordination are made to insure stability, when flexibility may be the more important requirement. Moreover, coordination and control become ends in themselves rather than means to an end. They are not seen in full perspective as adjusting the system to its environment but as desirable goals within a closed system. In fact, however, every attempt at coordination which is not functionally required may produce a host of new organizational problems.

One error which stems from this kind of misconception is the failure to recognize the equifinality of the open system, namely that there are more ways than one of producing a given outcome. In a closed physical system the same initial conditions must lead to the same final result. In open systems this is not true even at the biological level. It is much less true at the social level. Yet in practice we insist that there is one best way of assembling a gun for all recruits, one best way for the baseball player to hurl the ball in from the outfield and that we standardize and teach these best methods. Now it is true under certain conditions that there is one best way, but these conditions must first be established. The general principle, which characterizes all open systems, is that there does not have to be a single method for achieving an objective.

A second error lies in the notion that irregularities in the functioning of a system due to environmental influences are error variances and should be treated accordingly. According to this conception, they should be controlled out of studies of organizations. From the organization's own operations they should be excluded as irrelevant and should be guarded against. The decisions of officers to omit a consideration of external factors or to guard against such influences in a defensive fashion, as if they would go away if ignored, is an instance of this type of thinking. So is the now outmoded "public be damned" attitude of businessmen toward the clientele upon whose support they demand. Open system theory, on the other hand, would maintain that environmental influences are not sources of error variance but are integrally related to the functioning of a social system, and that we cannot understand a system without a constant study of the forces that impinge upon it.

Thinking of the organization as a closed system, moreover, results in a failure to develop the intelligence or feedback function of obtaining adequate information about the changes in environmental forces. It is remarkable how weak many industrial companies are in their market research departments when they are so dependent upon the market. The prediction can be hazarded that organizations in our society will increasingly move toward the improvements of the facilities for research in assessing environmental forces. The reason is that we are in the process of correcting our misconception of the organization as a closed system.

Emery and Trist have pointed out how current theorizing on organizations still reflects the older closed system conceptions. They write:

> In the realm of social theory, however, there has been something of a tendency to continue thinking in terms of a "closed" system, that is, to regard the enterprise as sufficiently independent to allow most of its problems to be analyzed with reference to its internal structure and without reference to its external environment. . . . In practice the system theorists in social science . . . did "tend to focus on the statics of social structure and to neglect the study of structural change." In an attempt to overcome this bias, Merton suggested that "the concept of dysfunction, which implied the concept of strain, stress and tension on the structural level, provides an analytical approach to the study of dynamics and change." This concept has been widely accepted by system theorists but while it draws attention to sources of

imbalance within an organization it does not conceptually reflect the mutual permeation of an organization and its environment that is the cause of such imbalance. It still retains the limiting perspectives of "closed system" theorizing. In the administrative field the same limitations may be seen in the otherwise invaluable contributions of Barnard and related writers.[18]

Summary

The open-system approach to organizations is contrasted with common-sense approaches, which tend to accept popular names and stereotypes as basic organizational properties and to identify the purpose of an organization in terms of the goals of its founders and leaders.

The open-system approach, on the other hand, begins by identifying and mapping the repeated cycles of input, transformation, output, and renewed input which comprise the organizational pattern. This approach to organizations represents the adaptation of work in biology and in the physical sciences by von Bertalanffy and others.

Organizations as a special class of open systems have properties of their own, but they share other properties in common with all open systems. These include the importation of energy from the environment, the through-put or transformation of the imported energy into some product form which is characteristic of the system, the exporting of that product into the environment, and the reenergizing of the system from sources in the environment.

Open systems also share the characteristics of negative entropy, feedback, homeostasis, differentiation, and equifinality. The law of negative entropy states that systems survive and maintain their characteristic internal order only so long as they import from the environment more energy than they expend in the process of transformation and exportation. The feedback principle has to do with information input, which is a special kind of energic importation, a kind of signal to the system about environmental conditions and about the functioning of the system in relation to its environment. The feedback of such information enables the system to correct for its own malfunctioning or for changes in the environment, and thus to maintain a steady state or homeostasis. This is a dynamic rather than a static balance, however. Open systems are not at rest but tend toward differentiation and elaboration, both because of subsystem dynamics and because of the relationship between growth and survival. Finally, open systems are characterized by the principle of equifinality, which asserts that systems can reach the same final state from different initial conditions and by different paths of development.

Traditional organizational theories have tended to view the human organization as a closed system. This tendency had led to a disregard of differing organizational environments and the nature of organizational dependency on environment. It has led also to an overconcentration on principles of internal organizational functioning, with consequent failure to develop and understand the processes of feedback which are essential to survival.

Notes

1. R. K. Merton, *Social Theory and Social Structure,* rev. ed. (New York: Free Press, 1957).
2. L. von Bertalanffy, "General System Theory," *General Systems,* Yearbook of the Society for the Advancement of General System Theory (1956), 1:1–10.
3. P. Solomon, et al., eds., *Sensory Deprivation* (Cambridge, Mass.: Harvard University Press, 1961).
4. R. A. Spitz, "Hospitalism: An Inquiry into the Genesis of Psychiatric Conditions in Early Childhood," *Psychoanalytic Study of the Child* (1945), 1:53–74.
5. W. Köhler and H. Wallach, "Figural After-Effects: An Investigation of Visual Processes," *Proceedings of the American Philosophical Society* 88 (1944), pp. 269–357; W. Köhler and D. Emery, "Figural After-Effects in the Third Dimension of Visual Space," *American Journal of Psychology* 60, (1947): 159–201.
6. R. Melzack and W. Thompson, "Effects of Early Experience on Social Behavior," *Canadian Journal of Psychology* 10 (1956): 82–90.

7. F. H. Allport, "A Structuronomic Conception of Behavior: Individual and Collective, I. Structural Theory and the Master Problem of Social Psychology," *Journal of Abnormal and Social Psychology* 64 (1962): 3–30.
8. E. F. I. Cohen, *Human Behavior in the Concentration Camp* (London: Jonathan Cape, 1954).
9. J. G. Miller, "Toward a General Theory for the Behavioral Sciences," *American Psychologist* 10 (1955): 513–531; quote from p. 529.
10. See D. F. Bradley and M. Calvin, "Behavior: Imbalance in a Network of Chemical Transformations," *General Systems*, yearbook of the Society for the Advancement of General System Theory (1956), 1:56–65.
11. D. Krech and R. Crutchfield, *Theory and Problems of Social Psychology* (New York: McGraw-Hill, 1948).
12. R. Stagner, "Homeostasis as a Unifying Concept in Personality Theory," *Psychological Review* 58 (1951): 5–17; quote from p. 5.
13. K. Lewin, "Frontiers in Group Dynamics," *Human Relations* (1947): 1:5–41.
14. Miller, op cit.
15. M. Haire, "Biological Models and Empirical Histories of the Growth of Organizations," in *Modern Organization Theory*, ed. M. Haire (New York: Wiley, 1959), pp. 272–306.
16. von Bertalanffy, 1956, op cit., p. 6.
17. L. von Bertalanffy, "Der Organismus als Physikalisches System Betrachtet," *Naturwissenschaften* 28 (1940): 521 ff.
18. F. E. Emery and E. L. Trist, "Sociotechnical Systems," in *Management Sciences Models and Techniques*, vol. 2 (London: Pergamon Press, 1960), quote from p. 84.

The Road to PPB: The Stages of Budget Reform

Allen Schick

Among the new men in the nascent PPB staffs and the fellow travelers who have joined the bandwagon, the mood is of "a revolutionary development in the history of government management." There is excited talk about the differences between what has been and what will be; of the benefits that will accrue from an explicit and "hard" appraisal of objectives and alternatives; of the merits of multiyear budget forecasts and plans; of the great divergence between the skills and role of the analyst and the job of the examiner; of the realignments in government structure that might result from changes in the budget process.

This is not the only version, however. The closer one gets to the nerve centers of budget life—the Divisions in the Bureau of the Budget offices in the departments and agencies—the more one is likely to hear that "there's nothing very new in PPB; it's hardly different from what we've been doing until now." Some old-timers interpret PPB as a revival of the performance budgeting venture of the early 1950's. Others belittle the claim that—before PPB—decisions on how much to spend for personnel or supplies were made without real consideration of the purposes for which these inputs were to be invested. They point to previous changes that have been in line with PPB, albeit without PPB's distinctive package of techniques and nomenclature. Such things as the waning role of the "green sheets" in the central budget process, the redesign of the appropriation structure and the development of activity classifications, refinements in work measurement, productivity analysis, and other types of output measurement, and the utilization of the Spring Preview for a broad look at programs and major issues.

Between the uncertain protests of the traditional budgeteer and the uncertain expectations of the *avant garde,* there is a third version. The PPB system that is being developed portends a radical change in the central function of budgeting, but it is anchored to half a century of tradition and evolution. The budget system of the future will be a product of past and emerging developments; that is, it will embrace both the budgetary functions introduced during earlier stages of reform as well as the planning function which is highlighted by PPB. PPB is the first budget system *designed* to accommodate the multiple functions of budgeting.

The Functions of Budgeting

Budgeting always has been conceived as a process for systematically relating the expenditure of funds to the accomplishment of planned objectives. In this important sense, there is a bit of PPB in every budget system. Even in the initial stirrings of budget reform more than 50 years ago, there were cogent statements on the need for a budget system to plan the objectives and activities of government and to furnish reliable data on what was to be accomplished with public funds. In 1907, for example, the New York Bureau of Municipal Research published a sample "program memorandum" that contained some 125 pages of functional accounts and data for the New York City Health Department.[1]

However, this orientation was not *explicitly* reflected in the budget systems—national, state, or local—that were introduced during the first decades of this century, nor is it *explicitly* reflected in the budget systems that exist today. The plain fact is that planning is not the only function that must be served by a budget system. The *management* of ongoing activities and the control of spending are two functions which, in the past, have been given priority over the planning function. (See Figure 1.) Robert Anthony identifies distinct administrative

---

processes, strategic planning, management control, and operational control.

> **Strategic planning** is the process of deciding on objectives of the organization, on changes in these objectives, on the resources used to attain these objectives, and on the policies that are to govern the acquisition, use, and disposition of these resources.
>
> **Management control** is the process by which managers assure that resources are obtained and used effectively and efficiently in the accomplishment of the organization's objectives.
>
> **Operational control** is the process of assuring that specific tasks are carried out effectively and efficiently.[2]

Every budget system, even rudimentary ones, comprises planning, management, and control processes. Operationally, these processes often are indivisible, but for analytic purposes they are distinguished here. In the context of budgeting, *planning* involves the determination of objectives, the evaluation of alternative courses of action, and the authorization of select programs. Planning is linked most closely to budget preparation, but it would be a mistake to disregard the management and control elements in budget preparation or the possibilities for planning during other phases of the budget year. Clearly, one of the major aims of PPB is to convert the annual routine of preparing a budget into a conscious appraisal and formulation of future goals and policies. Management involves the programming of approved goals into specific projects and activities, the design of organizational units to carry out approved programs, and the staffing of these units and the procurement of necessary resources. The management process is spread

FIGURE 1

Some Basic Differences between Budget Orientations

CHARACTERISTIC	CONTROL	MANAGEMENT	PLANNING
Personnel skill	Accounting	Administration	Economics
Information focus	Objects	Activities	Purposes
Key budget stage (central)	Execution	Preparation	Prepreparation
Breadth of measurement	Discrete	Discrete/activities	Comprehensive
Role of budget agency	Fiduciary	Efficiency	Policy
Decisional-flow	Upward-aggregative	Upward-aggregative	Downward-disaggregative
Type of choice	Incremental	Incremental	Teletic
Control responsibility	Central	Operating	Operating
Management responsibility	Dispersed	Central	Supervisory
Planning responsibility	Dispersed	Dispersed	Central
Budget-appropriations classifications	Same	Same	Different
Appropriations-organizational link	Direct	Direct	Crosswalk

over the entire budget cycle; ideally, it is the link between goals made and activities undertaken. *Control* refers to the process of binding operating officials to the policies and plans set by their superiors. Control is predominant during the executive and audit stages, although the form of budget estimates and appropriations often is determined by control considerations. The assorted controls and reporting procedures that are associated with budget execution—position controls, restrictions on transfers, requisition procedures, and travel regulations, to mention the more prominent ones—have the purpose of securing compliance with policies made by central authorities.

Very rarely are planning, management, and control given equal attention in the operation of budget systems. As a practical matter, planning, management, and control have tended to be competing processes in budgeting with no neat division of functions among the various participants. Because time is scarce, central authorities must be selective in the things they do. Although this scarcity counsels the devolution of control responsibilities to operating levels, the lack of reliable and relied-on internal control systems has loaded central authorities with control functions at the expense of the planning function. Moreover, these processes often require different skills and generate different ways of handling the budget mission, so that one type of perspective tends to predominate over the others. Thus, in the staffing of the budget offices, there has been a shift from accountants to administrators as budgeting has moved from a control to a management posture. The initial experience with PPB suggests that the next transition might be from administrators to economists as budgeting takes on more of the planning function.

Most important, perhaps, are the differential informational requirements of planning, control, and management processes. Informational needs differ in terms of time spans, levels of aggregation, linkages with organizational and operating units, and input-output foci. The apparent solution is to design a system that serves the multiple needs of budgeting. Historically, however, there has been a strong tendency to homogenize informational structures and to rely on a single classification scheme to serve all budgetary purposes. For the most part, the informational system has been structured to meet the purposes of control. As a result, the type of multiple-purpose budget system envisioned by PPB has been avoided.

An examination of budget systems should reveal whether greater emphasis is placed *at the central levels* on planning, management, or control. A *planning orientation* focuses on the broadest range of issues: What are the long-range goals and policies of the government and how are these related to particular expenditure choices? What criteria should be used in appraising the requests of the agencies? Which programs should be initiated or terminated, and which expanded or curtailed? A *management orientation* deals with less fundamental issues: What is the best way to organize for the accomplishment of a prescribed task? Which of several staffing alternatives achieves the most effective relationship between the central and field offices? Of the various grants and projects proposed, which should be approved? A control orientation deals with a relatively narrow range of concerns: How can agencies be held to the expenditure ceilings established by the legislature and chief executive? What reporting procedures should be used to enforce propriety in expenditures? What limits should be placed on agency spending for personnel and equipment?

It should be clear that every budget system contains planning, management, and control features. A control orientation means the subordination, not the absence, of planning and management functions. In the matter of orientations, we are dealing with relative emphases, not with pure dichotomies. The germane issue is the balance among these vital functions at the central level. Viewed centrally, what weight does each have in the design and operation of the budget system?

The Stages of Budget Reform

The framework outlined above suggests a useful approach to the study of budget reform. Every reform alters the planning-management control balance, sometimes inadvertently, usually deliberately. Accordingly, it is possible to identify three successive stages of reform. In the first stage, dating roughly from 1920 to 1935, the dominant emphasis was on developing a adequate system of expenditure control. Although planning and management considerations were not altogether absent (and indeed occupied a prominent role in the debates leading o the Budget and Accounting Act of 1921), they were pushed to the side by what was regarded as the first priority, a reliable system of expenditure accounts. The second stage came into the open during the New Deal and reached its zenith more than a decade later in the movement for performance budgeting. The management orientation, paramount during this period, made its mark in the reform of the appropriation structure, development of management improvement and work measurement programs, and the focusing of budget preparation on the work and activities of the agencies. The third stage, the full emergence of which must await the institutionalization of PPB, can be traced to earlier efforts to link planning and budgeting as well as to the analytic criteria of welfare economics, but its recent development is a product of modern informational and decisional technologies such as those pioneered in the Department of Defense.

PPB is predicated on the primary of the planning function; yet it strives for a multipurpose budget system that gives adequate and necessary attention to the control and management areas. Even in embryonic stages, PPB envisions the development of crosswalk grids for the conversion of data from a planning to a management and control framework, and back again. PPB treats the three basic functions as compatible and complementary elements of a budget system, though not as coequal aspects of central budgeting. In ideal form, PPB would centralize the planning function and delegate *primary* managerial and control responsibilities to the supervisory and operating levels respectively.

In the modern genesis of budgeting, efforts to improve planning, management, and control made common cause under the popular banner of the executive-budget concept. In the goals and lexicon of the first reformers, budgeting meant executive budgeting. The two were inseparable. There was virtually no dissent from Cleveland's dictum that "to be a budget it must be prepared and submitted by a responsible executive . . ."[3] Whether from the standpoint of planning, management, or control, the executive was deemed in the best position to prepare and execute the budget. As Cleveland argued in 1915, only the executive "could think in terms of the institution as a whole," and therefore, he "is the only one who can be made responsible for leadership."[4]

The executive budget idea also took root in the administrative integration movement, and here was allied with such reforms as functional consolidation of agencies, elimination of independent boards and commissions, the short ballot, and strengthening the chief executive's appointive and removal powers. The chief executive often was likened to the general manager of a corporation, the budget bureau serving as his general staff.

Finally, the executive budget was intended to strengthen honesty and efficiency by restricting the discretion of administrators in this role. It was associated with such innovations as centralized purchasing and competitive bidding, civil service reform, uniform accounting procedures, and expenditure audits.

The Control Orientation

In the drive for executive budgeting, the various goals converged. There was a radical parting of the ways, however, in the conversion of the budget idea into an operational reality. Hard choices had to be made in the design of expenditure accounts and in the orientation of the budget office. On both counts, the control orientation was predominant.

In varying degrees of itemization, the expenditure classifications established during the first wave of reform were based on objects-of-expenditure, with detailed tabulations of the myriad items required to operate an administrative unit—personnel, fuel, rent, office supplies, and other inputs. On these "line-itemizations" were built technical routines for the compilation and review of estimates and the disbursement of funds. The leaders in the movement for executive budgeting, however, envisioned a system of functional classifications focusing on the work to be accomplished. They regarded objects-of-expenditure as subsidiary data to be included for informational purposes. Their preference for functional accounts derived from their conception of the budget as a planning instrument, their disdain for objects from the contemporary division between politics and administration.[5] The Taft Commission vigorously opposed object-of-expenditure appropriations and recommended that expenditures be classified by class of work, organizational unit, character of expense, and method of financing. In its model budget, the Commission included several functional classifications.[6]

In the establishment of a budget system for New York City by the Bureau of Municipal Research, there was an historic confrontation between diverse conceptions of budgeting.

In evolving suitable techniques, the Bureau soon faced a conflict between functional and object budgeting. Unlike almost all other budget systems which began on a control footing with object classifications, the Bureau turned to control (and the itemization of objects) only after trial-and-error experimentation with program methods.

When confronted with an urgent need for effective control over administration, the Bureau was compelled to conclude that this need was more critical than the need for a planning functional emphasis. "Budget reform," Charles Beard once wrote, "bears the imprint of the age in which it originated."[7] In an age when personnel and purchasing controls were unreliable, the first consideration was how to prevent administrative improprieties.

> In the opinion of those who were in charge of the development of a budget procedure, the most important service to be rendered was the establishing of central controls so that responsibility could be located and enforced through elected executives. . . . The view was, therefore, accepted, that questions of administration and niceties of adjustment must be left in abeyance until central control has been effectively established and the basis has been laid for careful scrutiny of departmental contracts and purchases as well as departmental work.[8]

Functional accounts had been designed to facilitate rational program decisions, not to deter officials from misfeasance. "The classification by 'functions' affords no protection; it only operates as a restriction on the use which may be made of the services."[9] The detailed itemization of objects was regarded as desirable not only "because it provides for the utilization of all the machinery of control which has been provided, but it also admits to a much higher degree of perfection than it has at present attained."[10]

With the introduction of object accounts, New York City had a threefold classification of expenditures: (1) by organizational units; (2) by functions; and (3) by objects. In a sense, the Bureau of Municipal Research was striving to develop a budget system that would serve the multiple purposes of budgeting simultaneously. To the Bureau, the inclusion of more varied and detailed data in the budget was a salutary trend; all purposes would be served and the public would have a more complete picture of government spending. Thus the Bureau "urged from the beginning a classification of costs in as many different ways as there are stories to be told."[11] But the Bureau did not anticipate the practical difficulties which would ensue from the multiple classification scheme. In the 1913 appropriations act

> there were 3992 distinct items of appropriation. . . . Each constituted a distinct appropriation, besides which there was a further itemization of positions and salaries of personnel that multiplied this number several times, each of which operated as limitations on administrative discretion.[12]

This predicament confronted the Bureau with a direct choice between the itemization of objects and a functional classification. As a solution, the Bureau recommended retention of objects accounts and the total "defunctionalization" of the budget; in other words, it gave priority to the objects and the control orientation they manifested. Once installed, objects controls rapidly gained stature as an indispensable deterrent to administrative misbehavior. Amelioration of the adverse effects of multiple classifications was to be accomplished in a different manner, one which would strengthen the planning and management processes. The Bureau postulated a fundamental distinction between the purposes of budgets and appropriations, and between the types of classification suitable for each.

> . . . an act of appropriation has a single purpose—that of putting a limitation on the amount of obligations which may be incurred and the amount of vouchers which may be drawn to pay for personal services, supplies, etc. The only significant classification of appropriation items, therefore, is according to persons to whom drawing accounts are given and the classes of things to be bought.[13]

Appropriations, in sum, were to be used as statutory controls on spending. In its "Next Steps" proposals, the Bureau recommended that appropriations retain "exactly the same itemization so far as specifications of positions and compensations are concerned and therefore, the same protection."[14]

Budgets, on the other hand, were regarded as instruments of planning and publicity. They should include "all the details of the work plans and specifications of cost of work."[15] In addition to the regular object and organization classifications, the budget would report the "total cost incurred, classified by *functions*—for determining questions of policy having to do with service rendered as well as to be rendered, and laying a foundation for appraisal of results."[16] The Bureau also recommended a new instrument, a *work program,* which would furnish "a detailed schedule or analysis of each function, activity, or process within each organization unit. This analysis would give the total cost and the unit cost wherever standards were established."[17]

Truly a far-sighted conception of budgeting! There would be three documents for the three basic functions of budgeting. Although the Bureau did not use the analytic framework suggested above, it seems that the appropriations were intended for control purposes, the budget for planning purposes, and the work program for management purposes. Each of the three documents would have its specialized information scheme, but jointly they would comprise a multipurpose budget system not very different from PPB, even though the language of crosswalking or systems analysis was not used.

Yet the plan failed, for in the end the Bureau was left with object accounts pegged to a control orientation. The Bureau's distinction between budgets and appropriations was not well understood, and the work-program idea was rejected by New York City on the ground that adequate accounting backup was lacking. The Bureau had failed to recognize that the conceptual distinction between budgets and appropriations tends to break down under the stress of informational demands. If the legislature appropriates by objects, the budget very likely will be classified by objects. Conversely, if there are no functional accounts, the prospects for including such data in the budget are diminished substantially. As has almost always been the case, the budget came to mirror the appropriations act; in each, objects were paramount. It remains to be seen whether PPB will be able to break this interlocking informational pattern.

By the early 1920s the basic functions of planning and management were overlooked by those who carried the gospel of budget reform across the nation. First generation budget workers concentrated on perfecting and spreading the widely approved object-of-expenditure approach, and budget writers settled into a nearly complete preoccupation with forms and with factual descriptions of actual and recommended procedures. Although ideas about the use of the budget for planning and management purposes were retained in Buck's catalogs of "approved" practices,[18] they did not have sufficient priority to challenge tradition.

From the start, federal budgeting was placed on a control, object-of-expenditure footing, the full flavor of which can be perceived in reading Charles G. Dawes' documentary on *The First Year of the Budget of the United States.* According to Dawes,

> the Bureau of the Budget is concerned only with the humbler and routine business of Government. Unlike cabinet officers, it is concerned with no question of policy, save that of economy and efficiency.[19]

This distinction fitted neatly with object classifications that provided a firm accounting based for the routine conduct of government business, but no information on policy implications of public expenditures. Furthermore, in its first decade, the Bureau's tiny staff (40 or fewer) had to coordinate a multitude of well-advertised economy drives which shaped the job of the examiner as being that of reviewing itemized estimates to pare them down. Although Section 209 of the Budget and Accounting Act had authorized the Bureau to study and recommend improvements in the organization and administrative practices of Federal agencies, the Bureau was overwhelmingly preoccupied with the business of control.

The Management Orientation

Although no single action represents the shift from a control to a management orientation, the turning point in this evolution probably came with the New Deal's broadening perspective of government responsibilities.

During the 1920s and 1930s, occasional voices urged a return to the conceptions of budgeting advocated by the early reformers. In a notable 1924 article, Lent D. Upson argued vigorously that "budget procedure had stopped halfway in its development," and he proposed six modifications in the form of the budget, the net effect being a shift in emphasis from accounting control to functional accounting.[20] A similar position was taken a decade later by Wylie Kilpatrick who insisted that "the one fundamental basis of expenditure is functional, an accounting of payments for the services performed by government."[21]

Meanwhile, gradual changes were preparing the way for a reorientation of budgeting to a management mission. Many of the administrative abuses that had given rise to object controls were curbed by statutes and regulations and by a general upgrading of the public service. Reliable accounting systems were installed and personnel and purchasing reforms introduced, thereby freeing budgeting from some of its watchdog chores. The rapid growth of government activities and expenditures made it more difficult and costly for central officials to keep track of the myriad objects in the budget. With expansion, the bits and pieces into which the objects were itemized became less and less significant, while the aggregate of activities performed became more significant. With expansion, there was heightened need for central management of the incohesive sprawl of administrative agencies.

The climb in activities and expenditures also signaled radical changes in the role of the budget system. As long as government was considered a "necessary evil," and there was little recognition of the social value of public expenditures, the main function of budgeting was to keep spending in check. Because the outputs were deemed to be of limited and fixed value, it made sense to use the budget for central control over inputs. However, as the work and accomplishments of public agencies came to be regarded as benefits, the task of budgeting was redefined as the effective marshalling of fiscal and organizational resources for the attainment of benefits. This new posture focused attention on the problems of managing large programs and organizations, and on the opportunities for using the budget to extend executive hegemony over the dispersed administrative structure.

All these factors converged in the New Deal years. Federal expenditures rose rapidly from $4.2 billion in 1932 to $10 billion in 1940. Keynesian economics (the full budgetary implications of which are emerging only now in PPB) stressed the relationship between public spending and the condition of the economy. The President's Committee on Administrative Management (1937) castigated the routinized, control-minded approach of the Bureau of the Budget and urged that budgeting be used to coordinate Federal activities under presidential leadership. With its transfer in 1939 from the Treasury to the newly created Executive Office of the President, the Bureau was on its way to becoming the leading management arm of the Federal Government. The Bureau's own staff was increased tenfold; it developed the administrative management and statistical coordination functions that it still possesses; and it installed apportionment procedures for budget execution. More and more, the Bureau was staffed from the ranks of public administration rather than from accounting, and it was during the Directorship of Harold D. Smith (1939–46) that the Bureau substantially embraced the management orientation.[22] Executive Order 8248 placed the President's imprimatur on the management philosophy. It directed the Bureau:

> to keep the President informed of the progress of activities by agencies of the Government with respect to work proposed, work actually initiated, and work completed,

together with the relative timing of work between the several agencies of the Government; all to the end that the work programs of the several agencies of the executive branch of the Government may be coordinated and that the monies appropriated by the Congress may be expended in the most economical manner possible to prevent overlapping and duplication of effort.

Accompanying the growing management use of the budget process for the appraisal and improvement of administrative performance and the scientific management movement with its historical linkage to public administration were far more relevant applications of managerial cost accounting to governmental operations. Government agencies sought to devise performance standards and the rudimentary techniques of work measurement were introduced in several agencies including the Forest Service, the Census Bureau, and the Bureau of Reclamation.[23] Various professional associations developed grading systems to assess administrative performance as well as the need for public services. These crude and unscientific methods were the forerunners of more sophisticated and object techniques. At the apogee of these efforts, Clarence Ridley and Herbert Simon published *Measuring Municipal Activities: A Survey of Suggested Criteria for Appraising Administration,* in which they identified five kinds of measurement—(1) needs, (2) results, (3) costs, (4) effort, and (5) performance—and surveyed the obstacles to the measurement of needs and results. The latter three categories they combined into a measure of administrative efficiency. This study provides an excellent inventory of the state of the technology prior to the breakthrough made by cost-benefit and systems analysis.

At the close of World War II, the management orientation was entrenched in all but one aspect of Federal budgeting—the classification of expenditures. Except for isolated cases (such as TVA's activity accounts and the project structure in the Department of Agriculture), the traditional object accounts were retained though the control function had receded in importance. In 1949 the Hoover Commission called for alterations in budget classifications consonant with the management orientation. It recommended "that the whole budgetary concept of the Federal Government should be refashioned by the adoption of a budget based upon functions, activities, and projects."[24] To create a sense of novelty, the Commission gave a new label—performance budgeting—to what had long been known as functional or activity budgeting. Because its task force had used still another term—program budgeting—there were two new terms to denote the budget innovations of that period. Among writers there was no uniformity in usage, some preferring the "program budgeting" label, others "performance budgeting," to describe the same things. The level of confusion has been increased recently by the association of the term "program budgeting" (also the title of the Rand publication edited by David Novick) with the PPB movement.

Although a variety of factors and expectations influenced the Hoover Commission, and the Commission's proposals have been interpreted in many ways, including some that closely approximate the PPB concept, for purposes of clarity, and in accord with the control-management-planning framework, performance budgeting *as it was generally understood and applied* must be distinguished from the emergent PPB idea. The term "performance budgeting" is hereafter used in reference to reforms set in motion by the Hoover Commission and the term "program budgeting" is used in conjunction with PPB.

Performance budgeting is management-oriented; its principal thrust is to help administrators to assess the work efficiency of operating units by (1) casting budget categories in functional terms, and (2) providing work-cost measurements to facilitate the efficient performance of prescribed activities. Generally, its method is particularistic, the reduction of work-cost data into discrete, measurable units. Program budgeting (PPB) is planning-oriented; its main goal is to rationalize policy making by providing (1) data on the costs and benefits of alternative ways of attaining proposed public objectives, and (2) output measurements to facilitate the effective attainment of chosen objectives. As a policy device, program budgeting departs from simple engineering models of efficiency in which the objective is fixed and the quantity of inputs and outputs is adjusted to an optimal relationship. In PPB, the objective itself is variable; analysis may lead to a new statement of objectives. In order to enable budget makers to evaluate the costs and benefits of alternative expenditure options, program budgeting focuses on expenditure aggregates; the details come into play only as they contribute to an analysis of the total (the system) or marginal tradeoffs among competing proposals. Thus, in this macroanalytic approach, the accent is on comprehensiveness and on grouping data into categories that allow comparisons among alternative expenditure mixes.

Performance budgeting derived its ethos and much of its technique from cost accounting and scientific management; program budgeting has drawn its core ideas from economics and system analysis. In the performance budgeting literature, budgeting is described as a "tool of management" and the budget as a "work program." In PPB, budgeting is an allocative process among competing claims, and the budget is a statement of policy. Chronologically, there was a gap of several years between the bloom of performance budgeting and the first articulated conceptions of program budgeting. In the aftermath of the first Hoover report, and especially during the early 1950s, there was a plethora of writings on the administrative advantages of the performance budget. Substantial interest in program budgeting did not emerge until the mid-1950s when a number of economists (including Smithies, Novick, and McKean) began to urge reform of the Federal budget system. What the economists had in mind was not the same thing as the Hoover Commission.

In line with its management perspective the Commission averred that "the all-important thing in budgeting is the work of service to be accomplished, and what that work or service will cost."[25] Mosher followed this view closely in writing that "the central idea of the performance budget . . . is that the budget process be focused upon programs and functions—that is, accomplishments to be achieved, work to be done."[26] But from the planning perspective, the all-important thing surely is not the work or service to be accomplished but the objectives or purposes to be fulfilled by the investment of public funds. Whereas in performance budgeting, work and activities are treated virtually as ends in themselves, in program budgeting work and services are regarded as intermediate aspects, the process of converting resources into outputs. Thus, in a 1954 Rand paper, Novick defined a program as "the sum of the steps or interdependent activities which enter into the attainment of a specified objective. The program, therefore, is the end objective and is developed or budgeted in terms of all the elements necessary to its execution."[27] Novick goes on to add, "this is not the sense in which the government budget now uses the term."

Because the evaluation of performance and the evaluation of program are distinct budget functions, they call for different methods of classification which serves as an intermediate layer between objects and organizations. The activities relate to the functions and work of a distinct operating unit; hence their classification ordinarily conforms to organizational lines. This is the type of classification most useful for an administrator who has to schedule the procurement and utilization of resources for the production of goods and services. Activity classifications gather under a single rubric all the expenditure data needed by a manager to run his unit. The evaluation of programs, however, requires an end-product classification that is oriented to the mission and purposes of government. This type of classification may not be very useful for the manager, but it is of great value to the budget maker who has to decide how to allocate scarce funds among competing claims. Some of the difference between end-product and activity classifications can be gleaned by comparing the Coast Guard's existing activity schedule with the proposed program structure on the last page of Bulletin 66-3. The activity structure which was developed under the aegis of performance budgeting is geared to the operating responsibilities of the Coast Guard: Vessel Operations, Aviation Operations, Repair and Supply Facilities, and others. The proposed program structure is hinged to the large purposes sought through Coast Guard operations: Search and Rescue, Aids to Navigation, Law Enforcement, and so on.

It would be a mistake to assume that performance techniques presuppose program budgeting or that it is now possible to collect performance data without program classifications. Nevertheless, the view has gained hold that a program budget is "a transitional type of budget between the orthodox (traditional) character and object budget on the one hand and performance budget on the other."[28] Kammerer and Shadoan stress a similar connection. The former writes that "a *performance* budget car-ries the program budget one step further: into *unit costs*."[29] Shadoan "envisions 'performance budgeting' as an extension of . . . the program budget concept to which the element of unit work measurement has been added."[30] These writers ignore the divergent functions served by performance and program budgets. It is possible to devise and apply performance techniques without relating them to, or having the use of, larger program aggregates. A cost accountant or work measurement specialist can measure the cost or effort required to perform a repetitive task without probing into the purpose of the work or its relationship to the mission of the organization. Work measurement—"a method of establishing an equitable relationship between the volume of work performed and manpower utilized"[31]—is only distantly and indirectly related to the process of determining governmental policy at the higher levels. Program classifications are vitally linked to the making and implementation of policy through the allocation of public resources. As a general rule, performance budgeting is concerned with the *process of work* (what methods should be used) while program budgeting is concerned with the *purpose of work* (what activities should be authorized).

Perhaps the most reliable way to describe this difference is to show what was tried and accomplished under performance budgeting. First of all, performance budgeting led to the introduction of activity classifications, the management-orientation of which has already been discussed. Second, narrative descriptions of program and performance were added to the budget document. These statements give the budget-reader a general picture of the work that will be done by the organizational unit requesting funds. But unlike the analytic documents currently being developed under PPB, the narratives have a descriptive and justificatory function; they do not provide an objective basis for evaluating the cost-utility of an expenditure. Indeed, there hardly is any evidence that the narratives have been used for decision making; rather they seem best suited for giving the uninformed outsider some glimpses of what is going on inside.

Third, performance budgeting spawned a multitude of work-cost measurement explorations. Most used, but least useful, were the detailed workload statistics assembled by administrators to justify their requests for additional funds. On a higher level of sophistication were attempts to apply the techniques of scientific management and cost accounting to the development of work and productivity standards. In these efforts, the Bureau of the Budget had a long involvement, beginning with the issuance of the trilogy of work-measurement handbooks in 1950 and reaching its highest development in the productivity-measurement studies that were published in 1964. All these applications were at a level of detail useful for managers with operating or supervisory responsibilities, but of scant usefulness for top-level officials who have to determine organizational objectives and goals. Does it really help top officials if they know that it cost $0.07 to wash a pound of laundry or that the average postal employee processes 289 items of mail per hour? These are the main fruits of performance measurements, and they have an important place in the management of an organization. They are of great value to the operating official who has the limited function of getting a job done, but they would put a crushing burden on the policymaker whose function is to map the future course of action.

Finally, the management viewpoint led to significant departures from PPB's principal that the expenditure accounts should show total systems cost. The 1949 National Security Act (possibly the first concrete result of the Hoover report) directed the segregation of capital and operating costs in the defense budget. New York State's performance-budgeting experiment for TB hospitals separated expenditures into cost centers (a concept derived from managerial cost accounting) and within each center into fixed and variable costs. In most manpower and work measurements, labor has been isolated from other inputs. Most important, in many states and localities (and implicitly in Federal budgeting) the cost of continuing existing programs has been separated from the cost of new or expanded programs. This separation is useful for managers who build up a budget in terms of increments and decrements from the base, but is a violation of program budgeting's working assumption that all claims must be pitted against one another in the competition for funds. Likewise, the forms of separation previously mentioned make sense from the standpoint of the manager, but impair the planner's capability to compare expenditure alternatives.

The Planning Orientation

The foregoing has revealed some of the factors leading to the emergence of the planning orientation. Three important developments influenced the evolution from a management to a planning orientation.

1. Economic analysis—macro and micro—has had an increasing part in the shaping of fiscal and budgetary policy.
2. The development of new informational and decisional technologies has enlarged the applicability of objective analysis to policy making. And,
3. There has been a gradual convergence of planning and budgetary processes.

Keynesian economics with its macroanalytic focus on the impact of governmental action on the private sector had its genesis in underemployment economy of the Great Depression. In calling attention to the opportunities for attaining full employment by means of fiscal policy, the Keynesians set into motion a major restatement of the central budget function. From the utilization of fiscal policy to achieve economic objectives, it was but a few steps to the utilization of the budget process to achieve fiscal objectives. Nevertheless, between the emergence and the victory of the new economics, there was a lapse of a full generation, a delay due primarily to the entrenched balanced-budget idealology. But the full realization of the budget's economic potential was stymied on the revenue side by static tax policies and on the expenditure side by status spending policies.

If the recent tax policy of the Federal Government is evidence that the new economics has come of age, it also offers evidence of the longstanding failure of public officials to use the taxing power as a variable constraint on the economy. Previously, during normal times, the tax structure was accepted as given, and the task of fiscal analysis was to forecast future tax yields so as to ascertain how much would be available for expenditure. The new approach treats taxes as variable, to be altered periodically in accord with national policy and economic conditions. Changes in tax rates are not to be determined (as they still are in virtually all states and localities) by how much is needed to cover expenditures but by the projected impact of alternative tax structures on the economy.

It is more than coincidental that the advent of PPB has followed on the heels of the explicit utilization of tax policy to guide the economy. In macroeconomics, taxes and expenditures are mirror images of one another; a tax cut and an expenditure increase have comparable impacts. Hence, the hinging of tax policy to economic considerations inevitably led to the similar treatment of expenditures. But there were (and remain) a number of obstacles to the utilization of the budget as a fiscal tool. For one thing, the conversion of the budget process to an economic orientation probably was slowed by the Full Employment Act of 1946 which established the Council of Economic Advisers and transferred the Budget Bureau's fiscal analysis function to the Council. The institutional separation between the CEA and the BOB and between fiscal policy and budget making was not compensated by cooperative work relationships. Economic analysis had only a slight impact on expenditure policy. It offered a few guidelines (for example, that spending should be increased during recessions) and a few ideas (such as a shelf of public works projects), but it did not feed into the regular channels of budgeting. The business of preparing the budget was foremost a matter of responding to agency spending pressures, not of responding to economic conditions.

Moreover, expenditures (like taxes) have been treated virtually as givens, to be determined by the unconstrained claims of the spending units. In the absence of central policy instructions, the agencies have been allowed to vent their demands without prior restraints by central authorities and without an operational set of planning guidelines. By the time the Bureau gets into the act, it is faced with the overriding task of bringing estimates into line with projected resources. In other words, the bureau has had a budget-cutting function, to reduce claims to an acceptable level. The President's role has been similarly restricted. He is the *gatekeeper* of Federal budgeting. He directs the pace of spending increases by deciding which of the various expansions proposed by the agencies shall be included in the budget. But, as the gatekeeper, the President rarely has been able to look back at the items that have previously passed through the gate; his attention is riveted to those programs that are departures from the established base. In their limited roles, neither the Bureau nor the President has been able to inject fiscal and policy objectives into the forefront of budget preparation.

It will not be easy to wean budgeting from its utilization as an administrative procedure for financing ongoing programs to a decisional process for determining the range and direction of public objectives and the government's involvement in the economy. In the transition to a planning emphasis, an important step was the 1963 hearings of the Joint Economic Commission on *The Federal Budget as an Economic Document.* These hearings and the pursuant report of the JEC explored the latent policy opportunities in budget making. Another development was the expanded time horizons manifested by the multiyear expenditure projections introduced in the early 1960s. Something of a break-through was achieved via the revelation that the existing tax structure would yield cumulatively larger increments of uncommitted funds—estimated as much as $50 billion by 1970—which could be applied to a number of alternative uses. How much of the funds should be "returned" to the private sector through tax reductions and how much through expenditure increases? How much should go to the States and localities under a broadened system of Federal grants? How much should be allocated to the rebuilding of cities, to the improvement of education, or to the eradication of racial injustices. The traditional budget system lacked the analytic tools to cope with these questions, though decisions ultimately would be made one way or another. The expansion of the time horizon from the single year to a multiyear frame enhances the opportunity for planning and analysis to have an impact on future expenditure decisions. With a one-year perspective, almost all options have been foreclosed by previous commitments; analysis is effective only for the increments provided by self-generating revenue increases or to the extent that it is feasible to convert funds from one use to another. With a longer time span, however, many more options are open, and economic analysis can have a prominent part in determining which course of action to pursue.

So much for the macroeconomic trends in budget reform. On the microeconomic side, PPB traces its lineage to the attempts of welfare economists to construct a science of finance predicated on the principle of marginal utility. Such as science, it was hoped, would furnish objective criteria for determining the optimal allocation of public funds among competing uses. By appraising the marginal costs and benefits of alternatives (poor relief versus battleships in Pigou's classic example), it would be possible to determine which combination of expenditures afforded maximum utility. The quest for a welfare function provided the conceptual underpinning for a 1940 article on "The Lack of a Budgetary Theory" in which V. O. Key noted the absence of a theory which would determine whether "to allocate x dollars to activity A instead of activity B."[32] In terms of its direct contribution to budgetary practice, welfare economics has been a failure. It has not been possible to distill the conflicts and complexities of political life into a welfare criterion or homogeneous distribution formula. But stripped of its normative and formal overtones, its principles have been applied to budgeting by economists such as Arthur Smithies. Smithies has formulated a budget rule that "expenditure proposals should be considered in the light of the objectives they are intended to further, and in general final expenditure decisions should not be made until all claims on the budget can be considered."[33] PPB is the application of this rule to budget practice. By structuring expenditures so as to juxtapose substitutive elements within program categories, and by analyzing the cost and benefits of the various substitutes, PPB has opened the door to the use of marginal analysis in budgeting.

Actually, the door was opened somewhat by the development of new decisional and information technologies, the second item on the list of influences in the evolution of the planning orientation. Without the availability of the decisional-informational capability provided by cost-benefit and systems analysis, it is doubtful that PPB would be part of the budgetary apparatus today. The new technologies make it possible to cope with the enormous informational and analytic burdens imposed by PPB. As aids to calculation, they furnish a methodology for the analysis of alternatives, thereby expanding the range of decision-making in budgeting.

Operations research, the oldest of these technologies, grew out of complex World War II conditions that required the optimal coordination of manpower, material, and equipment to achieve defense objectives. Operations research is most applicable to those repetitive operations where the opportunity for quantification is highest. Another technology, cost-benefit analysis, was intensively adapted during the 1950s to large-scale water resource investments, and subsequently to many other governmental functions. Systems analysis is the most global of these technologies. It involves the skillful analysis of the major factors that go into the attainment of an interconnected set of objectives. Systems analysis has been applied in DOD to the choice of weapons systems, the location of military bases, and the determination of sealift-airlift requirements. Although the extension of these technologies across-the-board to government was urged repeatedly by members of the Rand Corporation during the 1950s, it was DOD's experience that set the stage for the current ferment. It cannot be doubted that the coming of PPB has been pushed ahead several years or more by the "success story" in DOD.

The third stream of influence in the transformation of the budget function has been a closing of the gap between planning and budgeting. Institutionally and operationally, planning and budgeting have run along separate tracks. The national government has been reluctant to embrace central planning of any sort because of identification with socialist management of the economy. The closest thing we have had to a central planning agency was the National Resources Planning Board in the 1939–1943 period. Currently, the National Security Council and the Council of Economic Advisors have planning responsibilities in the defense and fiscal areas. As far as the Bureau of the Budget is concerned, it has eschewed the planning units: in the States, because limitations on debt financing have encouraged the separation of the capital and operating budgets; in the cities, because the professional autonomy and land-use preoccupations of the planners have set them apart from the budgeteers.

In all governments, the appropriations cycle, rather than the anticipation of future objectives, tends to dictate the pace and posture of budgeting. Into the repetitive, one-year span of the budget is wedged all financial decisions, including those that have multiyear implications. As a result, planning, if it is done at all, "occurs independently of budgeting and with little relation to it."[34] Budgeting and planning, moreover, invite disparate perspectives: the one is conservative and negativistic; the other, innovative and expansionist. As Mosher has noted, "budgeting and planning are apposite, if not opposite. In extreme form, the one means savings; the other, spending."[35]

Nevertheless, there has been some *rapprochement* of planning and budgeting. One factor is the long lead-time in the development and procurement of hardware and capital investments. The multiyear projections inaugurated several years ago were a partial response to this problem. Another factor has been the diversity of government agencies involved in related functions. This has given rise to various *ad hoc* coordinating devices, but it also has pointed to the need for permanent machinery to integrate dispersed activities. Still another factor has been the sheer growth of Federal activities and expenditures and the need for a rational system of allocation. The operational code of planners contains three tenets relevant to these budgetary needs: (1) planning is future-oriented; it connects present decisions to the attainment of a desired future state of affairs; (2) planning, ideally, encompasses all resources involved in the attainment of future objectives. It strives for comprehensiveness. The *massive plan* is the one that brings within its scope all relevant factors; (3) planning is means-ends oriented. The allocation of resources is strictly dictated by the ends that are to be accomplished. All this is to say that planning is an economizing process, though planners are more oriented to the future than economists. It is not surprising that planners have found the traditional budget system deficient,[36] nor is it surprising that the major reforms entailed by PPB emphasize the planning function.

Having outlined the several trends in the emerging transition to a planning orientation, it remains to mention several qualifications. First, the planning emphasis is not predominant in Federal budgeting at this time. Although PPB asserts the paramountcy of planning, PPB itself is not yet a truly operational part of the budget machinery. We are now at the dawn of a new era in budgeting; high noon is still a long way off. Second, this transition has not been preceded by a reorientation of the Bureau of the Budget. Unlike the earlier change-over from control to management in which the alteration of budgetary techniques *followed* the revision of the Bureau's role, the conversion from management to planning is taking a different course—first, the installation of new techniques; afterwards, a reformulation of the Bureau's mission. Whether this sequence will hinder reform efforts is a matter that cannot be predicted, but it should be noted that in the present instance the Bureau cannot convert to a new mission by bringing in a wholly new staff, as was the case in the late 1930s and early 1940s.

What Difference Does It Make?

The starting point for the author was distinguishing the old from the new in budgeting. The interpretation has been framed in analytic terms, and budgeting has been viewed historically in three stages corresponding to the three basic functions of budgeting. In this analysis, an attempt has been made to identify the difference between the existing and the emerging as a difference between management and planning orientations.

In an operational sense, however, what difference does it make whether the central budget process is oriented toward planning rather than management? Does the change merely mean a new way of making decisions, or does it mean different decisions as well? These are not easy questions to answer, particularly since the budget system of the future will be a compound of all three functions. The case for PPB rests on the assumption that the form in which information is classified and used governs the actions of budget makers, and, conversely, that alterations in form will produce desired changes in behavior. Take away the assumption that behavior follows form, and the movement for PPB is reduced to a trivial manipulation of techniques—form for form's sake without any significant bearing on the conduct of budgetary affairs.

Yet this assumed connection between roles and information is a relatively uncharted facet of the PPB literature. The behavioral side of the equation has been neglected. PPB implies that each participant will behave as a sort of Budgetary Man, a counterpart of the classical Economic Man and Simon's Administrative Man.[37] Budgetary Man, whatever his station or role in the budget process, is assumed to be guided by an unwavering commitment to the rules of efficiency; in every instance he chooses that alternative that optimizes the allocation of public resources.

PPB probably takes an overly mechanistic view of the impact of form on behavior and underestimates the strategic and volitional aspects of budget making. In the political arena, data are used to influence the "who gets what" in budgets and appropriations. If information influences behavior, the reverse also is true. Indeed, data are more tractable than roles; participants are more likely to seek and use data which suit their preferences than to alter their behavior automatically in response to formal changes.

All this constrains, rather than negates, the impact of budget form. The advocates of PPB, probably in awareness of the above limitations, have imported into budgeting men with professional commitments to the types of analysis and norms required by the new techniques, men with a background in economics and systems analysis, rather than with general administrative training.

PPB aspires to create a different environment for choice. Traditionally, budgeting has defined its mission in terms of identifying the existing base and proposed departures from it—"This is where we are; where do we go from here?" PPB defines its mission in terms of budgetary objectives and purposes—"Where do we want to go? What do we do to get there?" The environment of choice under traditional circumstances is *incremental;* in PPB it is *teletic.* Presumably, these different processes will lead to different budgetary outcomes.

A budgeting process which accepts the base and examines only the increments will produce decisions to transfer the present into the future with a few small variations. The curve of government activities will be continuous, with few zigzags or breaks. A budget-making process which begins with objectives will require the base to compete on an equal footing with new proposals. The decisions will be more radical than those made under incremental conditions. This does not mean that each year's budget will lack continuity with the past. There are sunk costs that have to be reckoned, and the benefits of radical changes will have to outweigh the cost of terminating prior commitments. Furthermore, the extended time span of PPB will mean that big investment decisions will be made for a number of years, with each year being a partial installment of the plan. Most important, the political manifestations of sunk costs—vested interests—will bias decisions away from radical departures. The conservatism of the political system, therefore, will tend to minimize the decisional differences between traditional and PPB approaches. However, the very availability of analytic data will cause a shift in the balance of economic and political forces that go into the making of a budget.

Teletic and incremental conditions of choice lead to still another distinction. In budgeting, which is committed to the established base, the flow of budgetary decisions is upward and aggregative. Traditionally, the first step in budgeting, in anticipation of the call for estimates, is for each department to issue its own call to prepare and to submit a set of estimates. This call reaches to the lowest level capable of assembling its own estimates. Lowest level estimates form the building blocks for the next level where they are aggregated and reviewed and transmitted upward until the highest level is reached and the totality constitutes a department-wide budget. Since budgeting is tied to a base, the building-up-from-below approach is sensible; each building block estimates the cost of what it is already doing plus the cost of the increments it wants. (The building blocks, then, are decisional elements, not simply informational elements as is often assumed.)

PPB reverses the informational and decisional flow. Before the call for estimates is issued, top policy has to be made, and this policy constrains the estimates prepared below. For each lower level, the relevant policy instructions are issued by the superior level prior to the preparation of estimates. Accordingly, the critical decisional process—that of deciding on purposes and plans—has a downward and disaggregative flow.

If the making of policy is to be antecedent to the costing of estimates, there will have to be a shift in the distribution of budget responsibilities. The main energies of the Bureau of the Budget are now devoted to budget preparation; under PPB these energies will be centered on what we may term *prepreparation*—the stage of budget making that deals with policy and is prior to the preparation of the budget. One of the steps marking the advent of the planning orientation was the inauguration of the Spring Preview several years ago for the purpose of affording an advance look at departmental programs.

If budget making is to be oriented to the planning function, there probably will be a centralization of policy making, both within and among departments. The DOD experience offers some precedent for predicting that greater budgetary authority will be vested in department heads than heretofore, but there is no firm basis for predicting the degree of centralization that may derive from the relatedness of objectives pursued by many departments. It is possible that the mantle of central budgetary policy will be assumed by the Bureau; indeed, this is the expectation in many agencies. On the other hand, the Bureau gives little indication at this time that it is willing or prepared to take this comprehensive role.

Conclusion

The various differences between the budgetary orientations are charted in the table presented here. All the differences may be summed up in the statement that the ethos of budgeting will shift from justification to analysis. To far greater extent than heretofore, budget decisions will be influenced by explicit statements of objectives and by a formal weighing of the costs and benefits of alternatives.

NOTES

1. New York Bureau of Municipal Research, *Making a Municipal Budget* (New York: 1907), pp. 9–10.
2. Robert N. Anthony, *Planning and Control Systems: A Framework for Analysis* (Boston: 1965), pp. 16–18.
3. Frederick A. Cleveland, "Evolution of the Budget Idea in the United States," *Annals of the American Academy of Political and Social Science* 62 (1915): 16.
4. Ibid., p. 17.
5. See Frank J. Goodnow, "The Limit of Budgetary Control," *Proceedings, Am. Pol. Sci. Assoc.* (Baltimore: 1913), p. 72; William F. Willoughby, "Allotment of Funds by Executive Officials, An Essential Feature of Any Correct Budgetary System," ibid., pp. 78–87.
6. U.S. President's Commission on Economy and Efficiency, *The Need for a National Budget* (Washington: 1912), pp. 210–213.
7. Charles A. Beard, "Prefatory Note," ibid., p. vii.
8. New York Bureau of Municipal Research, "Some Results and Limitations of Central Financial Control in New York City," *Municipal Research* 81 (1917): 10.
9. "Next Steps," op. cit., p. 39.
10. "Next Steps," op. cit., p. 39.
11. New York Bureau, "Some Results and Limitations," op. cit., p. 9.
12. "Next Steps," op. cit., p. 35.
13. Ibid., p. 7.
14. "Next Steps," op. cit., p. 39.
15. New York Bureau, "Some Results and Limitations," op. cit., p. 7.
16. Ibid., p. 9.
17. "Next Steps," op. cit., p. 30.
18. See A. E. Buck, *Public Budgeting* (New York, 1929), pp. 181–188.
19. Charles G. Dawes, *The First Year of the Budget of the United States* (New York, 1923), preface, p. ii.
20. Lent D. Upson, "Half-Time Budget Methods," *The Annals of the American Academy of Political and Social Science* 113 (1924): 72.
21. Wylie Kilpatrick, "Classification and Measurement of Public Expenditure," *The Annals of the American Academy of Political and Social Science* 133 (1936): 20.
22. See Harold D. Smith, *The Management of Your Government* (New York, 1945).
23. Public Administration Service, *The Work Unit in Federal Administration* (Chicago, 1937).
24. U.S. Commission on Organization of the Executive Branch of the Government, *Budgeting and Accounting* (Washington, 1949) p. 8.
25. Ibid.
26. Frederick C. Mosher, *Program Budgeting: Theory and Practice* (Chicago, 1954), p. 79.
27. David Novick, *Which Program Do We Mean in "Program Budgeting?"* (Santa Monica, 1954), p. 17.
28. Lennex L. Meak and Kathryn W. Killian, *A Manual of Techniques for the Preparation, Consideration, Adoption, and Administration of Operating Budgets* (Chicago, 1963), p. 11.
29. Gladys M. Kammerer, *Program Budgeting: An Aid to Understanding* (Gainesville, 1959), p. 6.
30. Arlene Theuer Shadean, *Preparation, Review, and Execution of the State Operating Budget* (Lexington, 1963), p. 13.
31. U.S. Bureau of the Budget, *A Work Measurement System* (Washington, 1950), p. 2.
32. V. O. Key, Jr., "The Lack of a Budgetary Theory," *Am. Pol. Sci. Rev.* 34 (1940): 1138.
33. Arthur Smithies, *The Budgetary Process in the United States* (New York, 1955), p. 16.
34. Mosher, op. cit., pp. 47–48.
35. Ibid., p. 48.
36. See Edward C. Banfield, "Congress and the Budget: A Planner's Criticism," *Am. Pol. Sci. Rev.* 43 (1949): 1217–1227.
37. Herbert A. Simon, *Administrative Behavior* (New York, 1957).

Policy Analysts: A New Professional Role in Government Service

Yehezkel Dror

The main contemporary reform movement in the federal administration of the United States (and in some other countries as well) is based on an economic approach to public decision-making. The roots of this approach are in economic theory, especially microeconomics and welfare economics, and quantitative decision-theory; the main tools of this approach are operations research, cost-effectiveness and cost benefit analysis, and program budgeting and systems analysis; and the new professionals of this approach are the systems analysts. Together, these elements constitute main components of the Planning-Programming-Budgeting System, as first developed in the Department of Defense and now being extended to most executive departments and establishments.

In essence, these reforms constitute an invasion of public decision-making by economics. Going far beyond the domain of economic policy-making, the economic approach to decision-making views every decision as an allocation of resources between alternatives, that is, as an economic problem. Application of suitable tools of economic analysis should therefore, in this opinion, contribute to the improvement of decision-making, whatever the subject matter of the decision may be. This is the main innovation of the Planning-Programming-Budgeting System, which is in essence a restatement of earlier budgeting theory combined with systems analysis and put into a coherent and integrated framework.[1]

The invasion of public decision-making by economics is both unavoidable and beneficial, but fraught with danger. It is unavoidable because economics provides the only highly developed theoretical basis for improvement in highly critical decision-making processes. It is beneficial because the economic approach in the systems analysis and PPBS form can contribute to the improvement of public decision-making, if carefully utilized. It is fraught with dangers because of the inability to deal adequately with many critical elements of public policy-making and the possible distortion in decision-making resulting therefrom.

A main question is how to reap the full benefits of the economic approach and to improve public decision-making and policymaking while avoiding its pitfalls. This question becomes more and more acute with the present tendency to apply PPBS and systems analysis throughout governmental administration.

Systems Analysis and Decision-Making

In considering the dangers of system analysis (by itself and as a critical part of PPBS), we must keep in mind an important consideration: I accept as a fact that systems analysis has made very important, though limited contributions to better decision-making up to now, especially in the Department of Defense, but much of this contribution may have been due more to the wisdom, sophistication, and open-mindedness of the few outstanding practitioners of systems analysis and their readiness to fight organizational inertia and muddling-through tendencies than to their defined professional tools. Now systems analysis is to become a profession with defined job responsibilities throughout government, to be practiced by a larger group of specially trained staff officers. If this is so, we cannot rely any longer on the tacit qualities and multiple backgrounds (including, for instance, physics and engineering, in addition to economics) of the small number of highly gifted individuals who pioneered system analysis. Instead, we must develop institutional arrangements, professional training, and job definitions

---

which will provide the desired outputs with good and hopefully very good, but not necessarily outstanding, personnel.

When we look at the basic characteristics of systems analysis as a professional discipline (as distinguished from the personal wisdom of some of its pioneers), a number of weaknesses can be identified. These weaknesses are not transitory features of a new discipline, but seem to be endemic to the nature and origin of systems analysis and are introduced through it into PPBS.

Some of the important weaknesses of systems analysis from the point of view of public decision-making can be summed up as follows:[2]

1. Strong attachment to quantification and dependence upon it, including both need for quantitative models and for quantitative parameters for the variables appearing in the models.
2. Incapacity to deal with conflicting non-commensurate values (other than through neutralizing the issue when possible, by seeking out value-insensitive alternatives).
3. Requirement of clear-cut criteria of decision and well-defined missions.
4. Neglect of the problems of political feasibility and of the special characteristics of political resources (such as the power-producing effect of using political power).[3]
5. Lack of significant treatment of essential extra-rational decision elements, such as creativity, tacit knowledge, and judgment.
6. Inability to deal with large and complex systems other than through sub-optimization, which destroys the overall *Gestalt* of the more difficult and involved issues.
7. Lack of instruments for taking into account individual motivations, irrational behavior, and human idiosyncrasy.

As a result of these weaknesses, systems analysis as such is of doubtful utility for dealing with political decisions, overall strategic planning, and public policy-making. This does not disparage the importance of systems analysis for operational planning and control[4] or the essential contributions of systems analysis as one of the bases of a broader professional discipline of policy analysis. But by itself, or as a part of PPBS, systems analysis cannot deal with issues and situations where the problem is to move on from one appreciative system[5] or multidimensional space to another, or to get from one curve to a different curve.

Possible Boomerang Effects

Even so, a good prima facie argument can be made for taking systems analysis as it is and applying it to public decision-making. The principal claims in favor of this position are that systems analysis will at least permit some improvements in public decision-making. To paraphrase one of the founders of modern systems analysis, even in the situations where technology and objectives change very swiftly, good systems analysis will at least try to get on an entirely different curve and not look for a peak of a rather flat curve.[6] Furthermore, with the help of systems analysis and PPBS—so the argument may go—at the very least, we will begin to get out of the rote of inertia and incremental change onto the highway of doubting conventional wisdom and introducing desirable innovations.

These arguments would be valid if one condition is met, namely, that both the professional systems analysts and the senior staff and line of the agencies in which they serve are highly sophisticated in respect to the possibilities and limitations of systems analysis. But this is a completely unrealistic requirement. The successes of systems analysis in some domains in the Department of Defense, the brilliance of its main pioneers and first practitioners, and the exaggerated claims of some of its advocates and proponents combine to create an unrealistic level of expectation. Being evaluated in terms of such an unrealistic level of expectation, systems analysis and PPBS will often be judged as a failure. As a result, there is a great risk that the strong anti-innovation forces will be vindicated, will become stronger entrenched, and will be better able to oppose significant reforms in the future. Unsophisticated reliance on systems analysis in this way may also impair and indeed nullify the potential benefits of other important parts of PPBS, such as future orientation and multiple-year programming.

From Systems Analysis to Policy Analysis

What is needed is a more advanced type of professional knowledge, which can be used with significant benefits for the improvement of public decision-making. This professional knowledge should do for public decision-making in various issue-areas what systems analysis did in some areas of defense decision-making. To fill this rather difficult order, the various orientations, ideas, and tools of systems analysis must be developed so as to be applicable to complex and non-quantifiable issues and systems. Furthermore—and this is more important and more difficult—politics and political phenomena must be put into the focus of analysis. The term "policy analysis" seems to be suitable for the proposed professional discipline, as it combines affinity with systems analysis with the concept of policy in the broad and political sense.[7]

In essence, what is required is an integration between revised disciplines of political science and public administration on the one hand and systems analysis, decision theory, and economic theory on the other hand. This combination should be in the form of a compound rather than a mix, so as to provide a more advanced form of knowledge, rather than an eclectic collection of unrelated items. Care must be taken to achieve a real synthesis, rather than an uncritical subordination of the political to economic models, in which the specific features of politics may be lost.

To clarify the idea, let me point out some main features of policy analysis, as compared with system analysis.

1. Much attention would be paid to the political aspects of public decision-making and public policy-making (instead of ignoring or condescendingly regarding political aspects). This includes much attention to problems of political feasibility, recruitment of support, accommodations of contradicting goals, and recognition of diversity of values. Especially important are development of theories and construction of models which do full justice to the special characteristics of politics and political behavior and do not try to force them into a procrustean bed of economic terminology and theory.
2. A broad conception of decision-making and policy-making would be involved (instead of viewing all decision-making as mainly a resources allocation). Many types of critical decisions cannot be usefully approached from an economic resource allocation framework, e.g., determining the content of diplomatic notes or changing the selective draft to a randomized process. Here, qualitative exploration of new alternatives is necessary, beyond quantitative analysis and cost benefit estimation.
3. A main emphasis would be on creativity and search for new policy alternatives, with explicit attention to encouragement of innovative thinking (instead of comparative analysis of available alternatives and synthesis of new alternatives as one of the elements of analysis). A good example is the problem of reducing smoking—where the problem is clearly one of inventing new promising alternatives, rather than cost-benefit analysis of different known alternatives, none of which is good. The requirement of creativity and innovation of alternatives has far-reaching implications, as there is reason to suspect incompatibility between the personality traits, training, and organizational arrangements optimal for analysis (in the strict meaning of the term) and those optimal for invention of alternatives. The latter requires more "creative" personalities, structural tools to search for new ideas (for instance, through knowledge surveys), pro-innovating organizational arrangements (e.g., cross-fertilization and stimulation through brain trusts and interdisciplinary teams), imaginative and pro-risk entrepreneurship atmosphere, and changes in overall organizational climate (e.g., raising organizational levels of aspiration). Combining systems analysis with budgeting, as in PPBS, may be good for quantitative analysis, but it is not a way to encourage and stimulate new and risky and expensive-looking policy ideas.

4. There would be extensive reliance on tacit understanding, *Gestalt*-images, qualitative models, and qualitative methods (instead of main emphasis on explicit knowledge and quantitative models and tools). This involves imaginative thinking, systematic integration of trained intuition into policy analysis (e.g., through the Delphi Method), development of qualitative tools (such as metaphor construction, scenarios, counterfactual thinking), and construction of broad qualitative models of complex issues in cooperation with social scientists and other professionals (instead of ignoring the latter, in effect, or regarding them as passive sources of quantitative data).
5. There would be much more emphasis on "futuristic"[8] thinking with long-range predictions, alternative states-of-the-future, and speculative thinking on the future (in most areas up to the year 2000) as essential background for current policy-making.
6. The approach would be looser and less rigid, but nevertheless systematic, one which would recognize the complexity of means ends interdependence, the multiplicity of relevant criteria of decision, and the partial and tentative nature of every analysis (instead of striving for a clear-cut criterion and dominant solutions). In policy analysis, sequential decision-making and constant learning is dominant,[9] and clarification of issues, invention of new alternatives, more consideration of the future, and reduction of primary disagreements to secondary disagreements are main goals.

Policy Analysts as Government Staff Officers

To introduce urgently needed improvements in public decision-making, while avoiding the possible boomerang effects of systems analysis, policy analysis must become an important new professional role in government service. Policy analysis staff positions should be established in all principal administrative agencies and establishments, near the senior policy determining positions, operating, in general, formally as advisory staff to top executives and senior line positions and actually establishing with them a symbiotic cooperative relationship. Certainly, the professional staff of the federal planning-programming-budgeting system units should be trained also in policy analysis.

Policy analysis does not presume to bring about a radical change in policy-making. It does not presume to create omniscient units, which exist outside any socio-political-organizational framework and operate by a "downward and disaggregative flow" of top policy and policy directions.[10] Good policy analysis can at best become an additional component in aggregative policy-making, contributing to that process some better analysis, some novel ideas, some futuristic orientation, and some systematic thought. Policy analyses are one of the bridges between science and politics,[11] but they do not transform the basic characteristics of "the political" and of organization behavior.[12] In order to contribute to the improvement of policymaking, policy analysts should be dispersed throughout the higher echelons of government service (and, indeed, throughout the social guidance cluster) as part of the effort to improve aggregate policy-making through introducing into the clash and interaction between competing partisan interests[13] an additional element.[14] Such redundancy will increase the aggregate effect of policy analysis on policy-making, while also providing a safeguard against trained incapacities, one-sided value bias, and professional prejudices.

The main role of policy analysts in government—as parts of PPBS, in distinct high-level staff units, in separate independent advisory corporations, and in various other organizational locations—is to contribute to public decision-making a broad professional competence, based simultaneously on systems analysis and quantitative decision-theory and on a new outlook in political science and public administration. The aim of policy analysis is to permit improvements in decision-making and policy-making by permitting fuller consideration of a broader set of alternatives, within a wider context, with the help of more systematic tools. No metamorphosis of policy-making is aimed at, but improvements of, say, 10 to 15 percent in complex public decision-making and policy-making can be achieved through better integration of knowledge and policy-making

TABLE 1

A Tentative Comparison of Some Features of Systems Analysis and Policy Analysis

FEATURE	SYSTEMS ANALYSIS	POLICY ANALYSIS
Base discipline	Economics, operations research, quantitative decision sciences	As systems analysis, *plus*-political science, public administration, parts of the social sciences and psychology (in the future, new interdiscipline of policy sciences)
Main emphasis	Quantitative analysis	Qualitative analysis and innovation of new alternatives
Main desired qualities of professionals	Bright, nonconventional, high analytical capacities	As systems analysis, *plus* maturity, explicit and tacit knowledge of political and administrative reality, imagination, and idealistic realism
Main decision criteria	Efficiency in allocation of resources	Multiple criteria, including social, economic, and political
Main methods	Economic analysis, quantitative model construction	As systems analysis, *plus* qualitative models and analyses, imaginative and futuristic thought, and integration of tacit knowledge
Main location	In PPBS—in Bureau of the Budget and agency budget units	Throughout the social guidance cluster in different forms
Main outputs when applied to public decision-making	Clearly better decisions with respect to limited issues; possible boomerang effect if applied to highly complex political issues	Somewhat better decisions on highly complex and political issues; educational impact on political argumentation and long-range improvements in operation of public policymaking system
Requisites for development of knowledge and preparation of professionals	Already operational; further development requires some changes in university curricula	Changes in orientation of political science and public administration as academic disciplines—establishment of new university curricula and of new policy science interdisciplines

with the help of policy analysis—and this is a lot. This, I think, is certainly much more than can be achieved by systems analysis, outside relatively simple issue-areas and sub-systems.

It is premature to try and set down in detail the characteristics of the new professional role of policy analysis in government. These must be evolved largely through a careful process of learning and sequential decision-making. Nevertheless, some suggestive features can be presented tentatively in the form of a comparison between systems analysis and policy analysis (*see Table 1*).

Some Implications

The decision in 1965 to introduce PPBS in the federal administration and the preparation for including a social report in the State of the Union message[15] both provide in the United States an opportunity to introduce policy analysis as a new professional role in government service and create an urgent need to do so as expediently as possible. This involves a number of steps.

Immediately needed is a change in conception in respect to the introduction of PPBS, with explicit recognition of the necessity to move in the direction of policy analysis. As already pointed out, the main pioneers of systems analysis are highly sophisticated in their substantive work and often actually practice some policy analysis. This actual sophistication must be put into the formalized system and institutionalized directives. More important still, the schemes for training of staff for PPBS at the various special university programs must be changed, so as to move from nearly exclusive preoccupation with qualitative methods to full emphasis of quantitative and political analysis.[16] Later on, policy analysis units of different forms should be established at focal decision centers throughout the social guidance cluster.

The development of policy analysis depends on a number of transformations in the disciplines of political science and public adminis-tration. The one-sided invasion of public decision-making by economics was caused largely by the inability of modern political science and public administration to make significant contributions to governmental decision-making. Economics developed a highly advanced action-oriented theory and put it to the test of innovating economic policy-making. At the same time, the modern study of political science and public administration became sterilized by an escape from political issues into behavioral "value-free" research and theory, or exhausted itself in suggestions for insignificant incremental improvements on the technical level.

This trend must be revised. A new approach in political science and public administration, oriented towards the study and improvement of public policy-making, constitutes, in the longer run, a main avenue for the improvement of public decision-making.[17] A new interdiscipline of "policy science" may also be necessary to provide a sound theoretical and institutional basis for policy analysis knowledge and policy analysis professionals. In the meantime, serious boomerang effects and damage can and should be avoided and the foundations for such a study and profession can and should be laid by changing the present efforts to introduce systems analysis in government service in the direction of policy analysis.

Notes

1. This is brought out both from the papers published in "Planning-Programming-Budgeting System: A Symposium," *Pub. Adm. Rev.* (December 1966), pp. 243–310 (hereafter referred to as *Symposium*) and from the literature on program budgeting, e.g., David Novick, ed., *Program Budgeting* (Cambridge: Harvard University Press, 1965). The well-taken communication by Frederick C. Mosher in *Pub. Adm. Rev.* (March 1967), pp. 67–71, mentions this important innovation of PPBS, but does not give it the emphasis which it deserves.
2. Many of the pioneers of systems analysis are aware of some of these weaknesses. A number of them have left systems analysis and devote themselves to development of broad tools, mainly in the area of strategy and conflict studies (e.g., Herman Kahn and Albert

Wohlstetter). Others, at the Rand Corporation, continue to broaden systems analysis by developing non-quantitative tools, such as the Delphi Method and Operational Gaming. See, for instance, Olaf Helmer, *Social Technology* (New York: Basic Books, 1966). Recently, some important and able efforts have also been made to examine explicitly the relations between systems analysis and the political process, though without adequate attention to required and possible changes in the methods of systems analysis, so as to adjust them to broader political issues. See, for instance, James R. Schlesinger, *Systems Analysis and the Political Process* (Santa Monica: Rand Corp., 1967), p. 3464. These are important, though too timid, steps on the way from system analysis to policy analysis. But "systems analysis" as usually presented and as it appears in PPBS does not share the benefits of these first-step new advances.

3. The overwhelming influence of economic ideas influences even highly sophisticated political scientists to view political power as similar to economic resources while ignoring the critical differences—such as the often immediate power-producing effect of using political resources in the form of favors or coercive moves (see *Symposium*, p. 309). The economic models of resources which, for instance, can either be consumed or invented with continuous, concave, production possibility frontier curves do not apply to political power.
4. For the distinction between strategic planning, management control, and operational control, see Robert N. Anthony, *Planning and Control Systems: A Framework for Analysis* (Boston: Graduate School of Business Administration, Harvard University, 1965).
5. For the concept of "appreciative system" and its importance in public decision-making, see Sir Geoffrey Vickers, *The Art of Judgment: A Study of Policy Making* (New York: Basic Books, 1965), chap. 4.
6. See Albert Wohlstetter, "Analysis and Design of Conflict Systems," in *Analysis for Military Decisions,* ed. Edward S. Quade (Chicago: Rand McNally, 1964), p. 106.
7. One weakness of the term "analysis" is its calculative-logical connotation. In policy analysis a very important part of the job is to invent new alternatives and to engage in creative and imaginative thinking. Nevertheless, I prefer a concept which somewhat understates the role rather than too presumptuous, too "political," and too frightening a term, such as "policy advertiser" or "policy consultant."
8. E.g., see Dennis Gabor, *Inventing the Future* (New York: Alfred A. Knopf, 1964); Bertrand de Jouvenel, *The Art of Conjecture* (New York: Basic Books, 1967; French original published in 1964). For an application to political science, see Benjamin Akzin, "On Conjecture in Political Science," *Political Studies* (February 1966), pp. 1–14.
9. These methods are sometimes mentioned in passing, but are not at present actually integrated into systems analysis and PPBS, e.g., see *Symposium*, p. 262.
10. *Symposium*, p. 258.
11. For the concept, see Don K. Price, *The Scientific Estate* (Cambridge: Harvard University Press, Belknap Press, 1965), esp. pp. 123–126.
12. The tendency in systems analysis and PPBS to ignore organizational behavior is illustrated by the intention to rely on planned outputs as a standard for appraising actual outputs (*Symposium*, p. 275). As is well known, both from organization theory and from bitter experience, the defensive tendencies of organizations will operate to put planning output in line with expected output, well below optimal or even preferred outputs. The DOD may have been in some respects an exception as a result of its special structure, the personality of the Secretary of Defense, Presidential backing, and—perhaps most important of all—the external pressure of acute competition with active adversaries. But in ordinary organizations, cooperation by the senior executives is essential for significant changes in the quality of outputs. Interestingly enough, none of the papers in the *Symposium* mentions this requisite.
13. Compare Charles E. Lindblom, *The Intelligence of Democracy* (New York: Free Press, 1965).

14. The dangers of nonaggregative view of policy-making are illustrated by doubtful conclusions in respect to the effects of the establishment of the Council of Economic Advisors (*Symposium,* p. 254) and of unrestricted federal grants-in-aid (*Symposium,* p. 268). See Edward S. Flash, Jr., *Economic Advice and Presidential Leadership* (New York: Columbia University Press, 1965), esp. chap. 8 and 9; Walter W. Heller, *New Dimensions of Political Economy* (Cambridge: Harvard University Press, 1966), chap. 3.
15. See Bertram M. Gross, *The State of the Nation: Social Systems Accounting* (Tavistock Publications Ltd., 1966). An earlier version is "The State of the Nation: Social Systems Accounting," in *Social Indicators,* ed. Raymond A. Bauer (Cambridge: MIT Press, 1966), pp. 154–271. See also Bertram M. Gross, ed., "Social Goals and Indicators for American Society," *Annals of the American Academy of Political and Social Science* (May 1967). At present Senate hearings have already started on S-843, which proposes establishment of a council of social advisers and an annual social report of the President.
16. Some possibilities for doing so are illustrated by a seven-month graduate course for systems and policy-analysis staff officers organized by the Israeli government as part of an effort to improve decision-making and administrative planning. See Yehezkel Dror, "Improvement of Decision-Making and Administrative Planning in the Israel Government Administration," in *Public Administration in Israel and Abroad 1966* (Jerusalem, 1967), pp. 121–131.
17. For an effort in this direction see my book, *Public Policy-Making Reexamined* (San Francisco: Chandler, 1967).

The Life Cycle of Bureaus

Anthony Downs

How Bureaus Come into Being

Types of Bureau Genesis Bureaus are generally created in one of four different ways. First, a bureau can be formed by what Max Weber called the routinization of charisma.[1] A group of men brought together by their personal devotion to a charismatic leader may transform itself into a bureaucratic structure in order to perpetuate his ideas. Second, a bureau may be deliberately created almost out of nothing by one or more groups in society in order to carry out a specific function for which they perceive a need. Many of the agencies in the federal government formed during the New Deal years are of this type. Third, a new bureau can split off from an existing bureau, as the Air Force did from the Army after World War II. Fourth, a bureau may be created through "entrepreneurship" if a group of men promoting a particular policy (such as communism) gains enough support to establish and operate a large nonmarket organization devoted to that policy.

All of these geneses have three things in common: the bureau is initially dominated either by advocates or zealots, it normally goes through an early phase of rapid growth, and it must immediately begin seeking sources of external support in order to survive.

Dominance by Advocates or Zealots in New Bureaus In a vast majority of cases, a bureau starts as the result of aggressive agitation and action by a small group of zealots who have a specific idea they want to put into practice on a large scale. This is true by definition of bureaus created through "spontaneous entrepreneurship." Charismatic leaders also qualify as zealots. They attract a small group of disciples who eventually need to support themselves. This need tends to modify the original group into some more formal organization. In many cases, it becomes a predominantly bureaucratic organization. Thus, the Franciscan Order can be considered a bureaucratic offshoot from the leadership of St. Francis.

Almost every bureau formed by splitting off from an existing bureau is initially generated by the zealotry of a few members of the existing bureau. Some zealots are found in all bureaus—indeed, in almost all human organizations. This is true because the personal characteristics necessary for zealotry occur spontaneously in a certain fraction of any society's population. This fraction is higher in modern societies than in tradition-oriented societies, since the former encourage innovation in general. Also, the proportion of zealots in a given bureau may differ sharply from that in society as a whole, because some bureaus tend to attract zealots and others to repel them. As a result, the proportion of zealots in different bureaus varies widely. Nevertheless, a certain number appear spontaneously in every bureau.

When a group of such zealots somehow conceive a new function they believe their bureau should undertake, they form a nucleus agitating for change. Enthused by their idea, they persuade their superiors to give them some resources and manpower to develop it. If their efforts prove successful, they gradually enlarge their operations. For these operations to generate a new bureau, they must be technically distinct from the other activities of the parent bureau. As the practitioners of the new specialty become more immersed in it, their terminology, interests, and even policy outlooks become more unlike those of the remainder of the parent bureau. Hence a growing conflict usually springs up between these two groups. The new specialists eventually become convinced that they cannot fully exploit the potentialities of

---

Source: From Anthony Downs, Inside Bureaucracy, pp. 5–23

their operations within the parent bureau. This marks a critical stage in the life of the new section. It can either be suppressed by the traditionalists, or be successful in breaking off into a new bureau. The key factor is the amount of support the new section generates outside of the parent bureau. If the new section's leaders can establish a strong clientele or power base beyond the control of their immediate superiors, then they have some leverage in agitating for relative autonomy. In some cases, they will establish autonomy very quickly; in others it will take years of struggle and a strong push from the external environment. But in all cases, it is purposeful agitation by men specifically interested in promoting a given program that generates the splitting off of new bureaus from existing ones (or new sections within a bureau from existing sections). Hence the new bureau (or section) is initially dominated by the zealots whose efforts have brought it into being.

Only in bureaus created out of nothing by external agents is there initially no "small band of warriors" whose agitation has founded the bureau. In this case, politicians, existing bureaucrats, or members of private firms or unions have discerned the need for a new organization designed to accomplish a specific purpose. They round up the legal authority to establish this organization, select someone to run it, and give him an initial set of resources. Examples of such creation are the Commodity Credit Corporation[2] and the new campuses of the University of California.

However, new bureaus thus formed out of nothing usually behave very much like those formed around a nucleus of zealots. The ideas upon which a new bureau is based have generally originated with some group of zealots. In many cases, the leading proponents of these ideas are immediately put in charge of the bureau. In any case, whoever is running a bureau entrusted with a new function soon finds that his recruiting efforts are most successful with men who have a proclivity toward that function—including the zealots who started the idea, or their disciples. Moreover, since the top administrator and his staff will normally be judged by their success in carrying out this function, they also tend to become strong advocates themselves.

The Struggle for Autonomy No bureau can survive unless it is continually able to demonstrate that its services are worthwhile to some group with influence over sufficient resources to keep it alive. If it is supported by voluntary contributions, it must impress potential contributors with the desirability of sacrificing resources to obtain its services. If it is a government bureau, it must impress those politicians who control the budget that its functions generate political support or meet vital social needs.

Generation of such external support is particularly crucial for a new bureau. True, some "new" bureaus have already succeeded in gaining support, or else they would not have been able to split off from their parent agency. Similarly, an organization created by entrepreneurship can grow large enough to qualify as a bureau only if it has external support. Even bureaus formed by the routinization of charisma have attracted outside support because of the personal magnetism of their original leader. Thus only bureaus created almost out of nothing come into being without already having provided valuable services for "outsiders." Even they have some ready-made sources of external support, since their functions were being demanded by someone.

Yet the survival of new bureaus is often precarious. Their initial external sources of support are usually weak, scattered, and not accustomed to relations with the bureau. The latter must therefore rapidly organize so that its services become very valuable to the users. Only in this way can it motivate users to support it.

Once the users of the bureau's services have become convinced of their gains from it, and have developed routinized relations with it, the bureau can rely upon a certain amount of inertia to keep on generating the external support it needs. But in the initial stages of its life, it must concentrate on developing these "automatic" support generators. This critical drive for autonomy will determine whether or not it will survive in the long run.

This does not mean that members of the new bureau are interested solely in its survival. In fact, they are more interested in performing its social functions. This follows from the fact that the new bureau is initially dominated by advocates or zealots, who are not primarily motivated by self-interest.

In some cases, the social functions involved are inherently incapable of generating external support in the long run. For example, a bureau set up to plan a specific operation (such as the invasion of Normandy) eliminates its external support when it carries out its function. However, most bureaus have functions that cannot be adequately discharged in the long run if the bureaus do not continue to exist. Hence even pure altruism would lead their top officials to be vitally concerned about bureau survival.

To this motive must be added the motive of self-interest described by Peter Clark and James Wilson: "Few [organizations] disband willingly, as neither executives nor members are eager to end an activity that rewards them."[3] Thus officials in almost every new bureau place a high priority on creating conditions that will insure the bureau's survival.

As Clark and Wilson point out, bureau survival is closely related to the creation of relative autonomy by each bureau:

> The proliferation of associations and the division of labor in society has meant that there is almost no way for an organization to preserve itself by simply seeking ends for which there are no other advocates. Thus, the maintenance of organizational autonomy is a critical problem. By *autonomy* we refer to the extent to which an organization possesses a distinctive area of competence, a clearly demarcated clientele or membership, and undisputed jurisdiction over a function, service, goal, issue, or cause. Organizations seek to make their environment stable and certain and to remove threats to their identities. Autonomy gives an organization a reasonably stable claim to resources and thus places it in a more favorable position from which to compete for those resources. Resources include issues and causes as well as money, time, effort, and names.[4]

Rapid Growth of Young Bureaus Few bureaus ever achieve such perfect autonomy that they are immune from threats to their survival. However, a bureau can attain a certain initial degree of security as noted above. This presupposes that it has become large enough to render useful services, and old enough to have established routinized relationships with its major clients. We will refer to these minimal size and age levels as the bureau's *initial survival threshold.*

There is always a certain time interval between the beginnings of a bureau and the attainment of the initial survival threshold. Sometimes this period occurs before its formal "birth" as a separate organization. In other cases, a bureau's fight to reach the threshold begins with its formal establishment.

As a general rule, a bureau arrives at this threshold after a period of rapid growth in both its size and the relative social significance of its functions. This usually occurs in response to external environmental conditions favorable to the expansion of the bureau's functions. For example, the Army Air Force grew extremely rapidly during World War II in response to the need for military air power. This experience convinced Congress (stimulated by members of the Army Air Force seeking autonomy) that it should establish a separate Air Force. The formal birth of the Air Force thus marked the end of its critical creation period, which began in the 1920s.

For bureaus that do not develop by splitting off from existing agencies, rapid growth normally occurs immediately after they have been formally born as separate agencies. The leaders of such a new bureau must quickly serve enough customers to reach an initial survival threshold before their original allocation of resources is exhausted, or its replenishment is blocked.

Bureaus created through entrepreneurship are generally not successful until the zeal of the nucleus group coincides with environmental conditions favorable to the function they are promoting. Then other agents in society bestow enough resources on this nucleus so it can rapidly expand to meet the need its members have long been advocating.

Bureaus formed through the routinization of charisma generally do not experience rapid expansion until after the attraction of the charismatic leader has been transformed into organizational machinery. In most religions, this has not occurred until after the original leader's death.

Whatever its origin, a fledgling bureau is most vulnerable to annihilation by its enemies immediately before it attains it initial survival threshold. Then it has not yet generated enough external support to resist severe attacks.

Since most organizations have both functional and allocational rivals, the possibility that a bureau will be destroyed by its enemies is a real one. Its *functional* rivals are other agencies whose social functions are competitive with those of the bureau itself. Private power companies are competitive in this way with the Rural Electrification Administration. Its *allocational* rivals are other agencies who compete with it for resources, regardless of their functional relationships with it. In government, all bureaus supported by the same fund-raising agency (such as Congress) are allocationally competitive. In the private sector, allocational competition is usually indirect. The community fund, for example, competes with all forms of private expenditure for consumers' dollars. Thus the general scarcity of resources makes almost everyone an enemy of a new bureau unless it can demonstrate its usefulness to him. A bureau's infancy therefore nearly always involves a fight to gain resources in spite of this latent hostility.

If the new bureau has strong functional rivals, or if it is designed to regulate or inhibit the activities of powerful social agents, then it will be severely opposed from the start. These antagonists often seek to capture the new bureau's functions themselves, or suppress them altogether. Hence they try to block it from establishing a strong external power base. The bureau may have to fight strongly during its infancy to avoid being disbanded or swallowed by some larger existing bureau.

Some bureaus never succeed in reaching their initial survival threshold but may exist for years in a state of continuous jeopardy. An example is the Civilian Defense Agency, which has recently been swallowed by the Army. Such agencies have been unable to establish firm autonomy largely because they have no strong clientele with power in the U.S. political system. Their functions do not endow them with a host of well-organized domestic beneficiaries, or a powerful set of suppliers with no alternative markets (such as the suppliers of the Department of Defense). Thus, the single most important determinant of whether a bureau can establish autonomy (and how fast it can do so) is the character of its power setting. If its suppliers or beneficiaries are strong and well organized in comparison with its rivals and sufferers, then it will probably quickly gain a clearly autonomous position.

The Dynamics of Growth

The Cumulative Effects of Growth or Decline The major causes of both growth and decline in bureaus are rooted in exogenous factors in their environment. As society develops over time, certain social functions grow in prominence and others decline. Bureaus are inevitably affected more strongly by these external developments than by any purely internal changes. However, the interplay between external and internal development tends to create certain cumulative effects of growth or decline. They occur because bureaus can experience significant changes in the character of their personnel in relatively short periods of time. In spite of the career nature of bureau employment, there is often a considerable turnover of personnel in specific bureaus. Also, growth that doubles or triples the size of a bureau in a short time can swiftly alter its whole structure and character.

1. Dominance in bureaus. A shift in only a small proportion of the officials in a bureau can have a profound effect upon its operations. If most of the officials occupying key positions in a bureau are of one type (that is, conservers, climbers, and so on), then the bureau and its behavior will be *dominated* by the traits typical of that type. This relatively small group of key officials can exercise dominance even if a majority of bureau members are of other types.

The possibility of a few men dominating the activities and "spirit" of a whole bureau arises because its hierarchical structure tends to concentrate power disproportionately at the top. In some situations, however, it is difficult to tell whether a bureau really is dominated by one type, or is staffed by such a mixture of officials that no one type is dominant.

2. The growth accelerator effect. Let us imagine a bureau in a state of "perfect equilibrium" with a zero growth rate over time. Suddenly its social function becomes much more important than it had been. As a result, the bureau's sovereign and other agents in its environment direct it to expand its activities and staff rapidly, giving it the resources to do so. An example is NASA's experience shortly after Sputnik I.

Any organization experiencing rapid overall growth provides many more opportunities for promotion in any given time period than a static one. New supervisory positions are created, thereby attracting new personnel who are interested in rapid promotion; that is, climbers. At the same time conservers will not be drawn to fast-growing bureaus, or may even be repelled by them, because rapid growth is normally accompanied by uncertainty, constant shuffling of organizational structure, and hard work.[5] As a result, fast-growing bureaus will experience a rising proportion of climbers and a declining proportion of conservers. Moreover, this proportional increase in climbers will be larger in high-level positions than in the bureau as a whole. Climbers will rise faster because they deliberately pursue promotion more than others. They are much more innovation-prone than conservers, and the bureau needs innovators in order to carry out its newly expanded functions. Hence objective "natural selection" within the bureau, as well as the subjective selection caused by differences in personal motivation, will cause climbers to be selected for promotion faster than conservers. This means that the prominence of climbers (and other innovation-prone officials such as zealots and advocates) will increase in a fast-growing bureau, even if that bureau is initially dominated by conservers.

The bureau becomes continuously more willing and able to innovate and to expand its assigned social functions by inventing new ones or "capturing" those now performed by other less dynamic organizations. Such further expansion tends to open up even more opportunities for promotion. This in turn attracts more climbers, who make the bureau still more willing and able to innovate and expand, and so on. Rapid growth of a bureau's social functions thus leads to a cumulative change in the character of its personnel which tends to accelerate its rate of growth still further.

3. Brakes on acceleration. This growth acceleration soon runs into serious obstacles. First, even though the bureau's original social function expanded greatly in relative importance, that function must still compete allocationally with others for social attention and resources. Therefore, as the accelerating bureau grows larger, it encounters more and more resistance to further relative growth of this function at the expense of other activities in society. This has certainly happened to NASA.

Second, the ever-expanding bureau soon engenders hostility and antagonism from functionally competitive bureaus. Its attempt to grow by taking over their functions is a direct threat to their autonomy. Hence the total amount of bureaucratic opposition to the expansion of any one bureau rises the more it tries to take over the functions of existing bureaus.

Third, the bureau encounters the difficulty of continuing to produce impressive results as its organization grows larger and more unwieldy. The bureau cannot generate external support (except among its suppliers) without producing services beneficial to someone outside its own members. Therefore, a bureau must periodically come up with impressive results if it wishes to sustain its growth. NASA's staging of dramatic events at well-spaced intervals illustrates this concept. But as the bureau grows larger and takes on more functions, it often becomes increasingly difficult to produce such convincing results. Increased size and complexity cause greater difficulties of planning and coordination. Also, a higher proportion of the efforts of top echelon officials will be devoted to coordination and planning. This means that the best talent in the bureau will be diverted away from action into administration.

As the bureau gets larger, the average level of talent therein is likely to decline. This level may initially rise as ambitious and promotion-oriented climbers flow into it during the first phase of its fast growth. This is especially likely because of a certain "critical mass" effect. It is hard for a bureau to recruit one well-known physicist when it has none; but once it has two or three, others are attracted by the chance to work with this distinguished team. Nevertheless, the tendency for average talent to rise with growth eventually reverses itself. Once the bureau has all the high-level talent it can command during its first stages of growth, it must satisfy itself with lesser talent as it grows even larger. True, if the bureau expands into entirely different fields, it can start all over again at the top of the talent list. Hence, this growth-braking effect is less serious if the bureau grows by taking on new or different functions than if it grows by performing one set of functions more intensively.

Fourth, conflicts among the climbers who flood into a fast-growing bureau provide an internal check. As the proportion of climbers rises, a higher proportion of their efforts is devoted to internal politics and rivalry rather than performance of their social functions. This also tends to reduce the bureau's ability to provide impressive demonstrations of its efficiency.

The declining ability to produce impressive results as the bureau grows larger may be offset for a time by increasing economies of scale. Such economies may enable the bureau to produce more outputs per unit of input, but they do not reduce the amount of external opposition generated by every attempt to expand the bureau's total inputs. Eventually these factors choke off accelerated (or perhaps all) growth. This prevents the bureau from expanding indefinitely once it has experienced an initial spurt of high-speed growth.

4. ***The decelerator effort.*** Whenever the relative growth rate of a bureau declines below the average for all bureaus, its personnel may change in ways almost exactly opposite to those that make up the growth accelerator. This *decelerator effect* is most likely to occur when the bureau is forced to reduce its total membership because of a sharp drop in the relative significance of its social function. Such a decline, stagnation, or just slower than average growth tends to reduce the opportunity for promotion within the bureau to a level below that prevailing in comparable organizations. This will usually serve notice for climbers to depart. However, not all climbers have skills that are easily transferable to other organizations. Such transferability is an important factor determining the climber's mobility from bureau to bureau. Still, in most cases, many climbers will respond to a sharp decline in the bureau's growth rate by jumping to other bureaus. Also, those who have reached high positions in the bureau will lose hope of climbing much higher, and will tend to become conservers instead of climbers. Such changes reduce the proportion of climbers in the bureau and increase the proportion of conservers in key positions. As a result, the entire bureau will shift toward greater conserver dominance, thereby reducing its ability to innovate and the desire to expand its functions. Then, whenever opportunities for innovation of function-expansion do present themselves, the bureau will be less able, or willing, to take advantage of them. It may even lose functions to other more aggressive and innovation-prone bureaus. Thus, once a bureau starts to shrink, or even just experiences an abnormally slow growth rate over an extensive period, it sets in motion forces that tend to make it shrink even faster, or grow even more slowly.

However, this decelerator effect is not entirely symmetrical with the growth accelerator for the following reasons. First, the climbers who are left in the bureau will still tend to rise faster than nonclimbers. Second, the number of top jobs (which are soon occupied by climbers) will go up faster during acceleration periods than it goes down during deceleration periods. Third, since all types of officials, including conservers, resist shrinkage in their importance of resources, the resistance aroused by reductions in bureau size tends to be stronger than the enthusiasm caused by growth. Accelerators and decelerators cause more of a ratchet movement in the life of a single bureau than a smooth up-and-down curve.

These factors function as checks on the tendency of the decelerator to reduce the size of a bureau once it has stopped growing. The fact that reduction of a bureau's services below some minimal level will create strong protests from its direct beneficiaries serves as another check.

5. ***"Qualitative growth" without expansion.***[6] A logical deduction from our accelerator and decelerator principles is that

slow-growing or stable organizations of a certain type will generally be staffed by less talented personnel (in terms of innovation ability) than fast-growing organizations of the same type. However, this conclusion seems at variance with the experience of U.S. university faculties. In recent years, the fastest expansion in total faculty size has occurred at state-financed schools, yet nearly all measures of faculty quality show that the best-rated private universities have managed to maintain a higher caliber than their faster-growing state rivals. The reason for this is that these private universities have experienced rapid qualitative growth without quantitative expansion.

What really attracts climbers is not promotion *per se*, but increased power, income, and prestige. Normally, bureaus offer their members these perquisites primarily through promotion. They can usually promote many people rapidly only if fast growth creates more high-level positions. However, if the organization in essence promotes everyone simultaneously by increasing the power, income, and prestige of nearly all its members without growing larger, it can achieve the same effects. This is precisely what top-level private universities have accomplished. They have continued to offer both new recruits and existing faculty members higher salaries, more freedom from bureaucratic interference, and greater time for research than their state-financed rivals. Moreover, the extremely high turnover in most university faculties has made it possible to offer low-level members relatively rapid increases in rank without either expanding, forcibly ejecting present high-ranking members, or drastically increasing the ratio of high-ranking to low-ranking positions.

An organization can maintain high-quality personnel (in terms of innovation ability) even if it does not experience relatively rapid growth in size, so long as it experiences such growth in the incentives it offers its members. But this implies that it receives ever more resources from its environment for performing tasks requiring no more man-hours of input. This can happen only if the value of the members' outputs per man-hour of input rises sharply. Normally, such increased productivity occurs only when there is a dramatic increase in the relative social value of the organization's function. Again, this is precisely what has been going on at top-level private universities. As the total number of students seeking higher education has shot upward, the demand for education at the best-rated schools has zoomed even faster. Moreover, an increased emphasis on basic research occurred at the same time, thanks to the impact of Sputnik I. Therefore, top-level private universities have been able both to raise their tuitions and to attract larger research grants. These added funds have made it possible for them to up-grade the incentives offered to their faculties without experiencing rapid growth in size.

6. Some effects of rapid growth in a fragmentalized bureaucracy carrying out a single function. The above discussion of universities illustrates the operation of *fragmentalized systems* of bureaus all carrying out the same functions. Some bureaus enjoy a relative monopoly of responsibility for social functions in a given area. Examples are the U.S. Post Office Department and the Soviet Army. Other bureaus are individual units in much larger fragmentalized systems of organizations serving a single major social function. Relatively pure examples are universities and churches. Less pure examples are elementary and high schools and local governments in metropolitan areas. They have a monopoly in a given area, but their clients can and do move in order to be within the jurisdiction of the particular bureau whose services they desire.

When there is a rapid growth in the relative social importance of the function served by such a system, the system as a whole normally expands to meet this increased demand. This can involve the addition of new bureaus to the system, the expansion of existing bureaus, or both. Under such conditions, the "laws" of acceleration and deceleration we have set forth above apply to the system as a whole rather than just to individual units therein. Thus, the great relative increase in demand for university faculty members has resulted in the attraction of many climbers into this field whose counterparts in former years went into business or other fields.

The "top" of the system to which climbers rise rapidly consists of positions that provide the highest levels of income, prestige, power, and other perquisites. It is at least conceivable that these top positions may be disproportionately concentrated within a few bureaus. This is particularly likely if the demand for the highest quality of service provided by the system has risen even faster than the demand for its service as a whole. In such a case, the particular bureaus providing the highest quality of service may be able to increase their incomes (by getting more appropriations, more donations, and higher prices) faster than the system as a whole. Then they can offer their members a more rapid upgrading of incentives than the rest of the system. As a result, the most ambitious climbers will gravitate to these top-ranking bureaus, even if they do not individually expand in size. In fact, by deliberately refusing to expand, these bureaus can avoid the dilution of these top-quality personnel with the less-talented people necessary to staff rapid quantitative growth. This will reinforce their reputations for high quality, and thereby attract even higher demand for their services.

This is approximately what has happened among universities. The situation is complicated by the fact that universities depend significantly upon voluntary quid pro quo transactions for their incomes, and are therefore only quasi-bureaucratic in terms of our definition. However, the foregoing analysis illustrates that the basic conclusions made here about bureaus apply to those in fragmentalized systems too, but must sometimes be considered applicable to the system as a whole rather than individual bureaus therein.

Why Bureaus Seek to Expand C. Northcote Parkinson's famous first law states that, "Work expands so as to fill the time available for its completion."[7] Its major corollary further adds that, "In any public administrative department not actually at war, the staff increase . . . will invariably prove to be between 5.17 per cent and 6.56 per cent (per year), irrespective of any variation in the amount of work (if any) to be done."[8] These humorous views express a widely prevalent notion that bureaus have an inherent tendency to expand, regardless of whether or not there is any genuine need for more of their services. In fact, all organizations have inherent tendencies to expand. What sets bureaus apart is that they do not have as many restraints upon expansion, nor do their restraints function as automatically.

The major reasons why bureaus inherently seek to expand are as follows:

- An organization that is rapidly expanding can attract more capable personnel, and more easily retain its most capable existing personnel, than can one that is expanding very slowly, stagnating, or shrinking. This principle was examined in the preceding section.
- The expansion of any organization normally provides its leaders with increased power, income, and prestige; hence they encourage its growth. Conservers are the only exception, for they place little value on gaining more status for themselves.[9] This principle does not imply that larger organizations necessarily have more power or prestige than smaller ones. Rather, it implies that the leaders of any given organization can normally increase their power, income, and prestige by causing their organization to grow larger.
- Growth tends to reduce internal conflicts in an organization by allowing some (or all) of its members to increase their personal status without lowering that of others. Therefore, organizational leaders encourage expansion to maximize morale and minimize internal conflicts. Every bureau's environment changes constantly, thereby shifting the relative importance of the social functions performed by its various parts, and the resources appropriate to each part. Such shifts will be resisted by the sections losing resources. But these dissensions can be reduced if some sections are given more resources without any losses being experienced by others.
- Increasing the size of an organization may also improve the quality of its performance (per unit of output) and its chances for survival. Hence both loyalty and self-interest can encourage officials to promote organizational growth. As William H. Starbuck has pointed out in his analysis of organizational growth, there

may be significant operational advantages to being a very large organization.[10] Among these are the following:

— The organization may achieve economies of scale through greater specialization, ability to use up excess capacities, and reduction of stochastic errors through increasing sample sizes.
— Large organizations have a better chance of survival than small ones.
— Large organizations are harder to change than small ones (because they embody greater sunk costs); so they tend to be more resistant to external pressures. They also spend more on research and development (both in total and per employee), hence they can better develop new techniques useful in augmenting their power.
— Very large organizations can impose a certain degree of stability upon their external environment, whereas smaller ones cannot. Increased environmental stability reduces uncertainty and anxiety and solidifies the control of high-ranking officials.

- Finally because there is no inherent quid pro quo in bureau activity enabling officials to weigh the marginal return from further spending against its marginal cost, the incentive structure facing most officials provides much greater rewards for increasing expenditures than for reducing them. Hence officials are encouraged to expand their organization through greater spending. . . . Unlike the other sources of growth-pressure described above, this one is not found in most market-oriented organizations.

The Effects of Age upon Bureaus Bureaus, like men, change in predictable ways as they grow older. Following are the most important such changes, and their effects.

Bureaus learn to perform given tasks better with experience. Given the initial level of resources allocated to the bureau, this increased efficiency in effect allows the bureau to generate additional productive capacity just by growing older, without any added input of resources. The added capacity can be utilized by producing more of the same services, by absorbing the new capacity as organizational slack, or by devoting it to creating new functions or seeking to "capture" existing ones from other bureaus. Another possibility-cutting inputs—is unlikely, since all officials avoid reducing the resources under their control. It must be remembered that when a new process is undertaken, learning at first produces great economies, but the "learning curve" soon tends to flatten out.

As bureaus grow older, they tend to develop more formalized rule systems covering more and more of the possible situations they are likely to encounter. The passage of time exposes the bureau to a wide variety of situations, and it learns how to deal with most of them more effectively than it did in its youth. The desire for organizational memory of this experience causes the bureau's officials to develop more and more elaborate rules. These rules have three main effects. First, they markedly improve the performance of the bureau regarding situations previously encountered, and make the behavior of each of its parts both more stable and more predictable to its other parts. Second, they tend to divert the attention of officials from achieving the social functions of the bureau to conforming to its rules—the "goal displacement" described by sociologists. Third, they increase the bureau's structural complexity, which in turn strengthens its inertia because of greater sunk costs in current procedures. The resulting resistance to change further reduces the bureau's ability to adjust to new circumstances. Consequently, older bureaus tend to be more stable and less flexible than young ones.

As a bureau grows older, its officials tend to shift the emphasis of their goals from carrying out the bureau's social functions to insuring its survival and growth as an autonomous institution. When a bureau is first created, it is usually dominated by zealots or strong advocates who focus their attention upon accomplishing its social functions. As it grows older, its rules and administrative machinery become more complex and more extensive, demanding more attention from top officials. The conservers in the bureau tend to become more important because they are oriented toward preserving rules. Zealots become less important, because they are uninterested in administration and poor at allocating resources impartially.

As a bureau ages, its officials become more willing to modify the bureau's original formal goals in order to further the survival and growth of its administrative machinery.[11] This shift of emphasis is encouraged by the creation of career commitments among a bureau's more senior officials (in terms of service). The longer they have worked for the bureau, the more they wish to avoid the costs of finding a new job, losing rank and seniority, and fitting themselves into a new informal structure. Hence they would rather alter the bureau's formal goals than admit that their jobs should be abolished because the original goals have been attained or are no longer important.

As a bureau grows older, the number and proportion of administrative officials therein tends to rise. This tendency has been demonstrated by Starbuck in his analysis of the effects of longevity upon bureaus.[12] The main reasons why this shift to administration occurs as a function of age rather than size are as follows. First, administrators tend to have more job security and stability than production workers, partly because administrators are usually more senior in rank. Therefore, whenever attrition in personnel occurs, non-administrative officials are normally discharged first. The longer a bureau has survived, the more likely it is to have lived through a number of such shrinkages in the past. Second, the older a bureau is, the more different types of functions it is likely to carry out. As a result, a higher proportion of the bureau's personnel must be engaged in coordination. Third, until recent developments in the technology of business machines, production jobs were historically subject to a greater mechanization than administrative jobs. The older a bureau is, the more time it has been exposed to these effects of technical change.

If a bureau experiences a period of relative stability in total size following a period of rapid growth, the average age of its members tends to rise as the bureau grows older. This tends to increase the influence of conservers in the bureau, for many officials of other types are likely to become conservers as they grow older. The next section of this chapter discusses this in detail.

These effects of age upon a bureau lead to the Law of Increasing Conservatism: *All organizations tend to become more conservative as they get older, unless they experience periods of very rapid growth or internal turnover.* This principle is especially applicable to bureaus because they are relatively insulated from competition.

From this Law and the other effects of age examined, we can draw the following additional conclusions:

- The older a bureau is, the less likely it is to die. This is true because its leaders become more willing to shift major purposes in order to keep the bureau alive.
- The best time to "kill" a bureau is as soon as possible after it comes into existence.
- In general, the older a bureau is, the broader the scope of the social functions it serves. If a bureau is relatively long-lived, it has usually survived sizable fluctuations in the importance of its various social functions. Its initial functions declined in relative importance, pressuring its leaders to take on new functions. However, it probably did not relinquish its original ones. Therefore, as time passes, bureaus, like private firms, tend to diversify to protect themselves from fluctuations in demand.

The "Age Lump" Phenomenon and Its Effects One of the effects of increasing age upon a bureau is the tendency of the average age of the bureau's members to rise. Earlier, this chapter showed that almost every bureau goes through a period of rapid growth right before it reaches its initial survival threshold. During this period, it usually contains a high proportion of zealots (because they established it) and climbers (because they are attracted by fast growth). These people, moreover, tend to be relatively young, for youthful officials are more optimistic and full of initiative than older ones.

Soon after this initial spurt, the growth rate slows down, and the bureau is likely to enter a "growth plateau." This means that a high proportion of its total membership consists of the persons who joined it during the fast-growth period (unless it has a very high turnover). This group constitutes a "lump" of personnel, all about the same age. As they grow older, the average age of the bureau's members rises too, since they form such a large fraction of its total membership. This creates the following significant effects:

- There is a squeeze on the members of the age lump regarding promotions because so many of them attain the necessary qualifications all at once. Not all who are objectively suitable for promotion to the few high-level posts can be shifted upwards. Hence relatively low-level jobs continue to be occupied by very senior people.
- A high proportion of the bureau's membership tends to be changed into conservers because of increasing age and the frustration of ambitions for promotion. In any organization, officials tend to become conservers as they get older if they are not in the mainstream of promotion to the top. Hence the whole bureau tends to become more conserver-dominated as members of this lump become older.
- The squeeze on promotions tends to drive many climbers out of the organization into faster-growing organizations (if any alternatives are available). The proportion of conservers in the bureau tends to rise for this reason too. The most talented officials are the most likely to leave, since they naturally have more opportunities elsewhere. The bureau, therefore, becomes evermore dominated by mediocrity, unless there are really no alternative organizations to join (for example, the Russian Communist Party has no competitors within Russia).
- Up to the period just before most members of the age lump retire, it will be very difficult to attract able young people into the bureau. Climbers will be discouraged from joining because they see that the road upward is already clogged. Zealots will be discouraged by the conserver-domination of the bureau. However, when the main portions of the age lump are about to retire, the prospects of so many top-level jobs being suddenly vacated may attract both climbers and zealots.
- The bureau will experience a crisis of continuity when the age lump arrives at the normal retirement age. Almost all of the upper echelons will suddenly be vacated by members of the group that will have dominated the bureau's policies for many years. As a result, the bureau will go through a time of troubles as its remaining members struggle for control over its policies and resources.
- Many of these rather unfavorable consequences of age lumps can be offset by the following events:

— Additional spurts of rapid growth, which produce multiple age lumps within the bureau.
— Speeded-up retirement of bureau members who are not promoted. The U.S. Armed Forces used some version of this up-or-out system to counteract the lumps in their age structures resulting from World War II.
— Purges of upper level officials.
— Survival of the bureau over such a long period that the original age lump tends to be replaced by a more even age distribution.

- Because growth in many bureaus normally occurs in uneven spurts rather than at a steady pace, age lumps and their consequences are widespread phenomena.

The Death of Bureaus The ability of bureaus to outlive their real usefulness is part of the mythology of bureaucracy. Our theory supplies several reasons why bureaus—particularly government bureaus—rarely disappear once they have passed their initial survival thresholds.

Normally, organizations die because they fail to perform social functions of enough importance to make their members or clientele willing to sacrifice the resources necessary to maintain those functions. Such an inability can occur for three reasons: the specific functions performed by the organization decline in relative importance; the functions remain important but the organization is unable to perform them efficiently; or the functions remain important but some other organization performs them better. When the demise of a bureau is caused by the first two of these conditions, the bureau tends to disappear altogether. However, when its death is caused by the capture of its functions by another organization, the bureau's members are sometimes transferred to the other organization. In such cases, the bureau is swallowed and continues to live after a fashion.

There are several reasons why bureaus are unlikely to die once they have become firmly established:

- Bureaus are often willing to shift functions in order to survive; hence the relative decline of their initial social functions will not kill them if they are agile enough to undertake new and more viable functions before it is too late.
- The nature of bureaus leads their clients to create pressure to maintain them after their usefulness no longer justifies their costs. A bureau's clients normally receive its services without making full (or any) direct payments for them. These clients, therefore, pressure the central allocation agency to continue the bureau's services, even if they would be unwilling to pay for those services directly if they had to bear their full costs.
- A few of the clients or suppliers of nearly every bureau receive such large and irreplaceable net benefits from the bureau's services that they will continue to demand those services even if the marginal benefits thereof have declined below the marginal cost for most clients. Government bureaus are especially likely to have such zealous clients, since they usually perform services that cannot be duplicated by private agents acting alone. Defense contractors, for example, are unlikely to find any private buyers for missiles or space vehicles.
- The absence of any explicit quid pro quo relationship between bureau costs and benefits tends to conceal situations in which the costs of maintaining the bureau outweigh its benefits. This often allows the natural proclivity of any organization's members to keep the organization alive to function successfully even when the bureau really "ought" to die.
- Bureaus tend to be less willing to engage in all-out conflicts with each other than private profit-making firms; hence they are less likely to kill each other. Private firms are more willing to engage in struggles to the death than bureaus for two main reasons. First, in freely competitive markets containing a large number of small firms, intense competition is relatively impersonal and is a prerequisite to survival. In contrast, when one bureau "invades" the territory of another, this is a deliberate act aimed at a specific opponent. In essence, bureaus resemble large oligopolistic firms. Like such firms, they try to avoid all-out wars because they are too costly to all involved. Second, if two or more bureaus engage in a "war" concerning control over certain social functions, they inevitably attract the attention of the government's central allocation agencies (both executive and legislative). This is extremely hazardous because the bureau's opponents are sure to call attention to some of its major shortcomings. Moreover, top officials in every bureau fear any detailed investigation, since it is almost certain to uncover embarrassing actions.
- Experience shows that the "death rate" among both bureaus and large oligopolistic firms is extremely low. This demonstrates that the single most important reason why bureaus so rarely die is that they are large, and all large organizations have high survival rates. Large organizations can withstand greater absolute fluctuations in available resources than small ones, and they also enjoy certain other advantages set forth earlier in this chapter. Hence size, rather than type of function, is the number one determinant of survival. Since all bureaus are large by definition, and the vast majority of business firms are small, direct comparisons of the overall death rates among bureaus and private firms are bound to be misleading.
- Even if a bureau cannot muster sufficient external support to continue as an autonomous agency, it might survive by getting some other aggrandizing bureau to swallow it.
- Despite the low death rate of bureaus within their own cultures, very few bureaus—or organizations of any kind—have managed to survive for really long periods of time, that is, hundreds of years.

Most government bureaus disappear when the particular government that created them is replaced as did Roman bureaus. Similarly, private bureaus do not usually outlive the cultures that spawn them. Churches and universities seem to be the hardiest species, as the Roman Catholic Church and Oxford University illustrate.

Notes

1. Max Weber, *The Theory of Social and Economic Organization*, trans. A. M. Henderson and Talcott Parsons (New York: Free Press of Glencoe, 1947), p. 363 ff.
2. For an account of the origin of the Commodity Credit Corporation, see Arthur M. Schlesinger Jr., *The Coming of the New Deal* (Boston: Houghton Mifflin, 1959), pp. 61–67.
3. Peter B. Clark and James Q. Wilson, "Incentive Systems: A Theory of Organizations," *Administrative Science Quarterly* (September 1961), p. 157.
4. Ibid., p. 158.
5. Of course, if there is a great deal of unemployment, all types of officials who do not have jobs may be drawn to an expanding bureau.
6. I am indebted to Professor George Stigler of the University of Chicago for raising the problem of university faculties, and thereby stimulating the development of this section.
7. C. Northcote Parkinson, *Parkinson's Law and Other Studies in Administration* (Boston: Houghton Mifflin, 1962), p. 2.
8. Ibid., p. 12.
9. This inherent cause of bureau growth is essentially identical to William J. Baumol's argument that the managers of profit-making corporations try to maximize sales within a minimum-profit constraint. See William J. Baumol, "On the Theory of Expansion of the Firm," *American Economic Review* 52 (December 1962): 1078–1087.
10. William H. Starbuck, "Organizational Growth and Development," in *Handbook of Organizations*, ed. J. G. March (Chicago: Rand McNally, 1964).
11. Ibid., p. 303.
12. Ibid., pp. 366–376.

22

Rescuing Policy Analysis from PPBS

Aaron Wildavsky

Everyone knows that the nation needs better policy analysis. Each area one investigates shows how little is known compared to what is necessary in order to devise adequate policies. In some organizations there are no ways at all of determining the effectiveness of existing programs; organizational survival must be the sole criterion of merit. It is often not possible to determine whether the simplest objectives have been met. If there is a demand for information the cry goes out that what the organization does cannot be measured. Should anyone attempt to tie the organization down to any measure of productivity, the claim is made that there is no truth in numbers. Oftentimes this is another way of saying, "Mind your own business." Sometimes the line taken is that the work is so subtle that it resists any tests. On other occasions the point is made that only those learned in esoteric arts can properly understand what the organization does, and they can barely communicate to the uninitiated. There are men so convinced of the ultimate righteousness of their cause that they cannot imagine why anyone would wish to know how well they are doing in handling our common difficulties. Their activities are literally priceless; vulgar notions of cost and benefit do not apply to them.

Anyone who has weathered this routine comes to value policy analysis. The very idea that there should be some identifiable objectives and that attention should be paid to whether these are achieved seems a great step forward. Devising alternative ways of handling problems and considering the future costs of each solution appear creative in comparison to more haphazard approaches. Yet policy analysis with its emphasis upon originality, imagination, and foresight, cannot be simply described. It is equivalent to what Robert N. Anthony has called strategic planning: ". . . the process of deciding on objectives of the organization, on changes in these objectives, on the resources used to attain these objectives. . . . It connotes big plans, important plans, plans with major consequences."[1] While policy analysis is similar to a broadly conceived version of systems analysis,[2] Yehezkel Dror has pointed up the boundaries that separate a narrow study from one with larger policy concerns. In policy analysis,

1. Much attention would be paid to the political aspects of public decision-making and public policy-making (instead of ignoring or condescendingly regarding political aspects). . . .
2. A broad conception of decision-making and policy-making would be involved (instead of viewing all decision-making as mainly a resources allocation). . . .
3. A main emphasis would be on creativity and search for new policy alternatives, with explicit attention to encouragement of innovative thinking. . . .
4. There would be extensive reliance on . . . qualitative methods. . . .
5. There would be much more emphasis on futuristic thinking. . . .
6. The approach would be looser and less rigid, but nevertheless systematic, one which would recognize the complexity of means ends interdependence, the multiplicity of relevant criteria of decision, and the partial and tentative nature of every analysis. . . .[3]

Policy analysis aims at providing information that contributes to making an agency politically and socially relevant. Policies are goals, objectives, and missions that guide the agency. Analysis evaluates and sifts alternative means and ends in the elusive pursuit of policy recommendations. By getting out of the firehouse environment of day-to-day administration,

Source: Reprinted with permission from Public Administration Review.

policy analysis seeks knowledge and opportunities for coping with an uncertain future. Because policy analysis is not concerned with projecting the status quo, but with tracing out the consequences of innovative ideas, it is a variant of planning. Complementing the agency's decision process, policy analysis is a tool of social change.

In view of its concern with creativity, it is not surprising that policy analysis is still largely an art form; there are no precise rules about how to do it. The policy analyst seeks to reduce obscurantism by being explicit about problems and solutions, resources and results. The purpose of policy analysis is not to eliminate advocacy but to raise the level of argument among contending interests. If poor people want greater benefits from the government, the answer to their problems may not lie initially in policy analysis but in political organization. Once they have organized themselves, they may want to undertake policy analysis in order to crystallize their own objectives or merely to compete with the analyses put forth by others. The end result, hopefully, would be a higher quality debate and perhaps eventually public choice among better known alternatives.

A belief in the desirability of policy analysis—the sustained application of intelligence and knowledge to social problems—is not enough to insure its success, no more than to want to do good is sufficient to accomplish noble purposes. If grandiose claims are made, if heavy burdens are placed on officials without adequate compensation, if the needs of agency heads are given scant consideration, they will not desire policy analysis. It is clear that those who introduced the PPB system into the federal government in one fell swoop did not undertake a policy analysis on how to introduce policy analysis into the federal government.

In a paper called "The Political Economy of Efficiency"[4] written just as PPBS was begun in national government, I argued that it would run up against serious difficulties. There is still no reason to change a single word of what I said then. Indeed, its difficulties have been so overwhelming that there is grave danger that policy analysis will be rejected along with its particular manifestation in PPBS. In this essay I shall assess the damage that the planning-programming-budgeting system has done to the prospects of encouraging policy analysis in American national government. Then I would like to suggest some ways of enabling policy analysis to thrive and prosper.

Why Defense Was a Bad Model

A quick way of seeing what went wrong with PPBS is to examine the preconditions for the use of this approach in the Defense Department, from which it was exported throughout the federal government. The immediate origins of PPBS are to be found in the RAND Corporation,[5] where, after the Second World War, a talented group of analysts devoted years of effort to understanding problems of defense policy. It took five years to come up with the first useful ideas. Thus the first requisite of program budgeting in Defense was a small group of talented people who had spent years developing insights into the special problems of defense strategy and logistics. The second requisite was a common terminology, an ad hoc collection of analytical approaches, and the beginnings of theoretical statements to guide policy analysis. When Secretary of Defense Robert McNamara came into office, he did not have to search for men of talent nor did he have to wait for a body of knowledge to be created. These requisites already existed in some degree. What was further necessary was his ability to understand and to use analytical studies. Thus the third requisite of program budgeting is top leadership that understands policy analysis and is determined to get it and make use of it.

The fourth requisite was the existence of planning and planners. Planning was well accepted at the various levels of the Defense Department with the variety of joint service plans, long-range requirement plans, logistical plans, and more. Military and civilians believed in planning, in coping with uncertainty and in specifying some consequences of policy decisions. The problem as the originator of PPBS saw it was to introduce cost considerations into planning; they wanted to stop blue-sky planning and to integrate planning and budgeting. They wanted to use the program budget to bridge the gap between military planners, who cared about requirements but not about resources, and budget people, who were narrowly concerned with financial costs but not necessarily with effective policies.

Policy analysis is expensive in terms of time, talent, and money. It requires a high degree of creativity in order to imagine new policies and to test them out without requiring actual experience. Policy analysis calls for the creation of systems in which elements are linked to one another and to operational indicators so that costs and effectiveness of alternatives may be systematically compared. There is no way of knowing in advance whether the analysis will prove intellectually satisfying and politically feasible. Policy analysis is facilitated when: (a) goals are easily specified, (b) a large margin of error is allowable, and (c) the cost of the contemplated policy makes large expenditures on analysis worthwhile. That part of defense policy dealing with choices among alternative weapons systems was ideally suited for policy analysis. Since the cost of intercontinental missiles or other weapons systems ran into the billions of dollars, it was easy to justify spending millions on analysis.[6] The potential effectiveness of weapons like intercontinental missiles could be contemplated so long as one was willing to accept large margins of error. It is not unusual for analysts to assume extreme cases of damage and vulnerability in a context in which the desire for reducing risk is very great. Hence a goal like assuring sufficient destructive power such that no enemy strike could prevent devastation of one's country may be fuzzy without being unusable. If one accepts a procedure of imagining that possible enemies were to throw three times as much megatonnage as intelligence estimates suggest they have, he need not be overly troubled by doubts about the underlying theory. If one is willing to pay the cost of compensating against the worst, lack of knowledge will not matter so much. The point is not that this is an undesirable analytic procedure, quite the contrary, but the extreme cases were allowed to determine the outcomes.

Inertia The introduction of new procedures that result in new policies is not easy. Inertia is always a problem. Members of the organization and its clientele groups have vested interests in the policies of the past. Efforts at persuasion must be huge and persistent. But there are conditions that facilitate change. One of these is a rising level of appropriations. If change means that things must be taken away from people in the organization without giving them anything in return, greater resistance may be expected. The ability to replace old rewards with larger new ones helps reduce resistance to change. The fact that defense appropriations were increasing at a fast rate made life much easier for Mr. McNamara. The expected objections of clientele groups, for example, were muted by the fact that defense contractors had lots of work, even if it was not exactly what they expected. Rapid organizational growth may also improve the possibilities for change. The sheer increase in organizational size means that many new people can be hired who are not tied to the old ways. And speedy promotion may help convince members that the recommended changes are desirable.

The deeper change goes into the bowels of the organization, the more difficult it is to achieve. The more change can be limited to central management, the greater the possibility for carrying it out. The changes introduced in the Defense Department did not, for the most part, require acceptance at the lower levels. Consider a proposed change in the organization of fighting units that would drastically reduce the traditional heavy support facilities for ground forces. Such a change is not easily manipulated from Washington. But the choice of one weapons system over another is much more amen-able to central control. The kinds of problems for which program budgeting was most useful also turned out to be problems that could be dealt with largely at the top of the organization. The program budget group that McNamara established had to fight with generals in Washington but not with master sergeants in supply. Anyone who knows the Army knows what battle they would rather be engaged in fighting.

The ability of an organization to secure rapid change depends, of course, on the degree of its autonomy from the environment. I have argued elsewhere[7] that the President of the United States has much more control over America's foreign policy than over its domestic policy. In almost any area of domestic policy there is a well-entrenched structure of interests. In foreign and defense policy, excluding such essentially internal concerns as the National Guard, the territory within the American political system is not nearly so well defended; there are far fewer political fortifications, mines, and booby-traps.

Personnel Experienced personnel may be a barrier to change. They know something about the consequences of what they are doing. They may have tried a variety of alternatives and can point to reasons why each one will not work. If I may recall my low-level Army experience (I entered as a private first class and was never once demoted), the usual reply to a question about the efficacy of present practice was, "Have you ever been in combat, son?" But the most dramatic changes introduced in the Pentagon had to do with questions of avoiding or limiting nuclear war, in which no one had a claim to experience and in which the basic purpose of analysis is to make certain that we do not have to learn from experience. If the system fails, the game is over. And since McNamara's men possessed a body of doctrines on defense policy, they had an enormous advantage over regular military who were for a long time unable to defend themselves properly in the new field.[8]

The new policy analysts did not accept the currency of military experience. In their view, naked judgment was not a satisfactory answer to why a policy should be adopted. The Army might know the fire-power of an infantry division, but the fire-power was not "effectiveness." Competition among the services for appropriations, however, was favorable to PPBS. There was a defense budget that covered virtually all of the Department's subject matter. There were defense missions in which trade-offs could be made between the services. Resources could actually be diverted if the analysis "proved" a particular service was right. Programs could easily be developed because of the facile identification of program with weapons systems and force units. Once the military learned the jargon, they were willing to play the game for an extra division or carrier. So long as dollar losses in one program were more than made up by gains in another, the pain of policy analysis was considerably eased.

The favorable conditions for the limited use of program budgeting in the Department of Defense do not exist in most domestic agencies. There are no large groups of talented policy analysts expert in agency problems outside of the federal government. These nonexistent men cannot, therefore, be made available to the agencies. (The time has passed when eighth-rate systems engineers in aerospace industries are expected to solve basic social problems overnight.) Most agencies had few planners and even less experience in planning. There is no body of knowledge waiting to be applied to policy areas such as welfare and crime. A basic reason for wanting more policy analysis is to help create knowledge where little now exists. There are only a few agencies in which top managers want systematic policy analysis and are able to understand quantitative studies. Goals are not easily specified for most domestic agencies. Nor do they usually have handy equivalents for programs like expensive weapons systems. What Thomas Schelling has so pungently observed about the Department of State—it does not control a large part of the budget devoted to foreign policy—is true for the domestic departments and their lack of coverage as well.[9]

Except for a few individual programs like the proposals for income supplements or assessing the desirability of a supersonic transport, the cost of most domestic policies does not rise into the billions of dollars. Congress and interested publics are not disposed to allow large margins of error. Instead of increasing, the availability of federal funds began declining soon after the introduction of program budgeting. A higher level of conflict was inevitable, especially since the acceptance of proposed changes required the acquiescence of all sorts of people and institutions in the far-flung reaches of the agencies. Social workers, city officials, police chiefs, welfare mothers, field officers, and numerous others were involved in the policies. Program budgeting on the domestic side takes place in a context in which there is both less autonomy from the environment and a great deal more first-hand experience by subordinates. On these grounds alone no one should have been surprised that program budgeting in the domestic agencies did not proceed as rapidly or with as much ostensible success as in the Defense Department.[10]

No One Can Do PPBS

In past writings I argued that program budgeting would run up against severe political difficulties. While most of these arguments have been conceded, I have been told that in a better world, without the vulgar intrusion of political factors (such as the consent of the governed), PPBS would perform its wonders as advertised. Now it is clear that for the narrow purpose of predicting why program budgeting would not work there was no need to mention political problems at all. It would have been sufficient to say that the wholesale introduction of PPBS presented insuperable difficulties of calculation. All the obstacles previously mentioned, such as lack of talent, theory, and data, may be summed up in a single statement: *no one knows how to do program budgeting*. Another way of putting it would be to say that many know what program budgeting should be like in general, but no one knows what it should be in any particular case. Program budgeting cannot be stated in operational terms. There is no agreement on what the words mean, let alone an ability to show another person what should be done. The reason for the difficulty is that telling an agency to adopt program budgeting means telling it to find better policies and there is no formula for doing that. One can (and should) talk about measuring effectiveness, estimating costs, and comparing alternatives, but that is a far cry from being able to take the creative leap of formulating a better policy.

Pattern of Events On the basis of numerous discussions with would-be practitioners of program budgeting at the federal level, I think I can describe the usual pattern of events. The instructions come down from the Bureau of Budget. You must have a program budget. Agency personnel hit the panic button. They just do not know how to do what they have been asked to do. They turn, if they can, to the pitifully small band of refugees from the Pentagon who have come to light the way. But these defense intellectuals do not know much about the policy area in which they are working. That takes time. Yet something must quickly come out of all this. So they produce a vast amount of inchoate information characterized by premature quantification of irrelevant items. Neither the agency head nor the examiners in the Bureau of the Budget can comprehend the material submitted to them. Its very bulk inhibits understanding. It is useless to the Director of the Budget in making his decisions. In an effort to be helpful, the program analysis unit at the Budget Bureau says something like, "Nice try, fellows; we appreciate all that effort. But you have not quite got the idea of program budgeting yet. Remember, you must clarify goals, define objectives, relate these to quantitative indicators, project costs into the future. Please send a new submission based on this understanding."

Another furious effort takes place. They do it in Defense, so it must be possible. Incredible amounts of overtime are put in. Ultimately, under severe time pressure, even more data is accumulated. No one will be able to say that agency personnel did not try hard. The new presentation makes a little more sense to some people and a little less to others. It just does not hang together as a presentation of agency policies. There are more encouraging words from the Budget Bureau and another sermon about specifying alternative ways of meeting agency objectives, though not, of course, taking the old objectives for granted. By this time agency personnel are desperate. "We would love to do it," they say, "but we cannot figure out the right way. You experts in the Budget Bureau should show us how to do it." Silence. The word from on high is that the Bureau of the Budget does not interfere with agency operations; it is the agency's task to set up its own budget. After a while, cynicism reigns supreme.

PPBS must be tremendously inefficient. It resembles nothing so much as a Rube Goldberg apparatus in which the operations performed bear little relation to the output achieved. The data inputs into PPBS are huge and its policy output is tiny. All over the federal government the story is the same; if you ask what good has PPBS done, those who have something favorable to say invariably cite the same one or two policy analyses. At one time I began to wonder if the oil shale study[11] in the Interior Department and the maternal and child health care program[12] in Health, Education, and Welfare were all that had ever come out of the programming effort.

The orders to expand PPBS did not say, "Let us do more policy analysis than we have in the past." What it said was, "Let us make believe we can do policy analysis on everything." Instead of focusing attention on areas of policy amenable to study, the PPBS apparatus requires information on *all* agency policies.

Program Structure The fixation on program structure is the most pernicious aspect of PPBS. Once PPBS is adopted, it becomes necessary to have a program structure that provides a complete list of organization objectives and supplies information on the attainment of each one. In the absence of analytic studies for all or even a large part of an agency's operations, the structure turns out to be a sham that piles up meaningless data under vague categories.[13] It hides rather than clarifies. It suggests comparisons among categories for which there is no factual or analytical basis. Examination of a department's program structure convinces everyone acquainted with it that policy analysis is just another bad way of masquerading behind old confusions. A mere recitation of some program categories from the Department of Agriculture—Communities of Tomorrow, Science in the Service of Man, Expanding Dimensions for Living—makes the point better than any comment.

Even if the agency head does understand a data-reduction-summarization of the program budget, he still cannot use the structure to make decisions, because it is too hard to adjust the elaborate apparatus. Although the system dredges up information under numerous headings, it says next to nothing about the impact of one program on another. There is data but no causal analysis. Hence the agency head is at once over-supplied with masses of numbers and undersupplied with propositions about the impact of any action he might undertake. He cannot tell, because no one knows, what the marginal change he is considering would mean for the rest of his operation. Incremental changes at the Bureau of the Budget at the agency level are made in terms of the old budget categories. Since the program structure is meant to be part of the budget, however, it must be taken as a statement of current policy and it necessarily emerges as a product of organizational compromise. The program structure, therefore, does not embody a focus on central policy concerns. More likely, it is a haphazard arrangement that reflects the desire to manipulate external support and to pursue internal power aspirations. Being neither program nor budget, program structure is useless. It is the Potemkin Village of modern administration. The fact that generating bits of random data for the program structure takes valuable time away from more constructive concerns also harms policy analysis. The whole point of policy analysis is to show that what had been done intuitively in the past may be done better through sustained application of intelligence. The adoption of meaningless program structures, and their pervasion into slogans for supporting existing policies, does not—to say the least—advance the cause of policy analysis.

Gorham Testimony I do not mean to suggest that the introduction of PPBS has not led to some accomplishments. Before we consider the significance of these accomplishments, however, it is essential that we understand what PPBS has manifestly *not* done. One could hardly have better witness on this subject than William Gorham, formerly Assistant Secretary (Program Coordination), Department of Health, Education, and Welfare, and now head of the Urban Institute, who is widely acknowledged to be an outstanding practitioner of program budgeting.

At the highest level of generality, it is clear that PPBS does not help in making choices between vast national goals such as health and defense, nor is PPBS useful in making trade-offs between more closely related areas of policy such as health, education, and welfare. In his testimony before the Joint Economic Committee, Gorham put the matter bluntly:

> Let me hasten to point out that we have not attempted any grandiose cost-benefit analysis designed to reveal whether the total benefits from an additional million dollars spent on health programs would be higher or

> lower than that from an additional million spent on education or welfare. If I was ever naive enough to think this sort of analysis possible, I no longer am. The benefits of health, education, and welfare programs are diverse and often intangible. They affect different age groups and different regions of the population over different periods of time. No amount of analysis is going to tell us whether the Nation benefits more from sending a slum child to pre-school, providing medical care to an old man or enabling a disabled housewife to resume her normal activities. The "grand decisions"—how much health, how much education, how much welfare, and which groups in the population shall benefit—are questions of value judgments and politics. The analyst cannot make much contribution to their resolution.[14]

It turns out that it is extremely difficult to get consensus on goals within a single area of policy. As a result, the policy analysts attempt to find objectives that are more clearly operational and more widely acceptable. Gorham speaks with the voice of experience when he says:

> Let me give you an example. Education. What we want our kids to be as a result of going to school is the level of objective which is the proper and the broadest one. But we want our children to be different sorts of people. We want them to be capable of different sorts of things. We have, in other words, a plurality of opinions about what we want our schools to turn out. So you drop down a level and you talk about objectives in terms of educational attainment—years of school completed and certain objective measures of quality. Here you move in education from sort of fuzzy objectives, but very important, about what it is that you want the schools to be doing, to the more concrete, less controversial, more easily to get agreed upon objectives having to do with such things as educational attainment, percentage of children going to college, etc.
>
> I think the same thing is true in health and in social services, that at the very highest level objective, where in theory you would really like to say something, the difficulty of getting and finding a national consensus is so great that you drop down to something which is more easily and readily accepted as objectives.[15]

What can actually be done, according to Gorham, are analytic studies of narrowly defined areas of policy. "The less grand decisions," Gorham testified, "those among alternative programs with the same or similar objectives within health—can be substantially illuminated by good analysis. It is this type of analysis which we have undertaken at the Department of Health, Education, and Welfare."[16] Gorham gives as examples disease control programs and improvements in the health of children. If this type of project analysis is what can be done under PPBS, a serious question is raised: Why go through all the rigmarole in order to accomplish a few discrete studies of important problems?

A five-year budget conceived in the hodgepodge terms of the program structure serves no purpose.[17] Since actual budget decisions are made in terms of the old categories and policy analysis may take place outside of the program structure, there is no need to institutionalize empty labels. If a policy analysis has been completed, there is no reason why it cannot be submitted as part of the justification of estimates to the Bureau of the Budget and to Congress. For the few program memoranda that an agency might submit, changes could be detailed in terms of traditional budget categories. Problems of program structure would be turned over to the agency's policy analysts who would experiment with different ways of lending intellectual coherence to the agency's programs. There would be no need to foist the latest failure on a skeptical world. Nor would there be battles over the costs of altering a program structure that has achieved, if not a common framework, at least the virtue of familiarity. The difference is that stability of categories in the traditional budget has real value for control[18] while the embodiment of contradictions in the program structure violates its essential purpose.

Incentives for Policy Analysis

PPBS discredits policy analysis. To collect vast amounts of random data is hardly a serious analysis of public policy. The conclusion is obvious. The shotgun marriage between policy analysis and budgeting should be annulled. Attempts to describe the total agency program in program memoranda should be abandoned. It is hard enough to do a good job of policy analysis, as most agency people now realize, without having to meet arbitrary and fixed deadlines imposed by the budget process.[19] There is no way of telling whether an analysis will be successful. There is, therefore, no point in insisting that half-baked analyses be submitted every year because of a misguided desire to cover the entire agency program. The Budget Bureau itself has recently reorganized the difficulty by requiring agencies to present extensive memoranda only when major policy issues have been identified. It is easier and more honest just to take the program structure out of the budget.

The thrust of the argument thus far, however, forces us to confront a major difficulty. Policy analysis and budgeting were presumably connected in order to see that high quality analysis did not languish in limbo but was translated into action through the critical budget process. Removing policy analysis from the annual budget cycle might increase its intellectual content at the expense of its practical impact. While formal program structures should go—PPBS actually inhibits the prospects for obtaining good analysis that is worth translating into public policy—they should be replaced with a strong incentive to make policy analysis count in yearly budgetary decisions. I am therefore proposing a substitute for PPBS that maintains whatever incentive it provided for introducing the results of policy analysis into the real world without encouraging the debilitating effects.

The submission of program memoranda supported by policy analysis should be made a requirement for major dollar changes in an agency's budget. The Bureau of the Budget should insist that this requirement be met by every agency. Agency heads, therefore, would have to require it of subunits. The sequence could operate as follows:

1. Secretary of agency and top policy analysts review major issues and legislation and set up a study menu for several years. Additions and deletions are made periodically.
2. Policy analysts set up studies which take anywhere from six to 24 months.
3. As a study is completed for a major issue area, it is submitted to the Secretary of the agency for review and approval.
4. If approved, the implications of the study's recommendations are translated into budgetary terms for submission as a program memorandum in support of the agency's fiscal year budget.

No one imagines that a mechanical requirement would in and of itself compel serious consideration of policy matters. No procedure should be reified as if it had a life of its own apart from the people who must implement it. This conclusion is as true for my suggestion as for PPBS. We must therefore consider ways and means of increasing the demand for and supply of policy analysis.

Increasing Demand and Supply The first requirement of effective policy analysis is that top management want it. No matter how trite this criterion sounds, it has often been violated, as Frederick C. Mosher's splendid study of program budgeting in foreign affairs reveals.[20] The inevitable difficulties of shaking loose information and breaking up old habits will prove to be insuperable obstacles without steady support from high agency officials. If they do not want it, the best thing to do is concentrate efforts in another agency. Placing the best people in a few agencies also makes it more likely that a critical mass of talent will be able to achieve a creative response to emerging policy problems.

Policy analysis should be geared to the direct requirements of top management. This means that analysis should be limited to a few major issues. Since there will only be a few studies every year, the Secretary should have time to consider and understand each one. The analytical staff should be flexible enough to work on his priority interests. Consequently, one of the arguments by which program budgeting has been oversold has to be abandoned. Policy analysis will not normally identify programs of low priority. Top management is not interested in them. They would receive no benefit from getting supporters of these programs angry at them. Instead, agency heads want to know how to deal with emergent problems. Practitioners of policy analysis understand these considerations quite well. Harry Shooshan, Deputy Undersecretary for Programs, Department of the Interior, presents a perceptive analysis:

> . . . We have tried to more heavily relate our PPB work and our analytical work to the new program thrusts, and major issues, not because it is easier to talk about new programs, but rather, there is a good question of judgment, on how much time one should spend on ongoing programs that are pretty well set. So you restate its mission and you put it in PPB wrapping and what have you really accomplished?
>
> There are going to be new program proposals, new thrusts of doing something in certain areas. Let's relate our analyses to that and get the alternatives documented as well as we can for the decision-makers. So it is a combination of on the one hand it being difficult to identify low priorities in a manner that really means something and on the other hand, it is the fact of what have we really accomplished by simply putting old programs in new wrappings when new programs really should get the emphasis right now in terms of what are the decisions now before, in my case, the Secretary of the Interior, in terms of what should he know before he makes decisions relative to where he is attempting to go. If I can relate PPB to the decision on his desk today and the near future, I can sell him and in turn, our own Department on the contribution that we can make.[21]

The implications of Shooshan's point go beyond making policy analysis more desirable by having it meet the needs of top management. The subjects for policy analysis ought to be chosen precisely for their critical-fluidemergent character. These are the places where society is hurting. These are the areas in which there are opportunities for marginal gains. Indeed, a major role for top management is scanning the political horizon for targets of opportunity. Yet the characteristics of these new problems run counter to the criteria for selection that PPBS currently enforces, since they are identified by ambiguity concerning goals, lack of data upon which to project accurate estimates of costs and consequences, and pervasive uncertainty concerning the range of possible changes in program.

There would be a much larger demand for policy analysis if it were supplied in ways that would meet the needs of high level officials. Let us consider the example of the President of the United States. He can certainly use policy analysis to help make better decisions. Substantial policy studies would give him and his staff leverage against the bureaucracy. Knowledge is power. Indeed, command of a particular field would enable Presidents to exert greater control over the agenda for public decision and would give them advantages in competition with all sorts of rivals. Presidents could use perhaps a dozen major policy studies per year of their most immediate concerns. If even a few of these turn out well, the President may be motivated to make use of them. Contrast this with the present inundation of the Executive Office by endless streams of program "books," summaries, and memoranda that nobody ever looks at.

What is true of the President is also true for important executives in the agencies. Policy-oriented executives will want to get better analysis. Executives wishing to increase their resource base will be interested in independent sources of information and advice. Those who would exert power need objectives to fight for. It is neither fashionable nor efficient to appear to seek power for its own sake. In polite society the drive is masked and given a noble face when it can be attached to grand policy concerns that bring benefits to others as well as to power seekers. The way to gain the attention of leaders is not to flood them with trivia but to provide examples of the best kind of work that can be done. The last years of the Johnson Administration witnessed a proliferation of secret commissions to recommend new policies. The department secretary often became just another special pleader. If they have any interest in curbing this development, secretaries may find that producing their own policy analyses allows them to say that outside intervention is not the only or the best way to generate new policies.

Congressional Demand If strategically located Congressmen demanded more policy analysis, there is little doubt that we would get it. What can be done to make them want more of it? The answer does not lie in surrounding them with large staffs so that they lose their manifestly political functions and become more like bureaucrats. Nor does the answer lie in telling Congressmen to keep away from small administrative questions in favor of larger policy concerns. For many Congressmen get into the large questions only by feeling their way through the smaller details.[22] A threat to deprive Congressmen of the traditional line item appropriations data through which they exert their control of agency affairs also does not appear to be a good way of making Congressmen desire policy analysis.

Policy analysis must be made relevant to what Congressmen want. Some legislators desire to sponsor new policies and they are one clientele for analysis. For other Congressmen, however, policy is a bargainable product that emerges from their interactions with their fellows. These members must be appealed to in a different way. They often have a sense of institutional loyalty and pride. They know that Congress is a rare institution in this world—a legislative body that actually has some control over public policy. They are aware that the development of new knowledge and new techniques may freeze them out of many of the more serious decisions. Policy analysis should be proposed to these men as an enhancement of the power of Congress as an institution. The purpose of analysis would be, in its simplest form, to enable Congressmen to ask good questions and to evaluate answers. Oftentimes it is hardest for a layman to recognize the significant questions implicit in an area of policy. Are there other and better questions to be asked, other and better policies to be pursued?

A Congress that takes seriously its policy role should be encouraged to contract for policy analysis that would stress different views of what the critical questions are in a particular area of policy. Each major committee or subcommittee should be encouraged to hire a man trained in policy analysis for a limited period, perhaps two years. His task would be to solicit policy studies, evaluate presentations made by government agencies, and keep Congressmen informed about what are considered the important questions. In the past, chairmen have not always paid attention to the quality of committee staffs. Following the lead of the Joint Economic Committee, seminars might be held for a couple of weeks before each session. At these seminars discussions would take place between agency personnel, committee staff, and the academics or other experts who have produced the latest policy analysis. If all went well, Congressmen would emerge with a better idea of the range of issues and of somewhat different ways of tackling the problems, and the policy analysts would emerge with a better grasp of the priorities of these legislators.

Suppliers of Policy Analysis Thus far we have dealt solely with the incentive structure of the consumers who ought to want policy analysis—agency heads, Presidents, Congressmen. Little has been said about the incentive structure of the suppliers who ought to provide it—analysts, consultants, academics. Our premise has been that the supply of policy analysis would be a function of the demand. Now, the relationships between supply and demand have long been troublesome in economics because it is so difficult to sort out the mutual interactions. Upon being asked whether demand created supply or supply created demand, the great economist Marshall was reported to have said that it was like asking which blade of the scissors cuts the paper. There is no doubt, however, that changes in the conditions and quality of supply would have important effects on the demand for policy analysis.

Disengaging policy analysis from PPBS would help build the supply of policy analysis by:

1. Decreasing the rewards for mindless quantification for its own sake. There would be no requests from the Bureau of the Budget for such information and no premium for supplying it.

2. Increasing the rewards for analysts who might try the risky business of tackling a major policy problem that was obviously not going to be considered because everyone was too busy playing with the program structure. Gresham's Law operates here: programmed work drives out unprogrammed activity, make-work drives out analysis.

One way of increasing the supply of policy analysis would be to improve the training of people who work directly in the various areas of policy. Instead of taking people trained in policy analysis and having them learn about a particular policy area, the people in that area would be capable of doing policy analysis. Three-day or three-month courses will not do for that purpose. A year, and possibly two years, would be required. Since it is unlikely that the best people can be made available for so long a period, it is necessary to think in terms of education at an earlier period of their lives. There is a great need for schools of public policy in which technical training is combined with broader views of the social context of public policy. Although no one knows how to teach "creativity" it is possible to expose students to the range of subjects out of which a creative approach to public policy could come.

Another way of increasing the supply of policy analysis would be to locate it in an organizational context in which it has prestige and its practitioners are given time to do good work. Having the policy analysis unit report directly to the secretary or agency head would show that it is meant to be taken seriously.[23] But then it is bound to get involved in day-to-day concerns of the agency head, thus creating a classic dilemma.

Tactics The effective use of a policy analysis unit cannot be specified in advance for all agencies. There are certain tensions in its functions that may be mitigated on a case-by-case basis but cannot be resolved once and for all. Serious policy analysis requires months, if not years, of effort. A unit that spends its time solely on substantial policy analysis would soon find itself isolated from the operational concerns of the agency. There would be inordinate temptations on the part of its members to go where the action is. Before long, the policy unit might become more immediately relevant at the expense of its long-term impact. The frantic nature of day-to-day emergencies drives out the necessary time and quiet for serious study and reflection. What can be done? One tactic is for the policy unit to consider itself an educational as well as an action group. Its task should be to encourage analysis on the part of other elements of the organization. It should undertake nothing it can get subunits to do. The role of the policy unit would then be one of advising subunits and evaluating their output.

A second tactic would be to contract out for studies that are expected to take the longest period of time. The third tactic is the most difficult, because it calls for a balancing act. Immediate usefulness to top management may be secured by working on problems with short lead times while attempting to retain perhaps half of the available time for genuine policy analysis. To the degree that serious policy analysis enters into the life of the organization and proves its worth, it will be easier to justify its requirements in terms of release from everyday concerns, yet the demand for services of the analysts is certain to increase. Failures in policy analysis, on the other hand, are likely to give the personnel involved more time for reflection than they would prefer. Like headquarters-field relationships, line and staff responsibilities, and functional versus hierarchical command, the problems of the policy unit are inherent in its situation and can only be temporarily resolved.

These comments on incentives for increasing the supply and demand for policy analysis are plainly inadequate. They are meant merely to suggest that there is a problem and to indicate how one might go about resolving it. We do not really know how to make policy analysis fit in with the career requirements of Congressmen, nor can we contribute much beside proverbial wisdom to the structure and operation of policy analysis units. There are, however, opportunities for learning that have not yet been used. One of the benefits flowing from the experience with PPBS is that it has thrown up a small number of policy analyses that practitioners consider to be good. We need to know what makes some live in the world and others remain unused. Aside from an impressive manuscript by Clay Thomas Whitehead,[24] however, in which two recent policy analyses in defense are studied, there has been no effort to determine what this experience has to teach us. Despite the confident talk about policy analysis (here and elsewhere), a great deal of work remains to be done on what is considered "good" and why. The pioneering work by Charles E. Lindblom should not be wrongly interpreted as being anti-analysis, but as a seminal effort to understand what we do when we try to grapple with social problems.

Reexamination Critical aspects of policy analysis need to be reexamined. The field cries out for a study of "coordination" as profound and subtle as Martin Landau's forthcoming essay on "Redundancy."[25] That most elemental problem of political theory—the proper role of the government versus that of the individual—should be subject to a radical critique.[26] The fact that cost-benefit analysis began with water resource projects in which the contribution to national income was the key question has guided thought away from other areas of policy for which this criterion would be inappropriate. There are policies for which the willingness of citizens to support the activity should help determine the outcome. There are other policies in which presently unquantifiable benefits, like pleasure in seeing others better off or reduction of anxiety following a visible decrease in social hostility, should be controlling. Although social invention is incredibly difficult, the way is open for new concepts of the role of government to liberate our thoughts and guide our actions.

In many ways the times are propitious for policy analysis. The New Deal era of legislation has ended and has not yet been replaced by a stable structure of issues. People do not know where they stand today in the same way they knew how they felt about Medicare or private versus public electric power. The old welfare state policies have disenchanted former supporters as well as further enraged their opponents. Men have worked for 20 years to get massive education bills through Congress only to discover that the results have not lived up to their expectations; it takes a lot more to improve education for the deprived than anyone had thought. There is now a receptivity to new ideas that did not exist a decade ago. There is a willingness to consider new policies and try new ways. Whether or not there is sufficient creativity in us to devise better policies remains to be seen. If we are serious about improving public policy, we will go beyond the fashionable pretense of PPBS to show others what the best policy analysis can achieve.

NOTES

1. Robert N. Anthony, *Planning and Control Systems: A Framework for Analysis* (Cambridge, Mass.: Harvard University Press, 1965), p. 16.
2. Aaron Wildavsky, "The Political Economy of Efficiency," *Pub. Adm. Rev.* 26 (December 1966): 298–302.
3. Yehezkel Dror, "Policy Analysts: A New Professional Role in Government Service," *Pub. Adm. Rev.* 27 (September 1967): 200–201. See also Dror's major work, *Public Policy-Making Reexamined* (San Francisco: Chandler, 1968).
4. Aaron Wildavsky, op. cit.
5. See David Novick, "Origin and History of Program Budgeting," The RAND Corporation (October 1966), p. 3427.
6. I once tried to interest a graduate student who had experience with defense problems in doing research in the City of Oakland. He asked the size of Oakland's budget. "Fifty million dollars," I said. "Why, in the Air Force we used to round to that figure," was his reply.
7. Aaron Wildavsky, "The Two Presidencies," *Trans-Action* 4 (December 1966): 7–14.
8. For further argument along these lines see my article, "The Practical Consequences of the Theoretical Study of Defense Policy," *Pub. Adm. Rev.* 25 (March 1965): 90–103.
9. Senate Committee on Government Operations, Subcommittee on National Security and International Operations, "PPBS and Foreign Affairs," memorandum prepared by Thomas C. Schelling, 90th Congress, 1st sess., 1968.

10. Dr. Alain Enthoven, who played a leading role in introducing systems analysis to the Defense Department, has observed that: "The major changes in strategy, the step-up in production of Minutemen and Polaris and the build-up in our non-nuclear forces including the increase in the Army, the tactical air forces and the air lift . . . are being phased in at the same time that PPBS was being phased in. . . . We speeded up the Polaris and Minuteman programs because we believed it was necessary to have more land forces for limited non-nuclear wars. We speeded up the development of anti-guerrilla forces or special forces because we believed that was necessary for counter-insurgency. Those things would have happened with or without PPBS. PPBS does not make the strategy." Senate Committee on Government Operations, Subcommittee on National Security and International Operations, *Hearings, The Planning-Programming-Budgeting System,* 90th Congress, 1st sess., pt. 2, Sept. 27 and Oct. 18, 1967, p. 141.
11. *Prospects for Oil Shale Development* (Washington, D.C.: Department of the Interior, May 1968).
12. The study is presented in ibid., pp. 10–45.
13. Similar difficulties under similar conditions evidently occur in the business world. It is worth citing Anthony's comments: "Strategic planning [that is, policy analysis] is essentially *irregular*. Problems, opportunities, and 'bright ideas' do not arise according to some set timetable; they have to be dealt with whenever they happen to be perceived. . . . Failure to appreciate the distinction between regular and irregular processes can result in trouble of the following type. A company with a well-developed budgeting process decides to formalize its strategic planning. It prepares a set of forms and accompanying procedures, and has the operating units submit their long-range plans on these forms on one certain date each year. The plans are then supposed to be reviewed and approved in a meeting similar to a budget review meeting. Such a procedure does not work. . . . There simply is not time enough in an annual review meeting for a careful consideration of a whole batch of strategic proposals. . . . It is important that next year's operating budget be examined and approved as an entity so as to ensure that the several pieces are consonant with one another. . . . Except for very general check-lists of essential considerations, the strategic planning process follows no prescribed format or timetable. Each problem is sufficiently different from other problems so that each must be approached differently" (Anthony, op. cit., pp. 38–39).
14. Joint Economic Committee, *Hearings, The Planning-Programming-Budgeting System: Progress and Potentials,* 90th Congress, 1st sess., September 1967, p. 5.
15. Ibid., pp. 80–81. One might think that a way out of the dilemma could be had by adopting a number of goals for an area of policy. When Committee Chairman William Proxmire suggested that more goals should be specified, Gorham replied, "I would like to be the one to give the first goal. The first one in is always in the best shape. The more goals you have, essentially the less useful any one is, because the conflict among them becomes so sharp" (p. 83).
16. Ibid., p. 6
17. Anthony again supplies a useful comparison from private firms that makes a similar point: "An increasing number of businesses make profit and balance sheet projections for several years ahead, a process which has come to be know by the name 'long-range planning.' . . . A five-year plan usually is a projection of the costs and revenues that are anticipated under policies and programs *already approved,* rather than a device for consideration of, and decision on, new policies and programs. The five-year plan reflects strategic decisions already taken; it is not the essence of the process of making new decisions. . . . In some companies, the so-called five-year plan is nothing more than a mechanical extrapolation of current data, with no reflection of management decisions and judgments; such an exercise is virtually worthless" (Anthony, op. cit., pp. 57–58).
18. An excellent discussion of different purposes of budgeting and stages of budgetary development is found in Allen Schick, "The Road

to PPB: The Stages of Budget Reform," *Pub. Adm. Rev.* 26 (December 1966): 243–258.

19. In another paper ("Toward a Radical Incrementalism," op. cit.) I have proposed that policy analysis would be facilitated by abolishing the annual budget cycle. One of the great weaknesses of governmental policy making is that policies are formulated a good two years before funds become available. Given the difficulties of devising policies in the first place, the time lag wreaks havoc with the best analysis. Since no one seems disposed to consider this alternative seriously, I mention it merely in passing as a change that would fit in with what has been suggested.
20. Senate Committee on Government Operations, Subcommittee on National Security and International Operations, "Program Budgeting in Foreign Affairs: Some Reflections," memorandum prepared by Frederick C. Mosher, 90th Congress, 2nd sess., 1968.
21. Joint Economic Committee, *Hearings, The Planning-Programming-Budgeting System,* pp. 77–78.
22. "Toward a Radical Incrementalism," op. cit., pp. 27–29.
23. When Charles Hitch was Controller of the Defense Department, the policy analysis unit reported directly to him, as did the budget unit. One reported result is that the policy unit was able to do its work without being drawn into the daily concerns of the budget men. When policy analysis (called systems analysis) was given separate status, with its own assistant secretary, there was apparently a much greater tendency for its members to insist upon control of immediate budgetary decisions. Hence the distinction between longer-run policy analysis and shorter-run budgeting tended to be obscured. It would be interesting to know whether the participants saw it in this way. Optimal placement of a policy analysis unit is bound to be a source of difficulty and a subject of controversy.
24. Clay Thomas Whitehead, "Uses and Abuses of Systems Analysis," The RAND Corporation, September 1967.
25. See Martin Landau, "Redundancy," *Pub. Adm. Rev.,* scheduled for publication in vol. 29 (July–August 1969).
26. For a fine example of original thought on this question, see Paul Feldman, "Benefits and the Role of Government in a Market Economy," Institute for Defense Analysis, research paper, February 1968, p. 477.

23

The End of Liberalism: The Indictment

Theodore J. Lowi

The corruption of modern democratic government began with the emergence of interest-group liberalism as the public philosophy. Its corrupting influence takes at least four important forms, four counts, therefore, of an indictment for which most of the foregoing chapters are mere documentation. Also to be indicted, on at least three counts, is the philosophic component of the ideology, pluralism.

Summation I: Four Counts against the Ideology

1. Interest-group liberalism as public philosophy corrupts democratic government because it deranges and confuses expectations about democratic institutions. Liberalism promotes popular decision-making but derogates from the decisions so made by misapplying the notion to the implementation as well as the formulation of policy. It derogates from the processes by treating all values in the process as equivalent interests. It derogates from democratic rights by allowing their exercise in foreign policy, and by assuming they are being exercised when access is provided. Liberal practices reveal a basic disrespect for democracy. Liberal leaders do not wield the authority of democratic government with the resoluteness of men certain of the legitimacy of their positions, the integrity of their institutions, or the justness of the programs they serve.
2. Interest-group liberalism renders government impotent. Liberal governments cannot plan. Liberals are copious in plans but irresolute in planning. Nineteenth-century liberalism was standards without plans. This was an anachronism in the modern state. But twentieth-century liberalism turned out to be plans without standards. As an anachronism it, too, ought to pass. But doctrines are not organisms. They die only in combat over the minds of men, and no doctrine yet exists capable of doing the job. All the popular alternatives are so very irrelevant, helping to explain the longevity of interest-group liberalism. Barry Goldwater most recently proved the irrelevance of one. The *embourgeoisement* of American unions suggests the irrelevance of others.

The Departments of Agriculture, Commerce, and Labor provide illustrations, but hardly exhaust illustrations, of such impotence. Here clearly one sees how liberalism has become a doctrine whose means are its ends, whose combatants are its clientele, whose standards are not even those of the mob but worse, are those the bargainers can fashion to fit the bargain. Delegation of power has become alienation of public domain—the gift of sovereignty to private satrapies. The political barriers to withdrawal of delegations are high enough. But liberalism reinforces these through the rhetoric of justification and often even permanent legal reinforcement: Public corporations—justified, oddly, as efficient planning instruments—permanently alienate rights of central coordination to the directors and to those who own the corporation bonds. Or, as Walter Adams finds, the "most pervasive method . . . for alienating public domain is the certificate of convenience and necessity, or some variation thereof in the form of an exclusive franchise, license or permit. . . . [G]overnment has become increasingly careless and subservient in issuing them. The net result is a general legalization of private monopoly . . ."[1] While the best examples still are probably the 10 self-governing systems of agriculture policy, these are obviously only a

Source: Reprinted from The End of Liberalism: The Second Republic of the United States, 2nd Edition by Theodore J. Lowi. Copyright © 1979, 1969 by W. W. Norton & Company, Inc. Used by permission of W. W. Norton & Company, Inc.

small proportion of all the barriers the interest-group liberal ideology has erected to democratic use of government.

3. Interest group liberalism demoralizes government, because liberal governments cannot achieve justice. The question of justice has engaged the best minds for almost as long as there have been notions of state and politics, certainly ever since Plato defined the ideal as one in which republic and justice were synonymous. And since that time philosophers have been unable to agree on what justice is. But outside the ideal, in the realms of actual government and citizenship, the problem is much simpler. We do not have to define justice at all in order to weight and assess justice in government, because in the case of liberal policies we are prevented by what the law would call a "jurisdictional fact." In the famous jurisdictional case of *Marbury* v. *Madison* Chief Justice Marshall held that even if all the Justices hated President Jefferson for refusing to accept Marbury and the other "midnight judges" appointed by Adams, there was nothing they could do. They had no authority to judge President Jefferson's action one way or another because the Supreme Court did not possess such jurisdiction over the President. In much the same way, there is something about liberalism that prevents us from raising the question of justice at all, no matter what definition of justice is used.

Liberal governments cannot achieve justice because their policies lack the *sine qua non* of justice—that quality without which a consideration of justice cannot even be initiated. Considerations of the just in or achieved by an action cannot be made unless a deliberate and conscious attempt was made by the actor to derive his action from a general rule or moral principle governing such a class of acts. One can speak personally of good rules and bad rules, but a homily or a sentiment like liberal legislation, is not a rule at all. The best rule is one which is relevant to the decision or action in question and is general in the sense that those involved with it have no direct control over its operation. A general rule is, hence, *a priori*. Any governing regime that makes a virtue of avoiding such rules puts itself totally outside the context of justice.

Take the homely example of the bull and the china shop. Suppose it was an op art shop and that we consider op art worthy only of the junk pile. That being the case, the bull did us a great service, the more so because it was something we always dreamed of doing but were prevented by law from entering and breaking. But however much we may be pleased, we cannot judge the act. We can only like or dislike the consequences. The consequences are haphazard; the bull cannot have intended them. The act was a thoughtless, animal act which bears absolutely no relation to any aesthetic principle. We don't judge the bull. We only celebrate our good fortune. Without the general rule, the bull can reenact his scenes of creative destruction daily and still not be capable of achieving, in this case, aesthetic justice. The whole idea of justice is absurd.

The general rule ought to be a legislative rule because the United States espouses the ideal of representative democracy. However, that is merely an extrinsic feature of the rule.[2] All that counts is the character of the rule itself. Without the rule we can only like or dislike the consequences of the governmental action. In the question of whether justice is achieved, a government without good rules, and without acts carefully derived therefrom, is merely a big bull in an immense china shop.

4. Finally, interest-group liberalism corrupts democratic government in the degree to which it weakens the capacity of governments to live by democratic formalisms.[3] Liberalism weakens democratic institutions by opposing formal procedure with informal bargaining. Liberalism derogates from democracy by derogating from all formality in favor of informality. Formalism is constraining; playing it "by the book" is a role often unpopular in American war films and sports films precisely because it can dramatize personal rigidity and the plight of the individual in collective situations. Because of the impersonality of for-

mal procedures, there is inevitably a separation in the real world between the forms and the realities, and this kind of separation gives rise to cynicism, for informality means that some will escape their collective fate better than others. There has as a consequence always been a certain amount of cynicism toward public objects in the United States, and this may be to the good, since a little cynicism is the father of healthy sophistication. However, when the informal is elevated to a positive virtue, and hard-won access becomes a share of official authority, cynicism becomes distrust. It ends in reluctance to submit one's fate to the governmental process under any condition, as is the case in the United States in the mid-1960's.

Public officials more and more frequently find their fates paradoxical and their treatment at the hands of the public fickle and unjust when in fact they are only reaping the results of their own behavior, including their direct and informal treatment of the public and the institutions through which they serve the public. The more government operates by the spreading of access, the more public order seems to suffer. The more public men pursue their constituencies, the more they seem to find their constituencies alienated. Liberalism has promoted concentration of democratic authority but deconcentration of democratic power. Liberalism has opposed privilege in policy formulation only to foster it, quite systematically, in the implementation of policy. Liberalism has consistently failed to recognize, in short, that in a democracy forms are important. In a medieval monarchy all formalisms were at court. Democracy proves, for better or worse, that the masses like that sort of thing too.

Another homely parable may help. In the good old days, everyone in the big city knew the traffic tickets could be fixed. Not everyone could get his ticket fixed, but nonetheless a man who honestly paid his ticket suffered in some degree a dual loss: his money, and his self-esteem for having so little access. Cynicism was widespread, violations were many, but perhaps it did not matter, for there were so few automobiles. Suppose, however, that as the automobile population increased a certain city faced a traffic crisis and the system of ticket fixing came into ill repute. Suppose a mayor, victorious on the Traffic Ticket, decided that, rather than eliminate fixing by universalizing enforcement, he would instead reform the system by universalizing the privileges of ticket fixing. One can imagine how the system would work. One can imagine that some sense of equality would prevail, because everyone could be made almost equally free to bargain with the ticket administrators. But one would find it difficult to imagine how this would make the total city government more legitimate. Meanwhile, the purpose of the ticket would soon have been destroyed.

Traffic regulation, fortunately, was not so reformed. But many other government activities were. The operative principles of interest-group liberalism possess the mentality of a world of universalized ticket fixing: Destroy privilege by universalizing it. Reduce conflict by yielding to it. Redistribute power by the maxim of each according to his claim. Reserve an official place for every major structure of power. Achieve order by worshipping the process (as distinguished from the forms and the procedures) by which order is presumed to be established.

If these operative principles will achieve equilibrium—and such is far from proven—that is all they will achieve. Democracy will have disappeared, because all of these maxims are founded upon profound lack of confidence in democracy. Democracy fails when it lacks confidence in its own authority.

Democratic forms were supposed to precede and accompany the formulation of policies so that policies could be implemented authoritatively and firmly. Democracy is indeed a form of absolutism, but ours was fairly well contrived to be an absolutist government under the strong control of consent-building prior to taking authoritative action in law. Interest-group liberalism fights the absolutism of democracy but succeeds only in taking away its authoritativeness. Whether it is called "creative federalism" by President Johnson, "cooperation" by the farmers, "local autonomy" by the Republicans, or "participatory democracy" by the New Left, the interest-group liberal effort does not create democratic power but rather negates it.

Notes

1. Walter S. Adams and Horace Gray, *Monopoly in America* (N.Y.: Macmillan, 1955), pp. 47–48.
2. As argued in Chapter 5, there is a high probability that efforts to make rules will lead to the legislature. A general rule excites continuous efforts at reformulation, which tend to turn combatants toward the levels of highest legitimacy and last appeal. Contrary to the fears of pluralists, the statement of a good rule can produce more flexibility and more competition than the avoidance of the rule. These tendencies are still further developed under proposals for reform.
3. One aspect of this was dealt with at some length at the end of Chapter 3. Another was dealt with at the end of Chapter 6. Here, at the risk of some repetition, the various aspects of it are put together.

24

Redundancy, Rationality, and the Problem of Duplication and Overlap

Martin Landau

Not so long ago I experienced an emergency landing. We had been aloft only a short time when the pilot announced some mechanical failure. As we headed toward the nearest airport, the man behind me, no less frightened than I, said to his companion, "Here's where my luck runs out." A few minutes later we touched down to a safe landing amidst foam trucks and asbestos-clad fire fighters.

On the ground I ran into the pilot and asked him about the trouble. His response was vague, but he did indicate that something had been wrong with the rudder. How, then, was he able to direct and land the plane? He replied that the situation had not really been as ominous as it had seemed: the emergency routines we had followed were necessary precautions and he had been able to compensate for the impairment of the rudder by utilizing additional features of the aircraft. There were, he said, safety factors built into all planes.

Happily, such matters had not been left to chance, luck, as we say. For a commercial airliner is a very redundant system, a fact which accounts for its reliability of performance; a fact which also accounts for its adaptability.

A Paradox

The English language presents us with a striking curiosity. Its lexicons establish an instance of *redundancy* as a "liability" and yet it is precisely the liberal use of redundancy that provides linguistic expression with an extraordinary measure of "reliability."

The Definition In the context of ordinary language, redundancy is said to exist whenever there is an excess or superfluity of anything. The excess may be of parts, of rules, of words, . . . of anything. *Excess*, as defined lexically, is something which is more than the normal, the required, the usual, the specified. It is useless, superfluous, needless—terms which are variously employed to define redundancy.

This linguistic habit directs a negative judgment. It points to features of a situation which are of no value, which are wasteful, which are bad. The force of this habit is immediately to be seen by noting that the synonyms for the adjective "excessive" are: immoderate, intemperate, inordinate, extravagant, exorbitant, and extreme. If we need a time scale here, we can note that excessive has been used to define redundancy for some 400 years.

Accordingly, to say of a person's speech that it is redundant is not to extend a compliment. To observe an excess of parts is to observe an unnecessary duplication which, almost automatically, is seen as waste. To confront an excess of rules is, naturally, to make unhappy contact with red tape. And so on. In each case, more than is necessary is apparent, a condition which is sometimes regarded as affluent but more often as profligate. It is rarely regarded as economic and even less often as efficient. Indeed, there are many who seem to make *zero redundancy* the measure of both economy and efficiency. And if this condition is not fully realizable in practice, it nevertheless stands as the optimal state to be attained.

So powerful is this convention, that when Harry Nyquist introduced "redundancy" as a technical term in information theory, it referred to the useless portions of a message—those which could be eliminated without any loss of information. Nyquist sought a nonredundant system, one which would permit the transmission of information with the absolutely minimal number of signs that could possibly be employed.[1] Today, however, this goal is no longer entertained. It has been set aside: not because it is impossible of achievement, but because its realization would, in fact, increase the probability of failure—of false, misleading, and distorted messages.

Source: From Public Administration Review, July/August 1969. Reprinted by permission of Blackwell Publishing.

The Use of Redundancy Consider this essay. I write it because I have a statement to make, one which I think is deserving of interest. And, as befalls anyone who wishes to send a message of this kind, several doubts assail me. To begin with, it is possible that my statement is not worth sending, but upon reflection I think it is. Then, I may not be able to make myself understood. My thoughts and/or my phraseology may be quite unclear and I know that to be understood requires a clarity of expression. I am also aware that I know most about what I want to say, but I am not sure that I can present my position in such a way as to enable the reader to receive it exactly as I want him to. Nor am I any more certain of my reader who, for many reasons beyond my control, may misinterpret what I write and receive an erroneous impression.

These are some of the uncertainties which face me as I seek to communicate. The possibility of misunderstanding, of an inability to make contact, of breakdown, is inescapable. I anticipate this and I work to lessen the risk all along the line. It would be helpful, of course, if I could deploy a decision system specifically designed to do so; statistics perhaps. It does, after all, permit the making of decisions under conditions of uncertainty with the least possible error.[2] But I have not ordered this paper, nor can I, in such a manner as to make use of its powers. Happily, however, I am not without other resources.

Notice that the paragraphs I have written are quite repetitious. I repeat directly and indirectly, and I did this in all similar circumstances before I "knew" that simple repetition is the easiest way to introduce redundancy and that redundancy is a powerful device for the suppression of error. I employ more words than the "absolute minimum" and I arrange them according to a larger number of grammatical rules than are ideally necessary, all of this not to waste space but to insure reliability of communication.[3] If the overall uncertainty factor could be eliminated, I would (theoretically) write with zero redundancy. But then, strangely enough, there would be no way to detect error should one arise.[4] This, of course, is an idle speculation, because no language is without redundancy.[5] Even our most precise scientific languages contain redundancies, and this statement is true for purely formal languages as well.[6]

It is, thus, virtually impossible to eliminate all duplication. And given the state of my knowledge at this point, it is rather fortuitous that the language I must employ is loaded with both a semantic and syntactical redundancy that comes naturally to me. In time I may be able to communicate on this problem with more certainty, with a more logical and precise syntax, with less multiplicity of meanings; then, the type of redundancy needed would change, the amount would diminish, and the risk of inconsistency would lessen. Now, however, a resort to the vernacular and I need not apologize for this. On the contrary, "the rules we call grammar and syntax . . . supplement and duplicate each other, providing a great margin of safety."[7] While I must exercise care so as not to be incoherent, I can nevertheless break some of these rules without destroying or critically damaging the communication process itself. Nor need it be stressed that the redundancy of both our grammar and lexicon are sources of great creativity and innovation.

Public Administration and Redundancy

It is, however, the lexical evaluation of redundancy which prevails in public administration. Indeed, this view is to be seen as programmatic in such revitalization movements as Taylorism and scientific management. These demanded the wholesale removal of duplication and overlap as they pressed for "streamlined organizations" that would operate with the absolutely minimal number of units that could possibly be employed in the performance of a task. Zero redundancy constituted the measure of optimal efficiency and this ideal, fortified by a scarcity of resources and an abundance of precedent, has informed both the theory and practice of public administration since the earliest days of the reform movement. Now, of course, we possess new vocabularies, direct our attention to management control systems, and seize upon such new technologies as PPBS. But our perspective remains fully as Utopian as it was a half-century ago.[8]

For the plain fact is that no amount of effort has yet been able to produce, even for limited time-spans, the precise mutually exclusive differentiation of activity that administrative integrationists long for and that PPBS *requires.* In the last 30 years we have observed massive efforts to reduce duplication: we have moved from the radical reconstructions which followed upon the Roosevelt and Hoover commissions to the institution of continuous executive reorganization—only to find that duplication and overlap are as conspicuous today as they have ever been.

Nor will the introduction of PPBS alter this condition to any appreciable extent—if we follow the statements of its advocates (many of which, it must be said, could use a good dose of redundancy). Testimony varies from an unrestrained hyperbole to a caution that is tinged with pessimism, but it remains clear "that the functioning of a program budget will reveal wasteful duplications, overlaps and inconsistencies created or permitted by the scatter of related activities through numerous executive departments, agencies and bureaus."[9] Redressing this grievance, though necessary to effective program budgeting, is not likely to be an easy task and the proponents of PPBS know this. They fully anticipate that they will be unable to withstand the combined resistance of counterpart congressional committees and special-interest groups, "all mortgaged to the existing administrative structure."[10] Anshen then writes,

> One may conclude that the program budget could not function effectively in such an environment. Because *wholesale revision of the federal structure in accordance with the logic of a program budget* is clearly not going to be brought about in the near future, this judgment would be definitely negative for the budget's near term prospects.[11]

With such language before us, it is tempting to pursue Wildavsky's proposal that program budgeting is "an integral part of system politics,"[12] a contention that is unassailable. Engaged as we are, however, in an exploration of redundancy, it may suffice to suggest that the nation is not going to allow engineers to order its fundamental decision system "in accordance with the logic of program budgeting" now, or in the long term. That is, the probability that PPBS technicians will be given the authority to rewrite the constitution is zero. Hence they will have to settle for less—much less. And Anshen salvages what he can in the only way that he can; a compromise between the demands of the existing system and the requirements of program budgeting.[13] But if only such complication did not attend this scene: the nation's entire administrative complex could be transformed into one magnificent means-end chain with not an excess link in it.

Thus it is that the removal of redundancy is rarely, if ever, challenged in the technology of public administration. It is an article of faith, a commanding precept; and if its injunctions cannot be followed today, one can always dream of tomorrow. Those controversies that do arise generally concern the manner in which repair is to be effected and are not expressed any more differently than when Francis W. Coker cast a skeptical eye on the dogmas of administration. The doubts he raised turned on whether more might be accomplished through an incremental strategy than by a process of radical integration. But with respect to the need to "eliminate duplication and overlapping,"[14] he felt obliged to state, "No serious exception can be taken to this principle."[15]

In what follows, I shall exercise a theoretical option and take such exception. I cannot argue the case in full here, but I shall try to show that there are good grounds for suggesting that efforts to improve public administration by eliminating duplication and overlap would, if successful, produce just the opposite effect. That so many attempts have failed should perhaps alert us to what sociologists would call the "latent function" of this type of redundancy. This possibility alone is sufficient warrant for transforming a precept into a problem.

Redundancy and Error Suppression: Reliability

There is, however, an additional reason for doing so.

The reader will observe that the phenomenon of "duplication" is no longer left to chance in the study of language. Nor is it overlooked in the design of automobiles, computers, and aircraft; the latter are reliable to the extent that they are redundant—and we have all had occasion to note that a good deal of the controversy over "safe cars" has had to do with the introduction of this feature as a standard element of design, as with the dual braking system, for example. That is, there is now a developing theory of redundancy, and while it was originally conceived of in the domains of information science (including computer technology) and natural automata (neural networks), it appears to have very wide application. In many areas, therefore, "over-engineering," "reserve power," and "safety-factors" of all sorts need no longer be dealt with intuitively.

But what of large-scale formal organization: can it be engaged in terms of this theory? The answer, of course, cannot be had *a priori,* but the attempt to do so is well under way, precipitated quite naturally by our propensity to draw from such cognate languages as systems analysis, cybernetics, and information theory—in particular, the latter. Fashion aside, however, "this comparison need not be a sterile metaphorical analogy," as Rapoport and Horvath note, for all organizations have "neural physiologies" in the sense that they are unthinkable "without internal communication, integration and control."[16] Marschak, in the same vein, proposes that an organization is to be defined by the rules which determine the sets of messages that can be received by its different members. Any given system, thus, "states who should do what in response to what."[17]

Upon reflection, it makes a good deal of sense to regard a large-scale organization as a vast and complicated information system. It is, after all, necessarily and continuously engaged in the transmission and reception of messages. But it is an awfully noisy system. Its codes, classification rules, are not unambiguous; its internal arrangements are not perfect; the course of its messages are neither consistent nor constant—nor are the messages themselves. Error occurs at the point of origin, where a message is selected from a whole ensemble of signs (stimuli), and at the point of reception. The language which is employed is notoriously vague and the "variable human,"[18] acting both as sender and receiver, often transforms the relation between a sign and its referent into a mystery. In an organizational system one can never be sure that either members or clientele can be reached without error or distortion. The transmission of information is, indeed, a very risky business.[19] Against this backdrop, the demand for control by central officers can clearly be seen as a demand for increased reliability (predictability) of response—and this means a reduction of uncertainty.

In public administration the standard policy for improving the performance characteristics of an administrative agency has rested upon the classical axiom that the reliability and efficiency of an operating system, man or machine, is dependent on the reliability and efficiency of each of its parts, including linkages. Improvement, therefore, calls for a system to be broken down (decomposed or analyzed) into its most basic units, these to be worked on to the point of infallibility. So much success has attended this procedure, especially as regards machine-based systems, that it not only constitutes a sound problem-solving paradigm, but is often generalized into a good commonsense rule. About the only limitations which are imposed on its application are those which derive from market conditions, the law of diminishing returns, and the state of the art.

Yet it is doubtful that the risk of failure can be removed in this manner even in the most advanced technologies. No matter how much a part is perfected, there is always the chance that it will fail. In some cases, many in fact, this is a tolerable risk—the unit involved may not be a basic component and the consequences of failure may be minimal. But where a system is important, and where it is made dependent upon operating parts that are organized into a tight means-end chain, the problem becomes acute. In such systems, especially when large, there is a tendency for even minor errors to be so amplified along the length of the chain as to make the end-result quite unreliable. In formal organizations this tendency can be expressed in terms of "the absorption of uncertainty."[20] The failure, then, of a single part can mean the failure of the entire system: as when the breakdown of a switching circuit blacks out an entire region or the failure of a duty officer to heed radar readings permits a force of unidentified aircraft to attack Pearl Harbor with devastating success. The latter case, it will be recognized, constitutes a stark illustration of the uncertainty principle. Here it was not the *evidence* which was transmitted, only the *inferences*.[21] In complex and tightly ordered systems the cost of error can run very high.

This is the context in which the theory of redundancy bulks so large. For it sets aside the doctrine that ties the reliability of a system to the perfectibility of parts and thereby approaches the pragmatics of systems in action much more realistically. That is, it accepts the inherent limitations of any organization by treating any and all parts, regardless of their degree of perfection,[22] as risky actors. The practical implications of this shift in orientation is immediately to be seen when the following question is asked: Is it possible to take a set of individually unreliable units and form them into a system "with any arbitrarily high reliability"?[23] Can we, in other words, build an organization that is more reliable than any of its parts?

The answer, *mirabile dictu*, is yes. In what is now a truly classical paper, Von Neumann demonstrated that it could be done by adding sufficient redundancy.[24] Developments in this domain move swiftly and where before we could only resort to an intuitive and rather pragmatic redundancy, there now exist powerful theorems which can be applied with far greater certainty and much less waste.[25] This, it can be said, is a cardinal feature of "systems analysis"—all too often overlooked.

The theory itself is a rather complicated set of formulations and it serves no purpose to dwell upon it in any great detail. Yet there is one theorem that must be indicated because of the profound effect it can have on organizational design: that the probability of failure in a system decreases exponentially as redundancy factors are increased. Increasing reliability in this manner, of course, raises the price to be paid and if fail-safe conditions are to be reached, the cost may be prohibitive. But an immediate corollary of the theorem eases this problem for it requires only arithmetic increases in redundancy to yield geometric increases in reliability. Costs may then be quite manageable.

The application of this formula, however, depends upon the ability to construct a system so that it satisfies those conditions which permit the laws of probability to apply, in this case, the multiplication theorem or the product rule for independent events: alternatively, the failure of parts must be random and statistically independent (unrelated). In practical terms, therefore, a system must be so arranged that when parts fail, they do so unpredictably and in such manner *that they cannot and do not impair other parts*, as in the dual braking system of a car. If each braking assembly is not completely separated from the other, the redundancy is not only waste, it becomes a very dangerous addition: when it fails it is likely (perhaps certain) to damage the other assembly: So much for a theorem which has to do with duplication. We turn now to "overlapping."

"Overlapping" Generally employed to denote biological organisms (neural physiologies, in particular), "self-organizing systems" command fully as much attention in the study of redundancy as computing machines and communication networks. There is nothing surprising about this since the theory of redundancy is a theory of system reliability. And self-organizing systems exhibit a degree of reliability that is so far superior to anything we can build as to prompt theorists to suggest "that the richly redundant networks of biological organisms must have capabilities beyond anything our theories can yet explain."[26] In Von Neumann's phrasing, they "contain the necessary arrangements to diagnose errors as they occur, to readjust the organism so as to minimize the effects of errors, and finally to correct or to block permanently the faulty component." Error refers here to malfunction, and Von Neumann states that there is now little doubt that they are "able to operate even when malfunctions set in . . . [while] their subsequent tendency is to remove them."[27] Pierce adds that they are able to improve reliability when errors are common even as they improve their capabilities when errors are infrequent.[28]

Equipotentiality How, precisely, this works remains an object of inquiry. But it seems clear that such systems possess a fantastic number of parallel hookups of many different types. McCulloch, in commenting on the reliability of biological organisms, speaks of redundancies of codes, of channels, of calculation, and of potential command, noting that each serves differently. "The reliability you can buy with redundancy of calculation cannot be bought with redundancy of code or channel."[29] To these we can add the property of "equipotentiality" which provides the system with an extraordinary adaptive power.

Equipotentiality, interestingly enough, is often referred to as "overlapping."[30] It denotes the tendency of neural networks to resist that kind of precise differentiation of function which is mutually exclusive. Even in the case of highly specialized subsystems the tendency is restricted but not lost. There appears to be some "overlap" at all times which enables residual parts or subsidiary centers to "take over," though somewhat less efficiently, the functions of those which have been damaged. It is this overlap[31] that permits the organism to exhibit a high degree of adaptability, i.e., to change its behavior in accordance with changes in stimuli.

Duplication and Overlap: Politics

And this is why it may be quite *irrational* to greet the appearance of duplication and overlap by automatically moving to excise and redefine. To unify the defense departments, or the several independent information-gathering services of the government, or the large number of agencies engaged in technical assistance, or the various antipoverty programs, or the miscellany of agencies concerned with transportation, or the great variety of federal, state, and local administrations that function in the same areas may rob the system of its necessary supports. It can be hypothesized that it is precisely such redundancies that allow for the delicate process of mutual adjustment, of self-regulation, by means of which the whole system can sustain severe local injuries and still function creditably.

Hypothesis?—perhaps it is more than that. If, of course, "men were angels," the systems they constitute would be foolproof. But they are not; and this is the fact that stands at the foundation of the organization created in Philadelphia. For the charter of the national system is a patent illustration of redundancy. Look at it: separation of powers, federalism, checks and balances, concurrent powers, double legislatures, overlapping terms of office, the Bill of Rights, the veto, the override, judicial review, and a host of similar arrangements. Here is a system that cannot be described except in terms of duplication and overlap—of a redundancy of channel, code, calculation, and command.

These are the redundancies which prompt public administration theorists to regard this system as quite inefficient—if not irrational. Where they wish one unambiguous code, there are many and these are hardly unequivocal; where they seek a unity of command, there is a redundancy of command; and so on. As a decision system, the organization of government certainly appears to be inferior to that which underlays program budgeting—which is why we see an expressed longing for a "wholesale revision of the federal structure." After all, as some programmers see it, the objectives of the architects of the Constitution were as much political as economic, and their economics "had a philosophic rather than managerial or operational character. The decision-making structure came . . . under the influence of objectives other than rationality of choice."[32] And, as Smithies has noted, "It is fundamental to our culture that rational choice is better than irrational choice."[33]

It is not possible, however, to determine whether a choice is rational except in terms of systemic context and goal. A course of action may be perfectly rational in one sphere and perfectly silly in another. It is only when context and goal are rendered nonproblematical that objective evaluations of competing decision systems can be had. If these factors cannot be bracketed, then assessments of decision systems are of necessity assignments of priority to specific sets of values. To say, therefore, that rational choice is fundamental to our culture is either to say nothing or, as in the context of administration, to urge that economic rationality is intrinsically superior to political rationality. In this case it should be clear, economic rationality is equated to scientific rationality and we are being told, without restriction, that the rules of scientific decision making are not simply different, they are best. We need not wonder why scientific management programs have always had the appearance of an ideology.

But there is more than one kind of "rationality," including the rationality of redundancy. Theoretically, there can be as many rationalities as there are systems—which is why phenomenologists have urged that rationality not be treated solely as a methodological principle but as "empirically problematical material" as well. In this respect Garfinkle has demonstrated that there are profound differences between "common sense" and "scientific" rationalities—of such an order that the two cannot be ranked. Indeed, it might give us all pause to observe what happens when the maxims of ideal scientific procedure are introduced willy-nilly into the everyday situation; what they do is to disrupt its continuities and multiply its anomic features.[34] In short, they disorganize an organized state.

Moreover, there is an element of paradox in the effort to extend these maxims to government at large. Most of us are influenced, if not absorbed, by the notion of "system," and this statement obviously includes economizers. Among the most fundamental elements of systems analysis, however, is the concept of systemic relevance. And the criteria which establish relevance are the criteria which mark boundaries. This means that any methodology is to be valued only to the extent that it achieves systemically relevant goals and such goals, to be at all sensible, must be desired state conditions which are in reach and which are field determined. Otherwise, they are idle fantasies or simply Utopian. If, of course, boundaries enlarge so as to permit what was heretofore irrelevant, this can only be learned, by experience. Under such an expansion, methodologies which were once inappropriate may become extremely valuable. As Hamilton was known to say, "means ought to be proportional to the end."[35]

Auxiliary Precautions The constitution-makers, it appears, were eminently "rational." They chose wisely and they did so under hazardous conditions. They knew that they were "organizing" a system in the face of great uncertainty. We need not list the profound and abiding cleavages which existed nor the intense fears which were displayed: *The Federalist* alone makes this clear. But it also instructs that in fabricating the constitution, the architects were ever mindful of the grave possibility of failure and sought a system which could perform in the face of error—which could manage to provide a stable set of decision rules for an exceedingly unstable circumstance. And they found their answer in Newton's Third Law.[36] Experience, Madison wrote, has taught mankind the necessity for *auxiliary precautions:* these were to be had "by so contriving the internal structure of government so that its several constituent parts, may by their mutual relations, be the means of keeping each other in their proper places."[37] The principle of action and reaction, of checks and balances, turns out to have been, in organization terms, the principle of inter-woven and competing redundancies.

"That which is redundant is, to the extent that it is redundant, stable. It is therefore reliable."[38] One hundred and seventy-nine years have passed since the original design, and save for one massive failure, the system has withstood the severest of shocks—and may well continue to do so even in the face of today's unprecedented problems. We like to say that it is the oldest constitutional government in the world, yet it remains a novelty. It seems to have worked like a "self-organizing" system exhibiting both the performance reliability and adaptability that such systems display. Marked by a redundancy of law, of power and command, of structure and linkage—*the whole has appeared as more reliable than any of its parts.* Where one part has failed another has taken over, and even when duplicates were not there to be employed, the presence of equipotentiality, of overlapping functions, permitted the load to be assumed elsewhere, however imperfectly. Scholars have for years spoken of the "cyclical character" of intra-governmental arrangements, of a "pendulum of checks and balances," frequently pointing to this phenomenon as an adaptive response. The "uncertain content" (jurisdiction) of the various parts of government just will not allow it to sit still and the hyphenated phrases we are forced to use in describing government are indicative of the extent of its equipotentiality. Even when such reference is pejorative, as often happens in the instance of "judicial-legislation," such a concept points to an overlap which enables adaptation. *Baker* v. *Carr* is a recent illustration of this kind of self-regulation.[39] The boss, the historical master of an "invisible government," was a redundancy that developed to offset the failures of local government,[40] and this would not have been possible but for the redundancy of party. Senator Mike Mansfield, speaking on the floor of the Senate, warns his colleagues that if they do not act, other branches of government will:

> It is clear that when one road to this end fails, others will unfold as indeed they have unfolded. If the process is ignored in legislative channels, it will not necessarily be blocked in other channels—in the executive branch and in the courts.[41]

And the President has been severely criticized because he has radically curtailed the number of channels, formal and informal, that are employed for purposes of control. Richard Neustadt, after describing the extraordinary redundancy which marked FDR's administration, concludes the presidency cannot function effectively without competing information sources.[42]

Nor need any of this be gainsaid by the compelling movement toward centralization. Although this is an empirical problem which I have only begun to investigate, there is some basis for suggesting that this trend constitutes a replacement of historically accepted types of redundancies by those which may be more appropriate to the existent task environment. Because such changes involve command or control, they do not occur without sharp and often protracted conflict—as can be seen in the bitter controversy between the Senate Foreign Relations Committee and the President. This, to be sure, is exacerbated by differences over Vietnam policy, but it necessarily involves competing redundancies. However this is settled, the organization of government in this country, at least until now, demands attention: it seems to have brought an extraordinary amount of reliability and adaptability through its extensive parallel networks (duplication) and equipotential parts (overlap).

Indeed, it is a curiosity to observe the extent to which redundancy theorists resort to political metaphor. Their designs eschew single-line arrangements and they employ a system of multiplexing (multiple lines in parallel) which operates in accordance with the principle of "majority rule." Such devices are known as "vote-takers" which abide by the rules of "democratic suffrage." As Von Neumann put it, they are "majority organs." And Pierce remarks that, "It is as though there were a nation in which no citizen could be trusted, and accordingly, several citizens were required to act together in making decisions, executing orders or delivering messages."[43] But there are times when equally weighted votes are not as effective as one might desire. Under such circumstances, redundancy theorists provide for an "aristocratic suffrage" by assigning unequal weights to decision makers. What is most interesting here is that this assignment is made in proportion to a decision maker's reliability as tested under performance conditions and is adjusted continuously in accordance with the record.[44] More immediately, however, the use of such metaphor bespeaks an implicit grasp of the power of redundancy in politics.

Public Administration

Not so for public administration, however.

Its prevailing notions of organizational rationality are built upon contrary assumptions. Where the "rationality" of politics derives from the fact that a system can be more reliable (more responsive, more predictable) than any of its parts, public administration has postulated that a system can be no more than the sum of its parts: reliable components, thus, add up to a reliable system and *per contra*.

The logic of this position, to iterate, calls for each role to be perfected, each bureau to be exactly delimited, each linkage to articulate un-failingly, and each line of communication to be noiseless—all to produce one interlocking system, one means-end chain which possesses the absolutely minimum number of links, and which culminates at a central control point. For the public administration rationalist, the optimal organization consists of units that are wholly compatible, precisely connected, fully determined, and, therefore, perfectly reliable. The model which represents this dream is that of a linear organization in which everything is arrayed in tandem.[45] It is as if the entire house is to be wired in series.

If the analogy holds, and it does to a considerable extent—especially as regards communication processes, organizational systems of this sort are a form of administrative *brinkmanship.* They are extraordinary gambles. When one bulb blows, everything goes. Ordering parts in series makes them so dependent upon each other that any single failure can break the system. It is the old story of "For want of a nail . . . the battle was lost." Other illustrations: each of us can supply any number of instances of rather serious disruptions because of a faulty part, a malfunctioning actor, a noisy channel. Serial arrangements have the property of intensifying error.

In fact, they may be conducive to error—and to all sorts of problems. For they presuppose the human actor is a linear element and can, therefore, produce outputs in proportion to inputs, and on schedule. There is no doubt, of course, that the human actor can perform "indifferently" over a very wide task environment and under very diverse conditions: otherwise, large-scale formal organization as we know it would not be able to maintain itself.[46] But we have come to learn, and at sad cost, that even if serial demands fall within an actor's "zone of acceptance," there are limits to his linearity. The strains imposed can be too much, the burden of error can be too great—in short, he can be overloaded. A ready resort to a "rational calculus," which places actors in serial interdependence on the assumption of linearity, courts trouble. As against optimum performance, it may beget even less than a satisfying one. Indeed, it is more likely to breed a "resistance" which ultimately results in a sharply reduced zone of acceptance. And this reduction may be so severe as to constitute a direct challenge to organizational authority. In this circumstance, organizational expenditures to secure compliance may be far more than the cost of parallel hookups which do not require perfectibility to increase reliability and which, thereby, reduce strain.

There are additional risks as well—not the least of which is an intensification of the "displacement of goals."[47] Because each part assumes so weighty a responsibility in the system, exacting controls are required. Rules, therefore, assume even more importance than they ordinarily do. And the more precise they are, the better the control. There is, then, an even greater possibility that strict and slavish adherence to regulations will obtain. The burden of error is sufficient to prompt a refusal to exercise discretion when an untoward situation arises. This holds *a fortiori* in a government organization which is bound by rules that have the force of law, for a mistake in interpretation may place action outside the limits of the rule and render it *ultra vires.* Under such strictures there will neither be the "taking advantage of a technicality" or of a "loophole"—and it is a practice such as this one which often constitutes an adaptive response to an urgent problem.

But, beyond this, the "rationality of redundancy" assumes considerable praxiological force when it is noted that the typical organizational pattern which the administrative rationalist proposes is invariably the ideal organizational structure for synoptic or programmed decision making.[48]

To be sure, this type of decision process stands as the perfect form of problem solving. It is, on analysis, modeled on the deductive chain of a fully axiomatized theory. Where it holds, all that is needed to "decide" is to compute the solution—the correct course of action. It can only obtain, however, under conditions of certainty, in a circumstance that Herbert Simon has called a "closed set of variables."[49] For public administration, this means that the environment has been fully and correctly described, that preferred state conditions are unequivocal, and that the instruments necessary to produce preferred states are at hand. Said alternatively, certainty exists as to fact and value, instrumentation and outcome, means and ends. All that needs to be known is known and no ambiguities prevail. If there is any doubt on either side of the equation, then a forced programmed process is no more than an instance of "Gresham's Law." It will drive out the very activity which is needed to produce knowledge; in organizational terms, operational agencies that have not mastered their task environment will be sealed off from it.[50]

Now there are many areas of administration which admit of the logic of programming, with respect to which we can apply the rather powerful "closed decision systems" we already possess. Not to do so is a witless act, for it is an absurdity to refuse to deploy knowledge which is at hand. But there is a question as to how much of the domain of public administration can be covered in this manner.[51] Conditions of certainty, or near certainty, appear to be rare facts in the life of a public agency, and when they exist, their scope is likely to be severely restricted. If so, it is not very rational to design organizations to pursue decision strategies that can comprehend only a small portion of their activities. On the contrary, it is a very sensible rule to construct organizations so that they can cope with uncertainty as to fact and disagreement over values.

If facts are in question, then we simply do not have knowledge of the appropriate means to use in seeking an outcome. We may have hunches and rules of thumb and we may write elaborate plans which anticipate all conceivable outcomes, but these are only hypotheses. It is, therefore, an obvious and "rational calculus" to employ a pragmatic and experimental procedure—that is, a policy of redundancy which permits several, and competing, strategies to be followed both simultaneously and separately. Separately, because the moment a plan is put into effect it constitutes an experiment, and unless we introduce "controls" we cannot determine which course of action is best. And as difficult as it may be to apply this policy in an ongoing agency, so is it necessary. It can be seen, then, that any attempt to "program" solutions prematurely is the height of folly. Managements may do this in the interest of economy and control, but the economy will be false and the control a ritual—for we are acting, and organizing, as if we "know" when we do not. It is a striking phenomenon of organizational life (and elsewhere, of course) that we often present the appearance of "rationality" when we do not know what we are doing or why. Operating personnel will not find this last statement amiss.

Alternatives If the value side is open, we can either fight, slam it shut, or negotiate. It would take us too far afield to discuss conflict here, and we can dispatch the arbitrary closure of value differences by suggesting that it breeds conflict—up to and including "administrative sabotage"—a possibility that programmers must always be alert to. But if there exist differences as to preferences, and the parties involved value the existence of the organization, it makes good sense to compromise, to negotiate differences, to be "political" (a course of action, as noted earlier, that some PPBS spokesmen have had to urge upon their colleagues). This process, we know, is a widespread practice in public administration. The Inter-University Case Program, if it has demonstrated anything, points up "the intricate process of negotiation, mutual accommodation, and reconciliation of competing values . . ." which mark all of the agencies thus far studied.[52] As a decision system, negotiation avoids the precise, mutually exclusive definitions of value that are necessary to any synoptic procedure. This cardinal rule of bargaining has been generated by years of extensive experience, especially in labor-management relations, and is based upon the fact that such clarification of values serves only to extend and intensity disagreement.[53] It, therefore, requires the redundancy of ambiguity, surplus meaning, for it is precisely such surplus that permits values to overlap the parties in dispute providing thereby some common ground for agreement.

There are, then, a number of decision systems,[54] each of which calls for a different organizational perspective. None, however, can do without redundancy. Whatever claims are made for programmed decision making, it is to be recognized that if its organizational structure consisted only of the "absolutely minimal number of parts," error could not be detected. As against pragmatics and negotiation, there is little doubt that reliable performance requires lesser amounts of redundancy. But the task remains to learn to distinguish between inefficient redundancies and those that are constructive and reinforcing—and this includes the kind of knowledge which will permit the introduction of redundancies so that they can work to increase both reliability and adaptability. This task, needless to say, attends pragmatics and negotiation as well, for they are redundant by their nature.

A Final Note

The appearance, therefore, of duplication and overlap in administrative agencies are not necessarily signs of waste and inefficiency. On the contrary, it is becoming increasingly evident that large-scale organizations function as self-organizing systems and tend to develop their own parallel circuits, not the least of which is the transformation of such "residual" parts as "informal groups" into constructive redundancies. Where we are sometimes prone to regard such groups as sources of pathology, they may be compensating for the deficiencies of the formal organization in the same way that the "boss" once did.

At one and the same time, thus, redundancy serves many vital functions in the conduct of public administration. It provides safety factors, permits flexible responses to anomalous situations and provides a creative potential for those who are able to see it. If there is no duplication, if there is no overlap, if there is no ambiguity, an organization will neither be able to suppress error nor generate alternate routes of action.[55] In short, it will be most unreliable and least flexible, sluggish, as we now say.

"Streamlining an agency," "consolidating similar functions," "eliminating duplication," and "commonality" are powerful slogans which possess an obvious appeal. But it is just possible that their achievement would deprive an agency of the properties it needs most—those which allow rules to be broken and units to operate defectively without doing critical injury to the agency as a whole. Accordingly, it would be far more constructive, even under conditions of scarcity, to lay aside easy slogans and turn attention to a principle which lessens risks without foreclosing opportunity.

NOTES

1. J. R. Pierce, *Symbols, Signals and Noise* (New York: Harper, 1961), pp. 35–39. Also, see chapters 7 and 8.
2. Irwin D. J. Bross, *Design for Decision* (New York: Macmillan, 1953).
3. So, too, we repeat observations. The more observations, the less the uncertainty.
4. See J. R. Pierce, op. cit., chapters 7 and 8. Also, see Colin Cherry, *On Human Communication* (New York: Science Editions, 1961), pp. 180–185.
5. The English language is estimated to be between 50 to 65 per cent redundant. The language employed in control tower–pilot communication is about 95 per cent redundant.
6. It suffices to note that it is precisely the property of redundancy in a formal logic that permits deductive inference. Given a set of algebraic equations, e.g., we can deduce the solution by acting in accordance with the appropriate syntactical rules. This solution is *implicit* in the set of equations and can thereby be deduced. It contains "no more information" than the original equations and constitutes a redundancy (repetition) that is present but not obvious. See Cherry, op. cit., pp. 221–231. Also, see Herbert A. Simon, "The Architecture of Complexity," *Proceedings of the American Philosophical Society*, Vol. 106 (1962): pp. 478–479.
7. Cherry, ibid., p. 19.
8. Dwight Waldo, *The Administrative State* (New York: Ronald Press, 1948), pp. 37–38.
9. Melvin Anshen, "The Program Budget in Operation," in *Program Budgeting*, David Novick (ed.), (Cambridge, Mass.: Harvard University Press, 1965), p. 359. Anshen's essay summarizes the sense of the various papers in this volume.
10. Ibid.
11. Ibid., emphasis added.
12. Aaron Wildavsky, "The Political Economy of Efficiency," *Public Administration Review*, Vol. 24 (December 1966): pp. 304–305.
13. Anshen, op. cit., p. 359.
14. Once again this is a goal of the newly proposed "Hoover Commission" see *Public Administration News* (August 1967), p. 2.
15. "Dogmas of Administrative Reform," *American Political Science Review*, Vol. 16 (August 1922).
16. Anatol Rapoport and William J. Horvath, "Thoughts on Organization Theory and a Review of Two Conferences," *General Systems Yearbook*, Vol. IV (1959): p. 91.
17. Jacob Marschak, "Economic Planning and the Cost of Thinking," *Social Research*, Vol. 33 (Summer 1966): pp. 157–158. Also, see John T. Dorsey, Jr., "The Information-Energy Model," in F. Heady and

S. Stokes (eds.), *Papers in Comparative Public Administration* (Ann Arbor: Institute of Public Administration, 1962).

18. The phrase is James D. Thompson's. *Organizations in Action* (New York: McGraw-Hill, 1967), see chapter 8.
19. This, incidentally, is a redundant sentence.
20. James G. March, Herbert A. Simon, and Harold Guetzkow, *Organizations* (New York: John Wiley, 1958), pp. 164–166. I am indebted to Aaron Wildavsky for this suggestion.
21. Ibid., p. 165.
22. It is assumed, of course, that any component meets a specified standard of performance.
23. Jagjit Singh, *Information Theory, Language and Cybernetics* (New York: Dover Publications, 1966), p. 173.
24. John Von Neumann, "Probabilistic Logics and the Synthesis of Reliable Organizations from Unreliable Components," in C. E. Shannon and J. McCarthy (eds.), *Automata Studies* (Princeton: Princeton University Press, 1956). Also, see C. E. Shannon and W. Weaver, *The Mathematical Theory of Communication* (Urbana: University of Illinois Press, 1949). And see Pierce, op. cit., chapter 8; Singh, op. cit., chapters 4 and 5; and Cherry, op. cit., chapter 5.
25. W. H. Pierce, "Redundancy in Computers," *Scientific American*, Vol. 210 (February 1964). Also, see W. S. McCulloch, "The Reliability of Biological Systems," in M. G. Yovitz and S. Cameron (eds.), *Self-Organizing Systems* (New York: Pergamon Press, 1960); and Singh, op. cit., chapters 10–12. And see Robert Gordon, "Optimum Component Redundancy for Maximum System Reliability," *Operations Research*, Vol. 5 (1957).
26. Pierce, op. cit., p. 112.
27. John Von Neumann, "The General and Logical Theory of Automata," in James R. Newman, *The World of Mathematics* (New York: Simon and Schuster, 1956), Vol. IV, pp. 2085–2086.
28. Pierce, op. cit.
29. McCulloch, op. cit., p. 265.
30. Singh, op. cit., pp. 246–247, 323.
31. It is interesting to note that learning machines, machines which "interpret their environment," are built upon this principle. They are much more flexible than computers and "can rise to occasions not foreseen by programmed instructions." Ibid., p. 225.
32. Roland N. McKean and Melvin Anshen, "Limitations, Risks and Problems," in Novick, op. cit., p. 287.
33. Arthur Smithies, "Conceptual Framework for the Program Budget," ibid., p. 24.
34. Harold Garfinkle, "The Rational Properties of Scientific and Common-Sense Activities," *Behavioral Science*, Vol. 5 (1960), and *Studies in Ethnomethodology* (Englewood Cliffs, N.J.: Prentice-Hall, 1967), chapter 2.
35. *The Federalist*, No. 31.
36. Martin Landau, "On the Use of Metaphor in Political Analysis," *Social Research*, Vol. 28 (Autumn 1961).
37. *The Federalist*, No. 51, emphasis added; see also Nos. 47 and 48.
38. McCulloch, op. cit., p. 265.
39. See Martin Landau, "*Baker* v. *Carr* and the Ghost of Federalism," in G. Schubert (ed.), *Reapportionment* (New York: Scribner's, 1964).
40. Robert K. Merton, "Manifest and Latent Functions," in *Social Theory and Social Structure* (Glencoe, N.Y.: The Free Press, 1957).
41. Quoted by Marquis Childs, *New York Post*, May 10, 1962.
42. Richard E. Neustadt, *Presidential Power* (New York: John Wiley, 1960), chapter 7.
43. Pierce, op cit., p. 105–106. Also, see Singh, op. cit., p. 176.
44. Which appears as a sound principle for constituting "elites."
45. Thompson refers to this organizational pattern as the "long-linked technology" involving "serial interdependence," op. cit., pp. 18–19.
46. Ibid., pp. 105–106. Also, see Herbert Simon, *Administrative Behavior* (New York: Macmillan, 1947).
47. Robert Merton, "Bureaucratic Structure and Personality," in Merton et al., (eds.), *Reader in*

Bureaucracy (Glencoe, N.Y.: The Free Press, 1952).

48. I take both terms as synonyms for the same concept. See David Braybrooke and Charles E. Lindblom. *A Strategy for Decision* (New York: The Free Press, 1963), and Herbert Simon, *The New Science of Management Decision* (New York: Harper, 1960). "Computation decision is still another name employed by James Thompson and Arthur Tuden; see "Strategies, Structures, and Processes of Organizational Decision" in *Comparative Studies in Administration* (Pittsburgh: University of Pittsburgh Press, 1959).

49. If the situation is one in which we do not have certainty but we are able to measure (accurately) the probability distributions of the outcomes of each alternative course of action, the situation can be treated as "closed."

50. This is especially so with respect to serial designs, since they can only operate under closure. See Thompson, op. cit., p. 19, Prop. 2.1: Under norms of rationality, organizations seek to seal off their core technologies from environmental influences.

51. The history of science and technology indicates that as we gain more knowledge we open new areas of uncertainty. Which is why, I suspect, that Simon says that "many, perhaps most of the problems that have to be handled at middle and high levels of management" will probably never be amenable to mathematical treatment. Herbert Simon, *The New Science of Management Decision*, op. cit., p. 21.

52. Herbert Kaufman, "The Next Step in Case Studies," *Public Administration Review*, Vol. 18 (Winter 1958): p. 55.

53. Charles Lindblom offers an appropriate maxim in this regard: Do not try to clarify values if the parties can agree on policies. "Some Limitations on Rationality" in Carl J. Friedrich (ed.), *Rational Decision* (New York: Atherton Press, 1964).

54. The system of classification that I have employed is based upon Thompson and Tuden, op. cit. My own explication of their formulations is to be found in "Decision Theory and Comparative Public Administration," *Comparative Political Studies*, Vol. 1 (July 1968).

55. As an immediate illustration, an agency often encounters situations which require prompt and necessary action. Where rules duplicate, and overlap, safety factors exist. If one set of rules fails or does not cover the situation, an alternate route can be found or rules can be stretched—broadly interpreted. The problem, again, is to eliminate an inefficient profusion and to provide efficient redundancy.

Toward a New Public Administration

H. George Frederickson

In full recognition of the risks, this is an essay on new Public Administration. Its first purpose is to present my interpretation and synthesis of new Public Administration as it emerged at the Minnowbrook Conference on New Public Administration. Its second purpose is to describe how this interpretation and synthesis of new Public Administration relates to the wider world of administrative thought and practice. And its third purpose is to interpret what new Public Administration means for organization theory and vice versa.

To affix the label "new" to anything is risky business. The risk is doubled when newness is attributed to ideas, thoughts, concepts, paradigms, theories. Those who claim new thinking tend to regard previous thought as old or jejune or both. In response, the authors of previous thought are defensive and inclined to suggest that, "aside from having packaged earlier thinking in a new vocabulary there is little that is really new in so-called new thinking." Accept, therefore, this caveat. Parts of new Public Administration would be recognized by Plato, Hobbes, Machiavelli, Hamilton, and Jefferson as well as many modern behavioral theorists. The newness is in the way the fabric is woven, not necessarily in the threads that are used, and in arguments as to the proper use of the fabric—however threadbare.

The threads of the Public Administration fabric are well known. Herbert Kaufman describes them simply as the pursuit of these basic values: representativeness, politically neutral competence, and executive leadership.[1] In different times, one or the other of these values receivesthe greatest emphasis. Representativeness was preeminent in the Jacksonian era. The eventual reaction was the reform movement emphasizing neutral competence and executive leadership. Now we are witnessing a revolt against these values accompanied by a search for new modes of representativeness.

Others have argued that changes in Public Administration resemble a zero-sum game between administrative efficiency and political responsiveness. Any increase in efficiency results *a priori* in a decrease in responsiveness. We are simply entering a period during which political responsiveness is to be purchased at a cost in administrative efficiency.

Both the dichotomous and trichotomous value models of Public Administration just described are correct as gross generalizations. But they suffer the weakness of gross generalizations: They fail to account for the wide, often rich, and sometimes subtle variation that rests within. Moreover, the generalization does not explain those parts of Public Administration that are beyond its sweep. Describing what new Public Administration means for organization theory is a process by which these generalizations can be given substance. But first it is necessary to briefly sketch what this student means by new Public Administration.

What Is New Public Administration?

Educators have as their basic objective, and most convenient rationale, expanding and transmitting knowledge. The police are enforcing the law. Public-health agencies lengthen life by fighting disease. Then there are firemen, sanitation men, welfare workers, diplomats, the military, and so forth. All are employed by public agencies and each specialization or profession has its own substantive set of objectives and therefore its rationale.

What, then, is Public Administration?[2] What are its objectives and its rationale?

The classic answer has always been the efficient, economical, and coordinated management of the services listed above. The focus has

---

Source: Excerpt from Toward a New Public Administration: The Minnowbrook Perspective by Frank E. Marini.

been on top-level management (city management as an example) or the basic auxiliary staff services (budgeting, organization and management, systems analysis, planning, personnel, purchasing). The rationale for Public Administration is almost always better (more efficient or economical) management. New Public Administration adds *social equity* to the classic objectives and rationale. Conventional or classic Public Administration seeks to answer either of these questions: (1) How can we offer more or better services with available resources (efficiency)? or (2) how can we maintain our level of services while spending less money (economy)? New Public Administration adds this question: Does this service enhance social equity?

The phrase social equity is used here to summarize the following set of value premises. Pluralistic government systematically discriminates in favor of established stable bureaucracies and their specialized minority clientele (the Department of Agriculture and large farmers as an example) and against those minorities (farm laborers, both migrant and permanent, as an example) who lack political and economic resources. The continuation of widespread unemployment, poverty, disease, ignorance, and hopelessness in an era of unprecedented economic growth is the result. This condition is morally reprehensible and if left unchanged constitutes a fundamental, if long-range, threat to the viability of this or any political system. Continued deprivation amid plenty breeds widespread militancy. Militancy is followed by repression, which is followed by greater militancy, and so forth. A Public Administration which fails to work for changes which try to redress the deprivation of minorities will likely be eventually used to repress those minorities.

For a variety of reasons—probably the most important being committee legislatures, entrenched bureaucracies, nondemocratized political-party procedures, inequitable revenue-raising capacity in the lesser governments of the federal system—the procedures of representative democracy presently operate in a way that either fails or only very gradually attempts to reverse systematic discrimination against disadvantaged minorities. Social equity, then, includes activities designed to enhance the political power and economic well-being of these minorities.

A fundamental commitment to social equity means that new Public Administration attempts to come to grips with Dwight Waldo's contention that the field has never satisfactorily accommodated the theoretical implications of involvement in "politics" and policy-making.[3] The policy-administration dichotomy lacks an empirical warrant, for it is abundantly clear that administrators both execute and make policy. The policy-administration continuum is more accurate empirically but simply begs the theoretical question. New Public Administration attempts to answer it in this way: *Administrators are not neutral. They should be committed to both good management and social equity as values, things to be achieved, or rationales.*

A fundamental commitment to social equity means that new Public Administration is anxiously engaged in change. *Simply put, new Public Administration seeks to change those policies and structures that systematically inhibit social equity.* This is not seeking change for change's sake nor is it advocating alterations in the relative roles of administrators, executives, legislators, or the courts in our basic constitutional forms. Educators, agriculturists, police, and the like can work for changes which enhance their objectives and resist those that threaten those objectives, all within the framework of our governmental system. New Public Administration works in the same way to seek the changes which would enhance its objectives—good management, efficiency, economy, and social equity.

A commitment to social equity not only involves the pursuit of change but attempts to find organizational and political forms which exhibit a capacity for continued flexibility or routinized change. Traditional bureaucracy has a demonstrated capacity for stability, indeed, ultrastability.[4] New Public Administration, in its search for changeable structures, tends therefore to experiment with or advocate modified bureaucratic-organizational forms. Decentralization, devolution, projects, contracts, sensitivity training, organization development, responsibility expansion, confrontation, and client involvement are all essentially counter-bureaucratic notions that characterize new Public Administration. These concepts are designed to enhance both bureaucratic and policy change and thus to increase possibilities for social equity. Indeed, an important faculty member in one of the best-known and largest Master in Public Administration programs in the country described that degree program as "designed to produce change agents or specialists in organizational development."

Other organizational notions such as programming-planning-budgeting systems, executive inventories, and social indicators can be seen as enhancing change in the direction of social equity. They are almost always presented in terms of good management (witness McNamara and PPB) as a basic strategy, because it is unwise to frontally advocate change.[5] In point of fact, however, PPB can be used as a basic device for change (in McNamara's case to attempt to wrest control from the uniformed services, but in the name of efficiency and economy). The executive inventory can be used to alter the character of the top levels of a particular bureaucracy, thereby enhancing change possibilities. Social indicators are designed to show variation in socioeconomic circumstances in the hope that attempts will be made to improve the conditions of those who are shown to be disadvantaged.[6] All three of these notions have only a surface neutrality or good-management character. Under the surface they are devices by which administrators and executives try to bring about change. It is no wonder they are so widely favored in Public Administration circles. And it should not be surprising that economists and political scientists in the "pluralist" camp regard devices such as PPB as fundamentally threatening to their conception of democratic government.[7] Although they are more subtle in terms of change, PPB, executive inventories, and social indicators are of the same genre as more frontal change techniques such as sensitivity training, projects, contracts, decentralization, and the like. All enhance change, and *change is basic to new Public Administration.*

New Public Administration's commitment to social equity implies a strong administrative or executive government—what Hamilton called "energy in the executive." The policymaking powers of the administrative parts of government are increasingly recognized. In addition, a fundamentally new form of political access and representativeness is now occurring in the administration of government and it may be that this access and representativeness is as critical to major policy decisions as is legislative access or representativeness. *New Public Administration seeks not only to carry out legislative mandates as efficiently and economically as possible, but to both influence and execute policies which more generally improve the quality of life for all.* Forthright policy advocacy on the part of the public servant is essential if administrative agencies are basic policy battlefields. New Public Administrationists are likely to be forthright advocates for social equity and will doubtless seek a supporting clientele.

Classic Public Administration emphasizes developing and strengthening institutions which have been designed to deal with social problems. The Public Administration focus, however, has tended to drift from the problem to the institution. New Public Administration attempts to refocus on the problem and to consider alternative possible institutional approaches to confronting problems. The intractable character of many public problems such as urban poverty, widespread narcotics use, high crime rates, and the like lead Public Administrators to seriously question the investment of ever more money and manpower in institutions which seem only to worsen the problems. They seek, therefore, either to modify these institutions or develop new and more easily changed ones designed to achieve more proximate solutions. *New Public Administration is concerned less with the Defense Department than with defense, less with civil-service commissions than with the manpower needs of administrative agencies on the one hand and the employment needs of the society on the other, less with building institutions and more with designing alternate means of solving public problems. These alternatives will no doubt have some recognizable organizational characteristics and they will need to be built and maintained, but will seek to avoid becoming entrenched, nonresponsible bureaucracies that become greater public problems than the social situations they were originally designed to improve.*

The movement from an emphasis on institution building and maintenance to an emphasis on social anomalies has an important analogue in the study of Public Administration. The last generation of students of Public Administration generally accept both Simon's logical positivism and his call for an empirically based organization theory. They focus on generic concepts such as decision, role, and group theory to develop a generalizable body of organization theory. The search is for commonalities of behavior in all organizational settings.[8] The organization and the people within it are the empirical referent. The product is usually description, not prescription, and if it is prescription it prescribes how to better manage the organization internally. The subject matter is first *organization* and second the type of organization—private, public, voluntary.[9] The two main bodies of theory emerging from this generation of work are decision theory and human-relation theory. Both are regarded as behavioral and positivist. Both are at least as heavily influenced by sociology, social psychology, and economics as they are by political science.

New Public Administration advocates what could be best described as "second-generation behavioralism." Unlike his progenitor, the second-generation behavioralist emphasizes the *public* part of Public Administration. He accepts the importance of understanding as scientifically as possible how and why organizations behave as they do but he tends to be rather more interested in the impact of that organization on its clientele and vice versa. He is not antipositivist nor antiscientific although he is probably less than sanguine about the applicability of the natural-science model to social phenomena. He is not likely to use his behavioralism as a rationale for simply trying to describe how public organizations behave.[10] Nor is he inclined to use his behavioralism as a facade for so-called neutrality, being more than a little skeptical of the objectivity of those who claim to be doing science. He attempts to use his scientific skills to aid his analysis, experimentation, and evaluation of alternative policies and administrative modes. *In sum, then, the second-generation behavioralist is less "generic" and more "public" than his forebear, less "descriptive" and more "prescriptive," less "institution oriented" and more "client-impact oriented," less "neutral" and more "normative," and, it is hoped, no less scientific.*

This has been a brief and admittedly surface description of new Public Administration from the perspective of one analyst. If the description is even partially accurate it is patently clear that there are fundamental changes occurring in Public Administration which have salient implications for both its study and practice as well as for the general conduct of government. The final purpose of this chapter is a consideration of the likely impact of new Public Administration on organization theory particularly and the study of administration generally. (The term "theory" is used here in its loose sense, as abstract thought.)

Organization Theory and New Public Administration

Understanding of any phenomenon requires separating that phenomenon into parts and examining each part in detail. In understanding government this separation can reflect institutions such as the traditional "fields" in political science—Public Administration, legislative behavior, public law, and so forth. Or this separation can be primarily conceptual or theoretical such as systems theory, decision theory, role theory, group theory—all of which cut across institutions.

Public Administration has never had either an agreed upon or a satisfactory set of subfields. The "budgeting," "personnel administration," "organization and management" categories are too limiting, too "inside-organization" oriented, and too theoretically vacant. The middle-range theories—decisions, roles, groups, and the like—are stronger theoretically and have yielded more empirically, but still tend to focus almost exclusively on the internal dynamics of public organizations. The new Public Administration calls for a different way of subdividing the phenomenon so as to better understand it. This analyst suggests that there are four basic processes at work in public organizations and further suggests that these processes are suitable for both understanding and improving Public Administration. The four suggested processes are: the distributive process; the integrative process; the boundary-exchange process; and the socio-emotional process.

The Distributive Process New Public Administration is vitally concerned with patterns of distribution. This concern has to do first with the *external* distribution of goods and services to particular categories of persons, in terms of the benefits that result from the operation of publicly administered programs.

Cost-utility, or cost-benefit, analysis is the chief technique for attempting to understand the results of the distributive process. This form of analysis presumes to measure the utility to individuals of particular public programs. Because it attempts to project the likely costs and benefits of alternative programs it is a very central part of new Public Administration. It is central primarily because it provides a scientific or quasi-scientific means for attempting to "get at" the question of equity. It also provides a convenient or classic Public Administration rationale for redistribution. Take, for example, McNamara's justifications for decisions based on cost-utility analysis in the Department of Defense. These justifications were generally urged on the basis of substantive military criteria.

Because of the emergence of "program-planning-budgeting systems" we are beginning to see, in the policy advocacy of the various bureaus and departments of government, their attempts to demonstrate their impact on society in terms of utility. Wildavsky and Lindblom have argued that rational or cost-utility analysis is difficult if not impossible to do. Further, they contend, rational decision making fundamentally alters or changes our political system by dealing with basic political questions within the arena of the administrator. To date they are essentially correct, empirically. Normatively they are apologists for pluralism. Cost-benefit analysis can be an effective means by which inequities can be demonstrated. It is a tool by which legislatures and entrenched bureaucracies can be caused to defend publicly their distributive decisions. The inference is that a public informed of glaring inequities will demand change.

Like the executive budget, rational or cost benefit decision systems (PPB) enhance the power of executives and administrators and are, again, a part of new Public Administration. Because PPB is being widely adopted in cities and states, as well as the national government, it seems clear that new Public Administration will be highly visible simply by a look at the distributive processes of government over the next decade or two. The extent to which PPB will result in a redistribution which enhances social equity remains to be seen.

Benefit or utility analysis in its less prescriptive and more descriptive form, known in political science as "policy-outcomes analysis," attempts to determine the basic factors that influence or determine policy variation.[11] For example, "outcomes analysts" sketch the relationship between variations in public spending (quantity) and the quality of nonspending policy outcomes. The policy-outcomes analyst attempts to determine the relationship between the levels of spending in education and the IQ's, employability, college admissibility, and the like of the products of the educational process. This analysis is essentially after the fact, and indeed is commonly based on relatively out-of-date census data. It is, therefore, useful to new Public Administration, but only as a foundation or background.

A newer form of distributive analysis is emerging. This approach focuses on equity in the distribution of government services within a jurisdiction and asks questions such as: Does a school board distribute its funds equitably to schools and to the school children in its jurisdiction, and if not is inequity in the direction of the advantaged or disadvantaged? Are sanitation services distributed equitably to all neighborhoods in the city, and if not in what direction does inequity move and how is it justified? Is state and federal aid distributed equitably, and if not how are inequities justified?[12]

Patterns of internal-organization distribution are a traditional part of organization theory. The internal competition for money, manpower, status, space, and priorities is a staple in organization theory as any reading of the *Administrative Science Quarterly* indicates. We learn from this literature the extent to which many of the functions of government are in essence controlled by particular bodies of professionals—educators, physicians, attorneys, social workers, and the like. We learn how agencies age and become rigid and devote much of their energies to competing for survival purposes. We learn the extent to which distribution becomes what Wildavsky calls a triangulation between bureaus, legislatures (particularly legislative committees), and elected executives and their auxiliary staffs.[13] Finally, we have whole volumes of aggregated and disaggregated hypotheses which account for or attempt to explain the decision patterns involved in the internal distributive process.[14]

In new Public Administration the internal distributive process is likely to involve somewhat less readiness to make incremental compromises or "bargain" and somewhat more "administrative confrontation." If new Public Administrators are located in the staff agencies of the executive, which is highly likely, they will doubtless be considerably more tenacious than their predecessors. The spokesman for an established agency might have learned to pad his budget, to overstaff, to control public access to records, and to expand his space in preparation for the compromises he has learned to expect. He might now encounter a zealot armed with data which describe in detail padding, overstaffing, and suppressed records. Therefore an organization theory based primarily on the traditional administrative bargaining process is likely to be woefully inadequate. There is a need to develop a theory which accounts for the presence of public administrators considerably less willing to bargain and more willing to take political and administrative risks.

It is difficult to predict the possible consequences of having generalist public administrators who are prepared to rationalize their positions and decisions on the basis of social equity. Administrative theory explains relatively well the results of the use of efficiency, economy, or good management as rationale. We know, for instance, that these arguments are especially persuasive in years in which legislatures and elected executives do not wish to raise taxes. But we also know that virtually anything can be justified under the rubric "good management." When public administrators leave the safe harbor of this rhetoric, what might occur? The best guess is a more open conflict on basic issues of goals or purposes. Some administrators will triumph, but the majority will not; for the system tends to work against the man seeking change and willing to take risks for it. The result is likely to be highly mobile and relatively unstable middle-level civil service. Still, actual withdrawal or removal from the system after a major setback is likely to be preferred by new public administrators to the psychic withdrawal which is now common among administrators.

One can imagine, for instance, a city personnel director prepared to confront the chief of police and the police bureaucracy on the question of eligibility standards for new patrolmen. He might argue, backed with considerable data, that patrolman height and weight regulations are unrealistic and systematically discriminate against deprived minorities. He might also argue that misdemeanor convictions by minors should not prohibit adults from becoming patrolmen. If this were an open conflict, it would likely array deprived minorities against the majority of the city council, possibly against the mayor, and certainly against the chief and his men (and no doubt the Police Benevolent Association). While the new public administrator might be perfectly willing to take the risks involved in such a confrontation, present theory does not accommodate well what this means for the political system generally.

The Integrative Process Authority hierarchies are the primary means by which the work of persons in publicly administered organizations is coordinated. The formal hierarchy is the most obvious and easiest-to-identify part of the permanent and on-going organization. Administrators are seen as persons taking roles in the hierarchy and performing tasks that are integrated through the hierarchies to constitute a cohesive goal-seeking whole. The public administrator has customarily been regarded as the one who builds and maintains the organization through the hierarchy. He attempts to understand formal-informal relationships, status, politics, and power in authority hierarchies. The hierarchy is at once an ideal design and a hospitable environment for the person who wishes to manage, control, or direct the work of large numbers of people.

The counterproductive characteristics of hierarchies are well known.[15] New Public Administration is probably best understood as advocating modified hierarchic systems. Several means both in theory and practice are utilized to modify traditional hierarchies. The first and perhaps the best known is the project or matrix technique.[16] The project is, by definition, temporary. The project manager and his staff are a team which attempts to utilize the services of regularly established hierarchies in an ongoing organization. For the duration of the project, the manager must get his technical services from the technical hierarchy of the organization, his personnel services from the personnel agency, his budgeting services from the budget department, and so forth. Obviously the project technique would not be effective were it not for considerable top-level support for the project. When there are conflicts between the needs of the project and the survival needs of established hierarchies, top management must consistently decide in favor of the projects. The chief advantage of projects are of course their collapsible nature. While bureaucracies do not disestablish or self-destruct, projects do. The project concept is especially useful when associated with "one time" hardware or research and development, or capital improvement efforts. The concept is highly sophisticated in engineering circles and theoretically could be applied to a large number of less technical and more social problems.[17] The project technique is also useful as a device by which government contracts with industry can be monitored and coordinated.

Other procedures for modifying hierarchies are well known and include the group-decision-making model, the link pin function, and the so-called dialectical organization.[18] And, of course, true decentralization is a fundamental modification hierarchy.[19]

Exploration and experimentation with these various techniques is a basic part of new Public Administration. The search for less structured, less formal, and less authoritative integrative techniques in publicly administered organizations is only beginning. The preference for these types of organizational modes implies first a relative tolerance for variation. This includes variations in administrative performance and variations in procedures and applications based upon differences in clients or client groups. It also implies great tolerance for the possibilities of inefficiency and diseconomy. In a very general sense this preference constitutes a willingness to trade increases in involvement and commitment to the organization for possible decreases in efficiency and economy, particularly in the short run. In the long run, less formal and less authoritative integrative techniques may prove to be more efficient and economical.

There are two serious problems with the advocacy by new Public Administration of less formal integrative processes. First, there may develop a lack of Public Administration specialists who are essentially program builders. The new Public Administration man who is trained as a change agent and an advocate of informal, decentralized, integrative processes may not be capable of building and maintaining large, permanent organizations. This problem may not be serious, however, because administrators in the several professions (education, law enforcement, welfare, and the like) are often capable organization builders, or at least protectors, so a Public Administration specialist can concentrate on the change or modification of hierarchies built by others.

The second problem is in the inherent conflict between higher- and lower-level administrators in less formal, integrative systems. While describing the distributive process in Public Administration it was quite clear that top-level public administrators were to be strong and assertive. In this description of the integrative process there is a marked preference for large degrees of autonomy at the base of the organization. The only way to theoretically accommodate this contradiction is through an organizational design in which top-level public administrators are regarded as policy advocates and general-policy reviewers. If they have a rather high tolerance for the variations in policy application then it can be presumed that intermediate and lower levels in the organization can apply wide interpretive license in program application. This accommodation is a feeble one, to be sure, but higher-lower-level administrative relations are a continuing problem in Public Administration, and the resolution of these problems in the past had tended to be in the direction of the interests of upper levels of the hierarchy in combination with subdivisions of the legislative body and potent interest groups. New Public Administration searches for a means by which lower levels of the organization and less potent minorities can be favored.

The Boundary-Exchange Process The boundary-exchange process describes the general relationship between the publicly administered organization and its reference groups and clients. These include legislatures, elected executives, auxiliary staff organizations, clients (both organized and individual) and organized interest groups. The boundary-exchange process also accounts for the relationship between levels of government in a federal system. Because publicly administered organizations find themselves in a competitive political, social, and economic environment, they tend to seek support. This is done by first finding a clientele which can play a strong advocacy role with the legislature, then by developing a symbiotic relationship between the agency and key committees or members of the legislature, followed by building and maintaining as permanent an organization as possible.

The distributive and integrative processes which have just been described call for vastly altered concepts of how to conduct boundary exchange in new Public Administration.[20] Future organization theory will have to accommodate the following pattern of boundary exchange. First, a considerably higher client involvement is necessary on the part of those minorities who have not heretofore been involved. (It is unfair to assume that minorities are not already involved as clients: farmers, bankers, and heavy industries are minorities and they are highly involved clients. In this sense all public organizations are "client" oriented.) This change probably spells a different kind of involvement. A version of this kind of involvement is now being seen in some of our cities as a result of militancy and community-action programs, and on the campuses of some universities. A preferred form of deprived-minority-client involvement would be routinized patterns of communication with decentralized organizations capable of making distributive decisions that support the interests of deprived minorities, even if these decisions are difficult to justify in terms of either efficiency or economy.

In a very general way, this kind of decision making occurs in time of war with respect to military decision making. It also characterizes decision patterns in the Apollo program of the National Aeronautics and Space Administration. These two examples characterize crash programs designed to solve problems that are viewed as immediate and pressing. They involve a kind of backward budgeting in which large blocks of funds are made available for the project and wide latitude in expenditures is tolerated. The detailed accounting occurs after the spending, not before, hence backward budgeting. Under these conditions what to do and what materials are needed are decided at low levels of the organization. These decisions are made on the presumption that they will be supported and the necessary resources will be made available and accounted for by upper levels of the organization. This same logic could clearly be applied to the ghetto. A temporary project could be established in which the project manager and his staff work with the permanently established bureaucracies in a city in a crash program designed to solve the employment, housing, health, education, and transportation needs of the residents of that ghetto. The decisions and procedures of one project would likely vary widely from those of another, based on the differences in the circumstances of the clientele involved and the political-administrative environments encountered. The central project director would tolerate the variations both in decisions and patterns of expenditures in the same way that the Department of Defense and NASA cover their expenditures in time of crisis.

The danger will be in the tendency of decentralized projects to be taken over by local pluralist elites. The United States Selective Service is an example of this kind of take-over. High levels of disadvantaged-minority-client involvement are necessary to offset this tendency. Still, it will be difficult to prevent the new controlling minorities from systematic discrimination against the old controlling minorities.

From this description of a boundary-exchange relationship, it is probably safe to predict that administrative agencies, particularly those that are decentralized, will increasingly become the primary means by which particular minorities find their basic form of political representation. This situation exists now in the case of the highly advantaged minorities and may very well become the case with the disadvantaged.

The means by which high client involvement is to be secured is problematic. The maximum-feasible-participation notion, although given a very bad press, was probably more successful than most analysts are prepared to admit. Maximum feasible participation certainly did not enhance the efficiency or economy of OEO activities, but, and perhaps most important, it gave the residents of the ghetto at least the impression that they had the capacity to influence publicly made decisions that affected their well-being. High client involvement probably means, first, the employment of the disadvantaged where feasible; second, the use of client review boards or review agencies; and third, decentralized legislatures such as the kind sought by the Brownhill School District in the New York City Board of Education decentralization controversy.

The development of this pattern of boundary exchange spells the probable development of new forms of intergovernmental relations, particularly fiscal relations. Federal grants-in-aid to states and cities, and state grants-in-aid to cities will no doubt be expanded, and probably better equalized.[21] In addition, some form of tax sharing is probably called for. The fundamental weakness of the local governments' revenue capacity must be alleviated.

The use of the distributive and integrative processes described above probably also means the development of new means by which administrators relate to their legislatures. The elected official will probably always hold continuance in office as his number-one objective. This means that a Public Administration using less formal integrative processes must find means by which it can enhance the reelection probabilities of supporting incumbents. Established centralized bureaucracies do this in a variety of ways, the best known being building and maintaining of roads or other capital facilities in the legislators' district, establishing high-employment facilities, such as federal office buildings, county courthouses, police precincts, and the like, and distributing public-relations materials favorable to the incumbent legislator. The decentralized organization seems especially suited for the provision of this kind of service for legislators. As a consequence it is entirely possible to imagine legislators becoming strong spokesmen for less hierarchic and less authoritative bureaucracies.

The Socioemotional Process The Public Administration described herein will require both individual and group characteristics that differ from those presently seen. The widespread use of sensitivity training, T techniques, or "organizational development" is compatible with new Public Administration. These techniques include lowering an individual's reliance on hierarchy, enabling him to tolerate conflict and emotions, and indeed under certain circumstances to welcome them, and to prepare him to take greater risks. From the preceding discussion it is clear that sensitizing techniques are parallel to the distributive, integrative, and boundary-exchange processes just described.

Socioemotional-training techniques are fundamental devices for administrative change. These techniques have thus far been used primarily to strengthen or redirect on-going and established bureaucracies. In the future it is expected that the same techniques will be utilized to aid in the development of decentralized and possibly project-oriented organizational modes.

A recent assessment of the United States Department of State by Chris Argyris is highly illustrative of the possible impact of new Public Administration on organizational socioemotional processes.[22] Argyris concluded that "State" is a social system characterized by individual withdrawal from interpersonal difficulties and conflict; minimum interpersonal openness, leveling, and trust; a withdrawal from aggressiveness and fighting; the view that being emotional is being ineffective or irrational; leaders' domination of subordinates; an unawareness of leaders' personal impact on others; and very high levels of conformity coupled with low levels of risk taking or responsibility taking. To correct these organizational "pathologies" Argyris recommended that:

1. A long-range change program should be defined with the target being to change the living system of the State Department.
2. The first stage of the change program should focus on the behavior and leadership style of the most senior participants within the Department of State.
3. Simultaneously with the involvement of the top, similar change activities should be initiated in any subpart which shows signs of being ready for change.
4. The processes of organizational change and development that are created should require the same behavior and attitudes as those we wish to inculcate into the system (take more initiative, enlarge responsibilities, take risks).
5. As the organizational development activities produce a higher level of leadership skills and begin to reduce the system's defenses in the area of interpersonal relations, the participants should be helped to begin to reexamine some of the formal policies and activities of the State Department that presently may act as inhibitors to organizational effectiveness (employee evaluations and ratings, promotion process, inspections). The reexamination should be

conducted under the direction of line executives with the help of inside or outside consultants.

6. The similarities and interdependencies between administration and substance need to be made more explicit and more widely accepted.
7. The State Department's internal capacity in the new areas of behavioral-science based knowledge should be increased immediately.
8. Long-range research programs should be developed, exploring the possible value of the behavioral disciplines to the conduct of diplomacy.

The characteristics of the State Department are, sad to say, common in publicly administered organizations. While Argyris' recommendations are particular to "State," they are relevant to all highly authoritative hierarchy-based organizations.

While new Public Administration is committed to wider social equity, the foregoing should make it clear that a more nearly equitable internal organization is also an objective.

Conclusions

The search for social equity provides Public Administration with a real normative base. Like many value premises, social equity has the ring of flag, country, mother, and apple pie. But surely the pursuit of social equity in Public Administration is no more a holy grail than the objectives of educators, medical doctors, and so forth. Still, it appears that new Public Administration is an alignment with good, or possibly God.

What are the likely results for a *practicing* Public Administration working such a normative base? *First,* classic Public Administration on the basis of its expressed objectives commonly had the support of businessmen and the articulate and educated upper and upper-middle classes. The phenomenal success of the municipal-reform movement is testament to this. If new Public Administration attempts to justify or rationalize its stance on the basis of social equity, it might have to trade support from its traditional sources for support from the disadvantaged minorities. It might be possible for new Public Administration to continue to receive support from the educated and articulate if we assume that this social class is becoming increasingly committed to those public programs that are equity enhancing and less committed to those that are not. Nevertheless, it appears that new Public Administration should be prepared to take the risks involved in such a trade, if it is necessary to do so.

Second, new Public Administration, in its quest for social equity, might encounter the kinds of opposition that the Supreme Court has experienced in the last decade. That is to say, substantial opposition from elected officials for its fundamental involvement in shaping social policy. The Court, because of its independence, is less vulnerable than administration. We might expect, therefore, greater legislative controls over administrative agencies and particularly the distributive patterns of such agencies.

Third, new Public Administration might well foster a political system in which elected officials speak basically for the majority and for the privileged minorities while courts and the administrators are spokesmen for disadvantaged minorities. As administrators work in behalf of the equitable distribution of public and private goods, courts are increasingly interpreting the Constitution in the same direction. Legislative hostility to this action might be directed at administration simply because it is most vulnerable.

What of new Public Administration and academia? First, let us consider the theory, then the academy.

Organization theory will be influenced by new Public Administration in a variety of ways. The uniqueness of *public* organization will be stressed. Internal administrative behavior—the forte of the generic administration school and the foundation of much of what is now known as organization theory—will be a part of scholarly Public Administration, but will be less central. Its center position in Public Administration will be taken by a strong emphasis on the distributive and boundary-exchange processes described above.

Quantitatively inclined public-organization theorists are likely to drift toward or at least read widely in welfare economics. Indeed it is possible to imagine these theorists executing a model or paradigm of social equity fully as robust as the economist's market model. With social equity elevated to the supreme objective, in much the way profit is treated in economics, model building is relatively simple. We might, for example, develop theories of equity maximization, long- and short-range equity, equity elasticity, and so on. The theory and research being reported in the journal *Public Choice* provides a glimpse of this probable development. This work is presently being done primarily by economists who are, in the main, attempting to develop variations on the market model or notions of individual-utility maximization. Public-organization theorists with social-equity commitments could contribute greatly by the creation of models less fixed on market environments or individual utility maximization and more on the equitable distribution of and access to both public and private goods by different groups or categories of people. If a full-blown equity model were developed it might be possible to assess rather precisely the likely outcomes of alternative policies in terms of whether the alternative does or does not enhance equity. Schemes for guaranteed annual income, negative income tax, Head Start, Job Corps, and the like could be evaluated in terms of their potential for equity maximization.

The less quantitatively but still behaviorally inclined public-organization theorists are likely to move in the direction of Kirkhart's "consociated model." They would move in the direction of sociology, anthropology, and psychology, particularly in their existential versions, while the quantitatively inclined will likely move toward economics, as described above. And, of course, many public-organization theorists will stay with the middle-range theories—role, group, communications, decisions, and the like—and not step under the roof of the grand theories such as the consociated model, the social-equity model, or the so-called systems model.

What does new Public Administration mean for the academy? One thing is starkly clear: We now know the gigantic difference between "public administration" and "the public service." The former is made up of public-management generalists and some auxiliary staff people (systems analysis, budgeting, personnel, and so on) while the latter is made up of the professionals who man the schools, the police, the courts, the military, welfare agencies, and so forth. Progressive Public Administration programs in the academy will build firm and permanent bridges to the professional schools where most public servants are trained. In some schools the notion of Public Administration as the "second profession" for publicly employed attorneys, teachers, welfare workers will become a reality.

Some Public Administration programs will likely get considerably more philosophic and normative while others will move more to quantitative management techniques. Both are needed and both will contribute.

The return of policy analysis is certain in both kinds of schools. Good management for its own sake is less and less important to today's student. Policy analysis, both logically and analytically "hard-nosed," will be the order of the day.

Academic Public Administration programs have not commonly been regarded as especially exciting. New Public Administration has an opportunity to change that. Programs that openly seek to attract and produce "change agents" or "short-haired radicals" are light years away from the POSDCORB image. And many of us are grateful for that.

NOTES

1. Herbert Kaufman, "Administrative Decentralization and Political Power," *Pub. Adm. Rev.* (January–February, 1969): 3–15.
2. Frederick Mosher and John C. Honey wrestle with the question of the relative role of professional specialists as against the generalist administrator in public organizations. See Frederick Mosher, *Democracy and the Public Service* (New York: Oxford University Press, 1968), pp. 99–133. See also John C. Honey, "A Report: Higher Education for the Public Service," *Pub. Adm. Rev.* (November 1967).
3. Dwight Waldo, "Scope of the Theory of Public Administration," in *Theory and Practice of Public Administration: Scope, Objectives and Methods*, ed. James C. Charlesworth (Philadelphia: The American Academy of Political and Social Sciences, October, 1968), pp. 1–26.
4. Anthony Downs, *Inside Bureaucracy* (Boston: Little, Brown, 1967).

5. See especially Charles L. Schultze, *The Politics and Economics of Public Spending* (Washington, D.C.: Brookings Institution, 1969).
6. The general "social equity" concern expressed in the essays in Raymond A. Bauer, Social Indicators (Cambridge, Mass.: MIT Press, 1967) is clearly indicative of this.
7. Aaron Wildavsky, *The Politics of the Budgetary Process* (Boston: Little, Brown, 1964); Charles Lindblom, *The Intelligence of Democracy* (New York: Glencoe Free Press, 1966).
8. See especially James March and Herbert Simon, *Organizations* (New York: John Wiley and Sons, 1963).
9. See especially Amitai Etzioni, *A Comparative Analysis of Complex Organizations* (New York: Glencoe Free Press, 1961).
10. An exchange occurring at an informal rump session of the Minnowbrook Conference is especially illustrative of this. Several conferees were discussing errors in strategy and policy in the operations of the United States Office of Economic Opportunity. They were generalizing in an attempt to determine how organizations like OEO could be made more effective. Several plausible causal assertions were advanced and vigorously supported. Then a young but well-established political scientist commented that causal assertions could not be supported by only one case. True correlations of statistical significance required an "N" or "number of cases" of at least thirty. The reply was, "Has Public Administration nothing to suggest until we have had thirty O.E.O.'s? Can we afford thirty O.E.O.'s before we learn what went wrong with the first one? By ducking into our analytical and quantitative shelters aren't we abdicating our responsibilities to suggest ways to make the second O.E.O. or its equivalent an improvement on the first?"
11. For a good bibliographic essay on this subject see John H. Fenton and Donald W. Chamberlayne, "The Literature Dealing with the Relationships between Political Process, Socioeconomic Conditions and Public Policies in the American States: A Bibliographic Essay," *Polity* (spring, 1969): 388–404.
12. Equity is now a major question in the courts. Citizens are bringing suit against governments at all levels under the "equal protection of the laws" clause claiming inequities in distribution. Thus far the courts have taken a moderate equity stance in education and welfare. See John E. Coons, William H. Clune, and Stephen D. Sugerman, "Educational Opportunity: A Workable Constitutional Test for State Structures," *California Law Review* (April 1969): 305–421.
13. Aaron Wildavsky, op. cit.
14. March and Simon, op. cit.; Downs, op. cit.; James L. Price, *Organizational Effectiveness* (Homewood, Ill.: Richard D. Irwin, 1968).
15. See Victor Thompson, *Modern Organization* (New York: Alfred A. Knopf, 1961); Robert V. Presthus, *The Organizational Society* (New York: Alfred A. Knopf, 1962); Downs, op. cit.
16. David I. Cleland and William R. King, *Systems Analysis and Project Management* (New York: McGraw-Hill, 1968); David I. Cleland and William R. King, *Systems, Organizational, Analysis, Management: A Book of Readings* (New York: McGraw-Hill, 1969); George A. Steiner and William G. Ryan, *Industrial Project Management* (New York: Macmillan, 1968); John Stanley Baumgartner, *Project Management* (Homewood, Ill.: Richard D. Irwin, 1963).
17. H. George Frederickson and Henry J. Anna, "Bureaucracy and the Urban Poor," mimeographed.
18. See Rensis Likert, *New Patterns of Management* (New York: McGraw-Hill, 1961); Orion White, "The Dialectical Organization: An Alternative to Bureaucracy," *Pub. Adm. Rev.* (January–February, 1969): 32–42.
19. Kaufman, op. cit.
20. James Thompson, *Organizations in Action* (New York: McGraw-Hill, 1967).
21. Deil S. Wright, *Federal Grants-in-Aid: Perspectives and Alternatives* (Washington, D.C.: American Enterprise Institute for Public Policy Research, 1968).
22. Chris Argyris, "Some Causes of Organizational Ineffectiveness within the Department of State," [Center for International Systems Research, Occasional Paper No. 2] (Washington, D.C.: U.S. Government Printing Office, November, 1966).

26

Systematic Thinking for Social Action

Alice M. Rivlin

The two preceding chapters dealt with three strategies for finding more effective methods of producing education, health, and other social services: (1) analysis of the "natural experiment," (2) random innovation, and (3) systematic experimentation. The major conclusion was that all three strategies should be pursued with increased energy and greater methodological sophistication.

Analysis of the natural experiment has not yet turned up many clues to more effective ways of producing social services. But with time and more refined techniques, there is hope that it will. As a necessary first step to more effective services, all kinds of people should be encouraged to try out new ways of delivering services. But random innovation does not yield knowledge of what works best for whom or under what conditions. This requires systematic experimentation—with new curricula, new training techniques, new ways of delivering medical care. As the last chapter indicated, I believe systematic experimentation must be an important federal activity if we are to achieve breakthroughs in social service delivery.

But finding more effective methods is not enough. How do we know they will be used? What incentives are built into our social service systems to encourage effectiveness?

As the public sector of our economy grows larger, the problem of building incentives to effective performance into public programs becomes more and more crucial. As Schultze pointed out in his Gaither lectures, federal programs have often failed to reach their objectives because no thought was given to incentives:

> The failure of performance stems from two related causes. The first of these is "negative failure"—the failure to take account of private incentives that run counter to program objectives, and to provide for appropriate modifications in existing rewards and penalties that thwart social objectives. . . .
>
> The second cause is "positive failure"—the failure to build into federal programs a positive set of incentives to channel the activities of decentralized administrators and program operators toward the program objectives.[1]

In the social action area, the problem is both especially acute and especially difficult. Present arrangements for delivering social services provide few rewards for those who produce better education or health service, few penalties for those who fail to produce. School systems are big bureaucracies serving a largely captive clientele. Students and their parents have little freedom to move from one school to another in search of a "better" education, and hardly any information by which to judge the effectiveness of schools. Teachers, principals, and superintendents are rarely rewarded or promoted on the basis of the educational results they achieve. State and federal financing is not designed to reward effective performance of schools or school systems.

The health system *looks* different. There are far more small units—hospitals, clinics, and doctors in private practice—and the consumer seems to have choice. But in fact he has neither the time, the resources, nor the knowledge on which to base an intelligent choice. Moreover, in health as in education, payment mechanisms fail to reward efficiency or effectiveness. On the contrary, the present health insurance systems, both public and private, operate to encourage overuse of hospitals—the most expensive health facilities—and fail to encourage the development and use of less costly alternatives.

The diagnosis is clear, but what is the prescription? It is easy to talk loosely about holding producers of education and health services

Source: Alice M. Rivlin, Systematic Thinking for Social Action (Washington, D.C.: The Brookings Institution, 1971). Reprinted with permission.

"accountable" for their performance to those who consume the services and to those who pay for them. But it is hard to design a workable set of measures of performance, to decide exactly what accounts are to be rendered to whom and how rewards and penalties are to be meted out.

This chapter will deal with three models for improving the effectiveness with which social services are produced. One is decentralization—breaking up central administrative units, like school systems or federal programs, into more manageable units. The second is community control—a step beyond decentralization in which control of schools or other services is turned over to the community being served, in the hope of making producers more responsive to consumers. The last is the "market model," perhaps the most extreme form of decentralization. If the market model were applied to education, for one example, students would be given a choice among publicly, or privately, operated schools. Reliance would be placed on competition among schools to spur more effective educational methods.

Decentralization, community control, and a market system have all been advertised as panaceas. One or the other, it has been suggested, would solve the problem of incentives, even eliminate the need for central government efforts to discover and encourage more effective methods. The message of this chapter is that, while all three models hold out some promise, none is a cure-all. In particular, the success of all three depends on two conditions: (1) the development and use of better measures of the effectiveness of social services; and (2) vigorous and systematic attempts to find and test more effective methods and to publicize the results.

Decentralization

Decentralization of decision making, at least down to the state or city level, has always been popular with conservatives—those who generally oppose expansion of the public sector and changes in methods of delivering services. Rejecting "frills" and "new-fangled" devices in the school and clinging to fee-for-service medicine and traditional health facilities, these groups have always fought for local control and less interference from Washington or the state capital. But the remarkable political development of the last several years has been the conversion of liberals—those who favor more public services and newer methods—to the cause of decentralization. Why the switch?

One element is a new realism about the capacity of a central government to manage social action programs effectively. There was a time when those who believed in broader public commitment to social action pinned their hopes on centralization. Finding themselves stymied by conservatism, rigidity, and lack of resources at the local level, they turned to state government. Finding the states unresponsive, they turned—especially after 1933—to the federal government.

But the last several years have seen a marked shift in the attitude of liberals toward the federal role. I am not referring to the carping criticism of academics or of the party out of power about the "bungling and inefficiency" of federal executives. Those who happen not to be running the government at the moment have always griped, with more or less justification, about the ineptitude of those who were. Rather, I am talking about the change of attitude that occurred during the 1960s among those who helped design federal social action programs and tried to make them work.

I, for one, once thought that the effectiveness of a program like Headstart or Title I of the Elementary and Secondary Education Act could be increased by tighter management from Washington. Something was known about "good practices," or effective ways of reaching poor children; more could be learned and transmitted to the local level through federal guidelines and regulations and technical assistance. As knowledge accumulated, the guidelines could be tightened up, and programs would become more effective.

This view now seems to be naïve and unrealistic. The country is too big and too diverse, and social action is too complicated. There are over 25,000 school districts, and their needs, problems and capacities differ drastically. Universal rules are likely to do more harm than good. Nor, given the numbers of people involved, is it possible simply to rely on the judgment or discretion of federal representatives in the field.

Robert Levine, former planning officer for the Office of Economic Opportunity, has given a good description of the new realism:

> By and large, those programs which have stressed detailed planning and detailed administration have either not worked, or have worked only on a scale which was very small compared to the size of the problem.... The detailed administrative approach does not work for clear enough reasons—which start with the impossibility of writing detailed rules to fit every case, and end with the lack of highly trained people to administer every case, assuming even that an administrative solution is possible. . . . The setbacks of the War on Poverty arise, in part, from the difficulties of applying a specific and administered program to more than 30 million poor individuals. . . . What we might be able to achieve is a long-run redesign of the Poverty Program to reduce the amount of detailed administration, and to provide more incentives for individuals to develop their own programs.[2]

The new realists are not ready to give up on the federal government and turn social action programs back to state and local governments. One cogent reason is the inequality of state and local resources. The states with the greatest per capita needs for education, health, income maintenance, and other social action programs also have the lowest per capita resources. Even within states, resources are frequently concentrated where the problems are least acute. Central cities find themselves facing mounting needs for public services and falling tax bases, while the resources of the suburbs are far greater in relation to need. The intervention of the federal government is required to channel resources to areas of need, a task that, fortunately, it is well equipped to handle.

Two activities that the federal bureaucracy carries out with great efficiency are collecting taxes and writing checks. For all its faults, the federal tax system is certainly among the most equitable and efficient in the world. Federal taxation falls largely on income, and hence is more progressive than state and local taxation, which falls largely on property and sales and thus on the poor. The progressivity of the federal system, moreover, makes it more responsive to economic growth than state and local systems. Unless rates are lowered, federal revenues tend to rise faster than the national income—a fortunate fact in an age when the demand for public services is rising more rapidly than income. Finally, income taxes are easier and cheaper to collect than are property and sales taxes, and are far less subject to the whims and errors of individual assessors.

The efficiency with which the federal government collects money is matched by the efficiency with which it disburses it. The social security system, the Veterans Administration, and other federal agencies charged with making payments directly to individuals discharge their responsibilities apparently with a minimum of difficulty and confusion.

Since the federal government is good at collecting and handing out money, but inept at administering service programs, then it might make sense to restrict its role in social action mainly to tax collection and check writing and leave the detailed administration of social action programs to smaller units. This view implies cutting out categorical grants-in-aid with detailed guidelines and expenditure controls. Instead, the major federal domestic activity would be the distribution of funds to individuals and governments on the basis of need and other criteria. The mechanism for distributing funds to individuals would be social security, family assistance, or other forms of income maintenance. Lower levels of government would receive funds through revenue sharing or bloc grants for general purposes like education. The last two federal budgets, with their emphasis on income maintenance and revenue sharing, appear to be moving the federal government in this direction.

But a deep-seated fear that the money will be misused and misdirected has always made the liberals—and, indeed, most of the Congress—leery of turning over federal tax money to lower levels of government without strict guidelines. How does the federal taxpayer know that his funds will be spent efficiently and effectively? While it may be easier in principle to manage programs at the state or local level than to deal with the vastness and diversity of the nation as a whole, in practice state and local governments have hardly been models of efficiency, effectiveness, or even honesty. Moreover, not sharing national objectives, state and local governments may underfund such programs as higher education or pollution control whose benefits are likely to spill over into other jurisdictions. They may be dominated by a small, local power elite. The federal taxpayer clearly has grounds for insisting that lower levels of government be held "accountable" to the federal government for the uses they make of federal funds.

But stating the accountability in terms of inputs—through detailed guidelines and controls on objects of expenditure—spawns red tape and rigidity without introducing incentives to more outputs. Hence a new approach is in order: State the accountability in terms of outputs, and reward those who produce more efficiently. Free to vary the way they spend the money as long as they accomplish specified results, recipients of federal grants could be rewarded for producing beyond expectations. This procedure would liberate them from the straitjacket of input controls and promote vigorous and imaginative attempts to improve results, just as in large corporations plant managers are free to vary production methods, but are rewarded and promoted according to sales and profits.

This reasoning applies, of course, not just to federal relations with state and local governments, but to the broader question of productivity incentives in any large bureaucratic enterprise. Even in programs run by the federal government itself, productivity could be increased by allowing individual project managers—federal hospital administrators or training center heads, for example—more freedom of action and more incentive to achievement. Similar reasoning has led many to advocate decentralization of big-city school districts into semi-autonomous units that would be freed from rigid restrictions on curriculum, teaching methods, or mix of resources, and rewarded for producing better educational results.

The idea of accountability certainly sounds simple and sensible and right. Implementing it is harder. Most social action programs have vague and diverse goals, and agreement on how to measure their success is far from complete. Little serious work has been done to develop the objective measures of performance that are needed to implement this concept of accountability.

One might think, for example, that performance measures could be readily devised for manpower training programs. Their goals—to increase the employability and improve the earning capacity of trainees—are not esoteric. Success can be measured in rates at which trainees are placed in jobs, and retain and advance in them, and in differentials between what they earn and what they would have earned with-out the training. Good management practice suggests considerable freedom for project managers in designing programs suited to local conditions and to the needs of their trainees, and in rating the projects according to these objective criteria.

But even in manpower training, performance measures are difficult to devise. One problem is dealing with several different, albeit related, objectives. If manpower training projects were judged only on their success in job placement, there would be pressure to place trainees in jobs as quickly as possible regardless of the wage level, suitability, stability, or possibilities of advancement in the employment. The result would be a lot of placements in low-level, dead-end jobs, and little contribution to productivity. On the other hand, if increases in earnings were the sole criterion, programs would probably concentrate on people whose skills were already well developed and on younger workers with a longer earning life ahead of them. Some kind of weighted average of several success measures (job placements, earnings increases, retention rates, and so forth) would avoid distortion of the objectives of the program.

In addition, success measures have to be related to the difficulty of the problem. It is more difficult to find jobs for trainees if the local unemployment rate is high. It is harder and more expensive to train and place older people than younger people, poorly educated people than better educated people. Completion rates and wage rates are likely to be higher for men than for women. Such variations have to be taken into consideration in rating the performance of a project, both out of fairness to the project manager and to prevent "creaming," the tendency to enroll only those who will be easy to train and place. A rating system meeting these criteria was developed for assessing the effectiveness of projects under the Work Experience and Training Program in HEW, but was not used.[3]

Objectives are less easy to define in other social action areas than in manpower training, and work on performance measures is in an even more primitive stage. Incorporating performance incentives into education programs is intriguing, but a workable mechanism will be hard to design. A simple formula, based, for example, on high reading scores, might do more harm than good, by rewarding districts with easy-to-teach children, or by encouraging instruction solely for results on a specific test and overemphasis on reading at the expense of other educational values. The trick will be to develop measures that reflect the educational achievement of the schools without distorting programs in counterproductive directions.

Unless the effort is made to develop performance measures and use them as incentives, it is hard to see how decentralization by itself will lead to greater effectiveness. Without incentives to produce, small units are not obviously better than large ones.

Moreover, there are some governmental functions that would almost certainly suffer from decentralization. One is research and development. Small units are unlikely to invest in such a risky activity when most of the benefit is likely to go to other units. Moreover, for any hope of success, some problems demand a critical mass of talent and resources that only the federal government can mobilize. The atomic and hydrogen bombs, the lunar landings, and some of the federally sponsored breakthroughs in biomedical research are ample evidence of the federal ability to put the requisite resources to work on a scientific problem. Breakthroughs in social service delivery seem likely to require similar concentrations of effort.

Community Control

The push for decentralization comes at least partly from frustration at the top bred from the realization that very large units cannot manage social action programs effectively. The push for community control comes from frustration at the bottom. The supposed beneficiaries of social action programs, especially the poor and the black, feel themselves objects rather than participants in the process. The demand for community control, especially in the ghetto, reflects the feeling that schools and hospitals and welfare centers are alien institutions run by hostile members of another culture unable to understand the problems of the community they serve or to imagine their solution. If such institutions were controlled by and accountable to the community, the belief runs, they would be more effectively, or at least more sensitively, run. A ghetto community school board would hire teachers who believed in the capacity of black children to learn; it would revamp the curriculum to make it more relevant, and would assign books about black city children rather than about Dick and Jane in their suburban house. The result would be more learning. A ghetto community health board would find ways to reduce waiting times in clinics, hire personnel who did not patronize or insult patients, provide health instruction in the patient's own language. The result would be more effective health care. Moreover, community control of social action programs is also seen as a means of developing self-reliance in the community itself—feelings of competence and confidence and political power that will release energies and reduce despair.

At the moment, the movement for community control focuses on the process of gaining power. The vocal advocates of community control of schools and other social services feel that much of the problem lies in the negativism and hostility of the people who now run these institutions. Once the community assumed control, it could hold the managers accountable in some sense, fire those with hostile attitudes, and significantly improve the level of service. Community control advocates have not yet focused on new methods or organization, nor do they support experimentation or systematic testing of new models. On the contrary, one senses among ghetto militants a deep antagonism to experimentation, which is often viewed as an instrument of establishment control. "We do not want our children used as guinea pigs" typifies the attitude.

The word "accountability" is used frequently but vaguely by the advocates of community control. One searches the literature and the conversations in vain to learn what accounts are to be rendered and to whom, or how a community will know that its own administrators are doing a better job. So far, only limited attention has been paid to specific performance measures and that only with the view to dramatizing how bad the situation is. In the District of Columbia, for example, Julius W. Hobson induced the school system to publish reading scores by school in an effort to prove to the community that ghetto schools were not teaching children to read.

The vagueness about accountability seems likely to be temporary. If community control in big-city school systems, for example, becomes a reality, two things will probably happen. First, the community and its representatives will have to face up to the question: Now that we have control what shall we do? They will begin to search for proven models of more effective education, to demand the results of systematic experimentation. Second, improved measures of school performance will be called for. After all, no community can run a school directly. It has to elect a board, to appoint managers and teachers. Factions will develop and, along with them, disagreements about how well the school is being managed. One would expect a demand for performance measures to support one position or another, as well as community interest in test score changes, attendance rates, job and college placements, and, eventually, more subtle measures of student development and enthusiasm. But beyond this, there is almost certain to be a demand for performance measures from higher levels of government. In fact, development of reliable criteria may be the only condition on which states and cities will be willing to relinquish control to community boards and still pay the bills from the general tax system.

Those who favor community control of schools in cities, for example, are not arguing for financing schools out of neighborhood tax revenues. Even if it were practical to collect taxes at a neighborhood level, it would not be desirable to finance schools this way. Areas with low tax collections would often turn out to have high educational needs and vice versa. Ghetto areas with high concentrations of poor children would not have the resources necessary to support even average schools, let alone the more intensive and expensive education these children need. Clearly, school expenditures have to be redistributed in accordance with educational need if poor children are to have a chance at equal education.

But the general city taxpayer is likely to have little enthusiasm for turning over funds to community or neighborhood boards without some assurance that he will get his money's worth. The community board will have to be in some sense accountable to the central treasury as well as to the members of the community itself. At a minimum, city-wide rules to protect the health and safety of school children will have to be devised. Beyond this, accounts might be rendered in terms of either inputs or outputs. Input rules governing the qualifications of teachers, the hiring and firing of personnel, the duties of teachers, the size of classes, will be favored by teachers' unions. But these are exactly the kinds of rules that brought about the demand for community control in the first place. Community groups may well argue for shifting to an output or performance measure in rendering their accounts to the city taxpayer, on these grounds: If the children learn, why do you care how we do it? This approach would necessitate the development of test scores and other types of performance measures acceptable both to community boards and to the city administration. In order to retain their right to operate the schools, community boards might be required to meet certain minimum performance standards. In addition, part of the school budget might be used to reward better-than-expected gains in performance measures.

The New York City Board of Education and the Educational Testing Service are designing a system to measure the effectiveness of the city's teachers and supervisors and to make them accountable. Such a system might even help reconcile the United Federation of Teachers with the devotees of community control.[4]

The Market Model

The market model is essentially an extreme form of decentralization. It moves the locus of decisions about how services should be produced not simply to the community, but to the individual consumer.

The private sector of the economy relies on the profit motive to bring about improvement in the quality of goods and services offered to the consumer. If businesses want to survive, they have to attract customers by offering better products or lower prices than their competitors'—or both. The sanctions of the system are drastic: If the seller fails to produce what consumers want, he goes out of business. Success is also well rewarded. The firm that makes a "better" can opener or typewriter or lipstick can make millions.

Even economists know that this model does not work perfectly in the private sector. Sometimes there are too few sellers. They collude, overtly or tacitly. They may make profits—jointly—but the consumer loses. Antitrust laws and utility regulation exist to protect consumers against monopoly and oligopoly, but nobody really believes these laws and regulations work very effectively.

Moreover, even—or perhaps especially—when there are many sellers in the market, the level of public dissatisfaction with privately produced services can be high. Television and appliance repair, automobile servicing, laundering and dry cleaning are hardly objects of general consumer enthusiasm, even though they are privately produced by large numbers of competing sellers. True, the dissatisfied consumer can try another laundry, but he has little information to go on and may find the next place just as unsatisfactory as the last.

Despite these problems, some people believe that social services would be produced more effectively by private firms seeking to make a profit by pleasing the consumer. The argument is most frequently heard with respect to education. It runs thus: Children have to go to school and, in general, they have to go to the particular school in their neighborhood. Given this captive clientele, the school faculty and administration have little incentive to produce the kind of education that children and their parents want. The school management does not make money by producing more effective education, and nobody puts the school system out of business if the children fail to learn.

These observations have led some school reformers to the position that the only way to get effective education is to break the monopoly of public schools. They would not abolish public support of education, but they would channel it through the consumer rather than the producer.[5] Vouchers would entitle parents to buy education at whatever private or public school they found best for their children.

The voucher idea has attracted a spectrum of proponents that runs from the conservative economist Milton Friedman to liberal writer Christopher S. Jencks. Friedman's proposal was a simple one:

> . . . Governments would continue to administer some schools but parents who chose to send their children to other schools would be paid a sum equal to the estimated cost of educating a child in a government school, provided that at least this sum was spent on education in an approved school.[6]

The plan devised by a team headed by Jencks was a more complex proposal designed to meet some of the objections to the Friedman scheme.[7]

At the same time that they appealed to southern conservatives eager to escape public school integration, vouchers have also been seen as a way of improving the education of black children in the urban ghetto.[8] The proponents believe that a variety of private schools would spring up in and around the ghetto, many run by blacks for blacks. Since they would compete for students, schools that did not provide attractive facilities, relevant curricula, and teachers who believed in ghetto children and knew how to "turn them on" would not attract students. Many would try, but only those who gave the consumers what they wanted would survive. Ghetto parents, it is argued, want effective education for their children and will, with practice, know when they have found it.

One serious objection to a voucher system is that it might accentuate existing problems of income inequality.[9] Even if families received vouchers of the same value for each school-age child, schools offering more expensive education to those willing to pay a premium in addition to the voucher are likely to spring up. If experience is any guide, middle- and upper-income families will spend additional sums for what they believe to be superior education. After all, they do this now; some send their children to private schools and a great many more spend money on music lessons, summer camps, or "educational" family trips.

The result of an equal-size voucher system might well be expensive schools in the suburbs offering richer curricula, smaller classes, and more elaborate facilities to the children of the well-heeled, while the poor continued to study outmoded material in crowded classrooms in dismal schools. The suburban schools would be able to pay higher salaries and attract better teachers. Even if inner-city children were not discriminated against through entrance requirements, they would be effectively barred by higher tuition and the cost of commuting.

It would be possible, of course, to give larger vouchers to poor children on the grounds that their educational needs are greater. The differentials would have to be very large, however, to compensate for *both* the disposition of well-to-do families to spend more than their voucher and the greater real costs of teaching low-income children effectively. Such steep differentials in favor of the poor might be politically less palatable to the electorate than more subtle forms of income redistribution.

Under Jencks's proposal, the value of the voucher to the school would vary inversely with the family income of the student, and schools participating in the system would be prohibited from charging tuition beyond the voucher. Thus schools would have an incentive to enroll low-income children. The more expensive private schools would either have to cut their budgets or cater only to those rich enough to forgo the voucher and pay the full costs themselves. This may sound attractive on paper, but one wonders about the political saleability of a plan that would allow parents to shop around for the "best" school, but prohibit them from spending any additional funds on their children's education.

The other major problem with the voucher system is consumer ignorance. Unless he knows what he is buying, a consumer cannot choose rationally. Yet, in the social action area, it is very difficult for him to find out anything about the quality of a service before he uses it. Moreover, the costs of shopping around or sampling the merchandise of a hospital or a school may be prohibitive. In the medical area, they are obviously disastrous; one cannot shop around for a surgeon. But even in education, trial and error may be very costly. Parents cannot move a child around from one school to another until they find one they like, without endangering the child's educational and social progress. Moreover, even educated parents have trouble judging whether their child is progressing as rapidly as he could in school. How much greater, then, are the barriers to accurate parental judgment in the ghetto, where parents have little experience with books and learning.

If a voucher system is to increase the effectiveness of education, performance measures will have to be developed and made available so that parents can judge how much progress their children are making in school and how much they might make if they went to a different school. Hardly any schools, even private schools, provide anything resembling performance measures now. At best, a family considering alternative high schools may be able to find out where last year's graduates went to college, but this tells them little about the performance of the school. If a high proportion of graduates go to very selective colleges, it may mean only that the school tends to attract able and highly motivated students.

What kind of measures should schools produce for the information of current and potential consumers? First, a variety of measures, reflecting various objectives of education, should be developed and published. Publication of reading scores, for example, would prompt many parents to ask for evidence of other accomplishments, which might be poorly correlated with reading. What about mathematics and other cognitive skills? What about general ability to reason and oral expression and ability to get along with other children? What about leadership training and athletics and citizenship? Eventually, a variety of measures should be developed, validated, and published so that students and parents can choose intelligently among schools emphasizing the objectives of education they value most.

Second, to be useful, the measures have to reflect change in the student's performance over time rather than absolute levels of achievement. The absolute levels tell nothing about the effectiveness of the school. High reading scores may reflect only a student body selected for intelligence or verbal facility. The family of a child with a learning problem might well want to select a school with low absolute scores but higher rates of change at that level.

These two criteria raise the specter of constant testing and measurement, and of concentration on measurable skills to the detriment of the more subtle values of education. These are real dangers, but without serious effort to improve measures of education performance and to make them available, it is hard to see how a voucher system can lead to intelligent consumer choice and consumer pressure for effective education.

Moreover, reliance on the market would strengthen, not weaken, the case for public subsidy of research in education and systematic testing of new methods. Individual schools fighting for survival in the marketplace could not take risks with unproved methods or undertake expensive development of new curricula or approaches; nor could market competitors be expected to band together for systematic testing of innovations. Indeed, an atomistic private market for education might produce even less innovation than we have now. In general, in the normally private sectors of the economy, rapid technological change and increases in productivity occur in the large-firm, monopolized industries, not in those characterized by many sellers and intense inter-firm competition.

Perhaps major national manufacturers would invest considerable sums in new educational techniques, hoping that they could be proved more effective and then sold to schools seeking to enhance their attractiveness to students. These companies, however, would tend to invest in hardware and materials on which they could retain exclusive rights through patents and copyrights. There might be serious neglect of methods and approaches that, while conceivably more effective than hardware, could be easily copied without compensation to the original developer. For this reason, public as well as corporate investment in research and systematic testing of education methods would be necessary.

To sum up, experiments with market mechanisms in education are worth trying; indeed, the Office of Economic Opportunity has announced that it intends to experiment with voucher systems in a number of communities.[10] Nevertheless, the system has serious problems. It may not be possible to design a system that reduces rather than accentuates the differential between educational opportunities for the rich and the poor. Moreover, the problem of accountability remains. If the taxpayer is to provide subsidies for education, he must have some assurance that the money is not wasted, that some minimum standards are met by institutions cashing in the voucher. Beyond these considerations, the system will not work as intended to increase educational effectiveness unless performance measures are developed so that the consumer can choose intelligently, and unless an organized public effort is made to develop and test new and improved methods.

Where Do We Go from Here?

The point of the above discussion is that all the likely scenarios for improving the effectiveness of education, health, and other social services dramatize the need for better performance measures. No matter who makes the decisions, effective functioning of the system depends on measures of achievement. If federal, state, or city governments manage social service delivery directly, they need ways to gauge the success of different methods of delivering services so that they can choose the best ones. If social service management is decentralized, or even turned over to communities, both the community and higher levels of government will need performance measures on the basis of which to identify and reward more effective management. Even if social services are turned over to the private market in hope of harnessing competition and the profit motive to improvements in performance, consumers, to make wise choices, will need measures of what they are buying or might buy.

It therefore seems to me that analysts who want to help improve social service delivery should give high priority to developing and re- fining measures of performance. Relatively little effort has gone into devising such measures so far, despite their importance and the apparent intellectual challenge of the task. In education it will be necessary to move beyond standardized tests to more sensitive and less culturally biased measures that reflect not only the intellectual skills of children, but their creativity and faith in themselves and enthusiasm for learning. In health, it will be necessary to move beyond the conventional mortality and hospitalization statistics to more refined measures of health and vigor. Poverty cannot be measured by income alone. Job satisfaction is probably not closely related to earnings or hours of work. Considerable imagination will have to be brought to bear before performance measures can be developed for services like counseling and psychiatric care.

Two general rules can be suggested for the development of performance measures in the social action area. First, *single measures of social service performance should be avoided.* They will always lead to distortion, stultification, cheating to "beat the system," and other undesirable results. Schools cannot be judged by reading scores alone or mathematics scores alone or college placements alone or retention rates alone. Health service systems cannot be judged simply and solely by the number of patients treated or by the number of patients cured or even by health problems prevented. Manpower training programs cannot be weighted only by job placements or job retention or wage levels. Judging schools by reading scores would mean neglect of other skills and other dimensions of child development; judging a health center by the number of patients treated would encourage assembly line medicine; judging a man-power program on job placements would lead to hasty placement of trainees in low-level or unsuitable jobs.

Multiple measures are necessary to reflect multiple objectives and to avoid distorting performance. One can imagine schools developing and publishing a variety of measures of skills, knowledge, and satisfaction of students, some immediate and some based on longer-term follow-up. One can imagine health programs developing a variety of measures of health status and satisfaction of patients, also with different time lags. One can imagine manpower programs developing a variety of measures of skills acquired and subsequent job success of trainees.

For some purposes measures without any weights would be sufficient. In a voucher system for education, for example, one could simply make available a variety of performance measures for each school and let parents and students choose among them according to their own weighting systems. On the other hand, in a federal grant program designed to encourage effective manpower training, it would be necessary to assign weights to the various success measures being used. If several are being combined, the weights may not much matter, as long as no one measure is allowed to dominate and distort the reward system.

Second, *performance measures must reflect the difficulty of the problem.* If absolute levels of performance are rewarded, then schools will select the brightest students, training programs will admit only the workers who will be easiest to place in jobs, health centers will turn away or neglect the hopelessly ill. To avoid these distortions, social service effectiveness must always be measured in relation to the difficulty of the task. In general, measures of change are better than measures of absolute level, but even this approach may not solve the problem. It may be easier to bring about significant changes in the performance of bright children than in that of retarded children or to improve the health status of certain classes of patients. In this situation, the success of a social action activity can be measured only in relation to success of other activities with the same kind of student or patient or trainee. A considerable period of time will be necessary to collect experience and delineate above- and below-average performance with particular types of problems.

None of this sounds easy to accomplish. And it isn't. Nevertheless, we are unlikely to get improved social services (or, indeed, to know if we have them) until we make a sustained effort to develop performance measures suitable for judging and rewarding effectiveness. Current efforts to publish test scores or infant mortality rates in the name of "assessment" or "accountability" are only the first halting steps on the long road to better social services.

Performance measures for social services are not, of course, ends in themselves. They are prerequisites to attempts both to find more effective methods of delivering social services and to construct incentives that will encourage their use. But all the strategies for finding better methods discussed in these pages, especially social experimentation, depend for their success on improving performance measures. So do all the models for better incentives. Put more simply, to do better, we must have a way of distinguishing better from worse.

Notes

1. Charles L. Schultze, *The Politics and Economics of Public Spending* (Brookings Institution, 1968), pp. 104–105.
2. Robert A. Levine, "Rethinking Our Social Strategies," *Public Interest* 10 (winter 1968): 88, 89, 91, 92.
3. Worth Bateman, "Answering Program Effectiveness," U.S. Department of Health, Education, and Welfare, *Welfare In Review* 6 (January/February 1968): 1–10.
4. See *The New York Times*, February 9, 1971.
5. *Harvard Educational Review* 38 (winter 1968), devoted to equal educational opportunity, includes several articles on this subject. See also Theodore R. Sizer, "The Case for a Free Market," *Saturday Review* 52 (January 11, 1969): 34 ff.
6. Milton Friedman, "The Role of Government in Education," in *Economics and the Public Interest*, ed. Robert A. Folo (Rutgers University Press, 1955), p. 130.
7. The plan is described in Center for the Study of Public Policy, "Financing Education by Grants to Parents, A Preliminary Report," prepared for the Office of Economic Opportunity (The Center, March 1970), pp. 50–58.
8. Christopher Jencks, "Private Schools for Black Children," *New York Times Magazine*, November 3, 1968, sec. 6, p. 30 ff.
9. For a good critique of voucher plans, see Henry M. Levin, "The Failure of the Public Schools and the Free Market Remedy," *Urban Review* 2 (June 1968): 32–37 (Brookings Reprint 148).
10. Fred M. Hechinger, "School Vouchers: Can the Plan Work?" *The New York Times*, June 7, 1970; Eric Wentworth, "OEO Plans Test of Education Vouchers," *Washington Post*, December 26, 1970.

27

Implementation

Jeffrey L. Pressman and Aaron Wildavsky

Preface

Late in 1968 our attention was drawn to the Economic Development Administration's employment effort in Oakland by the appearance of a book with the arresting title, *Oakland's Not for Burning.* Written by a major participant in the EDA's Oakland venture,[1] the book appeared to suggest that the city had recently been saved from riot and ruin by the infusion of $23 million in federal funds. Because it created minority employment—thus sending out a beacon light of hope to a troubled nation—the EDA program was touted as a model worthy of imitation. Since Oakland Project members were not aware that the city had been delivered from evil, we inquired into the status of the program and discovered that in 1969, three years after it began, approximately $3 million had actually been spent. At that rate, another twenty years would pass before this emergency operation would have spent the money to create the jobs to employ the people who would prevent (or at least not participate in) riots. Part of the $3 million had gone to the city for the Hegenberger overpass to the coliseum (which we somehow thought would have been built anyway), and the rest had been spent on architects' fees. We indulged briefly in mild fantasies depicting local architects about to overthrow the Oakland City Council in a suave *coup d'etat,* only to be bought off at the last minute by EDA funds. But further investigation suggested that there were no easy targets or evident villains. Implementation of the EDA's program was just more difficult than any of us had thought.

This book begins at the end: We will concentrate on that part of a public program following the initial setting of goals, securing of agreement, and commitment of funds. A new agency called the Economic Development Administration (EDA) is established by Congress. The EDA decides to go into cities for the purpose of providing permanent new jobs to minorities through economic development. Oakland is chosen as an experiment in showing how the provision of public works and building loans can provide incentives for employers to hire minorities. Congress appropriates the necessary funds, the approval of city officials and employers is obtained, and the program is announced to the public amidst the usual fanfare. Years later, construction has only been partially completed, business loans have died entirely, and the results in terms of minority employment are meager and disappointing. Why?

Some programs are aborted because political agreement cannot be obtained. Others languish because funds cannot be secured. Still others die because the initial agreement of local officials or private concerns is not forthcoming. All these conditions were met in the EDA employment program in Oakland, but the program could not be implemented in time to secure the desired results.

In our study of implementation, we have deliberately chosen case material in which dramatic elements that are essentially self-explanatory are ruled out. There was no great conflict. Everyone agreed. There was only minimum publicity. The issue was not one of overriding political importance. Essential funds were on hand at the right time. The evils that afflicted the EDA program in Oakland were of a prosaic and everyday character. Agreements had to be maintained after they were reached. Numerous approvals and clearances had to be obtained from a variety of participants. Failure to recognize that these perfectly ordinary circumstances present serious obstacles to implementation inhibits learning. If one is always looking for unusual circumstances and dramatic events, he cannot appreciate how difficult it is to make the ordinary happen.

Source: From Implementation by J. L. Pressman and A. Wildavsky, pp. xi–xvii. Copyright © 1973 The Regents of the University of California. Reprinted by permission of the University of California Press.

People now appear to think that implementation should be easy; they are, therefore, upset when expected events do not occur or turn out badly. We would consider our effort a success if more people began with the understanding that implementation, under the best of circumstances, is exceedingly difficult. They would, therefore, be pleasantly surprised when a few good things really happened.

Implementation in recent years has been much discussed but rarely studied. Presidents and their advisers, department secretaries and their subordinates, local officials and groups in their communities complain that good ideas are dissipated in the process of execution. Yet, except for an excellent book by Martha Derthick,[2] we have not been able to locate any thoroughgoing analysis of implementation.[3] Complaints about implementation do not constitute serious efforts to grapple with the problem.

No doubt a comparative approach to problems of implementation would ideally be preferable to the one we have adopted. But not enough is known about the subject to develop appropriate categories, and there is no previous literature on which to rely for guidance. We do not make any claim to have undertaken a comprehensive analysis of implementation. We are not certain we know what all the problems are, let alone provide solutions to them. But a start must be made somewhere and we hope this is it.

Implementation, to us, means just what Webster and Roget say it does: to carry out, accomplish, fulfill, produce, complete. But what is it that is being implemented? A policy, naturally. There must be something out there prior to implementation; otherwise there would be nothing to move toward in the process of implementation. A verb like "implement" must have an object like "policy." But policies normally contain both goals and the means for achieving them. How, then, do we distinguish between a policy and its implementation?

In everyday discourse we use policy (when referring to decisions) in several strikingly different ways. Sometimes policy means a statement of intention: Our policy is to increase employment among minorities. Policy here is treated as a broad statement of goals and objectives. Nothing is said about what might be done or whether anything has been or will be done to accomplish that purpose. Other times we speak of policy as if it were equivalent to actual behavior: Our policy is to hire minorities, meaning that we actually do hire them. Policy in this sense signifies the goal and its achievement. Both these meanings of policy rule out the possibility of studying implementation. When policy remains a disembodied objective, without specifying actors or the acts in which they must engage to achieve the desired result, there is no implementation to study. When the statement of the objective includes its attainment, implementation is unnecessary.

We can work neither with a definition of policy that excludes any implementation nor one that includes all implementation. There must be a starting point. If no action is begun, implementation cannot take place. There must also be an end point. Implementation cannot succeed or fail without a goal against which to judge it.

Let us agree to talk about policy as a hypothesis containing initial conditions and predicted consequences. If X is done at time t_1, then Y will result at time t_2. If the federal government, through the Economic Development Administration, provides $23 million in loans and grants to enterprises in Oakland, and if these enterprises agree to hire minorities after spending the money, then facilities will be built leading to the creation of new jobs that will go to minorities. Implementation would here constitute the ability to achieve the predicted consequences after the initial conditions have been met.

Implementation does not refer to creating the initial conditions. Legislation has to be passed and funds committed before implementation takes place to secure the predicted outcome. Similarly, agreements with the local enterprises would have to be reached before attempts are made to carry them out. After all, the world is full of policy proposals that are aborted. You can't finish what you haven't started. Lack of implementation should not refer to failure to get going but to inability to follow through.

To emphasize the actual existence of initial conditions we must distinguish a program from a policy. A program consists of governmental action initiated in order to secure objectives whose attainment is problematical. A program exists when the initial conditions—the "if" stage of the policy hypothesis—have been met. The word "program" signifies the conversion of a hypothesis into governmental action. The initial premises of the hypothesis have been authorized. The degree to which the predicted consequences (the "then" stage) take place we will call implementation. Implementation may be viewed as a process of interaction between the setting of goals and actions geared to achieving them.

Considered as a whole, a program can be conceived of as a system in which each element is dependent on the other. Unless money is supplied, no facilities can be built, no new jobs can flow from them, and no minority personnel can be hired to fill them. A breakdown at one stage must be repaired, therefore, before it is possible to move on to the next. The stages are related, however, from back to front as well as from front to back. Failure to agree on procedures for hiring minorities may lead the government to withhold funds, thus halting the construction. Program implementation thus becomes a seamless web.

Policies imply theories. Whether stated explicitly or not, policies point to a chain of causation between initial conditions and future consequences. If X, then Y. Policies become programs when, by authoritative action, the initial conditions are created. X now exists. Programs make the theories operational by forging the first link in the causal chain connecting actions to objectives. Given X, we act to obtain Y. Implementation, then, is the ability to forge subsequent links in the causal chain so as to obtain the desired results. Once the funds are committed and the local agreements reached, the task is to build facilities to create new jobs so that minorities will be hired.

We oversimplify. Our working definition of implementation will do as a sketch of the earliest stages of the program, but the passage of time wreaks havoc with efforts to maintain tidy distinctions. As circumstances change, goals alter and initial conditions are subject to slippage. In the midst of action the distinction between the initial conditions and the subsequent chain of causality begins to erode. Once a program is underway implementers become responsible both for the initial conditions and for the objectives toward which they are supposed to lead.[4]

The longer the chain of causality, the more numerous the reciprocal relationships among the links and the more complex implementation becomes. The first four chapters illustrate the movement from simplicity to complexity. The reader interested in implementation should, therefore, be conscious of the steps required to accomplish each link in the chain. Who had to act to begin implementation? Whose consent was required to continue it? How many participants were involved? How long did they take to act? Each time an act of agreement has to be registered for the program to continue, we call a decision point. Each instance in which a separate participant is required to give his consent, we call a clearance. Adding the number of necessary clearances involved in decision points throughout the history of the program will give the reader an idea of the task involved in securing implementation. We will perform this chore for him in chapter 5.

When objectives are not realized, one explanation is the assertion of faulty implementation. The activities that were supposed to be carried out were not executed or were subject to inordinate delays. Another appropriate explanation may be that aspirations were set too high. Instead of asking why the process of implementation was faulty, we ask why too much was expected of it. Studying the process of implementation, therefore, includes the setting of goals (policy, according to its earlier meaning) toward which implementation is directed. By paying attention to the structural position of those who set targets—top federal officials who wish large accomplishments from small resources in a short time—and those who must implement them—career bureaucrats and local participants characterized by high needs and low cohesion—we seek in chapter 6 to uncover the causes of setting targets that are unlikely to be met.

The possibility of a mismatch between means and ends calls into question the adequacy of the original policy design. Perhaps implementation was good but the theory on which it was based was bad. Could a different set of initial conditions have achieved the predicted results? To explore this possibility, we end the book with an analysis of the economic theory underlying the EDA program in Oakland. Perhaps, we suggest in chapter 7, it might have been better to subsidize the wage bill of private firms directly in order to increase employment instead of the more roundabout method of providing grants and loans to construct facilities to create jobs for which minorities would then be hired.

The study of implementation requires understanding that apparently simple sequences of events depend on complex chains of reciprocal interaction. Hence, each part of the chain must be built with the others in view. The separation of policy design from implementation is fatal. It is no better than mindless implementation without a sense of direction. Though we can isolate policy and implementation for separate discussion, the purpose of our analysis is to bring them into closer correspondence with one another.

Notes

1. Amory Bradford, *Oakland's Not for Burning* (New York: McKay, 1968).
2. Martha Derthick, *New Towns In-Town* (Washington, D.C.: Urban Institute, 1972).
3. The splendid account of the Elementary and Secondary Education Act by Stephen Bailey and Edith Mosher reveals acute sensitivity to problems of implementation. But it is not their purpose to analyze implementation as a distinct phenomenon. See their *ESEA: The Office of Education Administers a Law* (Syracuse: Syracuse University Press, 1968). Jerome T. Murphy, in the article "Title I of ESEA: The Politics of Implementing Federal Education Before," *Harvard Educational Review* 41 (1971): 35–63, does address himself directly to the question of implementation. Although this article does not contain as thoroughgoing an analysis of implementation as is found in the Derthick study, the author does provide a number of insights into the problem.
4. After numerous discussions, we have come to understand why no one else has apparently tried to distinguish policy from implementation. One person says that he likes to think of implementation as problems that arise when goals are set at high levels of organizational decision but are not realized because of resistance or distortion at lower levels of organization performance. We cannot force anyone to accept our choice of words or concepts, but we do think it makes more sense to conceive of *organization* in an extended sense so that it encompasses those whose cooperation is necessary for a program to be carried out. To us, it seems strange to talk of a program as being implemented merely because lower level participants in the sponsoring organization attempted to carry it out though essential support from others was not forthcoming. Support for a program within an organization is but one stage of implementation as we understand it.

   Another person claims that policy and implementation are not distinguishable. Policy includes intended effects—i.e., policy includes implementation. Hence, a policy is not real until the intended changes have taken place. Again, we do not gainsay others the vocabulary with which they are comfortable. But we think that this choice of words confuses rather than clarifies. If policy includes its own implementation, then by definition alone it is not possible to carry out an investigation concerning the implementation of a policy. The important thing, we suppose, is that there are differences between deriving goals or objectives, working out a theory of how to achieve them, embodying that theory in governmental action, and executing it as intended. We think that Webster is on our side, but anyone else is welcome to translate his vocabulary into our concerns.

28

Representative Bureaucracy

Samuel Krislov

When this book began to take form, its topic—representative bureaucracy—was, at least in terms of general concern, of remote though hardly inconsequential importance. In recent months it has emerged among those who consider public policy as one of the bitterest and most discussed issues. The questions of quotas, of the merit of "compensatory justice," or (as I shall argue) of "remedial steps," have evoked much heated debate.

In many ways the light thrown on the subject has been disproportionately small. The reasons are not hard to find. Both sides feel there is an advantage in exaggeration and strongly stated positions, but these political techniques do tend to blur the fine points of the issues. This is borne out by a refreshingly candid comment by Christopher Jencks:

> For analytic purposes, it is therefore useful to distinguish between "equal opportunity" (i.e., treating everyone alike) and "compensatory opportunity" (i.e., helping the neediest). Unfortunately, conceptual clarity is precisely what the advocates of compensatory opportunity (including ourselves) feel they cannot afford. "Compensatory opportunity" is a slogan devoid of political appeal, while "equal opportunity" is still capable of rallying widespread support. Advocates of compensatory opportunity have therefore felt obliged to pretend that "equal opportunity" really implies compensatory opportunity. We see no reason for abandoning this sleight of hand, but it is also useful to recognize that treating everyone alike is not the same as helping the neediest.[1]

Similarly, those who are critical of what they see as a drive toward quotas as the system of selection throughout society tend to argue in terms of extreme examples as though these were the everyday standard. To the argument that these are untypical, such critics answer in terms of Alfred North Whitehead's "emergents"—the untypical is what is in process of becoming the general.

The issues of equality, merit, and reward are at the heart of current ideological conflict. One is as amused as amazed to read John Kenneth Galbraith's 1958 observation that "while it continues to have a large ritualistic role in the conventional wisdom of conservatives and liberals, inequality has ceased to preoccupy men's minds."[2] It is precisely as a preoccupation that it has survived. Irving Kristol has suggested that the shibboleths of inequality are used by elite "intellectuals" to attack bourgeois society; the real intention is not to elevate the poor so much as to demean the businessman and thus confirm the position of the snobbish counterculture. So, he argues, the criticism will perversely increase even as actual inequality wanes. Whether or not Kristol has accurately depicted the motives, it is clear that at the core of the ideological unity currently distinguishing the left in western society is the issue of inequality. It is, to employ an overused analogy, something of a secular religion, evoking devotion, sacrifice, and intensity.

The present study deals with these problems in terms of one set of social institutions—the public bureaucracy—and in terms of a single claim—to societal representativeness—offsetting those of "presumed merit" and "job-skill-related" criteria.

Part of the process of obfuscation has been the insistence of partisans that the issues can be clearly drawn on matters such as the above. This volume will acknowledge throughout the complexity involved in just such concepts—a complexity outlined in *The Negro in Federal Employment*.[3] It is perhaps wise to recapitulate and expand that argument here.

The fundamental fallacy encouraged by the practitioners of public and other "scientific"

Source: Samuel Krislov, Representative Bureaucracy. © 1974, pp. 1–6, 18–19. Reprinted by permission of Prentice-Hall, Englewood Cliffs, NJ.

administration is that job analysis is possible for most if not all of the positions in our society. The implicit models are elemental jobs, e.g., working on an assembly line or such powerful and seductive examples as that of the surgeon who literally can or cannot "cut it."

Of course it is realized that any particular example of ability—one day's effort, for example—is subject to error. The reliability of this kind of sample is in addition generally aggravated by the need to pick some surrogate for the requisite ability such as a paper and pencil test. In all of this it is assumed that there is a generally agreed-upon definition of what ideally should be measured.

In fact, the complexity far exceeds these obvious points. Expanding Blau—who in turn builds on Talcott Parsons and Robert F. Bales—I have suggested that merit and the criteria for selection and promotion can be approached as a series of "nesting" concepts with their appropriateness a matter of perspectives. In this sense, there are "multiple realities" in which criteria not only become less precise but encompass wider and wider viewpoints of what is an appropriate consideration.

Thus a surgeon's ability to diagnose is at least a second dimension of competence. His or her skill at organizing an office and the operating room team is even less esteemed, and yet it may be very consequential. The human relations involved in dealings with nurses may affect both the operation conditions and the aftercare, which is a significant aspect of the entire medical treatment—especially in cases such as the treatment of ulcers where poor attitudes transmitted to the patient can be immediately related to the recurrence of problems. The perennial TV plot involving the extra-operating room activity of the doctor who offends the clinic patron—usually by political or romantic activity—illustrates another set of problems complicating the supposedly simple job analysis. In fact, personal activities well beyond the simple task performance do impinge on successful operations of an institution. I am aware of an instance where a full-time administrator had to be hired to cope with the many-faceted activities of an inspiring and inspired idea man who didn't always observe the niceties of university rules before making what sometimes proved to be embarrassing commitments. There are extra costs that may result when one or more other physicians have to give up time that would otherwise be devoted to patients in order to rule on ethical questions, mediate, soothe ruffled feelings, or raise funds to substitute for sums lost through another's rudeness.

From the patient's viewpoint, only one set of considerations seems relevant—those that improve his care. From the standpoint of the physician's colleagues, fair use of nurses' time and such contributions as improvement of others' skill through keen analysis and awareness of new literature loom as worthy of consideration. The hospital administrator may value the individual who works well with others; the immediate community may esteem the TV celebrity; and society at large may value most the surgeon whose discoveries lead to further progress. All these perspectives are legitimate within their given context.

The point can be generalized. It is not simply that the physician's position, nominally the quintessence of a specific skill-oriented job, has complex ramifications. Rather, parallel observations can be made of the typical undergraduate's view of the professor as classroom teacher, the graduate student's emphasis on his creative helpfulness, the college's emphasis on his scholarship and the enhancement of departmental reputation, and his chairman's concern for his administrative contribution.

It is this multiple perspective that justifies "bumping," the practice of allowing unneeded employees in one office to displace employees with less seniority in another office. From the standpoint of the larger bureaucratic structure it is seen as a generalized procedure that helps induce everyone, including other members of the unit, adversely affected by the "bumping" to join and stay with the service, and to have some confidence in career lines. Similarly—and in a sense more grandiosely—veteran's preference is justified on the grounds that the soldier's defense of the social system is a prerequisite to the bureaucratic structure, and therefore a logical necessity for maintaining the operation as a whole.

The unfolding of such concepts is rather like an onion or artichoke in its nature. Essentially, taking a broader view is the assimilation of apparently extrinsic standards, which from the new perspective is quite reasonable and very much in order.

In short there is no natural dividing line between intrinsic and extrinsic criteria. And oddly enough, this makes it imperative that a line be drawn. If an institution is to perform its task, it must as a rule exclude external considerations that impinge on its own integrity. Such considerations as "private lives" or "non-job-connected background characteristics" are in modern and most premodern structures rigorously excluded from evaluation on the somewhat specious grounds that they do not affect performance—though they often do—or that they can be regulated through monitoring of performance—though performance is only crudely monitored in fact, and these criteria are realistically most relevant at point of hiring.

The tension between sets of criteria is greatest in connection with public service. On the one hand, the multiple perspectives, the variety of groupings that must be satisfied, is at maximum with respect to societally determined positions. A public office makes for public fuss. The process of preferring one or another set of criteria is one of policy making, of agenda setting, of preference ordering, of cue giving for the other sectors as well. Furthermore, the public sector has explicit need for extrinsic validation. A major task of governance is to gain support for policies. No matter how brilliantly conceived, no matter how artfully contrived, government action usually also requires societal support. And one of the oldest methods of securing such support is to draw a wide segment of society into the government to convey and to merchandise a policy.

Scholars in developmental administration have had to expand their concepts of administrative effectiveness to talk about "penetration," that is, the degree to which a government is able to move its policies into action outside the government halls. They were led to the concept by examination of former colonial civil services that continued to maintain their technical internal efficiency, but, having lost external military leverage, were increasingly ignored, isolated, and ineffectual. In most instances this was in part a product of the narrow base from which the colonial powers generally drew their native pen bearers. (The British often deliberately played off segments of society and entrusted bureaucratic power to groups heavily dependent on their foreign masters, for example, the Copts in Egypt. Such minorities were unlikely to seek or achieve independent power.)

All in all then, the pressure on government service to accommodate a wide variety of non-task considerations is great. But the threat of succumbing to the pressures, of sacrificing capacity to act, is also evident. While governments, like all institutions, succumb to pressures and trade off various boons for social peace, they are more vulnerable than many other institutions in that they act more publicly. This is especially true of Western democracies but is in essence true of all governments. The process of political selection is, other factors being equal, more open and deemed more a matter of general concern than, say, industrial recruitment. Special treatment for one group generates demands from other groups. (This is a group analogy with Ambrose Bierce's definition of patronage as the process of creating nine enemies and one ingrate.) Multiple effects from officially stated public policy can be salutary, or at least can be, as some have argued, the geometric diffusion of mediocrity.

This volume seeks to evaluate and mediate such claims regarding the public service, not in the popular terms of discourse, but in the light of the application of a quite different principle, that of "representative bureaucracy." That term suggests that administrative structures might be characterized by the presence or absence of such representativeness, and the degree to which the structures have in fact been representative agencies.

In exploring these issues we approach the whole problem of legitimacy and authority in government. In avoiding current cant we can, perhaps, at least avoid falling into popular ruts and old clichés. It is perhaps too much to hope to avoid all the new ones.

It has generally been assumed that the American political system first developed the prototype of a mass bourgeois party. This in turn was widely diffused and also engendered the mass proletarian party (see, e.g., Maurice

Duverger.)[4] It has also been suggested that the American bureaucracy was distinctive in its avoidance of class bias, and that this provides a unique opportunity for the radiating principle of representativeness to prevail.

The current argument has been less over this idealistic end than over means. To supporters of "guidelines" much of the argument is hypocritical or disguised racism; to critics the current effort is "reverse discrimination." By a more objective examination of the problem, I hope to clarify the issue and perhaps even to reconcile some of the differences among those of good will and fond hope. The sharing of world experience and historical perspective also seems to promise less heat and more light. . . .

V. The Emergence of the Issue in American Society

The issue of representative bureaucracy has, of course, been dramatized by the issue of Black rights in the United States; the Blacks were quickly joined in their demands by Puerto Ricans, Chicanos, and women. For Americans, as well as for foreign observers of the American scene, this has become a seminal challenge to the American dream.

How we solve the problem of Black participation in power and Black sharing of status and goods in American society will have a great effect on our self-image as well as on the image we project abroad. The American dream was built on several major themes, but its dominant one was its ability to cope effectively with diversity in society. The claim of a capacity to deal with inter-group conflicts that were in their native setting irrepressible lay at the heart of the romantic notion of America as the newfound and innocent land that could be a model for the world. Not shackled by the disabilities of the old feudal system, and freed from traditions of conflicts and feuds, American society was to be the paradigm for future societies of promise and worth—a United States of Europe, of Asia, of Africa, of the world itself.

This dream has taken sharply divergent forms without shattering that essential faith. The original notion was the "melting pot" concept made famous by Israel Zangwill.[5] The "tempest-tossed" and "homeless" were all tossed into the cauldron of American life and their dross thrown off, their character reformed. In this sociological equivalent of America's political motto of *E Pluribus Unum*, a common life-style and character were the expected result from this tempering process.

Horace Kallen's more complex program of "cultural pluralism" echoed William James's plea: "pluralism lets things really exist in the each-form or distributively. Monism thinks that the all-form or collective unit is the only form that is rational."[6] Kallen suggested that a polyglot culture would in fact be stronger than any enforced conformity. Kallen's arguments became the standard claim for unity-in-diversity—tolerating, even celebrating, the distinctiveness of subgroups as contributing to a synthesizing realization of the whole person as an American.[7]

This later version—a product of post–World War I days—had even greater attraction than the earlier program. The melting pot requires not just the taking on of a new identity but rejection of the old. The "cultural pluralistic" notion is not a jealous god, and rather resembles oriental religions that allow continued obeisance to the old, while granting absolution for accepting the new. Throughout the world the claim for social pluralism, perhaps in a politically federal system, has emerged as a potential solution to ethnic, religious, or local animosities, short of "final solutions" of physical or cultural annihilation.

The failure of American society over two centuries to deal with its indigenous Indian and forcibly imported Black populations became salient. In the nineteenth century they were excludable as "the troublesome presence," as President Grant so gracefully put it.[8] They were the essence of the problem, the proof of the pudding, in the twentieth century.

Whether it was this externally obvious contradiction, or the inexorable influence of the "American dilemma," the patent affront to our conscience noted by Gunnar Myrdal, or the changing geographic, political, economic, and educational status of the Negro, this past quarter-century has been marked by an extensive governmental, private, and morally directed effort to end this profound anomaly in our democratic order.

In this effort, governmental service has been important as both a symbol and a cause. As a major vehicle of social change, the occupation of its positions by minority-group members has been significant in policy outcomes and in the subtle transactions that cumulatively constitute policy. Advances in this area have some of the character of showcase achievements, encouraging changes in career aspirations and patterns among the minority, and inspiring new efforts and goals for majority elites in the private sector.

This new look at the relationship of Blacks to public service has raised for a highly developed and presumably integrated society many of the same questions about government service raised in newly independent and/or less united systems. The questions then seem universal—perhaps, in reality, timeless.

The emergence of new states as a product of dissolution of older more comprehensive ones—from empire to nation, in Rupert Emerson's provocative epigraph—has hidden the need for creation of more comprehensive subunit communities. In this respect the newer states share to a remarkable degree the problems that the more established states have also ignored. The merging of dual societies or dual polities—often a subdominant one merged into partnership with a senior partner—is a continuous fact of modern society, and all too often a painful one. Northern Ireland, Belgium, Canada, and the United States have more in common with and more to learn from polyethnic, polyglot, or polydeist communities like Lebanon, India, and Malaysia than appears on the surface. And the bureaucracy with its manifold significance, its need for variety, and its large sample size is a better microcosm of the total society than more commonly studied areas such as legislatures and a better laboratory for studying broad political action.

VI. Conclusion and Summary

The concept of representative bureaucracy was originally developed to argue for a less elite, less class-biased civil service. As such it was hardly of great interest in the United States because this country's problem then was to develop a respected administrative structure that could attract elite groups. The bureaucracy has since gained in prestige and power. More significantly, our society now sees other lines of division—race, ethnicity, and sex—as becoming even more relevant than class. These new lines of division in turn have particular relevance to contemporary bureaucratic structures.

Notes

1. Christopher Jencks, *Inequality* (New York: Basic Books, 1972), p. 75.
2. John K. Galbraith, *The Affluent Society* (Cambridge, Mass.: Houghton Mifflin, 1958), p. 82.
3. Samuel Krislov, *The Negro in Federal Employment* (Minneapolis, Minn.: University of Minnesota Press, 1967).
4. Maurice Duverger, *Political Parties* (New York: John Wiley, 1954).
5. Israel Zangwill, *The Melting Pot* (New York: Macmillan, 1913).
6. William James, *A Pluralistic Universe, Lecture 8* (New York: Longmans, Green and Co., 1909), p. 324.
7. Horace Kallen, *Cultural Pluralism and the American Idea* (Philadelphia: University of Pennsylvania Press, 1956).
8. See the book of that name by Eli Ginzberg and Alfred S. Eichner (New York: Free Press, 1964).

Intergovernmental Relations: An Analytical Overview

Deil S. Wright

William Anderson, one of the intellectual parents of the intergovernmental relations field, once claimed that "intergovernmental relations is, I believe, a term indigenous to the United States, of a relatively recent origin, and still not widely used or understood."[1] Since Anderson's assertion in 1960, the phrase intergovernmental relations (IGR) has experienced wider usage, but whether the term is clearly or adequately understood remains questionable. Brief attention to the definition and features of IGR is therefore appropriate if not mandatory.

Gaining Force by Unusualness: The Distinctive Features of IGR

We need look no further than the author quoted above for a starting point in clarifying IGR. Professor Anderson says that IGR is a term intended "to designate an important body of activities or interactions occurring between governmental units of all types and levels within the [United States] federal system."[2] It is possible to use his general definition as a starting point to elaborate the concept of IGR.

First and foremost, IGR occurs within the federal system. American federalism is the context, not the totality, of IGR. IGR encompasses more than is usually conveyed by the concept of federalism, where the emphasis is chiefly on national-state relationships with occasional attention to interstate relationships. IGR recognizes not only national-state and interstate relations, but also national-local, state-local, national-state-local, and interlocal relations. In short, IGR includes as proper objects of study all the permutations and combinations of relations among the units of government in the American system.

Anderson also assists us in making a second important point about IGR. "It is human beings clothed with office who are the real determiners of what the relations between units of government will be. Consequently the concept of intergovernmental relations necessarily has to be formulated largely in terms of human relations and human behavior . . ."[3] Strictly speaking, then, there are no intergovernmental relations, there are only relations among officials in different governing units. Individual interactions among public officials is at the core of IGR. In this sense it could be argued that federalism deals with the anatomy of the system, whereas IGR treats its physiology.

A third notion implicit in IGR is that relations are not one-time, occasional occurrences, formally ratified in agreements or rigidly fixed by statutes or court decisions. Rather, IGR is the continuous, day-to-day pattern of contacts, knowledge, and evaluations of government officials. A major concern is with the informal as well as with the formal, the practices as well as the principles, pursued in both competitive and cooperative interjurisdictional patterns. This third facet of IGR reads into the concept those activities—as well as research studies—that have previously gone under the title of cooperative federalism, which the late E. S. Corwin defined as one in which governmental units "are regarded as mutually complementary parts of a single governmental mechanism all of whose powers are intended to realize the current purposes of government according to their

Source: "Intergovernmental Relations: An Analytical Overview" by Deil Wright from Annals of the American Academy of Political & Social Science, Vol 416, Nov 1974, pp 1–16. Reprinted by permission.

applicability to the problem at hand."[4] These words from a constitutional law scholar provide the desirable emphasis on the working, problem-oriented informalities of IGR and at the same time are a reminder of the formal, legal, institutional context within which those relationships originate and flourish.

It has been shown that IGR recognizes multiple unit relationships, that it respects the primacy of public officials acting in an interjurisdictional context, and that it is concerned with informal working relationships in institutional contexts. A fourth distinguishing characteristic of IGR is its awareness of the role played by all public officials. Automatically assumed as integral and important to IGR are mayors, councilmen, governors, state legislators, members of Congress and others. But in recent years more attention has been paid to the actions, attitudes and roles of appointed administrators. The increased focus on administrators as relevant IGR participants is a natural outgrowth of the increasingly important role played by public bureaucracies in government. The concern for the administrative aspects of IGR also arises, however, from attention to informal working relationships and from the academic leanings of most of the writers who have staked out claims to the IGR field. A majority of these persons have been oriented toward public administration and have also held a strong interest in state and local government.

A fifth and final distinctive feature of IGR is its policy component. Federalism has, to a large extent, translated questions of policy into questions of law and relied upon the courts for their resolution. Economic and political complexities, combined with rapid rates of social and technological change, have greatly reduced the capacity of courts—and legislatures—to deal with continuous pressures for policy change. The secular shift from regulatory politics to distributive and redistributive politics signaled new power relationships and configurations to which the term federalism could be applied only with awkward and ambiguous modifiers, such as direct, private, functional, economic. From its origins in the 1930s, IGR was recognized as anchored in politics and suffused with policy. It retains those features in the 1970s.

IGR cut its teeth on the massive political and policy issues that remained following the Supreme Court decisions on the social welfare legislation of the New Deal. It reached early adolescence in grappling with federal aid to education, urban development and civil rights. It is now attempting to claim maturity on issues related to citizen participation and effective services delivery systems. Near the policy core of IGR have been fiscal issues. These have been dominated by allocational issues: Who shall raise what amounts by what method from which citizens, and who shall spend how much for whose benefit with what results? This "fiscal fixation" has sometimes skewed diagnoses of and prescriptions for IGR problems, but the main point stands: IGR is centrally concerned with policy. As the Kestnbaum Commission noted in 1955, "The crucial questions now are questions of policy: What level ought to move? Or should both?"[5] These questions, the commission added, are ones on which the criteria for judgment "are chiefly political, economic, and administrative rather than legal."[6]

The five distinctive features of IGR are summarized in table 1. These characteristics combine and interact to produce new directions, vectors, and results in the conduct of public affairs in the United States. A new term or phrase to describe these special features therefore seems amply justified. The term IGR alerts one to the multiple, behavioral, continuous and dynamic exchanges occurring between various officials in the political system. It may be compared to a different, novel and visual filter or concept that can be laid on the American political landscape. It permits one to observe, classify and cumulate knowledge without obscuring other relevant data which prior political concepts have provided.

TABLE 1

Distinctive Features of Intergovernmental Relations

1. All Units (Multiple Entities)	
National	Municipalities
States	Special districts
Counties	School districts
2. Interactions of Officials (Informal)	
Behavior	Perceptions
Beliefs	Preferences
3. Continuous and Cumulative (Regularities)	
Day-to-day contacts	
Working relationships	
Cumulative patterns	
4. All Public Officials (Administrators)	
Elected officials	Appointed administrators
a. legislators b. executives c. judges	a. generalists b. functional specialists or program professionals
5. Policy Emphasis (Fiscal Focus)	
Financial issues	
Anchored in politics	
Suffused with policy	

Phases of IGR

"To follow still the changes of the moon,"
Shakespeare

To say that the American political system has evolved and changed is trite. The significant questions in dealing with change are ones centering on the frequency, mechanisms, direction, and effects of change. It is possible, for example, to understand aspects of the solar system by studying carefully the phases of the moon. Similarly, a better grasp of the American political system may hopefully be gained by identifying and analyzing five phases of IGR.

In each of the five IGR phases, three main components are considered. First, what were the main problems dominating the public agenda during each phase? Second, what were the perceptions held by the main participants that seemed to guide or direct their behavior in each phase? Third, what mechanisms and techniques were used to implement intergovernmental actions and objectives during each period? Additional elements will help describe each phase, orient the reader, and reveal the effects of changing intergovernmental behavior patterns. These elements are a one-word descriptor, a metaphoric or graphic characterization, and an indication of the approximate dates in which each IGR phase peaked or climaxed.

The five phase descriptors employed here, together with rough date designations are: (1) conflict (pre-1937); (2) cooperative (1933–1953); (3) concentrated (1945–1960); (4) creative (1958–1968); and (5) competitive (1965-?). A condensed and summary chart of the successive phases is offered in table 2. Added to that overview are verbal and graphic expositions of the phases with important caveats. The phases are clearly indicated as successive ones with some overlapping of dates among the periods. While the dates have been selected with deliberateness, they are not sharp and arbitrary cutting points. Forces and tendencies bringing one or another phase to its climax were present or had antecedents in prior periods. Also, caution is necessary on terminal dates. None of the phases ends in any exact or literal sense. Each phase produces carryover effects beyond the years designated in table 2. Indeed, it is probably most accurate to think of the current state of intergovernmental affairs as resulting from overlaps of the cumulative and successive effects of each IGR phase.

Conflict (pre-1937)

The chief concern of the conflict phase of IGR was the effort to identify and implement "proper" spheres of governmental jurisdiction and neatly defined boundaries for officials' actions. This emphasis operated at the state-local level as well as between national and state governments. Dillon's rule, as a principle for interpreting narrowly the powers of local governments, was not only an assertion of state supremacy but also a consequence of the search for the exact limits of local power. Guiding this search was an expectation of exclusive powers. Public officials' perceptions reflected these adversary and antagonistic patterns of interaction.

These conceptions and attitudinal postures by participants were anchored in deeper societal values of competition, corporate organizational forms, profit and efficiency. Residual elements of this phase remain today on the urban-metropolitan scene in the so-called market models of metropolitanism and in the search for the political jurisdiction to perform most efficiently a particular function—for example, should an activity be assigned to a city or to an areawide body?

The manner in which problems of jurisdiction were resolved in the conflict model of IGR was through statutes and the courts. Growing social and economic complexity subsequently brought regulatory agencies and commissions into being to referee jurisdictional boundary disputes. The Interstate Commerce Act of 1887 created the first of the great regulatory commissions and was a major breach in the century-old "administrative settlement" between the national government and the states.[7] It broke the long-standing presumption against the creation and growth of a national administrative establishment. Attempts to locate the scope of federal regulatory power under the commerce clause and other authority have persisted to the point that under a recent court ruling *all* electric generating and transmission companies fall under the rate-making authority of the Federal Power Commission.

Other illustrations of the continued adversary, conflict-oriented pattern of national-state relations abound. Environmental and health concerns recently precipitated a jurisdictional dispute over the spheres of national and state power to regulate the safety levels of a nuclear generating plant in Minnesota. National standards set by the Atomic Energy Commission (AEC) specified one level of allowable millirems of radiation escaping from the reactor into the atmosphere. The Minnesota Pollution Control Agency set the permissible level of millirems at

TABLE 2

Phases of Intergovernmental Relations (IGR)

PHASE DESCRIPTOR	MAIN PROBLEMS	PARTICIPANTS PERCEPTIONS	IGR MECHANISMS	FEDERALISM METAPHOR	APPROXIMATE CLIMAX PERIOD
Conflict	Defining boundaries Proper spheres	Antagonistic Adversary Controversy Exclusivity	Statutes Courts Regulations	Layer cake federalism	pre-1937
Cooperative	Economic stress International threat	Collaboration Complementary Mutuality Supportive	Policy planning Broad formula grants Open-ended grants Tax credit	Marble cake federalism	1933–1953
Concentrated	Program needs Capital works	Professionalism Objectivity Neutrality Functionalism	Categorical grants Service standards	Focused or channelled federalism (water taps)	1945–1960
Creative	Urban-metropolitan Disadvantaged clients	National goals Great Society Grantsmanship	Program planning Project grants Participation	Fused-foliated federalism (proliferated)	1958–1968
Competitive	Coordination Program effectiveness Delivery systems Citizen access	Disagreement Tension Rivalry	Revenue sharing Reorganization Regionalization Grant consolidation	Picket fence federalism (fragmented)	1965- ?

only two percent of that sanctioned by the AEC. The Northern States Power Company brought suit in the federal court challenging the state standards and requesting permission to construct the nuclear power plant without regard for the Minnesota regulations. At issue in the case was the application and intent of federal statutes dealing with atomic energy. The court ruled in favor of the exclusive jurisdiction of the national government and invalidated the more restrictive state regulations.[8]

These recent court decisions probably come as close to reflecting current economic realities, social interdependencies, and technological necessity as pre-1937 courts and legislatures thought they were reflecting economic, social and technological separatism. That supposed separatism—however limited, qualified or restricted in practice—gave credence to the metaphor of "layer cake federalism" as a crude means of describing national, state and local disconnectedness.

Cooperation (1933–1953)

Several authors have ably argued and amply demonstrated that intergovernmental collaboration in the United States existed throughout the 19th and 20th centuries.[9] That such collaboration was of major significance or the dominant fact of our political history is less clear. It does seem possible, however, to point to one period in which complementary and supportive relationships were most prominent and had high political significance. That period is the cooperative phase from 1933–1953. The prime elements of national concern during those two decades were the alleviation of widespread economic distress and response to international threats. It seems logical and natural that internal and external challenges to national survival would bring us closer together.

The means by which increased collaboration occurred were several and varied. Most pertinent for our concerns were such approaches as national policy planning, tax credits, and categorical grants-in-aid. Most of the dozen or so grant programs enacted during the depression period were broad formula grants, with a few being open-ended. Special emergency funding arrangements were instituted during the depression years and repeated in selected federally-impacted areas in wartime. As one observer noted in 1943:

> Cooperative government by federal-state-local authorities has become a byword in the prodigious effort to administer civilian defense, rationing, and other war-time programs.... Intergovernmental administration, while it is a part of all levels of government, is turning into something quite distinct from them all.[10]

The IGR collaboration that persisted during these years was present on such unusual occasions as the 1952 steel seizure confrontation; prior to his seizure effort, President Truman polled state governors for their views.

The prime IGR mechanism, as well as the major legacy of this cooperative period, was fiscal. Substantial and significant fiscal links were firmly established. These established conduits were harbingers of more to come. They also served as important illustrations of a new and differently textured model of intergovernmental patterns, the well-publicized "marble cake" metaphor. The marble cake characterization appears to have been coined by Professor Joseph McLean of Princeton University in the early 1940s for the visual or contrast effect with the layer cake conception. Professor Morton Grodzins probably had the greatest impact in popularizing and elaborating the marble cake concept.

Concentrated (1945–1960)

The descriptor employed for this IGR phase stands for the specific, functional, highly focused nature of intergovernmental interaction that evolved and dominated the Truman-Eisenhower years. From 1946 to 1960, twenty-nine major new grant-in-aid programs were established, a number that doubled the total number of programs enacted before and during the depression and wartime eras. The expanded use of categorical grant programs was accompanied by increased attention to service standards and program measurement.

Guiding this growing functional emphasis were corps of program professionals in each of the specialized grant fields, such as airport construction, hospital construction, slum clearance and urban renewal, urban planning, waste treatment facilities, library construction, and so on. The pervasiveness of professionalism enhanced the service standards emphasis by covering the domain with a cloak of objectivity and neutrality. These fit comfortably into Professor Herbert Kaufman's conception of the autonomy accompanying "neutral competence" in public administration contrasted with the control over policy by a strong executive leader.[11] The professionalism, specialized grants and growing insulation also coincided neatly in time, as well as thematically, with Professor Frederick Mosher's view that the 1950s confirmed the triumph of the "professional state" in the public service.[12]

What aims or ends guided and provided the rationale for this surge of activity?

Two appear to be most prominent. One was a capital works, public construction push. Between 1946 and 1960, state and local capital outlays increased twelvefold while current operating expenses rose by a multiple of four. Federal grants for highways, hospitals, sewage plants, and airports underwrote much of the state-local effort to meet deferred wartime needs and respond to changing technology and population configurations, especially its suburbanization.

A second motive force propelling intergovernmental action in this period was the political realization that government generally, and IGR especially, was capable of responding to particularistic middle class needs. The New Deal may have had its most telling political effect in making the American middle class acutely aware of the positive and program-specific capabilities of governmental action. Effective political action based on this awareness came after World War II and was reinforced by several conditions.

One condition already mentioned was suburbanization. It constituted the urban frontier and reinforced the myth of Jeffersonian ward republics. Another was the predisposition for using intergovernmental mechanisms because they also meshed with the historical political tradition of localism. In addition, IGR techniques fitted middle class values of professionalism, objectivity and neutrality. It appeared that objective program needs rather than politics were being served. Like reform at the turn of the century, IGR appeared to take a program out of politics.

Those political values coincided with an important structural change at the national level: the legislative reorganization of Congress in 1946. The most significant result of this event for IGR was the creation and stabilization of standing committees with an explicit program emphasis. These congressional committee patterns soon became the leverage points and channels through which influence on program-specific grants flowed. Furthermore, the committees developed their own cadre of professional staff members with functional and programmatic inclinations.

The flow of influence combined with the concentrated or focused flow of funds in the 1946–1960 period prompts one to employ a hydraulic metaphor in depicting this phase of IGR. The national government had become an established reservoir of fiscal resources to which a rapidly increasing number of water taps were being connected. The functional flows of funds could be facilitated by those knowledgeable at turning on the numerous spigots, that is, the program professionals. Cooperation was prominent during this period, but it occurred in more concentrated and selectively channeled ways.

A crude effort to express the water tap phase of IGR is made in figure 1. The intergovernmental flow of funds for 1950 is shown by the lines connecting the national-state and state-local spending sectors. This phase of IGR confirmed the interconnected and interdependent nature of national-state-local relations.

Creative (1958–1968)

The foundations for the creative phase of IGR were formed and filled in the cooperative and concentrated periods. The dates delimiting this phase are again somewhat arbitrary, but they mark a decade of moves toward decisiveness rather than drift in American politics and public policy. The election of a heavily Democratic Congress in 1958 and the 1964 presidential results were the political pegs to which this phase of IGR was attached. An added input that contributed to direction and cohesiveness, if not decisiveness, was the report of the Eisenhower-appointed President's Commission on National Goals. The commission, appointed partially in response to the Russian challenge of Sputnik, was created in 1959 and reported in 1961.[13]

The term Creative Federalism is applied to this decade because of presidential usage and because of the novel and numerous initiatives in IGR during the period. Three

FIGURE 1

PUBLIC EXPENDITURES BY TYPE AND BY LEVEL OF GOVERNMENT AND THE INTERGOVERNMENTAL FLOW OF FUNDS, FISCAL YEAR 1950

(in billions of dollars)

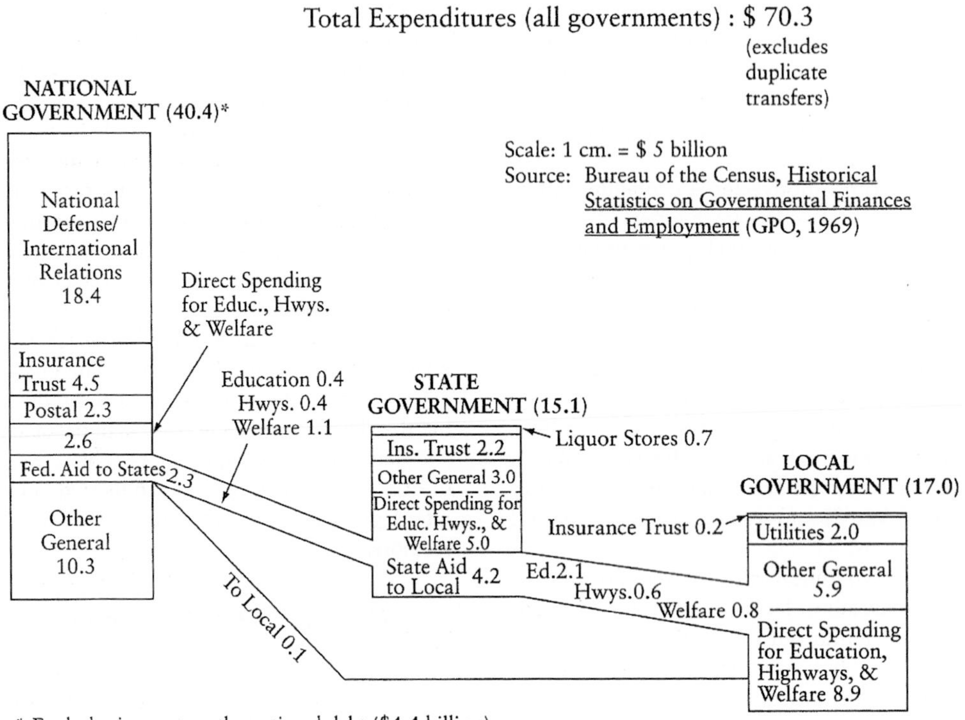

* Excludes interest on the national debt ($4.4 billion)

mechanisms are prominent: (1) program planning, (2) project grants, and (3) popular participation. The sheer number of grant programs alone is sufficient to set this decade apart from the preceding periods. In 1961 the Advisory Commission on Intergovernmental Relations (ACIR) identified approximately 40 major grant programs in existence that had been enacted prior to 1958. By 1969 there were an estimated 160 major programs, 500 specific legislative authorizations, and 1,315 different federal assistance activities, for which money figures, application deadlines, agency contacts, and use restrictions could be identified. Federal grants jumped in dollar magnitude from $4.9 billion in 1958 to $23.9 billion in 1970. At the state-local level, state aid to local governments rose from $8.0 billion to $28.9 billion over the 1958–1970 span.

Numbers and dollars alone are insufficient to distinguish the creative phase. Planning requirements, for example, were attached to 61 of the new grant programs enacted between 1961 and 1966. The tremendous growth in project grants as contrasted with formula grants increased the diversity of activities supported by federal funds and increased further the autonomy and discretion of program professionals. Project grant authorizations grew from 107 to 280 between 1962 and 1967, while formula grants rose from 53 to 99 in the same period. Finally, the public participation requirements tied to some grants increased the complexity, the calculations, and occasionally the chagrin of officials charged with grant allocation choices.

To what ends or aims were these federal initiatives directed? What were the chief problems addressed by this activism? At the risk of great oversimplification, two major policy themes are identified: (1) an urban-metropolitan emphasis and (2) attention to disadvantaged persons in the society through the anti-poverty programs and aid to education funds. The latter problem needs little documentation. Only one supporting item is mentioned for the former. Between 1961 and 1969 the percentage of all federal aid that went to urban areas increased from 55 percent to 70 percent, as total dollar amount so allocated went from $3.9 billion to $14.0 billion.[14]

Supporting the urban and disadvantaged emphases of this phase were selective but significant views held by important actors. President Johnson's speech first mentioning Creative Federalism also contained a phrase of larger and more popular political importance, that is, "The Great Society." As one observer has noted: "The Great Society was, by definition, one society; the phrase was singular, not plural."[15] How much this consensus politics push owed to the popularity of national goals efforts in the late 1950s and early 1960s is unknown. The unitary emphasis was evident, however. The president's preference on the need for centralized objective-setting made his 1965 moves toward planning-programming-budgeting a natural offshoot of views which held that our governmental system was a single system. Indeed, the basis for such revisionary thinking had been spelled out in a 1961 speech by Senator Joseph Clark entitled "Toward National Federalism."[16]

Accompanying these national and unitary sets of participants' perspectives was a subsidiary theme. It grew out of the expansion and proliferation of federal grants. This was the grantsmanship perspective that formed around the poverty and project grant programs. Playing the federal grant game became a well-known but time-consuming activity for mayors, managers, governors, universities, and, of course, for the program professionals.

This creative phase of IGR contains a paradox. Federal grants expanded massively in number, scope, and dollar magnitudes. The diversity that accentuated grantsmanship tendencies, however, moved from political and policy assumptions that were common—if not unitary—in their conception about the aims of society. The paradox is one of proliferation, participation, and pluralism amid convergence, consent, and concord. The prominence of the latter set suggests that "fused" is an appropriate metaphor by which this IGR phase can be characterized. An effort to show visually the coalesced character of IGR at the end of the creative period is provided in figure 2. The ties between national-state and state-local sectors are broad and weld the segments into a closely linked system. The visual contrast between figures 1 and 2 helps confirm the shift from a focused to a fused model of the IGR system.

The contrasting component present in this creative phase has not yet been noted. Figure 2 conveys the impression of intense interconnectedness and interdependence. What it does not convey is the diversity, proliferation, and fragmentation of the national-state fiscal links. There may be a superficial appearance of fusion, but the scores of specific and discrete categorical grants require additional adjectives to describe this period, such as the fused-foliated or proliferated phase.

Other, more crude metaphors that could be used are flowering federalism and spaghetti federalism. Both terms attempt to capture the elaborate, complex, and intricate features of IGR that developed in this phase.

Competitive (1965-?)

The proliferation of grants, the clash between professionals and participation-minded clients, the gap between program promises and proven performance, plus the intractability of domestic urban and international problems, formed a malaise in which IGR entered a new phase.

FIGURE 2

PUBLIC EXPENDITURES BY TYPE AND BY LEVEL OF GOVERNMENT AND THE INTERGOVERNMENTAL FLOW OF FUNDS, FY 1970

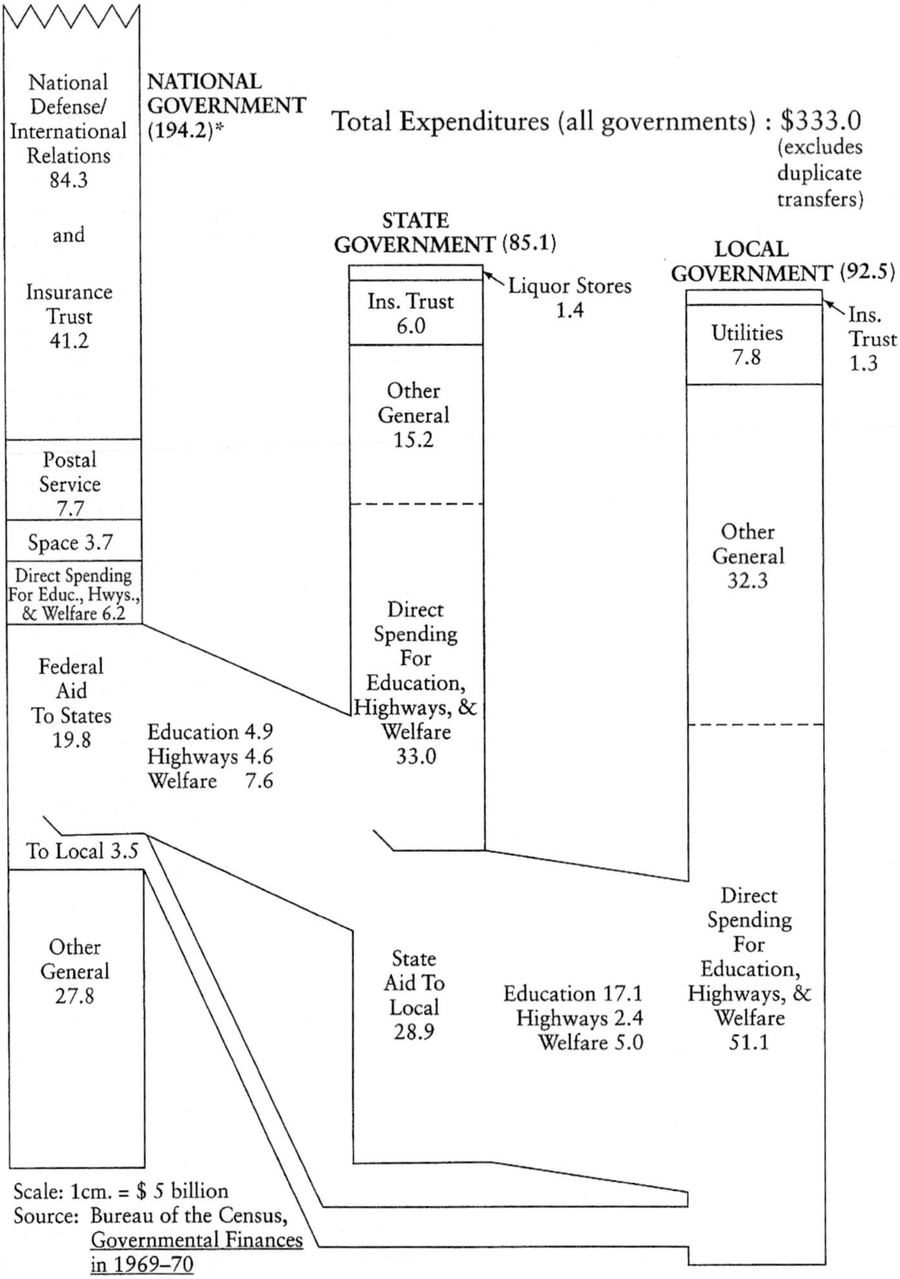

Scale: 1cm. = $ 5 billion
Source: Bureau of the Census, Governmental Finances in 1969–70

* Excludes interest on the national debt ($ 14.0 billion)

A different statement of central problems emerged when the administrative consequences of prior legislative whirlwinds became the center of attention. Issues associated with bureaucratic behavior and competence came to the forefront. One talisman earnestly sought was coordination. Others in close association were program accomplishment, effective service delivery systems and citizen access. Attention shifted to administrative performance and to organizational structures and relationships that either hindered or helped the effective delivery of public goods and services.

A sharply different tack was taken regarding appropriate IGR mechanisms. Pressure grew to alter and even reverse previous grant trends. Grant consolidation and revenue sharing were mentioned, popularized, and ultimately proposed by a Republican president on the basis of both program effectiveness and strengthening state and local governments. Some progress was made in the grant consolidation sphere, but as of 1973 the ACIR reported 69 formula grants and 312 project grants in existence. On the federal administrative scene, moves were made toward regionalization and reorganization. With the strong support of mayors, governors and county officials, general revenue sharing slipped through a divided Congress.

A flood of other developments in the late 1960s and early 1970s underscored the competition present in the system and also signaled efforts to reduce it. Perhaps the more visible actions and initiatives came at the national level, but in numerical terms and potential significance, important policy shifts occurred at the state and local levels. It is impossible to compress the numerous trends that were competition-inducing and to acknowledge some that eased competitive tendencies. Only three policy patterns will be mentioned as illustrations of tension-promoting developments: (1) economic opportunity programs and their chief implementation mechanisms—community action agencies; (2) "white flight" and the polarization of central city-suburban relationships, especially along racial lines; and (3) elimination or funding reductions in several grant programs by the Nixon administration in 1973 —some of which were achieved by the impounding of funds.

Countervailing tendencies in the direction of reduced tensions and increased cooperation appeared during this competition-dominated phase. At the local level, prompted and supported by national action, councils of governments sprang into existence in large numbers. One major aim was to foster metropolitan and regional coordination, especially through the A-95 grant review process. At the state level, herculean tax efforts were made to: (1) expand state services, (2) greatly increase state aid to local governments, and (3) meet the enlarged state-level funding requirements to match the vastly expanded federal grant monies.[17] Tension-reducing aims can also be attributed to such national-level actions as new departures with interstate compacts, the Partnership for Health Act (P.L.89–749), the Intergovernmental Cooperation Act of 1968 (P.L.90–577) and the Intergovernmental Personnel Act of 1970 (P.L.91–648).

The developments noted above reflected contrasting sets of perspectives that old as well as new participants brought to IGR. A statement by Senator Edmund Muskie—Democrat, Maine—in 1966 will serve as one example: "The picture, then, is one of too much tension and conflict rather than coordination and cooperation all along the line of administration—from top Federal policymakers and administrators to the state and local professional administrators and elected officials."[18] Similar views about the unwarranted degree of disagreement, tension, and rivalry among and between officials prompt the use of "competitive" for this phase of IGR.

The competition, however, is different in degree, emphasis, and configuration from the interlevel conflict of the older, layer cake phase. It is more modulated, and it acknowledges the lessons learned from the intervening periods of cooperation, concentration and creativity. For example, the current competitive phase appears reasonably realistic about the interdependencies within the system and the inability to turn the clock back in IGR. The three statutory enactments cited above bear witness to reasoned and reality-oriented approaches to IGR.

The nature of the competition in the present IGR phase is indicated in part by Senator Muskie's remarks. He mentions professional program administrators and state-local elected officials. It is the tension between the policy generalist, whether elected or appointed, and the program-professional-specialists that currently produces great static and friction

| FIGURE 3 |

PICKET FENCE FEDERALISM: A SCHEMATIC REPRESENTATION

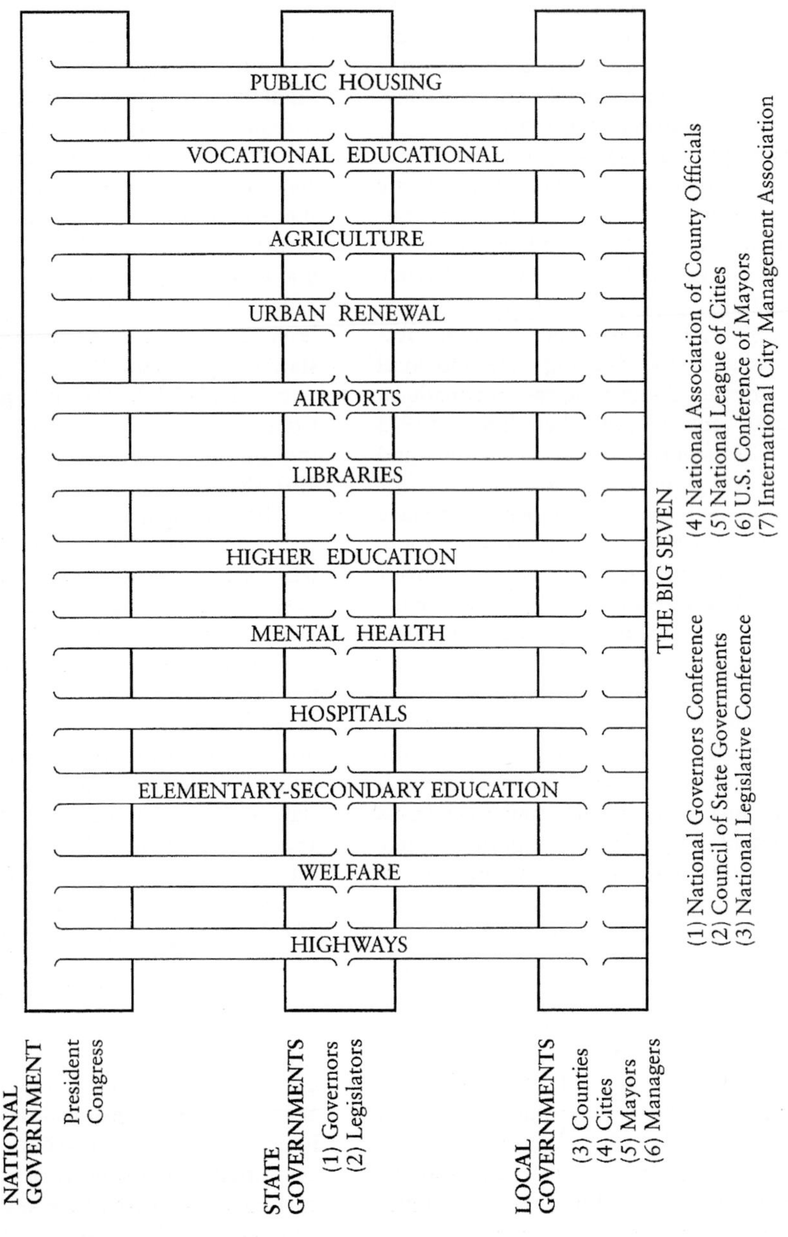

in IGR. This cleavage is another reason for describing this phase of IGR as competitive. A visual representation of the fractures and rivalry characterizing this phase is offered in figure 3. The metaphor of the picket fence, referred to in former Governor Sanford's book, *Storm Over the States,*[19] was the original stimulus for this formulation. The seven public interest groups, often called the Big Seven, have parted ways from the functional specialists. Their common interest in revenue sharing, grant consolidation and similar proposals represents a reassertion of the executive leadership doctrine and a challenge to the program professionals' doctrine of neutral competence.

A second type of competition can also be discerned from figure 3: the competition between the several functional program areas. Each vertical picket represents an alliance among like-minded program specialists or professionals, regardless of the level of government in which they serve. As early as the mid-1950s these interlevel linkages of loyalties were identified and criticized as "vertical functional autocracies."[20] Other epithets used against these patterns are: balkanized bureaucracies, feudal federalisms and autonomous autocracies. These terms emphasize not only the degree of autonomy that the program specialists have from policy control by political generalists, but also the separateness and independence that one program area has from another. This lack of horizontal linkage prompts interprogram, interprofessional and interagency competition. The cross-program competition combined with the generalist-specialist split helps confirm the contention that the competition depicted by the picket fence model best describes the current and most recent phase of IGR.

Both competitive patterns were captured in the words of local officials as quoted by James Sundquist. Speaking in the late 1960s, the director of a local model cities program contended that "Our city is a battleground among federal Cabinet agencies."[21] Similar sentiments came from mayors and city managers whose limited control and coordination powers over federal programs caused them to feel like spectators of the governmental process in their own cities. If, in fact, this competitive model is applicable to IGR today, then a recognition of these tensions and cleavages would seem to be the first-order task of those seeking changes and improvements in IGR.

Concluding Comment

IGR has become a distinctive dimension of activities in the American political system. It refers to a significant domain of political, policy and administrative actions by public officials. An acknowledged emphasis was made in this discussion on the meaning, features and trends in IGR (as a term or phrase). Concept explication and clarification have their uses; but they also have limits. There is much more to be said about the realities, practices and problems of IGR. Subsequent articles are appropriately addressed to these types of concerns.

One concluding comment on this exposition is offered in anticipation of the analyses that follow. This is an era when the *management* of IGR is a matter of major moment. James Sundquist observes that "The federal system is too important to be left to chance."[22] His book can be seen as an effort to critique and reconstruct the organizational philosophy undergirding effective intergovernmental action. Sundquist's treatment and the mood of this essay move toward a similar conclusion: intergovernmental achievements hinge on coping successfully with complexity. Complexity is an inherent and persistent characteristic of the several features of IGR. Accomplishments in the intergovernmental arena therefore depend on the successful management of complexity.

Notes

1. William Anderson, *Intergovernmental Relations in Review* (Minneapolis: University of Minnesota Press, 1960), p. 3.

2. Ibid., p. 3.
3. Ibid, p. 4.
4. E. S. Corwin, *The Passing of Dual Federalism,* Virginia Law Review 36 (February 1950), p. 19.
5. Commission on Intergovernmental Relations, A *Report to the President for Transmittal to the Congress* (Washington, D.C., June 1955), p. 33.
6. Ibid., p. 33.
7. Leonard D. White, *The States and The Nation* (Baton Rouge: Louisiana State University Press, 1953), pp. 9–10.
8. *Northern States Power Co.* v. *State of Minnesota,* 447 F. 2nd 1143 (1971); *see also, Science* 171 (8 January 1971), p. 45, and Harry Foreman, ed., *Nuclear Power and the Public* (Minneapolis: University of Minnesota Press, 1970).
9. Morton Grodzins, *The American System: A New View of Government in the United States* (Chicago: Rand McNally, 1966); Daniel J. Elazar, *The American Partnership: Intergovernmental Cooperation in the Nineteenth Century United States* (Chicago: University of Chicago Press, 1962).
10. Arthur W. Bromage, "Federal-State-Local Relations," *American Political Science Review* 37, no. 1 (February 1943), p. 35.
11. Herbert Kaufman, "Emerging Conflicts in the Doctrines of Public Administration," *American Political Science Review* 50, no. 4 (December 1956), pp. 1057–1073.
12. Frederick Mosher, *Democracy and the Public Service* (New York: Oxford University Press, 1968), esp. ch. 4, "The Professional State."
13. Report of the President's Commission on National Goals, *Goals for Americans* (Englewood Cliffs, N.J.: Prentice-Hall, Spectrum Series and the American Assembly of Columbia University, 1960).
14. *Special Analyses, Budget of the United-States, Fiscal Year 1971* (Washington, D.C., 1970), pp. 228–229.
15. James L. Sundquist, *Making Federalism Work: A Study of Program Coordination at the Community Level* (Washington, D.C.: The Brookings Institution, 1969), p. 12.
16. George Washington University, *The Federal Government and the Cities: A Symposium* (Washington, D.C.: George Washington University, 1961), pp. 39–49.
17. For example, state funds to match federal aid increased from $5.1 billion in 1964 to an estimated $18.4 billion in 1972; *see,* Deil S. Wright and David E. Stephenson, "The States as Middlemen: Five Fiscal Dilemmas," *State Government* 47, no. 2 (Spring 1974), pp. 101–107.
18. U.S., Congress, Senate, *Congressional Record,* 89th Cong., 2nd sess., 1966, 112, p. 6834.
19. Terry Sanford, *Storm Over the States* (New York: McGraw-Hill, 1967), p, 80.
20. Advisory Committee on Local Government, *An Advisory Committee Report on Local Government* (submitted to the Commission on Intergovernmental Relations, Washington, D.C., June 1955), p. 7.
21. Sundquist, *Making Federalism Work,* p. 27.
22. Ibid., p. 31.

Organizational Decline and Cutback Management

Charles H. Levine

Government organizations are neither immortal nor unshrinkable.[1] Like growth, organizational decline and death, by erosion or plan, is a form of organizational change; but all the problems of managing organizational change are compounded by a scarcity of slack resources.[2] This feature of declining organizations—the diminution of the cushion of spare resources necessary for coping with uncertainty, risking innovation, and rewarding loyalty and cooperation—presents for government a problem that simultaneously challenges the underlying premises and feasibility of both contemporary management systems and the institutions of pluralist liberal democracy.[3]

Growth and decline are issues of a grand scale usually tackled by only the most brave or foolhardy of macro social theorists. The division of scholarly labor between social theorists and students of management is now so complete that the link between the great questions of political economy and the more earthly problems of managing public organizations is rarely forged. This bifurcation is more understandable when one acknowledges that managers and organization analysts have for decades (at least since the Roosevelt Administration and the wide acceptance of Keynesian economics) been able to subsume their concern for societal level instability under broad assumptions of abundance and continuous and unlimited economic growth.[4] Indeed, almost all of our public management strategies are predicated on assumptions of the continuing enlargement of public revenues and expenditures. These expansionist assumptions are particularly prevalent in public financial management systems that anticipate budgeting by incremental additions to a secure base.[5] Recent events and gloomy forecasts, however, have called into question the validity and generality of these assumptions, and have created a need to reopen inquiry into the effects of resource scarcity on public organizations and their management systems. These events and forecasts, ranging from taxpayer revolts like California's successful Proposition 13 campaign and financial crises like the near collapse into bankruptcy of New York City's government and the agonizing retrenchment of its bureaucracy, to the foreboding predictions of the "limits of growth" modelers, also re-link issues of political economy of the most monumental significance to practices of public management.[6]

We know very little about the decline of public organizations and the management of cutbacks. This may be because even though some federal agencies like the Works Progress Administration, Economic Recovery Administration, Department of Defense, National Aeronautics and Space Administration, the Office of Economic Opportunity, and many state and local agencies have expanded and then contracted,[7] or even died, the public sector as a whole has expanded enormously over the last four decades. In this period of expansion and optimism among proponents of an active government, isolated incidents of zero growth and decline have been considered anomalous; and the difficulties faced by the management of declining agencies coping with retrenchment have been regarded as outside the mainstream of public management concerns. It is a sign of our times—labeled by Kenneth Boulding as the "Era of Slowdown"—that we are now reappraising cases of public organization decline and death as exemplars and forerunners in order to provide strategies for the design and management of *mainstream* public administration in a future dominated by resource scarcity.[8]

The decline and death of government organizations is a symptom, a problem, and a contingency. It is a symptom of resource scarcity at a societal, even global level that is creating the

---

Source: Reprinted with permission from Public Administration Review.

necessity for governments to terminate some programs, lower the activity level of others, and confront tradeoffs between new demands and old programs rather than to expand whenever a new public problem arises. It is a problem for managers who must maintain organizational capacity by devising new managerial arrangements within prevailing structures that were designed under assumptions of growth. It is a contingency for public employees and clients; employees who must sustain their morale and productivity in the face of increasing control from above and shrinking opportunities for creativity and promotion while clients must find alternative sources for the services governments may no longer be able to provide.

Organizational Decline and Administrative Theory

Growth is a common denominator that links contemporary management theory to its historical antecedents and management practices with public policy choices. William Scott has observed that ". . . organization growth creates organizational abundance, or surplus, which is used by management to buy off internal consensus from the potentially conflicting interest group segments that compete for resources in organizations."[9] As a common denominator, growth has provided a criterion to gauge the acceptability of government policies and has defined many of the problems to be solved by management action and organizational research. So great is our enthusiasm for growth that even when an organizational decline seems inevitable and irreversible, it is nearly impossible to get elected officials, public managers, citizens, or management theorists to confront cutback and decremental planning situations as anything more than temporary slowdowns. Nevertheless, the reality of zero growth and absolute decline, at least in some sectors, regions, communities, and organizations, means that management and public policy theory must be expanded to incorporate non-growth as an initial condition that applies in some cases. If Scott's assertions about the pervasiveness of a growth ideology in management are correct, our management and policy paradigms will have to be replaced or augmented by new frameworks to help to identify critical questions and strategies for action. Put squarely, without growth, how do we manage public organizations?

We have no ready or comprehensive answers to this question, only hunches and shards of evidence to serve as points of departure. Under conditions and assumptions of decline, the ponderables, puzzles, and paradoxes of organizational management take on new complexities. For example, organizations cannot be cut back by merely reversing the sequence of activity and resource allocation by which their parts were originally assembled. Organizations are organic social wholes with emergent qualities which allow their parts to recombine into intricately interwoven semi-lattices when they are brought together. In his study of NASA's growth and drawdown, Paul Schulman has observed that viable public programs must attain "capture points" of public goal and resource commitments, and these organizational thresholds or "critical masses" are characterized by their indivisibility.[10] Therefore, to attempt to disaggregate and cutback on one element of such an intricate and delicate political and organization arrangement may jeopardize the functioning and equilibrium of an entire organization.

Moreover, retrenchment compounds the choice of management strategies with paradoxes. When slack resources abound, money for the development of management planning, control, information systems, and the conduct of policy analysis is plentiful even though these systems are relatively irrelevant to decision making.[11] Under conditions of abundance, habit, intuition, snap judgments and other forms of informal analysis will suffice for most decisions because the costs of making mistakes can be easily absorbed without threatening the organization's survival.[12] However, in times of austerity, when these control and analytic tools are needed to help to minimize the risk of making mistakes, the money for their development and implementation is unavailable.

Similarly, without slack resources to produce "win-win" consensus-building solutions and to provide side payments to overcome resistance to change, organizations will have difficulty innovating and maintaining flexibility. Yet, these are precisely the activities needed to maintain capacity while contracting, especially when the overriding imperative is to minimize the perturbations of adjusting to new organizational equilibriums at successively lower levels of funding and activity.[13]

Lack of growth also creates a number of serious personnel problems. For example, the need to reward managers for directing organizational contraction and termination is a problem because without growth there are few promotions and rewards available to motivate and retain successful and loyal managers—particularly when compared to job opportunities for talented managers outside the declining organization.[14] Also, without expansion, public organizations that are constrained by merit and career tenure systems are unable to attract and accommodate new young talent. Without an inflow of younger employees, the average age of employees is forced up, and the organization's skill pool becomes frozen at the very time younger, more flexible, more mobile, less expensive and (some would argue) more creative employees are needed.[15]

Decline forces us to set some of our logic for rationally structuring organizations on end and upside down. For instance, under conditions of growth and abundance, one problem for managers and organizational designers is how to set up *exclusionary* mechanisms to prevent *"free riders"* (employees and clients who share in the consumption of the organization's collective benefits without sharing the burden that produced the benefit) from taking advantage of the enriched common pool of resources. In contrast, under conditions of decline and austerity, the problem for managers and organizational designers is how to set up *inclusionary* mechanisms to prevent organizational participants from avoiding the sharing of the *"public bads"* (increased burdens) that result from the depletion of the common pool of resources.[16] In other words, to maintain order and capacity when undergoing decline, organizations need mechanisms like long-term contracts with clauses that make pensions non-portable if broken at the employee's discretion. These mechanisms need to be carefully designed to penalize and constrain *"free exiters"* and cheap exits at the convenience of the employees while still allowing managers to cut and induce into retirement marginally performing and unneeded employees.

As a final example, inflation erodes steady states so that staying even actually requires extracting more resources from the organization's environment and effectuating greater internal economies. The irony of managing decline in the public sector is particularly compelling under conditions of recession or so called "stagflation." During these periods of economic hardship and uncertainty, pressure is put on the federal government to follow Keynesian dictates and spend more through deficit financing; at the same time, critical public opinion and legal mandates require some individual agencies (and many state and local governments) to balance their budgets, and in some instances to spend less.

These characteristics of declining public organizations are like pieces of a subtle jigsaw puzzle whose parameters can only be guessed at and whose abstruseness deepens with each new attempt to fit its edges together. To overcome our tendency to regard decline in public organizations as anomalous, we need to develop a catalogue of what we already know about declining public organizations. A typology of *causes* of public organizational decline and corresponding sets of *tactics* and *decision rules* available for managing cutbacks will serve as a beginning.

The Causes of Public Organization Decline

Cutting back any kind of organization is difficult, but a good deal of the problem of cutting back public organizations is compounded by their special status as authoritative, nonmarket extensions of the state.[17] Public organizations are used to deliver services that usually have no direct or easily measurable monetary value or when market arrangements fail to provide the necessary level of revenues to support the desired level

FIGURE 1

The Causes of Public Organization Decline

	Internal	*External*
Political	Political Vulnerability	Problem Depletion
Economic/ Technical	Organizational Atrophy	Environmental Entropy

or distribution of services. Since budgets depend on appropriations and not sales, the diminution or termination of public organizations and programs, or conversely their maintenance and survival, are political matters usually calling for the application of the most sophisticated attack or survival tactics in the arsenal of the skilled bureaucratic politician.[18] These strategies are not universally propitious; they are conditioned by the causes for decline and the hoped-for results.

The causes of public organization decline can be categorized into a four-cell typology as shown in Figure 1. The causes are divided along two dimensions: (a) whether they are primarily the result of conditions located either internal or external to the organization, or (b) whether they are principally a product of political or economic/technical conditions.[19] This is admittedly a crude scheme for lumping instances of decline, but it does cover most cases and allows for some abstraction.

Of the four types, *problem depletion* is the most familiar. It covers government involvement in short-term crises like natural disasters such as floods and earthquakes, medium-length governmental interventions like war mobilization and countercyclical employment programs, and longer-term public programs like polio research and treatment and space exploration—all of which involve development cycles. These cycles are characterized by a political definition of a problem followed by the extensive commitment of resources to attain critical masses and then contractions after the problem has been solved, alleviated, or has evolved into a less troublesome stage or politically popular issue.[20]

Problem depletion is largely a product of forces beyond the control of the affected organization. Three special forms of problem depletion involve demographic shifts, problem redefinition, and policy termination. The impact of demographic shifts has been vividly demonstrated in the closing of schools in neighborhoods where the school age population has shrunk. While the cause for most school closings is usually neighborhood aging—a factor outside the control of the school system—the decision to close a school is largely political. The effect of problem redefinition on public organizations is most easily illustrated by movements to *de*institutionalize the mentally ill. In these cases, the core bureaucracies responsible for treating these populations in institutions has shrunk as the rising per patient cost of hospitalization has combined with pharmaceutical advances in antidepressants and tranquilizers to cause public attitudes and professional doctrine to shift.[21]

Policy termination has both theoretical import and policy significance. Theoretically, it is the final phase of a public policy intervention cycle and can be defined as ". . . the deliberate conclusion or cessation of specific government functions, programs, policies, or organizations."[22] Its policy relevance is underscored by recent experiments and proposals for sunset legislation which would require some programs to undergo extensive evaluations after a period of usually five years and be reauthorized or be terminated rather than be continued indefinitely.[23]

Environmental entropy occurs when the capacity of the environment to support the public organization at prevailing levels of activity erodes.[24] This type of decline covers the now familiar phenomena of financially troubled cities and regions with declining economic bases. Included in this category are: market and technological shifts like the decline in demand for domestic textiles and steel and its effect on the economies and quality of life in places like New England textile towns and steel cities like Gary, Indiana, Bethlehem, Pennsylvania, and Youngstown, Ohio;[25] transportation changes that have turned major railroad hubs and riverports of earlier decades into stagnating and declining economies; mineral depletion which has crippled mining communities; and intra-metropolitan shifts of economic activity from central cities to their suburbs.[26] In these cases, population declines often have paralleled general economic declines which erode tax bases and force cities to cut services. One of the trade side effects of environmental entropy is that it most severely affects those who cannot move.[27] Caught in the declining city and region are the immobile and dependent: the old, the poor, and the unemployable. For these communities, the forced choice of cutting services to an ever more dependent and needy population is the cruel outcome of decline.[28]

Environmental entropy also has a political dimension. As Proposition 13 makes clear, the capacity of a government is as much a function of the willingness of taxpayers to be taxed as it is of the economic base of the taxing region. Since the demand for services and the supply of funds to support them are usually relatively independent in the public sector, taxpayer resistance can produce diminished revenues which force service reductions even though the demand and *need* for services remains high.

The *political vulnerability* of public organizations is an internal property indicating a high level of fragility and precariousness which limits their capacity to resist budget decrements and demands to contract from their environment. Of the factors which contribute to vulnerability, some seem to be more responsible for decline and death than others. Small size, internal conflict, and changes in leadership, for example, seem less telling than the lack of a base of expertise or the absence of a positive self-image and history of excellence. However, an organization's age may be the most accurate predictor of bureaucratic vulnerability. Contrary to biological reasoning, aged organizations are more flexible than young organizations and therefore rarely die or even shrink very much. Herbert Kaufman argues that one of the advantages of organizations over solitary individuals is that they do provide longer institutional memories than a human lifetime, and this means that older organizations ought to have a broader range of adaptive skills, more capacity for learning, more friends and allies, and be more innovative because they have less to fear from making a wrong decision than a younger organization.[29]

Organizational atrophy is a common phenomenon in all organizations but government organizations are particularly vulnerable because they usually lack market generated revenues to signal a malfunction and to pinpoint responsibility. Internal atrophy and declining performance which can lead to resource cutbacks or to a weakening of organizational capacity come from a host of system and management failures almost too numerous to identify. A partial list would include: inconsistent and perverse incentives, differentiation without integration, role confusion, decentralized authority with vague responsibility, too many inappropriate rules, weak oversight, stifled dissent and upward communication, rationalization of performance failure by "blaming the victim," lack of self-evaluating and self-correcting capacity, high turnover, continuous politicking for promotions and not for program resources, continuous reorganization, suspicion of outsiders, and obsolescence caused by routine adherence to past methods and technologies in the face of changing problems. No organization is immune from these problems and no organization is likely to be afflicted by them all at once, but a heavy dose of some of these breakdowns in combination can contribute to an organization's decline and even death.

Identifying and differentiating among these four types of decline situations provides a start toward cataloging and estimating the appropriateness of strategies for managing decline and cutbacks. This activity is useful because when undergoing decline, organizations face three decision tasks: first, management must decide whether it will adopt a strategy to resist decline or smooth it (i.e., reduce the impact of fluctuations in the environment that cause interruptions in the flow of work and poor performance); second, given this choice of maneuvering strategies it will have to decide what tactics are most appropriate;[30] and third, if necessary, it will have to make decisions about how and where cuts will occur. Of course, the cause of a decline will greatly affect these choices.

Strategic Choices

Public organizations behave in response to a mix of motives—some aimed at serving national (or state or local purposes), some aimed at goals for the *organization as a whole*, and others directed toward the particularistic goals of organizational subunits.

Under conditions of growth, requests for more resources by subunits usually can be easily concerted with the goals of the organization as a whole and its larger social purposes. Under decline, however, subunits usually respond to requests to make cuts in terms of their particular long-term survival needs (usually defended in terms of the injury which cutbacks would inflict on a program with lofty purposes or on a dependent clientele) irrespective of impacts on the performance of government or the organization as a whole.

The presence of powerful survival instincts in organizational subunits helps to explain why the political leadership of public organizations can be trying to respond to legislative or executive directives to cut back while at the same time the career and program leadership of subunits will be taking action to resist cuts.[31] It also helps to explain why growth can have the appearance of a rational administrative process complete with a hierarchy of objectives and broad consensus, while decline takes on the *appearance* of what James G. March has called a "garbage can problem"—a rational, polycentric, fragmented, and dynamic.[32] Finally, it allows us to understand why the official rhetoric about cutbacks—whether it be to "cut the fat," "tighten our belts," "preserve future options," or "engage in a process of orderly and programmed termination"—is often at wide variance with the unofficial conduct of bureau chiefs who talk of "minimizing cutbacks to mitigate catastrophe," or "making token sacrifices until the heat's off."

Retrenchment politics dictate that organizations will respond to decrements with a mix of espoused and operative strategies that are not necessarily consistent.[33] When there is a wide divergence between the official pronouncements about the necessity for cuts and the actual occurrence of cuts, skepticism, cynicism, distrust, and noncompliance will dominate the retrenchment process and cutback management will be an adversarial process pitting top and middle management against one another. In most cases, however, conflict will not be rancorous, and strategies for dealing with decline will be a mixed bag of tactics intended either to *resist* or to *smooth* decline. The logic here is that no organization accedes to cuts with enthusiasm and will try to find a way to resist cuts; but resistance is risky. In addition to the possibility of being charged with non-feasance, no responsible manager wants to be faced with the prospect of being unable to control where cuts will take place or confront quantum cuts with unpredictable consequences. Instead, managers will choose a less risky course and attempt to protect organizational capacity and procedures by smoothing decline and its effects on the organization.

An inventory of some of these cutback management tactics is presented in Figure 2. They are arrayed according to the type of decline problem which they can be employed to solve. This collection of tactics by no means exhausts the possible organizational responses to decline situations, nor are all the tactics exclusively directed toward meeting a single contingency. They are categorized in order to show that many familiar coping tactics correspond, even if only roughly, to an underlying logic. In this way a great deal of information about organizational responses to decline can be aggregated without explicating each tactic in great detail.[34]

The tactics intended to remove or alleviate the external political and economic causes of decline are reasonably straightforward means to revitalize eroded economic bases, reduce environmental uncertainty, protect niches, retain flexibility, or lessen dependence. The tactics for handling the internal causes of decline, however, tend to be more subtle means for strengthening organizations and managerial control. For instance, the management of decline *in the face of resistance* can be smoothed by changes in leadership. When hard unpopular decisions have to be made, new managers can be brought in to make the cuts, take the flak, and move on to another organization. By rotating managers into and out of the declining organization, interpersonal loyalties built up over the years will not interfere with the cutback process. This is especially useful in implementing a higher level decision to terminate an organization where managers will make the necessary cuts knowing that their next assignments will not depend on their support in the organization to be terminated.

FIGURE 2

Some Cutback Management Tactics

	TACTICS TO RESIST DECLINE	TACTICS TO SMOOTH DECLINE
External Political	(Problem Depletion) 1. Diversity programs, clients and constituents 2. Improve legislative liaison 3. Educate the public about the agency's mission 4. Mobilize dependent clients 5. Become "captured" by a powerful interest group or legislator 6. Threaten to cut vital or popular programs 7. Cut a visible and widespread service a little to demonstrate client dependence	1. Make peace with competing agencies 2. Cut low prestige programs 3. Cut programs to politically weak clients 4. Sell and lend expertise to other agencies 5. Share problems with other agencies
Economic/Technical	(Environmental Entropy) 1. Find a wider and richer revenue base (e.g., metropolitan reorganization) 2. Develop incentives to prevent disinvestment 3. Seek foundation support 4. Lure new public and private sector investment 5. Adopt user charges for services where possible	1. Improve targeting on problems 2. Plan with preservative objectives 3. Cut losses by distinguishing between capital investments and sunk costs 4. Yield concessions to taxpayers and employers to retain them
Internal Political	(Political Vulnerability) 1. Issue symbolic responses like forming study commissions and task forces 2. "Circle the wagons," i.e., develop a siege mentality to retain esprit de corps 3. Strengthen expertise	1. Change leadership at each stage in the decline process 2. Reorganize at each stage 3. Cut programs run by weak subunits 4. Shift programs to another agency 5. Get temporary exemptions from personnel and budgetary regulations which limit discretion
Economic/Technical	(Organizational Atrophy) 1. Increase hierarchical control 2. Improve productivity 3. Experiment with less costly service delivery systems 4. Automate 5. Stockpile and ration resources	1. Renegotiate long-term contracts to regain flexibility 2. Install rational choice techniques like zero-base budgeting and evaluation research 3. Mortgage the future by deferring maintenance and downscaling personnel quality 4. Ask employees to make voluntary sacrifices like taking early retirements and deferring raises 5. Improve forecasting capacity to anticipate further cuts 6. Reassign surplus facilities to other users 7. Sell surplus property, lease back when needed 8. Exploit the exploitable

The "exploit the exploitable" tactic also calls for further explanation. Anyone familiar with the personnel practices of universities during the 1970's will recognize this tactic. It has been brought about by the glutted market for academic positions which has made many unlucky recent Ph.D.'s vulnerable and exploitable. This buyers' market has coincided neatly with the need of universities facing steady states and declining enrollments to avoid long-term tenure commitments to expensive faculties. The result is a marked increase in part-time and non-tenure track positions which are renewed on a semester-to-semester basis. So while retrenchment is smoothed and organization flexibility increased, it is attained at considerable cost to the careers and job security of the exploited teachers.

Cutback management is a two-crucible problem: besides selecting tactics for either resisting or smoothing decline, if necessary, management must also select who will be let go and what programs will be curtailed or terminated. Deciding where to make cuts is a test of managerial intelligence and courage because each choice involves tradeoffs and opportunity costs that cannot be erased through the generation of new resources accrued through growth.

As with most issues of public management involving the distribution of costs, the choice of decision rules to allocate cuts usually involves the tradeoff between equity and efficiency.[35] In this case, "equity" is meant to mean the distribution of cuts across the organization with an equal probability of hurting all units and employees irrespective of impacts on the long-term capacity of the organization. "Efficiency" is meant to mean the sorting, sifting, and assignment of cuts to those people and units in the organization so that for a given budget decrement, cuts are allocated to minimize the long-term loss in total benefits to the organization as a whole, irrespective of their distribution.

Making cuts on the basis of equity is easier for managers because it is socially acceptable, easier to justify, and involves few decision-making costs. "Sharing the pain" is politically expedient because it appeals to common sense ideals of justice. Further, simple equity decision making avoids costs from sorting, selecting, and negotiating cuts.[36] In contrast, efficiency cuts involve costly triage analysis because the distribution of pain and inconvenience requires that the value of people and subunits to the organization have to be weighed in terms of their expected *future* contributions. In the public sector, of course, things are never quite this clear cut because a host of constraints like career status, veteran's preference, bumping rights, entitlements, and mandated programs limit managers from selecting optimal rules for making cuts. Nevertheless, the values of equity and efficiency are central to allocative decision making and provide useful criteria for judging the appropriateness of cutback rules. By applying these criteria to five of the most commonly used or proposed cutback methods—seniority, hiring freezes, even-percentage cuts-across-the-board, productivity criteria, and zero-base budgeting—we are able to make assessments of their efficacy as managerial tools.

Seniority is the most prevalent and most maligned of the five decision rules. Seniority guarantees have little to do with either equity or efficiency, *per se*. Instead, they are directed at another value of public administration; that is, the need to provide secure career-long employment to neutrally competent civil servants.[37] Because seniority is likely to be spread about the organization unevenly, using seniority criteria for making cuts forces managers to implicitly surrender control over the impact of cuts on services and the capacity of subunits. Furthermore, since seniority usually dictates a "last-in-first-out" retention system, personnel cuts using this decision rule tend to inflict the greatest harm to minorities and women who are recent entrants in most public agencies.

A *hiring freeze* is a convenient short-run strategy to buy time and preserve options. In the short run it hurts no one already employed by the organization because hiring freezes rely on "natural attrition" through resignations, retirements, and death to diminish the size of an organization's work force. In the long run, however, hiring freezes are hardly the most equitable or efficient way to scale down organizational size. First, even though natural and self-selection relieves the stress on managers, it also takes control over the decision of whom and where to cut away from management and thereby reduces the possibility of intelligent long-range cutback planning. Second, hiring freezes are more likely to harm minorities and women who are more likely to be the next hired rather than the next retired. Third, attrition will likely occur at different rates among an organization's professional and technical specialties. Since resignations will most likely come from those employees with the most opportunities for employment elsewhere, during a long hiring freeze an organization may find itself short on some critically needed skills yet unable to hire people with these skills even though they may be available.

Even-percentage-cuts-across-the-board are expedient because they transfer decision-making costs lower in the organization, but they tend to be insensitive to the needs, production functions, and contributions of different units. The same percentage cut may call for hardly more than some mild belt lightening in some large unspecialized units but when translated into the elimination of one or two positions in a highly specialized, tightly integrated small unit, it may immobilize that unit.

Criticizing *productivity criteria* is more difficult but nevertheless appropriate, especially when the concept is applied to the practice of cutting low-producing units and people based on their *marginal product* per increment of revenue. This method is insensitive to differences in clients served, unit capacity, effort, and need. A more appropriate criterion is one that cuts programs, organization units, and employees so that the *marginal utility* for a decrement of resources is equal across units, individuals, and programs thereby providing for *equal sacrifices* based on the *need* for resources. However, this criterion assumes organizations are fully rational actors, an assumption easily dismissed. More likely, cuts will be distributed by a mix of analysis and political bargaining.

Aggregating incompatible needs and preferences is a political problem and this is why *zero-base budgeting* gets such high marks as a method for making decisions about resource allocation under conditions of decline. First, ZBB is future directed; instead of relying on an "inviolate-base-plus-increment" calculus, it allows for the analysis of both existing and proposed new activities. Second, ZBB allows for tradeoffs between programs or units below their present funding levels. Third, ZBB allows a ranking of decision packages by political bargaining and negotiation so that attention is concentrated on those packages or activities most likely to be affected by cuts.[38] As a result, ZBB allows both analysis and politics to enter into cutback decision making and therefore can incorporate an expression of the *intensity of need* for resources by participating managers and clients while also accommodating estimates of how cuts will affect the *activity levels* of their units. Nevertheless, ZBB is not without problems. Its analytic component is likely to be expensive—especially so under conditions of austerity—and to be subject to all the limitations and pitfalls of cost-benefit analysis, while its political component is likely to be costly in political terms as units fight with each other and with central management over rankings, tradeoffs, and the assignment of decrements.[39]

These five decision rules illustrate how strategic choices about cutback management can be made with or without expediency, analysis, courage, consideration of the organization's long-term health, or the effect of cuts on the lives of employees and clients. Unfortunately, for some employees and clients, and the public interest, the choice will usually be made by managers to "go along" quietly with across-the-board cuts and exit as soon as possible. The alternative for those who would prefer more responsible and tough-minded decision making *to facilitate long-run organizational survival* is to develop in managers and employees strong feelings of organizational loyalty and loyalty to clients, to provide disincentives to easy exit, and to encourage participation so that dissenting views on the location of cuts could emerge from the ranks of middle management, lower level employees, and clients.[40]

Ponderables

The world of the future is uncertain, but scarcity and tradeoffs seem inevitable. Boulding has argued, "in a stationary society roughly half the society will be experiencing decline while the other half will be experiencing growth."[41] If we are entering an era of general slowdown, this means that the balance in the distribution between ending and contracting sectors, regions, and organizations will be tipped toward decline. It means that we will need a governmental capacity for developing tradeoffs between growing and declining organizations and for intervening in regional and sectorial economies to avoid the potentially harmful effects of radical perturbations from unmanaged decline.

So far we have managed to get along without having to make conscious tradeoffs between sectors and regions. We have met declines on a "crisis-to-crisis" basis through emergency legislation and financial aid. This is a strategy that assumes declines are special cases of temporary disequilibrium, bounded in time and space, that are usually confirmed to a single organization, community, or region. A broad scale long-run *societal level* decline, however, is a problem of a different magnitude and to resolve it, patchwork solutions will not suffice.

There seem to be two possible directions in which to seek a way out of immobility. First is the authoritarian possibility; what Robert L. Heilbroner has called the rise of "iron governments" with civil liberties diminished and resources allocated throughout society from the central government without appeal.[42] This is a possibility abhorrent to the democratic tradition, but it comprises a possible future—if not for the United States in the near future, at least for some other less affluent nations. So far we have had little experience with cutting back on rights, entitlements, and privileges; but scarcity may dictate "decoupling" dependent and less powerful clients and overcoming resistance through violent autocratic implementation methods.

The other possible future direction involves new images and assumptions about the nature of man, the state and the ecosystem. It involves changes in values away from material consumption, a gradual withdrawal from our fascination with economic growth, and more efficient use of resources—especially raw materials. For this possibility to occur, we will have to have a confrontation with our propensity for wishful thinking that denies that some declines are permanent. Also required is a widespread acceptance of egalitarian norms and of anti-growth and no growth ideologies which are now only nascent, and the development of a political movement to promote their incorporation into policy making.[43] By backing away from our obsession with growth, we will also be able to diminish the "load" placed on central governments and allow for greater decentralization and the devolvement of functions.[44] In this way, we may be able to preserve democratic rights and processes while meeting a future of diminished resources.

However, the preferable future might not be the most probable future. This prospect should trouble us deeply.

NOTES

1. The intellectual foundations of this essay are too numerous to list. Three essays in particular sparked my thinking: Herbert Kaufman, *The Limits of Organizational Change* (University, Ala.: University of Alabama Press, 1971); *Are Government Organizations Immortal?* (Washington, D.C.: Brookings Institution, 1976); Herbert J. Gans, "Planning for Declining and Poor Cities," *Journal of the American Institute of Planners* (September 1975): 305–307. The concept of "cutback planning" is introduced in the Gans article. My initial interest in this subject stemmed from my work with a panel of the National Academy of Public Administration (NAPA) on a NASA-sponsored project that produced *Report of the Ad Hoc Panel on Attracting New Staff and Retaining Capability During a Period of Declining Manpower Ceilings.*
2. For an explication of the concept of "organizational slack," see Richard M. Cyert and James G. March, *A Behavioral Theory of the Firm* (Englewood Cliffs, N.J.: Prentice-Hall, 1963), pp. 36–38. They argue that because of market imperfections between payments and demands "there is ordinarily a disparity between the resources available to the organization and the payments required to maintain the coalition. This difference between total resources and total necessary payments is what we have called *organizational slack.* Slack consists in payments to members of the coalition in excess of what is required to maintain the organization. . . . Many forms of slack typically exist: stockholders are paid

dividends in excess of those required to keep stockholders (or banks) within the organization; prices are set lower than necessary to maintain adequate income from buyers; wages in excess of those required to maintain labor are paid; executives are provided with services and personal luxuries in excess of those required to keep them; subunits are permitted to grow without real concern for the relation between additional payments and additional revenue; public services are provided in excess of those required. . . . Slack operates to stabilize the system in two ways: (1) by absorbing excess resources, it retards upward adjustment of aspirations during relatively good times; (2) by providing a pool of emergency resources, it permits aspirations to be maintained (and achieved) during relatively bad times."

3. See William G. Scott, "The Management of Decline," *The Conference Board RECORD* (June 1976): 56–59; idem, "Organization Theory: A Reassessment," *Academy of Management Journal* (June 1974): 242–253; also Rufus E. Miles, Jr., *Awakening from the American Dream: The Social and Political Limits to Growth* (New York: Universal Books, 1976).
4. See Daniel M. Fox, *The Discovery of Abundance: Simon N. Patten and the Transformation of Social Theory* (Ithaca, N.Y.: Cornell University Press, 1967).
5. See Andrew Glassberg's contribution to this symposium, "Organizational Responses to Municipal Budget Decreases," and Edward H. Potthoff Jr., "Pre-planning for Budget Reductions," *Public Management* (March 1975): 13–14.
6. See Donella H. Meadows, Dennis L. Meadows, Jorgen Randers, and William W. Behrens III, *The Limits to Growth* (New York: Universe Books, 1972); Robert L. Heilbroner, *An Inquiry into the Human Prospect* (New York: W. W. Norton, 1975); idem, *Business Civilization in Decline* (New York: W. W. Norton, 1976).
7. See Advisory Commission on Intergovernmental Relations, *City Financial Emergencies: The Intergovernmental Dimension* (Washington, D.C.: U.S. Government Printing Office, 1973).
8. Kenneth E. Boulding, "The Management of Decline," *Change* (June 1975): 8–9, 64. For extensive analyses of cutback management in the same field that Boulding addresses, university administration, see Frank M. Bowen and Lyman A. Glenny, *State Budgeting for Higher Education: State Fiscal Stringency and Public Higher Education* (Berkeley, Calif.: Center for Research and Development in Higher Education, 1976); Adam Yarmolinsky, "Institutional Paralysis," *Special Report on American Higher Education: Toward an Uncertain Future* 2 vols., *Daedalus* 104 (winter 1975): 61–67; Frederick E. Balderston, *Varieties of Financial Crisis* (Berkeley, Calif.: Ford Foundation, 1972); The Carnegie Foundation for the Advancement of Teaching, *More than Survival* (San Francisco: Jossey-Bass, 1975); Earl F. Cheit, *The New Depression in Higher Education* (New York: McGraw-Hill, 1975); idem, *The New Depression in Higher Education—Two Years Later* (Berkeley, Calif.: The Carnegie Commission on Higher Education, 1973); "The Illusions of Steady States," *Change* 6 (December/January 1974–1975): 24–28; John D. Millett, "What Is Economic Health?" *Change* 8 (September 1976): 27.
9. Scott, "Organizational Theory: A Reassessment," p. 245.
10. Paul R. Schulman, "Nonincremental Policy Making: Notes Toward an Alternative Paradigm," *Am. Pol. Sci. Rev.* (December 1975): 1354–1370.
11. See Naomi Caiden and Aaron Wildavsky, *Planning Budgeting in Poor Countries* (New York: John Wiley and Sons, 1974).
12. See James W. Vaupel, "Muddling through Analytically," in *Improving Urban Management*, ed. Willis D. Hawley and David Rogers (Newbury Park, Calif.: Sage Publications, 1976), pp. 124–146.
13. See Richard M. Cyert's contribution to this symposium, "The Management of Universities of Constant or Decreasing Size."
14. See NAPA, op. cit.; Glassberg, op. cit.
15. See NAPA, op. cit.; U.S. Senate Special Committee on Aging, *Cancelled Careers: Impact of Reduction-in-Force Policies on Middle-Aged*

Federal Employees, a report to the committee (Washington, D.C.: U.S. Government Printing Office, 1972).

16. See Albert O. Hirschman, *Exit, Voice, and Loyalty: Responses to Decline in Firms, Organizations, and States* (Cambridge, Mass.: Harvard University Press, 1970); Mancur Olson, *The Logic of Collective Action* (Cambridge, Mass.: Harvard University Press, 1965).
17. The distinctive features of public organizations are discussed at greater length in Hal G. Rainey, Robert W. Backoff, and Charles H. Levine, "Comparing Public and Private Organization," *Pub. Adm. Rev.* (March/April 1976): 223–244.
18. See Robert Behn's contribution to this symposium, "Closing a Government Facility"; Barry Mitnick, "Deregulation as a Process of Organizational Reduction"; and Herbert A. Simon, Donald W. Smithburg, and Victor A. Thompson, *Public Administration* (New York: Knopf, 1950) for discussions of the survival tactics of threatened bureaucrats.
19. This scheme is similar to those presented in Daniel Katz and Robert L. Kahn, *The Social Psychology of Organizations* (New York: John Wiley and Sons, 1966), p. 166; Gary L. Wamsley and Mayer N. Zald, *The Political Economy of Public Organizations: A Critique and Approach to the Study of Public Administration* (Lexington, Mass.: D. C. Heath, 1973), p. 20.
20. See Schulman, op. cit.; Charles O. Jones, "Speculative Augmentation in Federal Air Pollution Policy-Making," *Journal of Politics* (May 1974): 438–464.
21. See Robert Behn, "Closing the Massachusetts Public Training Schools," *Policy Sciences* (June 1976): 151–172; Valerie J. Bradley, "Policy Termination in Mental Health: The Hidden Agenda," *Policy Sciences* (June 1976): 215–224; David J. Rothman, "Prisons, Asylums, and Other Decaying Institutions," *The Public Interest* (winter 1972): 3–17. A similar phenomenon is occurring in some of the fields of regulation policy where deregulation is being made more politically feasible by a combination of technical and economic changes. See Mitnick, op. cit.
22. Peter deLeon, "Public Policy Termination: An End and a Beginning," an essay prepared at the request of the Congressional Research Service as background for the Sunset Act of 1977.
23. There are many variations on the theme of Sunset. Gary Brewer's contribution to this symposium, "Termination: Hard Choices–Harder Questions," identifies a number of problems central to most sunset proposals.
24. For two treatments of this phenomenon in the literature of organization theory see Barry M. Staw and Eugene Szwajkowski, "The Scarcity-Munificence Component of Organizational Environments and the Commission of Illegal Acts," *Administrative Science Quarterly* (September 1975): 345–354; Barry Bozeman and E. Allen Slusher, "The Future of Public Organizations under Assumptions of Environmental Stress" (paper presented at the annual meeting of the American Society for Public Administration, Phoenix, Arizona, April 9–12, 1978).
25. See Thomas Muller, *Growing and Declining Urban Areas: A Fiscal Comparison* (Washington, D.C.: Urban Institute, 1975).
26. See Richard P. Nathan and Charles Adams, "Understanding Central City Hardship," *Political Science Quarterly* (spring 1976): 47–62; Terry Nichols Clark, Irene Sharp Rubin, Lynne C. Pettler, and Erwin Zimmerman, "How Many New Yorks? The New York Fiscal Crisis in Comparative Perspective" (Report No. 72 of Comparative Study of Community Decision-Making, University of Chicago, April, 1976); David T. Stanley, "The Most Troubled Cities" (discussion draft prepared for a meeting of the National Urban Policy Roundtable, Academy for Contemporary Problems, summer 1976).
27. See Richard Child Hill, "Fiscal Collapse and Political Struggle in Decaying Central Cities in the United States," in *Marxism and the Metropolis,* ed. William K. Tabb and Larry Sawers (New York: Oxford University Press, 1978); H. Paul Friesema, "Black Control of Central Cities: The Hollow Prize," *Journal of the American Institute of Planners* (March 1969): 75–79.

28. See David T. Stanley, "The Most Troubled Cities" and "The Survival of Troubled Cities" (paper prepared for delivery at the 1977 Annual Meeting of the American Political Science Association, The Washington Hilton Hotel, Washington, D.C., September 1–4, 1977); Martin Shefter, "New York City's Fiscal Crisis: The Politics of Inflation and Retrenchment," *The Public Interest* (summer 1977): 98–127.

29. See Kaufman, *Are Government Organizations Immortal?* and "The Natural History of Human Organizations," *Administration and Society* (August 1975): 131–148. I have been working on this question for some time in collaboration with Ross Clayton. Our partially completed manuscript is entitled, "Organizational Aging: Progression or Degeneration." See also Edith Tilton Penrose, "Biological Analogies in the Theory of the Firm," *American Economic Review* (December 1952): 804–819; Mason Haire, Biological Models and Empirical Histories of the Growth of Organizations," in *Modern Organization Theory,* ed. Haire (New York: John Wiley and Sons, 1959), pp. 272–306.

30. For a fuller explanation of "smoothing" or "leveling," see James D. Thompson, *Organizations in Action* (New York: McGraw-Hill, 1967), pp. 19–24.

31. For recent analyses of related phenomena see Joel D. Aberbach and Bert A. Rockman, "Clashing Beliefs within the Executive Branch: The Nixon Administration Bureaucracy," *Am. Pol. Sci. Rev.* (June 1976): 456–468; Hugh Heclo, *A Government of Strangers: Executive Politics in Washington* (Washington, D.C.: Brookings Institution, 1977).

32. See James G. March and Johan P. Olsen, *Ambiguity and Choice in Organizations* (Bergen, Norway: Universitetsforlaget, 1976); Michael D. Cohen, James G. March, and Johan P. Olsen, "A Garbage Can Model of Organizational Choice," *Administrative Science Quarterly* (March 1972): 1–25.

33. See Charles Perrow, *Organizational Analysis: A Sociological View* (Belmont, Calif.: Wadsworth Publishing Company, 1970) and Chris Argyris and Donald A. Schon, *Theory in Practice: Increasing Professional Effectiveness* (San Francisco: Jossey-Bass, 1974) for discussions of the distinction between espoused and operative (i.e., "theory-in-use") strategies.

34. For extensive treatments of the tactics of bureaucrats, some of which are listed here, see Frances E. Rourke, *Bureaucracy, Politics, and Public Policy,* 2d ed. (Boston: Little, Brown, 1976); Aaron Wildavsky, *The Politics of the Budgetary Process,* 2d ed. (Boston: Little, Brown, 1974); Eugene Lewis, *American Politics in a Bureaucratic Age* (Cambridge, Mass.: Winthrop Publishers, 1977); Simon, Smithburg and Thompson, op. cit.

35. See Arthur M. Oken, *Equity and Efficiency: The Big Tradeoff* (Washington, D.C.: Brookings Institution, 1975).

36. For a discussion of the costs of interactive decision making see Charles R. Adrian and Charles Press, "Decision Costs in Coalition Formation," *Am. Pol. Sci. Rev.* (June 1968): 556–563.

37. See Herbert Kaufman, "Emerging Conflicts in the Doctrine of Public Administration," *Am. Pol. Sci. Rev.* (December 1956): 1057–1073; Frederick C. Mosher, *Democracy and the Public Service* (New York: Oxford University Press, 1968). Seniority criteria also have roots in the widespread belief that organizations ought to recognize people who invest heavily in them by protecting long-time employees when layoffs become necessary.

38. See Peter A. Pyhrr, "The Zero-Base Approach to Government Budgeting," *Pub. Adm. Rev.* (January/February 1977): 1–8; Graeme M. Taylor, "Introduction to Zero-Base Budgeting," *The Bureaucrat* (spring 1977): 33–35.

39. See Brewer, "Termination: Hard Choices—Harder Questions"; Allen Schick, "Zero-Base Budgeting and Sunset: Redundancy or Symbiosis?" *The Bureaucrat* (spring 1977): 12–32; idem, "The Road from ZBB," *Pub. Adm. Rev.* (March/April 1978): 177–180; Aaron Wildavsky, "The Political Economy of Efficiency," *Pub. Adm. Rev.* (December 1966): 292–310.

40. See Hirschman, op. cit., especially chap. 7, "A Theory of Loyalty," pp. 76–105. Despite the attractiveness of "responsible and tough-minded decision making" the constraints on managerial discretion in contradiction decisions should not be underestimated. At the local level, for example, managers often have little influence on what federally funded programs will be cut back or terminated. They are often informed after funding cuts have been made in Washington and they are expected to make appropriate adjustments in their local work forces. These downward adjustments often are also outside of a manager's control because in many cities with merit systems, veteran's preference, and strong unions, elaborate rules dictate who will be dismissed and the timing of dismissals.
41. Boulding, op. cit., p. 8.
42. See Heilbroner, op. cit.; Michael Harrington, *The Twilight of Capitalism* (New York: Simon and Schuster, 1976).
43. For a discussion of anti-growth politics see Harvey Molotch, "The City as a Growth Machine," *American Journal of Sociology* (September 1976): 309–332.
44. Richard Rose has made a penetrating argument about the potential of governments to become "overloaded" in "Comment: What Can Ungovernability Mean?" *Futures* (April 1977): 92–94. For a more detailed presentation, see his "On the Priorities of Government: A Developmental Analysis of Public Policies," *European Journal of Political Research* (September 1976): 247–290. This theme is also developed by Rose in collaboration with B. Guy Peters in *Can Governments Go Bankrupt?* (New York: Basic Books, forthcoming 1978).

Ethics for Bureaucrats: An Essay on Law and Values

John A. Rohr

Regime Values

As an alternative to political philosophy and humanistic psychology, I would suggest "regime values" as the most appropriate method for integrating the study of ethics into a public administration curriculum. At the outset, let us clarify the word "regime." As indicated earlier, it is not used here in the journalistic sense of the "Nixon regime," the "Carter regime," and so forth. Rather it is proposed as the most appropriate English word to suggest what Aristotle meant by "polity."[1] More specifically, "regime values" refer to the values of that political entity that was brought into being by the ratification of the Constitution that created the present American republic.

The method of regime values rests on three considerations:

1. That ethical norms should be derived from the salient values of the regime
2. That these values are normative *for bureaucrats* because they have taken an oath to uphold the regime[2]
3. That these values can be discovered in the public law of the regime[3]

The remainder of this chapter will be devoted to explaining and justifying these statements. The explanation and justification can be presented most coherently by recalling that the term "regime values" describes a method that addresses the ethical dimensions of *professional education for bureaucrats*. Let us begin by analyzing the implications of the three words "professional," "bureaucrats," and "education."

Professional Education for Bureaucrats

Professional If "professional" education means anything at all, it implies a narrower and more focused academic enterprise than education in general. Schools of law, for example, are not trade schools, but neither are they liberal arts colleges. The same can be said of schools of medicine, divinity, architecture, engineering, and so forth. These institutions, in conferring professional expertise and credentials, necessarily exact a price. The price is the relative narrowness of the curriculum. The narrowness will be reflected throughout the curriculum—including the treatment of professional ethics if it is taken seriously as part of the professional preparation of the student. In narrowing the curriculum to suit the goals of a professional school, certain questions that may be *of themselves* far more important than anything in the curriculum are nevertheless quite properly ignored. For example, a course in medical ethics would probably devote very little time to discussing whether life is better than nonlife or sickness better than health.[4] From an *absolute* point of view these questions are undoubtedly more important than the medical ethics of eugenics or practicing "defensive medicine" to avoid malpractice suits. However, one could hardly blame medical students who would prefer to learn more about ethical problems relating directly to their profession than about questions that in an *absolute* sense may be more important to them as human beings. Nor could one blame professors of medical ethics who conducted their courses on the presupposition that all their students believed that health is better than sickness

Source: From ETHICS FOR BUREAUCRATS, 1st Edition by John Rohr, pp. 59–67.

and life better than nonlife. In a word, professional education necessarily involves a canon of selectivity appropriate to its peculiar goals even at the expense of ignoring questions that may be inherently more interesting and important.

For Bureaucrats Because students of public administration either already hold or aspire to positions of leadership within the bureaucracy of a particular regime, the values of that regime are the most likely starting point for their ethical reflections. This is especially true in countries like our own where bureaucrats are expected to take an oath to uphold the Constitution. An oath is an important moral event in the personal history of an individual. This is especially true in a pluralistic society like the United States where there are myriad philosophical and religious starting points from which people derive their ethical norms. Pluralism of this nature makes it almost impossible to hope for an operational understanding of the public interest derived from some common metaphysical premise. Despite our pluralism, however, I think it is safe to assume that most of us would agree that one should adhere steadfastly to the oaths one has taken.[5] Because the Constitution of the United States is the preeminent symbol of our political values, an oath to uphold the Constitution is a commitment to uphold the values of the regime created by that instrument. Thus the oath of office provides for bureaucrats the basis of a moral community that our pluralism would otherwise prevent. It is the moral foundation of ethics for bureaucrats.[6]

In arguing the normative character of the values of the regime, we are, of course, avoiding the more important question of the fundamental justice of the regime itself.[7] Before one asks oneself, "How can I reinforce the values of the regime?" one should first ask, "Is the regime fundamentally just?" That is, "Can I be a good human being and a good citizen at the same time?" Although this is the more important question, it cannot be the focus of the course in ethics unless this course is simply to collapse into political philosophy. To say the justice of the regime cannot be the focus of the ethics course, however, does not mean the question is simply ignored. An argument might be made that one should not enter a career in government unless one is first convinced that the regime is fundamentally just. Once he or she is so convinced, the public servant can then investigate the full implications of the values of the regime whose justice he or she acknowledges.

Unfortunately, however, the moral universe is never this tidy. The very nature of judging the justice of a regime is an ongoing process rooted in contingency. Such a judgment cannot be made once and for all unless, of course, one is willing to acquiesce in the moral abdication symbolized by "my country right or wrong." Any serious consideration by a bureaucrat of how he or she might further the regime's values will continually invite higher questions of the moral authenticity of these values, and, therefore, of the justice of the regime itself. Nevertheless, the justice of the regime cannot be the focus of the course if it is to retain its identity as a course in ethics for bureaucrats. It must, however, remain the backdrop against which the course in ethics examines the less majestic questions of regime values.

The price, then, that the professional study of ethics for bureaucrats exacts from the curriculum is that questions of political philosophy ("Is the regime just?"[8]) must yield to less fundamental questions such as "How can I promote the values of the regime?" The method of regime values eschews metaphysics and addresses the students in the existential situation in which it finds them—persons who have taken or are about to take an oath to uphold values of a particular regime. It admonishes them that taking such an oath presupposes an acceptance of the fundamental justice of the regime[9] but does not inquire into how the students arrived at the conclusions that the regime is just.[10]

Education Certain consequences flow from the fact that the method of regime values deals with education. As indicated earlier, the word "education" is used in this book in such a way as to include most forms of management training as well. It will be helpful, however, to distinguish between inter- and intra-agency training. The former is more closely related to what is attempted in schools of public administration. Academic courses in the schools prepare students for careers in a wide variety of agencies. Similarly, interagency training sessions bring together practitioners with remarkably diverse working experiences. Both of these activities can be contrasted with intraagency training where relatively narrow and specific issues can be examined. As far as the study of ethics is concerned, it is only intraagency training that can afford to be specific, concrete, and directly operational in its objectives. Interagency training and the formal teaching of the schools must necessarily emphasize broad and general principles at the expense of concrete directives pertinent to one or only a few agencies. They should stress values rather than behavior and should aim at inviting reflection rather than providing answers.

Because of the broad and general nature of education, we must shift the direction of the argument we have developed up to this point. Hitherto we defended a relatively narrow focus for a course in ethics for bureaucrats as a consequence of the career orientation of education in public administration. This was the reason for rejecting political philosophy and humanistic psychology as foundation for a course in ethics. Now we must confess to the practitioner of public administration that the method of regime values is not "practical" in any immediate or operational sense. It is offered as an educational device and as such is necessarily somewhat removed from the "real" world of government.

There are several good reasons why the study of ethics for bureaucrats must not become too practical. We have already discussed the obvious consideration that the student population either already is or soon will be employed in many different agencies. The *practical* problems they will face are so varied that it would be impossible to discuss them seriously in a way that would be pertinent to all the students. Hence, it seems wise to retreat from the concrete problems in the agencies to the higher ground of regime values that cut across the entire administrative process—for example, "equality" as a salient value of the American regime should be of normative interest to any American administrator.

Secondly, an emphasis on practical ethical problems runs the risk of educating tomorrow's leaders with today's answers. Military academies have often been accused of preparing young officers to fight the last war rather than the next one. The same mistake could be made in the area of ethics. For example, if a course in ethics today tried to "solve" the problems associated with affirmative action, its educational value would be quite questionable. The student who completes the course in ethics with a "position" on affirmative action really has little to show for his or her efforts. For one thing, the student may find that this "position" is utterly unworkable and must be drastically revised (or even abandoned) in the light of what he or she learns at the experiential level after graduation. The student may also find that within a few years of graduation affirmative action is no longer a serious issue. By the time he reaches the middle-management level and begins to have a substantial impact on policy, his "practical" position on affirmative action will be hopelessly passé and he will not have developed the skills in ethical reflection that will enable him to address the new problems of the day. Had the student spent his time in school reflecting on affirmative action as an indicator of the meaning of equality as a regime value, he would be far better prepared to meet the short-term problems of affirmative action and the long-term problems of whatever lies ahead.

To conclude this discussion of professional education for bureaucrats, let us consider a brief example of the kind of ethical behavior we might hope the method of regime values would encourage once the student had begun to advance in his career.

Chester A. Newland served as director of the Federal Executive Institute (FEI) in

Charlottesville, Virginia. The purpose of FEI is to provide intensive, high-level training for federal executives (GS-16 then GS-18). On occasion during Newland's tenure, prominent political figures would be invited to FEI to address the executives on matters of administration policy and management. As the details of such visits were being worked out, the prominent guests would sometimes request accommodations outside the institute. Occasionally, they would ask for reservations at a nearby private club that excluded blacks.

Part of the training program at FEI was intended to ensure that the executives were made sensitive to the needs and feelings of minority groups. If FEI were to arrange accommodations for some of the top officials in government at an all-white club, the institute would undercut part of its own mission.

The problem was delicate. The racial exclusionary policy of the club broke no laws. An appointed official's choice of where he might want to spend the night was, at least ostensibly, a private matter. FEI was acting merely as a conduit of the VIP's personal choice. Those VIPs unfamiliar with the details of the institute's program—particularly its emphasis on human dignity—might have some difficulty seeing just how the choice of a night's lodging could harm FEI's mission.

Newland's solution was simple but effective. Whenever a visiting VIP asked for accommodations at the segregated club, Newland instructed his staff to reply along the following lines: "Oh, I'm sure the assistant secretary [or whoever] is not aware of the club's racial policies. We wouldn't want to cause him any embarrassment by booking him there." This solved the problem. No one ever replied that he knew perfectly well the club was segregated and wanted to stay there anyway.

This simple narrative illustrates several points developed previously in this book. First, Newland's decision was clearly discretionary; he could have ignored the whole problem. Second, the situation confronting Newland involved a *regime* value, equality, rather than values related to purely personal preferences. Thirdly, the ethical dimensions of the problem were positive rather than negative—that is, in classical terms, the decision involved an opportunity to "do good" rather than the necessity of "avoiding evil." Finally, the decision involved a routine matter of no dramatic significance. The fate of the Republic did not turn on Newland's decision but it was the kind of situation that occurs thousands of times every year through government at all levels. The sheer volume of such decisions made in routine situations influences at least the dominant tone, if not the ultimate fate, of the Republic.

A course in ethics for bureaucrats might well aim at developing in the student above all an ability to recognize the sort of problem Newland recognized and, second, an ability to evaluate the discretionary options available for solving the problem in a prudent and effective manner.

Law and Values In describing the method of regime values above, we stated that the values of a regime could be discovered in its public law and that this was particularly true of the United States. In developing this point we shall comment briefly on American values and then show how the study of Supreme Court opinions offers interpretations of values that are useful for our purposes. Before pursuing this matter further, two caveats are in order.

First, it should be recalled that no question can have an answer that is more precise than its subject matter admits. For example, a question asking the product of four and eight requires far more precision than a question calling for an explanation of the difference between jazz and rock, and both these questions require more precision than a question about the meaning of beauty.

In questions of ethics, classical moral doctrine has always recognized that reasoned judgments by the practical intellect become less certain as they become more specific: "Quanto magis ad propria descenditur, tanto magis invenitur defectus" ("The more we descend to particulars, the more defects we discover").[11] In contemporary terms, it is much easier to make the moral case for racial equality than for "forced" busing.

One who ignores the difference in the degree of precision demanded by different questions invites Procrusteam solutions to his or her problems. In constructing an ethic for bureaucrats, it is imperative that differences in degree of precision be kept in mind. Our purpose is to enable the bureaucrat to respond to the values of the American people. It is simply in the nature of things that such a response cannot be rigidly programmed into behavioral categories. Bureaucrats must not become discouraged if reflection on the values of the people in whose name they administer public affairs fails to yield the precise directives of a conflict-of-interest statute.

Secondly, bureaucrats should be cautioned against letting their consideration of American values harden into a rigid political orthodoxy. Reflection on salient values must not be used to justify a witch hunt for those who do not share these values. The point developed in the three previous paragraphs should safeguard against a quest for values degenerating into a witch hunt. One need only recall the imprecise nature of the questions involving American values to vanquish the temptation to become an arbiter of political orthodoxy. It should be clear that a bureaucrat's reflection on American values will not and should not lead to a dogmatic assertion that "the following are the values of the American people and this is what they must mean for all bureaucrats." Our concern is not to persuade bureaucrats that they should act in a certain way in the light of certain values. On the contrary, it is to provide them with a *method* for discovering these values themselves and putting them into practice as they see fit.

The starting point of such a method is the simple assertion that the American people have some values. I include earlier generations as well as our contemporaries within the term "American people." By "values" I mean beliefs, passions, and principles that have been held for several generations by the overwhelming majority of the American people.[12] A good example of what I mean appears in the final paragraph of the concurring opinion of Justice Frankfurter in *Cooper v. Aaron*. The case involved the painful experience surrounding the racial intergration of Little Rock's Central High School in the mid-1950s. The Supreme Court upheld a federal court order that had been defied by Governor Faubus. In closing his concurring opinion, Frankfurter said:

> Lincoln's appeal to "the better angels of our nature" failed to avert a fratricidal war. But the compassionate wisdom of Lincoln's First and Second Inaugurals bequeathed to the Union, cemented with blood, a moral heritage sure to find specific ways and means to surmount difficulties that may appear to be insurmountable.[13]

The "moral heritage" to which Frankfurter refers is an example of what I mean by a value. It is vague and imprecise but by no means meaningless unless one chooses to identify the meaningful with the empirically verifiable. In citing the moral heritage bequeathed by Lincoln's inaugural addresses, Frankfurter offers the nation a standard to which it can rally in a period of unrest.

The method of regime values involves two tasks. The first is to identify American values and the second is to look for meaningful statements about them. The first of these tasks is much easier than the second, provided one is content to identify just *some* values rather than attempting to provide an exhaustive list. Indications of the values of the American people can be found in a wide variety of sources. Among these are the writings and speeches of outstanding political leaders, major Supreme Court opinions, scholarly interpretations of American history, literary works of all kinds, religious tracts and sermons, and even the rhetoric of standard Fourth of July oratory. For example, it would seem that one could safely assert that freedom, property, and equality are values of the American people.[14] To be sure, these three are not *the* values of the American people but are simply among our many values. To safeguard their widespread appeal, they must be presented without any gloss on their meaning. The equality affirmed in the Declaration of Independence may be quite different from the equality underlying the equal protection clause of the Fourteenth Amendment, but we shall get ahead of ourselves if we make such distinctions now. For the present it is sufficient to offer freedom, property, and equality as examples of American values. Most Americans would have little trouble in saying they "believe" in such values as long as they were not pressed to say just what these values mean.

Far more difficult than simply *naming* some values of Americans is the task of infusing them with meaning suitable for ethical reflection. A good starting point might be to dwell on the fact that values like freedom, property, and equality command almost universal allegiance among our people. Perhaps this might be the beginning of a moral consensus. One might object, however, that splendid generalities like freedom, property, and equality are universally accepted only because they mean nothing. I do not think such an objection is sound. There is a difference between a word or a symbol that is vague and one that is meaningless. For example, the three symbols of the French Revolution, *liberté, fraternité, égalité,* are vague and indeterminate. They have been invoked by French citizens of remarkably diverse political persuasions for nearly two centuries. For many years these symbols appeared on French coins, but during the years of Marshall Pétain's Vichy regime the customary symbols disappeared from the coins and were replaced with *travail, famille, patrie.* These symbols, like the ones they replaced, were vague but they were not meaningless. They said something about the character of the Vichy regime. To be sure, a French citizen could be quite devoted to work, family, and fatherland without being a Nazi sympathizer. Nevertheless, the change in symbols had some significance. It represented an attempt by the Nazis to signal the arrival of a new order in France with a consequent change in traditional French values.

When Americans invoke symbols such as freedom, property, and equality—both in serious and trivial discourse—there is some minimal content to which these symbols point, and this content embodies some of the values of our society. These values may not be the highest values to which a regime might aspire, but nevertheless they carry some normative weight for American bureaucrats precisely because they are values of the American people. These values are normative because they are regime values, and bureaucrats have taken an oath to uphold the Constitution that brought this regime into being and continues to state symbolically its spirit and meaning.

The search for meaningful statements about our values is a more difficult task than simply naming them. At this point the consensus that would support certain values in a general, abstract way begins to fall apart. For example, some of those who would agree that equality is a fundamental value of the American people might not agree that this value should govern the relationships between the sexes as well as among the races and economic classes. Or, for some, equality might mean no more than equality of opportunity, while others would insist it means equality of income as well. Property might mean "big business" to one person, a modest dwelling to another, and a right to gainful employment to a third. Freedom could mean freedom for a woman to have an abortion on demand or Exxon's freedom from government regulation.

Thus, as the general values of the regime become sufficiently specific to have a practical effect on bureaucratic decision making, bureaucrats will have to decide which of many interpretations they will take seriously in their efforts to respond to the values of the American people. This is a very difficult undertaking. Eminent scholars after years of research reach very different conclusions on the "meaning of America."[15] This would seem to suggest that there is no one interpretation of the American tradition so compelling as to win the assent of all thoughtful persons. Further, we must recall that we are dealing with bureaucrats and not academicians. Bureaucrats are busy men and women whose energy and attention are focused primarily on the practical tasks of daily governmental routine. It would be unrealistic to expect them to interrupt their careers to undertake a profound study of American institutions and values. Students preparing themselves for careers in government could do more along these lines, but even for them other professional considerations will almost surely preclude a solid mastery of the American tradition.[16]

NOTES

1. For those who distinguish state and society, "regime," as used in this essay, is closer to society than state. Although the distinction of state and society is a philosophical question of the first order, I do not think it makes any difference for the purposes of this book just where one stands on this great issue. Those who, like Aristotle, do not distinguish state and society may perhaps feel more comfortable with the words "regime" or "polity" than those who make this distinction. The latter may prefer the somewhat ambiguous term "society values." It is important to note, however, that I am not talking exclusively about the values of the "state"—the authoritative and coercive agent of a political society.
2. I have not investigated just how widespread is the American custom of requiring an oath to uphold the Constitution. In nations where no such oath is required, I presume that some sort of adherence to the primary political symbols of the regime is implied in accepting public office.
3. This point is simply a corollary of the principle that laws reflect the values of the regime. Obviously, laws are not the only repository of public values. As political scientists have recognized for centuries, the study of a regime's laws must be supplemented by empirical findings—see Aristotle's *Politics*, Book 2. In the case of bureaucrats, it seems safe to assume they have some empirical awareness of public values.
4. Yet the issue of the relative importance of life and death is in itself of profound practical importance to many people. It is not uncommon to hear persons with serious religious beliefs say of a deceased loved one that "he is happier now." One can acknowledge the importance of such questions without dropping all other questions until the most important ones are solved.
5. Even Hobbes goes this far. See *De Cive* 3, 3.
6. It is unfortunate that the oath of office is administered in such a perfunctory way in most agencies. While not everyone can be sworn into office by the chief justice of the United States on the steps of the Capitol, it does seem a bit more imagination could be shown in accommodating the profound, human need to surround moral commitments with appropriate symbol and ritual. The failure of government to provide an appropriate ceremonial milieu may help to explain why the oath is seldom regarded as a moral commitment. Although ceremony and ritual can neither confer nor substitute for moral vigor, they can at least remind us of what it is we are becoming by our pledged word. Despite the sterility of the atmosphere in which the oath is administered, it can become meaningful after the fact when one is reminded of the pledge one has given. This is true of any ceremony that surrounds a moral commitment. Marriage vows are often given in a shallow and sentimental way, but after many years of loving dedication they become in retrospect the symbol of something that is now abiding and profound.
7. I must beg the readers' indulgence for continually repeating the word "fundamental." It is very important, however, that we distinguish between a regime that is fundamentally just and one that is perfectly just. To attempt to defend a theory of the meaning of fundamental justice would require nothing less than a recapitulation of the history of political thought.

To give the term some content, let me simply assert that the following questions might help one decide whether he or she considers a particular regime fundamentally just: (1) What are the professed values of the regime? (2) Are the professed values consistent with one's personal values? (3) To what extent does the regime achieve its professed values? (4) To the extent that it falls short of its professed values, are there corrective mechanisms that offer some hope of reform? It should be noted that these questions will lead to no more than a subjective understanding of justice that falls far short of the questions that philosophers have raised over the centuries.

8. Obviously, there are other questions in political philosophy, but few, if any, are more salient than the character of regimes. The fact that authors as diverse in time and content as Aristotle and Rawls are concerned primarily with the justice of regimes is a sound indication of the perennial importance of this issue.

9. If I may be permitted a personal aside, I have found that by simply announcing that I shall presuppose that the students in my course have settled to their own satisfaction the question of the fundamental justice of the regime, many students are sufficiently provoked (and at times outraged) that they soon find themselves giving serious thought to what they were told was presupposed.

10. See Abraham Kaplan, *American Ethics and Public Policy* (New York: Oxford University Press, 1963), pp. 8–10, for an argument that in matters of public values a conclusion is more important than the principles on which it is based. See also Maritain's position on Christian and secularist support for the Universal Declaration of Human Rights, *Man and the State*, p. 77. For a more recent and somewhat different approach to the same issue, see Albert R. Jonsen and Lewis H. Butler, "Public Ethics and Policy Making," *The Hastings Center Report* 5 (August 1975); 19-31. The authors attempt to rescue the ethics of policy choices from "metaethical" issues that necessarily spill over into epistemology and semantics.

11. Thomas Aquinas, *Summa Theologiae*, I–II, 94, 4c.

12. The definition of "values" given in the text is admittedly a bit thin when one considers the staggering quantity of literature available on this topic. A discussion of value theory, clarification of values, and so forth, is beyond the scope of this book. For a brief but lucid discussion of values, see Irving Kristol, "Can Values Do the Job Morals Used to Do? Namely: Keep People Moral," *Dividend*, Spring 1976. *Dividend* is the magazine of the Graduate School of Business Administration of the University of Michigan. The article consists of excerpts and summaries from an address given by Kristol at the business school's "Values Week" program. Kristol maintains the reason we speak of "values" rather then "morals" today is because the modern understanding of morality is divorced from religion. The word "morals" is just "too objective" for most moderns. "Values" is more subjective and creative. Instead of having his morality handed to him authoritatively, modern man prefers to "invent his own, individual, unique, appropriate morality." Kristol does not think this can be done. For him the urgent, practical question is given in the lengthy title of the article.

13. 358 U. S. 1 (1958).

14. I do not believe that anyone would contest the presence of freedom and property among American values. Equality might be somewhat controversial. See Willmore Kendall and George W. Carey, *The Basic Symbols of the American Political Tradition* (Baton Rouge: LSU Press, 1970).

15. Take, for example, the differences among scholars like Turner, Beard, Parrington, and Boorstin. On February 22, 1976, the *Washington Post's* "Book World" section featured an article in which six leading American historians were asked the

following two questions: (1) What books have had the greatest impact on the course of American history? (2) What books in American history would be most valuable for the general reader? The historians were Henry Steel Commager, Eugene D. Genovese, Samuel Eliot Morrison, J. H. Plumb, Arthur Schlesinger, Jr., and C. Vann Woodward. The responses were breathtakingly diverse.

16. The importance of the study of American history for high-ranking government personnel was underscored in William V. Shannon's editorial on "The Sad Young Men"—the White House officials who appeared before the Senate Watergate Committee in the summer of 1973. Shannon noted that "none of them seems to have ever studied any American history." *New York Times*, July 25, 1973, p. 39.

Part Four

FROM REAGAN TO REINVENTION

THE 1980S AND 1990S

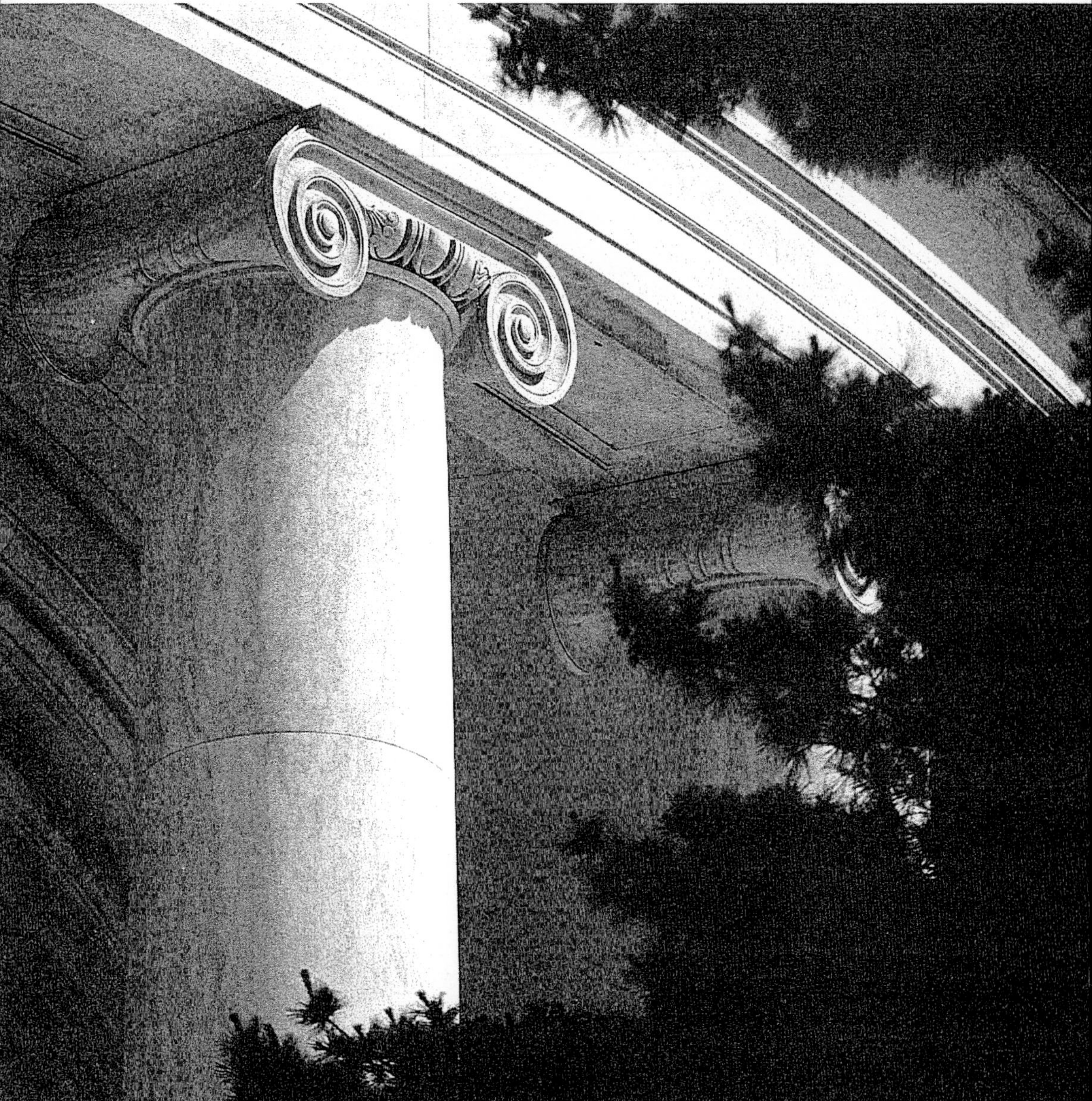

The 1980s ushered in another period of sweeping change, this time representing a major shift in political and economic values in the United States. Beginning with the election of President Ronald Reagan, a new path was charted at the federal level based on more conservative philosophies of less government and less regulation, new federalism, strength through defense, supply-side economics, and the realignment of public-sector and private-sector roles through "privatization." Some politically elected executives in previous decades had clamored for a more businesslike government, but this period of conservative activism would see much more decisive action. Fittingly, it was initiated by the Reagan administration's promise of a series of tax cuts and expenditure reductions that would lead to increased pressure to contract out increasingly more government functions and thus promote privatization of the public sector. These contractions in the domestic spending side within the public sector were also designed to place more responsibilities on state and local governments.

By the end of the twentieth century, a remarkable string of political and economic events would occur. Internationally, the Cold War ended with the collapse of the Soviet Union, replaced with now independent republics. The Berlin Wall fell and Germany reunited. The Eastern European states became independent republics pursuing free-market economic policies aimed ultimately at being included in the European Union. Apartheid was ended in South Africa after the release of Nelson Mandela and open elections in a transformation to a black majority government.

Politically, it seems also inconceivable that President George H. W. Bush, after an overwhelming Allied victory in the 1991 Gulf War ousting Iraq from Kuwait, could lose his 1992 reelection to a then little-known Southern governor, Democratic candidate Bill Clinton. Even more improbable, the Democrats in control of the legislature for most of the preceding several decades would lose both houses of the Congress to the Republicans in 1994.

RETHINKING THE ROLE AND SIZE OF GOVERNMENT

While the Reagan administration's political agenda was self-derived, it coincided with a period of new thought in public administration. In response to an economic philosophy generally called "public choice," public administration examined its own political values, assumptions, and limitations.[1] Essentially, public-choice theory challenged two fundamental and influential theories that had long dominated thinking about government and the economy. First, it rejected the concept of welfare economics that emerged out of the Great Depression of the 1930s. This approach held that when private markets fail, the government must step in to effectively carry out the public interest. Welfare economics also posited that the governmental level best suited to do this was the federal one. Second, public choice also rebutted pluralist political science, which advocated that competition among interest groups was the most effective process for ensuring that government adopt policy solutions that were best for the public good.[2]

Public choice means just what it says: more choice for the public. As a theoretical approach in both economics and politics, it is inherently reactive—almost reactionary. It is a reaction to large government and high taxation (to pay for it), which calls for less government and concomitant lower taxes. It harkens back to the ideal of self-reliance, the notion that citizens should take care of their own economic needs and not be dependent on the government for the necessities of life. This was President Herbert Hoover's philosophy of "rugged individualism," which called for economic freedom and opposed paternalistic government welfare programs—which he thought undermined character.

As an approach to public administration and politics, public-choice economics is based on microeconomic theory that views the citizen as a consumer of government goods and services. It attempts to maximize administrative responsiveness to citizen demands by creating a market system for government activities in which public agencies (and sometimes private corporations) compete to provide citizens with goods and services. This might replace a portion of the current system, under which most administrative agencies in effect act as monopolies under the influence of organized pressure groups, which, public choice economists argue, are institutionally incapable of representing the demands of individual citizens.

Public choice in its infinite variety of policy prescriptions (school vouchers, privately managed pensions, outsourcing of public services, etc.) is viewed as the avowed doctrine—the teaching and belief—of the Republican Party in the United States and of conservative parties throughout the world. It is also the foundation of the "third way"—the acceptance by the political left in the United States and Great Britain (the Democratic and Labour Parties, respectively) of many of the public-choice policy prescriptions initially espoused by the political right. So public choice, which was once right-wing doctrine, has become mainstream.

Public-choice theory seriously questioned whether decisions made in a traditional way really represented the wishes of the majority of citizens. But more emphatically, public choice denounced governments as being basically inefficient and completely lacking in incentives to perform well unless the expansion of their own programs and the increase of their budgets were involved.[3] The better solution, public-choice advocates urged, was to place as much governmental action (and expenditures) at the lowest possible levels—that is, local governments. The argument here was that local governments would provide more experimentation, true competition, and innovation. At the local level, citizens could "vote with their feet"—that is, if citizens had access to appropriate information, they would be able to readily compare the levels of taxation to the quality of services they received. They could then reject inefficient or unresponsive governments by voting down budgets, by voting out of office budgetary "big spenders," or even by moving elsewhere or choosing not to reside there.

Another tactic possible at the state and local levels was tax and expenditure limitations in which tax rates or expenditure levels were frozen at existing levels, rates of increase were curbed, or in some cases involving property taxes, assessment rates were actually rolled back to previous levels. Tax and expenditure limitations became prominent following California's successful passage in 1978 of the now famous Proposition 13.[4] Much of the impetus for taxpayers' revolts was caused by inflation, which drove up property values (and taxes) and put people in higher tax brackets in jurisdictions with progressive income-tax rate structures.[5] The Reagan administration's adoption of supply-side economics was premised on readjusting the role of government by cutting government expenditures and cutting taxes at the federal level to reduce the public sector's competition for scarce economic resources. This would free resources for private-sector investment and promote growth in the economy. The resulting growth, the supply-siders argued, would produce a trickle-down effect[6] that would benefit everyone (and even provide increasing resources for governments).[7] Accompanying this new economic picture of the role of governments was the reshaping of the boundary between the public and private sector.

Ironically, many public administration theorists had already noted by the 1980s that the role of government was changing. Frederick Mosher offered an initial assessment of these phenomena in 1980 in a *Public Administration Review* article in which he analyzed federal government expenditures and discussed how federal roles and responsibilities were changing.[8] But what was even more fundamental about the 1980s was the graying or blurring of distinctions between the public and private sector. This theme was addressed continuously during this period both by the federal government by design, with its movement toward contracting out and privatization, and by state and local governments by necessity, because they were increasingly hard pressed by fiscal crises and taxpayers' revolts.

Graham Allison's comparative work on public and private management captured perfectly the new themes for the era. Allison played off of an influential concept developed by Wallace S. Sayre who asserted that business administration and public administration were "fundamentally alike in all unimportant aspects." Allison[9] of Harvard University's Kennedy School of Government, turned Sayre's assertion into a question and tried to answer it. In his paper "Public and Private Management: Are They Fundamentally Alike in All Unimportant Aspects?" reprinted here, presented at a public management research conference he provided one of the most influential reviews of this proposition.

An often-voiced concern of the 1980s was to make government more businesslike or to use the most modern business techniques and theories to run government. Allison recognized that the gap between the private and public sector had narrowed and that the interactions between public managers and private managers had increased. In fact, many top politically appointed executives were basically top-level private-sector managers. In his paper, Allison compared the context and environments of public- and private-sector management. Then he assessed the perspectives of private-sector and public-sector top managers—how were they different, how did the orientation of one sector affect that person's management effectiveness and style?

Allison examined the implications of running government as a business as well as the interface between political executives and their administrative organizations. But even more fundamentally, he set the stage for understanding what public management is by examining the distinctive characteristics of public managers and the characteristics of their environments. Others, such as Laurence Lynn,[10] Hal Rainey,[11] Douglas Yates,[12] and Barry Bozeman and Jeffrey Straussman,[13] would tackle other dimensions of the difficult task of defining public management, a task that Harlan Cleveland once described as being as difficult as "nailing Jell-O to a tree."[14]

The implications are quite critical, as James Perry and Kenneth Kramer noted in the preface to an edited volume of articles on public management (one of the first readers on the subject). Perry and Kramer argued that from public administration's origins with Woodrow Wilson, a major goal was to help make the business of government "less unbusinesslike." Of course, public administration has to be able to see its differences from business administration. But at the same time it must understand how private-sector management ideas "have been imposed on public administration and how this process affects what is actually done in public organizations; . . . how appropriate are these ideas, and how well has the transfer worked?"[15]

Privatization of services usually is implemented in order to take advantage of one or more hoped for benefits: reduced costs, improved services, short-term access to expensive specialized services, avoidance of service start-up costs, greater flexibility in service policy (through reduced inflexibility of labor and equipment), increased responsiveness to consumer demand, and improved control. In addition, privatization sometimes is pursued on the ideological grounds that government should not provide goods and services that firms in the private for-profit or nonprofit sector are able and willing to provide. Government should limit itself to activities that firms in the private sector cannot or will not provide.

The debate over public and private-sector roles and comparable performance continues to be a major theme. Divested now of some of the political ideology and rhetoric it accumulated in the early part of the 1980s, "privatization" or "competitive sourcing" as it was called in the late 1990s will increasingly be viewed more simply as a policy choice or management decision. In this context, Ronald Moe's 1987 *Public Administration Review* article, "Exploring the Limits of Privatization," provided a thoughtful and legally based assessment of using private means to obtain public ends. Harkening first back to Allison's concerns about the blurring of the distinction between the public and private sectors, Moe reviewed the need for mutual coexistence and linkage between the two. Then he examined the limitations to privatization from a legal context as distinct from a managerial and economic perspective. The concept of sovereignty, he argued, must be considered in the privatization decision. Finally, he believed that public administration may be disregarding its "intellectual roots" in not presenting a legal perspective (based largely on the sovereignty argument) as opposed to a managerial or cost argument in determining the separation between public ends and public or private means.

Another excellent assessment about privatization was provided by John Donahue in his 1989 book entitled *The Privatization Decision*. Donahue declared that privatization brings good news and bad news. The good news is that while privatization is not a "universal corrective," it does present some real opportunities to make public undertakings more efficient and accountable by enlisting the private sector."[16] The bad news is that political pressures could just as easily "tend to retain for the public sector functions where privatization would make sense, and to privatize tasks that would be better left to government."

Still, the competitive sourcing story in the federal government is an old one. Efforts to have federal agencies use the commercial sector to purchase goods and services date back to 1955. The management issue has always created a division between the responsibility for creating a service or function (i.e., provision) and means for creating the service or function (i.e., production). However, the never simple but at least somewhat understandable process of comparing costs between public and private sector production of goods and services began following a more political path starting in the 1980s.

The Reagan administration promoted competitive sourcing through the OMB A-76 process as a means towards privatization—namely to outsource federal programs and services to business. With the Clinton administration, A-76 was also a vehicle, but to be primarily used in reaching downsizing goals for reducing the size of the federal workforce. But at the heart of these models is the dynamic relationship between the government jurisdiction and the business community and the need for growth and innovation. This is perhaps why the Department of Defense and NASA are so often cited as benchmarks for federal competitive sourcing—their use of private contracts is so extensive that they often are seen as basically contract management organizations.

It is also important to note that the federal processes were not the only model for introducing competition into government production process. State and local governments have an even longer history of using commercial goods/services for the public. Local governments also have a proven track record in using non-profit organizations extensively in producing a range of social, economic development, and health services. As non-profits have grown in importance, public administration has responded by developing non-profit administration curriculum and degree programs.

REASSESSING THE POLITICS OF BUDGETING

As the nation struggled politically to define public-, private-, and nonprofit-sector roles, a battle raged within the budgeting process for almost the entire two-decade period. (Indeed, it would continue even in the waning years of the Clinton administration, when the deficit turned to budget surpluses.) The first skirmish came with the acceptance of President Reagan's agenda when Congress passed a major tax cut to be implemented over a three-year period. President Reagan then began to push cutting domestic expenditures while increasing defense spending. At first the split Congress (Democratic House and Republican Senate) did little to resist, but gradually disputes intensified. The president threatened federal employee furloughs and announced a willingness to shut down the government by refusing to sign the various appropriation bills sent forward by the Congress. Reagan ridiculed the entire budget process, calling it "Mickey Mouse."[18] During the decade, the president and Congress would fight over spending cuts, increasing deficits, a deficit reduction act (the Gramm-Rudman-Hollings Act),[19] and repeated calls for either constitutional amendments to require balancing the federal budget or the adoption of a line-item veto that would allow the president to reject any proposed congressionally passed appropriation that exceeded the president's initial recommendations.

Of course, struggles between legislatures and executives over budgetary control are a constant theme in governance, but budget theorists recognized that something was different this time. Works by Naomi Caiden,[20] Lance LeLoup,[21] Irene Rubin,[22] and Alan Schick[23] set out to examine how budget theory and budget reform were being affected by the very different political and economic environment of the 1980s. Naomi Caiden's lead article in the first volume of a new journal, *Public Budgeting and Finance* (dedicated to the increased specialization and importance of public budgeting and its critical accounting-oriented counterpart, financial management), was one of the first significant efforts to interpret these developments. In "Public Budgeting amid Uncertainty and Instability," reprinted here, she noted that the budget environment was changing—its future was likely to (and would) be dominated by conditions of fiscal stress and political uncertainty.

The old debate between budget reformers (who stressed budget systems and rational decision making) and incrementalists (who stressed budget consensus through incremental decision making) was increasingly inappropriate. Useful in times when budget increases could be taken for granted and resource-raising capabilities were an assumed constant, neither would suffice in the new political milieu dominated by a lack of political consensus and growing federal budget deficits. For all of the Reagan administration's political economic conservatism, its principal budgeting legacy was huge federal budget deficits, reaching record heights in the 1980s—increasing from an average of 1.3 percent of the national income during the period 1950 to 1980 to 5 percent of the national income at the height of the U.S. recession in 1984 to 1985. The federal budget deficit would subside somewhat in the last half of the 1980s, but its vulnerability to recession and increasingly larger and larger percentages of spending on "uncontrollable entitlements" would return with a vengeance both in the1990s and in mid-decade after 2001.[25]

The mounting red ink of the federal debt and the federal deficit triggered a flurry of activities to control federal spending. Thus the second round of the budget battles began in 1990 with the Budget Enforcement Act agreed to by President George H. W. Bush and the Democratic Congress. This act blended some tax increases and spending cuts to produce $500 billion of deficit reduction. The problem, however, was that the economy was mired in recession so that the budget continued to bleed red ink. The Budget Enforcement Act also amended the infamous Gramm-Rudman-Hollings budget provisions of the late 1980s and created a number of procedural requirements such as "Paygo" (short for "pay as you go"), which meant that any new spending approved by the Congress and the president, such as disaster relief or extension of unemployment benefits, after the budget had been passed had to be compensated for by new sources of revenues or other spending reductions. In 1990, other important budget legislation was passed to include the Credit Reform Act, which tightened requirements on federal lending and loan guarantees (this largely in response to the massive federal bailout of the savings and loan industry failures in the unregulated 1980s), and the Chief Financial Officers Act, which added new financial management responsibilities for federal agencies including creating a CFO position to oversee agency financial practices.

However the deficit was the central story. By the time President Clinton, who had campaigned under a pledge for middle-class tax relief, presented his first budget, the deficit stood at over 5 percent of GDP. Clinton canceled his campaign-promised middle-class tax cut plans and crafted with the Democratic Congress another $500 billion deficit-reduction plan under the Omnibus Budget Reconciliation Act. This plan included major reductions in defense spending (the peace dividend) and tax increases for upper-income groups, and, of course, no tax cuts for the middle class. The Clinton budget plan passed the Congress by the closest margins in history: one vote in the House and the vice president's tie-breaking vote in the Senate. The deficit subsided after that, but largely because the economy came out of recession and high growth levels put the deficit back at more normal levels (back under 4 percent of national gross domestic product levels). But there was a political cost as the Republicans successfully used the 1992 tax increase deal to upset the Democratic majorities in the Congress and take control of both the House and Senate in the elections in 1994.

The next stage came with the Republican Congress and a Democratic president squabbling over a seven-year plan to reach a balanced budget by 2002. Republican plans called for major policy changes in entitlement and regulatory spending, a significant tax cut, and increases in defense spending. Democratic plans, at least those championed by President Clinton, demanded very minor cuts in entitlement spending with strong federal guarantees on policy aspects of Medicare and Medicaid, minor tax cuts, mostly for families, and level defense spending. While the differences in actual dollars between the $.9 and $1.2 trillion of deficit reduction over seven years were modest, the policy dimensions were not trivial.

Everything came to loggerheads with the attempted passage of the fiscal year 1996 budget. Fiscal year 1996 may well be remembered as the most difficult budget year in federal history. The federal government was shut down once for a week in late October 1995, and then over a third of the federal government was shut down a second time for almost a month beginning in December 1995. Both sides sought political leverage to show the American public that their view of the federal budget was the most appropriate one, while government agencies were held hostage, employees furloughed (both times with pay, but without any certainty that they would be paid), and costs in terms of late work and payments to contractors skyrocketed.

In the end, the Republicans lost the battle of public opinion and caved in. When the budget shutdown started to threaten assistance payments, processing of passports, and other highly visible federal services, the public blamed the Republicans. When President Clinton was reelected in 1996, it was clear that there were going to be some new limits on how budgeting war games would be played in the future. Congressional leaders and the President were going to have to compromise and they were going to have to learn how to keep the government open by using continuous spending resolutions. Ironically, the final years of the 1990s played out more tranquilly than anyone might have envisioned, given the budget history of these two decades. The budget prescriptions of the 1990 and 1993 budget agreements and the economic boom created massive federal budget surpluses and both parties clamored to take credit for having balanced the federal budget for the first time in a half century and for actually reducing the overall federal debt.

Ironically, in terms of public budgeting management reform, the most significant development may have been the one event that truly had true bipartisan approval; namely, the passage of the Government Performance Results Act (GPRA) in 1993. For several years, Senators William Roth (R-Del.) and John Glenn (D-Ohio) have pushed for reform in how agencies justify their spending requests. Most agencies focused on their work activities and workloads—higher outputs demanding high levels of funding. Roth and Glenn, with the active support of the public administration community, pushed through GPRA, which has been hailed as the first major budget systems reform since PPBS in the 1960s. GPRA, the federal version, or Performance Results Budgeting (PRB) as it is known in several states, demanded a new level of systems thinking about government programs; that is, what results or outcomes do they produce, and are these outcomes appropriate to the policy goals and strategic plans of government?[26]

GPRA came with a five-year implementation period, one of those rare instances when reformers recognized that it would take time for agency program managers and budgeting staff to transform their budget and reporting processes. In that ensuing period, federal agencies grappled with creating five-year strategic plans, performance assessments, and new "metrics"—the term of choice to describe new program outcome measurements. These transformation challenges were not trivial. For example, the U.S. Department of Interior with 70,000 employees has eight major bureaus or agencies with hundreds of programs that vary in terms of how they are connected and related to each other. Should Interior write one overarching strategic plan that aligns and connects all of these programs and their objectives (and the budget options behind them), or should it have each bureau and each major agency write its own distinct strategic plan?

The real impact of GPRA would be felt in the next decade as public managers and policy evaluators combined efforts to determine measurable outcomes for government programs and use that information to make choices.[27] One thing was apparent though: most budget theorists saw performance results management more as an evolution of the earlier 1960s-style PPBS budget reform (in the manner of Alan Schick's description) than a major reform breaking new ground. As the 1990s progressed with the first budget surplus in decades, performance results budgeting was not tested with the shifting resources across programs or agencies to meet hard fiscal choices.

CHANGE AND CONFLICT IN PERSONNEL—CHALLENGES IN LABOR RELATIONS AND EQUAL OPPORTUNITY

Turmoil in the budgeting arena was matched by conflict and confrontation in the personnel area. Personnel management was increasingly being renamed "human resources management" to reflect its new behavioral science orientation. New research appeared that emphasized equal opportunity, comparable worth, productivity (first) and (later) quality management, pay for performance and gain sharing, as well as developments in the basic elements of personnel management: classification, selection and examination, appraisal, compensation and benefits, and training and development. Playing a key role in delivering much of this new research was a new journal, *The Review of Public Personnel Administration*, which nicely complemented the International Personnel Management Association's long-standing *Public Personnel Management*. At the federal level, much of the new impetus for changes in personnel management or human resources management came from the Civil Service Reform Act of 1978 and the newly formed Office of Personnel Management (OPM).

Actual implementation of civil service reform had come in the waning months of the Carter administration.[28] Major changes included creation of the Senior Executive Service; delegation of many personnel regulatory responsibilities to the agencies themselves; and establishment of a new three-headed system for managing federal personnel: the U.S. Merit Systems Protection Board for adjudicating grievances and claims, the Federal Labor Relations Authority for working with unions and overseeing collective bargaining issues, and OPM itself for managing and working with agencies to affect modern human resources management.[29]

But the overall effects of privatization and the anti-public-service mood of the Reagan administration generated considerable conflict within the personnel community as a whole. Added to this was a major strike by air traffic controllers, who miscalculated their levels of support.[30] The Reagan administration broke both the strike and the air traffic controllers' union by firing and replacing the striking controllers and thus dealing a serious blow to public-sector union movements. Public-sector unionism had been strongly on the rise until that period.

After the ill-fated strike, many personnel theorists began to reexamine the relationship between collective bargaining principles and merit principles inherent in a civil service system. Public sector unions continued to grow, both in numbers and influence among public sector workforces, despite the decline of unions in the private sector. Perhaps the most persuasive and eloquent analysis of this conflicting and often tempestuous relationship is a chapter from the late Frederick C. Mosher's (1913–1990) *Democracy and the Public Service*. This book, originally published in 1968 and revised in 1982, is regarded as a classic in its own right. Mosher's history of the periods of development of the public service is standard recitation material for almost all graduate students in public administration. His overview of merit systems and equity issues is also important and frequently referenced. To choose any one selection over another is to slight something equally important. Nevertheless, we chose to reprint here his comparison of merit and collective systems (from his chapter on "The Collective Services"). It still provides the best foundation for understanding how this relationship must develop to advance the principles of democracy and public service in order to serve the public.

As part of his National Performance Review, President Clinton issued Executive Order 12871 (October 1, 1993); a new era in labor management relations was promised. The new Democratic administration considered the major federal employee unions allies and sought to include their advice for change from the outset. It should be said, though, that the first Bush administration had made some strides in improving the state of labor relations in the federal government since the nadir of the Reagan administration's firing of the air traffic controllers in the 1981 PATCO strike. Bush's Director of OPM Constance Newman had created several advisory committees on personnel issues and worked hard to include union representation and participation. Still, a key measure of the labor relations climate, namely the number of unfair labor practice charges and grievances, had almost doubled from 1986 to 1992.

Executive Order 12871 intended to create a new order as well as a new name for federal labor relations—namely partnership. Agencies were required to create labor-management committees or councils at appropriate levels and to see union representatives as full partners in organizational problem-solving and performance improvement. The scope of bargaining was extended to include performance appraisal issues, organizational restructuring, technology impacts, and work assignments. Last, a National Partnership Council (NPC) was established to oversee the development of partnerships and provide advice to the administration. And partnerships were created. At the midpoint of the Clinton administration, the NPC reported that the vast majority (over 70 percent) of federal bargaining units had labor management partnership councils and agreements. Furthermore, the numbers of unfair labor practice charges would be cut almost in half. While outcomes were harder to evaluate, the partnership effort certainly reversed the tide with the Clinton administration's effort to create "a partnership of equals" as opposed to a "struggle between adversaries."

Events in collective bargaining were not the only major personnel themes in the 1980s. Equal opportunity, which was highlighted by the Supreme Court's actions in the 1971 *Griggs* decision[31] and had been strongly supported throughout the 1970s, was also influenced by the new federal mood of conservatism. As more and more conservative judges were appointed during the eight years of the Reagan administration, the courts at the federal level slowly turned aside more and more equal opportunity challenges. The culmination was a series of Supreme Court rulings in the late 1980s, most specifically the *Wards Cove Packing* case of 1989, where a five-to-four divided Court basically set aside the longstanding burden-of-proof rule that had been established in the 1970s.[32] That rule held that if an organization's employment statistics showed that it was significantly out of line with regional percentages of minorities, the burden of proof was on the organization to show that its personnel practices were not discriminatory. By striking down this arrangement, the Court made it much more difficult for individuals to win discrimination cases. Congressional response was swift with the passage in 1990 of new civil rights legislation that basically incorporated some of the language of the *Griggs* case into law. However, President George H. W. Bush vetoed the bill, calling it a "jobs quota bill," and his veto was upheld. Two years later, President Bush signed a revised and bipartisan civil rights reform act that did effectively reverse these later Court decisions.[33] The 1980s, for the most part, sounded a harshly unsympathetic note for equal employment opportunity and portended more aggressive challenges yet to come.[34]

The other major personnel equity issue of the era was the attention given to women and organizational barriers to their advancement, termed the "glass ceiling."[35] Simply put, by the end of the 1980s, while women comprised 48 percent of all employees in the federal government, they held only 11 percent of the top management senior executive service positions. This caused a number of voices to argue that there was a "glass ceiling" preventing women from getting to the top.[36] Similar statistics for state and local governments showed that women were equally behind in obtaining equitable representation in the upper ranks.[37] In 1990, Canada released a study from a national commission on the status of women in government, "Beneath the Veneer,"[38] which found that there were a number of factors, some institutional and some caused by organizational, cultural, and attitudinal factors, that had created a barrier preventing women from getting to the top. In 1992, the U.S. federal government would follow suit with the issuance of a special Merit Systems Protection Board Study; "A Question of Equity" confirmed the impediments faced by women trying to move into the management ranks, including stereotypes and outmoded workplace expectations and organizational cultural factors that work to the detriment of women.[39]

In 1995, The Federal Glass Ceiling Commission (which was established as part of the 1991 Civil Rights Act) produced its report, "Good for Business," documenting the lack of representation in upper management ranks of women and minorities in the private sector at levels far above anything in the public sector.[40] More than a decade later, women are making some progress: while they now hold 45 percent of all federal jobs, they hold 25 percent of senior paying jobs in the federal government. Minorities now hold 19 percent of all senior pay-level jobs while making up 39 percent of GS federal jobs.[41]

But perhaps more important, within both the public and private sector a basic transformation was taking place. Equal opportunity was important, but affirmative action no longer seemed the best vehicle to get there. R. Roosevelt Thomas, a former Harvard Business School professor, is often credited for creating the term "managing diversity." That heralded a new approach, or perhaps it might be called the development of a new phase. Thomas's 1990 article in the *Harvard Business Review* (which is reprinted here) began with the prediction that "Sooner or later, affirmative action will die a natural death. Its achievements have been stupendous, but if we look at the premises that underlie it, we find assumptions and priorities that look increasingly shopworn." In his article, he instead advocated, "The goal is to manage diversity in such a way as to get from a diverse work force the same productivity we once got from a homogenous work force, and do it without artificial programs, standards—or barriers."

This article signaled more than a simple name change. It was extraordinarily influential in shaping new research and establishing a new literature on diversity that followed Thomas's lead in charting a path distinct from EEO and affirmative action. Thomas also drew a distinction between his methods and traditional approaches to EEO and affirmative action. He did so by defining "diversity" as focusing not just on race, ethnicity, gender, and so on but rather on all of the ways in which individuals may differ from one another, including age, background, education, and personality traits. Thomas's notion of diversity as including a wide variety of differences was widely adopted, in part because it helped avoid the image of "us versus them" that many believe had undermined the acceptance of traditional EEO and affirmative action programs.

REDISCOVERING PUBLIC ADMINISTRATION'S LEGAL FOUNDATION AND ETHICS

Another major theme sounded in the 1980s was the concern for law and accountability. In the 1970s, the experiences of Watergate started a basic reexamination of the role of public administration in government. John Rohr's 1978 work argued forcefully for a contemporary literature on ethics in the public service. David Rosenbloom (b. 1943), one of public administration's leading theorists, carried this concern a step further in his 1983 *Public Administration Review* article entitled "Public Administration Theory and the Separation of Powers," reprinted here. Rosenbloom challenged the dominance of the managerial model in modern conceptualizations of public administration. Traditionally, Rosenbloom argued, managerial theory was tied to the executive branch, political theory to the legislative branch, and legal theory to the judicial branch. But what happens when an administrative agency has responsibility for executive, legislative, and adjudicative decision powers? Rosenbloom's article compared managerial, political, and legal approaches to public administration and showed how each has separate values, origins, and structures. These three distinctly different approaches have become especially significant with the final development of the modern administrative state, whose chief characteristic seems to be the collapse of the classical separation of powers. Rosenbloom later developed the full integration of his three-part theory in an influential textbook appropriately entitled *Public Administration: Understanding Management, Politics, and Law in the Public Sector.*[42]

Attesting to the increasing significance of public administration's legal dimension were a number of other important works. Marshall E. Dimock wrote *Law and Dynamic Administration* in 1980 to evaluate the increasing influence of lawyers on governmental administrations.[43] Phillip J. Cooper provided one of the first major textbooks in 1988, *Public Law and Public Administration,* which analyzed in depth the regulatory aspects of administrative action and detailed the legal foundations and framework surrounding public administration.[44]

Yet the most extensive developments in public administration's legal dimension came in the area of ethics. Both the American Society for Public Administration and the International City Management Association developed or revised codes of ethics during the 1980s. Many civilian government agencies now have standards of conduct—formal guidelines—for ethical behavior. Their objective is to ensure that employees refrain from using their official positions for private gain. Typically, a variety of prohibited activities seek to ensure that employees conduct themselves in a manner that would not offer the slightest suggestion they will extract private advantage from public employment. All too frequently, standards of conduct are used to say the obvious. For example, the British Cabinet Office created a document meant to be helpful to new cabinet ministers. Paragraph 55 of "Questions of Procedure for Ministers" offers the unsurprising advice that ministers "have a duty to refrain from asking or instructing civil servants to do things they should not do."

Standards are often part of a state's formal legal code; thus violations can carry severe penalties. While standards of conduct are always related to a specific organization, codes of ethics are wide in scope and encompass a whole profession or occupational category. A code of ethics is a statement of professional standards of conduct to which the practitioners of a profession say they subscribe. Codes of ethics are usually not legally binding, so they may not be taken too seriously as constraints on behavior. They sometimes become significant factors in political campaigns when questionable behavior by one side or the other is attacked or defended as being within or without a professional code. Professional groups also hide behind codes as a way of protecting (or criticizing) a member subject to public attack. President Ronald Reagan took the attitude "that people should not require a code of ethics if they're going to be in government. They should determine, themselves, that their conduct is going to be beyond reproach." Nevertheless, the problem remains that some people need help in determining just what constitutes ethical behavior. So while codes are useful, standards have the kind of teeth that can put people in jail.

Major attention was now being given to ethics in the public administration literature. Indeed, it can fairly be said that there was an ethics explosion in terms of the volume of books and articles that appeared on the subject in the 1980s.[45] Dennis F. Thompson (b. 1940) in his *Public Administration Review* article, "The Possibility of Administrative Ethics," reprinted here, raised the radical and fundamental question of whether there is such a thing as administrative ethics at all. According to Thompson there are two commonly accepted administrative theories that undercut the possibility of ethics in government. The "ethic of neutrality" holds that administrators make their decisions on behalf of others and must remain morally neutral in doing so, if representative government is to work at all. But if administrators are indeed morally neutral when they make representative decisions, then it is not possible to hold them ethically accountable. Likewise, the "ethic of structure" claims that organizations and not individuals are responsible for the design, development, and implementation of public policies. Hence we cannot and should not cast moral judgments about government officials who merely find themselves somewhere in that structure. It would seem to follow that administrative accountability is a chimera if either of these two theories are completely valid. Administrators would not be liable for their actions. Administrative ethics that would seek to make moral judgments of those actions would be an impossibility. The only way to maintain the possibility of administrative ethics would be to demonstrate that these two theories are somehow mistaken. This is the task that Thompson set for himself.

By the early 1990s, public administration was well on its way in developing a true literature of ethics and public accountability. A keystone work was Carol W. Lewis's *The Ethics Challenge in Public Service*, published in 1991. Subtitled "A Problem-Solving Guide," this work helped codify the practical ethics movement in the sense that public administration (and public employees) had to actually understand how to do the right thing on the small, seemingly trivial situations. Codes of ethics and case study insights are all well and good, but Lewis noted a higher level of ethical reasoning is required to cope where "The public manager must act quickly in a gray marginal area where laws are silent or confusing, circumstances are ambiguous and complex, and the manager is responsible, well-meaning, and perplexed." A selection from Lewis's book, starting with the quote above, is reprinted here.

In the same vein, Lewis deconstructed larger headline-making situations like the Gerald Ford pardon of Richard Nixon, showing how ethical problems are inherent in most forms of specialized problem solving. The public employee—whether at the lowest level on the line doing the public's business or the highest, managing the agency and the myriad of interests and policy dilemmas that must be faced—is at the forefront whenever administrative discretion is involved. Describing the ethics challenge in the early days of the 1990s, Lewis also predicted that ethical problems would become more intricate and difficult in a future dominated by network relationships, matrix organizations, and intergovernmental and intersector collaborative relationships that she called the emerging "web like administrative environment." This prediction will be revisited in the closing section later in the discussion of the transformation of public administration from government to governance.

THE RISE OF PUBLIC POLICY ANALYSIS AND IGR

The most explosive growth in public administration as a field of academic study in the 1980s was in the area of public policy and analysis. Many schools of public affairs, following the example of the University of California at Berkeley, created or reoriented all or part of their programs toward a public-policy focus. A spate of works appeared during the decade on all aspects of public policy, including the politics of policy formulation; techniques of policy analysis; and policy implementation, planning, and evaluation. Attention was finally paid equally to the complementary issues of policy formulation (policy making) and policy content (policy analysis). Signs of the vitality of the policy field were the driving force behind excellent journals dedicated to policy matters, such as the *Journal of Policy Analysis and Management*, *Policy Studies Journal*, *Policy Studies Review*, and *Policy Sciences*.

In his 1984 book *Agendas, Alternatives, and Public Policies* (the first chapter from the second edition is reprinted here), John Kingdon makes many important contributions to the policy field. Kingdon explores how ideas find their way onto policy agendas and looks at how and why agendas change over time. Two categories that affect agenda setting and related policy alternatives include "the participants who are active, and the processes by which agenda items and alternatives come into prominence."

Kingdon uses an adjusted version of the "Cohen-March-Olsen[46] garbage can model of organizational choice to understand agenda setting and alternative generation." Cohen, March, and Olson's basic idea was that decision making in organizations could best be characterized as organized anarchies. Their view turned the classical premise of normative theory of organizations as "vehicles for solving well-defined problems or structures within which conflict is resolved through bargaining" on its head. Rather, they argued, organizations were more often a "collection of choices looking for problems and issues for which they might be the answer."

This would be portrayed by Kingdon in a public policy context where he conceives of "three process streams flowing through the system—streams of problems, policies, and politics." These separate streams, according to Kingdon, come together at critical junctures. When windows of opportunity are opened, problems and solutions are most likely to come together.

While it may seem odd to include intergovernmental relations (IGR) in this same introductory section as public policy, both fields were actively connected during the 1980s and 1990s. Public policy analysis fully recognized that any assessment of government programs and policy decisions would involve factoring in different roles and responsibilities for different levels of government. But as the levels of funding rose in terms of federal (and state support) grants for domestic programs (federal transfers as a percentage of state and local government had reached 25 percent by Reagan's first term), criticism mounted. Nixon had already advanced the term New Federalism to signal his intentions to shift the funding emphasis away from categorical grants to block grants where more flexibility and supposedly efficiencies would be possible. Reagan's New Federalism took this even further. First, federal funding levels were capped and a number of grant-in-aid programs even terminated. Subsequent steps led to consolidating many of the categorical grants into block grants and proposals to reorder federal and state roles.

In an even bolder move, the Reagan administration proposed a major realignment of federal and state responsibilities whereby the federal government would assume full responsibility for Medicare in return for states taking over the primary welfare functions such as AFDC and food stamps. While the motivation for this would be debated for years (Reagan asserted that he wanted federal aid focused more on individual entitlements, which the central government could administer best on a larger scale), suspicious states and local governments rejected the swap proposal. While the benefits of hindsight are always 20-20, in terms of current budget liabilities for state governments this probably represents the greatest missed opportunity of the century. As an example, California in 2009 paid 13 percent of its general fund revenues for Medicare (which is matched by federal funding) compared to less than 7 percent for all other general assistance programs combined.

But there was more to IGR than simply arguing over funding levels and fund granting mechanisms. The real debate was over the transformation of American Federalism and what would be the proper roles and alignment of the central government and the state and local government entities. In addition to the usual public policies involving distribution of public goods—supporting education, welfare, health care, and the like—there would be major government-led interventions in regulatory areas such as environmental protection, consumer protection, and public safety, to name only a few.

Martha Derthick has had a profound influence on this discussion of where federalism—now intergovernmental relations—was headed in this critical period at the end of the century. Her 1987 article in *Public Administration Review* aptly subtitled "Madison's Middle Ground in the 1980's" provides historical context for this debate, but it is more instrumental in pointing to the role of the judiciary in shaping the relationships between the federal and state governments. She argues that the courts have probably had more impact on the rise of centralization than the Congress.

NEW PERSPECTIVES ON ORGANIZATIONS

Budgeting issues and national policy reform initiatives may have dominated the headlines in the 1980s and 1990s, but within public administration, debates were occurring around other very fundamental issues. There continued to be significant debate about organizations. Organizational thinking has always been a main tenet of public administration—indeed, of business administration—but in this quarter of the century, new strands of thought were profoundly influencing public administration perspectives on organizational culture and organizational performance.

Part of the major reassessment of the role of government in the 1980s included the dilemmas posed by the power of the bureaucracy—specifically, the individual government workers at all levels of the public sector who, through specialization and involvement, had become synonymous with the various public policies they were responsible for implementing. Michael Lipsky wrote an insightful work at the start of the decade entitled *Street-Level Bureaucracy*, the first chapter of which is reprinted here. His central premise was that the public-sector employees who delivered goods and services were in many cases the policy-makers. Their range of discretion, their extensive level of contact with the public, and their control of the resource base of many public organizations made them the central force in public-sector decision making. Lipsky examined the implications for accountability, equity, and citizen access as well as the resulting controversy implicit in this reality. His arguments are even more important when one considers the impact of nonprofit organizations that have taken over major shares of human assistance and social services in the country and have even fewer political controls.

An organizational culture—the culture that exists within an organization—is a parallel but smaller version of a societal culture. It is made up of intangible things such as values, beliefs, assumptions, and perceptions. It is the pattern of these beliefs and attitudes that determines members' behaviors in and around the organization, persists over extended periods of time, and pervades all elements of the organization (albeit to different extents and with varying intensity). Organizational culture is transmitted to new members through socialization (or enculturation) processes; it is maintained and transmitted through a network of rituals and interaction patterns; it is enforced and reinforced by group norms and the organization's system of rewards and controls. It is the unseen and unobservable force that is always behind those organizational activities that can be observed.

Organizational culture is created by the attitudes and behaviors of the dominant or early organizational "shapers" and "heroes"; by the nature of the organization's work; and by the attitudes, values, and "willingness to act" of new members. It is transmitted by often-told stories and legends and by the formal and informal processes of socialization. An organization's culture provides a framework for shared understanding of events, defines behavioral expectations, and serves as a source of and focus for members' commitment and as an organizational "control system" (i.e., through group norms). But while a strong organizational culture can control organizational behavior, it can also block an organization from making those changes needed to adapt to a changing environment. Organizational culture is particularly useful as an intellectual construct because it helps us to understand or predict how an organization will behave under different circumstances. A cultural pattern is similar to a genetic inheritance: once you know the patterns of basic assumptions, you can anticipate how the organization will act in differing circumstances.

Every organizational culture is different. What has worked repeatedly for one organization may not work for another—so the basic assumptions differ. And each organizational culture is shaped by myriad factors—from the societal culture in which it resides to its technologies and competing organizations. Some organizations have strong, unified, pervasive cultures, whereas others have weaker cultures; often "subcultures" evolve in different functional or geographical areas. The most common example of this last phenomenon is the more formal culture of a headquarters office versus the informality of a field office.

More fundamental assessments of what was affecting organizations and the behavior of their members came in J. Steven Ott's 1989 book *The Organizational Culture Perspective* (first chapter reprinted here). The concept of culture within an organization is defined by Ott as the "unseen and unobservable force that is always behind organizational activities that can be seen and observed." Ott uses the organizational culture perspective as a "frame of reference for the way one looks at, attempts to understand, and works with organizations." The organizational culture perspective is based on the notion that there are basic patterns of assumptions that guide and influence behaviors and decisions within organizations. He explains that there are likely to be strong connections between the culture of an organization and its productivity. While this perspective is, admittedly, only one way of looking at organizations, it has become a permanent part of how we understand organizations. "People in organizations need culture for identity, purpose, feelings of belongingness, communication, stability, and cognitive efficiency."

The cultural analysis represents more than thoughts about how people behave and conform to rules and procedures. It is much more basic, because it brings into question how organizations view differences among people. One difference in question in the literature concerns gender, or more specifically, the recognition that men and women operate differently in organizations. Ideas of examining organizational theory from a gender perspective and applying them to management decision making, communication, and behavior interaction are now recognized as the feminist perspective.

Some may argue that much of this new perspective has been driven by the reality of demographics. Women have indeed made their presence felt in public organizations. By 1990, women constituted almost 60 percent of the total public-sector workforce, although, as noted, there were only minimal gains made in pay levels (comparable worth) and managerial representation (glass ceiling). Within public administration as a field of study, women now constitute the majority of the classroom, earning MPA degrees at twice the rate of men and doctorates at the same rate (although the rate is actually higher if international doctoral students are excepted from the degree-seeking population, since this group is almost exclusively male). Finally, perhaps the most significant economic indicator of the presence of women in the workforce came in the recession of 1990–1992, when, for the first time, American men and women lost jobs at about the same rate. The presence of women in the workforce is finally permanent.

But philosophically, the feminist perspective on organizations and public administration represents much more than a workforce participation issue. Feminist organizational analysts such as Joan Acker have argued that the long-standing male control of organizations has entailed almost exclusively male perspectives of organizational theory. In other words, the view of organizations dominated by males is through male lenses. Acker argues that at least four sets of gendered processes perpetuate this male reality of organizations:

1. Gender divisions that produce gender patterning of jobs.
2. Creation of masculine organizational symbols and images.
3. Interactions characterized by dominance and subordination.
4. "The internal mental work of individuals as they consciously construct their understandings of the organization's gendered structure of work and opportunity and the demands for gender-appropriate behaviors and attitudes."[47]

Even ordinary activities in organizations are not gender-neutral. They perpetuate the "gendered substructure within the organization itself and within the wider society"—as well as in organizational theory. But these differences are even more pronounced at managerial levels. As women increasingly climb the organizational ladders, they will leave their mark, and they will gradually change the culture. Substantial research has already shown that women tend to have different management styles than men. For example, Judy B. Rosener has shown women to be more cooperative and to share leadership; they are less apt to use the traditional authoritarian "command and control" militaristic style so favored by men.[48] The greatest beneficiaries of the last decades of affirmative-action hiring policies have been women. The seed has been planted. Organizational cultures, as they are increasingly impacted by feminine management styles, gradually change their approaches to something, if not feminine, at least less masculine. The alternative hypothesis is instead of making their organizations more hospitable to feminine management culture, the women managers—subject to the same stimuli for increased production as men have traditionally been—will become more like the men, will adapt more masculine attitudes because that is the way to thrive in the competitive environment of organizational life.

The feminist perspective on organizations and management will have profound impacts on public administration. Camilla Stivers, perhaps public administration's foremost feminist theorist, makes the following case: "As long as we go on viewing the enterprise of administration as genderless, women will continue to face their present Hobson's choice, which is either to adopt a masculine administrative identity or accept marginalization in the bureaucratic hierarchy."[49] So the leaders of today's organizations have three options:

1. Do nothing and wait for the problem to resolve itself over time.
2. Intervene to consciously create organizations more hospitable to feminine ways.
3. Hope that managerial women will be content to become more like men.

These options are not mutually exclusive. Time inexorably moves on. Considerable progress is constantly being made. In the end the best hope is that women will not necessarily become the organizational infighters that men traditionally have been, but that a mutual accommodation will evolve. Reprinted here is one of Stivers's first articles on the feminist perspective, which was published in 1990.

BUREAUCRATIC REFORM AND PUBLIC MANAGEMENT

Public management emerged in the 1980s and 1990s as a significant field in its own right in public administration. Management has always included two main subfields, budget and personnel, which have already been discussed. With increasing attention being given to privatization and outsourcing of government services (already discussed) procurement or contracting developed more fully as a third subfield. Behind all three of these subfields was the rapid pace of new technology and how it would influence the production, delivery, and management of government services. In the 1980s and 1990s, there was a critical concern about information management. Three rapid periods of growth—first with mainframe computers, then microcomputers, and finally networks and the Internet—in the public sector, as well as in every other sector, have been truly remarkable. Harlan Cleveland, one of public administration's luminaries, wrote some of the early articles on information management.[50] Other pioneers were Ken Kraemer, John King, and James Danziger at the University of California at Irvine, who surveyed and assessed how extensively governments were using computers and technology and what would be the implications on work and the workforce.[51] In November 1986, a special issue of *Public Administration Review* was devoted to the concerns of information management.

Of course, that early activity would be deemed pretty primitive by current standards. In today's Internet environment, public administration is grappling with a range of issues about e-government, e-governance, and even the issue of who has computers (and access) and who does not—what is called the *digital divide*. When historians look back at the twentieth century, they will note a true divide in administrative and management practices centered on the advent of the computer revolutions. Some levels of government will surely be seen as having been slow to realize the potential of technology and the ability to provide a greater range of services at lower costs. Concerns about personal privacy and security and serving all the public, not just those with the best access, will be the prominent excuses.

Perhaps the larger reason that public sector agencies have not developed an e-management model is the larger concern with governance. The bulk of the research about information technology has been about institutional change, policy, and potential impacts on democratic functions like voting or civic participation. Even seminal works like Jane Fountain's *Building the Virtual State* devoted only a chapter to discussing how IT will change bureaucracy and by inference management functions. Some might argue that this is exactly right.[52] First, agencies should figure out how governance is going to work in cyberspace in terms of impacting citizens, interest groups, and society; then, they should construct a new model for virtual management. But others argue that IT fundamentally alters business processes, organizational structures, workforce capabilities, and knowledge management and must be developed concurrently. This is perhaps the final irony. As the debate in the new century shifts to whether or not IT provides strategic advantage and whether it is just a basic utility like electricity, it subsumes the e-management model developed by business.

Certainly, there is more to public management than just the functional domains of personnel, budgets, and information systems. Robert Anthony's seminal work on planning systems[53] and Alan Walter Steiss's research on management control helped illustrate the many different dimensions of public management during this period.[54] Other useful works served as guides for denoting the progress made in public management. A baseline work can be found in *Managing the Public Organization* by Cole Graham and Steven Hays.[55] Graham and Hays dedicated their book to Luther Gulick and organized it loosely around POSDCORB, which they argue is a greatly misunderstood and underappreciated framework for understanding the management functions common to all public organizations. The other—a benchmark work for what public management aspires to be—is the work of Laurence Lynn of the University of Chicago, whose 1996 work *Public Management as Art, Science, and Profession* nicely integrates the theory and practice dimensions of public management.[56] But by the mid-1990s, generic public management was being supplanted by the performance management movement in the United States and the new public management movement overseas.

Of course, organizational performance was not neglected in the 1980s, either. One of the most significant concerns was organizational productivity, which generated new interest in measurement and motivation. A host of work on quality circles, work redesign, worker humanism, and participative management appeared. But these themes were captured in the last major management movement of the 1980s—*total quality management*, or TQM. As a management movement, TQM has been inspired by a circle of private-sector quality "gurus" such as W. Edwards Deming and Joseph M. Juran, who emphasized the need for organizations to rethink their major management strategies, organizational structures, and, even more basic, their workforce values and culture.[57] Productivity improvement, cost reduction, and performance management were, to a large degree, all pushed aside in this new commitment to improve work quality. The federal government even established the Federal Quality Institute to educate federal agencies about TQM.[58] Many state and local governments would soon follow suit, led by the pioneering example of then governor of Arkansas Bill Clinton, who saw quality as simply "good government." By the mid-1990s, however, quality management would fade away in importance.[59]

By the 1990s, it was abundantly clear that new visions for managing were having significant impacts on how organizations should be managed, how workers should be supervised, and how consumers of government programs should be treated. The first challenge came from the new public management movement. New public management was international in origin,[60] developing in the United Kingdom, Australia, New Zealand, and other countries that have parliamentary forms of government. It advocated a different model for providing public services—essentially seeing public agencies being split into small policy oversight boards and larger performance-based managed organizations that delivered services and products. This model would heavily influence the reinvention movement under Clinton.

The American response to new public management was reflected in a number of innovation efforts. One of the most prominent was a series of experiments designed to radically rethink government performance in Minnesota. In 1992, Michael Barzelay and Babak Armajani published their book *Breaking Through Bureaucracy*, which looked at the innovative experiments in Minnesota that attempted to transform public programs by emphasizing customer service, employee empowerment, selective competition, and administrative deregulation. This "new vision for managing in government," as the book was subtitled, argued that government did not have to be bureaucratic, rule-bound, control-focused, and inflexible. Excerpts from the book are reprinted here to show the thrust of this frontal challenge to traditional Weberian thinking about organizations and how they must operate.

It would be incorrect to interpret the management and budget struggles of the 1990s as simply a struggle over resource control, or who gets what, or concerns about waste, fraud, and red tape. By the 1990s, it was clear to both politicians and the public that government programs often were ineffective and public funds were being poorly used because the public policies that government efforts were founded on were fundamentally flawed. Nowhere was this more apparent than with the large-scale social service programs on which governments at all levels (federal, state, and local) were increasingly spending public funds. Indeed, from a policy perspective, perhaps the most significant budgetary date in the last quarter century was in 1990, when the federal spending on Social Security surpassed defense spending as the top outlay category.

Of course, national and state-level elections regularly raised the banner of "government failure" as challengers confronted incumbents about unintended consequences and social welfare dependency. The 1990s saw all this come to a head. Many state and local governments became involved in new policy experiments to change public education funding or transportation and infrastructure financing. Crime and prisons, welfare, child support, job training, and environmental regulation and protection became significant policy issues in different states. At the federal level, the Clinton administration would try to tackle and fail miserably in pursuing fundamental reform of health care. But it would cobble together enough support to pass welfare reform legislation, which was based more on dissatisfaction with the old system than on any assurance that the new solution was any better. Real reform, however, remained elusive.

THE CHALLENGE OF REINVENTION?

The fiscal and organizational performance challenges facing public administration were only symptoms for a much larger set of concerns about government itself. Public confidence in government continued to decline. The "trust deficit"—the lack of public confidence that the government could be trusted to do the right thing most of the time—was a major factor in the Clinton administration's effort to make government reform itself a major thrust of his administration. During the campaign, Clinton had promised to reduce the size of the federal government by 100,000 employees. Once elected, he went much further.

Within 90 days of his inauguration, he announced a major initiative to "reinvent government" to be led by the vice president under the title National Performance Review, or NPR. Of course, management reform initiatives in government are not new ideas. Indeed, depending on which historian or administrative expert one consults, there have been no fewer than ten major federal government reform initiatives in the twentieth century alone, beginning with the Taft Commission in 1910 that produced the first blueprints for a federal executive budget to the National Performance Review, which called for reinvention or revolution.

In fall 1993, the Clinton administration unveiled its report *From Red Tape to Results: Creating a Government That Works Better and Costs Less,*[61] which spoke directly to the goals the administration set for its reform effort. Given the comprehensiveness of the National Performance Review, it is useful to look briefly at the "process" of the reform effort and the "principles" that guided the reformers. Much of the guiding philosophy for the National Performance Review and, indeed, the term reinvention itself came from the management book *Reinventing Government* by columnist David Osborne and consultant and former city manager Ted Gaebler. Osborne and Gaebler's *Reinventing Government*[62] decried the bankruptcy of bureaucracy and heralded entrepreneurialism as the solution to transforming government. Using primarily examples of innovative practices and experiments in state and local governments, they called for a series of radical changes in the public sector.[63]

The National Performance Review was no copy of the blueprint offered by *Reinventing Government.* But the guiding influence of *Reinventing Government* is unmistakable from the introductory chapter, which touts "Creating Entrepreneurial Organizations" as "The Solution" to the massive emphasis on deregulating federal management control systems (that is, budget, personnel, procurement, support and information services, and so on). In calling for a revolution in government, the National Performance Review was offering its own set of guiding principles, which ranged from "cutting unnecessary spending and eliminating red tape" to "fostering excellence with incentives and customer service measures."

The National Performance Review was touted as an "internal reform process" primarily because it has been staffed by a large group of federal employees who constituted the bulk of the task force. This was in sharp contrast to the major executive reform effort under President Reagan in 1982—the Grace Commission, which was headed by an outsider, business executive J. Peter Grace. The National Performance Review was an inside federal effort beginning with the vice president as chair and approximately 200 federal employees who were either detailed or given part-time assignments to the project team. Following the issuance of the report and to show that the NPR was but the first step in a continuous improvement process, the president issued a series of executive orders and presidential memorandums detailing the next steps in the reform process. A presidential memorandum entitled "Streamlining the Bureaucracy" was issued on September 11, 1993, detailing requirements to cut the federal workforce by 12 percent. In the spirit of the first principle—"to make do with less"—the NPR called for $108 billion in budget savings over five years led by a reduction in the federal workforce of 252,000 workers.

The Clinton administration started out with a major problem of being unable to convince the Congress to make a number of these system-wide reforms, such as procurement, budgeting, and civil service reforms. The then-Democratic Congress was not very keen on the NPR prescriptions other than to accept the personnel reduction of 252,000 federal job cuts and wrap the savings into the crime bill to pay for the new costs of federal support for more police officers on the street and new crime reduction programs.[64] Ultimately, the Congress passed a first stab at procurement reform and a modified form of budget reform. The major provisions for entrepreneur budget reform would be rejected.

With the election of a Republican Congress, the NPR had to switch from offense to defense. Republican plans for reform, sometimes referred to as "De-Invention," called for much more drastic change. Privatization, terminating entire cabinet departments, moving to block grants, and devolution were the new challenges issued by the 104th Congress. NPR responded by stepping up its review of programs in an exercise entitled "REGO II" in which substantial savings and cuts in several agencies were announced. More intense efforts were launched on the customer service initiative, including new steps to benchmark government services against the private sector.

So, under a heavy political crossfire, NPR continued on in its pursuit of a very ambitious reform agenda. Interestingly, within public administration, NPR, or reinvention, was attacked on both sides. On one side it was rejected by "traditionalists" who felt that the principles of NPR did not fit the values of public administrations or misdiagnosed the problem, or failed to deal adequately with the politics of public policy and public management.[65] On the other side were the radicals who felt that the NPR did not go far enough and would fail to dramatically reengineer the core processes and structures of government.

If there is a final lasting statement about the reform efforts in government during the 1980s and 1990s, it is probably the work of Mark Moore. In 1995, Moore's book on strategic management in government entitled *Creating Public Value* was published; an excerpt from the second chapter of that book on defining public value is reprinted here. Moore proposed to develop a philosophy for "new public managers," who now faced rising expectations for delivering results, being efficient and accountable, and being customer service focused, but who also were expected to build trust and make government more legitimate.

Some have argued that this fusion of different roles and premises masks competing themes and priorities that are more contradictory than complementary. But Moore argues that public managers must begin with the idea that their purpose is to create public value, just as private sector managers seek to create private return on investment for their stakeholders. His assessment of different perspectives of what constitutes public value in the "political marketplace" requires that politics be at center to resolve conflicts and to ensure that what government does is perceived as having public value.

The defeat of Vice President Gore in the 2000 presidential election ended reinvention. But it could be said that by the end of its eight years, reinvention was desperately in need of being reinvented. Its slogan—"making government work better and cost less"—was no longer connecting with the public, who were increasingly uncertain of the value of what government was doing. As David Rosenbloom wrote in an editorial in *Public Administration Review* on the themes of reform: "In their zeal to promote visions of the public interest, American administrative reformers sometimes seek to remake the political system to serve the needs of better management rather than to develop better management to serve the purposes of the political system.... This is an old lesson: if we want better government, we better talk politics."[66]

NOTES

1. Public-choice political economists work out of various academic centers in the United States, one of the most notable being George Mason University, which houses the Center for the Study of Public Choice and publishes the journal *Public Choice.*
2. According to *The Dorsey Dictionary of American Government and Politics* (Chicago: Dorsey Press, 1988): "pluralism is a theory of government that attempts to reaffirm the democratic character of society by asserting that open, multiple, competing, and responsive groups preserve traditional democratic values in a mass industrial state.... Pluralism assumes that power will shift from group to group as elements in the mass public transfer their allegiance in response to their perceptions of their individual interests. However, power-elite theory argues that, if democracy is defined as popular participation in

public affairs, then pluralist theory is inadequate as an explanation of modern U.S. government. Pluralism, according to this view, offers little direct participation, since the elite structure is closed, pyramidal, consensual, and unresponsive. Society is divided into two classes: the few who govern and the many who are governed; that is, pluralism is covert elitism instead of a practical solution to preserve democracy in a mass society."

3. This argument was first made by Nobel laureate James M. Buchanan, "Why Does Government Grow?" in *Budgets and Bureaucrats: The Sources of Government Growth*, ed. Thomas Borcherding (Durham, N.C.: Duke University Press, 1977), pp. 3–18.
4. See Jerry McCaffery and John H. Bowman, "Participatory Democracy and Budgeting: The Effects of Proposition 13," *Public Administration Review* 38 (November–December 1978): 530–538. Proposition 13 was a revolt by the middle class over rising taxes, especially on real estate, which were increasing dramatically in a period of double-digit inflation. By 1980, the tax revolt movement forced 38 states to reduce or at least stabilize tax rates. When California passed Proposition III in 1990, which, among other things, would double the state gasoline tax over five years to pay for new highways, many analysts hailed this as the end of the "tax revolt." According to former Speaker of the House Thomas Foley: "The tax revolt, which allegedly started in California, has been tempered by a realization that we have to make investments in the country," *USA Today* (June 8, 1990).
5. The best analysis of taxation and inflation issues during the period is the work of Joseph A. Pechman, *Federal Tax Policy*, 5th ed. (Washington, D.C.: Brookings Institution, 1987). For a definitive history of change in the federal income tax during the decade of the 1980s, see Eugene Steurle, *The Tax Decade* (Washington, D.C.: Urban Institute Press, 1991).
6. The trickle-down effect held that government policies should benefit the wealthy whose prosperity will then "trickle down" to the middle and lower economic classes. The term was first coined by humorist Will Rogers when he analyzed some of the Great Depression remedies of the Hoover administration and noted that "the money was all appropriated for the top in the hopes it would trickle down to the needy." However, this sentiment was also expressed by William Jennings Bryan, in his famous "Cross of Gold" speech at the Democratic National Convention in Chicago, July 8, 1896: "Mere are those who believe that if you will only legislate to make the well-to-do prosperous, their prosperity will leak through on those below. The Democratic idea, however, has been that if you make the masses prosperous, their prosperity will find its way up through every class which rests upon them."
7. There are many accounts of supply-side economic theory but few are as revealing as the Reagan administration's first budget director, David Stockman's memoirs, *The Triumph of Politics* (New York: Harper and Row, 1986).
8. Fredrick C. Mosher, "The Changing Responsibilities and Tactics of the Federal Government," *Public Administration Review* 40 (November–December 1980): 541–548.
9. Allison is best known as the author of a classic study of government policy-making, *Essence of Decision: Explaining the Cuban Missile Crisis* (Boston: Little, Brown, 1971), which demonstrated the inadequacies of the view that the decisions of a government are made by a "single calculating decision-maker" who has control over the organizations and officials within the government. Instead, as Allison showed, different bureaucratic viewpoints contend and conflict over policy. Allison first described his thesis in "Conceptual Models and the Cuban Missile Crisis," *American Political Science Review* 63 (September 1969): 698–718.
10. Laurence Lynn, *Managing the Public's Business* (New York: Basic Books, 1981).
11. Hal G. Rainey has written numerous articles on this topic, but a good summation of his research in this period is found in "Public Management: Recent Research on the Political Context and Managerial Roles, Structures, and Behaviors," *Journal of Management* 15, no. 2 (1989): 229–250.
12. Douglas Yates, *The Politics of Management* (San Francisco: Jossey-Bass, 1985).
13. Barry Bozeman and Jeffrey Straussman, eds. *New Directions in Public Administration* (Pacific Grove, Calif.: Brooks/Cole, 1984).

14. The quote was first attributed to Harlan Cleveland by the late Selma Mushkin.
15. James L. Perry and Kenneth L. Kraemer, *Public Management: Public and Private Perspectives* (Palo Alto, Calif.: Mayfield, 1983).
16. The opening salvo on privatization was sounded by E. E. Savas in a number of articles written during the 1980s. The best collections of his ideas are first in *Privatization: The Key to Better Government* (Chatham, N.J.: Chatham House, 1987) and *Privatization and Public-Private Partnerships* (Chatham, N.J.: Chatham House, 2000). For John M. Donahue, see *The Privatization Decision: Public Ends, Private Means* (New York: Basic Books, 1989).
17. In this decade, public administration as a field of study was just beginning to sort out what part it would play in the academic study of nonprofit management. For most of the 1980s, the study of nonprofits was a blend of social-work education (since much of the functional emphasis of nonprofits is human services), business administration (since the financial management and fundraising aspects were oriented toward the private sector), and public administration (since the organizational theory and management roots were primarily focused on public-sector values).
18. From the Associated Press, June 4, 1982, which quoted President Reagan as saying: "The United States government's program for arriving at a budget is about the most irresponsible Mickey Mouse arrangement that any government body has ever practiced."
19. For more definitive treatment of these themes, see Lance T. LeLoup, Barbara Luck Graham, and Stacy Barwick, "Deficit Politics and Constitutional Government: The Impact of Gramm-Rudman-Hollings," *Public Budgeting and Finance* (spring 1987): 83–103; Glen Abney and Thomas P. Lauth, "The Line Item Veto in the States: An Instrument for Fiscal Restraint or an Instrument for Partisanship?" *Public Administration Review* 45 (May–June 1985): 372–377; William R. Kew, "A Theoretical Analysis of the Case for a Balanced Budget Amendment," *Policy Sciences* 18 (1985): 157–168.
20. Naomi Caiden, "Guidelines to Federal Budget Reform," *Public Budgeting and Finance* 3 (winter 1983): 4–22. For a comprehensive overview of the budgeting field, see Caiden, "Public Budgeting in the United States," in *Public Administration: The State of the Discipline,* ed. Naomi Lynn and Aaron Wildavsky (Chatham, N.J.: Chatham House, 1990).
21. Lance LeLoup, *The Fiscal Congress* (Westport, Conn.: Greenwood Press, 1980). LeLoup also wrote the definitive critique of budgetary incrementalism in "The Myth of Incrementalism: Analytical Choices in Budgetary Theory," *Polity* 10 (1978): 488–509.
22. Irene Rubin, *Running in the Red: The Political Dynamics of Urban Fiscal Stress* (Albany: State University of New York Press, 1982). Rubin also wrote a later volume, *The Politics of Public Budgeting: Getting and Spending, Borrowing, and Balancing* (Chatham, N.J.: Chatham House, 1990), which examined budgeting from a true multilevel perspective: federal, state, and local.
23. Alan Schick's contributions to budgeting are too numerous to illustrate in a footnote. His most significant work is probably his definitive study *Congress and Money: Budgeting, Spending, and Taxing* (Washington, D.C.: Urban Institute, 1980). For a look at his perspective on the development of budget reform, see his "Incremental Budgeting in a Decremental Age," *Policy Sciences* 16 (September 1983): 1–25.
24. Aaron Wildavsky began the 1980s with an interesting study, *How to Limit Government Spending* (Berkeley: University of California Press, 1980), and with the fourth edition of his classic, *The Politics of the Budgetary Process* (Boston: Little, Brown, 1984). In 1988, he completely revised this classic and published *The New Politics of the Budgetary Process* (Boston: Little, Brown, 1988). In his preface, he explained that the budgetary process was no longer capable of going back to where it was before.
25. The most detailed account of the federal deficit problem in this era was written by Joseph White and Aaron Wildavsky, *The Deficit and the Public Interest: The Search for Responsible Budgeting in the 1980s* (Berkeley: University of California Press and Russell Sage Foundation, 1989). For an economic perspective (and the source for the deficit percentage statistics quoted), see Charles L. Schultze, "The Federal Budget and the Nation's Economic Health" in *Setting National Priorities: Policy for the Nineties,* ed., Henry J. Aaron (Washington, D.C.: Brookings Institution, 1990), pp. 19–63.

26. Perhaps the best early assessment of GPRA in the 1990s was by Philip Joyce, then of the CBO and a principal researcher in a key CBO study of performance results management, in an article for *Public Budgeting and Finance* (Winter 1993, pp. 3–17).
27. The federal government was not the only performance results budgeting story. For a superb assessment of state government experiences (indeed, 47 of the 50 states instituted some form of PRB or PBB, which is performance based budgeting), see Katherine Willoughby and Julia Melkers, "Implementing PBB—Conflicting Views of Success," *Public Budgeting and Finance* (spring 2000).
28. A good source of information on civil-service reform is the testimony of former Civil Service Commission Chair Alan K. Campbell before the U.S. House Committee on the Post Office and Civil Service. It is excerpted along with provisions for the act in Frank Thompson, *Classics of Public Personnel Policy*, 2d ed. (Pacific Grove, Calif.: Brooks/Cole, 1990), pp. 82–104.
29. Fundamental reform in personnel has remained elusive. Patricia Ingraham, who served on the Volcker Commission as a staffer, has written extensively about civil service reform and its politics. Her book, *The Foundation of Merit*, provides a superb summary of the issues and stakes involved in personnel reform and what it means to the notion of public service.
30. The strike of the Professional Air Traffic Controllers Organization (PATCO) in 1981 resulted in the complete destruction of their union and the dismissal of 11,000 controllers. On July 29, 1981, 95 percent of PATCO's 13,000 members went on strike. In response, the U.S. government cut back scheduled flights and reduced staff at small airports. Then it brought supervisors and retired controllers into service and ordered military controllers to civilian stations. Also, President Reagan addressed the nation on television. After reminding viewers that it is illegal for federal government employees to strike and that each controller had signed an oath asserting that he or she would never strike, the president proclaimed: "They are in violation of the law, and if they do not report for work within forty-eight hours, they have forfeited their jobs and will be terminated." Only a thousand controllers reported back. Most thought that the president was bluffing, but he was not. See Herbert R. Northrup, "The Rise and Demise of PATCO," *Industrial and Labor Relations Review* 37 (January 1984): 167–184.
31. *Griggs et al. v. Duke Power Co.*, 401 U.S. 424 (1970). This was the most significant single U.S. Supreme Court decision concerning the validity of employment examinations. The Court unanimously ruled that Title VII of the Civil Rights Act of 1964 "proscribes not only overt discrimination but also practices that are discriminatory in operation." Thus if employment practices operating to exclude minorities "cannot be shown to be related to job performance, the practice is prohibited." The ruling dealt a blow to restrictive credentialism, stating that while diplomas and tests are useful, "Congress has mandated the commonsense proposition that they are not to become masters of reality." In essence, the Court held that the law requires that tests used for employment purposes, "must measure the person for the job and not the person in the abstract." The *Griggs* decision applied only to the private sector until the Equal Employment Opportunity Act of 1972 extended the provisions of Title VII to cover public employees.
32. *Wards Cove Packing Company v. Antonio*, 109 Sup. Ct. 2115 (1989). The Supreme Court held that the burden of proof is on the plaintiff in equal employment opportunity cases to prove that employer practices that result in racial imbalance are not justified by legitimate business reasons. This ruling made it more difficult for workers to make a *prima facie* case of discrimination by simply citing statistics that demonstrate underrepresentation of various racial minorities in the workforce. For an early but well-developed analysis, see James Ledvinka and Vida G. Scarpello, *Federal Regulation of Personnel and Human Resources Management* (Boston: PWS-Kent Publishing, 1991).
33. Under the provisions of the Civil Rights Act of 1991. For a comprehensive assessment, see Harold S. Hartman, Gregory W. Homer, and John E. Menditto, "Human Resources Management Legal Issues: An Overview" in Stephen Condrey's *Handbook of Human Resources Management in Government* (San Francisco: Jossey-Bass, 1998).
34. A superb assessment of court decisions following the passage of the 1991 Civil Rights Act can be found in J. Edward Kellough's book *Understanding Affirmative Action*, specifically Chapter 6, "Cases from

1995 to 2003: Challenges, Uncertainty and the Survival of Affirmative Action." (Washington DC: Georgetown University Press, 2007).

35. For a summary of the issues and the statistical case for the Glass Ceiling, see Chapter 4 in Katherine C Naff, *To Look Like America: Dismantling Barriers for Women and Minorities* (Boulder, Co.: Westview Press: 2001).
36. One of the first voices raised in this area was that of Debra Stewart, "Women in Top Jobs: An Opportunity for Federal Leadership," *Public Administration Review* 36 (July-August 1976): 357–364.
37. See a comparative study by The Center for Women in Government at the State University of New York at Albany in 1991 and 1992. The Center however would refer to the disparity in women in top positions as "the sticky floor."
38. *Beneath the Veneer—The Report of the Task Forces on Barriers to Women in the Public Service* (Ottawa: Canadian Government Publishing Centre, 1990).
39. The U.S. Merit Systems Protection Board study was entitled "A Question of Equity: Women and the Glass Ceiling in the Federal Government" (Washington, DC: USMSPB, 1992). It would become one of their most cited reports, perhaps second in influence only to their 1980 and 1987 reports on sexual harassment in the federal government.
40. The Federal Glass Ceiling Commission would issue their report in two parts: their environmental scan entitled "Good for Business: Making Full Use of the Nation's Human Capital (March 1995), followed by "A Solid Investment," which was a November 1995 report providing recommendations for change. The U.S. Department of Labor, however, was active on glass-ceiling issues throughout the 1990s, having first issued "A Report on the Glass Ceiling Initiative" in 1991.
41. Two excellent sources for assessments and perspectives on representative bureaucracy are Julie Dolan and David H Rosenbloom (editors), *Representative Bureaucracy* (Armonk, NY: M. E. Sharpe, 2003), and Katherine C. Naff, *To Look Like America* (Boulder, Colorado: Westview Press, 2001).
42. David Rosenbloom, *Public Administration: Understanding Management, Politics, and Law in the Public Sector* (New York: Random House, 1986; 3rd edition, 1996). Rosenbloom had earlier developed some of these themes in *Public Administration and Law* (New York: Marcel Dekker, 1983). His most current work in this area is *Administrative Law for Public Managers* (Boulder, Colorado: Westview Press, 2003).
43. Marshall E. Dimock, *Law and Dynamic Administration* (New York: Praeger, 1980). Phillip J. Cooper, *Public Law and Public Administration* (Englewood Cliffs, N.J.: Prentice-Hall, 1988).
44. Cooper also wrote the lead article in *Public Administration Review*'s 1985 special issue: "Law and Public Affairs." The article is entitled "Conflict or Constructive Tension: The Changing Relationship of Judges and Administrators," *Public Administration Review* 45 (November 1985): 643–652.
45. For representative works, see Joel Fleishman, Lance Liebman, and Mark H. Moore, eds. *Public Duties: The Moral Obligations of Government Officials* (Cambridge, Mass.: Harvard University Press, 1981); Terry L Cooper, *The Responsible Administrator* (Port Washington, N.Y.: Kennikat Press, 1982); Peter French, *Ethics in Government* (Englewood Cliffs, N.J.: Prentice-Hall, 1983); Dennis F. Thompson, *Political Ethics and Public Office* (Cambridge, Mass.: Harvard University Press, 1987).
46. Michael Cohen, James March, and Johan Olsen, "A Garbage Can Model of Organizational Choice," *Administrative Science Quarterly* 17 (March 1972): 1–25.
47. Joan Acker, "Gendering Organizational Theory" in *Gendering Organizational Analysis*, ed. A. J. Mills and P. Tancred (Newbury Park, CA: Sage, 1992).
48. Judy B. Rosener, *America's Competitive Secret: Utilizing Women As a Management Strategy* (New York: Oxford University Press, 1995).
49. Camilla Stivers, *Gender Images in Public Administration: Legitimacy and the Administrative State* (Newbury Park, CA: Sage, 1993).
50. For an overview of Cleveland's work, see "The Twilight of Hierarchy: Speculations on the Global Information Society," *Public Administration Review* 45 (January–February 1985): 185–195.

51. See, for example, James Danziger et al., *Computers and Politics: High Technology in American Local Governments* (New York: Columbia University Press, 1982); Kenneth L. Kraemer and John King, "Computing and Public Organizations," *Public Administration Review* 46 (special issue, November 1986): 488–496.
52. Of course, information technology has virtually become its own subfield in management. For assessments, see Jane Fountain's *Building the Information State* (Washington DC, Brookings: 2001) and the more internationally focused *Reinventing Government in the Information Age*, edited by Richard Heeks (London: Routledge, 1999).
53. Robert N. Anthony and Regina Herzlinger, *Management Control in Nonprofit Organizations* (Homewood, Ill.: Irwin, 1980).
54. Alan Walter Steiss, *Management Control in Government* (Lexington, Mass.: Lexington Books, 1982).
55. Cole Blease Graham and Steven W. Hays, *Managing the Public Organization* (Washington, D.C.: CQ Press, 1986).
56. Laurence Lynn, *Public Management as Art, Science, and Profession* (Chatham, NJ: Chatham House, 1996).
57. See W. Edwards Deming, *Out of the Crises* (Cambridge, Mass.: Center for Advanced Engineering Study, 1986) or J. M Juran, *Juran on Leadership for Quality* (New York: McGraw-Hill, 1988).
58. The Federal Quality Institute would itself be dismantled and finally abandoned in the mid-1990s and reconstituted as a contract consulting organization. For an account of its demise, see "TQM and the Invisible Man" in *Personnel Management in Government*, 5th edition by Shafritz, Rosenbloom, Riccucci, Naff, and Hyde (New York: Marcel Dekker, 2001).
59. One journal, *Public Productivity and Management Review*, took the lead in analyzing and assessing organizational change from the perspective of organizational performance and quality improvement. This journal essentially provided public administration with an abundance of case studies and theoretical and qualitative reviews about how organizations improve and how they introduce, adapt, and sustain continuous incremental improvement through quality, led by editor Marc Holzer. But by the mid-1990s, it was abundantly clear that TQM had become subsumed as part of the basic public management approach. Its core features—process statistical measurements, customer feedback, employee participation in quality improvement, and supplier cooperation—are now viewed by most managers as "commonsense management." Quality has essentially become part of the public management foundation.
60. The best assessment of new public management remains Christopher Hood, "A Public Management for All Seasons," *Public Administration* 69 (spring 1991): 3–19. It remains the definitive statement, and according to a recent literature survey of public management by the International Public Management Journal, the most referenced article in public management—both internationally and in the United States.
61. *From Red Tape to Results: Creating a Government That Works Better and Costs Less*, Report of the National Performance Review (Washington, D.C.: U.S. Government Printing Office, September 1993).
62. David Osborne and Ted Gaebler, *Reinventing Government* (Reading, Mass.: Addison Wesley Publishers, 1992).
63. The public sector, according to Osborne and Gaebler's book, must seek to restructure itself by vigorously pursuing a "new form of governance." But the root of Osborne and Gaebler's prescription was entrepreneurialism. The authors explained that the original idea of entrepreneur went beyond business risk-taking normally associated with the private sector. Entrepreneurial government follows a broader model that "uses resources in new ways to maximize productivity and effectiveness." Osborne summarized the importance of this philosophy in testimony before the U.S. Senate a week after the National Performance Review had been launched: "We must restructure the basic incentives that drive public managers, public employees, and elected officials. Our federal bureaucracies grow so large and so sluggish not because those who work for them want it that way, but because the basic incentives operating on those bureaucracies literally demand it be that way. For example, most public programs are monopolies whose customers cannot go elsewhere for a better deal. Most are funded according to

their inputs—how many children qualify, how many farmers are poor enough—rather than their outcomes or results. Most are considered important not because they achieve tremendous results but because they spend tremendous sums of money. Their managers earn greater stature and higher pay not because they have demonstrated superior performance, but because they have built up a larger bureaucracy. With such incentives embedded within all our major control systems—our budget system, our personnel system, our reward system—is it any wonder that we get bureaucratic behavior rather than entrepreneurial behavior?" Excerpts taken from testimony before the Senate Governmental Affairs Committee, March 11, 1993, by David Osborne.

64. The original number of federal positions to be cut as an objective of the NPR was slightly over 250,000, but in the fall debates over the crime bill, the Congress increased the target number to 272,000-plus and "locked" the projected savings from this cut in federal employment into the needed offset for funding the crime bill, which among other things promised federal aid to put 100,000 new police officers in the street.

65. For samples of the Reinvention Critique, see James Carroll, "The Rhetoric of Reform and Political Reality in the National Performance Review," *Public Administration Review* (May–June 1995): 302–312; Ronald Moe, "The Reinventing Government Exercise: Misinterpreting the Problem, Misjudging the Consequences," *Public Administration Review* (March–April 1994): 111–122; and Charles Goodsell, "Did NPR Reinvent Government Reform?" *The Public Manager* (Fall 1993): 7–11.

66. David Rosenbloom, "Have an Administrative Rx? Don't Forget the Politics," *Public Administration Review* (November–December 1993): 507.

Public and Private Management: Are They Fundamentally Alike in All Unimportant Respects?

Graham T. Allison

My subtitle puts Wallace Sayre's oft quoted "law" as a question. Sayre had spent some years in Ithaca helping plan Cornell's new School of Business and Public Administration. He left for Columbia with this aphorism: public and private management are fundamentally alike in all unimportant respects.

Sayre based his conclusion on years of personal observation of governments, a keen ear for what his colleagues at Cornell (and earlier at OPA) said about business, and a careful review of the literature and data comparing public and private management. Of the latter there was virtually none. Hence, Sayre's provocative "law" was actually an open invitation to research.

Unfortunately, in the 50 years since Sayre's pronouncement, the data base for systematic comparison of public and private management has improved little. Consequently, when Scotty Campbell called six weeks ago to inform me that I would make some remarks at this conference, we agreed that I would, in effect, take up Sayre's invitation to *speculate* about similarities and differences among public and private management in ways that suggest significant opportunities for systematic investigation.

To reiterate: this paper is not a report of a major research project of systematic study. Rather, it is a response to a request for a brief summary of reflections of a dean of a school of government who now spends his time doing a form of public management—managing what Jim March has labeled an "organized anarchy"—rather than thinking, much less writing.[1] Moreover, the speculation here will appear to reflect a characteristic Harvard presumption that Cambridge either is the world, or is an adequate sample of the world. I say "appear" since as a North Carolinian, I am self-conscious about this parochialism. Nevertheless, I have concluded that the purposes of this conference may be better served by providing a deliberately parochial perspective on these issues—and thereby presenting a clear target for others to shoot at. Finally, I must acknowledge that this paper plagiarizes freely from a continuing discussion among my colleagues at Harvard about the development of the field of public management, especially from Joe Bower, Hale Champion, Gordon Chase, Charles Christenson, Richard Darman, John Dunlop, Phil Heymann, Larry Lynn, Mark Moore, Dick Neustadt, Roger Porter, and Don Price. Since my colleagues have not had the benefit of commenting on this presentation, I suspect I have some points wrong, or out of context, or without appropriate subtlety or amendment. Thus I assume full liability for the words that follow.

This paper is organized as follows:

- Section 1 frames the issue: What is public management?
- Section 2 focuses on similarities: How are public and private management basically alike?
- Section 3 concentrates on differences: How do public and private management differ?
- Section 4 poses the question more operationally: How are the jobs and responsibilities of two specific managers, one public and one private, alike and different?
- Section 5 attempts to derive from this discussion suggestions about promising research directions and then outlines one research agenda and strategy for developing knowledge of and instruction about public management.

Source: Proceedings of the Public Management Research Conference, November 19-20, 1979 (Washington, D.C.: Office of Personnel Management, OPM Document 127-53-1, February 1980), pp. 27–38.

Section 1
Framing the Issue: What Is Public Management?

What is the meaning of the term "management" as it appears in Office of *Management* and Budget, or Office of Personnel *Management?* Is "management" different from, broader or narrower than "administration"? Should we distinguish between management, leadership, entrepreneurship, administration, policymaking, and implementation?

Who are "public managers"? Mayors, governors, and presidents? City managers, secretaries, and commissioners? Bureau chiefs? Office directors? Legislators? Judges?

Recent studies of OPM and OMB shed some light on these questions. OPM's major study of the "Current Status of Public Management Research" completed in May 1978 by Selma Mushkin of Georgetown's Public Service Laboratory starts with this question. The Mushkin report notes the definition of "public management" employed by the Interagency Study Committee on Policy Management Assistance in its 1975 report to OMB. That study identified the following core elements:

(1) *Policy Management*	The identification of needs, analysis of options, selection of programs, and allocation of resources on a jurisdiction-wide basis.
(2) *Resource Management*	The establishment of basic administrative support systems, such as budgeting, financial management, procurement and supply, and personnel management.
(3) *Program Management*	The implementation of policy or daily operation of agencies carrying out policy along functional lines (education, law enforcement, etc.).[2]

The Mushkin report rejects this definition in favor of an "alternative list of public management elements." These elements are:

- Personnel Management (other than work force planning and collective bargaining and labor management relations)
- Work Force Planning
- Collective Bargaining and Labor Management Relations
- Productivity and Performance Measurement
- Organization/Reorganization
- Financial Management (including the management of intergovernmental relations)
- Evaluation Research, and Program and Management Audit.[3]

Such terminological tangles seriously hamper the development of public management as a field of knowledge. In our efforts to discuss public management curriculum at Harvard, I have been struck by how differently people use these terms, how strongly many individuals feel about some distinction they believe is marked by a difference between one word and another, and consequently, how large a barrier terminology is to convergent discussion. These verbal obstacles virtually prohibit conversation that is both brief and constructive among individuals who have not developed a common language or a mutual understanding of each others' use of terms. (What this point may imply for this conference, I leave to the reader.)

This terminological thicket reflects a more fundamental conceptual confusion. There exists no over-arching framework that orders the domain. In an effort to get a grip on the phenomena—the buzzing, blooming confusion of people in jobs performing tasks that produce results—both practitioners and observers have strained to find distinctions that facilitate their work. The attempts in the early decades of this century to draw a sharp line between "policy" and "administration," like more recent efforts to make a similar divide between "policymaking" and "implementation," reflect a common search for a simplification that allows one to put the value-laden issues of politics to one side (who gets what, when and how), and focus on the more limited issue of how to perform tasks more efficiently.[4] But can anyone really deny that the "how" substantially affects the "who," the "what," and the "when"? The basic categories now prevalent in discussions of public management—strategy, personnel management, financial management, and control—are mostly derived from a business context in which executives manage hierarchies. The fit of these concepts to the problems that confront public managers is not clear.

Finally, there exists no ready data on what public managers do. Instead, the academic literature, such as it is, mostly consists of speculation tied to bits and pieces of evidence about the tail or the trunk or other manifestation of the proverbial elephant.[5] In contrast to the literally thousands of cases describing problems faced by private managers and their practice in solving these problems, case research from the perspective of a public manager is just beginning.[6] Why the public administration field has generated so little data about public management, my fellow panelist Dwight Waldo will explain. But the paucity of data on the phenomena inhibits systematic empirical research on similarities and differences between public and private management, leaving the field to a mixture of reflection on personal experience and speculation.

For the purpose of this presentation, I will follow Webster and use the term management to mean the organization and direction of resources to achieve a desired result. I will focus on *general managers,* that is, individuals charged with managing a whole organization or multifunctional sub-unit. I will be interested in the general manager's full responsibilities, both *inside* his organization in integrating the diverse contributions of specialized sub-units of the organization to achieve results, and *outside* his organization in relating his organization and its product to external constituencies. I will begin with the simplifying assumption that managers of traditional government organizations are public managers, and managers of traditional private businesses, private managers. Lest the discussion fall victim to the fallacy of misplaced abstraction, I will take the Director of EPA and the Chief Executive Officer of American Motors as, respectively, public and private managers. Thus, our central question can be put concretely: in what ways are the jobs and responsibilities of Doug Costle as Director of EPA similar to and different from those of Roy Chapin as Chief Executive Officer of American Motors?

Section 2
Similarities: How Are Public and Private Management Alike?

At one level of abstraction, it is possible to identify a set of general management functions. The most famous such list appeared in Gulick and Urwick's classic *Papers in the Science of Administration.*[7] Gulick summarized the work of the chief executive in the acronym POSDCORB. The letters stand for:

- Planning
- Organizing
- Staffing
- Directing
- Coordinating
- Reporting
- Budgeting

With various additions, amendments, and refinements, similar lists of general management functions can be found through the management literature from Barnard to Drucker.[8]

I shall resist here my natural academic instinct to join the intramural debate among proponents of various lists and distinctions. Instead, I simply offer one composite list (see Table 1) that attempts to incorporate the major functions that have been identified for general managers, whether public or private.

These common functions of management are not isolated and discrete, but rather integral components separated here for purposes of analysis. The character and relative significance of the various functions differ from one time to another in the history of any organization, and between one organization and another. But whether in a public or private setting, the challenge for the general manager is to integrate all these elements so as to achieve results.

Section 3
Differences: How Are Public and Private Management Different?

While there is a level of generality at which management is management, whether public or private, functions that bear identical labels take on rather different meaning in public and private settings. As Larry Lynn has pointed out,

TABLE 1

Functions of General Management

STRATEGY

1. **Establishing Objectives and Priorities** for the organization (on the basis of forecasts of the external environment and the organization's capacities).

2. **Devising Operational Plans** to achieve these objectives.

MANAGING INTERNAL COMPONENTS

3. **Organizing and Staffing:** In organizing the manager establishes structure (units and positions with assigned authority and responsibilities) and procedures (for coordinating activity and taking action); in staffing tries to fit the right persons in key jobs.*

4. **Directing Personnel and the Personnel Management System:** The capacity of the organization is embodied primarily in its members and their skills and knowledge, the personnel management system recruits, selects, socializes, trains, rewards, punishes, and exits the organization's human capital, which constitutes the organization's capacity to act to achieve its goals and to respond to specific directions from management.

5. **Controlling Performance:** Various management information systems—including operating and capital budgets, accounts, reports and statistical systems, performance appraisals, and product evaluation—assist management in making decisions and in measuring progress towards objectives.

MANAGING EXTERNAL CONSITITUENCIES

6. **Dealing with "External" Units** of the organization subject to some common authority: Most general managers must deal with general managers of other units within the larger organization—above, laterally, and below—to achieve their unit's objectives.

7. **Dealing with Independent Organizations:** Agencies from other branches or levels of government, interest groups, and *private enterprises* that can importantly affect the organization's ability to achieve its objectives.

8. **Dealing with the Press and Public** whose action or approval or acquiescence is required.

*Organizations and staff are frequently separated in such lists, but because of the interaction between the two, they are combined here. See Graham Allison and Peter Szanton, *Remaking Foreign Policy* (Basic Books, 1976), p.14.

one powerful piece of evidence in the debate between those who emphasize "similarities" and those who underline "differences" is the nearly unanimous conclusion of individuals who have been general managers in both business and government. Consider the reflections of George Schultz (former director of OMB, Secretary of Labor, Secretary of the Treasury; now president of Bechtel), Donald Rumsfeld (former congressman, director of OEO, director of the Cost of Living Council, White House chief of staff, and Secretary of Defense; now president of GD Searle and Company), Michael Blumenthal (former chairman and chief executive officer of Bendix, Secretary of the Treasury; and now vice chairman of Burrows), Roy Ash (former president of Litton Industries, director of OMB; now president of Addressograph), Lyman Hamilton (former budget officer in BOB, high commissioner of Okinawa, division chief in the World Bank, and president of ITT), and George Romney (former president of American Motors, governor of Michigan, and Secretary of Housing and Urban Development).[9] All judge public management different from private management—and harder!

Three Orthogonal Lists of Differences My review of these recollections, as well as the thoughts of academics, has identified three interesting, orthogonal lists that summarize the current state of the field: one by John Dunlop; one major *Public Administration Review* survey of the literature comparing public and private organizations by Hal Rainey, Robert Backoff and Charles Levine; and one by Richard E. Neustadt prepared for the National Academy of Public Administration's Panel on Presidential Management.

John T. Dunlop's "impressionistic comparison of government management and private business" yields the following contrasts.[10]

1. Time perspective. Government managers tend to have relatively short time horizons dictated by political necessities and the political calendar, while private managers appear to take a longer time perspective oriented toward market developments, technological innovation and investment, and organization building.

2. Duration. The length of service of politically appointed top government managers is relatively short, averaging no more than 18 months recently for assistant secretaries, while private managers have a longer tenure both in the same position and in the same enterprise. A recognized element of private business management is the responsibility to train a successor or several possible candidates while the concept is largely alien to public management since fostering a successor is perceived to be dangerous.

3. Measurement of performance. There is little if any agreement on the standards and measurement of performance to appraise a government manager, while various tests of performance—financial return, market share, performance measures for executive compensation—are well established in private business and often made explicit for a particular managerial position during a specific period ahead.

4. Personnel constraints. In government there are two layers of managerial officials that are at times hostile to one another: the civil service (or now the executive system) and the political appointees. Unionization of government employees exists among relatively high-level personnel in the hierarchy and includes a number of supervisory personnel. Civil service, union contract provisions, and other regulations complicate the recruitment, hiring, transfer, and layoff or discharge of personnel to achieve managerial objectives or preferences. By comparison, private business managements have considerably greater latitude, even under collective bargaining, in the management of subordinates. They have much more authority to direct the employees of their organization. Government personnel policy and administration are more under the control of staff (including civil service staff outside an agency) compared to the private sector in which personnel are much more subject to line responsibility.

5. Equity and efficiency. In governmental management great emphasis tends to be placed on providing equity among different constituencies, while in private business management relatively greater stress is placed upon efficiency and competitive performance.

6. Public processes versus private processes. Governmental management tends to be exposed to public scrutiny and to be more open, while private business management is more private and its processes more internal and less exposed to public review.

7. Role of press and media. Governmental management must contend regularly with the press and media; its decisions are often anticipated by the press. Private decisions are less often reported in the press, and the press has a much smaller impact on the substance and timing of decisions.

8. Persuasion and direction. In government, managers often seek to mediate decisions in response to a wide variety of pressures and must often put together a coalition of inside and outside groups to survive. By contrast, private management proceeds much more by direction or the issuance of orders to subordinates by superior managers with little risk of contradiction. Governmental managers tend to regard themselves as responsive to many superiors while private managers look more to one higher authority.

9. Legislative and judicial impact. Governmental managers are often subject to close scrutiny by legislative oversight groups or even judicial orders in ways that are quite uncommon in private business management. Such scrutiny often materially constrains executive and administrative freedom to act.

10. Bottom line. Governmental managers rarely have a clear bottom line, while that of a private business manager is profit, market performance, and survival.

The *Public Administration Review*'s major review article comparing public and private organizations, by Rainey, Backoff and Levine, attempts to summarize the major points of consensus in the literature on similarities and differences among public and private organizations.[11] Table 2 presents that summary.

Third, Richard E. Neustadt, in a fashion close to Dunlop's, notes six major differences between Presidents of the United States and Chief Executive Officers of major corporations.[12]

1. Time-horizon. The private chief begins by looking forward a decade, or thereabouts, his likely span barring extraordinary troubles. The first-term President looks forward four years at most, with the fourth (and now even the third) year dominated by campaigning for reelection. (What second-termers look toward we scarcely know, having seen but one such term completed in the past quarter century.)

2. Authority over the enterprise. Subject to concurrence from the Board of Directors which appointed and can fire him, the private executive sets organization goals, shifts structures, procedure, and personnel to suit, monitors results, reviews key operational decisions, deals with key outsiders, and brings along his Board. Save for the deep but narrow sphere of military movements, a President's authority in these respects is shared with well-placed members of Congress (or their staffs); case by case, they may have more explicit authority than he does (contrast authorizations and appropriations with the "take-care" clause). As for "bringing along the Board," neither the Congressmen with whom he shares power or the primary and general electorates which "hired" him have either a Board's duties or a broad view of the enterprise precisely matching his.

3. Career-system. The model corporation is a true career system, something like the Forest Service after initial entry. In normal times the chief himself is chosen from within, or he is chosen from another firm in the same industry. He draws department heads et al. from among those with whom he's worked, or whom he knows in comparable companies. He and his principal associates will be familiar with each other's roles—indeed he probably has had a number of them—and also usually with one another's operating styles, personalities, idiosyncrasies. Contrast the President who rarely has had much experience "downtown," probably knows little of most roles there (much of what he knows will turn out wrong) and less of most associates whom he appoints there, willy-nilly, to fill places by inauguration day. Nor are they likely to know one another well, coming as they do from "everywhere" and headed as most are toward oblivion.

4. Media relations. The private executive represents his firm and speaks for it publicly in exceptional circumstances; he and his associates judge the exceptions. Those aside, he neither sees the press nor gives its members access to internal operations, least of all in his own office, save to make a point deliberately for public-relations purposes. The President, by contrast, is routinely on display, continuously dealing with the White House press and with the wider circle of political reporters, commentators, columnists. He needs them in his business, day by day, nothing exceptional about it, and they need him in theirs: the TV Network News programs lead off with him some nights each week. They and the President are as mutually dependent as he and Congressmen (or more so). Comparatively speaking, these relations overshadow most administrative ones much of the time for him.

5. Performance measurement. The private executive expects to be judged, and in turn to judge subordinates, by profitability, however the firm measures it (a major strategic choice). In practice, his Board may use more subjective measures; so may he, but at risk to morale and good order. The relative virtue of profit, of "the bottom line" is its legitimacy, its general acceptance in the

TABLE 2

Public Administration Review Research Developments

SUMMARY OF LITERATURE ON DIFFERENCES BETWEEN PUBLIC AND PRIVATE ORGANIZATIONS: MAIN POINTS OF CONSENSUS

The following table presents a summary of the points of consensus by stating them as propositions regarding the attributes of a public organization, relative to those of a private organization.

Topic	*Proposition*
I. ENVIRONMENTAL FACTORS	
I.1. Degree of market exposure (reliance on appropriations)	I.1.a. Less market exposure results in less incentive cost reduction, operating efficiency, effective performance.
	I.1.b. Less market exposure results in lower allocational efficiency (reflection of consumer preferences, proportioning supply to demand, etc.)
	I.1.c. Less market exposure means lower availability of market indicators and information (prices, profits, etc.)
I.2. Legal, formal constraints (courts, legislature, hierarchy)	I.2.a. More constraints on procedures, spheres of operations (less autonomy of managers in making such choices)
	I.2.b. Greater tendency to proliferation of formal specifications and controls
	I.2.c. More external sources of formal influence, and greater fragmentation of those sources
I.3. Political influences	I.3.a. Greater diversity of intensity of external informal influences on decisions (bargaining, public opinion, interest group reactions)
	I.3.b. Greater need for support of "constituencies"—clientgroups, sympathetic formal authorities, etc.
II. ORGANIZATION-ENVIRONMENT TRANSACTIONS	
II.1. Coerciveness ("coercive," "monopolistic," unavoidable nature of many government activities)	II.1.a. More likely that participation in consumption and financing of services will be unavoidable or mandatory (Government has unique sanctions and coercive powers.)
II.2. Breadth of impact	II.2.a. Broader impact, greater symbolic significance of actions of public administrators (Wider scope of concern, such as "public interest.")
II.3. Public scrutiny	II.3.a. Greater public scrutiny of public officials and their actions
II.4. Unique public expectations	II.4.a. Greater public expectations that public officials act with more fairness, responsiveness, accountability, and honesty

(*continued*)

TABLE 2 | ***continued***

III. INTERNAL STRUCTURES AND PROCESSES	
III.1. Complexity of objectives, evaluation and decision criteria and criteria	III.1.a. Greater multiplicity and diversity of objectives
	III.1.b. Greater vagueness and intangibility of objectives and criteria
	III.1.c. Greater tendency of goals to be conflicting (more "tradeoffs")
III.2. Authority relations and the role of the administrator	III.2.a. Less decision-making autonomy and exibility on the part of the public administrators
	III.2.b. Weaker, more fragmented authority over subordinates and lower levels (1. Subordinates can bypass, appeal to alternative authorities. 2. Merit system constraints.)
	III.2.c. Greater reluctance to delegate, more levels of review, and greater use of formal regulations (Due to difficulties in supervision and delegation, resulting from III.1.b.)
	III.2.d. More political, expository role for top managers
III.3. Organizational performance	III.3.a. Greater cautiousness, rigidity, less innovativeness
	III.3.b. More frequent turnover of top leaders due to elections and political appointments results in greater disruption of implementation of plans
III.4. Incentives and incentive structures	III.4.a. Greater difficulty in devising incentives for effective and efficient performance
	III.4.b. Lower valuation of pecuniary incentives by employees
III.5. Personal characteristics of employees	III.5.a. Variations in personality traits and needs, such as higher dominance and flexibility, higher need for achievement, on part of government managers
	III.5.b. Lower work satisfaction and lower organization commitment

(III.5. and III.5.b. represent results of individual empirical studies, rather than points of agreement among authors.)

Source: Public Administration Review (March–April, 1976), pp. 236–237.

business world by all concerned. Never mind its technical utility in given cases, its apparent "objectivity," hence "fairness," has enormous social usefulness; a myth that all can live by. For a President there is no counterpart (expect *in extremis* the "smoking gun" to justify impeachment). The general public seems to judge a President, at least in part, by what its members think is happening to them, in their own lives; Congressmen, officials, interest groups appear to judge by what they guess, at given times, he can do for or to their causes. Members of the press interpret both of these and spread a simplified criterion affecting both, the legislative box-score, a standard of the press's own devising. The White House denigrates them all except when it does well.

6. *Implementation.* The corporate chief, supposedly, does more than choose a strategy and set a course of policy; he also is supposed to

oversee what happens after, how in fact intentions turn into results, or if they don't to take corrective action, monitoring through his information system, acting, and if need be, through his personnel system. A President, by contrast, while himself responsible for budgetary proposals, too, in many spheres of policy, appears ill-placed and ill-equipped, to monitor what agencies of state, of cities, corporations, unions, foreign governments are up to or to change personnel in charge. Yet these are very often the executants of "his" programs. Apart from defense and diplomacy the federal government does two things in the main: it issues and applies regulations and it awards grants in aid. Where these are discretionary, choice usually is vested by statute in a Senate-confirmed official well outside the White House. Monitoring is his function, not the President's except at second-hand. And final action is the function of the subjects of the rules and funds; they mostly are not federal personnel at all. In defense, the arsenals and shipyards are gone; weaponry comes from the private sector. In foreign affairs it is the *other* governments whose actions we would influence. From implementors like these a President is far removed most of the time. He intervenes, if at all, on a crash basis, not through organizational incentives.

Underlying these lists' sharpest distinctions between public and private management is a fundamental *constitutional difference.* In business, the functions of general management are centralized in a single individual: the Chief Executive Officer. The goal is authority commensurate with responsibility. In contrast, in the U.S. government, the functions of general management are constitutionally spread among competing institutions: the executive, two houses of Congress, and the courts. The constitutional goal was "not to promote efficiency but to preclude the exercise of arbitrary power," as Justice Brandeis observed. Indeed, as *The Federalist Papers* make starkly clear, the aim was to create incentives to compete: "the great security against a gradual concentration of the several powers in the same branch, consists in giving those who administer each branch the constitutional means and personal motives to resist encroachment of the others. Ambition must be made to counteract ambition."[13] Thus, the general management functions concentrated in the CEO of a private business are, by constitutional design, spread in the public sector among a number of competing institutions and thus shared by a number of individuals whose ambitions are set against one another. For most areas of public policy today, these individuals include at the federal level the chief elected official, the chief appointed executive, the chief career official, and several congressional chieftains. Since most public services are actually delivered by state and local governments, with independent sources of authority, this means a further array of individuals at these levels.

Section 4 An Operational Perspective: How Are the Jobs and Responsibilities of Doug Costle, Director of EPA, and Roy Chapin, CEO of American Motors, Similar and Different?

If organizations could be separated neatly into two homogeneous piles, one public and one private, the task of identifying similarities and differences between managers of these enterprises would be relatively easy. In fact, as Dunlop has pointed out, "the real world of management is composed of distributions, rather than single undifferentiated forms, and there is an increasing variety of hybrids." Thus for each major attribute of organizations, specific entities can be located on a spectrum. On most dimensions, organizations classified as "predominantly public" and those "predominantly private" overlap.[14] Private business organizations vary enormously among themselves in size, in management structure and philosophy, and in the constraints under which they operate. For example, forms of ownership and types of managerial control may be somewhat unrelated. Compare a family-held enterprise, for instance, with a public utility and a decentralized conglomerate, a Bechtel with ATT and Textron. Similarly, there are vast differences in management of governmental organizations. Compare the Government Printing Office or TVA or the police department of a small town with the Department of Energy or the Department of Health and Human Services. These distributions and varieties should encourage penetrating comparisons within both business and governmental organizations, as well as contrasts and comparisons across these broad categories, a point to which we shall return in considering directions for research.

Absent a major research effort, it may nonetheless be worthwhile to examine the jobs and responsibilities of two specific managers, neither polar extremes, but one clearly public, the other private. For this purpose, and primarily because of the availability of cases that describe the problems and opportunities each confronted, consider Doug Costle, Administrator of EPA, and Roy Chapin, CEO of American Motors.[15]

Doug Costle, Administrator of EPA, January 1977 The mission of EPA is prescribed by laws creating the agency and authorizing its major programs. That mission is "to control and abate pollution in the areas of air, water, solid wastes, noise, radiation, and toxic substances. EPA's mandate is to mount an integrated, coordinated attack on environmental pollution in cooperation with state and local governments."[16]

EPA's organizational structure follows from its legislative mandates to control particular pollutants in specific environments: air and water, solid wastes, noise, radiation, pesticides and chemicals. As the new Administrator, Costle inherited the Ford Administration's proposed budget for EPA of $802 million for federal 1978 with a ceiling of 9,698 agency positions.

The setting into which Costle stepped is difficult to summarize briefly. As Costle characterized it:

- "Outside there is a confusion on the part of the public in terms of what this agency is all about: what it is doing, where it is going."
- "The most serious constraint on EPA is the inherent complexity in the state of our knowledge, which is constantly changing."
- "Too often, acting under extreme deadlines mandated by Congress, EPA has announced regulations, only to find out that they knew very little about the problem. The central problem is the inherent complexity of the job that the agency has been asked to do and the fact that what it is asked to do changes from day to day."
- "There are very difficult internal management issues not amenable to quick solution: the skills mix problem within the agency; a research program with laboratory facilities scattered all over the country and cemented in place, largely by political alliances on the Hill that would frustrate efforts to pull together a coherent research program."
- "In terms of EPA's original mandate in the bulk pollutants we may be hitting the asymptotic part of the curve in terms of incremental clean-up costs. You have clearly conflicting national goals: energy and environment, for example."

Costle judged his six major tasks at the outset to be:

- assembling a top management team (six assistant administrators and some 25 office heads);
- addressing EPA's legislative agenda (EPA's basic legislative charter—the Clean Air Act and the Clean Water Act—were being rewritten as he took office; the pesticides program was up for reauthorization also in 1977);
- establishing EPA's role in the Carter Administration (aware that the Administration would face hard tradeoffs between the environment and energy, energy regulations and the economy, EPA regulations of toxic substances and the regulations of FDA, CSPS, and OSHA, Costle identified the need to build relations with the other key players and to enhance EPA's standing);
- building ties to constituent groups (both because of their role in legislating the agency's mandate and in successful implementation of EPA's programs);
- making specific policy decisions (for example, whether to grant or deny a permit for the Seabrook Nuclear Generating Plant cooling system. Or how the Toxic Substance Control Act, enacted in October 1976, would be implemented: this act gave EPA new responsibilities for regulating the manufacture, distribution, and use of chemical substances so as to prevent

unreasonable risks to health and the environment. Whether EPA would require chemical manufacturers to provide some minimum information on various substances, or require much stricter reporting requirements for the 1,000 chemical substances already known to be hazardous, or require companies to report all chemicals, and on what timetable, had to be decided and the regulations issued);
- rationalizing the internal organization of the agency (EPA's extreme decentralization to the regions and its limited technical expertise).

No easy job.

Roy Chapin and American Motors, January 1977 In January 1967, in an atmosphere of crisis, Roy Chapin was appointed Chairman and Chief Executive Officer of American Motors (and William Luneburg, President and Chief Operating Officer). In the four previous years, AMC unit sales had fallen 37 percent and market share from over 6 percent to under 3 percent. Dollar volume in 1967 was off 42 percent from the all-time high of 1963 and earnings showed a net loss of $76 million on sales of $656 million. Columnists began writing obituaries for AMC. *Newsweek* characterized AMC as "a flabby dispirited company, a product solid enough but styled with about as much flair as corrective shoes, and a public image that melted down to one unshakable label: loser." Said Chapin: "We were driving with one foot on the accelerator and one foot on the brake. We didn't know where the hell we were."

Chapin announced to his stockholders at the outset that "we plan to direct ourselves most specifically to those areas of the market where we can be fully effective. We are not going to attempt to be all things to all people, but to concentrate on those areas of consumer needs we can meet better than anyone else." As he recalled: "There were problems early in 1967 which demanded immediate attention, and which accounted for much of our time for several months. Nevertheless, we began planning beyond them, establishing objectives, programs, and timetables through 1972. Whatever happened in the short run, we had to prove ourselves in the marketplace in the long run."

Chapin's immediate problems were five:

- The company was virtually out of cash and an immediate supplemental bank loan of $20 million was essential.
- Car inventories—company owned and dealer owned—had reached unprecedented levels. The solution to this glut took five months and could be accomplished only by a series of plant shutdowns in January 1967.
- Sales of the Rambler American series had stagnated and inventories were accumulating; a dramatic merchandising move was concocted and implemented in February, dropping the price tag on the American to a position midway between the VW and competitive smaller U.S. compacts, by both cutting the price to dealers and trimming dealer discounts from 21 percent to 17 percent.
- Administrative and commercial expenses were much too high and thus a vigorous cost reduction program was initiated that trimmed $15 million during the first year. Manufacturing and purchasing costs were also trimmed significantly to approach the most effective levels in the industry.
- The company's public image had deteriorated: the press was pessimistic and much of the financial community had written it off. To counteract this, numerous formal and informal meetings were held with bankers, investment firms, government officials, and the press.

As Chapin recalls "with the immediate fires put out, we could put in place the pieces of a corporate growth plan—a definition of a way of life in the auto industry for American Motors. We felt that our reason for being, which would enable us not just to survive but to grow, lay in bringing a different approach to the auto market—in picking our spots and then being innovative and aggressive." The new corporate growth plan included a dramatic change in the approach to the market to establish a "youthful image" for the company (by bringing out new sporty models like the Javelin and by entering the racing field), "changing the product line from one end to the other" by 1972, acquiring Kaiser Jeep (selling the company's non-transportation assets and concentrating on specialized transportation, including Jeep, a company that had lost money in each of the preceding five years, but that Chapin believed could be turned around by substantial cost reductions and economies of scale in manufacturing, purchasing, and administration).

Chapin succeeded: for the year ending September 30, 1971, AMC earned $10.2 million on sales of $1.2 billion.

Recalling the list of general management functions in Table 1, which similarities and differences appear salient and important?

Strategy Both Chapin and Costle had to establish objectives and priorities and to devise operational plans. In business, "corporate strategy is the pattern of major objectives, purposes, or goals and essential policies and plans for achieving these goals, stated in such a way as to define what businesses the company is in or is to be in and the kind of company it is or is to be."[17] In reshaping the strategy of AMC and concentrating on particular segments of the transportation market, Chapin had to consult his Board and had to arrange financing. But the control was substantially his.

How much choice did Costle have at EPA as to the "business it is or is to be in" or the kind of agency "it is or is to be"? These major strategic choices emerged from the legislative process which mandated whether he should be in the business of controlling pesticides or toxic substances and if so on what timetable, and occasionally, even what level of particulate per million units he was required to control. The relative role of the President, other members of the administration (including White House staff, Congressional relations, and other agency heads), the EPA Administrator, Congressional committee chairmen, and external groups in establishing the broad strategy of the agency constitutes an interesting question.

Managing Internal Components For both Costle and Chapin, staffing was key. As Donald Rumsfeld has observed "the single, most important task of the chief executive is to select the right people. I've seen terrible organization charts in both government and business that were made to work well by good people. I've seen beautifully charted organizations that didn't work very well because they had the wrong people."[18]

The leeway of the two executives in organizing and staffing were considerably different, however. Chapin closed down plants, moved key managers, hired and fired, virtually at will. As Michael Blumenthal has written about Treasury, "if you wish to make substantive changes, policy changes, and the Department's employees don't like what you're doing, they have ways of frustrating you or stopping you that do not exist in private industry. The main method they have is Congress. If I say I want to shut down a particular unit or transfer the function of one area to another, there are ways of going to Congress and in fact using friends in the Congress to block the move. They can also use the press to try to stop you. If I at Bendix wished to transfer a division from Ann Arbor to Detroit because I figured out that we could save money that way, as long as I could do it decently and carefully, it's of no lasting interest to the press. The press can't stop me. They may write about it in the local paper, but that's about it."[19]

For Costle, the basic structure of the agency was set by law. The labs, their locations and most of their personnel were fixed. Though he could recruit his key subordinates, again restrictions like the conflict of interest law and the prospect of a Senate confirmation fight led him to drop his first choice for the Assistant Administrator for Research and Development, since he had worked for a major chemical company. While Costle could resort to changes in the process for developing policy or regulations in order to circumvent key office directors whose views he did not share, for example, Eric Stork, the deputy assistant Administrator in charge of Mobile Source Air Program, such maneuvers took considerable time, provoked extensive infighting, and delayed significantly the development of Costle's program.

In the direction of personnel and management of the personnel system, Chapin exercised considerable authority. While the United Auto Workers limited his authority over workers, at the management level he assigned people and reassigned responsibility consistent with his general plan. While others may have felt that his decisions to close down particular plants or to drop a particular product were mistaken, they complied. As George Schultz has observed: "One of the first lessons I learned in moving from government to business is that in business you must be very careful when you tell someone who is working for you to do something because the probability is high that he or she will do it."[20]

Costle faced a civil service system designed to prevent spoils as much as to promote productivity. The Civil Service Commission exercised much of the responsibility for the personnel function in his agency. Civil service rules severely restricted his discretion, took long periods to exhaust, and often required complex maneuvering in a specific case to achieve any results. Equal opportunity rules and their administration provided yet another network of procedural and substantive inhibitions. In retrospect, Costle found the civil service system a much larger constraint on his actions and demand on his time than he had anticipated.

In controlling performance, Chapin was able to use measures like profit and market share, to decompose those objectives to sub-objectives for lower levels of the organization and to measure the performance of managers of particular models, areas, divisions. Cost accounting rules permitted him to compare plants within AMC and to compare AMC's purchases, production, and even administration with the best practice in the industry.

Managing External Constituencies As Chief Executive Officer, Chapin had to deal only with the Board. For Costle, within the executive branch but beyond his agency lay many factors critical to the achievement of his agency's objectives: the President and the White House, Energy, Interior, the Council on Environmental Quality, OMB. Actions each could take, either independently or after a process of consultation in which they disagreed with him, could frustrate his agency's achievement of its assigned mission. Consequently, he spent considerable time building his agency's reputation and capital for interagency disputes.

Dealing with independent external organizations was a necessary and even larger part of Costle's job. Since his agency's mission, strategy, authorizations, and appropriations emerged from the process of legislation, attention to Congressional committees, and Congressmen, and Congressmen's staff, and people who affect Congressmen and Congressional staffers rose to the top of Costle's agenda. In the first year, top level EPA officials appeared over 140 times before some 60 different committees and subcommittees.

Chapin's ability to achieve AMC's objectives could also be affected by independent external organizations: competitors, government (the Clean Air Act that was passed in 1970), consumer groups (recall Ralph Nader), and even suppliers of oil. More than most private managers, Chapin had to deal with the press in attempting to change the image of AMC. Such occasions were primarily at Chapin's initiative, and around events that Chapin's public affairs office orchestrated, for example, the announcement of a new racing car. Chapin also managed a marketing effort to persuade consumers that their tastes could best be satisfied by AMC products.

Costle's work was suffused by the press: in the daily working of the organization, in the perception by key publics of the agency and thus the agency's influence with relevant parties, and even in the setting of the agenda of issues to which the agency had to respond.

For Chapin, the bottom line was profit, market share, and the long-term competitive position of AMC. For Costle, what are the equivalent performance measures? Blumenthal answers by exaggerating the difference between appearance and reality: "At Bendix, it was the reality of the situation that in the end determined whether we succeeded or not. In the crudest sense, this meant the bottom line. You can dress up profits only for so long—if you're not successful, its going to be clear. In government there is no bottom line, and that is why you can be successful if you appear to be successful—though, of course, appearance is not the only ingredient of success."[21] Rumsfeld says: "In business, you're pretty much judged by results. I don't think the American people judge government officials this way. . . . In government, too often you're measured by how much you seem to care, how hard you seem to try—things that do not necessarily improve the human condition. . . . It's a lot easier for a President to get into something and end up with a few days of good public reaction than it is to follow through, to pursue policies to a point where they have a beneficial effect on human lives."[22] As George Shultz says: "In government and politics, recognition and therefore incentives go to those who formulate policy and maneuver legislative compromise. By sharp contrast, the kudos and incentives in business go to the persons who can get something done. It is execution that counts. Who can get the plant built, who can bring home the sales contract, who can carry out the financing, and so on."[23]

This casual comparison of one public and one private manager suggests what could be done—if the issue of comparisons were pursued systematically, horizontally across organizations and at various levels within organizations. While much can be learned by examining the chief executive officers of organizations, still more promising should be comparisons among the much larger numbers of middle managers. If one compared, for example, a regional administrator of EPA and an AMC division chief, or two comptrollers, or equivalent plant managers, some functions would appear more similar, and other differences would stand out. The major barrier to such comparisons is the lack of cases describing problems and practices of middle-level managers.[24] This should be a high priority in further research.

The differences noted in this comparison, for example, in the personnel area, have already changed with the Civil Service Reform Act of 1978 and the creation of the Senior Executive Service. Significant changes have also occurred in the automobile industry: under current circumstances, the CEO of Chrysler may seem much more like the Administrator of EPA. More precise comparison of different levels of management in both organizations, for example, accounting procedures used by Chapin to cut costs significantly as compared to equivalent procedures for judging the costs of EPA mandated pollution control devices, would be instructive.

Section 5
Implications for Research on Public Management

The debate between the assimilators and the differentiators, like the dispute between proponents of convergence and divergence between the U.S. and the Soviet Union reminds me of the old argument about whether the glass is half full or half empty. I conclude that public and private management are at least as different as they are similar, and that the differences are more important than the similarities. From this review of the "state of the art," such as it is, I draw a number of lessons for research on public management. I will try to state them in a way that is both succinct and provocative:

- First, the demand for performance from government and efficiency in government is both real and right. The perception that government's performance lags private business performance is also correct. But the notion that there is any significant body of private management practices and skills that can be transferred directly to public management tasks in a way that produces significant improvements is wrong.
- Second, performance in many public management positions can be improved substantially, perhaps by an order of magnitude. That improvement will come not, however, from massive borrowing of specific private management skills and understandings. Instead, it will come, as it did in the history of private management, from an articulation of the general management function and a self-consciousness about the general public management point of view. The single lesson of private management most instructive to public management is the prospect of substantial improvement through recognition of and consciousness about the public management function.

Alfred Chandler's prize winning study, *The Visible Hand: The Managerial Revolution in American Business*,[25] describes the emergence of professional management in business. Through the 19th century most American businesses were run by individuals who performed management functions but had no self-consciousness about their management responsibilities. With the articulation of the general management perspective and the refinement of general management practices, by the 1920s, American businesses had become competitive in the management function. Individuals capable at management and self-conscious about their management tasks—setting objectives, establishing priorities, and driving the organization to results—entered firms and industries previously run by family entrepreneurs or ordinary employees and brought about dramatic increases in product. Business schools emerged to document better and worse practice, largely through the case method, to suggest improvements, and to refine specific management instruments. Important advances were made in technique. But the great leaps forward in productivity stemmed from the articulation of the general management point of view and the self-consciousness of managers about their function. (Analogously, at a lower level, the articulation of the salesman's role and task, together with the skills and values of salesmanship made it possible for individuals with moderate talents at sales to increase their level of sales tenfold.)

The routes by which people reach general management positions in government do not assure that they will have consciousness or competence in management. As a wise observer of government managers has written, "One of the difficult problems of schools of public affairs is to overcome the old-fashioned belief—still held by many otherwise sophisticated people—that the skills of management are simply the application of 'common sense' by any intelligent and broadly educated person to the management problems which are presented to him. It is demonstrable that many intelligent and broadly educated people who are generally credited with a good deal of 'common sense' make very poor managers. The skills of effective management require a good deal of uncommon sense and uncommon knowledge."[26] I believe that the most significant aspect of the Civil Service Reform Act of 1978 is the creation of the Senior Executive Service; the explicit identification of general managers in government. The challenge now is to assist people who occupy general management positions in actually becoming general managers.

- Third, careful review of private management rules of thumb that can be adapted to public management contexts will pay off. The 80–20 rule—80 percent of the benefits of most production processes come from the first 20 percent of effort—does have wide application, for example, in EPA efforts to reduce bulk pollutants.
- Fourth, Chandler documents the proposition that the categories and criteria for identifying costs, or calculating present value, or measuring the value added to intermediate products are not "natural." They are invented: creations of intelligence harnessed to operational tasks. While there are some particular accounting categories and rules, for example, for costing intermediate products, that may be directly transferable to public sector problems, the larger lesson is that dedicated attention to specific management functions can, as in the history of business, create for public sector managers accounting categories, and rules, and measures that cannot now be imagined.[27]
- Fifth, it is possible to learn from experience. What skills, attributes, and practices do competent managers exhibit and less successful managers lack? This is an empirical question that can be investigated in a straight-forward manner. As Yogi Berra noted: "You can observe a lot just by watching."
- Sixth, the effort to develop public management as a field of knowledge should start from problems faced by practicing public managers. The preferences of professors for theorizing reflects deep-seated incentives of the academy that can be overcome only by careful institutional design.

In the light of these lessons, I believe one strategy for the development of public management should include:

- *Developing a significant number of cases on public management problems and practices.* Cases should describe typical problems faced by public managers. Cases should attend not only to top-level managers but to middle and lower-level managers. The dearth of cases at this level makes this a high priority for development. Cases should examine both general functions of management and specific organizational tasks, for example, hiring and firing. Public management cases should concentrate on the job of the manager running his unit.

- *Analyzing cases to identify better and worse practice.* Scientists search for "critical experiments." Students of public management should seek to identify "critical experiences" that new public managers could live through vicariously and learn from. Because of the availability of information, academics tend to focus on failures. But teaching people what not to do is not necessarily the best way to help them learn to be *doers.* By analyzing relative successes, it will be possible to extract rules of thumb, crutches, and concepts, for example, Chase's "law": wherever the product of a public organization has not been monitored in a way that ties performance to reward, the introduction of an effective monitoring system will yield a 50 percent improvement in that product in the short run. GAO's handbooks on evaluation techniques and summaries suggest what can be done.
- *Promoting systematic comparative research:* management positions in a single agency over time; similar management positions among several public agencies; public management levels within a single agency; similar management functions, for example, budgeting or management information systems, among agencies; managers across public and private organizations; and even cross-nationally. The data for this comparative research would be produced by the case development effort and would complement the large-scale development of cases on private management that is ongoing.
- *Linking to the training of public managers.* Intellectual development of the field of public management should be tightly linked to the training of public managers, including individuals already in positions of significant responsibility. Successful practice will appear in government, not in the university. University-based documentation of better and worse practice and refinement of that practice, should start from problems of managers on the line. The intellectual effort required to develop the field of public management and the resources required to support this level of effort are most likely to be assembled if research and training are vitally linked. The new Senior Executive Service presents a *major* opportunity to do this.

The strategy outlined here is certainly not the only strategy for research in public management. Given the needs for effective public management, I believe that a major research effort should be mounted and that it should pursue a number of complementary strategies. Given where we start, I see no danger of overattention to, or overinvestment in the effort required in the immediate future.

Any resemblance between my preferred strategy and that of at least one school of government is not purely coincidental.

NOTES

1. In contrast to the management of structured hierarchies, for which the metaphor of a traditional football game in which each team attempts to amass the larger number of points is apt, an organized anarchy is better thought of as a soccer game played on a round field, ringed with goals; players enter and leave the field sporadically, and while there vigorously kick various balls of sundry sizes and shapes towards one or another of the goals, judging themselves and being judged by assorted, ambiguous scoring systems. See Michael Cohen and James March, *Leadership and Ambiguity* (McGraw-Hill, 1974).
2. Selma J. Mushkin, Frank H. Sandifer, and Sally Familton, *Current Status of Public Management: Research Conducted by or Supported by Federal Agencies* (Public Services Laboratory, Georgetown University, 1978), p. 10.
3. Ibid, p. 11.
4. Though frequently identified as the author who established the complete separation between "policy" and "administration," Woodrow Wilson has in fact been unjustly accused. "It is the object of administrative study to discover, first, what government can properly and successfully do, and, secondly, how it can do these proper things with the utmost possible efficiency . . ." (Wilson, "The Study of Public Administration," published as an essay in 1888 and reprinted in *Political Science Quarterly* [December 1941]: 481.) For another statement of the same point, see

Brooks Adams, *The Theory of Social Revolutions* (Macmillan, 1913), pp. 207–208.

5. See Dwight Waldo, "Organization Theory: Revisiting the Elephant," *Pub. Adm. Rev.* (November–December 1978). Reviewing the growing volume of books and articles on organization theory, Waldo notes that "growth in the volume of the literature is to be equated with growth in knowledge."
6. See *Cases in Public Policy and Management,* spring 1979, of the Intercollegiate Case Clearing House for a bibliography containing descriptions of 577 cases by 366 individuals from 79 institutions. Current casework builds on and expands earlier efforts of the Inter-University Case Program. See, for example, Harold Stein, ed., *Public Administration and Policy Development: A Case Book* (Harcourt, Brace, and Jovanovich, 1952); Edwin A. Bock and Alan K. Campbell, eds., *Case Studies in American Government* (Prentice-Hall, 1962).
7. Luther Gulick and Al Urwick, eds., *Papers in the Science of Public Administration* (Institute of Public Administration, 1937).
8. See, for example, Chester I. Barnard, *The Functions of the Executive* (Harvard University Press, 1938); Peter F. Drucker, *Management: Tasks, Responsibilities, Practices* (Harper and Row, 1974). Barnard's recognition of human relations added an important dimension neglected in earlier lists.
9. See, for example, George Romney, "A Businessman in a Political Jungle," *Fortune,* April 1964; Michael Blumenthal, "Candid Reflections of a Businessman in Washington," *Fortune,* January 29, 1979; Donald Rumsfeld, "A Politician Turned Executive," *Fortune,* September 10, 1979; George Shultz, "The Ambitions Interface," *Harvard Business Review* (November–December 1979).
10. John T. Dunlop, "Public Management" (draft of an unpublished paper and proposal, summer 1979).
11. Hal G. Rainey, Robert W. Backoff, and Charles N. Levine, "Comparing Public and Private Organizations," *Pub. Adm. Rev.* (March–April 1976).
12. Richard E. Neustadt, "American Presidents and Corporate Executives" (paper prepared for a meeting of the National Academy of Public Administration's Panel on Presidential Management, October 7–8, 1979).
13. *The Federalists Papers,* no. 51. The word "department" has been translated as "branch," which was its meaning in the original papers.
14. Failure to recognize the fact of distributions has led some observers to leap from one instance of similarity between public and private to general propositions about similarities between public and private institutions or management. See, for example, Michael Murray, "Comparing Public and Private Management: An Exploratory Essay," *Pub. Adm. Rev.* (July–August 1975).
15. These examples are taken from Bruce Scott, "American Motors Corporation" (Intercollegiate Case Clearing House #9-364-001); Charles B. Weigle, with the collaboration of C. Roland Christensen, "American Motors Corporation II" (Intercollegiate Case Clearing House #6-372-350); Thomas R. Hitchner and Jacob Lew, under the supervision of Philip B. Heymann and Stephen B. Hitchner, "Douglas Costle and the EPA (A)" (Kennedy School of Government Case #C94-78-216); and Jacob Lew and Stephen B. Hitchner, "Douglas Costle and the EPA (B)" (Kennedy School of Government Case #C96-78-217). For an earlier exploration of a similar comparison, see Joseph Bower, "Effective Public Management," *Harvard Business Review* (March–April 1977).
16. *U.S. Government Manual* (1978/1979), p. 507.
17. Kenneth R. Andrews, *The Concept of Corporate Strategy* (Dow Jones-Irwin, 1971), p. 28.
18. Rumsfeld, op. cit., p. 92.
19. Blumenthal, op. cit., p. 39.
20. Shultz, op. cit., p. 95.
21. Blumenthal, op. cit., p. 36
22. Rumsfeld, op. cit., p. 90.
23. Shultz, op. cit., p. 95.
24. The cases developed by Boston University's Public Management Program offer a promising start in this direction.
25. Alfred Chandler, *The Visible Hand: The Managerial Revolution in American Business,* (Cambridge, Mass.: Harvard University Press, Belknap Press, 1977).
26. Rufus Miles, "The Search for Identity of Graduate Schools of Public Affairs," *Pub. Adm. Rev.* (November 1967).
27. Chandler, op. cit., pp. 277–279.

33

Street-Level Bureaucracy: The Critical Role of Street-Level Bureaucrats

Michael Lipsky

Public service workers currently occupy a critical position in American society. Although they are normally regarded as low-level employees, the actions of most public service workers actually constitute the services "delivered" by government. Moreover, when taken together the individual decisions of these workers become, or add up to, agency policy. Whether government policy is to deliver "goods"—such as welfare or public housing—or to confer status—such as "criminal" or "mentally ill"—the discretionary actions of public employees are the benefits and sanctions of government programs or determine access to government rights and benefits.

Most citizens encounter government (if they encounter it at all) not through letters to congressmen or by attendance at school board meetings but through their teachers and their children's teachers and through the policeman on the corner or in the patrol car. Each encounter of this kind represents an instance of policy delivery.

Public service workers who interact directly with citizens in the course of their jobs, and who have substantial discretion in the execution of their work are called *street-level bureaucrats* in this study. Public service agencies that employ a significant number of street-level bureaucrats in proportion to their work force are called *street-level bureaucracies.* Typical street-level bureaucrats are teachers, police officers and other law enforcement personnel, social workers, judges, public lawyers and other court officers, health workers, and many other public employees who grant access to government programs and provide services with them. People who work in these jobs tend to have much in common because they experience analytically similar work conditions.[1]

The way in which street-level bureaucrats deliver benefits and sanctions structure and delimit people's lives and opportunities. These ways orient and provide the social (and political) context in which people act. Thus every extension of service benefits is accompanied by an extension of state influence and control. As providers of public order, street-level bureaucrats are the focus of political controversy. They are constantly torn by the demands of service recipients to improve effectiveness and responsiveness and by the demands of citizen groups to improve the efficacy and efficiency of government services. Since the salaries of street-level bureaucrats comprise a significant proportion of non-defense governmental expenditures, any doubts about the size of government budgets quickly translate into concerns for the scope and content of these public services. Moreover, public service workers have expanded and increasingly consolidated their collective strength so that in disputes over the scope of public services they have become a substantial independent force in the resolution of controversy affecting their status and position.

Street-level bureaucrats dominate political controversies over public services for two general reasons. First, debates about the proper scope and focus of governmental services are essentially debates over the scope and function of these public employees. Second, street-level bureaucrats have considerable impact on people's lives. This impact may be of several kinds. They socialize citizens to expectations of government services and a place in the political community. They determine the eligibility of citizens for government benefits and sanctions. They oversee the treatment (the service) citizens receive in those programs. Thus, in a sense street-level bureaucrats implicitly mediate aspects of the constitutional relationship of citizens to the state. In short, they hold the key to a dimension of citizenship.

Conflict over the Scope and Substance of Public Services

In the world of experience we perceive teachers, welfare workers, and police officers as members of separately organized and motivated public agencies. And so they are from many points of view. But if we divide public employees according to whether they interact with citizens directly and have discretion over significant aspects of citizens' lives, we see that a high proportion and enormous number of public workers share these job characteristics. They comprise a great portion of all public employees working in domestic affairs. State and local governments employ approximately 3.7 million in local schools, more than 500,000 people in police operations, and over 300,000 people in public welfare. Public school employees represent more than half of all workers employed in local governments. Instructional jobs represent about two-thirds of the educational personnel, and many of the rest are former teachers engaged in administration, or social workers, psychologists, and librarians who provide direct services in the schools. Of the 3.2 million local government public employees not engaged in education, approximately 14 percent work as police officers. One of every sixteen jobs in state and local government outside of education is held by a public welfare worker.[2] In this and other areas the majority of jobs are held by people with responsibility for involvement with citizens.

Other street-level bureaucrats comprise an important part of the remainder of local government personnel rolls. Although the U.S. Census Bureau does not provide breakdowns of other job classifications suitable for our purposes, we can assume that many of the 1.1 million health workers,[3] most of the 5,000 public service lawyers,[4] many of the employees of the various court systems, and other public employees also perform as street-level bureaucrats. Some of the nation's larger cities employ a staggering number of street-level bureaucrats. For example, the 26,680 school teachers in Chicago are more numerous than the populations of many of the Chicago suburbs.[5]

Another measure of the significance of street-level bureaucrats in public sector employment is the amount of public funds allocated to pay them. Of all local government salaries, more than half went to public education in 1973. Almost 80 percent of these monies was used to pay instructional personnel. Police salaries comprised approximately one-sixth of local public salaries not assigned to education.[6]

Much of the growth in public employment in the past 25 years has occurred in the ranks of street-level bureaucrats. From 1955 to 1975 government employment more than doubled, largely because the baby boom of the postwar years and the growing number of elderly, dependent citizens increased state and local activity in education, health, and public welfare.[7]

Street-level bureaucracies are labor-intensive in the extreme. Their business is providing service through people, and the operating costs of such agencies reflect their dependence upon salaried workers. Thus most of whatever is spent by government on education, police, or other social services (aside, of course, from income maintenance, or in the case of jails and prisons, inmate upkeep) goes directly to pay street-level bureaucrats. For example, in large cities over 90 percent of police expenditures is used to pay for salaries.[8]

Not only do the salaries of street-level bureaucrats constitute a major portion of the cost of public services, but also the scope of public services employing street-level bureaucrats has increased over time. Charity was once the responsibility of private agencies. The federal government now provides for the income needs of the poor. The public sector has absorbed responsibilities previously discharged by private organizations in such diverse and critical areas as policing, education, and health. Moreover, in all these fields government not only has supplanted private organizations but also has expanded the scope of responsibility of public ones. This is evident in increased public expectations for security and public safety, the extension of responsibilities in the schools to concerns with infant as well as post-adolescent development, and public demands for affordable health care services.[9]

Public safety, public health, and public education *may* still be elusive social objectives, but in the past century they have been transformed into areas for which there is active governmental responsibility. The transformation of public responsibility in the area of social welfare has led some to recognize that what people "have" in modern American society often may consist primarily of their claims on government "largesse," and that claims to this "new property" should be protected as a right of citizens.[10] Street-level bureaucrats play a critical role in these citizen entitlements. Either they directly provide public benefits through services, or they mediate between citizens and their new but by no means secure estates.

The poorer people are, the greater the influence street-level bureaucrats tend to have over them. Indeed, these public workers are so situated that they may well be taken to be part of the problem of being poor. Consider the welfare recipient who lives in public housing and seeks the assistance of a legal services lawyer in order to reinstate her son in school. He has been suspended because of frequent encounters with the police. She is caught in a net of street-level bureaucrats with conflicting orientations toward her, all acting in what they call her "interest" and "the public interest."[11]

People who are not able to purchase services in the private sector must seek them from government if they are to receive them at all. Indeed, it is taken as a sign of social progress that poor people are granted access to services if they are too poor to pay for them.

Thus, when social reformers seek to ameliorate the problems of the poor, they often end up discussing the status of street-level bureaucrats. Welfare reformers move to separate service provision from decisions about support payments, or they design a negative income tax system that would eliminate social workers in allocating welfare. Problems of backlog in the courts are met with proposals to increase the number of judges. Recognition that early-childhood development largely established the potential for later achievement results in the development of new programs (such as Head Start) in and out of established institutions, to provide enriched early-childhood experiences.

In the 1960s and early 1970s the modal governmental response to social problems was to commission a corps of street-level bureaucrats to attend to them. Are poor people deprived of equal access to the courts? Provide them with lawyers. Equal access to health care? Establish neighborhood clinics. Educational opportunity? Develop preschool enrichment programs. It is far easier and less disruptive to develop employment for street-level bureaucrats than to reduce income inequalities.

In recent years public employees have benefited considerably from the growth of public spending on street-level bureaucracies.[12] Salaries have increased from inadequate to respectable and even desirable. Meanwhile, public employees, with street-level bureaucrats in the lead, have secured unprecedented control over their work environments through the development of unions and union-like associations.[13] For example, teachers and other instructional personnel have often been able to maintain their positions and even increase in number, although schools are more frequently under attack for their cost to taxpayers. The ratio of instructional personnel in schools has continued to rise despite the decline in the number of school-age children.[14] This development supplements general public support for the view that some street-level bureaucrats, such as teachers and police officers, are necessary for a healthy society.[15]

The fiscal crisis that has affected many cities, notably New York and more recently Cleveland and Newark, has provided an opportunity to assess the capacity of public service workers to hold onto their jobs in the face of enormous pressures. Since so much of municipal budgets consists of inflexible, mandated costs—for debt service, pension plans and other personnel benefits, contractually obligated salary increases, capital expenditure commitments, energy purchases, and so on—the place to find "fat" to eliminate from municipal budgets is in the service sector, where most expenditures tend to be for salaries. While many public employees have been fired during this crisis period, it is significant that public service workers often have been able to lobby, bargain, and cajole to minimize this attrition.[16] They are supported in their claims by a public fearful of a reduced police force on the street and resentful of dirtier streets resulting from fewer garbage pickups. They are supported by families whose children will receive less instruction from fewer specialists than in the past if teachers are fired. And it does not hurt their arguments that many public employees and their relatives vote in the city considering force reductions.[17]

The growth of the service sector represents the furthest reaches of the welfare state. The service sector penetrates every area of human needs as they are recognized and defined, and it grows within each recognized area. This is not to say that the need is met, but only that the service state breaches the barriers between public responsibility and private affairs.

The fiscal crisis of the cities focuses on the service sector, fundamentally challenging the priorities of the service state under current perceptions of scarcity. Liberals have now joined fiscal conservatives in challenging service provision. They do not do so directly, by questioning whether public services and responsibilities developed in this century are appropriate. Instead, they do it backhandedly, arguing that the accretion of public employees and their apparently irreversible demands upon revenues threaten the autonomy, flexibility, and prosperity of the political order. Debates over the proper scope of services face the threat of being overwhelmed by challenges to the entire social service structure as seen from the perspective of unbalanced public budgets.

Conflict over Interactions with Citizens

I have argued that street-level bureaucrats engender controversy because they must be dealt with if policy is to change. A second reason street-level bureaucrats tend to be the focus of public controversy is the immediacy of their interactions with citizens and their impact on people's lives. The policy delivered by street-level bureaucrats is most often immediate and personal. They usually make decisions on the spot (although sometimes they try not to) and their determinations are focused entirely on the individual. In contrast, an urban renewal program might destroy a neighborhood and replace and substitute new housing and different people, but the policy was prolonged, had many different stages, and was usually played out in arenas far removed from the daily life of neighborhood residents.

The decisions of street-level bureaucrats tend to be redistributive as well as allocative. By determining eligibility for benefits they enhance the claims of some citizens to governmental goods and services at the expense of general taxpayers and those whose claims are denied. By increasing or decreasing benefits availability to low-income recipient populations they implicitly regulate the degree of redistribution that will be paid for by more affluent sectors.

In another sense, in delivery policy street-level bureaucrats make decisions about people that affect their life chances. To designate or treat someone as a welfare recipient, a juvenile delinquent, or a high achiever affects the relationships of others to that person and also affects the person's self-evaluation. Thus begins (or continues) the social process that we infer accounts for so many self-fulfilling prophecies. The child judged to be a juvenile delinquent develops such a self-image and is grouped with other "delinquents," increasing the chances that he or she will adopt the behavior thought to have been incipient in the first place. Children thought by their teacher to be richly endowed in learning ability learn more than peers of equal intelligence who were not thought to be superior.[18] Welfare recipients find or accept housing inferior to those with equal disposable incomes who are not recipients.[19]

A defining facet of the working environment of street-level bureaucrats is that they must deal with clients' personal reactions to their decisions, however they cope with their implications. To say that people's self-evaluation is affected by the actions of street-level bureaucrats is to say that people are reactive to the policy. This is not exclusively confined to subconscious processes. Clients of street-level bureaucracies respond angrily to real or perceived injustices, develop strategies to ingratiate themselves with workers, act grateful and elated or sullen and passive in reaction to street-level bureaucrats' decisions. It is one thing to be treated neglectfully and routinely by the telephone company, the motor vehicle bureau, or other government agencies whose agents know nothing of the personal circumstances surrounding a claim or request. It is quite another thing to be shuffled, categorized, and treated "bureaucratically" (in the pejorative sense), by someone to whom one is directly talking and from whom one expects at least an open and sympathetic hearing. In short, the reality of the work of street-level bureaucrats could hardly be farther from the bureaucratic ideal of impersonal detachment in decision making.[20] On the contrary, in street-level bureaucracies the objects of critical decisions—*people*—actually change as a result of the decisions.

Street-level bureaucrats are also the focus of citizen reactions because their discretion opens up the possibility that they will respond favorably on behalf of people. Their general and diffuse obligation to the "public interest" permits hope to flourish that the individual worker will adopt a benign or favorable orientation toward the client. Thus, in a world of large and impersonal agencies that apparently hold the keys to important benefits, sanctions, and opportunities, the ambiguity of work definitions sustains hope for a friend in court.

This discussion helps explain continued controversy over street-level bureaucracies at the level of individual service provision. At the same time, the peculiar nature of government service delivery through street-level bureaucrats helps explain why street-level bureaucracies are apparently the primary focus of community conflict in the current period, and why they are likely to remain the focus of such conflict in the foreseeable future. It is no accident that the most heated community conflicts since 1964 have focused on schools and police departments, and on the responsiveness of health and welfare agencies and institutions.[21] These are the sites of the provision of public benefits and sanctions. They are the locus of individual decisions about the treatment of citizens, and thus are primary targets of protest. As Frances Fox Piven and Richard Cloward explain:

> . . . people experience deprivation and oppression within a concrete setting, not as the end product of large and abstract processes, and it is the concrete experience that molds their discontent into specific grievances against specific targets. . . . People on relief [for example] experience the shabby waiting rooms, the overseer or caseworker, and the dole. They do not experience American social welfare policy. . . . In other words, it is the daily experience of people that shapes their grievances, establishes the measure of their demands, and points out the targets of their anger.[22]

While people may experience these bureaucracies as individuals, schools, precinct houses, or neighborhood clinics are places where policy about individuals is organized collectively. These administrative arrangements suggest to citizens the possibility that controlling, or at least affecting, their structures will influence the quality of individual treatment. Thus we have two preconditions for successful community organization efforts: the hope and plausibility that individual benefits may accrue to those taking part in group action and a visible, accessible, and blamable, collective target.[23]

Community action focused on street-level bureaucracies is also apparently motivated by concerns for community character. The dominant institutions in communities help shape community identity. They may be responsive to the dominant community group (this has been the traditional role of high schools in Boston) or they may be unresponsive and opposed to conceptions of community and identity favored by residents, as in the case of schools that neglect the Spanish heritage of a significant minority. Whether people are motivated by specific grievances or more diffuse concerns that become directed at community institutions, their focus in protesting the actions of street-level bureaucracies may be attributed to the familiarity of the agency, its critical role in community welfare, and a perception at some level that these institutions are not sufficiently accountable to the people they serve.

Finally, street-level bureaucrats play a critical role in regulating the degree of contemporary conflict by virtue of their role as agents of social control. Citizens who receive public benefits interact with public agents who require certain behaviors of them. They must anticipate the requirements of these public agents and claimants must tailor their actions and develop "suitable" attitudes both toward the services they receive and toward the street-level bureaucrats themselves. Teachers convey and enforce expectations of proper attitudes toward schooling, self, and efficacy in other interactions. Policemen convey expectations about public behavior and authority. Social workers convey expectations about public benefits and the status of recipients.

The social control function of street-level bureaucrats requires comment in a discussion of the place of public service workers in the larger society. The public service sector plays a critical part in softening the impact of the economic system on those who are not its primary beneficiaries and inducing people to accept the neglect or inadequacy of primary economic and social institutions. Police, courts, and prisons obviously play such a role in processing the junkies, petty thieves, muggers, and others whose behavior toward society is associated with their economic position. It is a role equally played by schools in socializing the population to the economic order and the likely opportunities for different strata of the population. Public support and employment programs expand to ameliorate the impact of unemployment or reduce the incidence of discontent; they contract when employment opportunities improve. Moreover, they are designed and implemented to convey the message that welfare status is to be avoided and that work, however poorly rewarded, is preferable to public assistance. One can also see the two edges of public policy in the "war on poverty" where the public benefits of social service and community action invested neighborhood institutions with benefits for which potential dissidents could compete and ordinary citizens could develop dependency.[24]

What to some are the highest reaches of the welfare state are to others the furthest extension of social control. Street-level bureaucrats are partly the focus of controversy because they play this dual role. Welfare reform founders on disagreements over whether to eliminate close scrutiny of welfare applications in order to reduce administrative costs and harassment of recipients, or to increase the scrutiny in the name of controlling abuses and preventing welfare recipients from taking advantage. Juvenile corrections and mental health policy founder on disputes over the desirability of dismantling large institutions in the name of cost effectiveness and rehabilitation, or retaining close supervision in an effort to avoid the costs of letting unreconstructed "deviants" loose. In short, street-level bureaucrats are also at the center of controversy because a divided public perceives that social control in the name of public order and acceptance of the status quo are social objectives with which proposals to reduce the role of street-level bureaucrats (eliminating welfare checkups, reducing parole personnel, decriminalizing marijuana) would interfere.

Public controversy also focuses on the proper kind of social control. Current debates in corrections policy, concerning automatic sentencing and a "hard-nosed" view of punishment or more rehabilitative orientations, reflect conflict over the degree of harshness in managing prison populations. In educational practice the public is also divided as to the advisability of liberal disciplinary policies and more flexible instruction or punitive discipline and more rigid, traditional approaches. The "medicalization" of deviance, in which disruptive behavior is presumed cause for intervention by a doctor rather than a disciplinarian, is another area in which there is controversy over the appropriate kind of social control.

From the citizen's viewpoint, the roles of street-level bureaucrats are as extensive as the functions of government and intensively experienced as daily routines require them to interact with the street ministers of education, dispute settlement, and health services. Collectively, street-level bureaucrats absorb a high share of public resources and become the focus of society's hopes for a healthy balance between provision of public services and a reasonable burden of public expenditures. As individuals, street-level bureaucrats represent the hopes of citizens for fair and effective treatment by government even as they are positioned to see clearly the limitations on effective intervention and the constraints on responsiveness engendered by mass processing.

Notes

1. These definitions are analytical. They focus not on nominal occupational roles but on the characteristics of the particular work situations. Thus not every street-level bureaucrat works for a street-level bureaucracy [for example, a relocation specialist (a type of street-level bureaucrat) may work for an urban renewal agency whose employees are mostly planners, builders, and other

technicians]. Conversely, not all employees of street-level bureaucracies are street-level bureaucrats (for example, file clerks in a welfare department or police officers on routine clerical assignments).

The conception of street-level bureaucracy was originally proposed in "Toward a Theory of Street-Level Bureaucracy," a paper prepared for the Annual Meeting of the American Political Science Association in 1969. It was later revised and published in Willis Hawley and Michael Lipsky, eds., *Theoretical Perspectives on Urban Politics* (Englewood Cliffs, N.J.: Prentice-Hall, 1977), pp. 196–213.

2. U.S. Bureau of the Census, Public Employment in 1973, Series GE 73, no. 1 (Washington, D.C.: Government Printing Office, 1974), p. 9, presented in Alan Baker and Barbara Grouby, "Employment and Payrolls of State and Local Governments, by Function: October 1973," *Municipal Year Book, 1975* (Washington D.C.: International City Managers Association, 1975), pp. 109–112, table 4/3; Marianne Stein Kah, "City Employment and Payrolls: 1975," *Municipal Year Book, 1977* (Washington, D.C.: International City Managers Association, 1977), pp. 173–179. These figures have been adjusted to represent full-time equivalents. For purposes of assessing public commitments to providing services, full-time equivalents are more appropriate statistics than total employment figures, which count many part-time employees.
3. Jeffry H. Galper, *The Politics of Social Services* (Englewood Cliffs, N.J.: Prentice-Hall, 1975), p. 56.
4. Lois Forer, *Death of the Law* (New York: McKay, 1975), p. 191.
5. The *New York Times*, April 4, 1976, p. 22.
6. Baker and Grouby, op. cit.
7. The *New York Times*, July 10, 1977, p. F13.
8. Of four cities with populations over one million responding to a *Municipal Year Book* survey, the proportion of personnel expenditures to total expenditures in police departments averaged 94 percent and did not go beyond 86 percent. Cities with smaller populations showed similar tendencies. These observations are derived from David Lewin, "Expenditure, Compensation, and Employment Data in Police, Fire, and Refuse Collection and Disposal Departments," *Municipal Year Book, 1975*, pp. 39–98, table 1/21. However, the variation was much greater in the less populous cities because of smaller base figures and the fact that when cities with smaller bases make capital investments, the ratio of personnel to total expenditures changes more precipitously.

   That public expenditures for street-level bureaucracies go to individuals primarily as salaries may also be demonstrated in the case of education. For example, more than 73 percent of all non-capital education expenditures inside Standard Metropolitan Statistical Areas goes toward personal services (i.e., salaries). See Government Finances, Number 1, Finances of School Districts, 1972 U.S. Census of Government (Bureau of the Census, Social and Economic Statistics Administration, U.S. Department of Commerce), table 4.
9. Many analysts have discussed the increasing role of services in the economy. See Daniel Bell, *The Coming of the Post-Industrial Society: A Venture in Social Forecasting* (New York: Basic Books, 1973); Alan Gartner and Frank Reissman, *The Service Society and the Consumer Vanguard* (New York: Harper and Row, 1974); Victor Fuchs, *The Service Economy* (New York: Columbia University Press, 1968). On transformations in public welfare, see Gilbert Steiner, *Social Insecurity* (Chicago: Rand McNally, 1966), chap. 1; on public safety, see Allan Silver, "The Demand for Order in Civil Society," in *The Police: Six Sociological Essays*, ed. David Bordua (New York: John Wiley, 1967), pp. 1–24.
10. Charles Reich, "The New Property," *Yale Law Journal* 72 (April 1964): 733–787.
11. Carl Hosticka, "Legal Services Lawyers Encounter Clients: A Study in Street-Level Bureaucracy" (Ph.D. diss., Massachusetts Institute of Technology, 1976), pp. 11–13.
12. See Frances Piven's convincing essay in which she argues that social service workers were the major beneficiaries of federal programs concerned with cities and poor people in the 1960s. Piven, "The Urban Crisis: Who Got What and Why," in Richard Cloward and Piven, *The Politics of Turmoil* (New York: Vintage Books, 1972), pp. 314–351.

13. J. Joseph Loewenberg and Michael H. Moskow, eds., *Collective Bargaining in Government* (Englewood Cliffs, N.J.: Prentice-Hall, 1972); A. Laurence Chickering, ed., *Public Employee Unions* (Lexington, Mass.: Lexington Books, 1976); Margaret Levi, *Bureaucratic Insurgency* (Lexington, Mass.: Lexington Books, 1977).
14. The decline is a function of the lower birthrate and periodicity in the size of the school-age population originally resulting from the birth explosion following World War II. See Baker and Grouby, op. cit., p. 109 ff., on serviceability ratios.
15. This perspective remains applicable in the current period. However, in reaction to this tendency, programs that would eliminate service mediators and service providers, such as negative income taxation and housing allowances, have gained support. Fiscal scarcity has brought to public attention questions concerning the marginal utility of some of these service areas.
16. Consider the New York City policemen who, in October 1976, agreed to work overtime without pay so that a crop of rookie patrolmen would not be eliminated (The *New York Times,* October 24, 1976, p. 24).
17. There can be no better illustration of the strength of the organized service workers and their support by relevant interests than the New York State Assembly's overriding of Gov. Hugh Carey's veto of the so-called Stavisky bill. This legislation, written in a period of massive concern for cutting the New York City budget, required the city to spend no less on education in the three years following the fiscal collapse than in the three years before the crisis, thus tying the hands of the city's financial managers even more (The *New York Times,* April 4, 1976, p. E6; ibid., April 18, 1976, p. E6).
18. The seminal work here is Robert Rosenthal and Lenore Jacobson, *Pygmalion in the Classroom* (New York: Holt, Rinehart and Winston, 1968).
19. Martin Rein, "Welfare and Housing," Joint Center Working Paper Series, no. 4 (Cambridge Mass.: Joint Center for Urban Studies, spring 1971, rev. Feb. 1972).
20. On the alleged importance of bureaucratic detachment in processing clients see Peter Blau, *Exchange and Power in Social Life* (New York: John Wiley, 1964), p. 66.
21. See National Advisory Commission on Civil Disorders, *Report* (New York: Bantam, 1968); Peter Rossi et al., *Roots of Urban Discontent* (New York: John Wiley, 1974).
22. Frances Fox Piven and Richard Cloward, *Poor People's Movements* (New York: Pantheon, 1977), pp. 20–21.
23. Michael Lipsky and Margaret Levi, "Community Organization as a Political Resource," in *People and Places in Urban Society,* ed. Harlan Hahn, Urban Affairs Annual Review, vol. 6 (Newbury Park, Calif.: Sage Publications, 1972), pp. 175–199.
24. See James O'Connor's discussion of "legitimation" and his general thesis concerning the role of the state service sector, in O'Connor, *The Fiscal Crisis of the State* (New York: St. Martin's, 1973). On social control functions in particular policy sectors see Samuel Bowles and Herbert Gintis, *Schooling in Capitalist America* (New York: Basic Books, 1976); Frances Fox Piven and Richard Cloward, *Regulating the Poor* (New York: Pantheon, 1971); Galper, op. cit.; Richard Quinney, *Criminology* (Boston: Little, Brown, 1975); Ira Katznelson, "Urban Counterrevolution," in *1984 Revisited,* ed. Robert P. Wolff (New York: Alfred Knopf, 1973), pp. 139–164.

34

Public Budgeting Amidst Uncertainty and Instability

Naomi Caiden

The world of budgeting which we had grown to know well in the past fifty years, since the advent of the Keynesian revolution in public economics and the rapid expansion of the administrative state, is fast being disoriented by new and unexpected events. Familiar landmarks are being obliterated. The rules of the budgeting game are rapidly changing, and many public authorities are in danger of losing their way unless they adjust to the new context. The credibility of secure public financing which has for so long been taken for granted is at stake. Certainty and stability are giving way to uncertainty and instability.

Budgeting processes may be said to thrive on stability. Since budgeting is concerned with making financial provision for future activities, it depends on accurate prediction of the amount of revenues available and of the cost of expenditures. In its more sophisticated forms, it demands knowledge of future output or achievement related to given resources, preferably over a long period of time. Budgeting works best where year-to-year adjustments are marginal, where it is possible to make firm commitments in advance of expenditures, where the recent past is a good guide to the immediate future, and where results may be easily and promptly evaluated.

Classical budget theory tried to keep uncertainties within bounds through insistence on annual budgets (foreshortening the time period), budget unity (keeping all expenditures under a single control), strict appropriation (preventing unauthorized changes), and timely audit (checking past performance). The budget process in itself brought a measure of stability and predictability previously lacking in state finance, but its efforts to impose order could never entirely make the world according to its own rules or exclude all uncertainties. Budgeters have traditionally guarded against surprises by such informal strategies as underestimating revenues and overestimating costs of expenditures, and limiting spending in the first part of the year. Policies of incrementalism, or regular additions to the budget base, have also helped to accommodate change and increase predictability from year to year. Generally buoyant revenues for many jurisdictions have provided a measure of redundancy, cushioning uncertainties, and allowing for flexibility and correction of errors.

Now the traditional means of coping with uncertainty appear inadequate, while the uncertainties themselves are multiplying to an unprecedented extent. The symptoms are marked. The value of the American dollar has been declining for nearly two decades and no relief is in sight. State and local governments are increasingly dependent on federal subventions without which many would face bankruptcy; already several have had to be rescued from the brink. Growing resistance to rising public expenditures and taxes is being translated into expenditure ceilings and tax revolts. Public authorities cannot predict from one year to the next what they will have to spend and where they will find the money. They still cannot prove convincingly that they spend money wisely and that the public receives value from public expenditures.

The task of public budgeting has become infinitely more complex, complicated and worrisome. Current budget theory and practice lag behind operational requirements. A new agenda is urgently needed to bridge the gap and provide better instruments to cope with uncertainty and instability. Its items should avoid rehashing traditional proposals that fail to reflect the changing environment of public budgeting.

Source: "Public Budgeting Amidst Uncertainty and Instability" by Naomi Caiden from PUBLIC BUDGETING & FINANCE (Spring 1981), pp. 409–419. Reprinted by permission of Blackwell Publishing Ltd.

The Changing Environment of Budgeting

For a long time, it was believed that the major challenges in public budgeting had been met and that all that remained was some tinkering around with the form of the budget to match inputs and outputs, costs and benefits, resources and results. Public needs were conceived as finite and public resources infinite. The ability of governments to raise revenues and manage large expenditures was accepted as a matter of course. Given modern techniques of taxation and borrowing, the amounts of money that could be generated seemed virtually limitless, while social problems seemed amenable to solution through the mechanisms of the administrative state. It is now quite apparent that the administrative state often merely encourages new public demands, without ensuring that effective use is made of public resources at its disposal or dispelling resentment of taxation. We now have to work on a different assumption, namely, that public resources are finite and public needs infinite.

The ability of public authorities to raise any given level of revenues without serious resistance can no longer be taken for granted. Historically, the ability to tax on a substantial scale has been a function of industrialization and democratization. It has depended on maintaining a high level of economic activity and retaining public confidence in an efficient, effective and accountable public administration capable of delivering quality public goods and services. Lately, concern about the amount of equity of taxation, fears that the public sector is reaching its limits in a mixed economy, and mistrust of proliferating public bureaucracy indicate that the era of expanding public revenues may be coming to a close. Inflation temporarily obscures the longer-term effects of greater financial pressures on taxpayers, demands for tax relief and a decline in the real value of tax receipts relative to the costs of expected services. All these make rising real revenues more problematical, particularly if taxpayers succumb under inflationary pressure to temptations to avoid or evade paying taxes, and more people join the underground economy beyond the reach of government control and taxation.

If these complications were not enough, a dramatic new factor has arisen to affect governmental capacity to raise revenues, namely, numerous public initiatives to restrict revenues and/or expenditures constitutionally. They immediately impact on expected fund levels because of speculation whether they will pass and their unpredictable effects. Administrators have to prepare several budgets to meet different possible outcomes. Even without formal limitations, politicians, responding to what they believe is the mood of the public, put tax relief and lower budgets near the top of their priorities, restricting expenditure growth to the rate of inflation or below.

In contrast, demands for public goods and services do not abate. They can be expected to rise in the future. America's aging population will entail large increases in social expenditures on the elderly just when the labor force will decline. Hopes that poverty would be susceptible to a one-time solution have given way to somber realization that it is a structural problem that will take generations to resolve. Burgeoning technology requires heavy public investment in research and development and increasing public expenditures on safety measures and environmental protection. The hardening habit of turning to the administrative state to fulfill needs unmet by the market system is creating new legal rights. Consequently, in many areas of public administration, such as health, education, social welfare, urban renewal, crime control and consumer protection, there is no clearly defined and acceptable level of public expenditure. Money can be poured indefinitely into defense, environmental protection, police, schools, hospitals, job retraining and recreation facilities. They are all open-ended expenditures in the sense that there is no limit to the potential amount of public funds which may be devoted to improving them.

More and more public administrators find themselves working in conditions of fiscal stress in which they must try to accomplish unlimited goals with fewer real resources. It is increasingly difficult for them to provide for contingencies through disguised surpluses and reserves, or compensate for mistakes and faulty judgment, or spread resources to satisfy as many parties as possible. They cannot avoid hard choices any longer. Already they find it harder to forecast revenues and costs, and their budget plans are upset by economic problems. With potential resource levels more variable and objectives more complex, past experience is less relevant in budgeting. Meantime competition for resources intensifies among pressure groups, levels of government and public agencies. Alignments disintegrate, shift and reform with baffling fluidity. The budget game is being played with more conflict and the rules are giving way under the strain. It becomes more difficult to agree on and stick to budgets.

When the environment becomes increasingly uncertain and more stringent, budgets are more complex, more difficult to control and less predictable. Revenue uncertainties promote multiple budgets and dysfunctional tactics by administrators protecting themselves. As programs have to be undertaken and maintained without guarantee of funding until the last minute, administrators have to take countervailing protective action. They seek out new revenue resources, switch expenditures between categories, pad estimates, cut essential items to favor others knowing that cuts will have to be made up later, and engage in a whole host of ploys familiar to students of budgetary politics. Unfortunately in trying to create more certainty for themselves, they probably compound uncertainty for everybody else as the general pool diminishes and information becomes increasingly suspect.

Imbalances of resources and responsibilities at different government levels vastly complicate the intergovernmental system and make it virtually impossible to track funding through the maze. Once a fairly clear-cut stratification of types of government matched to specific functions, the intergovernmental system has become an inextricable jumble of interdependent responsibilities and finances. Budgets at all levels now reflect a complex maze of intergov-ern-mental grants, subsidies and reimbursements designed for different purposes and disbursed according to different criteria and formulae. It is hard to discover just what is being spent and by whom on any particular function. Further, because many intergovernmental programs are funded conditionally or subject to frequent renewal, continued funding is not assured. Recipients have to deal with the red tape engendered by efforts of donors to target funds to areas of greatest need and to ensure that funds are used effectively and for the purposes for which they are intended. Meantime, the donors discover that existing techniques are inadequate to prevent seepage and that their intelligence is soon overtaken by events. To discipline apparently "uncontrollable" budgets, they devise new and increasingly sophisticated methods which further compound complexity and uncertainty in formulating and carrying through budget policies.

The injection of new values such as forward planning, participation, formal program evaluation, prioritizing and zero base considerations into the budget process has enormously complicated the life of budget formulators. Budget documents have expanded from single binders to sets of volumes occupying several feet in shelving. Participation has added to the number of steps and pairs of hands through which a budget must travel.

Technical innovations entail conversations from one system of budgeting and accounting to another, and then back again. With integrated budgeting systems, a change in one figure requires wholesale alterations across the board. To meet requirements of formal planning and lengthier budget processes, the lead time of federal budgets has been extended two years or more in advance of the budget year. Budget formulators find they have to work on three future budgets at once, using information that is bound to be outdated before they finish.

Even when the budget has been passed, uncertainties continue to plague implementation and execution. In the past we could assume that once a budget document had been approved, expenditures would follow the printed figures. A routine audit at year's end would ensure correspondence of purpose and expenditure. In a turbulent environment, the predictions of an annual budget cannot keep pace. Transfers of appropriations between categories have considerably increased and are now routine in some agencies. Spending toward the end of the budget year is common as agencies hold on to money at the beginning, fearing later overruns, or financial management authorities refuse to release it or agencies overestimate and then panic in fear of cuts the following year. Thus even the agencies themselves find it more difficult to track expenditures, to know what is spent and to control funds. The growth of intergovernmental disbursements, multi-pocket budgeting, contracting and third party payments poses major problems for control.[1]

It should hardly surprise that budget formulators and financial managers should evince a mood of doubt and pessimism. Even in the best of times, they have come to realize that a substantial portion of governmental budgets is uncontrollable, or that is what budget experts tell them.[2] But they have been thrown off balance by the disappearance of certainty and stability. They do not have adequate hard data on which to base realistic forecasts of revenues and expenditures. They do not have clear benchmarks for expenditure categories. They can barely link the achievement of social objectives with the public money spent on them. Problems of control and tracking expenditures in a complex budgeting system create new opportunities for fraud, abuse, waste, extravagance and corruption. Yet they are mindful that many proposals now being made to remedy the situation may actually aggravate it further. They are challenging traditional theories which have structured our ways of looking at budgeting and produced these suspect solutions, because they feel that they are not the only ones overtaken by current events.

The Quest for Budget Reform

Even before budgeting concepts were upset by recent events, budgeting was the focus for reform efforts. Although traditional budgeting was acceptable, it suffered several defects that advocates of PPB and ZBB were quick to point out. In any event, it has always been a target for reformers. Budget management is an activity in which all governments must engage, for in a money economy it is the crucial element in carrying out public policies. The budget represents the outcome of competition for political power. As success is having one's claims written into the budget, the structure and process of budgeting must concern any interest group attempting to influence governmental policy. Further, budgets are also major weapons for controlling governments. After all, the wresting of financial power from arbitrary rulers was a key constitutional issue in the evolution of representative governmental institutions.

As a result of all this interest in budgeting, there now exists an impressive array of budget reforms that cover:

1. The mobilization of resources for public use and employment;
2. The consolidation and control of available resources to prevent seepage and monitor their location at all times;
3. The allocation of resources among competing demands;
4. The prompt and economic disbursement of public funds;
5. The improvement of skillful and proficient financial management;
6. The institutionalization of honest, open and careful accounting practices;
7. The establishment of independent audit; and
8. The scientific evaluation of public expenditures and projects.

Many have been incorporated successfully into practice with impressive results. Others are being tried out with more variable success. Cost benefit analysis, for example, is still in its infancy. Performance auditing is proving fertile ground for budget innovations. Too much attention has been focused on the novelties, such as PPB and ZBB, which are only a small portion of current contemporary efforts to improve budgeting.

Many budget experiments disclose a distressing gap between theory and practice. As with other administrative reforms, it is difficult to convince conservative administrators to try something different and to get them to persist with new ways of doing things when they hanker after the old with which they were comfortable no matter what the evidence shows. They cherish the hallowed principles of accountability—annuality, unity, appropriation, balance and audit—even though they are observed in the breach as governments grow. In the massive budgets of contemporary national government detailed accountability to the public or the public's representatives is largely a fiction. Even leaving aside hidden accounting for secret intelligence agencies and other politically sensitive areas, budgets are too complex for ready understanding. Off-budget trust funds and multi-year appropriations create large uncontrollable accounts which infringe annuality and budget unity. Balancing the budget has virtually been abandoned in practice, given consistent deficits at the federal level and the extensive use of capital budgeting and borrowing powers of special districts by public authorities at state and local levels. Similarly, external auditing has given way to internal checks. Yet public administrators continue to pay lip service to principles on which they no longer operate. They are reluctant to replace them with principles that better suit the new reality.

This reluctance has been partially responsible for recent failures to gain acceptance for more sophisticated techniques designed to accomplish efficiency, rationality and planning in the budget process. The most elaborate effort along these lines, program budgeting or PPB, has been largely abandoned at the federal level. Its successor, zero base budgeting or ZBB, is fading from the scene. Accumulating evidence suggests that its effectiveness in influencing decision making and outcomes is in doubt.[3] The history of these new budget concepts has been told too many times to bear recounting here.[4] Suffice it to say that the great expectations raised by across-the-board changes in budgeting methods have been punctured, leaving behind a skeptical mood in the face of an intractable budget situation seemingly beyond control.

The failure of such budget reforms cannot be attributed to lack of willingness to experiment, or lack of appreciation of what the reforms were supposed to achieve, or sheer obstinacy by smug, complacent bureaucrats too set in their ways to try something new. Reviewing the welter of specific circumstances which may have defeated these particular reforms, some major reservations can be drawn. One is that the whole notion of budget reform may be misconceived and doomed to failure. A second is that budgeting goals have been misunderstood and that reform has over-concentrated on form without considering that ultimate goals may be unattainable or in conflict. A third is that budget systems are intrinsically fragile and cumulative reform cannot be expected. Finally, reformers pay insufficient attention to the environment in which budgeting, conceived as a purely technical process, is conducted. If the mistakes of the past are to be avoided in coping with uncertainty in public budgeting, these reservations should be carefully considered.

Budget Reform Is Misconceived Budget reform has often been conceived as the rationalization of budget outcomes through the incorporation of programming and planning techniques and restructuring of budget processes. Emphasis has been placed on formal determination of objectives, evaluation of alternatives and authorization of programs on the basis of systematic analysis. The aim of budgeting is seen as the maximization of societal return from public expenditures.

Budgets may also be seen somewhat differently as a reflection of politics.[5] Budgets are put together by political and bureaucratic actors pursuing their own strategies and reacting to their perceptions of public needs and priorities. The process follows certain rules, expressed formally in regulations but more importantly in informal practices, the foremost of which has been incrementalism, that is, basing each budget on that of the previous year with regular, limited additions. Incrementalism describes both decision processes and outcomes. If budgeting is politics in the raw, its forms reflect current political realities and enable political processes, such as competition bargaining, accommodation and compromise, to work.

These two views are often juxtaposed. Procedural rationality is contrasted with incrementalism and political dynamics. Reforms of techniques and processes, it is alleged, will inevitably be undermined by the rationale of politics and bureaucratic behavior. Moreover, it is asserted that budget reform represents an improper dictation of policies and purposes of government which should be the prerogative of democratic politics. Budget reform might therefore be regarded not only as foredoomed to failure, but in some measure as illegitimate.

Such a sharp dichotomy is misleading. There is no reason why improved budget techniques should not inform, clarify and strengthen political financial decision making. Similarly, a rationality which takes no account of political conditions or subordinates the practicality of budget outcomes to formal processes is not really rational at all. But successful budget reform has to elucidate its aims over and beyond incorporation of techniques and processes. It must also heed the political climate and take into account the inertia and rationale of existing budget methods.

Process Subordinates Substance Budget reformers seem to believe that behavior follows form since they concentrate so much on the formal processes of budgeting and rarely deal with budgeting behavior. The trouble with this view is that new procedures may simply be subverted by old ways instead of mandating real changes in decision-making behavior. Reforms are formally instituted but the old ways continue in practice. Further, alterations in the formal processes may miss the real aim of budget reform which is a change in budget allocations. Process reforms, such as PPB and ZBB, are only intermediate steps. Through them, it is hoped to incorporate certain values (rationality, planning, prioritizing) into budgetary decision making. Unfortunately, in the effort to get the formal processes right the values are subordinated. Should good budgetary decision making be judged by the process by which it is arrived at or by the substantive outcomes? Even if process goals are conceded, they may be inconsistent. For example, the continuity and predictability required for planning may clash with the need for management flexibility.[6]

Reforms Are Not Cumulative Reformers appear to believe that new reforms build on earlier ones. Reform resembles a path marked with regular signposts which indicate the right direction and the progress so far made toward it. Reforms once accomplished, stay accomplished. Unfortunately, this is not so. The path requires constant repair and maintenance. We cannot assume, for instance, that once we have learned how to structure budget systems for control purposes that control in practice is an accomplished fact which requires no further attention. Circumstances may so change that older methods for maintaining control or management efficiency no longer suffice. The very introduction of new methods cannot be achieved without changing existing emphases or outcomes. Budgeting is a dynamic process depending as much on habits of thought and mutual expectations as on formal regulations. Budget institutions are built on trust, probity and a spirit of public service and guardianship of the public purse, none of which can be legislated. These qualities are not constant. They change according to popular morality, perceptions of public role, institutional reactions to external pressures, and a host of other imprecise and poorly understood factors. In short, budget processes cannot be conceived as a set of fixed techniques which remain in place irrespective of what is happening around them. Constant monitoring and reevaluation is needed to ensure that well-tried methods are still appropriate for reaching desired ends.

Reforms Are Not Universal Because budgeting is such a pervasive activity of governments, reformers have readily assumed that a single set of prescriptions applies in all circumstances. Reform failures have been blamed on faulty implementation. Little attention has been paid to contextual supports of budget systems. For instance, the part played by complex redundancy in the smooth working of budgeting in rich countries has been inadequately appreciated. Such redundancy provides greater reliability, allows for looser estimating and calculation, and increases the number of current and future options. Now that such redundancy is diminishing and cannot cushion an increasingly uncertain budgeting environment, public authorities in rich countries are beginning to experience problems similar to those of their counterparts in poor countries.[7] Budgets disappear as earmarked funds and special authorities are established to gain and hold revenues. Cash flow management in the form of repetitive budgeting or preauditing of expenditures replaces the regular budgeted flow of funds. In the frenzied scramble for funds, the apparently neutral and universal stipulations of budgetary technology fail to work. Successful budgeting techniques seem to depend as much on their environment as on their own internal perfection.

We have not inherited an encouraging legacy to help us with current budget problems. So-called rationalists and incrementalists are locked in combat. Significant reform failures have brought disillusion, cynicism and exhaustion. Practitioners are suspicious of innovative budget theorists. The immediate outlook is not promising. But the dawning realization that there is no quick fix through mechanical changes may enhance receptivity to a more realistic agenda for public budgeting and aid adaptation to uncertainty and instability.

Coping with Uncertainty and Instability

Clearly budgeting should move beyond sterile exercises in the application of techniques. Budgeting should be seen again as an integral part of a complex learning process through which public administrators come to understand the constraints and opportunities of their environment. When contemporary budgeting systems emerged in the early nineteenth century with the advent of the administrative state, they were seen by their progenitors as instruments both of control and choice. Before then, governments had been at the mercy of their financial environments. They had little control or choice over methods. Their finances were a jumble of indiscriminate taxes levied opportunistically, a maze of debts, and a variety of mind-boggling expedients. All the elements of modern budgeting—forecasting, planning, balancing revenues and expenditures, calculation of tax burdens or worth of expenditures—were missing.

As government administration became accountable to elected legislatures, the annual budget became an instrument of deliberate choice. Expenditures were forecast and provided for by revenue measures. Taxes were levied according to criteria of relative yield and equity. Through the budget, public finance became a matter for public debate, and gradually by experience the limits and possibilities of public revenues and expenditures came to be appreciated. Such knowledge was never exact; errors and misjudgments were made. But there was confidence that the public budget was an effective tool manipulable in the public interest. Such confidence is lacking today.

Nevertheless budget officials have to cope with the effects of these uncertainties in carrying out their functions. The following list of some of these uncertainties and possible ways of dealing with them may be of some aid. At this point suggestions are necessarily generalized; they represent areas to which attention should be directed, not a set of solutions for all times and places. Their development or application would require further research diagnosis, discussion and cooperation on the part of those concerned.

1. Uncertainties Arising from Novelty
A major source of uncertainty in budgeting today is the feeling that we are coping with unique and unprecedented problems. The future is unclear and policy choices have to be made without benefit of previous experience. Hence a persistent casting around for novel solutions.

This preoccupation with the novel may be exaggerated, particularly in the area of budgeting where knowledge of how other budget systems work is often fragmentary. Systematic studies among several jurisdictions are a rarity.[8] This valuable tool for research has been neglected. Yet if we want to learn about what works in budgeting and what doesn't, it is indispensable and preferable to constructing systems a priori and imposing them in blanket fashion irrespective of circumstances. The comparative approach, marred in the past by collections of descriptions of formal budget processes from exotic places, broadens the learning experience by focusing on how finance officials deal with their problems and reviewing their diverse experiences to discover apposite lessons of wider applicability. There is no need to travel far to do this. Cities, counties, states and government corporations can pool ideas and learn from one another. A wealth of historical evidence waits to be tapped. It should provide valuable insights into the relationship between changes in formal structures and budgeting behavior and outcomes, and between environmental changes and budget processes. Analysis should not be confined solely to the public sector, for valuable lessons can also be obtained from comparing private and public practices. For example, public administrators can study the possibilities of applying such concepts as flow of funds, opportunity costs in capital budgeting, and accounting indicators of future financial problems. By studying environments other than their own, budget theorists and practitioners may find similarities to their own experiences and be encouraged to innovate and experiment.

2. Uncertainties Arising from an Annual Perspective Financing the activities of governments is continuous process, which budgeting fits into an annual framework for purposes of accountability, assessment of past and future expenditures and orderly provision of funding and fiscal policy. Annual budgeting brings greater certainty to government financing by imposing periodic check and review upon transactions, ensuring appropriation of funds in advance of obligations, and allowing comprehensive oversight of the financial position.

But precisely because annual budgeting uses a static framework to control a continuous and dynamic flow of activities, it may become a source of uncertainty. Where, as is commonly the case today, programs extend beyond a single year, the annual period of accounting and review is too short. Such programs require stable long-term commitment of funds so that persons, agencies and authorities depending on them can plan ahead in the knowledge that the end of each budget year will not bring about a sudden cut-off in funds.

In practice provision is made to deal with programs which extend beyond a single year through setting up entitlements, multi-year authorizations and permanent appropriations. But these practices create a different kind of uncertainty relating to control of programs for which provision has already been made in advance of the annual budget. These form an "uncontrollable" budget, which lies outside the discretion of legislators formally responsible for deciding annual allocations of funds.

This uneasy dilemma between the uncertainties of commitment and control[9] arises from reliance on an annual framework to impose accountability where the majority of government programs extend over a number of years. The appropriateness of repetitive annual budgeting in such cases seems open to question. It is possible that adoption of differential time spans for program review according to need may be a more realistic response to this problem. Such periodic appropriations and reviews might allow greater concentration on fewer areas, different kinds of scrutiny over the life of a program and better monitoring of program progress and effectiveness.[10]

3. Uncertainties Arising from Problems in Forecasting The literature on budgeting often gives the misleading impression that once a budget has received assent according to due process, there is nothing more to be discussed. The grand debates about budgeting are concerned mainly with how budget totals are arrived at, not with what happens to them after that. But in a fast changing environment and high inflation, forecasts of costs and revenues become more difficult. At the beginning of the year, it is harder to envisage the financial position at the end. Increasingly budget allocations require readjustment during the year. Programs which have been underestimated may run out of money and require supplementary appropriations. Alternatively where attempts have been made to do too much too quickly, unrealistic overallocations to popular programs may result in underspending and large balances at the end of the year. The changed nature of government outlays no longer fits into an even and regular apportionment schedule.[11] Irregular disbursements, frequent adjustments, under or over spending in various categories, all represent divergences from initial budgetary intentions and may involve serious inefficiencies in the use of public funds. The initial allocation of funds through the annual budget process can no longer be relied upon to ensure that spending will be exactly in accordance with its mandates.

The implementation phase of the budget should not be ignored. The annual budget can no longer be expected to last in unaltered form for a whole year. It is therefore essential that serious consideration be given to planning budget implementation processes, reviewing how officials work with budgets during the year, the arrangements made for ensuring cash flow at critical periods, self-pacing disbursement schedules and incentives for compliance with budget mandates.

4. Uncertainties Arising from Centralization and Bureaucratic Controls One of the major changes in budgeting in recent years is that few budgets are made in isolation. Local governments in particular have become heavily dependent on resources distributed by other levels of government. Federal agencies increasingly find themselves in a donor role, while state governments are sometimes donors and sometimes recipients. This financial interdependence has been productive of a number of new uncertainties. Recipient governments have suffered loss of control over their budgets where financial transfers are channeled into ear-marked funds beyond local decision making, though they may have ramifications on other local government activities. They also suffer from uncertainties of commitment where donor governments hold up transfers for one reason or another, or will not commit funds for more than a limited period. Donor governments for their part have trouble determining eligibility requirements or need for aid, and also in tracking the use and effectiveness of indirect outlays.

The response to these uncertainties by donor governments has generally been toward increased bureaucratic control, which has been regarded as the lynchpin of financial accountability. But particularly in the case of intergovernmental financial relations, bureaucratic controls have become increasingly hard to administer, and often seem counterproductive. The redoubling of efforts at control and integration increases red tape and makes information more difficult to obtain and interpret. It may be that this approach is misconceived. Now that accounting techniques and computerized operations offer new possibilities for comparing, tracking and assessing expenditures, it may be feasible to achieve greater decentralization as well as more effective accountability by means other than centralized controls.

5. Uncertainties Arising from Size and Complexity The explosive growth in size and complexity of government budgets in recent years is an obvious source of uncertainty. Both bureaucratic and legislative oversight become more difficult because of the sheer volume of transactions involved. Efforts to maintain independence from budget discipline have created a tendency to separate budgets and accounts which conceal more than they reveal.

In several jurisdictions considerable effort has gone into simplifying presentations and processes for purposes of clarification, and also into bringing all relevant accounts into the budget. Special analyses, and special budgets to deal with fringe areas such as regulatory costs and tax expenditures, have been undertaken or suggested. Legislative research efforts and new legislative procedures have provided more information and a sharper focus for legislators. Yet size and complexity often obfuscate, and simplification should remain on the agenda. The need is particularly urgent in view of growing attempts to boost program staff participation in the budget process. If these financial amateurs are to understand what they are doing, procedures should be designed for maximum clarity and precision.

6. Uncertainties Arising from Erosion of Accountability A major problem undermining public confidence in government is the difficulty in ensuring that public money is spent wisely and efficiently. The vogue for public expenditure controls is an indication of this unease. But these may prove a blunt instrument for achieving official responsibility in handling public resources. They penalize both good and bad areas alike, and the avoidance techniques they encourage may actually make for worse decision making. Yet if legitimate public purposes are to be fulfilled, it is essential that steps be taken to ensure that the public feels that it is getting its money's worth.

It is imperative to examine government budgets to determine what has been achieved for given revenue outlays. We need to find out the total amounts which have been spent on various government functions, and establish indicators of performance. We need more exact ideas about how much of a public service can be provided for a given outlay. Some work of this kind has already been undertaken, but all too often a simple inquiry about levels of expenditure and results cannot be answered. Measures for ensuring accountability need to be built into program design. New incentives for good performance should be instituted. At the same time, it is necessary to cut down the probability of waste or corruption by examination of procedures for contracting, disbursements and auditing.

On the other side of the budget, questions of revenue need to be tied into issues of expenditure. For too long, the literature of budgeting has tended to separate the two. While budget discussions have concentrated on expenditure policies and classification, revenue raising has been regarded as the Province of public finance experts. Budget management needs to be regarded as a unitary function in which revenues and expenditures figure in a single equation. Further, as pressures mount on budgets, attention has to be given to finding new sources of revenues (new kinds of taxes or loans) and restructuring taxation to accord with economic goals, yet meet public demands for greater equity and fairness. Existing sources of revenues should be made more effective. The growth of a significant underground economy represents an important loss of tax revenues and adds to the burden of those who do not participate in it. It also corrupts public administration and worsens the seepage of public funds. Research into the underground economy and illegal markets and their impact on public finance is long overdue.

Conclusion

These six areas of uncertainty and suggestions for their alleviation, by no means exhaustive of what needs to be done in public budgeting, are merely manifestations of a deeper crisis in American society. We cannot agree about the nature and ends of government in post-industrial society. Public finance is the center of the controversy over the future role of the administrative state. An agenda for public budgeting amidst uncertainty and instability cannot be drawn without reference to the public purposes it serves. As long as these are in doubt, the proper allocation of public funds will remain beyond the grasp of public budgeting. Financial administrators will continue to receive mixed and perplexing signals. They will not know how to prioritize let alone make sense out of the confusion that passes for budget formulation and execution or satisfy conflicting and contradictory claims on them. They won't even know what direction to take. However, if they assess their own practices in the areas presented here, they may be better able to find their bearings and realize not only the real constraints upon their actions but also what new opportunities are open to them.

Public administrators cannot solve by themselves the bigger issues raised here. They can do much better in the special field of their own competence. To improve budgeting, a good look has to be taken at current budget institutions. Are they adaptive enough to apparent changes in the environment? Are they performing well enough? Are they capable of assuming new roles? Do they take advantage of all available techniques?

In particular, we need to encourage innovation and creativity in public finance as the traditional landmarks fade amidst uncertainty and instability. We still do not have sufficient incentives in the public sector to prevent waste and encourage economy. We still do not have adequate means of dealing with large-scale capital expenditures on risky, long-term public projects. We still do not know how to manage what amount to open-ended contracts to private organizations to deliver important public goods and services. We still do not have proper tools to tackle tax evasion and expenditure seepage. We have numerous momentary fads and fancies, many half-baked and untested theories, and a continuous flow to refinements to traditional budgeting, when what really may be needed is a new budgetary system more in keeping with the new context of public finance, more appropriate to current technological capability, and more attuned to public expectations, not managerial convenience.

Notes

1. Allen Schick, "Contemporary Problems in Financial Control," *Pub. Adm. Rev.* 38 (November/December 1978): 513–519.
2. Joseph A. Pechman and Robert W. Hartman, "The 1980 Budget and the Budget Outlook," in *Setting National Priorities: The 1980 Budget*, ed. Joseph A. Pechman (Washington, D.C.: Brookings Institution, 1979), p. 54.
3. Allen Schick, *Zero Base '80* (Washington, D.C.: National Governors Association, 1980).

4. Allen Schick, "The Road to PPB: The Stages of Budget Reform," *Pub. Adm. Rev.* 26 (December 1966): 243–258; Allen Schick, "The Road from ZBB," *Pub. Adm. Rev.* 38 (March/April 1978): 177–180.
5. See Aaron Wildavsky, *The Politics of the Budgetary Process,* 3d ed. (Boston: Little, Brown, 1979).
6. Aaron Wildavsky, "A Budget for All Seasons? Why the Traditional Budget Lasts," *Pub. Adm. Rev.* 38 (November/December 1978): 501.
7. Naomi Caiden and Aaron Wildavsky, *Planning and Budgeting in Poor Countries* (New York: Wiley, 1974; Transaction Books, 1980).
8. See Aaron Wildavsky, *Budgeting: A Comparative Theory of Budgetary Processes* (Boston: Little, Brown, 1975). See also the section on "Comparative Budgeting" in Albert C. Hyde and Jay M. Shafritz, *Government Budgeting: Theory, Process and Politics* (Oak Park, Ill.: Moore Publishing Company, 1978).
9. Statement of Elmer B. Staats, Comptroller General of the United States, before the Budget Process Task Force Committee on the Budget, House of Representatives, *The Federal Budget Process,* December 11, 1979, p. 24.
10. See scheme for biennial review for R&D activities in Statement of Elmer B. Staats, Comptroller General of the United States, before the Committee on Science and Technology, House of Representatives, *H.R. 7178, The Research and Development Authorization Estimates Act,* June 4, 1980.
11. Elmer B. Staats, *Effectiveness of the Federal Apportionment Process and Implications for Budget Execution* (Washington, D.C.: General Accounting Office, November 1979), p. 5.

35

Democracy and the Public Service: The Collective Services

Frederick C. Mosher

In state and local governments, unionization and collective bargaining were little developed until quite recently. In some, the employees never won the battle for security in tenure against political spoils. In others, civil service became so strongly entrenched as to inhibit the development of powerful employee unions. In most, unions were discouraged by the essentially conservative cast of state legislatures, city councils, county boards, and boards of education. Unions did, however, develop in parts of the federal establishment, and had a growing influence on federal employment policies. Starting soon after passage of the Pendleton Act, the postal unions played an important part in the passage of the eight-hour-workday law for federal employees in 1881[1] and later, of the Lloyd-LaFollette Act of 1912, which for 65 years remained the most important—indeed almost the only—law asserting and protecting rights of federal unions. Later joined by a service-wide union—the National Federation of Federal Employees (NFFE)—the unions were influential in the passage of the Retirement Act of 1920 and the Classification Act of 1923.

Subsequently union influence seems not to have grown except in certain pockets of the federal service. Federal unions have contributed support to a number of measures designed to strengthen the merit system and benefit civil servants (such as the Welch Act of 1928, the Postmaster Act of 1938, the revisions of the Retirement Act, and a variety of fringe benefits and pay acts). Federal unions have also dampened a number of efforts to damage the civil service. Their aims were fundamentally the same as those of the civil service; unions had with civil service the common enemy of partisan patronage. Civil service provided a guarantee of tenure and security and an orderly, predictable system for personnel decisions. Government unions therefore worked within the civil service system, contributed their support to its extension, and sought to maximize their influence in the civil service organizations. Few of them were in any sense radical.

In some organizations the unions came to exercise great influence on employment practices. Largest among these was the Post Office (since 1970, the U.S. Postal Service) with its tremendous, widely scattered, and politically influential labor force, the great majority of whom have long been unionized. Second were the industrial establishments of military and a few other agencies where the craft unions of the private sector have been active. Third were a few federal agencies in which management deliberately encouraged unionization and collective bargaining. Notable among these was the Tennessee Valley Authority (TVA).

Yet for the bulk of federal employees outside the Post Office Department, employee organization was weak if not totally unknown. President Kennedy's Task Force, discussed below, reported in 1962 that one third of all federal employees belonged to labor organizations—a proportion almost exactly equal at that time to that of non-agricultural employees in the private sector. About three fifths of the federal union members were postal workers, and more than half of the others were blue-collar workers. Obviously the unions had made only minor inroads among the main body of white-collar federal employees outside the Post Office—something in the order of 15 percent.

This apparently low level of unionization in the federal government is illusory. White-collar employees were not widely unionized in the private sector either. Employee organizations have not thrived in the service industries, and much of government is service oriented. On balance, one would guess that among comparable groups of employees (blue collar, clerical, professional, and administrative), unionization

Source: From Democracy and the Public Service, 2nd ed., by Frederick C. Mosher. Copyright © 1968, 1982 by Oxford University Press, Inc. Reprinted by permission.

of federal employees was no less common than in private organizations. But government unions lacked the collective bargaining guarantees of a Wagner Act; most of them disavowed the use of the ultimate weapon—the strike; few could assure prospective members of effective influence upon the central issues of labor relations: wages and hours.

If union membership in federal employment was equivalent to that in the private sector, the acceptance of collective bargaining was not. Mrs. B. V. H. Schneider attributed this not to any theory of sovereignty or other peculiarity of public employment, but to a simple behavioral fact: "At no time have a sufficient number of federal civil servants believed that bargaining rights were desirable or necessary and been prepared to press for such rights."[2] The statement is no doubt true, but it does not explain *why*. I would hazard as one reason that the bulk of federal employees were professional or clerical, and these categories had nowhere been aggressive in collective bargaining. A second reason is that the middle and lower grades of the federal service have, on the whole, done pretty well with their wages, hours, and fringe benefits without the necessity of labor organization. For political reasons, and perhaps partly as a spin-off from the aggressiveness of the postal unions, personnel in the lower levels of the federal service have for many years been in a favorable position relative to other employees. Their pay has been relatively high, their hours reasonably low, their vacations relatively generous, their positions secure. The incentives for unionization and collective bargaining in such circumstances would almost certainly be minimal. The personnel who were relatively disadvantaged in federal (and much state and local) employment were those in middle- and upper-level professional, scientific, and administrative positions, mainly because of the well-known compression of salary rates.

A third reason is found in the linking, by the public and by prospective union members, of labor organization with its more extreme weapons, particularly the strike, coupled with the general fear and disapproval of their use against "vital" public activities.[3]

In any case until the 1950s and 1960s there was a relatively quiescent labor presence in most of government, one which—with sporadic exceptions—made modest demands and little public noise. Effective systems of collective bargaining, systems in which both parties had sufficient power to influence settlements, were few and far between.

The Labor Explosion of the 1960s and 1970s

Against so sleepy a backdrop, the recent development of labor organization and collective bargaining in government was both sudden and unexpected. It was probably fed in part by the rapid growth of state and local employment, in part by the increasing disposition of subprofessional and professional personnel to organize and endeavor to improve their lot. But behind it also has been the fundamental anomaly of governments' supporting and requiring practices in the private sector, which they discouraged or denied for their own employees. In the words of the American Bar Association in 1955:

> A government which imposes upon private employers certain obligations in dealing with their employees may not in good faith refuse to deal with its own public servants on a reasonably similar basis, modified of course to meet the exigencies of public service.[4]

Changes began, as has so often been true of public reform movements in the past, at the municipal level. Several of the larger cities piece by piece negotiated agreements with unions of various kinds and coverage during the fifties and early sixties: Philadelphia, Cincinnati, Hartford, Detroit, New York, and many others. In 1959, Wisconsin by state law launched its now-famous program authorizing and prescribing methods for collective bargaining in cities (though not then in the state government itself) and providing that a state agency, the Wisconsin Employment Relations Board, supervise its operations. The Wisconsin system was the nearest approach in the nation for public personnel to that provided by the National Labor Relations Act for private employees.

The federal government came along a little later. In fact, Congress had under consideration, in almost every session from 1948 on, one or more bills which would have recognized federal employee organizations. Most of them would have guaranteed union recognition and collective bargaining with relatively severe penalties for administrative officers who infringed upon such rights. Lacking administration support, the bills made no headway.

Senator John F. Kennedy strongly supported these bills and testified in their behalf. But soon after he became President in 1961, he moved to preempt authority over labor-management relations in the executive branch and effectively undercut the Congressional initiative. His undercut would silence the Congress in this field for more than fifteen years. Kennedy's first move was to establish a task force to study and make recommendations on labor-management relations in the federal service. In his memorandum setting up the task force, the President made it very clear that in his view federal employees had a *right* to organize and to bargain; and by his appointments to the task force, including particularly then Labor Secretary Arthur J. Goldberg—long-time counsel to the CIO and the Steelworkers Union—its chairman. Kennedy made it clear that he expected an approach fundamentally similar to that in private industry. The task force report, issued on November 30, 1961,[5] contained an expectably enthusiastic endorsement of the right of federal employees to organize and through their organizations to negotiate with their managers, along with a variety of recommendations as to how this right should be exercised. Most of its recommendations were embodied six weeks later in President Kennedy's Executive Orders 10987 and 10988 of January 17, 1962. The Kennedy orders provided a highly decentralized system for union recognition and negotiation in the departments and agencies under very general guidance from the Civil Service Commission and the Department of Labor. In most respects these orders were pale reflections of what was even then standard and required practice in private industry; the scope of negotiation—i.e., what was negotiable; union security; powers of unions; management rights; absence of a supervisory and appellate agency in any sense comparable to the National Labor Relations Board (NLRB). In fact, the Kennedy orders contained no provisions that were not already practiced by one or more different agencies in the federal establishment.

Nonetheless, these orders were probably the most significant event in the history of labor relations of American governments. They established the general legitimacy of the unionization of public employees and of collective bargaining between such employees and public management even though for years the words "collective bargaining" and even "unions" were carefully avoided in federal pronouncements; the preferred terms were "employee management cooperation" and "employee organizations." They sparked a tremendous growth in the unionization of federal employees which continued through the 1970s; an expansion of the political power of government unions and their leaders; an increase in employee influence upon employment policies and actions in individual agencies; and a growing threat to the principles and practices of both civil service and other types of merit personnel administration.

Every President after Kennedy, at least to the close of the 1970s, took or tried to take some action with regard to collective bargaining in the federal government, and most of the changes were in the direction of increasing the voice and influence of organized labor. Lyndon Johnson in 1967 designated a President's Review Committee on Federal Employee-Management Relations, headed by then Secretary of Labor W. Willard Wirtz. That committee's proposals, perhaps the most far-reaching of any before 1978, were vigorously resisted by Secretary of Defense Clark Clifford, principally because the report's proposed Federal Labor Relations Panel would be authorized to make final decisions, binding on his own department. The report was published in early 1969 as a draft in the annual report of the Labor Department, but, for want of consensus, it never reached the President's desk.

Soon after his inauguration, Richard Nixon appointed a Study Committee to make recommendations in this area. Many of the recommendations of this group's report, which was transmitted in August 1969, were similar to those of the Wirtz group though distinctly more conservative and more negative toward labor. They were largely incorporated in Nixon's Executive Order 11491, October 29,

1969, which superseded Kennedy's order 10988. The Nixon action provided for greater centralization over collective bargaining, which virtually everyone agreed was needed, by establishing a general oversight and policymaking body, the Federal Labor Relations Council (FLRC), consisting of top federal officials.[6] Among many other changes, the Nixon order provided only one form of recognition—exclusive—for unions, and this could be gained only by a majority vote in a secret election. The FLRC was empowered to issue binding arbitration decisions. The Kennedy order had provided only for mediation to settle unresolved disputes. Nixon's order also established a Federal Service Impasse Panel within the FLRC and empowered it to issue binding arbitration rulings, subject to appeal to the FLRC. The 1969 order also gave the assistant Secretary of Labor for Labor Management Relations authority to resolve disagreements over representation rights, the composition of bargaining units, supervision of representation elections, rulings on alleged unfair labor practices, and certain other matters.

Although Executive Order 11491 provided significant advances for organized labor, it was soon under criticism from the unions as well as other groups, including the American Bar Association. Labor was dissatisfied with the absence of opportunity for judicial review (because the executive order was not a statute) and limitations on the areas of negotiation, severe strike restrictions, prohibition of the union shop, and perhaps most of all, the relationship of the FLRC to the President. Labor leaders believed that the FLRC could not administer a fair program because it was created and appointed by, and reported and was answerable to, the President. A few years later, the FLRC conducted an intensive review of the operations of the labor relations program, which resulted in Executive Order 11838, issued on February 6, 1975, by President Ford. This order clarified and strengthened the system as set up by Nixon's earlier order and broadened the scope of issues permitted for bargaining. It did not, however, alter the fundamental organizational problem posed by the FLRC as a management-oriented arbiter and decider.

This problem was one of the central issues attacked by President Carter's civil service reform task forces, described earlier in Chapter 4. His Reorganization Plan No. 2 of 1978 and the Civil Service Reform Act which followed it did not greatly change the rights, the procedures, and the practices which had developed in labor-management relations over the preceding fifteen years. But the Reorganization Plan and the Act did fundamentally change the central structure for overseeing those matters. They replaced the FLRC with an independent, fulltime, three-member Federal Labor Relations Authority (FLRA), to be appointed by the President with confirmation by the Senate. They transferred to this new organization the responsibilities of the FLRC and also of the Assistant Secretary of Labor for Labor-Management Relations. They created a General Counsel to the FLRA who would investigate and, when appropriate, prosecute alleged unfair labor practices before the FLRA. And they authorized judicial review of FLRA decisions in most cases.

Labor leaders did not get all they wanted, which included repeal of the Hatch Act and a union shop. But they did pretty well. Further, the ambiguous mission of the old Civil Service Commission was clarified. As the Office of Personnel Management (OPM), it was made quite definitely the director and coordinator of administrative policies toward organized labor; it now became unequivocally the arm of management in matters of labor relations.

This sporadic but consistent growth in the influence of unions was accompanied by a steady increase in federal union membership, which nearly doubled between 1960 and 1980. By the latter year, almost three fifths of all federal civilian employees were members of unions or comparable employee associations, and nearly nine tenths of those members were covered under collective bargaining agreements. These figures do not include about 600,000 employees of the U.S. Postal Service, almost all of whom are unionized. When the Postal Service was created in 1970 to replace the Post Office Department, the postal employees were separated from regular federal coverage and placed under the jurisdiction of the National Labor Relations Act.

Very probably, an important spin-off of the federal decisions to recognize and encourage unions and collective bargaining was the impetus they gave to the movements already under way in state and local governments, particularly local. Since World War II, these have grown at a faster rate than any other sector of the country, although their growth rate is now leveling off. With the federal government, state and local governments have also been the fastest growing group in the proportions of employees who hold membership in unions and in employee associations, most of which behave like unions. The proportion of unionized state and local employees was recently estimated at 35.5 percent.[7] The rapid growth in public sector unionism has accompanied stability or relative decline in union membership in the private sector. A recent study revealed that between 1968 and 1976, bargaining organizations in manufacturing industries lost 755,000 members while those in other parts of the private sector gained 781,000 members and public sector membership grew by two million.[8] For a good many years, the fastest growing union in the country has been the American Federation of State, County, and Municipal Employees (AFSCME). Closely following has been the American Federation of Government Employees (AFGE, mainly federal). Both are affiliated with the AFL-CIO, as is the American Federation of Teachers. The National Education Association, which like a number of other professional associations has become a de facto labor union, now has nearly two million members. Among these four organizations alone are nearly four million members, virtually all of whom are government employees.

By the time of this writing, most of the states, particularly in industrial areas, have gone well beyond the federal government in encouraging and extending the limits of collective bargaining, especially for their local governments. A few, mainly in the south, prohibit or severely limit it. Yet in recent years, the fastest growing, the most articulate, and frequently the most militant of labor organizations have been in the public sector. It is at least interesting, whatever one wishes to make of it, that while the size, importance, and political influence of the labor movement in this country have apparently declined in the last couple of decades, public service unions have risen in all these dimensions. Union membership in the private sector, following the National Labor Relations Act in 1935, grew from 6.7 percent of the work force to a peak of 25.5 percent in 1953. Since then, while its numbers have remained steady, its proportion of the work force has steadily declined to 16.2 percent in 1978. Meanwhile, since the late 1950s, membership in public sector unions and associations has been rising sharply, reaching a proportion of the total labor force in 1978 of 5.8 percent, about one third of all employees in the public sector.[9] With the growth in membership has come a growth in the militancy of public employee unions. In defiance of prohibiting laws, they have indulged in strikes, sit-ins, and walkouts. And for the most part, they were not penalized for such illegal activities until President Reagan cracked down on the air traffic controllers in the summer of 1981.

How Is Public Service Different?

In the social sphere it often takes theory and principle a long time to catch up with practice and "common sense." Scholars and most of the rest of us have long accepted the proposition that public employment is different from private, that the approved norms of the industrial sphere cannot apply to civil servants. The argument was usually buttressed by a number of reasons, among which sovereignty was central. The growing public-private mix of social enterprise through a vast array of mechanisms makes it difficult to draw lines, as the aspirations of workers make it difficult to differentiate rights and expectations of workers in public or private employ. The current rapidity and disparity of change make observation unreliable, prediction risky. The paragraphs that follow undertake no theoretic analysis of sovereignty and the rights of labor. Rather, they are meant to elucidate the practical problems in the governmental realm of labor organization and collective bargaining that are visible today and that demand resolution in the future. One thing is clear: civil service systems and collective bargaining are different. They arise from different ideologies, espouse different aims and values, pursue different procedures. How are they to be reconciled?

A first category of problems centers on the question: *What is negotiable?* The National Labor Relations Act prescribes for the private sector bargaining in good faith over "wages, hours, and other terms and conditions of employment"—a blanket stipulation which has been interpreted to cover a very large portion of the labor front. In most American governments at every level, hours, most wages, and some other conditions are determined by a legislative body, not by management. There is legal doubt as to what part of these prerogatives a legislature *can* delegate away (though practice differs among different jurisdictions and among different kinds of employees in the same jurisdiction). In the national government, salary scales for the bulk of employees are established by law or by the President, subject to possible disapproval by the Congress.[10] The same is true of most large jurisdictions. This means that unless the employee organizations bargain directly with the legislatures, their negotiations with management on salary levels can be advisory at the most, for the power to make binding decisions lies elsewhere. Management cannot make commitments in this field, which constitutes the central issue of most labor activity in the private sector. Unions could, theoretically and indirectly, affect salaries on a selective basis through negotiations on position classification. But if there is any sacrosanct element in public personnel administration, it is the integrity of the classification plan, objective and free from pressure. Can classification be made negotiable without shaking the roots of civil service itself?

As a matter of fact, other conditions of employment are often legislated, sometimes in such precise detail as to leave little or no discretion to administrators: criteria for appointments and promotions, hours of work, vacations and other leave, retirement, reductions in force, fringe benefits. It is significant too that most of the causes that employees pursue cost money. Almost everywhere in American governmental life the appropriating power resides in legislative bodies—city councils, school boards, county boards of supervisors, state legislatures, Congress.[11]

In addition to the legislative problems, there are constraints on the administrative side which limit the area of employee negotiation. Some of these, not too unlike those that weighed on the rugged individualists in the private sector five decades ago, relate to the powers and responsibilities of management, its accountability to the people, its exercise of sovereignty. Others stem from the ideology and procedures of civil service. To the extent these are detailed in statute, there is not much that labor can do beyond accepting them or going to the legislature to seek changes in the law. As one city manager put it: "Perhaps most important [of the differences between public and private employment] is that public administrators do not have the same freedom of action which their counterparts in the private sector enjoy. Their authority is conferred on them by public law and by the definition of that law is limited and cannot be delegated or contracted away."[12]

The original Kennedy orders had specified a rather broad range of management rights, which were not negotiable in collective bargaining. These were repeated in the Nixon order of 1969 and later in the Carter Civil Service Reform Act of 1978 with some changes in wording but fundamentally the same substance. According to the Carter legislation, management officials are authorized "to determine the mission, budget, organization, number of employees, and internal security practices of the agency . . . to hire, assign, direct, layoff, and retain employees . . . or to suspend, remove, reduce in grade or pay, or take other disciplinary action . . . to assign work . . . [and] to make selections for appointments" from proper promotion lists or from other appropriate sources.[13] But a section was added to the law which authorized agencies at their discretion to negotiate "on the numbers, types, and grades of employees or positions assigned to any organizational subdivision, work project, or tour of duty or on the technology, methods and means of performing work. . . ."[14]

It should be observed, however, that substantial rights are often reserved to management in private industry, and that individual federal agencies can permit, and have permitted, some or many of these subjects to be covered under collective bargaining agreements. Experience has shown that, even within these limitations, there is an impressive array of subjects that are negotiable.

Clearly, the push of public employee organizations as they grow stronger will be toward exercising greater influence over personnel activities heretofore considered nonnegotiable and retained within the unilateral prerogatives of civil service commissions and other public personnel agencies. Indeed, this movement is already well under way in some places and in certain areas of personnel activity. These areas include appointments, position classification, establishment of minimum examination requirements and class specifications, and promotions. But if these issues, together with others in the legislative domain, remain "off limits" to labor representatives, what is in their domain will not likely satisfy them and their union members very long. Grievance procedures and working conditions not covered by law and the traditional merit system constitute a foot in the door; and the door to effective collective bargaining in most public agencies is gradually opening.

In comparing labor activity in the public service with that in private, a second category of problems concerns the *tools* or *weapons* which employee organizations may use. Here, too, there are vital historic and ideological differences, but many of these are now under union attack. Labor organization and collective bargaining were themselves frowned upon in government for most of our history, and they are still forbidden in some jurisdictions. The strike, the anchor power of most unions outside of government, is still forbidden in the national government and a large number of states. So is picketing. Compulsory arbitration of unresolved disputes is not legal in some places. The closed or union shop is not permitted in most jurisdictions; it is probably one of the most difficult of labor's potential tools to square with the principle of equal treatment, long a central tenet of America's merit systems.

In the federal government, employee organizations have won the right to negotiate, to reach written agreements with management, to represent employees in grievance cases, and to have union dues checked off from payrolls. But they lack some of the legal weapons to back up their demands that are available to kindred organizations in private employ. In some local jurisdictions and among some kinds of employees the ultimate weapon, the strike, has been utilized, whether or not legally, without severe penalty. In fact, strikes among local employees have sharply increased. Public sector strikes grew from 15 in 1958 to 481 in 1978; the great majority of them were in school districts and cities.[15] The federal ban on strikes has occasionally been defied; but on the whole it does not appear to be under serious challenge, even by the more aggressive labor leaders. In fact, many seem to regard it as a necessary safety valve in the event of particularly damaging strikes in the private sector, which the federal government can terminate through the process of nationalizing a whole industry.

But labor in the public sphere has political weapons not generally available in the private sector. It can and does carry its problems to legislatures and legislative committees. In the federal government and in the large industrial states it can usually expect sympathetic consideration of its views, and through affiliation with larger sectors of the labor movement it can pack a considerable political punch. A major reason that strikes on the local scene have increased so sharply is that local legislative bodies in most jurisdictions have been predominantly conservative. At the national level and in the industrialized states, legislatures are at least as amenable to labor organizations as are the executive branches, and usually more so.

In short, the powers and weapons of labor unions in the public sector are different from those in the private. They are primarily political rather than economic. At the local level the absence of legislative responsiveness has in many places forced employee organizations to utilize the weapons of unions in the private sector. But even there, the major weapon of the strike is essentially a political one. One need not judge whether labor organizations have been more or less effective in the public service than elsewhere, or whether employees have been better treated in government than outside. But clearly their instruments for betterment are different, and it seems reasonable to expect that they will continue to be different.

In comparing collective bargaining in the public and private sectors, the third question is,

Who negotiates for whom? On the employee side, the situation in government is not unlike that in the private sector forty years ago. There are many different types of organizations operating from different principles with different aspirations, and often they are at war among themselves. They include unions affiliated with the labor movement; unaffiliated unions; craft unions, usually comparable to and affiliated with the same crafts in the private sector; industrial-type unions (like the American Federation of Government Employees and the American Federation of State, County, and Municipal Employees); general employee associations (which are commonly likened by unionists to company unions in the private sector); and professional associations. In general, governments seem to be moving toward the principle of exclusive recognition, long established in the private sector. But uncertainties remain about the definition of the bargaining unit, the handling of situations in which no organization commands a majority, the inclusion of supervisory officials within bargaining organizations, and other issues. With a few exceptions the employee associations—strongest in some of the states—have supported and worked through normal civil service machinery. The industrial-type affiliated unions have been most aggressive and have posed the gravest threat to accustomed public employment practices. Recently, professional associations and unions of professionals in a number of fields have contested bitterly for the right to represent the interests of their professional groups. The unionization of professionals is a relatively recent phenomenon in both the public and the private sectors, and the problems seem to be roughly similar in both.

The question of who will represent labor thus seems not greatly different in the public and the private sectors, except that the former has run several decades behind the latter in crystallizing the issues. One would guess that, in most fields below the professional and supervisory level, affiliated unions will gradually assume primacy as they have for the most part in private industry. Among the professional and sub-professional employees, whatever the outcome of the current struggles between unions and associations, clearly the former are driving the latter toward more aggressive demands and tactics, including strikes.

A difference, even more difficult and crucial, concerns the question of who will represent the employer—i.e., the government—in labor-management negotiations. As we have seen above, the problem here arises first from the separation of powers between executive and legislature. It is complicated, secondly, by the varying degrees of identity and autonomy of individual public agencies, with respect to both the executive and the legislature. Thirdly, the role, power, and degree of autonomy of the civil service organization are a source of ambiguity. Our experience to date at all levels suggests that labor organizations, as they acquire self-identity and recognition, are not greatly influenced by the niceties of political and constitutional theory. They approach the sources of real authority through whatever devices are most promising of results. If present trends toward larger and more influential public sector unions continue, particularly at lower levels of government, we may expect increasing—and increasingly direct—demands upon local legislative bodies. Insofar as these demands are frustrated, the unions will turn to state legislatures to provide guarantees of negotiating rights, minimum standards, and mediating and appellate machinery. Within limits, legislative bodies may delegate, and in many cases have delegated, negotiating powers to administrative officers and special agencies. But the possibilities of appeal back to the legislature can hardly be foreclosed for any organization with potential political power.

The Dilemmas of Civil Service

The rapid growth of labor organizations, like that of the professions, is clouding the already hazy role of civil service agencies. Historically these agencies were the protectors of the public service against the machinations of politics; later, the defenders of efficiency as well as security in the management of public personnel. Public employees turned to the civil service agencies in both roles as their principal representatives and as proponents of employee interests. The trend toward legal recognition of employee organizations and of rights to collective bargaining confronts the civil service agencies with grave problems. Are those agencies properly instruments of management with whom labor organizations should negotiate (short of legislative appeal)? Are they properly representatives of employees in seeking benefits, participation, and adjustment of grievances? Or are they properly mediators, bringing to bear an objective and disinterested view and with power to impose, or exert major influence upon, final judgment? Or are they defenders of traditional merit system principles against all who challenge those principles?

The inconsistencies and the conflicts among these roles of civil service agencies have piecemeal forced differentiation and separation of roles and functions, a process which is likely to be extended. This is the logic and the basic merit of the Carter reforms of the civil service in 1978. The principles of the merit system and appeals against violations of the system would be decided and defended by an independent agency, the Merit Systems Protection Board. The fairness of labor-management relations would be judged by an independent Federal Labor Relations Authority. Both of these would be collegial, quasi-judicial groups. The development and enforcement of plans, rules, and standards governing federal personnel matters would be lodged in an office with a single head, the Director of the Office of Personnel Management, who would be the agent of the President. He would also be the principal representative of management in dealing with federal employees and unions.

It seems very likely that, as public employees organize and become more militant, they are almost bound to cast civil service organizations in the role of staff arms to management, whatever independence and impartiality may be claimed. Few at any level of government are likely to be perceived as NLRB equivalents. Labor organizations may prove a more potent force in driving public personnel administration into the arms of management than the "management movement," epitomized by the Brownlow Committee, ever was. This view was affirmed years ago by a principal public employee union leader: "The role of the civil service commission is not regarded by the workers as that of a third, impartial party; to most of them, the commission is felt to represent the employer."[16]

The organizational question discussed above is but a reflection of a more profound dilemma: the relations between the traditional principles and practices of the merit system and those of collective bargaining. Can the two be made compatible? If public employees are to bargain equally on the conditions of their employment, does this by definition authorize bargaining on the very principles of merit? Obviously, the students and authors who gave rise to the various federal executive orders and the Civil Service Reform Act thought that the two were not in conflict—though they quite consistently opposed provisions for union security (e.g., the closed or union shop) as being threats to merit. It may be noted too that, unlike many state and local jurisdictions, collective bargaining in the federal government does not extend to pay levels, fringe benefits, and a good many other matters considered to be management rights. John W. Macy, Jr., Chairman of the U.S. Civil Service Commission under both Presidents Kennedy and Johnson, wrote that the 1961 Task Force which started it all "faced up to the basic issue of the relationship of the merit system to collective bargaining. It determined that there could be an acceptable compatibility and that the negotiation of agreements with unions gaining exclusive recognition could be developed without violating basic merit principles."[17] Others have been less sanguine, one going so far as to say that: "To destroy merit systems . . . is a perfectly logical objective of unions. . . ."[18] In fact, there is a wide divergence of opinion on this question among the many people who have expressed themselves on it. Most would probably agree that if unions took over all the activities to which some of them aspire, which will probably never happen, collective bargaining would replace civil service as we have known it; we would have a quite different definition of merit.

Some of the issues on which there have been or may be collisions between collective bargaining and traditional merit principles are illustrated in Table 1.

In essence, these differences may be reduced to two related issues: first, the extent

TABLE 1

SUBJECT	COLLECTIVE BARGAINING	MERIT PRINCIPLES
Management rights	Minimal or none; bilateralism	Maximal or total; unilateralism
Employee participation and rights	Union shop or maintenance of membership Exclusive recognition	Equal treatment to each employee Open shop (if any recognition)
Recruitment and selection	Union membership and/or occupational license Entrance at bottom only	Open competitive examination Entrance at any level
Promotion	On basis of seniority	Competitive on basis of merit (often including seniority)
Classification of positions	Negotiable as to classification plan; subject to grievance procedure as to allocation	Intrinsic as to level of responsibilities and duties on basis of objective analysis
Pay	Negotiable and subject to bargaining power of union	On basis of analytically balanced pay plan and, for some fields, subject to prevailing rates
Hours, leaves, conditions of work	Negotiable	On basis of public interest as determined by legislature and management
Grievances	Appealed with union representation to impartial arbitrators	Appealed through management with recourse to civil service agency

to which the conditions of employment will be determined on the basis of a bilateral philosophy, which accords the employees a voice equal to that of the employing government; second, the extent to which the terms of employment will be based upon collective as distinguished from individual considerations. The first of these involves basic concessions in the historic concept of sovereignty, the concept that a public job is a privilege and not a right, to the extent that a private job is a right. The second calls for modifications in the ideal of individualism in the merit system as it developed in this country: that each person would be considered on his or her distinctive merits in comparison and competition with all others. The wishes of the individual in relations with his or her employing institution—the government—give way to those of the group acting in concert, a more equal confrontation.

How far and how fast public employment will move in the direction of collective bargaining is problematical. But the directions are unmistakable. Somewhat surprisingly, among the most aggressive are organizations of professionals or emergent professionals, especially those principally employed by and therefore principally dependent upon public employers: school teachers, social workers, nurses, and other hospital specialists, police and fire fighters. It is worth noting that the concessions now being demanded by the labor movement against unilateralism and individualism are essentially parallel to those demanded by the organized professions and their career services (as described in the preceding chapters). Both constitute challenges to the traditional civil service as we have come to know it. So far, and in most places, the professions have made the greater inroads. But the development of each presents the fundamental confrontation of political and administrative generalism and of personnel specialism by collectivized, organized, occupational groupings.

What does all of this mean for democracy and the public service? A principal argument for collective bargaining, in fact, emphasizes democracy. Bargaining provides the opportunity for participation by those most concerned in determining the conditions and the rewards of their work, for maintaining human dignity in the work situation, for actualizing the self against the stultifying effects of authoritarian rule. In the words of former Secretary of Labor Willard Wirtz: "Collective bargaining is industrial democracy."[19]

Few would challenge the Wirtz definition or argue that, in principle, public employees should be deprived of industrial democracy any more than private employees. Yes . . . but! The defenders of government hegemony and of civil service urge that collective bargaining, unless circumscribed by narrow boundaries, threatens political democracy, the ultimate power of the citizen through his political representatives to control the destinies of government and the conditions whereby it employs its personnel.

NOTES

1. The first permanent union in the Post Office, the National Association of Letter Carriers, was formed in 1888.
2. "Collective Bargaining and the Federal Civil Service," *Industrial Relations,* May 3, 1964, p. 98.
3. Though Leonard White showed long ago that many services in the private sector were as vital as some in the public—or more so. See his "Strikes in the Public Service," *Public Personnel Review* (January 1949): 3–10.
4. *Second Report of the Committee on Labor Relations of Governmental Employees,* 1955, p. 125.
5. President's Task Force on Employee-Management Relations in the Federal Service, *Report.*
6. After 1971, the ERC was chaired by the chairman of the Civil Service Commission and included the Secretary of Labor and the Director of the Office of Management and Budget. Such a board might compare, in the private sector, with a National Labor Relations Board consisting of the chairmen of the boards of the Chamber of Commerce, the National Association of Manufacturers, and the Chase Manhattan National Bank.
7. U.S. Department of Labor, Bureau of Labor Statistics (Washington, D.C., 1980). Figures are for 1980 as quoted by Myron Lieberman, *Public Sector: A Policy Bargaining Reappraisal* (Lexington, Mass., Lexington Books, 1980), p. 4.
8. John F. Burton, Jr., "The Extent of Collective Bargaining in the Public Sector," in *Public Sector Bargaining,* ed. Benjamin Aaron, Joseph R. Grodin, and James L. Stern (Washington, D.C., The Bureau of National Affairs, 1979), p. 36.
9. Ibid, p. 2.
10. Exceptions are the blue-collar workers known as wage-board employees, whose wages can be, and in fact are, negotiated in a limited sense; i.e., against the criterion of the prevailing rate.
11. There are exceptions, especially in the semiautonomous, self-supporting enterprises such as the Port Authority of New York and New Jersey. The Tennessee Valley Authority is very nearly in this category, and this may have been a necessary condition for the success of its collective bargaining system.
12. Elder Gunter, City Manager of Pasadena, California, in a letter in *Public Personnel Review* (January 1966): 57.
13. Public Law 95-454, October 13, 1978. Section 7106.
14. Ibid.
15. Lieberman, op. cit., p. 35.
16. Jerry Wurf, International President, American Federation of State, County, and Municipal Employees, AFL-CIO, in a letter to *Public Personnel Review* (January 1966): 52.
17. John W. Macy, Jr., *Public Service: The Human Side of Government* (New York: Harper and Row, 1971), p. 124.
18. Nelson Watkins in a letter published in *Public Personnel Review* (January 1966): 58.
19. W. Willard Wirtz, *Labor and the Public Interest* (New York: Harper and Row, 1964), p. 57.

36

Public Administrative Theory and the Separation of Powers

David H. Rosenbloom

It has been recognized for some time that the discipline of public administration is plagued by a weak or absent theoretical core. This has led some to conclude, along with Robert Parker,[1] that "there is really no such subject as 'public administration.' No science or art can be identified by this title, least of all any single skill or coherent intellectual discipline." Others, including Frederick C. Mosher,[2] have considered it a "resource," that public administration "is more an area of interest than a discipline," since this enables the field to draw upon a variety of disciplines. Still others, such as Herbert Kaufman[3] and James Q. Wilson,[4] have argued that public administration faces a serious and seemingly irresolvable problem in continually seeking to maximize the attainment of mutually incompatible values. The contention of this essay is that the central problem of contemporary public administrative theory is that it is derived from three disparate approaches to the basic question of what public administration is. Each of these approaches has a respected intellectual tradition, emphasizes different values, promotes different types of organizational structure, and views individuals in markedly distinct terms. These approaches are conveniently labeled "managerial," "political," and "legal." They have influenced one another over the years, and at some points they overlap. Yet, their primary influence on public administration has been to pull it in three separate directions. Furthermore, these directions tend to follow the pattern of the separation of powers established by the Constitution. Consequently, it is unlikely that the three approaches can be synthesized without violating values deeply ingrained in the United States political culture.[5]

The Managerial Approach to Public Administration

Origin and Values In the United States the managerial approach to public administration grew largely out of the civil service reform movement of the late 19th century. In the reformers' words, "What civil service reform demand[ed], [was] that the business part of the government shall be carried on in a sound businesslike manner."[6] The idea of "businesslike" public administration was most self-consciously and influentially discussed by Woodrow Wilson in his essay on "The Study of Administration."[7] There, Wilson considered public administration to be "a field of business" and consequently largely a managerial endeavor. He also set forth the three core values of the managerial approach to public administration: "It is the object of administrative study to discover, first, what government can properly and successfully do, and, secondly, how it can do these proper things with the utmost possible efficiency and at the least possible cost either of money or of energy."[8] Thus, public administration was to be geared toward the maximization of effectiveness, efficiency, and economy.

The managerial approach was strengthened by Frederick Taylor and the scientific management movement.[9] Taylorism sought to enshrine the values of efficiency and economy in a world view that promised to achieve harmony and affluence among mankind. Later, Leonard White's influential *Introduction to the Study of Public Administration*[10] asserted that "the study of administration should start from the base of management rather than the foundation of law, and is, therefore, more absorbed in the affairs of the American Management Association than in the decisions of the courts." When the managerial approach to public administration was at the pinnacle of its

---

influence in the 1930s, it was widely held, along with Luther Gulick, that "efficiency" was "axiom number one in the value scale of administration" and that politics could not enter "the structure of administration without producing inefficiency."[11]

The essence of the managerial approach's values was captured by Simmons and Dvorin in the following terms: "The 'goodness' or 'badness' of a particular organizational pattern was a mathematical relationship of 'inputs' to 'outputs.' Where the latter was maximized and the former minimized, a moral 'good' resulted. Virtue or 'goodness' was therefore equated with the relationship of these two factors, that is, 'efficiency,' or 'inefficiency.' Mathematics was transformed into ethics."[12]

Organizational Structure The managerial approach to public administration promotes organization essentially along the lines of Max Weber's "ideal-type bureaucracy."[13] It stresses the importance of functional specialization for efficiency. Hierarchy is then relied upon for effective coordination.[14] Programs and functions are to be clearly assigned to organizational units. Overlap are to be minimized. Positions are to be classified into a rational scheme and pay scales are to be systematically derived in the interests of economy and motivating employees to be efficient. Selection of public administrators is to be made strictly on the basis of merit. They are to be politically neutral in their competence. Relationships among public administrators and public agencies are to be formalized in writing and, in all events, the public's business is to be administered in a smooth, orderly fashion.[15]

View of the Individual The managerial approach to public administration promotes an impersonal view of individuals. This is true whether the individuals in question are the employees, clients, or the "victims"[16] of public administrative agencies. One need not go so far as Max Weber in considering "dehumanization" to be the "special virtue" of bureaucracy or to view the bureaucrat as a "cog" in an organizational machine over which he/she has virtually no control.[17] Yet there can be no doubt that a strong tendency of scientific management was to turn the individual worker into an appendage to a mechanized means of production. By 1920, this view of the employee was clearly embodied in the principles of position classification in the public sector: "The individual characteristics of an employee occupying a position should have no bearing on the classification of the position."[18] Indeed, the strong "position-orientation" of the managerial approach to public administration continues to diminish the importance of the individual employees to the overall organization.

Clients, too, have been "depersonalized" and turned into "cases" in an effort to promote the managerial values of efficiency, economy, and effectiveness. Ralph Hummel explains,

> At the intake level of the bureaucracy, individual personalities are converted into cases. Only if a person can qualify as a case, is he or she allowed treatment by the bureaucracy. More accurately, a bureaucracy is never set up to treat or deal with persons: it "processes" only "cases."[19]

"Victims" may be depersonalized to such an extent that they are considered sub-human, especially where physical force or coercion is employed as in mental health facilities and police functions.[20]

The human relations approach to organization theory and some contemporary views argue that reliance on impersonality tends to be counter-productive because it generates "bureau pathologies."[21] Nevertheless, the managerial approach's impersonal view of individuals is deeply ingrained and considered essential to the maximization of efficiency, economy, and effectiveness.

The Political Approach to Public Administration

Origins and Values The political approach to public administration was perhaps most forcefully and succinctly stated by Wallace Sayre:

> Public administration is ultimately a problem in political theory: the fundamental problem in a democracy is responsibility to popular control; the responsibility and

> responsiveness of the administrative agencies and the bureaucracies to the elected officials (the chief executives, the legislators) is of central importance in a government based increasingly on the exercise of discretionary power by the agencies of administration.[22]

This approach grew out of the observation of some, such as Paul Appleby, that public administration during the New Deal and World War II was anything but devoid of politics.[23] Thus, unlike the origin of the managerial approach, which stressed what public administration ought to be, the political approach developed from an analysis of apparent empirical reality.

Once public administration is considered a political endeavor, emphasis is inevitably placed on a different set of values than those promoted by the managerial approach. "Efficiency," in particular, becomes highly suspect, as Justice Brandeis pointed out in dissent in *Myers* v. *United States* (1926):

> The doctrine of the separation of powers was adopted by the Convention of 1787, not to promote efficiency but to preclude the exercise of arbitrary power. The purpose was, not to avoid friction, but, by means of the inevitable friction incident to the distribution of governmental powers among three departments, to save the people from autocracy.[24]

Rather, the political approach to public administration stresses the values of representativeness, political responsiveness, and accountability through elected officials to the citizenry. These are viewed as crucial to the maintenance of constitutional democracy, especially in view of the rise of the contemporary administrative state, which may be likened unto "bureaucratic government."[25]

One can find many examples of governmental reforms aimed at maximizing the political values of representativeness, responsiveness, and accountability within public administration. For instance, the wide ranging academic controversy concerning the concept of "representative bureaucracy"[26] notwithstanding, the Federal Civil Service Reform Act of 1978 made it "the policy of the United States . . . to provide a Federal work force reflective of the Nation's diversity" by endeavoring "to achieve a work force from all segments of society."[27] The Federal Advisory Committee Act of 1971 sought to enhance responsiveness through the use of "representative" advisory committees.[28] Earlier, the poverty and model cities programs of the 1960s sought to use "citizen participation" as a means of promoting political responsiveness in administrative operations. The quest for responsiveness has also blended into attempts to promote the accountability of public administrators to political officials through a variety of measures including greater use of the General Accounting Office,[29] the creation of the federal Senior Executive Service, and structural changes such as the establishment of the Office of Management and Budget, the Office of Personnel Management, and the Congressional Budget Office. "Sunshine" provisions such as the Freedom of Information Act and "sunset" requirements are also examples of the attempt to promote political accountability. There is also a growing academic literature on the need to promote representativeness, responsiveness, and accountability in the modern administrative state.[30]

It is important to note that the values sought by the political approach to public administration are frequently in tension with those of the managerial approach. For instance, efficiency in the managerial sense is not necessarily served through sunshine regulations which can dissuade public administration from taking some courses of action, though they may be the most efficient, and can divert time and resources from program implementation to the deliverance of information to outsiders. Consultation with advisory committees and "citizen participants" can be time consuming and costly. A socially representative public service may not be the most efficient one.[31] Nor is the intended shuffling of Senior Executive Servants from agency to agency likely to enhance efficiency in the managerial sense. Rather it is thought that by providing this cadre of top public administrators a wider variety of experience, they may come to define the public interest in more comprehensive terms and therefore become more responsive to the nation's overall political interests. Moreover, while various budgeting strategies and sunset provisions can promote economy in one sense, the amount of paperwork they generate and the extent to which they may require agencies to justify and argue on behalf of their programs and expenditures can become quite costly. Indeed, a quarter century ago, Marver Berstein reported that "many officials complain that they must spend so much time preparing for appearing at Congressional hearings and in presenting their programs before the Bureau of the Budget and other bodies that it often leaves little time for directing the operations of their agencies."[32] Managerial effectiveness is difficult to gauge, of course, but federal managers have long complained that their effectiveness is hampered by the large congressional role in public administration and the need to consult continually with a variety of parties having a legitimate concern with their agencies' operations.[33]

Organizational Structure Public administration organized around the political values of representativeness, responsiveness, and accountability also tends to be at odds with the managerial approach to organization. Rather than emphasizing clear lines of functional specialization, hierarchy, unity, and recruitment based on politically neutral administrative competence, the political approach stresses the extent and advantages of political pluralism within public administration. Thus, Harold Seidman urges that, "Executive branch structure is in fact a microcosm of our society. Inevitably it reflects the values, conflicts, and competing forces to be found in a pluralistic society. The ideal of a neatly symmetrical, frictionless organization structure is a dangerous illusion."[34] Norton Long makes a similar point: "Agencies and bureaus more or less perforce are in the business of building, maintaining, and increasing their political support. They lead and in large part are led by the diverse groups whose influence sustains them. Frequently they lead and are themselves led in conflicting directions."[35] Roger Davidson finds a political virtue where those imbued with the managerial approach might see disorder: "In many respects, the civil service represents the American people more comprehensively than does Congress."[36]

The basic concept behind pluralism within public administration is that since the administrative branch is a policy-making center of government, it must be structured to enable faction to counteract faction by providing political representation to a comprehensive variety of the organized political, economic, and social interests that are found in the society at large. To the extent that the political approach's organizational scheme is achieved, the structure comes to resemble political party platform that promises something to almost everyone without establishing clear priorities for resolving conflicts among them. Agency becomes adversary of agency and the resolution of conflict is shifted to the legislature, the office of the chief executive, interagency committees, or the courts. Moreover, the number of bureaus and agencies tends to grow over time, partly in response to the political demands of organized interests for representation. This approach to administrative organization has been widely denounced as making government "unmanageable," "costly," and "inefficient,"[37] but, as Seidman argues, it persists because administrative organization is frequently viewed as a political question that heavily emphasizes political values.

View of the Individual The political approach to public administration tends to view the individual as part of an aggregate group. It does not depersonalize the individual by turning him or her into a "case," as does the managerial approach, but rather identifies the individual's interests as being similar or identical to those of others considered to be within the same group or category. For example, affirmative action within the government service is aimed at specific social groups such as blacks and women without inquiry as to the particular circumstances of any individual member of these broad and diverse groups. Similarly, farmers growing the same crops and/or located in the same national geopolitical subdivisions are considered alike, despite individual differences among them. The same is true in any number of areas of public administration where public policies dealing with people are implemented. This is a tendency, of course, that fits the political culture well—politicians tend to think in terms of group, e.g., the "black" vote, the "farm" vote, labor, and so forth. Indeed, this approach is so strong that some, such as David Truman,[38] consider it the main feature of government in the United States. Theodore Lowi argues that a central tenet of the contemporary American "public philosophy" is that "organized interests are homogeneous and easy to define, sometimes monolithic. Any 'duly elected' spokesman for an interest is taken as speaking in close approximation for each and every member."[39] In this view of the individual, then, personality exists, but it is conceptualized in collective terms.

The Legal Approach to Public Administration

Origins and Values In the United States, the legal approach to public administration has historically been eclipsed by the other approaches, especially the managerial. Nevertheless, it has a venerable tradition and has recently emerged as a full-fledged vehicle for defining public administration. It is derived primarily from three interrelated sources. First is administrative law. As early as 1905, Frank Goodnow, a leading contributor to the development of public administrative theory generally, published a book entitled *The Principles of the Administrative Law of the United States.*[40] There he defined administrative law as "that part of the law which fixes the organization and determines the competence of the authorities which execute the law, and indicates to the individual remedies for the violation of his rights."[41] Others have found this broad conception of administrative law adequate for defining much of the work of public administrators and the nature of public agencies. For instance, Marshall Dimock writes:

> To the public administrator, law is something very positive and concrete. It is his authority. The term he customarily uses to describe it is "my mandate." It is "his" law, something he feels a proprietary interest in. It does three things: tells him what the legislature expects him to accomplish, fixes limits to his authority, and sets forth the substantive and procedural rights of the individual and group. Having a positive view of his mandate, the administrator considers himself both an interpreter and a builder. He is a builder because every time he applies old law to new situations he builds the law. Therefore law, like administration, is government in action.[42]

Taking a related view, Kenneth Davis argues that public agencies are best defined in terms of law: "An administrative agency is a governmental authority, other than a court and other than a legislative body, which affects the rights of private parties through either adjudication, rulemaking, investigating, prosecuting, negotiating, settling, or informally acting."[43]

A second source of the legal approach has been the movement toward the "judicialization"[44] of public administration. Judicialization falls within the purview of Goodnow's definition of administrative law, but tends to concentrate heavily upon the establishment of procedures designed to safeguard individual rights. Dimock succinctly captures the essence of judicialization:

> Before the Administrative Procedure Act [1946] came into existence, decisions were made by the regular administrative staff, with the ultimate decision being entrusted to the head of the agency. Characteristically, it was a collective or institutional decision, each making his contribution and all checking each other. The decisions were made on the basis of statutory law, plus agency sub-legislation, plus decided court cases. The system worked, and in most cases worked well. Then the idea arose of using "hearing examiners" in certain cases where hearings were long and technical, as in railroad cases coming under the Interstate Commerce Commission. . . .
>
> When the Administrative Procedure Act . . . was enacted, however, judicialization was speeded up, and now, like a spreading fog, it has become well-nigh universal. It began with hearing officers who were recruited by the U.S. Civil Service Commission and put in a pool, from which they were assigned to various agencies. . . . [T]he idea of courtroom procedure was still further enlarged when Congress created the office of "Administrative Judge," this being one who operates inside the agency instead of outside it, as in the case of the European administrative courts.
>
> . . . In actual practice . . . the longer the system has been in existence, the more frequently the hearing examiner's

recommended decision becomes the final decision.[45]

Thus, judicialization brings not only law but legal procedure as well to bear upon administrative decision making. Agencies begin to function more like courts and consequently legal values come to play a greater role in their activities.

Constitutional law provides a third source of the contemporary legal approach to public administration. Since the 1950s, the federal judiciary has virtually redefined the procedural, equal protection, and substantive rights and liberties of the citizenry *vis-à-vis* public administrators.[46] The old distinction between rights and privileges, which had largely made the Constitution irrelevant to individuals' claims with regard to the receipt of governmental benefits, met its demise. Concomitantly, there was a vast expansion in the requirement that public administrators afford constitutional procedural due process to the individuals upon whom they specifically acted. A new stringency was read into the Eighth Amendment's prohibition of cruel and unusual punishment. Wholly new rights, such as the right to treatment and habilitation, were created, if not fully ratified by the Supreme Court, for those confined to public mental health facilities. The right to equal protection was vastly strengthened and applied in a variety of administrative matters ranging from public personnel merit examinations to the operation of public schools and prisons.

The expansion of the constitutional rights of individuals *vis-à-vis* public administrators has been enforced primarily in two ways, both of which enhance the relevance of the legal approach to contemporary public administration. The courts have sought to force public administrators scrupulously to avoid violating individuals' constitutional rights by reducing public officials' once absolute immunity from civil suits for damages to a qualified immunity.[47] With some exceptions, public administrators are now liable for damages if they "knew or reasonably should have known" that an action taken abridged someone's constitutional rights.[48] In the Supreme Court's view, this approach "in addition to compensating victims, serves a deterrent purpose"[49] that "should create an incentive for officials who may harbor doubts about the lawfulness of their intended actions to err on the side of protecting citizens' constitutional rights."[50] Consequently, the concept of administrative competence is expanded to include reasonable knowledge of constitutional law. In addition, in suits challenging the constitutionality or legality of public institutions such as schools, prisons, and mental health facilities, the courts have frequently decreed on-going relief requiring institutional reforms that place the judges in the role of "partner"[51] with public administrators. Indeed, in some instances judges clearly become supervisors of vast administrative undertakings.[52]

The legal approach to public administration embodies three central values. One is procedural due process. It has long been recognized that this value cannot be confined to any single set of requirements or standards.[53] Rather, the term stands for the value of fundamental fairness and is viewed as requiring procedures designed to protect individuals from malicious, arbitrary, capricious, or unconstitutional harm at the hands of the government. A second value concerns individual substantive rights as embodied in evolving interpretations of the Bill of Rights and the Fourteenth Amendment. In general, the judiciary views the maximization of individual rights and liberties as a positive good and necessary feature of the United States political system. Breaches of these rights may be tolerated by the courts when, on balance, some essential governmental function requires their abridgment. However, the usual presumption is against the government in such circumstances and, consequently, judicial doctrines place a heavy burden on official administrative action that infringes upon the substantive constitutional rights of individuals.[54] Third, the judiciary values equity, a concept that like due process is subject to varying interpretation. However, in terms of public administration in general, equity stands for the value of fairness in the result of conflicts between private parties and the government. It militates against arbitrary or invidious treatment of individuals, encompasses much of the constitutional requirement of equal protection, and enables the courts to fashion relief for individuals whose constitutional rights have been violated by administrative action.

One of the major features of the values of the legal approach to public administration is the downgrading of the cost/benefit reasoning associated with the managerial approach. The judiciary is not oblivious to the costs of its decisions, but its central focus tends to be on the nature of the individual's rights, rather than on the costs to society of securing those rights. This is especially evident in cases involving the reform of public institutions. As one court said, "inadequate resources can never be an adequate justification for the state's depriving any person of his constitutional rights."[55]

Organizational Structure As suggested in the discussion of judicialization, the preferred structure of the legal approach to public administration is one that will maximize the use of adversary procedure. The full-fledged judicial trial is the archetypical model of this structure. In terms of public administration, however, it is generally modified to allow greater flexibility in the discovery of facts. Juries are not used and hearing examiners often play a more active role in bringing out relevant information. Although this structure is often associated with regulatory commissions, its general presence within public administration should not be underestimated. For example, it is heavily relied upon in contemporary public personnel management, especially in the areas of adverse actions, equal employment opportunity, and labor relations.[56] It is also common in instances where governmental benefits, such as welfare or public school education, are being withheld or withdrawn from individuals.[57] The precise structure varies from context to context, but the common element running through it is the independence and impartiality of the hearing examiner. As Dimock points out, to a large extent this independence undermines the managerial approach's reliance on hierarchy. Hearing examiners stand outside administrative hierarchies in an important sense. Although they can be told what to do, that is, which cases to hear, they cannot be told how to rule or decide. Moreover, for all intents and purposes, their rulings may be binding upon public agencies. This may introduce serious limitations on administrative coordination as the hearing examiner's interpretation of law and agency rules may differ from that of the agency's managerial hierarchy. Dimock summarizes the impact of the adjudicatory structure as follows:

> The hearing officers and administrative judges are on a different payroll. Moreover, unlike other officials in his department or agency, the executive is expressly forbidden to fire, discipline, or even communicate with the administrative judge except under very special circumstances, which usually means when the judge submits his proposed order. Under the new system, the judge is isolated in the same manner as a judicial judge, for fear that improper influence will be brought to bear upon him.[58]

To a considerable extent, therefore, this model is at odds with all the values embodied in the other two approaches: It militates against efficiency, economy, managerial effectiveness, representativeness, responsiveness, and political accountability. It is intended, rather, to afford maximum protection of the rights of private parties against illegal, unconstitutional, or invidious administrative action.

View of the Individual The legal approach's emphasis on procedural due process, substantive rights, and equity leads it to consider the individual as a unique person in a unique set of circumstances. The notion that every person is entitled to a "day in court" is appropriate here. The adversary procedure is designed to enable an individual to explain his or her unique and particular circumstances, thinking, motivations, and so forth to the governmental decision maker. Moreover, a decision may turn precisely upon such considerations, which become part of the "merits" of the case. There are some outstanding examples of this in the realm of public administration. For instance, in *Cleveland Board Education* v. *LaFleur* (1974),[59] the Supreme Court ruled that before a mandatory maternity leave could be imposed upon a pregnant public school teacher, she was entitled to an individualized medical determination of her illness to continue on the job. In *Wyatt* v. *Stickney* (1971),[60] a federal district court requires that an individual treatment plan be developed for each person involuntarily confined to Alabama's public mental health facilities. Emphasis on the individual *qua* individual does not, of course, preclude the aggregation of individuals into broader groups, as in the case of class action suits. However, while such a suit may be desirable to obtain widespread change, it does not diminish the legal approach's concern with the rights of specific individuals.

The Separation of Powers

Reflection upon these opposing approaches to public administration suggests that they cannot be synthesized for the simple reason that they are an integral part of a political culture that emphasizes the separation of powers rather than integrated political action. Thus, it is largely true that each of these approaches is associated with the values embodied in a different branch of government. The managerial approach is most closely associated with the executive. The presidency has taken on a vast number of roles and functions, but a major feature of its constitutional power is to make sure that the laws are faithfully executed. This is largely the role of implementation, which is the focus of the managerial approach's definition of public administration. The political approach, by contrast, is more closely associated with legislative concerns. It views public administrators as supplementary law makers and policy makers generally. Hence its emphasis on representativeness, responsiveness, and accountability. The legal approach is very closely related to the judiciary in its concern with individual rights, adversary procedure, and equity.

As Justice Brandeis pointed out, the founders' purpose in creating the constitutional branches was not simply to facilitate efficiency, coordination, and a smooth functioning of government generally. The purpose was also to create a system that would give each branch a motive and a means for preventing abuses or misguided action by another. This would prevent the "accumulation of all powers, legislative, executive, and judiciary, in the same hands," which, as Madison wrote in *Federalist #47*, the founders considered to be "the very definition of tyranny." But the separation of powers would also create a tendency toward inaction. Not only would each branch check the others, but a system of checks and balances would also serve as a check on popular political passions. Thus, the terms of office and the constituencies of members of the House of Representatives and the Senate differ from each other and from those of the president. The judiciary, being appointive, has no constituency *per se* and serves at good behavior, subject to removal by impeachment. Changing the staffing of the government as a whole, therefore, is something that can be accomplished only gradually. Altering its policy initiatives and direction drastically requires widespread consensus among the citizenry. Importantly, some actions of the legislature, such as approving treaties, over-riding vetoes, and proposing constitutional amendments, require extraordinary majorities. This can enable a political minority to protect itself from a majority passion.[61] Overall, the government was designed to be responsive slowly to relatively long-term public demands and to require the development of relatively broad agreement among the electorate prior to taking action.

This model of government has not seemed well-suited to public policy aimed at widespread penetration of the economic and social life of the political community. It is weighted in favor of inertia and inflexibility. In answer to this problem, during the past century or so, the United States developed a large administrative apparatus to facilitate specialized, positive, and flexible governmental action.[62] This phenomenon is commonly referred to as the "rise of the administrative state" and is hardly confined to the United States.[63] However, in this country it represents an effort to reduce the inertial qualities of the system of separation of powers. In essence, all three governmental functions have been collapsed into the administrative branch. Thus, public administrators make rules (legislation), implement these rules (an executive function), and adjudicate questions concerning their application and execution (a judicial function). The collapsing of the separation of powers has been well recognized. As Justice White wrote in *Buckley* v. *Valeo* (1976), "There is no doubt that the development of the administrative agency in response to modern legislative and administrative need has placed severe strain on the separation-of-powers principle in its pristine formulation."[64] This strain has also contributed to a "crisis of legitimacy"[65] in public administration because the accumulation of legislative, executive, and judicial functions in administrative agencies runs counter to the deeply ingrained desire within the political culture for a system of checks and balances.

In a very real fashion, however, a system of checks and balances has devolved to the administrative branch along with the three governmental functions. Thus, as has been argued in this essay, the values associated with each function have been transmuted into distinctive theoretical approaches toward public administration. These approaches have different origins, stress different values and structural arrangements, and view individuals in remarkably different ways. This is precisely because each stresses a different function of public administration. Consequently, although there may be room for greater synthesis of these approaches, seeking to unify theory by allowing one approach to drive out the others would promote public bureaucracy in the most invidious sense of the term. Rather, the task is to develop a distinctive theoretical core suitable to the political culture by building around the need to maintain values, organizational structure, and perspectives on the individual that tends to check and balance each other.

Precisely how such theory may be derived is, of course, not immediately evident or predictable. However, a few ideas come to mind. First, public administrative theorists must recognize the validity and utility of each of the approaches discussed here. Perhaps others can be added in the future, but the legitimacy of each of these is beyond question. Consequently, definition of the field of public administration must include a consideration of managerial, political, and legal approaches. Second, it is necessary to recognize that each approach may be more or less relevant to different agencies, administrative functions, and policy areas. For example, regulation stresses adjudication and, consequently, probably should not be organized primarily according to the managerial or political approaches. Likewise, overhead operations most clearly fall within the purview of the managerial approach. Distributive policy *may* be best organized according to the political approach. Much more thought and research must be devoted to these matters before any firm conclusions can be reached. But clearly it is an administrative fallacy to try to treat all agencies and programs under a universal standard. This is one reason why the much vaunted "rational" budgeting techniques of PPBS and ZBB failed.[66] Third, as heretical as it will sound to some, public administrative theory must make greater use of political theory. As is argued here, the separation of powers goes well beyond the issues of legislative delegation and agency sub-delegation—it reaches to the core of the leading theories of public administration. Finally, attention must be paid to the practical wisdom of the public administrative practitioners whose action is circumscribed by internal considerations of checks, balances, and administrative and political pressures generally. Individual public administrators are often called upon to integrate the three approaches to public administration and much can be learned from their experience.

NOTES

1. Robert Parker, "The End of Public Administration," *Pub. Adm. Rev.* 34 (June 1965): 99, quoted in Richard Stillman, *Public Administration: Concepts and Cases* (Boston: Houghton, Mifflin, 1976), p. 3.
2. Frederick C. Mosher, "Research in Public Administration," *Pub. Adm. Rev.* 16 (summer 1956): 177; Stillman, op. cit., p. 3.
3. Herbert Kaufman, "Emerging Conflicts in the Doctrines of Public Administration," *Am. Pol. Sci. Rev.* 50 (December 1956): 1057–1073.
4. James Q. Wilson, "The Bureaucracy Problem," *The Public Interest* 6 (winter 1976): 3–9.
5. See Gabriel Almond and Sidney Verba, *The Civic Culture* (Boston: Little, Brown, 1965), whose findings provide a useful outline of the values forming the core of the U.S. political culture.
6. Carl Schurz, *The Necessity and Progress of Civil Service Reform* (Washington, D.C.: Good Government, 1894), p. 3.
7. Woodrow Wilson, "The Study of Administration," *Political Science Quarterly*

56 (December 1941): 481–506 (originally copyrighted in 1887).

8. Ibid., p. 481.
9. Frederick Taylor, *The Principles of Scientific Management* (New York: Harper and Bros., 1917).
10. Leonard D. White, *Introduction to the Study of Public Administration* (New York: Macmillan, 1926), pp. vii–viii. See also Herbert J. Storing, "Leonard D. White and the Study of Public Administration," *Pub. Adm. Rev.* 25 (March 1965): 38–51.
11. Luther Gulick and L. Urwick, eds., *Papers on the Science of Administration* (New York: Institute of Public Administration, 1937), pp. 192, 10.
12. Robert Simmons and Eugene Dvorin, *Public Administration* (Port Washington, N.Y.: Alfred Publishing, 1977), p. 217.
13. Max Weber, from *Max Weber: Essays in Sociology,* trans. and ed. H. H. Gerth and C. W. Mills (New York: Oxford University Press, 1958), pp. 196–244.
14. Peter Blau and Marshall Meyer, *Bureaucracy in Modern Society,* 2d ed. (New York: Random House, 1971), esp. p. 8. See also Victor Thompson, *Modern Organization* (New York: Knopf, 1961), pp. 58–80.
15. See Harold Seidman, *Politics, Position, and Power* (New York: Oxford University Press, 1970), chap. 1.
16. See Eugene Lewis, *American Politics in a Bureaucratic Age: Citizens, Constituents, Clients, and Victims* (Cambridge, Mass.: Winthrop, 1977).
17. Weber, op. cit., p. 228.
18. Jay Shafritz et al., *Personnel Management in Government* (New York: Marcel Dekker, 1978), p. 94.
19. Ralph Hummel, *The Bureaucratic Experience* (New York: St. Martin's, 1977), pp. 24–25.
20. See Erving Goffman, *Asylums* (Garden City, N.Y.: Doubleday, 1961), esp. pp. 1–24; *Halderman* v. *Pennhurst State School,* 244 F. Supp. 1295 (1977); *Holt* v. *Sarver,* 304 F. Supp. 362 (1970); John Hersey, *The Algiers Motel Incident* (New York: Knopf, 1968).
21. See Amitai Etzioni, *Modern Organizations* (Englewood Cliffs, N.J.: Prentice-Hall, 1964), chap. 4, for a brief, cogent description of the human relations approach. Victor Thompson, op. cit., discusses bureau pathology at pp. 152–177.
22. Wallace Sayre, "Premises of Public Administration: Past and Emerging," in *Classics of Public Administration,* ed. Jay Shafritz and Albert Hyde (Oak Park, Ill.: Moore, 1978), p. 201. Dwight Waldo, *The Administrative State* (New York: Ronald Press, 1948), demonstrates how the basic value choices of managerial public administration are ultimately statements of political preference.
23. Paul Appleby, *Policy and Administration* (University, Ala.: University of Alabama Press, 1949); see also Theodore Lowi, *The End of Liberalism* (New York: W. W. Norton, 1969).
24. *Myers* v. *U.S.,* 52, 293 (1926).
25. David Nachmias and David H. Rosenbloom, *Bureaucratic Government, U.S.A.* (New York: St. Martin's, 1980).
26. The literature here is too vast to cite in its entirety. See Samuel Krislov and David H. Rosenbloom, *Representative Bureaucracy and the American Political System* (New York: Praeger, 1981) for a recent discussion.
27. Public Law 95-454, sect. 3 and sect. 2301 (b) (1). See also *Givhan* v. *Western Line Consolidated School District,* 99 S. Ct. 693 (1979), which enunciates constitutional conditions permitting a public employee to act as a "representative" within a public administrative structure.
28. Public Law 92-463.
29. See William Keefe and Morris Ogul, *The American Legislative Process,* 4th ed. (Englewood Cliffs, N.J.: Prentice-Hall, 1977), p. 407.
30. See Frederick Mosher, *Democracy and the Public Service* (New York: Oxford University Press, 1968); Ralph Hummel, *The Bureaucratic Experience;* Morris Janowitz, Deil Wright, and William Delany, *Public Administration and the Public* (Westport, Conn.: Greenwood, 1977); Lowi, op. cit.; William Morrow, *Public Administration* (New York: Random House, 1975); Bruce Smith and James D. Carroll, eds., *Improving the Accountability and Performance of*

Government (Washington, D.C.: Brookings, 1982).

31. This was an implicit assumption of the 19th-century civil service reformers, who argued that "as the functions of government grow in extent, importance and complexity, the necessity grows of their being administered not only with honesty, but also with trained ability and knowledge" (Carl Schurz, *Congress and the Spoils System* [New York: George Peck, 1895], p. 4). See Harry Kranz, *The Participatory Bureaucracy* (Lexington, Mass.: Lexington Books, 1976); Samuel Krislov, *Representative Bureaucracy* (Englewood Cliffs, N.J.: Prentice-Hall, 1974), for discussions of social representativeness and efficiency.
32. Marver Bernstein, *The Job of the Federal Executive* (Washington, D.C.: Brookings, 1958), p. 30.
33. Ibid., pp. 26–37. See also Herbert Kaufman, *The Administrative Behavior of Federal Bureau Chiefs* (Washington, D.C.: Brookings, 1981), esp. chap. 2.
34. Seidman, op. cit., p. 13.
35. Norton Long, "Power and Administration," in *Bureaucratic Power in National Politics*, ed. Francis Rourke (Boston: Little, Brown, 1965), p. 18.
36. Roger Davidson, "Congress and the Executive: The Race for Representation," in *Congress: The First Branch of Government*, ed. A. DeGrazia (New York: Anchor, 1967), p. 383.
37. See Seidman, op. cit., chap. 1.
38. David Truman, *The Government Process* (New York: Knopf, 1951); see also Arthur Bentley, *The Process of Government* (Chicago: University of Chicago, 1908).
39. Lowi, op. cit., p. 71. See also Grant McConnell, *Private Power and American Democracy* (New York: Knopf, 1966), chaps. 4 and 5.
40. Frank Goodnow, *The Principles of the Administrative Law of the United States* (New York: G. P. Putnam's Sons, 1905).
41. Ibid., p. 17.
42. Marshall Dimock, *Law and Dynamic Administration* (New York: Praeger, 1980), p. 31.
43. Kenneth Davis, *Administrative Law and Government* (St. Paul: West, 1975), p. 6.
44. Dimock, op. cit., chap. 10.
45. Ibid., p. 113. According to Charles Dullea, "Development of the Personnel Program for Administrative Law Judges," *Administrative Law Review* 25 (winter 1973): 41–47, the title "Administrative Law Judge" was created by the U.S. Civil Service Commission.
46. The case law and literature are too voluminous to cite. See David H. Rosenbloom, *Public Administration and Law:* Bench *v.* Bureau *in the United States* (New York: Marcel Dekker, 1983).
47. See *Scheuer* v. *Rhodes*, 416 U.S. 322 (1974). See also Rosenbloom, op. cit., chap. 6.
48. *Wood* v. *Strickland*, 420 U.S. 308, 322 (1975); *Harlow* v. *Fitzgerald*, 50 Law Week 4815 (1982).
49. *Carlson* v. *Green*, 446 U.S. 14 (1980).
50. *Owen* v. *City of Independence*, 445 U.S. 622, 652 (1980).
51. David Bazelon, "The Impact of the Courts on Public Administration," *Indiana Law Journal* 52 (1976): 101–110.
52. Abram Chayes, "The Role of the Judge in Public Law Litigation," *Harvard Law Review* 89 (1976): 1281–1316; Roger Cramton, "Judicial Lawmaking in the Leviathan State," *Pub. Adm. Rev.* 36 (September/October 1976): 551–555.
53. *Hannah* v. *Larche*, 363 U.S. 420 (1960).
54. See for instance, *Branti* v. *Finkel*, 445 U.S. 507, 518 (1980), which requires the public employer to "demonstrate that party affiliation is an appropriate requirement for the effective performance of the public office involved" when making a patronage dismissal.
55. *Hamilton* v. *Love*, 328 F. Supp. 1182, 1194 (1971).
56. See Robert Vaughn, *The Spoiled System* (New York: Charterhouse, 1975); Richard A. Merrill, "Procedure for Adverse Actions against Federal Employees," *Virginia Law Review* 59 (1973): 196–287.
57. *Goldberg* v. *Kelly*, 397 U.S. 254 (1970); *Goss* v. *Lopez*, 419 U.S. 565 (1975).
58. Dimock, op. cit., p. 114.

59. *Cleveland Board of Education* v. *LaFleur,* 414 U.S. 632 (1974). Argued and decided with *Cohen* v. *Chesterfield Co. School Board.*

60. *Wyatt* v. *Stickney,* 325 F. Supp. 781 (1971); 334 F. Supp. 387 (1972).

61. See *Federalist* No. 10.

62. See Peter Woll, *American Bureaucracy,* 2d ed. (New York: Norton, 1977). Woll is among several scholars with a constitutional focus who argue cogently that the administrative process is far more flexible than government according to the original constitutional scheme could be. See also Davis, op. cit. James O. Freedman, *Crisis and Legitimacy* (New York: Cambridge University Press, 1978), chap. 2, provides a brief description of the rise of the contemporary administrative state and the tension between its operation and the founders' concept of the separation of powers.

63. Henry Jacoby, *The Bureaucratization of the World* (Berkeley and Los Angeles: University of California Press, 1978).

64. *Buckley* v. *Valeo,* 424 U.S. 1, 280–281 (1976).

65. Freedman, op. cit.

66. Allen Schick, "A Death in the Bureaucracy," *Pub. Adm. Rev.* 33 (March/April 1973): 146–156; "Budgeting Expert Calls Carter Plan 'Disaster,'" *Houston Post,* April 8, 1977, p. 14A, quotes Peter Phyrr, originator of zero based budgeting, as calling the federal effort to institute ZBB all-at-once "absolute folly."

37

How Does an Idea's Time Come? Agendas, Alternatives, and Public Policies

John W. Kingdon

Greater than the tread of mighty armies is an idea whose time has come.

Victor Hugo

The phrase "an idea whose time has come" captures a fundamental reality about an irresistible movement that sweeps over our politics and our society, pushing aside everything that might stand in its path. We feel that such an event can be recognized by signs like sustained and marked changes in public opinion, repeated mobilization of people with intensely held preferences, and bandwagons onto which politicians of all persuasions climb.

Members of Congress are fond of trotting out the phrase whenever they are advocating a piece of landmark legislation. And policy activists of all kinds often attempt to account for the emergence of an issue to the forefront of attention with such comments as, "I don't know—it was an idea whose time had come, I guess." But what makes an idea's time come? That question is actually part of a larger puzzle: What makes people in and around government attend, at any given time, to some subjects and not to others? Political scientists have learned a fair amount about final enactment of legislation, and more broadly about authoritative decisions made at various locations in government.

But predecision processes remain relatively uncharted territory. We know more about how issues are disposed of than we know about how they came to be issues on the governmental agenda in the first place, how the alternatives from which decision makers chose were generated, and why some potential issues and some likely alternatives never came to be the focus of serious attention.

If academics find these subjects rather murky, practitioners of the art of government scarcely have a clearer understanding of them.

They are able to describe the subjects occupying their attention with some precision, and, in specific instances, can set forth a convincing account of the reasons for their focus on those subjects. But with some exceptions, they are neither inclined nor obliged to develop a more general understanding of the forces that move policy formation processes in one direction or another. As I was reminded by respondents in the study reported in this book, "You're the political scientist, not me" and, "It's your job to put this thing together, so that's not my worry." Yet the subject remains an absolutely critical puzzle for them. As one well-informed individual high in the federal executive branch put it:

> It's a fascinating question that you're dealing with. Why do decision makers pay attention to one thing rather than another? I've seen situations in which the secretary has been dealing with absolute junk when he should be working on some really significant issue. I've always wondered why.

. . . Let no reader begin with the illusion that the journey is easy. In contrast to many areas of study in the social sciences, this one is particularly untidy. Subjects drift onto the agenda and drift off, and it is difficult even to define agenda status. When a subject gets hot for a time, it is not always easy even in retrospect to discern why. The researcher thinks one case study illuminates the process beautifully, only to discover another case study that behaves very differently.

Conceptual difficulties often rise up to ensnare the traveler.

But the journey is also rewarding because the phenomena involved are so central to our comprehension of public policy outcomes and

Source: Excerpt pp. 1–22 from AGENDAS, ALTERNATIVES, AND PUBLIC POLICIES, 2nd ed. by John W. Kingdon.

governmental processes, yet they are so incompletely understood. The patterns of public policy, after all, are determined not only by such final decisions as votes in legislatures, or initiatives and vetoes by presidents, but also by the fact that some subjects and proposals emerge in the first place and others are never seriously considered.[1] This book tries to contribute to a more complete understanding of these predecision public policy processes.

Though a drastic oversimplification, public policy making can be considered to be a set of processes, including at least (1) the setting of the agenda, (2) the specification of alternatives from which a choice is to be made, (3) an authoritative choice among those specified alternatives, as in a legislative vote or a presidential decision, and (4) the implementation of the decision.[2] Success in one process does not necessarily imply success in others. An item can be prominently on the agenda, for instance, without subsequent passage of legislation; passage does not necessarily guarantee implementation according to legislative intent. This study concentrates on the first two processes. We seek to understand why some subjects become prominent on the policy agenda and others do not, and why some alternatives for choice are seriously considered while others are neglected. . . .

Consider Table 1, which shows some subjects in health and transportation that were discussed very infrequently. These figures present several interesting puzzles. Why do items that deserve attention never receive it? Everybody realizes that the population is aging, and that long-term medical care will increasingly be a pressing problem for the society. In view of these demographic projections, why was the subject of long-term care discussed so infrequently by health specialists in the late 1970s?

In view of the tremendous amount of attention the media gave to fraud and abuse during this very period, why did health policy makers and those around them refer so little to that subject when discussing issues that were occupying their attention? Why are intercity buses so far out of sight? Why does a subject like transportation safety, so prominent only a few years earlier, fade so quickly from high agenda status?

By contrast, the cost of medical care was prominently discussed in over 80 percent of my health interviews in most of these years. Why does a subject like cost come to dominate an agenda like health so completely?

Some subjects receive a lot of attention, while others are neglected. This book tries to understand why.

Some Explanations

. . . In general, two categories of factors might affect agenda setting and the specification of alternatives: the participants who are active, and the processes by which agenda items and alternatives come into prominence.

Participants The president, the Congress, bureaucrats in the executive branch, and various forces outside of government (including the media, interest groups, political parties, and the general public) could all be sources of agenda items and alternatives. Thus agenda setting may involve the transfer of items from a nongovernmental, "systemic" agenda to a governmental, "formal" agenda, partly through the mobilization of the relevant publics by leaders.[3]

Or issues may reach the agenda through diffusion of ideas in professional circles and among policy elites, particularly bureaucrats.[4]

Or changes in the agenda may result from a change in party control or in intraparty ideological balances brought about by elections.[5]

Thus a critical locus of initiative may be parties and elected officials. One of the purposes of this study is to ascertain how frequently and under what conditions each of these participants is important, and to determine what sorts of interactions there might be among them.

This book sheds some light on the long-smoldering topic of the sources of initiative, partly by tracking the progression of ideas from one place to another over the years under observation, and partly by learning how seriously the people close to policy making treat these possible influences. What is the relative importance of president and Congress? Within the executive branch, how important are political appointees as opposed to career civil servants? In Congress, what are the respective contributions of staff and members? Do agenda items well up from the public, or is the process better understood as a "top-down"

TABLE 1

Subjects Discussed Infrequently*

HEALTH	
Maternal and child care	14%
Long-term care	13
Government delivery (Community Centers, Veterans Administration, Public Health Service)	11
Fraud and abuse	11
FDA and drugs	9
Mental health	5
TRANSPORTATION	
Environmental impact	16
Pipeline (including coal slurry)	15
Safety	14
Buses	13
Rail nationalization	7

**For each subject, the number is the percentage of health or transportation respondents who treated the subject as very or somewhat prominent, adding across all four years, for the highest-valued variable associated with the subject. . . . Health N = 133: Transportation N = 114.*

sequence? Within the public, what is the place of general public opinion, as contrasted with organized interest groups? How often do ideas come from people like policy analysts, researchers, academics, and consultants, or are such people regarded as quaint irrelevancies? How important are the mass media in focusing officials' attention on some problems and contributing to their neglect of other problems, or do media report attention rather than create it?

Processes of Agenda Setting and Alternative Specification It would surely be unsatisfying to end the story with the importance of various players in the game. We want to know something about the game itself. So aside from the participants, we are interested in the processes by which agendas are set and alternatives are specified. We will deal in this book with three kinds of processes: problems, policies, and politics.

One influence on agendas might be the inexorable march of problems pressing in on the system. A crisis or prominent event might signal the emergence of such problems. The collapse of the Penn Central Railroad or the crash of a DC-10, for example, result in some focus on the financial problems of the railroads or on issues in air safety. Another way of becoming aware of a problem might be change in a widely respected indicator: costs of medical care or the size of the Medicare budget increase; energy consumed per ton mile decreases with the application of a given technology; the incidence of rubella or polio inches up; the number of highway deaths per passenger mile rises or falls. How often is governmental attention to problems driven by such indicators, by dramatic events, or by other suggestions that there might be a problem which needs addressing? Indeed, how does a given condition get defined as a problem for which government action is an appropriate remedy?

A second contributor to governmental agendas and alternatives might be a process of gradual accumulation of knowledge and perspectives among the specialists in a given policy area, and the generation of policy proposals by such specialists. Academics' arguments that economic regulation of trucking or airlines only produces inefficiencies, or studies that suggest a greater supply of doctors increases rather than decreases medical costs might gradually diffuse among policy makers, producing perspectives that might make them more receptive to some proposals than to others. The development of a new technology, such as a shunt making renal dialysis possible or a markedly more efficient storage battery for electric automobiles, might create considerable pressure for policy change. But independent of science or knowledge, ideas may sweep policy communities like fads, or may be built gradually through a process of constant discussion, speeches, hearings, and bill introductions. What part does each of these communication or diffusion processes play in agenda setting and alternative specification?[6]

The foregoing suggests that at some points in this book we will forsake the usual political science preoccupation with pressure and influence, and instead take excursions into the world of ideas. One inquiry of the study, indeed, is the extent to which arm-twisting, muscle, and other such metaphors of pressure realistically describe the forces that drive the agenda, and the extent to which persuasion and the diffusion of ideas, good or bad, affect the subjects of attention.

How much do ideas like equity or efficiency affect the participants? More broadly, what values affect the processes, and how much are people motivated by their desire to change the existing order to bring it into line with their conception of the ideal order? How much do they acquire new ideas by studying situations similar to their own in states or other countries? How much do they learn through experimentation, either formally designed experiments or cruder personal experiences? How much does feedback from the operation of existing programs affect the agenda?

Third, political processes affect the agenda.

Swings of national mood, vagaries of public opinion, election results, changes of administration, and turnover in Congress all may have powerful effects. How much change in the agenda and in the seriously considered alternatives is produced by a change of administration, a change of congressional committee chairs, or a marked turnover of personnel in Congress through retirement or defeat at the polls? How much does politicians' receptivity to certain ideas depend on such considerations as maintaining or building electoral coalitions, being reelected, or running for higher office? How much do important people compete for policy turf, and what effect does such competition have? How do important people judge such a vague phenomenon as a shift in national mood?

Each of the three processes—problem recognition, generation of policy proposals, and political events—can serve as an impetus or as a constraint. As an impetus, items are promoted to higher agenda prominence, as when a new administration makes possible the emergence of a new battery of proposals. As a constraint,[7] items are prevented from rising on the agenda, as when a budget constraint operates to rule out the emergence of items that are perceived as being too costly. Some items may not rise on the agenda because of the financial cost, the lack of acceptance by the public, the opposition of powerful interests, or simply because they are less pressing than other items in the competition for attention.

Finally, the study began with several general musings on the nature of the processes to be examined.

Does change take place incrementally, in gradual, short steps, or does one observe sudden, discontinuous change? If both are present, does one pattern describe one part of the process better than another part? Do the participants seem to proceed in an orderly process of planning, in which they identify problems, specify goals, and attend to the most efficient means of achieving these goals? Even if some single participants proceed in this orderly, rational manner, does the process involving many participants take on a less orderly character, with the outcome a product of bargaining among the participants? Or is the process even more free form than that, with problems, proposals, and politics floating in and out, joined by fortuitous events or by the appearance on the scene of a skillful entrepreneur who assembles the previously disjointed pieces? Instead of problem solving, do advocates first generate their pet solutions and then look for problems coming along to which to attach their proposals?

How often is plain dumb luck responsible?

A Brief Preview of the Book

The last few pages have presented a rather formidable array of puzzles. Not all of them will be completely assembled in the pages of this book. But answers to many of these questions and partial answers to others, combined with attempts to build theory about these processes from careful empirical observation, will advance our understanding.

We are now ready to begin our journey through the labyrinth of policy formation.

We first distinguish between participants and processes.

In principle, each of the active participants can be involved in each of the important processes—problem recognition, policy generation, and politics. Policy is not the sole province of analysts, for instance, nor is politics the sole province of politicians. In practice, as we will see, participants specialize to a degree in one or another process, but participants can be seen as conceptually different from processes.

... We will discover, perverse as it might sound to some readers, that textbooks are not always wrong: If any one set of participants in the policy process is important in the shaping of the agenda, it is elected officials and their appointees, rather than career bureaucrats or nongovernmental actors. We will also discuss the clusters of the actors which emerge, arguing that a visible cluster made up of such actors as the president and prominent members of Congress has more effect on the agenda, while a hidden cluster that includes specialists in the bureaucracy and in professional communities affects the specification of the alternatives from which authoritative choices are made.

We will then turn our attention in the remaining chapters of the book to the processes which govern the system.... We first discuss the limitations of three common approaches. A search for origins of public policies turns out to be futile. Comprehensive, rational policy making is portrayed as impractical for the most part, although there are occasions where it is found.

Incrementalism describes parts of the process, particularly the gradual evolution of proposals or policy changes, but does not describe the more discontinuous or sudden agenda change.

Instead of these approaches, we use a revised version of the Cohen-March-Olsen garbage can model of organizational choice to understand agenda setting and alternative generation.[8]

We conceive of three process streams flowing through the system—streams of problems, policies, and politics. They are largely independent of one another, and each develops according to its own dynamics and rules. But at some critical junctures the three streams are joined, and the greatest policy changes grow out of that coupling of problems, policy proposals, and politics.

... [We then] consider how problems come to be recognized and how conditions come to be defined as problems. Problems are brought to the attention of people in and around government by systematic indicators, by focusing events like crises and disasters, or by feedback from the operation of current programs. People define conditions as problems by comparing current conditions with their values concerning more ideal states of affairs, by comparing their own performance with that of other countries, or by putting the subject into one category rather than another.

The generation of policy proposals ... resembles a process of biological natural selection.

Many ideas are possible in principle, and float around in a "policy primeval soup" in which specialists try out their ideas in a variety of ways—bill introductions, speeches, testimony, papers, and conversation. In that consideration, proposals are floated, come into contact with one another, are revised and combined with one another, and floated again. But the proposals that survive to the status of serious consideration meet several criteria, including their technical feasibility, their fit with dominant values and the current national mood, their budgetary workability, and the political support or opposition they might experience. Thus the selection system narrows the set of conceivable proposals and selects from that large set a short list of proposals that is actually available for serious consideration.

The political stream ... is composed of such factors as swings of national mood, administration or legislative turnover, and interest group pressure campaigns. Potential agenda items that are congruent with the current national mood, that enjoy interest group support or lack organized opposition, and that fit the orientations of the prevailing legislative coalitions or current administration are more likely to rise to agenda prominence than items that do not meet such conditions. In particular, turnover of key participants, such as a change of administration, has powerful effects on policy agendas. The combination of perceived national mood and turnover of elected officials particularly affects agendas, while the balance of organized forces is more likely to affect the alternatives considered.

The separate streams of problems, policies, and politics come together at certain critical times. Solutions become joined to problems, and both of them are joined to favorable political forces. This coupling is most likely when policy windows—opportunities for pushing pet proposals or conceptions of problems—are open. As we argue . . . windows are opened either by the appearance of compelling problems or by happenings in the political stream. Thus agendas are set by problems or politics, and alternatives are generated in the policy stream.

Policy entrepreneurs, people who are willing to invest their resources in pushing their pet proposals or problems, are responsible not only for prompting important people to pay attention, but also for coupling solutions to problems and for coupling both problems and solutions to politics. While governmental agendas are set in the problems or political streams, the chances of items rising on a *decision* agenda—a list of items up for actual action—are enhanced if all three streams are coupled together. Significant movement, in other words, is much more likely if problems, policy proposals, and politics are all coupled into a package. . . .

The processes we will discuss are extraordinarily complex, and the telling of the story is thus complicated. Unlike the juggler who keeps several bowling pins in the air at once, we will concentrate on one pin at a time, allowing the rest to clatter to the floor. If readers are patient, they will notice that the seemingly neglected pins will each receive attention in their turn, and that we will finally assemble them into a pattern as coherent as is allowed by the actual character of the observed processes. We will follow Einstein's sage advice: "Everything should be made as simple as possible, but not simpler."

Notes

1. Schattschneider's oft-quoted statement, "The definition of the alternatives is the supreme instrument of power," aptly states the case. See E. E. Schattschneider, *The Semi-Sovereign People* (New York: Holt, Rinehart, and Winston, 1960), p. 68.
2. When discussing decision-making models, Simon distinguishes between directing attention, discovering or designing possible courses of action, and selecting a particular course of action. These categories roughly correspond to agendas, alternatives and choice. See Herbert Simon, "Political Research: The Decision-Making Framework," in David Easton, ed., *Varieties of Political Theory* (Englewood Cliffs: Prentice-Hall, 1966), p. 19. For another use of similar distinctions, see John W. Kingdon, *Congressmen's Voting Decisions,* 2nd ed. (New York: Harper and Row, 1981), Chapter 12.
3. For a statement of this perspective, see Roger W. Cobb and Charles D. Elder, *Participation in American Politics: The Dynamics of Agenda-Building* (Boston: Allyn and Bacon, 1972), pp. 14–16, 34–35, 85–89.
4. For a treatment of such a process, see Jack L. Walker, "The Diffusion of Innovations Among the American States," *American Political Science Review* 68 (September 1969): 880–899.
5. For treatments of the effects of realignments on policy agendas, see Benjamin Ginsberg, "Elections and Public Policy," *American Political Science Review* 70 (March 1976): 41–49; Barbara Deckard Sinclair, "Party Realignment and the Transformation of the Political Agenda," *American Political Science Review* 71 (September 1977): 940–953; and David Brady, "Congressional Party Realignment and Transformations of Public Policy in Three Realignment Eras," *American Journal of Political Science* 26 (May 1982): 333–360.
6. On diffusion in policy communities, see Walker, "Diffusion of Innovations," op. cit.; and Hugh Heclo, "Issue Networks and the Executive Establishment," in Anthony King, ed., *The New American Political System* (Washington, D.C.: American Enterprise Institute, 1978), pp. 87–124.
7. An excellent summary of constraints on agenda change is in Roger W. Cobb and Charles D. Elder, "Communications and Public Policy," in Dan Nimmo and Keith Sanders, eds., *Handbook of Political Communications* (Beverly Hills: Sage, 1981), Chapter 14, particularly pp. 402–408.
8. Michael Cohen, James March, and Johan Olsen, "A Garbage Can Model of Organizational Choice," *Administrative Science Quarterly* 17 (March 1972): 1–25.

38

The Possibility of Administrative Ethics

Dennis F. Thompson

Is administrative ethics possible? The most serious objections to administrative ethics arise from two common conceptions of the role of individuals in organizations—what may be called the ethic of neutrality and the ethic of structure. Both of these views must be rejected if administrative ethics is to be possible.

Administrative ethics involves the application of moral principles to the conduct of officials in organizations.[1] In the form with which we are primarily concerned here (ethics-in public organizations), administrative ethics is a species of political ethics, which applies moral principles to political life more generally. Broadly speaking, moral principles specify (a) the rights and duties that individuals should respect when they act in ways that seriously affect the well-being of other individuals and society; and (b) the conditions that collective practices and policies should satisfy when they similarly affect the well-being of individuals and society. Moral principles require a disinterested perspective. Instead of asking how an action or policy serves the interest of some particular individual or group, morality asks whether the action or policy serves everyone's interest, or whether it could be accepted by anyone who did not know his or her particular circumstances, such as race, social class, or nationality. Moral judgments presuppose the possibility of a person to make the judgment and a person or group of persons to be judged.

The most general challenge to administrative ethics would be to deny the possibility of ethics at all or the possibility of political ethics. Although a worthy challenge, it should not be the primary concern of defenders of administrative ethics. Theorists (as well as practitioners when they think about ethics at all) have been so preoccupied with general objections to ethics that they have neglected objections that apply specifically to ethics in administration. They have not sufficiently considered that even if we accept the possibility of morality in general and even in politics, we may have doubts about it in organizations.

To isolate more specifically the objections to administrative ethics, we should assume that the moral perspective can be vindicated and that some moral principles and some moral judgments are valid. Despite disagreement about how morality is to be justified and disagreement about its scope and content, we nevertheless share certain attitudes and beliefs to which we can appeal in criticizing or defending public actions and policies from a moral perspective.[2]

The more direct challenge to administrative ethics comes from those who admit that morality is perfectly possible in private life but deny that it is possible in organizational life. The challenge is that by its very nature administration precludes the exercise of moral judgment. It consists of two basic objections—the first calls into question the subject of the judgment (who may judge); the second, the object of judgment (who is judged). The first asserts that administrators ought to act neutrally in the sense that they should follow not their own moral principles but the decisions and policies of the organization. This is the ethic of neutrality. The second asserts that not administrators butthe organization (and its formal officers) should be held responsible for its decisions and policies. This is the ethic of structure. Each is called an ethic because it expresses certain norms and prescribes conduct. But neither constitutes an ethic or a morality because each denies one of the presuppositions of moral judgment—either a person to judge or a person to be judged.

Source: Reprinted with permission from Public Administration Review. © 1985 by the American Society for Public Administration (ASPA), 1120 G Street, NW, Suite 700, Washington, D.C. 20005. All rights reserved. Reprinted by permission of Blackwell Publishing.

I. The Ethic of Neutrality

The conventional theory and practice of administrative ethics holds that administrators should carry out the orders of their superiors and the policies of the agency and the government they serve.[3] On this view, administrators are ethically neutral in the sense that they do not exercise independent moral judgment. They are not expected to act on any moral principles of their own, but are to give effect to whatever principles are reflected in the orders and policies they are charged with implementing. They serve the organization so that the organization may serve society. Officials are morally obliged to serve the organization in this way because their acceptance of office is voluntary: it signifies consent. Officials know in advance what the duties of office will be, and if the duties (or their minds) change, officials can usually leave office.

The ethic of neutrality does not deny that administrators often must use their own judgment in the formulation of policy. But their aim should always be to discover what policy other people (usually elected officials) intend or would intend; or in the case of conflicting directives to interpret legally or constitutionally who has the authority to determine policy. The use of discretion on this view can never be the occasion for applying any moral principles other than those implicit in the orders and policies of the superiors to whom one is responsible in the organization. The ethic of neutrality portrays the ideal administrator as a completely reliable instrument of the goals of the organization, never injecting personal values into the process of furthering these goals. The ethics thus reinforces the great virtue of organization—its capacity to serve any social end irrespective of the ends that individuals within it favor.

A variation of the ethic of neutrality gives some scope for individual moral judgment until the decision or policy is "final." On this view, administrators may put forward their own views, argue with their superiors, and contest proposals in the process of formulating policy. But once the decision or policy is final, all administrators fall into line, and faithfully carry out the policy. Furthermore, the disagreement must take place within the agency and according to the agency's rules of procedure. This variation puts neutrality in abeyance, but "suspended neutrality" is still neutrality, and the choice for the administrator remains to "obey or resign."[4]

Three sets of criticisms may be brought against the ethic of neutrality. First, because the ethic underestimates the discretion that administrators exercise, it impedes the accountability of administrators by citizens. The discretion of administrators goes beyond carrying out the intentions of legislators or the superiors in the organization, not only because often there are no intentions to discover, but also because often administrators can and should take the initiative in proposing policies and mobilizing support for them.[5] The ethic of neutrality provides no guidance for this wide range of substantive moral decision making in which administrators regularly engage. By reinforcing the illusion that administrators do not exercise independent moral judgment, it insulates them from external accountability for the consequences of many of their decisions.

A second set of objections centers on the claim that office-holding implies consent to the duties of office as defined by the organization. While it may be easier to resign from office than from citizenship, it is for many officials so difficult that failure to do so cannot be taken to indicate approval of everything the organization undertakes. For the vast majority of governmental employees, vested rights (such as pensions and seniority) and job skills (often not transferable to the private sector) supply powerful incentives to hold on to their positions. Even if on their own many would be prepared to sacrifice their careers for the sake of principle, they cannot ignore their responsibilities to their families. Higher level officials usually enjoy advantages that make resignation a more feasible option. They can return to (usually more lucrative) positions in business or in a profession. But their ability to do so may depend on their serving loyally while in government, demonstrating that they are the good "team players" on whom any organization, public or private, can rely.

Furthermore, the dynamics of collective decision making discourage even conscientious officials from resigning on principle. Many decisions are incremental, their objectionable character apparent only in their cumulative effect. An official who is involved in the early stages of escalations of this kind (such as aid increases, budget cuts, troop commitments) will find it difficult to object to any subsequent step. The difference between one step and the next is relatively trivial, certainly not a reason to resign on principle. Besides, many decisions and policies represent compromises, and any would-be dissenter can easily be persuaded that because his opponents did not get everything they sought, he should settle for less than what his principles demand. For these and other reasons, an official may stay in office while objecting to the policies of government; a failure to resign therefore does not signify consent.

Proponents of the ethic of neutrality may still insist that officials who cannot fulfill the duties of their office must resign, however difficult it may be to do so. But as citizens we should hesitate before endorsing this as a general principle of administrative ethics. If this view were consistently put into practice, public offices would soon be populated only by those who never had any reason to disagree with anything the government decided to do. Men and women of strong moral conviction would resign rather than continue in office, and we would lose the services of the persons who could contribute most to public life.

Because we do not want to drive persons of principle from office, we should recognize that there may be good moral reasons for staying in office even while disagreeing with the policies of the government. This recognition points to a third set of objections to the ethic of neutrality—that it simplifies the moral circumstances of public office. It tends to portray officials as assessing the fit between their moral principles and the policies of the organization, obeying if the principles and policies match, resigning if they diverge too much. What is important on this view is that in resigning, the individual express "ethical autonomy," which Weisband and Franck, in their otherwise valuable plea for resignations in protest, define as "the willingness to assert one's own principled judgment, even if that entails violating rules, values, or perceptions of the organization, peer group or team."[6] "The social importance of ethical autonomy," they write, "lies not in what is asserted but in the act of asserting." The ethic of neutrality encourages this and similar portrayals of an isolated official affirming his or her own principles against the organization at the moment of resignation. The ethic thereby neglects important considerations that an ethical administrator should take into account in fulfilling the duties while in office.

First of all, as an official you have obligations to colleagues, an agency, and the government as a whole. By accepting office and undertaking collective tasks in an organization, you give others reason to rely on your continued cooperation. Your colleagues begin projects, take risks, make commitments in the expectation that you will continue to play your part in the organization. If you resign, you disappoint these expectations, and in effect break your commitments to your colleagues. A resignation may disrupt many organizational activities, some of which may be morally more important than the policy that occasions the resignation. Presidential Assistant Alexander Haig deployed this kind of argument in October 1973 in an effort to persuade Attorney-General Elliot Richardson to fire Special Prosecutor Archibald Cox. Richardson claimed that he would resign rather than dismiss Cox. Haig argued that resignation or disobedience at this time would jeopardize the president's efforts, which were at a critical stage, to reach a peace settlement in the Middle East.[7] The argument understandably did not convince Richardson (his commitment to Congress and Cox were too clear, and the connection between his resignation and the Middle East settlement too tenuous), but the *form* of the argument Haig invoked was sound. An official must consider his commitments to all of his associates in government and the effect of his intended resignation on the conduct of government as a whole. Officials also have more general obligations to the public. Officials should not decide simply whether they can in good conscience continue to associate themselves with the organization. This could be interpreted as merely wanting to keep one's own hands clean—a form of what some have called "moral self-indulgence."[8]

A third way in which the ethic of neutrality distorts the duties of public administrators is by limiting their courses of action to two—obedience or resignation. Many forms of dissent may be compatible with remaining in office, ranging from quiet protest to illegal obstruction. Some of these, of course, may be morally wrong except under extreme circumstances, but the ethic of neutrality provides no guidance at all here because it rules out, in advance, the possibility of morally acceptable internal opposition to decisions of the organization, at least "final decisions."

The problem, however, is how we can grant officials scope for dissent without undermining the capacity of the organization to accomplish its goals. If the organization is pursuing goals set by a democratic public, individual dissent in the organization may subvert the democratic process. We should insist, first of all, that would-be dissenters consider carefully the basis of their disagreement with the policy in question. Is the disagreement moral or merely political? This is a slippery distinction since almost all important political decisions have moral dimensions. But perhaps we could say that the more directly a policy seems to violate an important moral principle (such as not harming innocent persons), the more justifiable dissent becomes. An official would be warranted in stronger measures of opposition against decisions to bomb civilian targets in a guerrilla war than against decisions to lower trade barriers and import duties.[9] In cases of political disagreement of the latter sort, straightforward resignation seems the most appropriate action (once the decision is final). Dissenters must also consider whether the policy they oppose is a one-time incident or part of a continuing pattern and whether the wrongness of the policy is outweighed by the value of the other policies the organization is pursuing. Furthermore, dissenters must examine the extent of their own involvement and own role: how (formally and informally) responsible are they for the policy? What difference would their opposition make to the policy and to the other policies of the organization? To what extent does the policy violate the ethics of groups to which they are obligated (such as the canons of the legal or medical professions)?

These considerations not only determine whether an official is justified in opposing the organization's policy, but they also help to indicate what methods of dissent the official may be justified in using to express opposition. The more justified an official's opposition, the more justified the official is in using more extreme methods. The methods of dissent may be arrayed on a continuum from the most extreme to the most moderate. Four types of dissent will illustrate the range of this continuum and raise some further issues that any would-be dissenter must consider.

First, there are those forms of dissent in which an official protests within the organization but still helps implement the policy, or (a slightly stronger measure) asks for a different assignment in the organization. In its weakest form, this kind of dissent does not go much beyond the ethic of neutrality. But unlike that ethic, it would permit officials to abstain from active participation in a policy they oppose and to continue their protest as long as they do so in accordance with the accepted procedures of the organization.[10]

One danger of this form of protest is what has been called the "domestication of dissenters."[11] A case in point is George Ball, who as undersecretary of state in the Johnson administration persistently argued against the government's Vietnam policy in private meetings:

> Once Mr. Ball began to express doubts, he was warmly institutionalized: he was encouraged to become the in-house devil's advocate on Vietnam. . . . The process of escalation allowed for periodic requests to Mr. Ball to speak his peace; Ball felt good . . . (he had fought for righteousness); the others felt good (they had given a full hearing to the dovish option); and there was minimal unpleasantness.[12]

In this way dissenters can be "effectively neutralized," and contrary to their intentions, their dissent can even help support the policy they oppose. It is important therefore to consider whether this effect is inevitable, and, if not, to discover the conditions under which it can be avoided.

In a second form of dissent, officials, with the knowledge of, but against the wishes of their superiors, carry their protest outside the organization while otherwise performing their jobs satisfactorily. This is the course of action taken by most of the 65 Justice Department attorneys who protested the decision to permit delays in implementing desegregation decrees in Mississippi in August of 1969.[13] The attorneys signed and publicized a petition denouncing the attorney-general and the president for adopting a policy the attorneys believed violated the law and would require them to act contrary to the ethical canons of the legal profession. They also believed that resignation would not fulfill their obligation to act affirmatively to oppose illegality. Several of the dissenters argued for stronger actions that would directly block the policy, and some gave information to the NAACP Legal Defense Fund, which was opposing the Justice Department in court. Most of the attorneys declined to engage in these stronger actions, however, on the grounds that obstruction would weaken public support for their dissent.

This kind of dissent usually depends, for its efficacy as well as its legitimacy, on the existence of some widely accepted standards to which the dissenters can appeal outside the organization. Professional ethics or even the law may not be sufficient, since people disagree on how to interpret both, but appealing to such standards may at least reassure the public that the dissenters are not using their office to impose the dictates of their private consciences on public policy. When dissenters oppose democratically elected officials, they must find ways to show that they are defending principles that all citizens would endorse.

The third form of dissent is the open obstruction of policy. Officials may, for example, withhold knowledge or expertise that the organization needs to pursue the policy, refuse to step aside so that others can pursue it, or give information and other kinds of assistance to outsiders who are trying to overturn the policy. A few officials may adopt this strategy for a short time, but organizations can usually isolate the dissenters, find other officials to do the job, and mobilize its own external support to counter any opposition that arises outside the organization. In any such event, the dissenters are not likely to retain much influence within the organization. Effective and sustained opposition has to be more circumspect.

We are therefore led to a fourth kind of dissent: covert obstruction. Unauthorized disclosure—the leak—is the most prominent example. Leaks vary greatly in purpose and effect. Some simply provide information to other agencies that are entitled to receive it; others embarrass particular officials within an agency but do not otherwise subvert the agency's policies; others release information to the press or public ultimately reversing a major government policy; and at the extreme, still others give secrets to enemy agents and count as treason. Short of that extreme, we still may want to say that unauthorized disclosure is sometimes justified even when it breaches government procedures or violates the law, as in the release of classified documents.

An analogy is sometimes drawn between official disobedience and civil disobedience. Many democratic theorists hold that citizens in a democracy are justified in breaking the law with the aim of changing a law or policy, but only in certain ways and under certain conditions. Citizens must (1) act publicly; (2) commit no violence; (3) appeal to principles shared by other citizens; (4) direct their challenge against a substantial injustice; (5) exhaust all normal channels of protest before breaking a law; and (6) plan their disobedience so that it does not, in conjunction with that of other citizens, disrupt the stability of the democratic process.[14]

Even if one thinks that civil disobedience is justifiable, one may not agree that official disobedience is warranted. Officials cannot claim the same rights as citizens can, and, it may be said, the analogy does not in general hold. But the analogy may not hold for the opposite reason. In extreme cases of governmental wrongdoing, so much is at stake that we should give officials greater scope for disobedience than we allow citizens. In these cases we might be prepared to argue that the standard conditions for civil disobedience are too restrictive for officials. If we insist, for example, that disobedience always be carried out in public, we may in effect suppress much valuable criticism of government. Fearful of the consequences of public action, dissenting officials may decide against providing information that their superiors have declared secret but that citizens ought to know. The point of relaxing the requirement of publicity would be not to protect the rights of dissenters for their own sake but to promote public discussion of questionable actions of government. We may wish to retain some form of the requirement of publicity, perhaps by establishing an authority to whom a dissenter must make his or her identity known. But this requirement, as well as the others, should be formulated with the goal of maximizing the responsibility of governmental officials, not with the aim of matching exactly the traditional criteria of civil disobedience.

The important task, with respect to disobedience as well as the other forms of dissent, is to develop the criteria that could help determine when each is justifiable in various circumstances. The ethic of neutrality makes that task unnecessary by denying that ethics is possible in administration. But, as we have seen, that administrative neutrality itself is neither possible nor desirable.

II. The Ethic of Structure

The second major obstacle to administrative ethics is the view that the object of moral judgment must be the organization or the government as a whole. This ethic of structure asserts that, even if administrators may have some scope for independent moral judgment, they cannot be held morally responsible for most of the decisions and policies of government. Their personal moral responsibility extends only to the specific duties of their own office for which they are legally liable.

Moral judgment presupposes moral agency. To praise or blame someone for an outcome, we must assume that the person is morally responsible for the action. We must assume (1) that the person's actions or omissions were a cause of the outcome; and (2) that the person did not act in excusable ignorance or under compulsion. In everyday life, we sometimes withhold moral criticism because we think a person does not satisfy one or both of these criteria. But since usually so few agents are involved and because the parts they play are obvious enough, we are not normally perplexed about whether anyone can be said to have brought about a particular outcome. The main moral problem is what was the right thing to do, not so much who did it. In public life, especially organizations, the problem of identifying the moral agents, of finding the persons who are morally responsible for a decision or policy, becomes at least as difficult as the problem of assessing the morality of the decision or policy. Even if we have perfect information about all the agents in the organizational process that produced an outcome, we may still be puzzled about how to ascribe responsibility for it. Because many people contribute in many different ways to the decisions and policies of an organization, we may not be able to determine, even in principle, who is morally responsible for those decisions and policies. This has been called "the problem of many hands,"[15] and the assumption that it is not soluble underlies the ethic of structure.

Proponents of the ethic of structure put forward three arguments to deny the possibility of ascribing individual responsibility in organizations and thereby to undermine the possibility of administrative ethics. First, it is argued that no individual is a necessary or sufficient cause of any organizational outcome.[16] The contributions of each official are like the strands in a rope. Together they pull the load: no single strand could do the job alone, but the job could be done without any single strand. Suppose that for many decades the CIA has had a policy of trying to overthrow third-world governments that refuse to cooperate with their operatives, and suppose further that many of these attempts are morally wrong. No one presently in the agency initiated the practice, let us assume, and no one individual plays a very important role in any of the attempts. If any one agent did not do his or her part, the practice would continue, and even particular attempts would still often succeed. How could we say that any individual is the cause of the practice?

A second argument points to the gap between individual intention and collective outcomes. The motives of individual officials are inevitably diverse (to serve the nation, to help citizens, to acquire power, to win a promotion, to ruin a rival). Many praiseworthy policies are promoted for morally dubious reasons, and many pernicious policies are furthered with the best of intentions. In many organizations today, for example, we may well be able to say that no official intends to discriminate against minorities in the hiring and promoting of employees; yet the pattern of appointments and advancements still disadvantages certain minorities. Here we should want to condemn the pattern or policy (so the argument goes), but we could not morally blame any individual official for it.

A third argument stresses the requirements of role. The duties of office and the routines of large organizations require individual actions which, in themselves harmless or even in some sense obligatory, combine to produce harmful decisions and policies by the organization. Although the policy of the organization is morally wrong, each individual has done his or her moral duty according to the requirements of office. The collective sum is worse than its parts. In a review of the policies that led to financial collapse of New York City in the mid-1970s and endangered the welfare and livelihoods of millions of citizens, one writer concludes that no individuals can be blamed for the misleading budgetary practices that helped bring about the collapse: "The delicately balanced financial superstructure was a kind of evolutionary extrusion that had emerged from hundreds of piecemeal decisions."[17]

If we were to accept these arguments, we would let many guilty officials off the moral hook. Without some sense of personal responsibility, officials may act with less moral care, and citizens may challenge officials with less moral effect. Democratic accountability is likely to erode. How can these arguments be answered so that individual responsibility can be maintained in organizations?

First, we should not assess an official's moral responsibility solely according to the proportionate share he or she contributes to the outcome. "Responsibility is not a bucket in which less remains when some is apportioned out."[18] If a gang of 10 thugs beats an old man to death, we do not punish each thug for only one-tenth of the murder (even if no single thug hit him hard enough to cause his death). Further, in imputing responsibility we should consider not only the acts that individuals committed but also the acts they omitted. Even though in the CIA example no one initiated the wrongful policy, many officials could be blamed for failing to try to halt the practice. Admittedly, there are dangers in adopting a notion of "negative responsibility."[19] One is that such a notion can make individuals culpable for almost anything (since there seems to be no limit to the acts that an individual did not do). But in the context of organizations we can more often point to specific omissions that made a significant difference in the outcome and that are ascribable to specific persons. Patterns of omissions can be predicted and specified in advance.

The force of the second argument, which points to the gap between individual intention and collective outcome, can be blunted if we simply give less weight to intentions than to consequences in assessing moral culpability of officials, at least in two of the senses that "intention" is commonly understood—as motive and as direct goal. It is often hard enough in private life to interpret the motives of persons one knows well; in public life it may be impossible to discover the intentions of officials, especially when the motives of so many of those questioning the motives of officials are themselves questionable. Insofar as we can discover motives, they are relevant in assessing character and may sometimes help in predicting future behavior, but administrative ethics does better to concentrate on actions and results in public life.[20]

What about officials who directly intend only good results but, because of other people's mistakes or other factors they do not foresee, contribute to an unjust or harmful policy? Here the key question is not whether the officials actually foresaw this result, but whether they should have foreseen it.[21] We can legitimately hold public officials to a higher standard than that to which we hold ordinary citizens. We can expect officials to foresee and take into account a wider range of consequences, partly because of the general obligations of public office. Where the welfare of so many are at stake, officials must make exceptional efforts to anticipate consequences of their actions.

Moreover, the nature of organization itself often forestalls officials from plausibly pleading that they did not foresee what their actions would cause. Organizations tend to produce patterned outcomes; they regularly make the same mistakes in the same ways. While officials may once or twice reasonably claim they should not have been expected to foresee a harmful outcome to which their well-intentioned actions contributed, there must be some (low) limit to the number of times they may use this excuse to escape responsibility. In the example of discrimination in employment, we would say that officials should recognize that their organizational procedures (combined with social forces) are still producing unjust results in personnel decisions; they become partly responsible for the injustice if they do not take steps to overcome it as far as they can.

The requirements of a role insulate an official from blame much less than the earlier argument implied.[22] The example of the New York City fiscal crisis actually tells against that argument as much as for it. Mayor Beame was one of the officials who disclaimed responsibility for the allegedly deceptive accounting practices on the grounds that they were part of organizational routines established many years earlier and could not be changed in the midst of a crisis. But Beame had also served as comptroller and in the budget office during the years when those accounting practices were initiated.[23] In ascribing responsibility to public officials, we should keep in mind that it attaches to persons, not offices. It cannot be entirely determined by any one role a person holds, and it follows a person through time. These features of personal responsibility are sometimes ignored. Public officials are blamed for an immoral (or incompetent) performance in one role but then appear to start with a clean slate once they leave the old job and take up a new one. This recycling of discredited public figures is reinforced by the habit of collapsing personal responsibility into role responsibility. Another way that officials may transcend their roles should also be emphasized. Even when a role fully and legitimately constrains what an official may do, personal responsibility need not be completely extinguished. Officials may escape blame for a particular decision, but they do not thereby escape responsibility for seeking to change the constraints of role and structure that helped produce that decision, and they do not escape responsibility for criticizing those constraints. Criticism of one's own past and current performance, and the structures in which that performance takes place, may be the last refuge of moral responsibility in public life.

Administrative ethics is possible—at least, the two major theoretical views that oppose its possibility are not compelling. We are forced to accept neither an ethic of neutrality that would suppress independent moral judgment, nor an ethic of structure that would ignore individual moral agency in organizations. To show that administrative ethics is possible is not of course to show how to make it actual. But understanding why administrative ethics is possible is a necessary step not only toward putting it into practice but also toward giving it meaningful content in practice.

NOTES

1. It may be assumed that there is no important philosophical distinction between "ethics" and "morality." Both terms denote the principles of right and wrong in conduct (or the study of such principles). When we refer to the principles of particular professions (e.g., legal ethics or political ethics), "ethics" is the more natural term; and when we refer to personal conduct (e.g., sexual morality), "morality" seems more appropriate. But in their general senses, the terms are fundamentally equivalent. For various definitions of the nature of morality or ethics, see William Frankena, *Ethics*, 2d ed. (Englewood Cliffs, N.J.: Prentice-Hall, 1973), pp. 1–11; Alan Donagan, *The Theory of Morality* (Chicago: University of Chicago Press, 1977), pp. 1– 31; G. J. Warnock, *The Object of Morality* (London: Methuen and Co., 1971), pp. 1–26.
2. Cf. the method of "reflective equilibrium" presented by John Rawls, *A Theory of Justice* (Cambridge, Mass.: Harvard University Press, 1971), pp. 48–51.
3. For citations and analysis of some writers who adopt part or all of the ethic of neutrality, see Joel L. Fleishman and Bruce L. Payne, eds., *Ethical Dilemmas and the Education of Policymakers* (Hastings-on-Hudson, N.Y.: The Hastings Center, 1980), pp. 36–38. Cf. John A. Rohr, *Ethics for Bureaucrats* (New York: Dekker, 1978), pp. 15–47.
4. Cf. George Graham, "Ethical Guidelines for Public Administrations," *Pub. Adm. Rev.* 34 (January/February 1974): 90–92.
5. Donald Warwick, "The Ethics of Administrative Discretion," in *Public Duties,*

ed. Joel Fleishman et al. (Cambridge, Mass.: Harvard University Press, 1981), pp. 93–127.

6. Edward Weisband and Thomas M. Franck, *Resignation in Protest* (New York: Penguin, 1976), p. 3.
7. J. Anthony Lukas, *Nightmare: The Underside of the Nixon Years* (New York: Bantam, 1977), p. 588.
8. On "complicity," see Thomas E. Hill, "Symbolic Protest and Calculated Silence," *Philosophy & Public Affairs* (fall 1979): 83–102. For a defense against the charge of moral self-indulgence, see Bernard Williams, *Moral Luck* (Cambridge: Cambridge University Press, 1981), pp. 40–53.
9. For an example of the latter, see Weisband and Franck, op. cit., p. 46.
10. Cf. Graham, op. cit., p. 92.
11. James C. Thomson, "How Could Vietnam Happen?" *Atlantic*, April 1968, p. 49. Also see Albert Hirschman, *Exit, Voice, and Loyalty* (Cambridge, Mass.: Harvard University Press, 1970), pp. 115–119.
12. Thomson, op. cit., p. 49.
13. Gary J. Greenberg, in *Inside the System*, eds. Charles Peters and T. J. Adams (New York: Praeger, 1970), pp. 195–209.
14. See Rawls, op. cit., pp. 363–391.
15. Dennis F. Thompson, "Moral Responsibility of Public Officials: The Problem of Many Hands," *Am. Pol. Sci. Rev.* 74 (December 1980): 905–916.
16. John Ladd, "Morality and the Ideal of Rationality in Formal Organizations," *Monist* 54 (October 1970): 488–516.
17. Charles R. Morris, *The Cost of Good Intentions* (New York: W. W. Norton, 1980), pp. 239–240. For some other examples of structuralist analyses, see Herbert Kaufman, *Red Tape* (Washington, D.C.: Brookings, 1977), pp. 27–28; Richard J. Stillman, *Public Administration: Concepts and Cases,* 2d ed. (Boston: Houghton Mifflin, 1980), p. 34.
18. Robert Nozick, *Anarchy, State, and Utopia* (New York: Basic Books, 1974), p. 130.
19. Cf. Bernard Williams, "A Critique of Utilitarianism," in *Utilitarianism,* by J. J. C. Smart and Williams (Cambridge: Cambridge University Press, 1973), pp. 93–118.
20. But cf. Joel L. Fleishman, "Self-Interest and Political Integrity," in *Public Duties,* ed. Joel Fleishman et al. (Cambridge, Mass.: Harvard University Press, 1981), pp. 52–92.
21. But cf. Charles Fried, *Right and Wrong,* (Cambridge, Mass.: Harvard University Press, 1978), esp. pp. 21–22, 26, 28, 202–205. More generally on "intention," see Donagan, op. cit., pp. 112–142, and J. L. Mackie, *Ethics* (New York: Penguin, 1977), pp. 203–226.
22. On role responsibility, see H. L. A. Hart, *Punishment and Responsibility* (New York: Oxford University Press, 1968), pp. 212–214; R. S. Downie, *Roles and Values* (London: Methuen, 1971), pp. 121–145.
23. Dennis F. Thompson, "Moral Responsibility and the New York City Fiscal Crisis," in *Public Duties,* ed. Joel Fleishman et al. (Cambridge, Mass.: Harvard University Press, 1981), pp. 266–285.

Understanding Organizational Culture

J. Steven Ott

This book is about organizational culture, a phrase that means two different but related things. First, it is the culture that exists in an organization. When the phrase is used in this sense, it means something similar to the culture in a society and consists of such things as shared values, beliefs, assumptions, perceptions, norms, artifacts, and patterns of behavior. It is the unseen and unobservable force that is always behind organizational activities that can be seen and observed. According to Kilmann and associates (1985), organizational culture is a social energy that moves people to act. "Culture is to the organization what personality is to the individual—a hidden, yet unifying theme that provides meaning, direction, and mobilization."

Second, organizational culture is a way of looking at and thinking about behavior of and in organizations, a perspective for understanding what is occurring. When used in this sense, organizational culture refers to a collection of theories that attempt to explain and predict how organizations and the people in them act in different circumstances. For clarity, *organizational culture* is used in this book to mean the culture of an organization, and *the organizational culture perspective* means the use of organizational culture as a frame of reference for the way one looks at, attempts to understand, and works with organizations.

The organizational culture perspective represents a counterculture within organization theory. Its assumptions, theories, and approaches are very different from those of the dominant structural and systems perspectives. The organizational culture perspective is challenging the views of the structural and systems perspectives about basic issues: for example, how organizations make decisions, and how and why people in organizations behave as they do.

Organizational culture is . . . perhaps the most controversial of the organization theory perspectives. Its theories are based on assumptions about organizations and people that depart radically from those of the mainline perspectives. One important difference is that the organizational culture perspective does not believe that quantitative, experimental-type, logical-positivist, scientific research is especially useful for studying organizations.

In the structural and systems perspectives of organization theory, organizations are assumed to be institutions whose primary purposes are to accomplish established goals. Goals are set by people in positions of formal authority. In these two schools of thought, the primary questions for organization theory involve how best to design and manage organizations so that they achieve their declared purposes effectively and efficiently. The personal preferences of organizational members are restrained by systems of formal rules, by authority, and by norms of rational behavior. In a 1982 article Karl Weick, a leading writer about symbolic management, argues that four organizational conditions must exist in order for the basic assumptions of the structuralists and systemists to be valid:

1. A self-correcting system of interdependent people.
2. Consensus on objectives and methods.
3. Coordination is achieved through sharing information.
4. Organizational problems and solutions must be predictable.

However, Weick is forced to conclude that these conditions seldom exist in modern organizations.

Source: Understanding Organizational Culture by J. Steven Ott. Reprinted by permission of the author.

Assumptions of the Organizational Culture Perspective

The organizational culture school rejects the assumptions of the modern structural and systems schools. Instead, it assumes that many organizational behaviors and decisions are almost predetermined by the patterns of basic assumptions existing in the organization. Those patterns of assumptions have continued to exist and influence behaviors because they have repeatedly led people to make decisions that usually worked for the organization. With repeated use, the assumptions slowly drop out of people's consciousness but continue to influence organizational decisions and behaviors—even when the organization's environment changes. They become the underlying, unquestioned—but virtually forgotten—reasons for "the way we do things here," even when the ways are no longer appropriate. They are so basic, so pervasive, and so totally accepted as the truth that no one thinks about or remembers them. Thus a strong organizational culture controls organizational behavior; for example, it can block an organization from making changes needed to adapt to a changing environment.

From the organizational culture perspective, the personal preferences of organizational members are not restrained by systems of formal rules, authority, and norms of rational behavior. Instead, they are controlled by cultural norms, values, beliefs, and assumptions. In order to understand or predict how an organization will behave under different circumstances, one must know what its patterns of basic assumptions are—its organizational culture.

Every organizational culture is different for several reasons. First, what has worked repeatedly for one organization does not for another, so the basic assumptions differ. Second, an organization's culture is shaped by many factors, including, for example, the societal culture in which it resides; its technologies, markets, and competition; and the personality of its founder(s) or most dominant early leaders. Some organizational cultures are more distinctive than others. Some organizations have strong, unified, pervasive cultures, whereas others have weaker cultures; some organizational cultures are quite pervasive, whereas others have many subcultures in different functional or geographical areas.

Research Bias of the Organizational Culture Perspective

Knowledge of an organization's structure, information systems, strategic planning processes, markets, technology, goals, etc., provides clues about an organizational culture—but not accurately or reliably. As a consequence, an organization's behavior cannot be understood or predicted by studying its structural or systems elements: its organizational culture must be studied. And, the quantitative quasi-experimental research methods used by the structural and systems perspectives *cannot* identify or measure unconscious, virtually forgotten basic assumptions. Van Maanen, Dabbs, and Faulkner (1982) describe a growing wave of disenchantment with the use of quantitative quasi-experimental research methods for studying organizations, mainly because such methods have produced very little useful knowledge about organizations over the last twenty years. Yet quantitative research using quasi-experimental designs, control groups, computers, multivariate analyses, heuristic models, and the like are the essential "tools" of the structural and systems perspectives. More and more the organizational culture perspective is turning to qualitative research methods such as ethnography and participant observation.

The reasons for terming the organizational culture perspective a *counterculture* within the field of organization theory should be becoming evident. The organizational culture perspective believes that the mainstream structural and systems perspectives of organization theory are using the wrong "lenses" to look at the wrong organizational elements in their attempts to understand and predict organizational behavior. Their tools are as ineffective as a hammer is for fixing a leaking pipe. In effect, they are wasting their time.

Radical Change in Organizations

It takes courage to challenge the basic views of a mainstream perspective in any profession or academic discipline. Yet this is just what the organizational culture perspective is doing when it advocates radically different ways of looking at and working with organizations. . . .

The organizational culture perspective is especially useful for describing, explaining, and, to a limited extent, predicting behavior when organizations are facing fundamental changes, particularly changes involving their identities. This is what I refer to in this book as *radical change*. . . .

The usefulness of the organizational culture perspective is not limited to radical change in organizations. It also is helpful for understanding and predicting a host of other types of holistic organizational phenomena and behaviors involving, for example, employee commitment and loyalty, leadership effectiveness, leadership succession, creativity, and innovation and organizational survival strategies. Furthermore, it seems logical to expect that there are strong relationships between aspects of organizational culture and an organization's productivity and quality of outputs—but the existence of culture-productivity relationships has yet to be established.

Other perspectives of organizations (in other words, other groupings of organization theories) are not well suited for explaining or predicting these kinds of holistic organizational phenomena. Moreover, they are least useful during periods of major organizational change, especially when change in an organization's identity is involved. For now, please accept the unsubstantiated and oversimplified assertion that other existing perspectives of organizations do not provide the correct "lenses" through which to "see" organizational culture nor the analytical methods for working with it. By analogy, using any other perspective to work with organizational culture is like trying to watch a three-dimensional movie without those special "3-D glasses."

The organizational culture perspective is important to practicing managers as well as students of organizations, for it provides a new approach for viewing, thinking about, analyzing, understanding, explaining, and predicting organizational behavior. . . .

Despite its usefulness, the organizational culture perspective has major problems and limitations. First, it is only one of many ways of looking at organizations. It is not the ultimate answer—the magic key for understanding all complexities of organizations. Second, the organizational culture perspective has many problems that reflect its youthfulness. Although the phrase "culture of a factory" was used by Elliott Jaques as long ago as 1952, and "organizational culture" was used by Philip Selznick in 1957, few students of management or organizations paid much attention to organizational culture until about 1978. Even then, the subject typically was addressed narrowly, and the writings did not receive much notice. The turning point for the organizational culture perspective came in 1981 and 1982, when it suddenly became a very "hot" topic in books, journals, and periodicals aimed at both management practitioners and academicians.

The perspective's problems and limitations of youthfulness remain today. Minimal consensus exists about much of anything concerned with organizational culture, even among its proponents. The disagreements start with what an organizational culture is. So, it is no surprise that the debates are even more pronounced and heated about its nature, components, and the appropriate situations and methods for applying the perspective. Lack of agreement about these very basic issues causes serious problems for those inclined to use the organizational culture perspective for managing or studying organizations. It creates doubts about the very legitimacy of the perspective.

To be more concrete: consider a few conflicting views about changing an organizational culture. Should a manager even try to do so? If so, what change strategy should be used? For example, Allen and Kraft (1982) are proponents of changing organizational cultures by changing behavioral norms. Davis (1984) disagrees, arguing for chief executive officer–imposed, top-to-bottom, organization-wide change efforts. Schein (1985); Sathe (1985); and Martin and Siehl (1983) all predict failure for any single-strategy organizational culture change program. Schein (1985) cautions that attempts to change organizational cultures can be harmful and, in many situations, should not even be tried.

Leadership provides an excellent second example of the debates. Can a manager change existing leadership styles and practices in an organization by changing the organizational culture, or does one modify the organizational culture by changing leadership practices? Or both? Some writers, including Davis (1984), postulate that dominant, charismatic, organizational founders and chief executive officers are the primary sources, transmitters, and maintainers of organizational cultures. On the other hand, Sergiovanni (1984) describes organizational leadership and the leaders' decision patterns as cultural artifacts. He believes that leaders, leadership styles and practices, and patterns of decisions are created and shaped more by organizational culture than by the leaders themselves.

The youthfulness of the organizational culture perspective is evident in the dearth of comprehensive and integrative writing about it.[1] Schein (1985) and Sathe (1985) bemoaned the problem:

> Unfortunately, most of the writers on organizational culture use different definitions, different methods of determining what they mean by culture, and different standards for evaluating how culture affects organizations. These conceptual and methodological differences make it almost impossible to assess the various claims made. (Schein, 1985, p. x)
>
> Although the importance of corporate culture is now widely acknowledged in both business and academic circles, the available literature leaves something to be desired. . . . This literature is also generally not well grounded in systematic theory and research. (Sathe, 1985, p. 1)

Depending on one's viewpoint, the first comprehensive and integrative studies of organizational culture did not appear until 1984 or 1985. There are now only a few such studies. Schein's (1985) *Organizational Culture and Leadership* is the most notable. Sathe's (1985) *Culture and Related Corporate Realities* is a theoretically sound textbook with readings and cases. Sergiovanni and Corbally's (1984) *Leadership and Organizational Culture* is a stimulating collection of theoretical papers mostly concerned with educational administration.[2] There are several excellent chapters in H. P. Sims, D. A. Gioia, and Associates' (1986) reader, *The Thinking Organization: Dynamics of Organizational Social Cognition.*

As useful as these works are, there has been no serious attempt to present a historical analytical study of the organizational culture perspective in its totality. The situation is equally bleak relative to methods for identifying or deciphering organizational cultures.[3]

Why is there a dearth of good comprehensive integrative writing about organizational culture? The answer requires some reasoned speculation. The first reason has been discussed previously. The perspective is young, and there are few good precedents for researchers and writers to follow and build on. Second, since the late 1960s, the dominant, mainstream perspectives on organizations have assumed that organizations are rational, goal-oriented institutions whose behaviors can be understood by studying their goals, structures, and processes for making decisions. For example, the dominant mainstream perspective, usually termed the *structural and systems school* or the *structural/systems framework* (Bolman and Deal, 1984, chs. 9, 10, and 12), relies on quantitative analytical methods to analyze structures, information, information systems, and decision processes. In contrast, the organizational culture perspective does not assume that organizations are necessarily rational, goal-oriented entities. Whereas the mainstream perspectives tend to work with hard, tangible, quantifiable, organizational variables—often using computer models—the organizational culture perspective focuses on soft, less tangible, more ethereal variables such as basic assumptions, cognitive patterns, values, myths, and unspoken beliefs. Using another analogy, organizational culture is like ordinary air. Usually, it cannot be touched, felt, or seen. It is not noticed unless it changes suddenly. The mainstream perspectives of organizations are not comfortable with air-like variables and concepts. Computerized information systems and statistical, quasi-experimental research methods of the structural and systems perspectives are not designed to measure ethereal concepts such as values, myths, and preconscious underlying assumptions.

Thus, the organizational culture perspective is a counterculture within organization theory. The assumptions, theories, and approaches of countercultures are not readily accepted by members of dominant cultures (Kuhn, 1970, ch. II). They are challenging existing assumptions and beliefs about what is important, how organizations function, and ways of designing and conducting research. It takes courage to advocate new and different ways of looking at and working with organizations—just as the organizational culture perspective is doing.

Third, a comprehensive and integrative study of organizational culture requires analyzing and synthesizing theories and research findings from a wide array of academic disciplines. The task is formidable. Just for starters, the fields of organization theory, archaeology, anthropology, psychology, social psychology, sociology, organizational communication, and even biology contain knowledge, theories, and research methods that are important for understanding organizational culture and using the organizational culture perspective. When one also considers contributions from sub-disciplines such as material anthropology, cultural anthropology, learning theory, cognitive social psychology, social constructionism, clinical psychology, and transactional analysis, it becomes readily apparent why few attempts have been made to synthesize it, to "pull it all together."

Despite the problems, or, more important, because of the problems, the need for an integrative, pulling-it-all-together study is evident. The perspective holds too much potential to be ignored or to remain in its current state of rampant disagreement about even its most basic concepts. . . .

Conclusion

. . . Children must crawl before they walk, walk before they run. They also must develop through a sequence of levels of moral reasoning ability (Kohlberg, 1968, 1969) and psychological or intellectual development (Piaget, 1973).

> Any development . . . supposes duration, and the childhood lasts longer as the species becomes more advanced; the childhood of a kitten and that of a chick are much shorter than that of the human infant since the human infant has much more to learn. (Piaget, 1973, p. 1)

The development of schools of organization theory appears to go through analogous stages. The organizational culture perspective will need to pass through a sequence of developmental steps before it achieves its full potential or becomes a mature perspective. Reaching agreement about what organizational culture is, is the first level—akin to an infant crawling. A definition does not accomplish very much in and of itself, but just like crawling before walking, it is a necessary precondition for advancing to the second developmental level, the level at which organizational cultures can be identified other than through lengthy participant observation.

Once it has become possible to identify or decipher organizational culture with a reasonable amount of effort, the perspective's ability to explain and predict organization behavior—as well as its array of "action tools" for leading effectively and managing organizational change—should expand rapidly. Results of efforts to date to "run" with the organizational culture perspective (to apply it in complex practical situations) while it is still in an early stage of development are predictable (Allen & Kraft, 1982; Davis, 1984; Kilmann, 1984). As with a toddler, its legs are not strong enough; and its sense of balance is not adequate for the task. The organizational culture perspective per se usually is not the problem. Rather, the problem lies in attempting to use the perspective to accomplish that which is beyond its current stage of development.

While a child is in an early stage of moral development, he or she cannot comprehend moral reasoning from more advanced stages—it is beyond the child's mental grasp (Kohlberg, 1968, 1969). Likewise, not enough is known yet about organizational culture and its perspective to appreciate their full potential and, thus, to grasp all that we do not know about them. This book attempts to decrease what is not yet known. . . .

Although this may sound good, it isn't easy to achieve in practice. Systems of homogeneous organizational values, beliefs, and basic assumptions are functional. Multiple viewpoints may be desirable for long-term flexibility and adaptability, but they often create short-term inefficiencies and divisiveness.

Of the many unanswered questions associated with organizational culture, this one may have the most immediate need for answers. Especially considering our social constructionist leanings, how can an organization balance its simultaneous needs for a strong pervasive culture and diverse realities? . . .

With organizational culture, it seems as though every issue raised or question asked only generates one more set of unanswered questions or one more chain of related issues to ponder. Some of the questions raised above in the discussions about "Selecting and Shaping Organizational Leadership" and "Rigidity and Overconformance" almost seem to argue for leaving culture alone. Yet the potential implications of being able to predict organizational decision patterns are too great—too heady—to permit blissful ignorance of the subject.

When the subject is organizational culture, few things or assertions are absolute. Nevertheless, there is one such certainty. Regardless of the future of the organizational culture perspective, organizational cultures themselves are and will remain permanent parts of organizations' realities. Organizational culture is here to stay. It serves necessary purposes. People in organizations need culture for identity, purpose, feelings of belongingness, communication, stability, and cognitive efficiency.

NOTES

1. The term *integrative* is used throughout this study in its ordinary sense, meaning multidisciplinary in approach, sources, and methods, and not directed toward justifying, supporting, or proving a single viewpoint.
2. Bolman and Deal (1984) provides an excellent but brief overview of the "symbolic framework." Kilmann, Saxton, Serpa, and Associates (1985) contains excellent articles but makes no effort to integrate the information.
3. Martin and Siehl (1983); Siehl and Martin (1984); Sathe (1985); Harrison (1972); Pettigrew (1979); Van Maanen, Dabbs, and Faulkner (1982); and Van Maanen (1983) have contributed usefully to aspects of the issue.

REFERENCES

Allen, R. F., & Kraft, C. (1982). *The organizational unconscious: How to create the corporate culture you want and need.* Englewood Cliffs, NJ: Prentice-Hall.

Bolman, L. G., & Deal, T. E. (1984). *Modern approaches to understanding and managing organizations.* San Francisco: Jossey-Bass.

Davis, S. M. (1984). *Managing corporate culture.* Cambridge, MA: Ballinger.

Harrison, R. (1972, May–June). Understanding your organization's character. *Harvard Business Review,* 119–128.

Jaques, Elliott. (1952). *The changing culture of a factory.* New York: Dryden Press.

Kilmann, R. H. (1984). *Beyond the quick fix.* San Francisco: Jossey-Bass.

Kilmann, R. H., Saxton, M. J., Serpa, R., & Associates (Eds.), (1985). *Gaining control of the corporate culture.* San Francisco: Jossey-Bass.

Kohlberg, L. (1968) The child as a moral philosopher. *Psychology Today,* 7, 25–30.

Kohlberg, L. (1969). Stage and sequence: The cognitive-developmental approach to socialization. In D. Goslin (Ed.), *Handbook of socialization theory and research* (ch. 6). Chicago: Rand McNally.

Kuhn, T. S. (1970). *The structure of scientific revolutions.* Chicago: University of Chicago Press.

Martin, J., & Siehl, C. (1983, Autumn). Organizational culture and counterculture: An uneasy symbiosis. *Organizational Dynamics,* 52–64.

Pettigrew, A. M. (1979). On studying organizational cultures. *Administrative Science Quarterly,* 24, 579–581.

Piaget, J. (1973). *The child and reality: Problems of genetic psychology* (trans. by A. Rosin). New York: Grossman Publishers. (Original work published in 1972.)

Sathe, V. (1985). *Culture and related corporate realities: Text, cases, and readings on organizational entry, establishment, and change.* Homewood, IL: Irwin.

Schein, E. H. (1985). *Organizational culture and leadership.* San Francisco: Jossey-Bass.

Selznick, P. (1957). *Leadership in administration: A sociological interpretation.* New York: Harper & Row.

Sergiovanni, T. J., & Corbally, J. E. (1984a). Preface. In T. J. Sergiovanni & J. E. Corbally (Eds.), *Leadership and organizational culture* (pp. vii–x). Urbana, IL: University of Illinois Press.

Sergiovanni, T. J., & Corbally, J. E. (1984b). Theory of practice in educational administration and organizational analysis. In T. J. Sergiovanni & J. E. Corbally (Eds.), *Leadership and organizational culture* (pp. 207–213). Urbana, IL: University of Illinois Press.

Siehl, C., & Martin, J. (1984). The role of symbolic management: How can managers effectively transmit organizational culture? In J. G. Hunt, D. M. Hosking, C. A. Schriesheim, & R. Stewart (Eds.), *Leaders and managers: International perspectives on managerial behavior and leadership* (pp. 227–269). New York: Pergamon Press.

Sims, H. P., Jr., Gioia, D. A., & Associates. (1986). *The thinking organization: Dynamics of organizational social cognition.* San Francisco: Jossey-Bass.

Van Maanen, J. (1982a). Introduction. In J. Van Maanen, J. M. Dabbs, Jr., & R. R. Faulkner (Eds.), *Varieties of qualitative research* (pp. 7–10). Beverly Hills, CA: Sage Publications.

Van Maanen, J. (1982b). Fieldwork on the beat. In J. Van Maanen, J. M. Dabbs, Jr., & R. R. Faulkner (Eds.), *Varieties of qualitative research* (pp. 103–151). Beverly Hills, CA: Sage Publications.

Van Maanen, J. (1983). People processing: Strategies of organizational socialization. In R. W. Allen and L. W. Porter (Eds.), *Organizational influence processes* (pp. 240–259). Glenview, IL: Scott, Foresman & Company.

Weick, K. E. (1982, June). Administering education in loosely coupled schools. *Phi Delta Kappan,* 673–676.

40

From Affirmative Action to Affirming Diversity

R. Roosevelt Thomas, Jr.

Sooner or later, affirmative action will die a natural death. Its achievements have been stupendous, but if we look at the premises that underlie it, we find assumptions and priorities that look increasingly shopworn. Thirty years ago, affirmative action was invented on the basis of these five appropriate premises:

1. Adult, white males make up something called the U.S. business mainstream.
2. The U.S. economic edifice is a solid, unchanging institution with more than enough space for everyone.
3. Women, blacks, immigrants, and other minorities should be allowed in as a matter of public policy and common decency.
4. Widespread racial, ethnic, and sexual prejudice keeps them out.
5. Legal and social coercion are necessary to bring about the change.

Today all five of these premises need revising. Over the past six years, I have tried to help some 15 companies learn how to achieve and manage diversity, and I have seen that the realities facing us are no longer the realities affirmative action was designed to fix.

To begin with, more than half the U.S. work force now consists of minorities, immigrants, and women, so white, native-born males, though undoubtedly still dominant, are themselves a statistical minority. In addition, white males will make up only 15% of the increase in the workforce over the next ten years. The so-called mainstream is now almost as diverse as the society at large.

Second, while the edifice is still big enough for all, it no longer seems stable, massive, and invulnerable. In fact, American corporations are scrambling, doing their best to become more adaptable, to compete more successfully for markets and labor, foreign and domestic, and to attract all the talent they can find....

Third, women and minorities no longer need a boarding pass, they need an upgrade. The problem is not getting them in at the entry level; the problem is making better use of their potential at every level, especially in middle-management and leadership positions. This is no longer simply a question of common decency, it is a question of business survival.

Fourth, although prejudice is hardly dead, it has suffered some wounds that may eventually prove fatal. In the meantime, American businesses are now filled with progressive people—many of them minorities and women themselves—whose prejudices, where they still exist, are much too deeply suppressed to interfere with recruitment. The reason many companies are still wary of minorities and women has much more to do with education and perceived qualifications than with color or gender. Companies are worried about productivity and well aware that minorities and women represent a disproportionate share of the undertrained and undereducated.

Fifth, coercion is rarely needed at the recruitment stage. There are very few places in the United States today where you could dip a recruitment net and come up with nothing but white males. Getting hired is not the problem—women and blacks who are seen as having the necessary skills and energy get into the work force relatively easily. It's later on that many of them plateau and lose their drive and quit or get fired. It's later on that their managers' inability to manage diversity hobbles them and the companies they work for.

In creating these changes, affirmative action had an essential role to play and played it very well. In many companies and communities it still plays that role. But affirmative action is an artificial, transitional intervention intended to give managers a chance to correct an imbalance, an injustice, a mistake. Once the numbers mistake has been corrected, I don't think affirmative action alone can cope with the remaining long-term task of creating a work setting geared to the upward mobility of all kinds of people, including white males. It is difficult for affirmative action to influence upward mobility even in the short run, primarily because it is perceived to conflict with the meritocracy we favor. For this reason, affirmative action is a red flag to every individual who feels unfairly passed over and a stigma for those who appear to be its beneficiaries.

Moreover, I doubt very much that individuals who reach top positions through affirmative action are effective models for younger members of their race or sex. What, after all, do they model? A black vice president who got her job through affirmative action is not necessarily a model of how to rise through the corporate meritocracy. She may be a model of how affirmative action can work for the people who find or put themselves in the right place at the right time.

If affirmative action in upward mobility meant that no person's competence and character would ever be overlooked or undervalued on account of race, sex, ethnicity, origins, or physical disability, then affirmative action would be the very thing we need to let every corporate talent find its niche. But what affirmative action means in practice is an unnatural focus on one group, and what it means too often to too many employees is that someone is playing fast and loose with standards in order to favor that group. Unless we are to compromise our standards, a thing no competitive company can even contemplate, upward mobility for minorities and women should always be a question of pure competence and character unmuddled by accidents of birth.

And that is precisely why we have to learn to manage diversity—to move beyond affirmative action, not to repudiate it. Some of what I have to say may strike some readers—mostly those with an ax to grind—as directed at the majority white males who hold most of the decision-making posts in our economy. But I am speaking to all managers, not just white males, and I certainly don't mean to suggest that white males somehow stand outside diversity. White males are as odd and as normal as anyone else.

The Affirmative Action Cycle

If you are managing diverse employees, you should ask yourself this question: Am I fully tapping the potential capacities of everyone in my department? If the answer is no, you should ask yourself this follow-up: Is this failure hampering my ability to meet performance standards? The answer to this question will undoubtedly be yes.

Think of corporate management for a moment as an engine burning pure gasoline. What's now going into the tank is no longer just gas, it has an increasing percentage of, let's say, methanol. In the beginning, the engine will still work pretty well, but by and by it will start to sputter, and eventually it will stall. Unless we rebuild the engine, it will no longer burn the fuel we're feeding it. As the work force grows more and more diverse at the intake level, the talent pool we have to draw on for supervision and management will also grow increasingly diverse. So the question is: Can we burn this fuel? Can we get maximum corporate power from the diverse work force we're now drawing into the system?

Affirmative action gets blamed for failing to do things it never could do. Affirmative action gets the new fuel into the tank, the new people through the front door. Something else will have to get them into the driver's seat. That something else consists of enabling people, in this case minorities and women, to perform to their potential. This is what we now call managing diversity. Not appreciating or leveraging diversity, not even necessarily understanding it. Just managing diversity in such a way as to get from a heterogeneous work force the same productivity, commitment, quality, and profit that we got from the old homogeneous work force.

The correct question today is not "How are we doing on race relations?" or "Are we promoting enough minority people and women?" but rather "Given the diverse work force I've got, am I getting the productivity, does it work as smoothly, is morale as high, as if every person in the company was the same sex and race and nationality?" Most answers will be, "Well, no, of course not!" But why shouldn't the answer be, "You bet!"?

When we ask how we're doing on race relations, we inadvertently put our finger on what's wrong with the question and with the attitude that underlies affirmative action. So long as racial and gender equality is something we grant to minorities and women, there will be no racial and gender equality. What we must do is create an environment where no one is advantaged or disadvantaged, an environment where "we" is everyone. What the traditional approach to diversity did was to create a cycle of crisis, action, relaxation, and disappointment that companies repeated over and over again without ever achieving more than the barest particle of what they were after.

Affirmative action pictures the work force as a pipeline and reasons as follows: "If we can fill the pipeline with *qualified* minorities and women, we can solve our upward mobility problem. Once recruited, they will perform in accordance with our promotional criteria and move naturally up our regular developmental ladder. In the past, where minorities and women have failed to progress, they were simply unable to meet our performance standards. Recruiting qualified people will enable us to avoid special programs and reverse discrimination."

This pipeline perspective generates a self-perpetuating, self-defeating, recruitment-oriented cycle with six stages:

1. *Problem Recognition.* The first time through the cycle, the problem takes this form—We need more minorities and women in the pipeline. In later iterations, the problem is more likely to be defined as a need to retain and promote minorities and women.
2. *Intervention.* Management puts the company into what we may call an Affirmative Action Recruitment Mode. During the first cycle, the goal is to recruit minorities and women. Later, when the cycle is repeated a second or third time and the challenge has shifted to retention, development, and promotion, the goal is to recruit *qualified* minorities and women. Sometimes, managers indifferent or blind to possible accusations of reverse discrimination will institute special training, tracking, incentive, mentoring, or sponsoring programs for minorities and women.
3. *Great Expectations.* Large numbers of minorities and women have been recruited, and a select group has been promoted or recruited at a higher level to serve as highly visible role models for the newly recruited masses. The stage seems set for the natural progression of minorities and women up through the pipeline. Management leans back to enjoy the fruits of its labor.
4. *Frustration.* The anticipated natural progression fails to occur. Minorities and women see themselves plateauing prematurely. Management is upset (and embarrassed) by the failure of its affirmative action initiative and begins to resent the impatience of the new recruits and their unwillingness to give the company credit for trying to do the right thing. Depending on how high in the hierarchy they have plateaued, alienated minorities and women either leave the company or stagnate.
5. *Dormancy.* All remaining participants conspire tacitly to present a silent front to the outside world. Executives say nothing because they have no solutions. As for those women and minorities who stayed on, calling attention to affirmative action's failures might raise doubts about their qualifications. Do they deserve their jobs, or did they just happen to be in the right place at the time of an affirmative action push? So no one complains, and if the company has a good public relations department, it may even wind up with a reputation as a good place for women and minorities to work.

   If questioned publicly, management will say things like "Frankly, affirmative action is not currently an issue," or "Our numbers are okay," or "With respect to minority representation at the upper levels, management is aware of this remaining challenge."

   In private and off the record, however, people say things like "Premature plateauing is a problem, and we don't know what to do," and "Our top people don't seem to be interested in finding a solution," and "There's plenty of racism and a sexism around this place—whatever you may hear."
6. *Crisis.* Dormancy can continue indefinitely, but it is usually broken by a crisis of competitive pressure, governmental intervention, external pressure from a special interest group, or internal unrest. One company found that its pursuit of a Total Quality program was hampered by the alienation of minorities and women. Senior management at another corporation saw the growing importance of minorities in their customer base and decided they needed minority participation in their managerial ranks. In another case, growing expressions of discontent forced a break in the conspiracy of

silence even after the company had received national recognition as a good place for minorities and women to work.

Whatever its cause, the crisis fosters a return to the Problem Recognition phase, and the cycle begins again. This time, management seeks to explain the shortcomings of the previous affirmative action push and usually concludes that the problem is recruitment. This assessment by a top executive is typical: "The managers I know are decent people. While they give priority to performance, I do not believe any of them deliberately block minorities or women who are qualified for promotion. On the contrary, I suspect they bend over backward to promote women and minorities who give some indication of being qualified.

"However, they believe we simply do not have the necessary talent within those groups, but because of the constant complaints they have heard about their deficiencies in affirmative action, they feel they face a no-win situation. If they do not promote, they are obstructionists. But if they promote people who are unqualified, they hurt performance and deny promotion to other employees unfairly. They can't win. The answer, in my mind, must be an ambitious new recruitment effort to bring in quality people."

And so the cycle repeats. Once again blacks, Hispanics, women, and immigrants are dropped into a previously homogeneous, all-white, all-Anglo, all-male, all native-born environment, and the burden of cultural change is placed on the newcomers. There will be new expectations and a new round of frustration, dormancy, crisis, and recruitment.

Ten Guidelines for Learning to Manage Diversity

The traditional American image of diversity has been assimilation: the melting pot, where ethnic and racial differences were standardized into a kind of American puree. Of course, the melting pot is only a metaphor. In real life, many ethnic and most racial groups retain their individuality and express it energetically. What we have is perhaps some kind of American mulligan stew; it is certainly no puree.

At the workplace, however, the melting pot has been more than a metaphor. Corporate success has demanded a good deal of conformity, and employees have voluntarily abandoned most of their ethnic distinctions at the company door.

Now those days are over. Today the melting pot is the wrong metaphor even in business, for three good reasons. First, if it ever was possible to melt down Scotsmen and Dutchmen and Frenchmen into an indistinguishable broth, you can't do the same with blacks, Asians, and women. Their differences don't melt so easily. Second, most people are no longer willing to be melted down, not even for eight hours a day—and it's a seller's market for skills. Third, the thrust of today's nonhierarchical, flexible, collaborative management requires a ten- or twenty fold increase in our tolerance for individuality.

So companies are faced with the problem of surviving in a fiercely competitive world with a work force that consists and will continue to consist of *unassimilated diversity*. And the engine will take a great deal of tinkering to burn that fuel.

What managers fear from diversity is a lowering of standards, a sense that "anything goes." Of course, standards must not suffer. In fact, competence counts more than ever. The goal is to manage diversity in such a way as to get from a diverse work force the same productivity we once got from a homogeneous work force, and to do it without artificial programs, standards—or barriers.

Managing diversity does not mean controlling or containing diversity, it means enabling every member of your work force to perform to his or her potential. It means getting from employees, first, everything we have a right to expect, and, second—if we do it well—everything they have to give. If the old homogeneous work force performed dependably at 80% of its capacity, then the first result means getting 80% from the new heterogeneous work force too. But the second result, the icing on the cake, the unexpected upside that diversity can perhaps give as a bonus, means 85% to 90% from everyone in the organization.

For the moment, however, let's concentrate on the basics of how to get satisfactory performance from the new diverse work force. There are few adequate models. So far, no large company I know of has succeeded in managing diversity to its own satisfaction. But any number have begun to try.

On the basis of their experience, here are my ten guidelines:

1. *Clarify Your Motivation.* A lot of executives are not sure why they should want to learn to manage diversity. Legal compliance seems like a good reason. So does community relations. Many executives believe they have a social and moral responsibility to employ minorities and women. Others want to placate an internal group or pacify an outside organization. None of these are bad reasons, but none of them are business reasons, and given the nature and scope of today's competitive challenges, I believe only business reasons will supply the necessary long-term motivation. In any case, it is the business reasons I want to focus on here.

In business terms, a diverse work force is not something your company ought to have; it's something your company does have, or soon will have. Learning to manage that diversity will make you more competitive.

2. *Clarify Your Vision.* When managers think about a diverse work force, what do they picture? Not publicly, but in the privacy of their minds?

One popular image is of minorities and women clustering on a relatively low plateau, with a few of them trickling up as they become assimilated into the prevailing culture. Of course, they enjoy good salaries and benefits, and most of them accept their status, appreciate the fact that they are doing better than they could do somewhere else, and are proud of the achievements of their race or sex. This is reactionary thinking, but it's a lot more common than you might suppose.

Another image is what we might call "heightened sensitivity." Members of the majority culture are sensitive to the demands of minorities and women for upward mobility and recognize the advantages of fully utilizing them. Minorities and women work at all levels of the corporation, but they are the recipients of generosity and know it. A few years of this second-class status drives most of them away and compromises the effectiveness of those that remain. Turnover is high.

Then there is the coexistence-compromise image. In the interests of corporate viability, white males agree to recognize minorities and women as equals. They bargain and negotiate their differences. But the win-lose aspect of the relationship preserves tensions, and the compromises reached are not always to the company's competitive advantage.

"Diversity and equal opportunity" is a big step up. It presupposes that the white male culture has given way to one that respects difference and individuality. The problem is that minorities and women will accept it readily as their operating image, but many white males, consciously or unconsciously, are likely to cling to a vision that leaves them in the driver's seat. A vision gap of this kind can be a difficulty.

In my view, the vision to hold in your own imagination and to try to communicate to all your managers and employees is an image of fully tapping the human resource potential of every member of the work force. This vision sidesteps the question of equality, ignores the tensions of coexistence, plays down the uncomfortable realities of difference, and focuses instead on individual enablement. It doesn't say, "Let *us* give *them* a chance." It assumes a diverse work force that includes us and them. It says, "Let's create an environment where everyone will do their best work."

Several years ago, an industrial plant in Atlanta with a highly diverse work force was threatened with closing unless productivity improved. To save their jobs, everyone put their shoulders to the wheel and achieved the results they needed to stay open. The senior operating manager was amazed.

For years he had seen minorities and women plateauing disproportionately at the lower levels of the organization, and he explained that fact away with two rationalizations. "They haven't been here that long," he told himself. And "This is the price we pay for being in compliance with the law."

When the threat of closure energized this whole group of people into a level of performance he had not imagined possible, he got one fleeting glimpse of people working up to their capacity. Once the crisis was over, everyone went back to the earlier status quo—white males driving and everyone else sitting back, looking on—but now there was a difference. Now, as he put it himself, he had been to the mountaintop. He knew that what he was getting from minorities and women was nowhere near what they were capable of giving. And he wanted it, crisis or no crisis, all the time.

3. *Expand Your Focus.* Managers usually see affirmative action and equal employment opportunity as centering on minorities and women, with very little to offer white males. The diversity I'm talking about includes not only race, gender, creed, and ethnicity but also age, background, education, function, and personality differences. The objective is not to assimilate minorities and women into a dominant white male culture but to create a dominant heterogeneous culture.

The culture that dominates the United States socially and politically is heterogeneous, and it works by giving its citizens the liberty to achieve their potential. Channeling that potential, once achieved, is an individual right but still a national concern. Something similar applies in the workplace, where the keys to success are individual ability and a corporate destination. Managing disparate talents to achieve common goals is what companies learned to do when they set their sights on, say, Total Quality. The secrets of managing diversity are much the same.

4. *Audit Your Corporate Culture.* If the goal is not to assimilate diversity into the dominant culture but rather to build a culture that can digest unassimilated diversity, then you had better start by figuring out what your present culture looks like. Since what we're talking about here is the body of unspoken and unexamined assumptions, values, and mythologies that make your world go round, this kind of cultural audit is impossible to conduct without outside help. It's a research activity, done mostly with in-depth interviews and a lot of listening at the water cooler.

The operative corporate assumptions you have to identify and deal with are often inherited from the company's founder. "If we treat everyone as a member of the family, we will be successful" is not uncommon. Nor is its corollary "Father Knows Best."

Another widespread assumption, probably absorbed from American culture in general, is that "cream will rise to the top." In most companies, what passes for cream rising to the top is actually cream being pulled or pushed to the top by an informal system of mentoring and sponsorship.

Corporate culture is a kind of tree. Its roots are assumptions about the company and about the world. Its branches, leaves, and seeds are behavior. You can't change the leaves without changing the roots, and you can't grow peaches on an oak. Or rather, with the proper grafting, you *can* grow peaches on an oak, but they come out an awful lot like acorns—small and hard and not much fun to eat. So if you want to grow peaches, you have to make sure the tree's roots are peach friendly.

5. *Modify Your Assumptions.* The real problem with this corporate culture tree is that every time you go to make changes in the roots, you run into terrible opposition. Every culture, including corporate culture, has root guards that turn out in force every time you threaten a basic assumption.

Take the family assumption as an example. Viewing the corporation as a family suggests not only that father knows best; it also suggests that sons will inherit the business, that daughters should stick to doing the company dishes, and that if Uncle Deadwood doesn't perform, we'll put him in the chimney corner and feed him for another 30 years regardless. Each assumption has its constituency and its defenders. If we say to Uncle Deadwood, "Yes, you did good work for 10 years, but years 11 and 12 look pretty bleak; we think it's time we helped you find another chimney," shock waves will travel through the company as every family-oriented employee draws a sword to defend the sacred concept of guaranteed jobs.

But you have to try. A corporation that wants to create an environment with no advantages or disadvantages for any group cannot allow the family assumption to remain in place. It must be labeled dishonest mythology.

Sometimes the dishonesties are more blatant. When I asked a white male middle manager how promotions were handled in his company, he said, "You need leadership capability, bottom-line results, the ability to work with people, and compassion." Then he paused and smiled. "That's what they say. But down the hall there's a guy we call Captain Kickass. He's ruthless, mean-spirited, and he steps on people. That's the behavior they really value. Forget what they say."

In addition to the obvious issue of hypocrisy, this example also raises a question of equal opportunity. When I asked this young middle manager if he thought minorities and women could meet the Captain Kickass standard, he said he thought they probably could.

But the opposite argument can certainly be made. Whether we're talking about blacks in an environment that is predominantly white, whites in one predominantly black, or women in one predominantly male, the majority culture will not readily condone such tactics from a member of a minority. So the corporation with the unspoken kickass performance standard has at least one criterion that will hamper the upward mobility of minorities and women.

Another destructive assumption is the melting pot I referred to earlier. The organization I'm arguing for respects differences rather than seeking to smooth them out. It is multicultural rather than culture blind, which has an important consequence: When we no longer force people to "belong" to a common ethnicity or culture, then the organization's leaders must work all the harder to define belonging in terms of a set of values and a sense of purpose that transcend the interests, desires, and preferences of any one group.

6. *Modify Your Systems.* The first purpose of examining and modifying assumptions is to modify systems. Promotion, mentoring, and sponsorship comprise one such system, and the unexamined cream-to-the-top assumption I mentioned earlier can tend to keep minorities and women from climbing the corporate ladder. After all, in many companies it is difficult to secure a promotion above a certain level without a personal advocate or sponsor. In the context of managing diversity, the question is not whether this system is maximally efficient but whether it works for all employees. Executives who only sponsor people like themselves are not making much of a contribution to the cause of getting the best from every employee.

Performance appraisal is another system where unexamined practices and patterns can have pernicious effects. For example, there are companies where official performance appraisals differ substantially from what is said informally, with the result that employees get their most accurate performance feedback through the grapevine. So if the grapevine is closed to minorities and women, they are left at a severe disadvantage. As one white manager observed, "If the blacks around here knew how they were really perceived, there would be a revolt." Maybe so. More important to your business, however, is the fact that without an accurate appraisal of performance, minority and women employees will find it difficult to correct or defend their alleged shortcomings.

7. *Modify Your Models.* The second purpose of modifying assumptions is to modify models of managerial and employee behavior. My own personal hobgoblin is one I call the Doer Model, often an outgrowth of the family assumption and of unchallenged paternalism. I have found the Doer Model alive and thriving in a dozen companies. It works like this:

Since father knows best, managers seek subordinates who will follow their lead and do as they do. If they can't find people exactly like themselves, they try to find people who aspire to be exactly like themselves. The goal is predictability and immediate responsiveness because the doer manager is not there to manage people but to do the business. In accounting departments, for example, doer managers do accounting, and subordinates are simply extensions of their hands and minds, sensitive to every signal and suggestion of managerial intent.

Doer managers take pride in this identity of purpose. "I wouldn't ask my people to do anything I wouldn't do myself," they say. "I roll up my sleeves and get in the trenches." Doer managers love to be in the trenches. It keeps them out of the line of fire.

But managers aren't supposed to be in the trenches, and accounting managers aren't supposed to do accounting. What they are supposed to do is create systems and a climate that allow accountants to do accounting, a climate that enables people to do what they've been charged to do. The right goal is doer subordinates, supported and empowered by managers who manage.

8. *Help Your People Pioneer.* Learning to manage diversity is a change process, and the managers involved are change agents. There is no single tried and tested "solution" to diversity and no fixed right way to manage it. Assuming the existence of a single or even a dominant barrier undervalues the importance of all the other barriers that face any company, including, potentially, prejudice, personality, community dynamics, culture, and the ups and downs of business itself.

While top executives articulate the new company policy and their commitment to it, middle managers—most or all of them still white males, remember—are placed in the tough position of having to cope with a forest of problems and simultaneously develop the minorities and women who represent their own competition for an increasingly limited number of promotions. What's more, every time they stumble they will themselves be labeled the major barriers to progress. These managers need help, they need a certain amount of sympathy, and, most of all, perhaps, they need to be told that they are pioneers and judged accordingly.

In one case, an ambitious young black woman was assigned to a white male manager, at his request, on the basis of her excellent company record. They looked forward to working together, and for the first three months, everything went well. But then their relationship began to deteriorate, and the harder they worked at patching it up, the worse it got. Both of them, along with their superiors, were surprised by the conflict and seemed puzzled as to its causes. Eventually, the black woman requested and obtained reassignment. But even though they escaped each other, both suffered a sense of failure severe enough to threaten their careers.

What could have been done to assist them? Well, empathy would not have hurt. But perspective would have been better yet. In their particular company and situation, these two people had placed themselves at the cutting edge of race and gender relations. They needed to know that mistakes at the cutting edge are different—and potentially more valuable—than mistakes elsewhere. Maybe they needed some kind of pioneer training. But at the very least they needed to be told that they were pioneers, that conflicts and failures came with the territory, and that they would be judged accordingly.

9. *Apply the Special Consideration Test.* I said earlier that affirmative action was an artificial, transitional, but necessary stage on the road to a truly diverse work force. Because of its artificial nature, affirmative action requires constant attention and drive to make it work. The point of learning once and for all how to manage diversity is that all that energy can be focused somewhere else.

There is a simple test to help you spot the diversity programs that are going to eat up enormous quantities of time and effort. Surprisingly, perhaps, it is the same test you might use to identify the programs and policies that created your problem in the first place. The test consists of one question: Does this program, policy, or principle give special consideration to one group? Will it contribute to everyone's success, or will it only produce an advantage for blacks or whites or women or men? Is it designed for *them* as opposed to us? Whenever the answer is yes, you're not yet on the road to managing diversity.

This does not rule out the possibility of addressing issues that relate to a single group. It only underlines the importance of determining that the issue you're addressing does not relate to other groups as well. For example, management in one company noticed that blacks were not moving up in the organization. Before instituting a special program to bring them along, managers conducted interviews to see if they could find the reason for the impasse. What blacks themselves reported was a problem with the quality of supervision. Further interviews showed that other employees too—including white males—were concerned about the quality of supervision and felt that little was being done to foster professional development. Correcting the situation eliminated a problem that affected everyone. In this case, a solution that focused only on blacks would have been out of place.

Had the problem consisted of prejudice, on the other hand, or some other barrier to blacks or minorities alone, a solution based on affirmative action would have been perfectly appropriate.

10. *Continue Affirmative Action.* Let me come full circle. The ability to manage diversity is the ability to manage your company without unnatural advantage or disadvantage for any member of your diverse work force. The fact remains that you must first have a work force that is diverse at every level, and if you don't, you're going to need affirmative action to get from here to there.

The reason you then want to move beyond affirmative action to managing diversity is because affirmative action fails to deal with the root causes of prejudice and inequality and does little to develop the full potential of every man and woman in the company. In a country seeking competitive advantage in a global economy, the goal of managing diversity is to develop our capacity to accept, incorporate, and empower the diverse human talents of the most diverse nation on earth. It's our reality. We need to make it our strength.

41

Toward a Feminist Perspective in Public Administration Theory

Camilla Stivers

At present there is virtually no published theoretical work from a feminist perspective in the field of public administration. I hope to make clear in this essay what I mean by a "feminist perspective," to offer from this base some questions that have occurred to me, and to begin to sketch out some initial ideas about what a feminist approach to public administration theory might be like.

To begin requires reviewing some background on the nature of feminist thinking, in order to make clear what I mean by a feminist perspective. I then suggest four current areas in public administration theory[1] where feminist thought might be productively used: the question of administrative knowledge; the model of the ideal public servant; the nature of administrative discretion; and the dimensions of the administrative state. Each of these issues might—and I hope one day will—serve as the focus of in-depth feminist treatment. My purpose in touching on all four in a single essay is to indicate that there are many possible applications of feminist theory to public administration (no doubt many more than the ones I offer here), and to try to stimulate dialogue on this general topic.

Feminist Theory

Most if not all feminist theorists agree that, whatever else it is, feminist theory is critical of existing reality. Feminists view women's historical exclusion from certain human pursuits (such as politics) and confinement to others (such as homemaking) as, if not always deliberate on the part of individual men, certainly not "natural." Feminists argue that such arrangements make women more likely than men to encounter neglected perspectives and to ask submerged questions about the terms and characteristics of our common existence. Feminists are in general agreement that to be a feminist means to bring up these left out or ignored ideas. Understandably, these tend to be experienced by those who take existing reality for granted in the way they usually are intended: as criticism of business-as-usual.

Under the general rubric of criticism fall a host of different perspectives, ranging from liberal-incremental to quite radical ideas about the proper focus and scope of the critique and the extent of the remedies thought necessary. Over the course of a dialogue that has been going on in the feminist community for some 20 years, two very general sorts of perspective have emerged. One, typically but not exclusively associated with liberal feminists, addresses the historical dichotomy in sex roles by seeking to wipe it out to various degrees. This perspective treats perceived differences in men's and women's behavior as largely a side effect of societal sex roles and argues that, by opening up existing arrangements to women, such differences, or at least our feelings that they are important, will largely disappear. Existing values such as those on which liberal politics is based are largely accepted. Individual rights, procedural justice, and so on form the basis for critique (hoisting the system on its own petard, so to speak) rather than being the object of it. The Equal Rights Amendment, affirmative action, and comparable worth policies are products of critique from the liberal feminist perspective.

The second perspective, which has emerged somewhat in reaction to the first, takes the position that perceived differences between men and women, whether natural or not, *matter.* Existing societal systems and norms are seen not as "human" but as the products of male experiences and values. In this view, women's experiences and the values emerging from them are not only different, they are worthy in

Source: Women and Politics, 10, no. 4 (1990).

their own right, and need to be injected in one way or another into existing arrangements, which are seen as unnecessarily one-sided. Presumptive "feminine" values such as nurturance, connectedness, and intuition are to be celebrated, even idealized, rather than left behind in the quest for equality. The work of theorists like Nancy Chodorow (1978), Carol Gilligan (1982), and Mary O'Brien (1981) generally reflect this point of view. Some feminists, such as Mary Daly (1978), even see these values as the basis for a complete paradigm shift.

Recently, a third feminist perspective has made an appearance. It, too, is in response to previous thinking, but attempts to transcend the tension set up by the first two. This perspective suggests that while the celebratory view of women's experiences provides important support for neglected values and capacities, it glosses over real differences among women, which have been produced by influences of race, class, history, and culture. These theorists ask, for example, whether the experiences of poor black women and upper middle class white women may not be significantly different rather than (or possibly as well as) basically alike. In addition, feminists in this framework point to the fact that many if not most feminine values and behaviors have developed within—and continue to be used to support and justify—a context of male dominance. If so, they say, it may not be safe to assume that "women's values," if they do exist, are what they might have been if history and culture had developed differently. Given the shortcomings of the celebratory perspective, the question becomes whether there is a sense of difference that involves neither idealizing nor canceling out women's varied experiences, which are still seen as the source of important neglected questions and problems, but which offer no easy "better way." The direction taken by these arguments is that in proposing a "different" view or standard, the aim should not be to *replace* one framework with another but *to call into question the very terms that constitute the difference between them* and, hence, "to write what cannot be written" (Mary Jacobus, "The Difference of View," quoted in Heilbrun 1988, p. 41). The standpoint that would make this possible is still emerging; but clearly it requires a process of evolution rather than whole-cloth discovery. The work of theorists like Wendy Brown (1988), Joan Landes (1988), Jean Grimshaw (1986), and Lynne Segal (1987) is rich with material suggestive of possible directions.

My intent in thinking about public administration from a feminist perspective is to work from this potentially evolutionary perspective. Within it, I believe, a conversation could develop that might suggest or support new ways of thinking about important issues, concepts and questions in public administration: ways that use rather than ignore the neglected perspectives reflected in particular experiences of particular groups of women. Ultimately, a conversation that takes this sort of direction can transform the field in a positive way. But such a project will not be easily accomplished even if there could be universal agreement about its desirability—and I do not fool myself about the possibility that such a consensus may emerge. The requirements include trying to open up the discourse of public administration to these perspectives; being willing to be radically critical in doing so; but also building from, rather than casting aside, ideas that are already central and valued in the field. I believe that to reject, cast aside, or treat as irrelevant the central issues in the field would amount not to constructing a "feminist perspective on public administration" but to advocating a revolution rather than a transformation. Nevertheless, I am prepared to admit that if public administration deals seriously with feminist theory, the result is likely to strike many as a revolution, albeit, I trust, a bloodless one.

With these initial thoughts about a feminist perspective sketched out, we can move on to the more central part of the discussion: What might a feminist perspective in public administration theory be like? Obviously the development of such a framework is a much more ambitious exercise than one paper, or one person, can encompass. But simply to get a discussion going, I want to suggest some apparently promising avenues along which to approach this work: to sound familiar public administration themes, but, in line with the feminist project, to raise neglected aspects and suggest possible new approaches. Many public administration theorists will note that not all these ideas are "new."

A feminist perspective in many cases supports theoretical trends already at work in the field.

The Quest for Neutrality

Woodrow Wilson's (1978 [1887]) groundbreaking essay argued that administration was legitimate only if it was apolitical, taking its orders from the representative legislature and executing them according to dictates of rationality, comprehensiveness, and efficiency. It may be true, as Paul Van Riper (1984) suggests, that nobody paid much attention to Wilson's essay for the first 50 years or so after its appearance. Clearly, however, the issue Wilson raised has been and is still at the center of the field. The idea that administration can and should be neutral, and with it the notion that a politics-administration dichotomy legitimates the activities of public bureaucracies, today seem simplistic and unrealistic to many. Despite numerous attempts to sound its death knell, however, the culture of neutral expertise is alive and well, as Rosenbloom (1987)—to just take one example—argues.

This is a many-sided dilemma; but one particularly vexing aspect appears to be that we can neither live with the idea of neutral technique nor do without it. Administrators long for right answers in the form of incontrovertible facts at the same time as they recognize the undeniably value-laden nature of their enterprise. No one is naive enough to cling to the idea of a simple fact-value dichotomy any longer; yet we all do obeisance to apparent objectivity.

What can a feminist perspective bring to this problem? No easy answers, surely. But feminism does appear to me to offer some different, potentially fruitful, ways of looking at the situation. For one thing, feminist theorists have argued that the importance of the idea of neutrality can be traced to liberal individualism's insistence that the state maintain moral neutrality with respect to the preferences of autonomous persons. They suggest that the notion of a state—or a state of nature—made up of isolated individuals is an idea foreign to the experiences of most women, whose child bearing and child rearing responsibilities make them acutely aware of the extent to which human beings must depend upon each other to survive. If, instead, we had predicated the nature of modern state upon the essential interconnectedness of human beings, we might be able to conceptualize public values somewhat differently. For example, we might base the public interest dimensions of administrative decision-making as much on the discovery of mutual needs as on the adjudication of competing claims among disconnected utility maximizers. Indeed, mothering (see Chodorow, 1978) and "maternal thinking" (Ruddick, 1989)—despite the neologism "parenting," the activities in question are still largely women's province—are principal counterfactuals to the notion that human behavior can be adequately summarized as self-interested. We have yet, however, to develop a political understanding of interconnectedness, or community, which does not depend for its coherence on an explicitly apolitical view of traditionally feminine activities such as is reflected in the works of Aristotle and Rousseau, and thus on an implicitly masculine understanding of politics (an issue I expand upon below).

On the question of objectivity, feminists have criticized for their masculinity both linear rational thinking and the attempt to achieve unbiased knowledge by means of detached observation. To be sure, human systems organized according to and seemingly dependent upon this mode of thought have been historically male. Sandra Harding (1987) and Evelyn Fox Keller (1985) have each written compellingly in this vein. Keller's treatment of the Baconian metaphor linking the inductive acquisition of knowledge about nature with the act of taking a woman by force exemplifies this stream of thinking in a vivid way. (According to Bacon, the scientific method has "the power to conquer and subdue [Nature], to shake her to her foundations.") In an intensification of recent tendencies in the philosophy of science, Harding argues that there is no such thing as unbiased knowledge in the sense of knowledge unaffected by the characteristics of the knower. She suggests that feminist claims may actually be scientifically preferable because they originate in a more complete, therefore less distorting, social experience.

This work is of great interest, but I approach it with some caution because of its tendency to neglect the diversity of women's—and men's—experiences. What I do think feminism usefully emphasizes is the *partiality of the dominant.* In other words, it seems counterproductive to assume that there is something inherently masculine about linear thinking or the quest for objectivity, as it appears both that women are as capable of such thinking as men and that men are similarly able to think intuitively and wholistically. In a similar way, talk of an essential "women's experience" or "women's values" cancels out the great variety in perspectives, life chances, behaviors, and so on of people of different races, classes, and cultures. But it does seem misguided to take values as universal simply because they are pervasive, and to assume that the men who set up and still predominate in social systems, and their demonstrated values whatever they may be in particular settings, represent the human norm. Although there may not be universal male or female experiences, clearly there *are* in every society socially constructed genders, which carry with them propensities to look at the world in quite different ways. We can use this awareness to expose the incompleteness of our understandings: to undercut, for example, the taken-for-grantedness of values like efficiency, comprehensiveness, and objectivity. From this perspective, a substitute for or way of moving beyond neutrality of technique and standards might be to take steps to assure that the full diversity of perspectives reflected in the field of concern become ingredients in the administrative process. I suggest, further, that it is similarly one-sided to *assume* that out of diversity must come conflict rather than collaboration, or that, when conflict does occur, it must be solved by reference to "objective" standards or techniques.[2]

The Model of the Ideal Public Servant

Because of the decade-long epidemic of bureaucrat-bashing characterizing the public conversation, public administration has been preoccupied with restoring the public servant to a position of societal respect. In the community of theorists, this effort has taken the form of trying to reconceptualize the nature of public service. According to Mitchell and Scott (1987), the American people are disenchanted not so much with their institutions as with the people who run them; in particular, they note, the trustworthiness of people in public life has been called into question. Out of this sort of awareness have come examinations of the ideal personal characteristics or "image" of the public administrator. For example, the 1988 meeting of the American Society for Public Administration featured a symposium on the image of the public administrator and a panel dealing with the life stories of several "exemplary" public servants. The sense of need for this dialogue can be traced to the argument made by the framers of the Constitution, that men [sic] of virtue would be attracted to public life by the possibility of winning public honor and fame, a motivation not only considered noble at the time but perhaps even heroic. Fame is a *public* virtue, one that must be earned through the effort to be a force in history, one bestowed by an audience of the wise and the good (Adair, 1974). In his examination of the lives of Alexander, Wellington, and Ulysses Grant, John Keegan (1987) argues that heroic leadership is a public performance, which validates the hero's authority through the display of virtue. Hero worship, or recourse to exemplars as guidance, becomes structural, a way of stabilizing the political order. Given this, it is understandable that public administration should be seeking an exemplary—even heroic—image. While the typical public servant may have to continue to labor in anonymity, at least the public service as a whole might take on heroic qualities and in so doing validate its authority.

The question of what this image ought to be, however, remains an open one. Feminists have not been slow to take up the question of the nature of heroism, nor to point to its essential masculinity, at least in traditional terms. Certainly most of us would agree that our administrative heroes need not all be men, but we have not yet begun to think about the extent to which the inclusion of women in the pantheon of administrative heroes changes the canons based on which we decide what an exemplary public servant is. Feminist examinations of heroism (e.g., Edwards, 1984; Pearson, 1986) stress the masculinity of the traditional physical mode dating back to ancient Greece, which emphasizes culturally male characteristics such as aggressiveness, physical prowess, and the performance of visible deeds—including actual battle—as the basis for meriting public glory and honor. This heroic image is still not far beneath the surface of our understanding of public life; an example is Garry Wills's mocking reference in a recent review of Larry Speakes's book on life in the Reagan administration: "This is a world, like the Greek poem's, where heroes buckle on bean-pod greaves before they thump the foe with mock epithets, inflicting pygmy terrors on each other." (Wills's review is entitled, "All the President's Mice.")

A feminist approach to the question of heroism, on the other hand, makes it possible to emphasize the challenging, even transformative, potential of the heroic figure—one who explains us to ourselves not so much by reasons as by imaginative projection, and in so doing transforms consciousness. From this perspective the function of the heroic symbol is embodiment of a wide range of otherwise in-effable qualities, rather than performance in the public eye of a narrow set of capacities. If we can come to see women as heroes (rather than as heroines, whom heroes rescue), this calls into question at least a couple of accepted ways of thinking. One is the relationship between gender and behavior. If women do classically heroic—for example, physically courageous—things, then the link between physical courage and masculinity is attenuated. Similarly, the connection between heroism and maleness is weakened when we recognize that traditionally female acts of compassion and nurturance can also be heroic. As Wendy Brown (1988, p. 206) puts it: "In the terms of manliness, courage is overcoming bodily fears and overcoming concerns for life. In contrast, I am suggesting that we need courage to sustain life, to fight for freedom as bearers of life and hence of possibility."

It may well be that, because women's societal position is still marginal in a way that men's isn't, the female hero figure is a particularly potent challenge to existing consciousness and institutions. But, its persistence in myth suggests that the heroic quest is a lesson of the deepest spiritual significance (see, for example—though I take issue with some of its interpretations—Campbell's [1968] great *The Hero with a Thousand Faces*). Thus the feminist challenge to the idea of heroism is positive in essence, though stress may be attached to the social transformation that could result.

Among the possible implications for public administration of reshaping our understanding of heroism may be the need to rethink the desirability of public honor and fame. The framers of the Constitution believed that only a minority of men [sic]—the "better sort"— were qualified to lead the nation. Are the "best" public administrators attracted to public service, as the founders thought, by the opportunity to act before an audience of the wise and the good? Should they be? It appears that many of the modern images of the public administrator, such as the entrepreneur, the advocate, the decision-maker, derive their legitimacy and their appeal from their potential for individual visibility—for glory. Yet it may be that glory is possible for only a few and less widely attractive than might be thought. The need to re-win the public's trust may call for more broadly interactive images.

Administrative Discretion

Theorists who reject the notice of public administration as a neutral technique view it instead as a form of governance. They see governance in the exercise of discretion, when administrators, in order to breathe life into vague legislative mandates, make substantive judgments about the nature of the public interest in particular situations, decisions that have impacts for good or ill on people's lives. The "Blacksburg Manifesto" (Wamsley et al., 1987), to take one example, is an attempt to substantiate the legitimacy of administrative governance. As the Blacksburg theorists point out, the exercise of public authority is an inescapable fact of post-industrial life. Administrative governance is the use of bureaucratic authority for the purpose of system steering; the Manifesto takes the position that the fragmented nature of our system of government makes this a positive opportunity. Norton Long (1981) has also argued along these lines, to the effect that it is a good thing that administrators see themselves to be governing, because no one else is.

The key question is the basis on which discretion shall be exercised. The Blacksburg theorists argue that legitimate administrative discretion is informed and guided by an agency-specific set of normative elements, including the Constitution, laws, regulations, history, agency culture, and a commitment to the "widest possible interpretation of the public interest."

The Blacksburg and similar perspectives do much to counter public administration's overly technocratic tendencies, but their vulnerability to charges of elitism still seems significant. Clearly the Manifesto is meant as a thoughtful reply to the charge that, because administrators are not elected and cannot take detailed orders from the legislature, their decisions are not legitimate. The issue remains a live one, however. In addition, justifications of administrative governance have a hollow ring unless they confront the essentially undemocratic nature of bureaucratic hierarchy.

Questions of power, authority, and hierarchy are central to a growing body of feminist literature, although no one writing in this vein has yet taken up the issue of administrative governance. (Kathy Ferguson's *The Feminist Case against Bureaucracy* [1984], to my mind, despite its virtues neglects fundamental differences between public and private organizations.) But clearly certain feminist ideas appear relevant to an understanding of administrative governance that is less hierarchical and more interactive, therefore less elitist and more democratic. Feminist theories, for example, support a view of power not only as a mode of domination but also as a form of enabling capacity. Similarly, they emphasize the possibility of leadership as facilitation rather than the giving of orders, and authority as accountable expertise rather than as chain of command. Ultimately, working within such a perspective, we should be able to ground administrative legitimacy in accountability that not only is exercised in the privacy of the individual conscience or in the internal processes of a particular agency, but is also tangibly enacted in substantive collaboration with affected others, including members of the general public. The strengthening of these kinds of interpretations should reinforce arguments already being heard in the field to the effect that efforts at centralized control over societal—including administrative—processes appear more and more tenuous and misguided in a world of increasing complexity and unpredictability (a good example is Korten [1981]). If this is true, then the inclusion of a more diverse range of perspectives is one possible way to avoid what Dunn (1981) calls a "Type III" error—incorrect interpretation of the nature of the problem. Collaboration and participation thus become protection against bureaucratic pathology rather than a source of inefficiency.

The Administrative State

Dwight Waldo's classic *The Administrative State* (1948) first introduced the idea that public administration theory is a theory of the state and administrative practice a form of statecraft. Waldo wanted to show how seemingly neutral techniques and principles have normative implications where applied in a public context. But in addition, he called our attention to the existence of *the state* in American society, a problematic insight to many whose political comfort depends upon viewing the United States as an exception to the inevitable development—at least in industrializing countries—of institutional capacity for system steerage. Since Waldo, we have had to acknowledge the substantive, organized exercise of (presumably) legitimate coercion by an "integrated network of institutions, procedures, and human talents . . ." (Skowronek, 1982, p. 15). The persistence of work in the field stressing the fractionated nature of the American system of governance and the need for administration as a balance wheel or fulcrum, attests to our continuing ambivalence about the American administrative state (as Skowronek points out, an institution built *around* administrative capacity rather than one presuming its absence): we want it to be an entity capable of significant power; but as administrators we are reluctant to see this power as oppressive, even potentially. Therefore we stress its necessity. Critics to the right and left of mainstream public administration, of course, remind us of this potential continually, though the nature of the oppression is viewed differently from the two vantage points.

It seems to me that our mixed feelings about the existence of a positive state have to do with our ambivalence about the nature of freedom and what sort of state is required in order to ensure it. I see two problems, and feminist thinking helps to shed light on both.

The first has to do with the dichotomy between the public and private realms on which our liberal heritage depends. The liberal state, as we know, developed in opposition to monarchy, a patriarchal system if ever there was one.

Feminist political theorists join with others in pointing out that the liberal case against monarchy depended on justifying a societal space beyond the reach of *"l'etat c'est moi,"* but they see the development of that space as resting on the exclusion of women from it. From their perspective, we are still operating within an intellectual inheritance in which freedom for some (i.e., men) is profoundly dependent on limiting the freedom of others (women).

For example, Joan Landes' (1988) study of the French Revolution argues that monarchy feminized men by keeping men and women equally helpless in the face of the king's power. Her account portrays an age in which a performative public sphere, while ultimately controlled by the king, offered, in the institution of the *salon,* opportunities for both men and women to be and act in public. The *salon,* known literally as *"le monde"* (the world) was a social institution and cultural terrain controlled by women, who hosted the gatherings. There, new individuals were taught the style, language, and art necessary in order to operate in public—to be seen, to have access to the public conversation. Landes argues that men came to see women's power in the *salons* as analogous to the king's monopoly on the terms of political life. The challenge to patriarchy thus came to be equated in men's minds with the silencing and banishment of women.

This vision has deep roots, of course, dating back to ancient Greece. The *polis,* idealized by so many as the quintessential public space, depended for its existence on the simultaneous presence of a household where women were confined and where the necessities of life could be taken care of by women and slaves, thus freeing men for the life of action-beyond-purpose portrayed so glowingly by Hannah Arendt (1963). (For a devastating critique of this aspect of the Athenian city-state, see Keuls [1985].)

The political theory that freedom depends on a separation between public and private life was reinforced in the modern era by economic restructuring. Numerous observers, feminist and otherwise, have delineated the widening of the gap between the public and private worlds that took place during industrialization; work became something done outside the home, so that women's traditional duties were no longer carried out alongside men's but in isolation. The spread of wage labor, of course, also meant that women's domestic labor was no longer viewed as "work." The banished activities of women were imbued with public purpose by viewing home and family as responsible for developing [male] citizens for their proper place in the state and women as responsible for keeping male aggressiveness in check. Thus the extent to which the state depended on women's silence was masked by assigning them a political "role."

Landes argues that once banished in order that a masculine public sphere can be constructed, women who attempt to fashion public languages violate the code of natural behavior. Having become, because of their exclusion, unutterably different, women's voices can only be heard as partial, while the discourse that constructs the public sphere can be viewed by those taking part in it as universal. Landes suggests that, once the terms of this development are understood, it becomes clear that women (unless they "become men," i.e., obliterate their difference) cannot take possession of a public sphere constructed on masculine lines. We must transform discourse in order to authorize women's participation.

There has been a great deal of attention in public administration, particularly recently, to its essential publicness and what this implies for the nature of administrative practice in the public sector. We have yet to turn our attention, however, to the sense of difference obscured by our taken-for-granted notion of the public. For example, we tend to see intrusion of the state into family life as a violation of privacy, or at least as not Constitutionally mandated (for example, the Supreme Court recently ruled in a child abuse case that the 14th Amendment protects us from the state but does not imply any positive obligation on the part of the state to protect us from violent family members). From women's vantage point, however, the "haven in a heartless world" is frequently cruel, almost always fundamentally limiting.

Let me push this line of thought one notch further by turning to the second of the two problems referred to above, that is, regarding our notions of freedom. Here I draw on Wendy Brown's (1988) critique of our understanding of freedom as existing in a plane beyond necessity. Using material from Aristotle, Arendt, Machiavelli, and Weber, Brown lays out the development and persistence of a culturally masculine idea of politics. She points out the gender origins and dimensions of state-creating: political action (that is, virtue, from *vir* = man), giving form to matter (from *mater*, or mother/woman). By taking political action, men achieve mastery over circumstances (in Machiavelli's terms, they outwit *fortuna*—as Hanna Pitkin [1984] has shown, a woman); they rise above necessity. Forming and controlling the body politic, which becomes an instrument, they can move into the realm where freedom means not being confined by the body. In essence, they can (at least for a time) cheat death. Women meanwhile, as we saw above, remain in the realm of necessity, the world of food, dirt, blood, crying children, and soiled clothing: in sum, the world of subsistence.

As Brown points out, Arendt's form of political action takes this dichotomy to such extremes—any connection whatever with purpose, for Arendt, contaminates action—that her public sphere is completely empty of content: what, then, is all this action to be about? In this view, the true politician lives for, rather than as a result of, politics. He [sic] becomes disembodied by rising above necessity, that is, by relegating it to the care of women. He becomes pure mind, dominating the body, giving it form and purpose but also standing beyond these. As a result, Brown suggests, politics can legitimize the pursuit of aims higher than life (such as "the national interest"). She argues that instead we need to recognize that freedom is embodied: that living things cannot overcome themselves, but must engage with the materials of existence to draw forth possibilities rather than to try to impose form on them (childrearing is Brown's partial model here).

If, as Skowronek suggests, statecraft is institution-building, perhaps this is not too far from Brown's idea of imposing form on matter. I would argue, however, that our emphasis on the administrative state as virtue and administrative discretion as an "opportunity" for positive action in a fragmented polity, is our bid to establish and reserve to ourselves a sphere of freedom: constrained, it is true, by the Constitution, laws, and agency norms, but nonetheless action not fully resolvable to following a set of rules and therefore, at its core, "free." Beguiled by this freedom, we may be slow to ask ourselves the extent to which its exercise depends on the unfreedom of others and our distaste for challenging it, or to look for a mode of action that accepts its embodied nature (that is, its grounding in The People not as an abstraction but as a group of real human beings) and thereby begins to rejoin the body politic with its head and putative mind: the administrative state.

Feminist theory sees the barrier between public and private, erected ostensibly to protect the freedom of all, as supportive of the oppression of many. In a space constructed out of the exclusion of half the human race, as long as this exclusion remains unexamined no heroism of practice is possible. Nor can women be counted in without changing the terms of the dialogue, since in order to enter the public sphere as given, women must leave behind part of ourselves—as must men. The transformation suggested by feminist thought is the opportunity to become whole in the process of writing what has not yet been written. It seems to me that we public administrators need to consider the challenges represented in feminist theory, and use them as a source of creativity. Let us begin the conversation.

Notes

1. By "theory," of course, I mean something much closer to political philosophy than what is arrived at by linking empirically tested hypotheses. I view public administration as a form of governance. As such, its most interesting questions are inherently value-laden and must therefore be dealt with by means of reasoned argument rather than proof.
2. The only well-known woman among classic public administration theorists, Mary Parker Follett, made an argument along these lines that was strikingly different from the perspectives of her contemporaries (see Follett [1918] 1965, [1924] 1951). The field has yet to deal with the radical political implications of Follett's ideas.

REFERENCES

Adair, Douglass. 1974. *Fame and the Founding Fathers,* ed. Trevor Colbourn. New York: W. W. Norton.

Arendt, Hannah. 1963. *The Human Condition.* Chicago: University of Chicago Press.

Campbell, Joseph. 1968. *The Hero with a Thousand Faces.* 2nd ed. Princeton: Princeton University Press.

Brown, Wendy. 1988. *Manhood and Politics: A Feminist Reading in Political Theory.* Totowa, N.J.: Rowman and Littlefield.

Chodorow, Nancy. 1978. *The Reproduction of Mothering.* Berkeley and Los Angeles: University of California Press.

Daly, Mary. 1978. *Gyn-Ecology: The Metaethics of Radical Feminism.* Boston: Beacon Press.

Dunn, William. 1981. *Public Policy Analysis: An Introduction.* Englewood Cliffs, N.J.: Prentice- Hall.

Edwards, Lee R. 1984. *Psyche as Hero: Female Heroism and Fictional Form.* Middlebury, Conn.: Wesleyan University Press.

Ferguson, Kathy. 1984. *The Feminist Case Against Bureaucracy.* Philadelphia: Temple University Press.

Follett, Mary Parker. [1918] 1965. *The New State: Group Organization the Solution of Popular Government.* Gloucester, Mass.: Peter Smith.

Follett, Mary Parker. [1924] 1951. *Creative Experience.* New York: Peter Smith.

Gilligan, Carol. 1982. *In a Different Voice.* Cambridge, Mass.: Harvard University Press.

Grimshaw, Jean. 1986. *Philosophy and Feminist Thinking.* Minneapolis: University of Minnesota Press.

Harding, Sandra. 1987. *Feminism and Methodology: Social Science Issues.* Bloomington: Indiana University Press.

Heilbrun, Carolyn G. 1988. *Writing a Woman's Life.* New York: W. W. Norton.

Keegan, John. 1987. *The Mask of Command.* New York: Viking.

Keller, Evelyn Fox. 1985. *Reflections on Gender and Science.* New Haven: Yale University Press.

Keuls, Eva. 1985. *The Reign of the Phallus: Sexual Politics in Ancient Athens.* New York: Harper and Row.

Korten, David. 1981. "The Management of Social Transformation." *Pub. Adm. Rev.* (Nov.–Dec.): 609–618.

Landes, Joan. 1988. *Women in the Public Sphere in the Age of the French Revolution.* Ithaca: Cornell University Press.

Long, Norton. 1981. "S.E.S. and the Public Interest." *Pub. Adm. Rev.* (May–June): 305–312.

Mitchell, Terence R., and William G. Scott. 1987. "Leadership Failures, the Distrusting Public, and Prospects of the Administrative State." *Pub. Adm. Rev.* (Nov.–Dec.): 445–452.

O'Brien, Mary. 1981. *The Politics of Reproduction.* London: Routledge.

Pearson, Carol. 1986. *The Hero Within: Six Archetypes We Live By.* San Francisco: Harper and Row.

Pitkin, Hanna. 1984. *Fortune Is a Woman: Gender and Politics in the Thought of Niccolo Machiavelli.* Berkeley and Los Angeles: University of California Press.

Rosenbloom, David H. 1987. "Public Administrators and the Judiciary: The 'New Partnership.'" *Pub. Adm. Rev.* (Jan.–Feb.): 75–83.

Ruddick, Sara. 1989. *Maternal Thinking: Toward a Politics of Peace.* Boston: Beacon Press.

Segal, Lynne. 1987. *Is The Future Female?* London: Virago Press.

Skowronek, Stephen. 1982. *Building a New American State: The Expansion of National Administrative Capacities, 1877–1920.* Cambridge: Cambridge University Press.

Van Riper, Paul P. 1984. "The Politics-Administration Dichotomy: Concept or Reality?" In *Politics and Administration: Woodrow Wilson and American Public Administration,* ed. Jack Rabin and James S. Bowman. New York: Marcel Dekker.

Waldo, Dwight. 1948. *The Administrative State.* New York: Ronald Press.

Wamsley, Gary L., Charles T. Goodsell, John A. Rohr, Camilla M. Stivers, Orion F. White, and James F. Wolf. 1987. "The Public Administration and the Governance Process: Refocusing the American Dialogue." In *A Centennial History of the American Administrative State,* ed. Ralph Clark Chandler. New York: Free Press.

Wilson, Woodrow. [1887] 1978. "The Study of Administration." In *Classics of Public Administration,* ed. Jay M. Shafritz and Albert C. Hyde. Oak Park, Ill.: Moore.

42

The Ethics Challenge in Public Service

Carol W. Lewis

The public manager must act quickly in a gray, marginal area where laws are silent or confusing, circumstances are ambiguous and complex, and the manager is responsible, well-meaning, and perplexed. Consider an example from John F. (Jack) Azzaretto, director of the Institute of Public Service at the University of Connecticut (unpublished cases provided to author, May 1990): "In order to avoid dealing with an almost certain grievance and a probable law suit, are you [ethically] correct in taking your superior's advice to overlook the marginal to poor performance of a minority employee?" This example summons honesty, justice, impartiality, loyalty, and prudence, which pull the manager in different directions.

Where does the manager turn? Ethics commissions or designated agency ethics officers are not available in all jurisdictions; where they do exist, their emphasis on compliance means that the legal staff may not be able to help, and they take time to respond. What other resources are there? A friend? The boss? Religion? Philosophy? A survey conducted by the *Wall Street Journal* (1988) asked 1,000 corporate executives to name their most trusted confidant when faced with an ethical situation. The single largest category, 44 percent of all responses, was "myself." Although this kind of self-sufficiency may be popularly admired and what ethical integrity boils down to, it is inadequate in a head-on collision over contending ethical values and principles. Accountability precludes public managers from playing cowboy, shooting from the hip and roaming where they please. Ethical benchmarks and philosophical sounding boards keep managers in tune with public service.

Source: From THE ETHICS CHALLENGE IN PUBLIC SERVICE by Carol W. Lewis. Reprinted by permission of John Wiley & Sons, Inc.

Common Sense

The manager may prefer to rely on character and upbringing for a commonsense, visceral choice between right and wrong. In fact, we make most of our ethical choices this way: in the pit of the stomach, automatically, reflexively, intuitively in the popular sense, by common sense, and in tune with the first category in Exhibit 1. We must do this, or contemplative demands would bring the office to a standstill and suspend our daily lives.

A good start, going with how it "feels" is a suitable and efficient method for making relatively straightforward, routine choices. Having faced these predicaments before, we reliably use our experience again. The best-seller *All I Really Need to Know I Learned in Kindergarten* (Fulghum, 1988) resolves life's muddles with childhood lessons. Of course, this problem-solving approach can only be as good as the character and common sense of the decision maker.

A commonsense approach works well on routine problems. These are the ones amenable to President Bush's advice, "It's not really very complicated. It's a question of knowing right from wrong, avoiding conflicts of interest, bending over backwards to see that there's not even a perception of conflict of interest" (Volcker Commission, 1989, p. 14). This is the approach presumed in the report of the President's Commission on Federal Ethics Law Reform (the Volcker Commission), which argues, "Ethical government means much more than laws. It is a spirit, an imbued code of conduct. It is a climate in which, from the highest to the lowest ranks of policy and decision-making officials, some conduct is *instinctively sensed* as correct and other conduct as being beyond acceptance" (1989, p. 1; emphasis added).

EXHIBIT 1

How Do I Make Ethical Choices?

If I believe
I learned to tell right from wrong as a child and that does not change
an itch, warning bell, or uncomfortable feeling tells me it is wrong
What is there to think about? I have to live with myself and my conscience
sophisticated arguments are used to justify unethical behavior
then I may be using a commonsense approach.

If I believe
some principles like the sanctity of human life must not be compromised
fundamental right and wrong never change, only excuses change
the way we do something is more important than what we do
there are certain things I would never do or condone, for any reason
it is my responsibility and no other reason is needed; it is that simple
then I may be using a principle-based approach.

If I believe
it is not fair to treat people in different circumstances the same
rules are rigid; we need flexibility to respond to changing situations
what matters is people; we do not agree on principles anyway
government should be efficient and effective; it is results that count
noble principles are fine, but I have to be practical when I spend taxpayers' money
then I may be using a results-oriented approach.

Philosophical Perspectives at Work

Well-meaning managers sometimes find themselves sincerely baffled and needing to bounce decisions off someone or something else. The philosophical concepts that have penetrated our society and culture over thousands of years are rich resources. An unfashionable topic? Yes. An annual survey conducted since 1966 by the American Council on Education shows a decline in the proportion of college freshmen for whom developing "a meaningful philosophy of life" is essential or very important ("Fact File," 1990, pp. A33–A34). With the proportion falling from three-fifths in 1976 to two-fifths in 1989, new recruits into public service are unlikely to bring philosophical proficiency with them. Granted, a busy manager may dismiss philosophy as artificial, impractical—as an abuser's guide to reality. Then, too, agency problems do not fit neatly into predrawn ethical categories.

Sometimes the administrative world is complex, circumstances ambiguous, the situation new, and thoughtful reflection is needed for an ethically sound decision. Then, bumping against a true dilemma, we need expert advice. Philosophy is the expert in ethics, a "systematic attempt to understand, establish, or defend basic moral principles or rules of conduct, judgments about what is right and wrong" (American Society for Public Administration, 1989, p. 101). Our thinking about right and wrong rests on two broad philosophical traditions, one based on duty or principle underlying action (deontological) and the other on consequences of action (teleological). A brief review serves as a reminder of their main features. There is no need to repeat at length what is readily available in many philosophy and ethics texts. (For further exploration, see Bok, 1978; French, 1983; and Strauss and Cropsey, 1987.)

Duty or Principle. According to deontological frameworks based on duty or principle, some types of behavior or acts are either good or bad in themselves, and the outcome is irrelevant to moral judgment. As its name implies, this approach uses duties or moral rules or principles as guides to action. The Golden Rule is a familiar example. Another comes from Le Chambon, France, whose residents, community leaders, and public officials defied Nazi orders and saved thousands of people. According to the pastor's wife (recorded in Johnson, 1989–1990, p. 19), "Sometimes people ask me, 'How did you make a decision?' There was no decision to make. The issue was: 'Do you think we are all brothers or not?' "

Immanuel Kant (1724–1804) provides the categorical imperative, a rational rather than a religious formulation whereby one should only act as if one were legislating a universal law for everyone to follow in a preferred world; people are never treated instrumentally, as a means, but only as ends in themselves. An insistence on human beings' dignity and worth is central to Kant's ethical perspective.

Deontological reasoning comes in many shades, depending upon whether the rules of behavior are seen as permanent and universal; knowable or unknowable; derived from revelation, human law, or community norms; and so on. All permutations dictate that there are certain underlying rules according to which behavior is judged, and no matter how desirable the consequences, there are certain things the manager (and government) may not do.

Results. The results-based or teleological approach judges ethical worth by an action's consequences. Because this standard is frequently applied to international affairs, U.S. power on a global scale makes it especially important to understand. An illustration comes from Lieutenant Colonel Oliver North, who played a leading role in the Iran-Contra affair during the second Reagan administration; North explained his lying to Congress this way: "Lying does not come easily to me. But we all had to weigh in the balance the difference between lies and lives."

In results-based reasoning's most familiar form, *utilitarianism,* ethical action means utility maximization, defined as society's net benefit over harm. An excessively simplistic formulation would have it that the ends justify the means, but Figure 1 sounds the necessary warning against this caricature. More sophisticated formulations speak on behalf of impartiality and benefiting all concerned. John Stuart Mill argued, "As between his own happiness and that of others, utilitarianism requires him to be strictly impartial as a disinterested and benevolent spectator." Variations within the results-based approach stem from the good to maximize (happiness? pleasure?) and other factors.

Accommodating the Two Traditions. Our democratic society has been unable or unwilling to reconcile the deontological and teleological traditions or choose between them. So our ideology accommodates both. The American political system operates according to two different ethical standards within constitutional and legal limits. Teleology's utilitarian principle is deeply imbedded in American culture and politics, as illustrated by the widespread use of formal and informal cost-benefit analysis. The Bill of Rights represents deontology's alternative of underlying rules. Their joint role in political discourse is invoked by the remark of Representative Lee H. Hamilton of Indiana at the congressional hearings on Iran-Contra: "A great power cannot base its policy on an untruth, without a loss of credibility." Over a quarter-century earlier, President Kennedy appealed to both duty and results in his 1961 inaugural address: "To those peoples in the huts and villages of half the globe struggling to break the bonds of mass misery, we pledge our best efforts to help them help themselves, for whatever period is required—not because the communists may be doing it, not because we seek their votes, but because it is right. If a free society cannot help the many who are poor, it cannot save the few who are rich."

The result is to burden each elected, appointed, and career public official with responsibility for deciding which standard applies and when. The scope for disagreement was evident during congressional hearings on the Iran-Contra affair, which was in many respects a nationally televised argument over fundamental ethical premises. A principal figure in the intrigue, Lieutenant Colonel Oliver L. North, was deputy director of the political-military affairs bureau at the National Security Council (NSC) from 1981 until November 1986, when President Reagan dismissed him. While the questions asked during his testimony were often phrased in terms of underlying duties, such as to tell the truth, North appealed to the opposing, results-based standard in his answers.

John W. Nields, Jr., the House committee's chief counsel, asserted the ethical principle of truth telling by asking, "Did you ever say, 'You can't do that, it's not true and you cannot commit the President of the United States to a lie'?" North replied, "I don't believe that I ever said that to anyone, no." Nields pressed on, "So none of these people, director of central intelligence, two national security advisers, attorney general, none of them ever made the argument, 'It's not true, you can't say it'?" Again, North replied, "No."

While Nields used the principle of truth, North responded in terms of results. North argued that Congress should be investigated for a "fickle, vacillating, unpredictable" policy toward the Nicaraguan Contras. He, on the other hand, did what was necessary to accomplish the administration's policy goals, irrespective of underlying ethical boundaries (or law). That Nields and North did not agree is hardly surprising; different ethical standards lead to different views of acceptable behavior.

The two ways of thinking induce different responses to problems and offer competing premises upon which to make decisions. This is why changing decision-making premises (meaning the philosophical framework) is so useful in thinking through ethical dilemmas. A series of questions triggers the open-mindedness that incorporates both impartiality and responsibility.

1. What philosophical tradition underlies your proposal or posture?
2. What other moral principles could guide action and alter the proposal or decision?
3. What considerations emerge from alternative philosophical positions?
4. Why would a public manager try to design a proposal that reconciles different philosophical perspeclives?
5. Should anything else be thought about?
6. In your view, is the proposal personally acceptable and ethically persuasive?

(Try applying these questions to the cases that conclude subsequent chapters in this book.) In the end, the individual decision maker is left with the judgment and the responsibility for exercising it.

Views on Public Service

Examining different ideas enriches our thinking by providing nuance and depth. At the same time, these ideas complicate matters by offering different views of public service and behavior befitting different roles. Ideologically, contemporary public service follows the Platonic tradition that stresses public interest as distinguishable from self-interest. According to Bruce Jennings (1989a, p. 175), this is precisely what judgment entails in the political arena within which public service operates. "Political judgment, in the classical sense of the term, is the capacity to tell the difference between public and private ends. It is also the ability to spot a private interest masquerading as a public good." Machiavelli's very name has come to signify the opposite: rational, self-interested decision making conducted in the long and short term. (In contrast to the classical Platonic tradition of abandoning personal interests, the rational self-interest theory underlies arguments for pay parity with private-sector counterparts.)

Contrasting notions of organizational and professional roles complicate matters further. Again, American democratic and bureaucratic practice combines both main ideas, the trustee and the delegate, associated with philosophers such as Locke, Bentham, and Mill. The trustee, an interpreter, acts statesmanlike in the community's best interest as the decision maker sees it. The U.S. Supreme Court, the U.S. Senate, political executives, and senior administrative generalists fit this category, as do claims of electoral mandate. A famous speech by English philosopher Edmund Burke coincided with the American Revolution: "Your representative owes you, not his industry only, but his judgment." The delegate, on the other hand, is more like a conduit who purposefully brings the constituency's views to bear and faithfully reflects them. This stance is typified by public opinion polls and some elements of populist and representative bureaucracy.

In sum, we have an ethics stew simmering on the back burner for every public manager. Ethical choices bubble up from ideas about morality, about public service, and about organizational and professional roles derived from classical philosophy and political thought. The sheer number of options drawn from philosophical traditions indicates that philosophy will not make our choices for us. Instead, it clarifies the reasoning behind those choices. The burden of multiple sets of ethical standards is all the heavier because the public manager uses public authority and enormous government power to back up decisions. As a result, the obligation for *informed* ethical reasoning—thinking through a dilemma and making a morally reasonable decision—falls on the shoulders of the individual public manager.

References

American Society for Public Administration. *Ethics Resource Notebook*. Washington, D.C. Nov 12, 1989.

Bok, S. *Lying: Moral Choice in Public and Private Life* (New York: Vintage Books, 1978).

"Fact File: Attitudes and Characteristics of this Year's Freshmen." Survey by American Council on Education and Higher Education Research Institute at the University of California, Los Angeles. *Chronicle of Higher Education* Jan 24, 1990 pp. A33–A34.

French, P.A. *Ethics in Government* (Englewood Cliffs, N.J.: Prentice Hall, 1983).

Fulghum, R. *All I Really Need to Know I Learned in Kindergarten* (New York: Ivy Books, 1988).

Jennings, B. "Ethics in Government: There Still Is Hope." Reprinted in American Society for Public Administration, *Ethics Resource Notebook*, Washington, D.C. Nov 12, 1989.

Johnson, M. "A Filmmaker's Odyssey." *Facing History and Ourselves News*, Winter 1989–90 pp. 18–21.

Strauss, L. and Cropsey, J. (editors) *History of Political Philosophy* (3rd Ed) (Chicago: University of Chicago Press, 1987).

Volcker Commission. *Leadership for America: Rebuilding the Public Service*, Report of the National Commission on the Public Service, Washington, D.C. 1989.

Wall Street Journal, "Oliver North, Businessman? Many Bosses Say That He's Their Kind of Employee," July 14, 1987 p. 35.

Wall Street Journal, "Survey of 1,000 Corporate Executives," April 6, 1988 p. 27.

43

Breaking Through Bureaucracy

Michael Barzelay
with Babak J. Armajani

Imagine how government would work if almost every operating decision—including the hiring and firing of individuals—were made on partisan political grounds; if many agencies spent their entire annual appropriations in the first three months of the fiscal year; if appropriations were made to agencies without anyone having formulated a spending and revenue budget for the jurisdiction as a whole; and if no agency or person in the executive branch had authority to oversee the activities of government agencies.

This state of affairs was, in fact, the norm in the United States in the nineteenth century. That it sounds so chaotic and backward to us is due to the success of early twentieth-century reformers in influencing politics and administration at the city, state, and federal levels. As a result of their influence, most Americans take for granted that administrative decisions should be made in a businesslike manner, that the executive branch should be organized hierarchically, that most agency heads should be appointed by the chief executive, that the appropriations process should begin when the chief executive submits an overall budget to the legislature, that most positions should be staffed by qualified people, that materials should be purchased from responsible vendors based on objective criteria, and that systems of fiscal control and accountability should be reliable.[1]

The political movements favoring this form of bureaucratic government emerged partly in response to the social problems created by the transformation of the United States from an agrarian and highly decentralized society to an urban, industrial, and national society.[2] For government to address social problems in an efficient manner, reformers said repeatedly, government agencies needed to be administered much like the business organizations that, at the time, were bringing about the industrial transformation.[3] For Americans supporting the reform and reorganization movements, bureaucracy meant efficiency and efficiency meant good government.[4]

Bureaucratically minded reformers also placed a high value on the impersonal exercise of public authority. To this end, they argued that actions intended to control others should be based on the application of rules and that no action should be taken without authorization. When officials' actions could not be fully determined by applying rules, professional or technical expertise was to be relied on to make official action impersonal.[5] This outlook extended to hiring and purchasing. The consistent application of universal rules embodying the merit principle was expected to assure that government officials would act competently on behalf of the public interest, while simultaneously undermining the power of the party machines that dominated politics *and* administration.[6] The consistent application of universal rules in purchasing was expected to reduce government's operating costs and to have similar political consequences.[7]

The values of efficiency and impersonal administration along with prescriptions for putting them into practice in government constituted a compelling system of beliefs in the early twentieth century. This system may be termed the *bureaucratic reform vision.*

Persistence of The Bureaucratic Paradigm

The bureaucratic reform vision lost its hold on the political imagination of the reform constituency once civil service and executive budgeting had been put into place and the Great Depression posed new and pressing collective problems. As a belief system about public administration, by contrast, the bureaucratic

---

Source: From *Breaking through Bureaucracy* by M. Barzelay with B. J. Armajani, pp. 3–9; 115–133.

reform vision survived—although not wholly intact—such political changes as the Great Society and Reaganism and a series of efforts to improve management in government including systems analysis, management by objectives, and zero-based budgeting. Among the legacies of the bureaucratic reform movements are deeply ingrained habits of thought.[8] These habits of thought and the belief system that supports them are referred to in this book as the bureaucratic paradigm.[9]

In order to probe whether the bureaucratic paradigm is a good guide to public management a century after the reform movements began, it is important to be aware of the key beliefs it contains. The following beliefs are among those embedded in the *bureaucratic paradigm* that deserve close scrutiny.

- Specific delegations of authority define each role in the executive branch. Officials carrying out any given role should act only when expressly permitted to do so either by rule or by instructions given by superior authorities in the chain of command. Employees within the executive branch are responsible to their supervisors.
- In exercising authority, officials should apply rules and procedures in a uniform manner. The failure to obey rules should be met with an appropriate penalty.
- Experts in substantive matters—such as engineers, law-enforcement personnel, and social service providers—should be assigned to line agencies, while experts in budgeting, accounting, purchasing, personnel, and work methods should be assigned to centralized staff functions.
- The key responsibilities of the financial function are to prepare the executive budget and to prevent actual spending from exceeding appropriations. The key responsibilities of the purchasing function are to minimize the price paid to acquire goods and services from the private sector and to enforce purchasing rules. The key responsibilities of the personnel function include classifying jobs, examining applicants, and making appointments to positions.[10]
- The executive branch as a whole will operate honestly and efficiently as long as the centralized staff functions exercise unilateral control over line agencies' administrative actions.

Unraveling the Bureaucratic Paradigm

The bureaucratic paradigm has been criticized by intellectuals since the 1930s. Some criticized the idea that the formal organization is the principal determinant of efficiency and effectiveness.[11] Some urged that control be viewed as a process in which all employees strive to coordinate their work with others.[12] Some voices criticized the idea that the exercise of unilateral authority within hierarchies was a recipe for good government.[13] More argued that the meaning of economy and efficiency within the bureaucratic paradigm was conceptually muddled.[14] Many came to recommend that budgeters analyze social benefits and costs of government programs instead of focusing attention only on expenditures.[15] Some raised concerns about the tendency of line agency employees to adjust to staff agency's administrative systems by becoming constraint-oriented rather than ission-oriented.[16] A few intellectuals also found evidence for the proposition that the workings of some administrative systems contradicted common sense.[17] Many of these insights and arguments have been incorporated into mainstream practitioner and academic thinking about public management. Nonetheless, many of the beliefs of the bureaucratic paradigm have escaped serious challenge.[18]

The most important recent conceptual challenge to the bureaucratic paradigm arising in the world of practice is the notion that government organizations should be customer-driven and service-oriented. A recurring aspiration of public managers and overseers using these concepts is to solve operational problems by transforming their organizations into responsive, user-friendly, dynamic, and competitive providers of valuable services to customers. Thinking in terms of customers and service helps public managers and overseers articulate their concerns about the performance of the government operations for which they are accountable. When supplemented by analysis of how these concepts have been put into practice in other settings, reasoning about customers and service helps managers generate alternative solutions to the particular problems they have defined as meriting attention. In many instances, the range of alternatives generated in this fashion is substantially different from that yielded by reasoning within the bureaucratic paradigm.[19]

Many public officials, alert to the power of these conceptual resources in the contemporary United States, are identifying those whom they believe to be their customers and are using methods of strategic service management to improve their operations.[20] For example, the U.S. Army Recruiting Command has developed an extremely sophisticated strategy to attract its external customers—qualified young Americans—to join the military.[21] This strategy is designed to satisfy these customers' needs for guaranteed future employment, occupational training, immediate income, self-esteem, individuality, and fair treatment so as to meet the internal customers' needs for a high-quality workforce. The Army recruiting operation's key service concept—reinforced by television advertising—is to provide external customers a "guaranteed reservation" for "seats" in training programs for specific military occupations. To support this service concept, Army contractors engineered a sophisticated information system known as REQUEST. Operated by specialized recruiters referred to as guidance counselors, the REQUEST system customizes the Army's offer of multiyear membership, employment, training, immediate cash, and other benefits. The more attractive the recruit—as judged from a battery of standardized tests—the better the offer. This example plainly illustrates how one government organization, in attempting to implement public policies—in this case, maintaining a large standing army capable of fighting wars and staffing it with volunteers—puts the customer-service approach into practice.[22]

Strategic service management is also practiced in situations where the government/citizen transaction is involuntary and when obligations are being imposed. An example of this kind of situation is the operation of taxation systems. Some revenue agencies now identify taxpaying individuals and businesses as their customers; others identify the collective interests of the people who pay taxes and receive government services as the customer, while conceiving of service provision as a way of cost-effectively facilitating voluntary compliance.[23] Such revenue agencies are making operational changes—for example, simplifying tax forms, writing instructions in plain English, providing taxpayers assistance, and building the capacity to produce timely refunds—with the aim of making it easier and more rewarding for people to comply with their obligations. This approach to managing revenue agencies puts into practice in a compliance context two key principles of service operations management: first, that customers participate in the production and delivery of services, and, second, that the service-delivery process tends to operate more smoothly when customers understand what is expected of them and feel that the organization and its service providers are making a reasonable effort to accommodate their needs.

Formulating an Alternative

The concept of a customer-driven service organization is thus a tool used increasingly by public officials to define and solve problems.[24] At a higher level of generality, this concept also provides many of the resources needed to formulate a coherent alternative to the bureaucratic paradigm.[25] The outlines of this alternative and its mode of identifying and attacking the vulnerabilities of the bureaucratic paradigm are already coming into focus. The following paired statements highlight the main rhetorical battle lines:[26]

- A bureaucratic agency is focused on its own needs and perspectives. A customer-driven agency is focused on customer needs and perspectives.
- A bureaucratic agency is focused on the roles and responsibilities of its parts. A customer-driven agency is focused on enabling the whole organization to function as a team.
- A bureaucratic agency defines itself both by the amount of resources it controls and by the tasks it performs. A customer-driven agency defines itself by the results it achieves for its customers.
- A bureaucratic agency controls costs. A customer-driven agency creates value net of cost.

- A bureaucratic agency sticks to routine. A customer-driven agency modifies its operations in response to changing demands for its services.
- A bureaucratic agency fights for turf. A customer-driven agency competes for business.
- A bureaucratic agency insists on following standard procedures. A customer-driven agency builds choice into its operating systems when doing so serves a purpose.
- A bureaucratic agency announces policies and plans. A customer-driven agency engages in two-way communication with its customers in order to assess and revise its operating strategy.
- A bureaucratic agency separates the work of thinking from that of doing. A customer-driven agency empowers front-line employees to make judgments about how to improve customer service and value.[27]

The fact that this kind of rhetoric is coming into common use suggests that a new alternative to the bureaucratic paradigm—one that builds on much prior practical and intellectual work—is now available. As this alternative becomes well-formulated and well-accepted, it may become the frame of reference for most efforts to diagnose operational problems in the public sector and to find solutions to them. The time is ripe, therefore, to define as carefully as possible what this alternative is. *Breaking Through Bureaucracy* takes on this task.[28]

The Post-Bureaucratic Paradigm in Historical Perspective

The increasingly common use of such terms as *customers, quality, service, value, incentives, innovation, empowerment,* and *flexibility* by people trying to improve government operations indicates that the bureaucratic paradigm is no longer the only major source of ideas and argumentation about public management in the United States.[29] In the search for better performance, some argue for deregulating government.[30] Others make the case for reinventing government, a concept that encourages Americans to take note of marked changes in operating practices taking place in an array of public activities.[31] As a challenge to conventional thinking, many government agencies are investing millions of dollars in training programs structured by a conceptual system that includes customers, quality, value, process control, and employee involvement.[32] To increase flexibility and financial responsibility, some advocate a vast expansion of exchange and payment relationships in place of general fund financing; many also argue for utilizing competition as a device for holding operating units of government accountable to their customers.[33] Among the programmatic concepts that have arisen from studied criticism of the ways in which the bureaucratic reform vision and bureaucratic paradigm have played out in compliance and service organizations are market-based incentives in environmental regulation,[34] promoting voluntary compliance in tax administration, community policing,[35] social service integration,[36] the one-day or one-trial jury system,[37] school-based management,[38] and school choice.[39]

Is there a single core idea—perhaps reducible to a sound bite—behind this ferment in thinking and practice? Some readers will respond that the core idea is service. Or customer focus. Or quality. Or incentives. Or creating value. Or empowerment. But the major concepts of emerging practice are not organized hierarchically, with one master idea at the top. As an indication, the concept of incentives does not subsume the equally useful idea of empowerment, which can be defined as a state of affairs in which individuals and groups feel psychologically responsible for the outcomes of their work. Since emerging argumentation and practice are structured by a paradigm rather than by any single core idea, those who want to make the most of the new conceptual resources should understand how various components of the system are related to one another.[40]

To understand the structure and workings of the newer paradigm well enough to improve public management requires attention and thoughtfulness but not the honed skills of an analytic philosopher or social linguist. The new paradigm, we suggest, can readily be understood by working with the metaphor of an extended family of ideas. The image of an extended family is helpful because it indicates that each idea is somehow related to every other, and it implies that some concentration is required to identify just how. The same metaphor can be pushed much further.[41] Think of the new paradigm, as well as the bureaucratic one, as a generation within an extended family. Although the members of each generation may not enjoy equal standing, their relationships—like those between concepts in either paradigm—are not hierarchical. All the cousins may be compatible in many situations, but their personalities—much like the entailments of the concepts of incentives and empowerment—are likely to differ markedly. Furthermore, just as siblings and cousins seek to prove that they are individually and collectively different from their parents' generation, self-definitions of the new paradigm emphasize divergences from the bureaucratic paradigm. Generational differences in extended families and paradigms also reflect changes in the social, economic, and political environments in which they have lived. To pursue the metaphor one more step, just as the siblings and cousins are influenced more by the preceding generation than they care to see or admit, concepts in the new paradigm are deeply conditioned by their lineal relationships to concepts in the bureaucratic predecessor.

The most appropriate term for the new generation of the extended family of ideas about how to make government operations productive and accountable is the *post-bureaucratic paradigm.* This term implies that the post-bureaucratic paradigm is as multifaceted as its predecessor. An unrelated name would hide the fact that as a historical matter, the younger generation of ideas has evolved from the bureaucratic paradigm.

Table 1 depicts this evolution. This framework guides the effort to identify the post-bureaucratic paradigm and to place it in historical perspective.

Shifting Paradigms

From the Public Interest to Results Citizens Value The purpose of the bureaucratic reforms was to enable government to serve the public interest.[42] Government would serve the public interest, reformers argued, if it were honest and efficient. By honest, they meant a government cleansed of particularism, featherbedding, and outright stealing of public funds. By efficient, they meant a government that improved urban infrastructure, provided education, and promoted public health.[43]

In time, the reformers' strategy for serving the public interest came to define the public interest. A central element of that strategy was to recruit, develop, and retain experts in such fields as accounting, engineering, and social work. This strategy was designed not only to achieve results, but also to use expertise as a way to legitimate the actions of unelected officials in an administrative state. As an unintended but unsurprising consequence, these officials came to presume that the public interest was served whenever they applied their various bodies of knowledge and professional standards to questions within their respective domains of authority.

In the age of bureaucratic reform, when the effective demand for combating disease, building civil works, and accounting for public funds had just become significant, the presumption that decisions made in accord with professional standards were congruent with citizens' collective needs and requirements was reasonably defensible. This presumption is no longer reasonable to make. Government often fails to produce desired results from the standpoint of citizens when each professional community within government is certain that its standards define the public interest.

To stimulate more inquiry and better deliberation about how the work of government actually bears on citizens' volitions, the post-bureaucratic paradigm suggests that the specific rhetorical phrase "the public interest" should be confined to books on the history of American politics and administration. A desirable substitute expression is "results citizens value." Compared with its predecessor, the newer expression can be used to motivate more inquiry, clearer argumentation, and more productive deliberation about what results citizens collectively value. This rhetorical construction also conjures up the network of ideas about customer-focused organizations, emphasizes results over inputs and process, and implies that what citizens value cannot be presumed by professional communities in government.[44]

From Efficiency to Quality and Value Leaders of the scientific management movement in the early twentieth century crafted and popularized a commonsense theory about the causes, nature, and significance of efficiency.[45] This commonsense theory rang true because it explained the industrial progress that characterized the age and because information about the workings of modern

TABLE 1

Comparing the Paradigms

BUREAUCRATIC PARADIGM	POST-BUREAUCRATIC PARADIGM
Public interest	Results citizens value
Efficiency	Quality and value
Administration	Product
Control	Winning adherence to norms
Specify functions, authority, and structure	Identify mission, services, customers, and outcomes
Justify costs	Deliver value
Enforce responsibility	Building accountability Strengthen working relationships
Follow rules and procedures	Understand and apply norms Identify and solve problems Continuously improve processes
Operate administrative systems	Separate service from control Build support for norms Expand customer choice Encourage collective action Provide incentives Measure and analyze results Enrich feedback

factories was widely known. It is a small step to infer that reformers used their knowledge of efficient industrial administration to inform their conception of efficient public administration.[46]

What did reformers know about factory administration? They knew that an efficient factory system succeeded in producing ever-increasing quantities of goods while reducing the cost of production.[47] They also knew recipes for achieving such success. In factories, managers controlled production in great detail through hierarchical supervisory structures. They knew that production and administrative systems were designed and operated by experts, who staffed offices responsible for personnel, accounting, inspection, power and works, engineering, product design, methods, production efficiency, and orders.[48] Bureaucratic reformers also knew that factory managers and experts applied their authority and expertise to industrial administration without partisan political interference.

Thus, industry was not just a source of rhetoric about efficient government; reformers' understanding of the main ingredients of efficient government—reorganization, accounting systems, expertise, and cost control—was rooted in their knowledge about industry.[49] Reformers elaborated some ingredients into specific processes and techniques, such as careful delineation of roles and responsibilities, centralized scrutiny of budget estimates, centralized purchasing, work programming, reporting systems, and methods analysis. However, one key concept—the product—did not make the journey from industry to government.[50]

Since it excluded the concept of product, reformers' influential conception of efficient government was trouble waiting to happen. It encouraged the notorious bureaucratic focus on inputs to flourish and it permitted specialized functions to become worlds unto themselves. More specifically, an increase in efficiency could be claimed in government whenever spending on inputs was reduced, whereas it was much easier to argue in an industrial setting that cost reduction improved efficiency only when it led to a reduction in the cost per unit of output. Industrial managers may not have had an easy time keeping every specialized member of the organization focused on the product, but in this concept—embodied in the goods moving through the production stream and out the door—they at least had a way to think precisely and meaningfully about how integration of differentiated functions could achieve efficiency. For reasons discussed above, the concept of the public interest did not possess the product concept's powers of integration; indeed, the strategy of sharply delineating roles and responsibilities and exalting specialized expertise cut in the other direction.[51] The bottom line—illustrated by the horror stories told in chapter 2—is that the pursuit of efficiency without adequate tendencies toward functional integration was a sham.[52]

Efficiency should be dropped from the lexicon of public administration, as it has from sophisticated practical theories of manufacturing and service enterprise management.[53] Public officials, like their counterparts in nongovernmental organizations, instead should make use of such interrelated concepts as product or service, quality, and value when deliberating about the nature and worth of government activities. The claim is that deliberation in these terms is as useful in the public sector as elsewhere.[54]

The post-bureaucratic paradigm does not try to settle most of the controversies about the general definitions of the concepts of product or service, quality, and value.[55] Legislating the precise definition of such rhetorical and analytical categories is probably futile; in any event, what is important for our purposes here is how well people in practice make use of such concepts in formulating and deliberating over made-to-measure or ad hoc arguments about how the performance of particular organizations should be evaluated and improved.[56]

To make the most of such deliberation efforts, some minimal agreement on terms is necessary. First, the appropriate perspective from which these concepts should be defined is that of the customer. By this rule, the recurring definition of quality as conformance to customer requirements is acceptable. Second, net value should be distinguished from value by taking costs into account. By this rule, the claim that reducing expenditures is desirable needs to be scrutinized in terms of the effect on the cost *and* value of products and services. Third, the non-pecuniary costs borne by customers when co-producing services or complying with norms should be taken into account. By this rule, costs measured by conventional accounting systems should be adjusted in service or compliance contexts.

From Administration to Production The bureaucratic reformers had a theory of how individual public servants contributed to efficient administration. The theory claimed that the purpose of administration was to solve public problems by implementing laws efficiently. Agencies performed their functions by subdividing responsibilities and assigning them to positions. Public servants, assigned to positions on the basis of merit, performed their responsibilities competently by applying their expertise.[57] This theory promised order and rationality in that new domain of public affairs denominated as administration[58] and nicely combined a political argument about administrative legitimacy with an organizational argument about efficiency. The theory also provided a reason to believe that the work of public servants served the public interest.

To some degree, this theory of work in the administrative branch of government lives on. Ask public servants to describe their work and many will relate facts about their organization's functions and their own responsibilities. In order to communicate what the incumbent of a position does, some agencies compose titles mimicking the chain of command. For exam-ple, one senior manager in the Veterans Administration carried the title of Assistant Associate Deputy Chief Medical Director.

This strategy of defining work is failing to satisfy public servants.[59] Younger members of the workforce are less than willing to accept close supervision.[60] It is a reasonable inference that specifying organization positions is an unsatisfactory way to characterize their identity and purpose at work. Another problem with the standard account is that citizens are skeptical about the value of work public servants do—and public servants know it.[61] The bureaucratic paradigm offers late-twentieth-century public servants few tools for explaining to themselves and others why their work counts.

The accumulating evidence that production is a powerful alternative to the idea of administration comes from the total quality management (TQM) movement. TQM provides employees with methods—such as process flow analysis—for identifying and improving production processes.[62] Most government employees whose experience with TQM concepts and methods has been positive are deeply committed to the idea of process analysis and control.[63]

Why is production a powerful idea? One reason is that operating-level employees are typically involved in decision making, another is that formalized methods of reasoning are considered—often for the first time—in deliberations about how the production process should be organized. Both employee involvement and objective analysis mitigate the sense of powerlessness among employees in organizational hierarchies.[64] Furthermore, by using methods of process analysis, employees can develop a shared visual representation of the organization without making any reference to its hierarchical structure or boundaries. What is more important is that through process analysis, individual employees can visualize and describe for others how their work leads to the delivery of a valuable service or product. And coworkers develop an understanding of—and appreciation for—the work each does.[65]

To guard against mistaken analogies between production in government and manufacturing, the post-bureaucratic paradigm suggests that the concept of production be rendered as service delivery.[66] This terminology reminds public servants of the complex and intimate relationship between process and product in service delivery: whereas the production of goods is a separate process from distribution and consumption, many services are produced, delivered, and consumed in the same process, often with customers participating as co-producers.[67]

From Control to Winning Adherence to Norms Within the bureaucratic reformers' vision of government, control was the lifeblood of efficient administration. Control was considered to be so vital that the intention to strengthen it served as an effective major premise in arguments supporting a wide array of practices that deepened and extended the bureaucratic reforms. These practices included accounting systems, budgetary freezes, reorganizations, reporting requirements, and countless measures to reduce the exercise of discretion by most public servants.

Why did such a cold, mechanical idea become revered by advocates of efficient administration? The answer lies in the fact that control was an important concept in each of the several lines of thought that became interwoven in the bureaucratic reform vision.[68] Control was essential to realize the aim of a unified executive branch. Control needed to be exercised to purge administrative decisions of particularistic influences. Control was the basis for the efficient operation of large-scale organizations.[69] And control assured the public that someone, namely the chief executive, was in charge of administration.

Influenced by ideas of rational-legal bureaucracy and industrial practice, the formulators of the bureaucratic paradigm pursued the aims of order, rationality, impersonal administration, efficiency, and political accountability by instituting centrally controlled systems of rules. The focus on rules, commitment to centralization, and emphasis on enforcement spawned worrisome consequences, which have tended to make bureaucracy a pejorative rather than a descriptive term.

Rules. The bureaucratic paradigm encouraged control activities to develop ever-denser networks of rules in response to changing circumstances or new problems.[70] When rules systems became extremely complex, staff operations of substantial size—located in both staff and line agencies—were needed to understand, administer, and update them.

Centralization. The bureaucratic paradigm urged overseers to centralize responsibility and authority for making administrative decisions in the hands of staff agencies. Centralized staff operations generally lacked the capacity to process incoming requests quickly, either because their power in the budget process was slight or because they were committed to the idea of saving taxpayers money. As a further consequence, decisions made centrally did not take into account the complexity and variability of the situations confronted by line agencies.

Enforcement. Staff agencies focused on enforcement were typically blind to opportunities to correct problems at their source.[71] For instance, agencies were often unable to comply with norms because their employees did not know how to apply them to specific situations. Many such compliance problems could have been solved by providing education and specific advice about how to improve administrative or production processes; however, compliance organizations stressing enforcement tended to under-invest in problem solving. Furthermore, an emphasis on enforcement unnecessarily set up adversarial relationships between control activities and compilers. This kind of relationship discouraged efforts to comply voluntarily with norms.[72]

In our view, after more than a half-century of use, the concept of control is so bound up with the obsolete focus on rules, centralization, and enforcement that continued use of the term is an obstacle to innovative thinking about how to achieve results citizens value. Alternative terms currently in use, such as *delegation, decentralization, streamlining, incentive-based regulation,* and *voluntary compliance,* are not wholly adequate as substitutes. Whatever term comes to structure post-bureaucratic thinking, the concept should serve to (1) illuminate means other than rules, such as principles, to frame and communicate the norms to which agencies should adhere; (2) recognize the complexity and ambiguity of the choice situations faced by compliers; and (3) underscore the role that rewards and positive working relationships can play in motivating compliers to make good decisions. The term *winning adherence to norms* is designed to fulfill this function. This concept indicates several lines of post-bureaucratic thinking about organizational strategies of compliance activities—one of which deserves to be highlighted here.

Since achieving adherence to norms requires people to make choices among alternatives under conditions of complexity and ambiguity, compliance strategies should empower compliers to apply norms to their particular circumstances. Compliers become empowered, by definition, when they feel personally responsible for adhering to the norms and are psychologically invested in the task of finding the best way to comply. Taking personal responsibility for results is as crucial to making good compliance decisions as to delivering quality goods and services.

As analysts have discovered in studying the sources of productivity and quality in organizations, taking personal responsibility is substantially influenced by the work setting. In particular, researchers argue that employees are most likely to take personal responsibility at work when they receive clear direction about purposes and desired outcomes, education, coaching, material resources, feedback, and recognition.[73] These findings suggest that taking personal responsibility for adhering to norms is likely to be enhanced when compliers understand the purpose of the norms, obtain education and coaching about how to apply the norms to the situations they face, receive timely and useful information about the extent to which compliance is being achieved, and are recognized for their accomplishments.

The willingness to take personal responsibility for complying with norms also depends on several other factors, including the extent to which the community of compliers supports the norms; whether other members of the community are assuming their obligations; whether compliance organizations seek to streamline the compliance process; and whether the capacity to enforce the norms upon those who fail to live by them is apparent.[74] The post-bureaucratic paradigm recognizes that some people may not respond adequately to efforts to win their compliance. For this reason, enforcement remains an indispensable function even when the focus is on winning adherence to norms.[75] These factors are increasingly recognized by tax administrations and other agencies that rely for their success principally on the willingness and ability of people and organizations to bring themselves into compliance with norms.[76]

Beyond Functions, Authority, and Structure

The bureaucratic paradigm defined organizations in terms of their assigned functions, delegated authority, and formal structure. Functions were abstract categories of work to be performed within the larger organizational machinery of government. Authority was the right to make decisions and demand obedience from subordinates on matters related to the grant of authority. Formal structure referred to the system of superior-subordinate relationships, which matched delegated authority with subdivided functions ultimately to the level of individual positions.

The critiques of this outlook are legendary. The focus on functions made organizations seem like technical instruments rather than institutions whose members are committed to achieving purposes.[77] The focus on authority concealed the power of other methods of social calculation and control, including persuasion and exchange.[78] The focus on formal structure put the cart of organization means before the horse of organizational purpose and strategy.[79]

From a post-bureaucratic perspective, the central challenge of organizations is to channel human energies into thinking about and doing socially useful work. Public servants need better categories than functions, authority, and structure to meet this challenge. The concepts of mission, services, customers, and outcomes are valuable because they help public servants articulate their purposes and deliberate about how to adapt work to achieve them.[80] Missions are claims about the distinctive contribution an organization makes to the public good.[81] Services are the organization's products.[82] Customers are individuals or collective bodies—whether internal or external to the organization—to whom employees are accountable as parties to customer relationships.[83] Outcomes are precisely defined states of affairs that the organization intends to bring about through its activities.[84]

From Enforcing Responsibility to Building Accountability According to the bureaucratic paradigm, a key role of administrators was to use their authority to enforce responsibility upon their subordinates.[85] As a mandate for managing people in organizations, this formalistic, hierarchical, and remedial conception of accountability left much to be desired. Formalism neglected the roles that emotions, commitments, and peer group norms play in shaping intrinsic motivation and behavior. The focus on hierarchy steered attention away from managing the network of interdependencies between subordinates and employees reporting to different superiors. And the notion of enforcing responsibility gave accountability a retrospective and defect-finding cast.

From a post-bureaucratic perspective, the most effective way to hold employees accountable is to make them feel accountable.[86] This route to accountability is attractive, in part, because employees want to be accountable. They want to be accountable because it is the only way for them, as for us all, to be important. According to a noted contemporary philosopher:

> Importance has two aspects. The first involves having external impact or effect, being the causal source of external effects, a place from which effects flow so that other people or things are affected by your actions. The second aspect of importance involves having to be taken account of, counting. If the first aspect of importance involves being a causal source from which effects flow, the second involves being a place toward which responses flow, responses to your actions, traits, or presence. In some way they pay attention to you and take you into account. Simply being paid attention to is something we want.[87]

Psychologists specializing in the study of work argue that employees feel accountable when they believe intended work outcomes are consequential for other people, receive information about outcomes, and can attribute outcomes to their own efforts, initiatives, and decisions.[88] Informed by this kind of argument, the post-bureaucratic paradigm values efforts by public managers and their overseers to bring about states of affairs in which public servants feel accountable for achieving desired results.

As a way to overcome the hierarchical and remedial thrust of accountability in the bureaucratic paradigm, attention should focus on the spectrum of working relationships, including the customer relationship, through which public servants create results citizens value. (Table 2 shows a classification scheme of working relationships.) From a post-bureaucratic perspective, accountability between the parties engaged in such working relationships should be a two-way street. For example, providers should be accountable to customers for meeting their needs for quality and value, while customers should be accountable to providers for clarifying their own needs and for giving feedback. More generally, in thinking and deliberating about accountability to customers and others, public managers should call to mind all the ingredients of well-functioning relationships: a consistent understanding of the purpose and character of the relationship; a detailed understanding of what behaviors and results the parties believe would be satisfactory; the provision of feedback about how well the parties are performing and how they could make improvements; responsiveness to feedback; and reconsideration of the working relationship in light of changing circumstances and cumulative experience.

From Justifying Costs to Delivering Value Budgeting, according to the bureaucratic paradigm, was a process of arriving at annual spending plans. As part of the budgeting process, administrators were charged with the task of developing process estimates of their organization's needs.[89] In practice, administrators assumed the task of developing convincing arguments that their needs in the upcoming budget year were greater than in the current one. The major categories of acceptable evidence for arguments about needs included current spending, expected increases in the cost of doing business, and the estimated cost of expanding the organization's level of activity. Upon receiving estimates of needs, central budget offices built arguments for the claim that the agency's costs were less than the estimated ones as part of an effort to judge whose claims for resources were most justified.[90]

The bureaucratic paradigm of budgeting was congruent with its many other aspects. For example, the rhetoric of need was consistent with reformers' idea that government was supposed to satisfy citizens' wants without wasting taxpayers' dollars. It was also consistent with the belief that the responsibility for making government efficient should be vested primarily in the hands of overseers and their budget staffs. And the task of making government efficient meant scrutinizing costs.

Some advocates of the post-bureaucratic paradigm raise provocative questions about this conception.[91] They speculate that citizens are much more interested in the quality and value of public services than they are in costs; hence, it is mistaken for overseers to scrutinize costs during budget deliberations. They envision a world in which budget deliberations enable overseers to make informed purchases of services from agencies on behalf of the public. They further contend that improving the quality and value of public services can be achieved on a routine basis if agencies are expected to track changes in customer requirements and to improve productivity through better management of production processes; they point out that budget processes under the bureaucratic paradigm instead motivate public managers to spend their limited time justifying costs. From a post-bureaucratic perspective, it is urgent to work out the implications of these claims and speculations in theory and practice.

Beyond Rules and Procedures The premise of countless arguments made from the bureaucratic paradigm is that the proposed course of action (or inaction) is consistent with existing rules and procedures. The prior discussions of the concepts of efficiency, administration, and control explain why such arguments were generally persuasive.

From a post-bureaucratic angle, arguments premised on existing rules and procedures should be greeted with a reasonable degree of skepticism. Arguments premised on rules should be challenged and the issue reframed in terms of achieving the best possible outcome, taking into account the intention behind the rules, the complexity and ambiguity of the situation, and the ability to secure support from those who would enforce the norms. In this way, problem solving rather than following bureaucratic routines can become the dominant metaphor for work. Similarly, arguments premised on current procedures should be countered by instigating deliberation about how process improvements could enhance service quality and value.

Beyond Operating Administrative Systems Centralized staff agencies were institutional embodiments of the bureaucratic reform vision. By operating administrative systems, these organizations put into practice the concepts of efficiency, administration, and control. Their cultures and routines spawned many of the constraints and incentives facing line agencies, which from a post-bureaucratic vantage point now detract from government's ability to deliver results citizens value.

If the time has come to break through bureaucracy, centralized staff operations must be part of the process. In serving this purpose, centralized staff operations need to transform their organizational strategies. Just like line

TABLE 2

Working Relationships

CUSTOMER RELATIONSHIPS

Individual or organizational customers
- within the organization
- within government
- outside government

Collective customers
- within the organization
- within government
- outside government

PRODUCTION RELATIONSHIPS

Coproduction relationships with customers

Complier relationships
- within government
- between government and the public

Relationships with providers
- within government
- vendors

Team relationships
- between individuals
- between task groups
- between functions

Partner relationships
- within government
- between public and private sectors

OVERSIGHT RELATIONSHIPS

Relationships with executive branch leadership and their staffs

Relationships with legislative bodies, legislators, and staff

Relationships with courts

MEMBERSHIP RELATIONSHIPS

Employment relationships
- between employees and their organizational leaders
- between employees and their immediate superiors
- between employees and the employer

Communitywide relationships
- among agencies
- among public servants

Peer group relationships
- among executives
- among members of a professional specialty

agencies, they can benefit from using the concepts of mission, services, customers, quality, value, production, winning adherence to norms, building accountability, and strengthening working relationships. More specifically, central staff operations should separate service from control, build support for norms, expand customer choice, encourage collective action, provide incentives, measure and analyze results, and enrich feedback in the context of all working relationships. What this extended family of concepts means in practice should constantly evolve through deliberation and incremental innovation. A starting point for both processes is the information and argumentation contained in this book.

Role of Public Managers The bureaucratic paradigm informed public administrators that their responsibilities included planning, organizing, directing, and coordinating. Planning meant looking beyond the day-to-day operations of each function in order to determine how the work of the organization as a whole should evolve. Organizing meant dividing work responsibilities and delegating to each position requisite authority over people and subject matter. Directing meant informing subordinates of their respective roles in implementing plans and ensuring that they carried out their roles in accordance with standards. Coordinating meant harmonizing efforts and relations among subordinates.[92] The deficiencies of this role conception have been amply and ably catalogued by management writers for more than forty years.

The post-bureaucratic paradigm values argumentation and deliberation about how the roles of public managers should be framed. Informed public managers today understand and appreciate such varied role concepts as exercising leadership, creating an uplifting mission and organizational culture, strategic planning, managing without direct authority, pathfinding, problem setting, identifying customers, groping along, reflecting-in-action, coaching, structuring incentives, championing products, instilling a commitment to quality, creating a climate for innovation, building teams, redesigning work, investing in people, negotiating mandates, and managing by walking around.[93] As a contribution to current deliberation, we suggest that breaking through bureaucracy is a useful supplement to this stock of ideas. This concept alerts public managers to the need to take seriously the profound influence of the bureaucratic paradigm on standard practices, modes of argumentation, and the way public servants derive meaning from their work.

Historically aware public managers, committed to breaking through bureaucracy, will help coworkers understand that the bureaucratic paradigm mistakenly tended to define organizational purpose as doing assigned work. They will argue that a crucial challenge facing all organizations is to imbue work effort with purpose while thwarting the tendency to presume that current practices deliver as much value as possible. They will build capacity within and around organizations to deliberate about the relationships between results citizens value and the work done.

Public managers guided by the idea of breaking through bureaucracy should employ not only a combination of historical knowledge and post-bureaucratic ideas as tools to diagnose unsatisfactory situations and to spot inadequacies in arguments rooted in the bureaucratic paradigm, but should also deal creatively with the fact that many public servants are emotionally invested in the bureaucratic paradigm. Public servants, in our experience, are generally willing to move on to a newer way of thinking and practicing public management if they are convinced that the efforts they expended in past years will not become depreciated by the move. An effective way to overcome resistance to change stemming from this source is to make an informed argument that the presuppositions of the bureaucratic paradigm as played out in the organization's particular field of action were reasonable during most of the twentieth century, but that times have changed.[94]

NOTES

1. William F. Willoughby, *The Movement for Budgetary Reform in the States* (New York: D. Appleton, 1918); Leonard D. White, *Trends in Public Administration and Finance* (New York: McGraw-Hill, 1933); Lloyd M. Short and Carl W. Tiller, *The Minnesota Commission on Administration and Finance,*

1925–39: An Administrative History (Minneapolis: University of Minnesota Press, 1942); Fritz Morstein Marx, ed., *Elements of Public Administration,* 2d ed. (Englewood Cliffs, N.J.: Prentice-Hall, 1959); Barry Dean Karl, *Executive Reorganization and Reform in the New Deal* (Cambridge, Mass.: Harvard University Press, 1963); Aaron Wildavsky, *The New Politics of the Budgetary Process* (Glenview, Ill.: Scott, Foresman, 1988), pp. 53–63.

2. Stephen Skowronek, *Building a New American State: The Expansion of National Administrative Capacities, 1877–1920* (Cambridge, England: Cambridge University Press, 1982).
3. See, generally, Jack H. Knott and Gary J. Miller, *Reforming Bureaucracy: The Politics of Institutional Choice* (Englewood Cliffs, N.J.: Prentice-Hall, 1987); Robert B. Reich, *The Next American Frontier* (New York: Times Books, 1983). According to Yale sociologist Charles Perrow, "The founders of organizations of all types and reformers of those that existed repeatedly held the industrial organization model—factories, by and large—as the important social innovation of the time. And it truly was" ("A Society of Organizations," *Estudios del Instituto Juan March de Estudios e Investigaciones* [Madrid] [October 1990]: 33).
4. In the words of historian Barry Deal Karl, these movements' beliefs and actions (as well as those of many New Dealers) were "in many respects a consequence of both industrialism and nationalism. The chief value of centralization rested on the increase in efficiency which it invariably seemed to bring to the growing urban and industrial chaos. But efficiency could also become identified with national purpose. The idea that human effort could be wasted when undirected and uncontrolled . . . was central to the growing concern with efficiency, leadership, and planning." Op. cit., pp. 182–183.
5. An excellent contemporary restatement of this outlook is contained in Jerry L. Mashaw, *Bureaucratic Justice: Managing Social Security Disability Claims* (New Haven, Conn.: Yale University Press, 1983). For a discussion of the concept of impersonal administration from a sociological and historical perspective, see Charles Perrow, *Complex Organizations: A Critical Essay,* 3d ed. (New York: Random House, 1986), pp. 1–29.
6. See Woodrow Wilson, "The Study of Public Administration," *Political Science Quarterly* (June 1887): 197–202. See also Skowronek, op. cit., pp. 47–84.
7. See Steven Kelman, *Procurement and Public Management: The Fear of Discretion and the Quality of Government Performance* (Washington, D.C.: American Enterprise Institute, 1990), pp. 11–15.
8. Other key legacies are institutional arrangements, including hierarchical executive branches and staff agencies, and organizational routines. These arrangements, agencies, and routines embed certain habits of thought into people who work in government.
9. A definition of paradigm that fits this usage is "the basic way of perceiving, thinking, valuing, and doing associated with a particular vision of reality. A dominant paradigm is seldom if ever stated explicitly; it exists as unquestioned, tacit understanding that is transmitted through culture and in succeeding generations through direct experience rather than being taught" (Willis Harmon, *An Incomplete Guide to the Future* [New York: Norton, 1970], quoted in Joel Arthur Barker, *Discovering the Future: The Business of Paradigms* [St. Paul, Minn.: ILI Press, 1985], pp. 13–14). A similar locution can be found in the literature on public administration: "Each of us lives with several paradigms at any given time. . . . As it appears appropriate, each of us moves in and out of paradigms throughout any work day, and with scarcely a thought about the belief and values systems that undergird them" (Yvonna S. Lincoln, introduction in *Organizational Theory and Inquiry: The Paradigm Revolution,* ed. Yvonna S. Lincoln [Beverly Hills, Calif.: Sage, 1985], p. 30). The word *paradigm* began to be used in natural scientific and social scientific communities after publication of Thomas S. Kuhn's *Structure of Scientific Revolutions* (Chicago: University of Chicago Press, 1962).
10. Institute of Government Research, "A Proposal for a National Service of General

Administration" (Washington, D.C., 1929). See also Short and Tiller, op. cit. See discussion of administrative management in Karl, op. cit., pp. 195–210.

11. For a summary of this literature, see Perrow, op. cit., pp. 62–118.

12. Mary Parker Follett, "The Process of Control," in *Papers on the Science of Administration,* ed. L. Gulick and L. Urwick (New York: Institute of Public Administration, 1937), pp. 161–169.

13. Charles E. Lindblom, "Bargaining: The Hidden Hand of Government (1955)," chap. 7 in *Democracy and Market System* (Oslo: Norwegian University Press, 1988), pp. 139–170; Charles E. Lindblom and David Braybrooke, *The Strategy of Decision* (New York: Free Press, 1963); Charles E. Lindblom, *The Intelligence of Democracy* (New York: Free Press, 1965). A related criticism was made by Martin Landau, "Redundancy, Rationality, and the Problem of Duplication and Overlap," *Pub. Adm. Rev.* (July–August 1969): 346–358.

14. Herbert A. Simon, *Administrative Behavior,* 3d ed. (New York: Free Press, 1976), pp. 61–78; Herbert A. Simon, Donald W. Smithburg, and Victor A. Thompson, *Public Administration* (New York: Knopf, 1950); Robert A. Dahl and Charles E. Lindblom, *Politics, Economics, and Welfare* (New York: Harper Brothers, 1953); Karl, op. cit., pp. 224–226; James Q. Wilson, *Bureaucracy: What Government Agencies Do and Why They Do It* (New York: Basic Books, 1989), pp. 315–332.

15. See, for example, Guy Black, *The Application of Systems Analysis to Government Operations* (New York: Praeger, 1968); Robert Haveman, ed., *Public Expenditures and Policy Analysis,* 3d ed. (Boston: Houghton Mifflin, 1983); Ida R. Hoos, *Systems Analysis in Public Policy: A Critique,* rev. ed. (Berkeley and Los Angeles: University of California Press, 1983).

16. Wilson, op. cit., pp. 113–136.

17. Kelman, op. cit., p. 52.

18. The belief that politics and public administration are separate domains of social action was central to the bureaucratic reform vision. This notion has been criticized for decades by academics and educators. According to Wilson, "Political scientists never fail to remind their students on the first day of class [that] in this country there is no clear distinction between policy and administration" (op. cit., p. 241). We suppose that these teachings have had sufficient influence to merit focusing attention elsewhere. The bureaucratic paradigm's prescribed separation between substance and institutional administration *within* the administration component of the politics/administration dichotomy has received inadequate notice and scrutiny.

19. Strictly speaking, in the public sector the concepts of *customer* and *service* are typically structural metaphors. Introducing new metaphorically structured concepts into an existing conceptual system makes a difference in how people reason. According to George Lakeoff and Mark Johnson, "New metaphors have the power to create a new reality. This can begin to happen when we start to comprehend our experience in terms of a metaphor, and it becomes a deeper reality when we begin to act in terms of it. If a new metaphor enters the conceptual system that we base our actions on, it will alter that conceptual system and the perceptions and actions that the system gives rise to. Much of cultural change arises from the introduction of new metaphorical concepts and the loss of old ones. For example, the Westernization of cultures throughout the world is partly a matter of introducing the 'time is money' metaphor into those cultures." *Metaphors We Live By* (Chicago: University of Chicago Press, 1980), p. 145.

20. The forces making customer service attractive as a conceptual scheme include the emergence of services as the nation's leading sector, a climate that makes privatization in its various forms an ever-present possibility, public discontent with bureaucracy, renewed appreciation for market-oriented forms of social coordination, technological innovation (especially in information systems), directives from the Office of Management and Budget and the Office of the Secretary of Defense, and the availability of training monies. The list could be extended. The social and intellectual history of the movement under way has yet to be written.

21. See the John F. Kennedy School of Government case study "The Army and REQUEST," by Steven Kelman.

22. The point of the example is not that the substitution of a customer orientation for the bureaucratic approach necessarily improves the operation of government; rather, it suggests that applying the customer approach is likely to alter what government agencies do, thereby changing the results of government operations. To evaluate whether the altered outcome constitutes an improvement requires an act of judgment and will. As an empirical matter, the judgment of the Army and its authorizers is that this application is desirable, on the whole.
23. Massachusetts took the first approach—see Massachusetts Department of Revenue, *Annual Reports* (Boston, 1983–1984)—while Minnesota took the second (see "A Strategy for the 1990s," n.p., nfid., St. Paul, Minn.).
24. See Ron Zemke, "Putting Service Back into Public Service," *Training* (November 1989): pp. 42–49, on improvements in motor vehicle licensing and registration services. See Mary Faulk, "Customer Service and Other Unbureaucratic Notions" (Olympia: Department of Licensing, State of Washington, nfid., mimeographed). The John F. Kennedy School of Government case study "Middlesex County Jury System," C16-86-656, is another illustration.
25. Excellent academic critiques of more general versions of the bureaucratic paradigm can be found in Perrow, op. cit.; Gareth Morgan, *Images of Organization* (Beverly Hills, Calif.: Sage, 1986); Wilson, op. cit. The service approach is not used by these prominent organizational theorists to critique the theory or practice of bureaucracy. Among the works we draw on in synthesizing the conceptual system of customer service are those written by business school academics and consultants: Theodore Levitt, "The Industrialization of Service," *Harvard Business Review* (September–October 1976): 63–74; Richard B. Chase, "Where Does the Customer Fit in a Service Operation?" *Harvard Business Review* (November–December 1978): 137–142; Thomas J. Peters and Robert H. Waterman, Jr., *In Search of Excellence: Lessons from America's Best-Run Companies* (New York: Warner, 1982); Geoffrey M. Bellman, *The Quest for Staff Leadership* (Glenview, Ill.: Scott, Foresman, 1986); James L. Heskett, *Managing in the Service Economy* (Boston: Harvard Business School Press, 1986); James L. Heskett, "Lessons in the Service Sector," *Harvard Business Review* (March–April 1987): 118–126; Karl Albrecht, *At America's Service* (Homewood, Ill.: Dow Jones-Irwin, 1988); Christian Grönroos, *Service Management and Marketing: Managing the Moment of Truth in Service Competition* (Lexington, Mass.: Lexington Books, 1990); David E. Bowen, Richard B. Chase, Thomas G. Cummings, and Associates, *Service Management Effectiveness* (San Francisco: Jossey-Bass, 1990); James L. Heskett, W. Earl Sasser, Jr., and Christopher W. L. Hart, *Service Breakthroughs* (New York: Free Press, 1990). The public sector literature on service management includes Charles C. Goodsell, ed., *The Public Encounter: Where State and Citizens Meet* (Bloomington: Indiana University Press, 1981).
26. The term *rhetorical* is not meant to be disparaging. On the contrary, rhetoric is a valuable way of mobilizing conceptual resources and evidence. See Giandomenico Majone, *Evidence, Argument, and Persuasion in the Policy Process* (New Haven, Conn.: Yale University Press, 1989). See also Alasdair Roberts, "The Rhetorical Problems of the Manager," paper presented at the Annual Research Conference of the Association for Public Policy Analysis and Management, San Francisco, October 1990.
27. The rhetoric of customer service is becoming ubiquitous in statements of mission and strategy by government organizations. See, for example, U.S. General Services Administration, "1991 Strategic Plan" (Washington, D.C.: 1990). It is also becoming commonplace in articles written for public managers. See, for example, Organization for Economic Cooperation and Development, *Administration as Service: The Public as Client* (Paris, 1987); Zemke, op. cit.; Steven Kelman, "The Renewal of the Public Sector," *American Prospect* (summer 1990): 51–57; David Osborne, "Ten Ways to Turn D.C. Around," *Washington Post Magazine*, December 9, 1990, pp. 19–42; Barbara Bordelon and Elizabeth Clemmer,

"Customer Service, Partnership, Leadership: Three Strategies That Work," *GAO Journal* (winter 1990–91): 36–43; Monte Ollenburger and Jeff Thompson, "A Strategy for Service?" *Public Management* (April 1990): 21–23; George D. Wagenheim and John H. Reurink, "Customer Service in Public Administration," *Pub. Adm. Rev.* (May–June 1991): 263–270; Tom Glenn, "The Formula for Success in TQM," *Bureaucrat* (spring 1991): 17–20; Joseph Sensenbrenner, "Quality Comes to City Hall," *Harvard Business Review* (March–April 1991): 64–75. Professional associations of public administrators are bringing these ideas to the attention of their members. See, for example, the papers presented at the 1990 National Conference of the American Society for Public Administration, published in the fall 1990 issue of *The Bureaucrat.* Executive education programs, furthermore, are increasingly using the concepts of customers and service. See Michael Barzelay and Linda Kaboolian, "Structural Metaphors and Public Management Education," *Journal of Policy Analysis and Management* (fall 1990): 599–610.

28. In undertaking this task, it is well to bear in mind two observations made many years ago by legal theorist Karl N. Llewellyn. First, "it is hard to take things which are unconventional or otherwise unfamiliar to the addressee and to get them said so that they come through as intended. . . . I say we all know this, and we all try to canvass and prepare, to choose words well and to arrange them better, so that they may become true messengers." Second, "there are no panaceas" (*The Common Law Tradition: Deciding Appeals* (Boston: Little, Brown, 1960), pp. 401–403.

29. The concepts of program budgeting, program evaluation, and policy analysis broadened and improved the bureaucratic paradigm and provided some of the seeds for the post-bureaucratic paradigm, but they did not challenge the bureaucratic paradigm's conception of administration, production, organization, and accountability.

30. James Q. Wilson, *Bureaucracy: What Government Agencies Do and Why They Do It* (New York: Basic Books, 1989), pp. 369– 376.

31. David Osborne and Ted Gaebler, *Reinventing Government: How the Entrepreneurial Spirit Is Transforming the Public Sector* (Reading, Mass.: Addison-Wesley, 1992). The term was used in the 1991 inaugural address of Massachusetts Governor William Weld. See "What 'Entrepreneurial Government' Means to Governor Weld," *Boston Globe,* January 8, 1991, pp. 17–18.

32. On the quality movement in government, see Christopher Farrell, "Even Uncle Sam Is Starting to See the Light," *Business Week,* Special 1991 Bonus Issue: "The Quality Imperative," October 25, 1991, pp. 132–137. On the origins of quality management concepts and practices, see David A. Garvin: *Managing Quality: The Strategic and Competitive Edge* (New York: Free Press, 1988). TQM's influence in the defense department can be seen in, e.g., Tom Varian, "Beyond the TQM Mystique: Real-World Perspectives on Total Quality Management" (Arlington, Va.: American Defense Preparedness Association, 1990); Defense Communications Agency, "Vision 21/TQM: Venturing Forth into the 21st Century," 2d ed. (Washington, D.C., March 1989); Navy Personnel Research and Development Center, "A Total Quality Management Process Improvement Model" (San Diego, Calif., December 1988). Any scholarly literature on total quality management in government has yet to appear.

33. Donald B. Shykoff, "Unit Cost Resourcing Guidance," (Washington, D.C.: Department of Defense, n.p., October 1990), cited in Fred Thompson and L. R. Jones, "Management Control and the Pentagon," book manuscript, October 1991, p. 16.

34. Project 1988, "Round II: Incentives for Action: Designing Market-based Environmental Strategies" (Washington, D.C., 1991), Robert N. Stavins, "Clean Profits: Using Economic Incentives to Protect the Environment," *Policy Review* (spring 1989): 58–63.

35. Malcolm K. Sparrow, Mark H. Moore, and David M. Kennedy, *Beyond 911: A New Era for Policing* (New York: Basic Books, 1990).

36. Beth A. Stroul and Robert M. Friedman, "A System of Care for Severely Emotionally

Disturbed Children and Youth" (Washington, D.C.: Georgetown University Child Development Center, July 1986).

37. "Middlesex County Jury System," John F. Kennedy School of Government case C16–86–656.0.

38. Theodore R. Sizer, *Horace's Compromise: The Dilemma of the American High School* (Boston: Houghton Mifflin, 1984); Paul T. Hill and Josephine Bonan, "Decentralization and Accountability in Public Education" (Santa Monica, Calif.: RAND, 1991).

39. John E. Chubb and Eric A. Hanushek, "Reforming Educational Reform," in *Setting National Priorities,* ed. Henry Aaron (Washington, D.C.: Brookings Institution, 1990), pp. 213–247; John E. Chubb and Terry M. Moe, *Politics, Markets, and America's Schools* (Washington, D.C.: Brookings Institution, 1990), pp. 185–229. For a critical book review of Chubb and Moe by Richard F. Elmore, see *Journal of Policy Analysis and Management* (fall 1991): 687–694.

40. A paradigm is an experientially grounded conceptual system. More specifically, a paradigm might be thought of as a system of awareness, mental schemes, commonsense theories, and general reasons for action. To see how such a system is structured, consider an important concept in the paradigm of modern society: production. The concept of production heightens awareness of certain kinds of work processes (such as factory work) and downplays others (such as domestic work). The concept entails a complex mental scheme, which includes such other concepts as workers, tasks, machines, specialization, skills, organization, supervision, throughput, work-in-process inventory, bottlenecks, defects, inspection, rework, costs, and efficiency. This complex mental scheme structures commonsense theories about production. A historically important commonsense theory held that modern prosperity and convenience required efficiency; efficiency required reducing production costs; and costs could be reduced through task specialization, close supervision of workers, and rational organization. Out of this commonsense theory came a general reason for action in industrial society: efficiency.

41. On mappings from source to target domains, see George Lakoff and Mark Turner, *More Than Cool Reason* (Chicago: University of Chicago Press, 1989), pp. 57–65.

42. These reforms included introduction of civil service protections, and short ballot, reorganization, the executive budget process, and competitive purchasing.

43. The concept of the public interest has been ably scrutinized by political scientists over the years. See, for example, Charles E. Lindblom, "Bargaining: The Hidden Hand in Government (1955)," chap. 7 in *Democracy and Market System* (Oslo: Norwegian University Press, 1988), pp. 139–170. Historian Richard Hofstadter points out that in general the public interest was what reformers—principally middle-class professionals and elites who had lost power to political machines —thought would make America a better society. See *The Age of Reform: From Bryan to F.D.R.* (New York: Vintage, 1955), pp. 174–214.

44. Some may criticize the use of any concept such as the public interest. Arguments can be found in the literature on public deliberation and public management to support our premise that if the public interest rhetorical category is suppressed, it should be replaced by a functionally similar idea. See Steven Kelman, *Making Public Policy: A Hopeful View of American Government* (New York: Basic Books, 1987), p. 215. See also Robert B. Reich, ed., *The Power of Public Ideas* (Cambridge, Mass.: Harvard University Press, 1990); Dennis F. Thompson, "Representatives in the Welfare State," in *Democracy and the Welfare State,* ed. Amy Gutmann (Princeton, N.J.: Princeton University Press, 1988, pp. 136–143); and Mark H. Moore, "Creating Value in the Public Sector," book manuscript in progress. Support for the premise that rhetoric contributes to deliberation can be found in such diverse works as Donald N. McCloskey, *The Rhetoric of Economics* (Madison: University of Wisconsin Press, 1985); Warren Bennis and Richard Nanus, *Leaders: Strategies for Taking Charge* (New York: Harper and Row, 1985); David Johnston, *The Rhetoric of Leviathan* (Princeton, N.J.: Princeton

University Press, 1986); Giandomenico Majone, *Evidence, Argument, and Persuasion in the Policy Process* (New Haven, Conn.: Yale University Press, 1989).

45. We simplify here by omitting discussion of the concept of economy. Economy was the watchword of those who wanted to reduce government expenditures and taxes; efficiency was highlighted by those who wanted to improve government performance. We also simplify the discussion of efficiency here by focusing on the scientific management movement and factory administration. For a more complete discussion of the concept of efficiency in early public administration, see Dwight Waldo, *The Administrative State,* 2d ed. (New York: Holmes and Meier, 1984).
46. By knowledge in this context we mean ordinary knowledge as discussed in Charles E. Lindblom and David K. Cohen, *Usable Knowledge: Social Science and Social Problem Solving* (New Haven, Conn.: Yale University Press, 1979), pp. 12–14. On mappings from source to target domains, see Lakoff and Turner, op. cit., pp. 57–65.
47. Robert B. Reich, *The Next American Frontier* (New York: Times Books, 1983), pp. 22–82.
48. Alfred D. Chandler, Jr., "Mass Production and the Beginnings of Scientific Management," in *The Coming of Managerial Capitalism: A Case Book in the History of American Economic Institutions,* ed. Chandler and Richard S. Tedlow (Homewood, Ill.: Richard D. Irwin, 1985), p. 465.
49. "Systematic bookkeeping was revolutionizing control over industrial production, pointing out the direction not only of efficiency and greater profit but honesty as well" (Barry Dean Karl, *Executive Reorganization and Reform in the New Deal* (Cambridge, Mass.: Harvard University Press, 1963), p. 35). In stressing the role of industry as a source domain of knowledge about efficient government, we do not claim that other sources of knowledge were irrelevant. Indeed, Karl points out that early reformers were influenced by city management in Germany and the British parliamentary system, although the influence of these models was mediated by knowledge of business and industry in the United States. See op. cit., pp. 95–96. Karl also argues that the power of arguments about industrial practice was enhanced by moral outrage against corruption and waste. See op. cit., pp. 141–143.
50. What explains this puzzle? One argument might be that the outputs of government are different from the outputs of factories. But that argument fails because the concept of product could have served as a structural metaphor—as it does today—in efforts to conceptualize the relation between organizational goals and organizational work. One might argue, against this view, that reformers did not know how to think metaphorically. But the concept of an efficient government entails the use of the structural metaphor "Government is industry." Whether reformers knew they were speaking metaphorically is largely irrelevant. We conjecture that the concept of product was left out because reformers were committed to rationalism and professionalism and shunned market processes and commercial values in the context of government. The influence of legal conceptions of organizations was also felt.
51. See Herbert A. Simon, *Administrative Behavior,* 3d ed. (New York: Free Press, 1976), pp. 134–145. Simon restates arguments for respecting lines of authority irrespective of the merits of the particular decision.
52. On the importance of integrating functions and adapting organizations to the environment, see Kenneth R. Andrews, *The Concept of Corporate Strategy,* rev. ed. (Homewood, Ill.: R. D. Irwin, 1980).
53. The word *efficiency* does not appear in the index of either Michael E. Porter, *Competitive Advantage: Creating and Sustaining Superior Performance* (New York: Free Press, 1985), or of James L. Heskett, W. Earl Sasser Jr., and Christopher W. L. Hart, *Service Breakthroughs* (New York: Free Press, 1990).
54. The information provided in chapters 3–5 of this book is evidence for this claim.
55. On rival definitions of the concept of product, see Derek Abell, *Defining the Business: The Starting Point of Strategic Planning* (Englewood Cliffs, N.J.: Prentice-Hall, 1980). For discussions of the concept of value creation, see Porter, op. cit., pp. 33–61; David A. Lax and James K.

Sebenius, *The Manager as Negotiator* (New York: Free Press, 1986), pp. 63–116. The concept of value creation in both works fits in the broad tradition of welfare consequentialism. See Amartya Sen and Bernard Williams, eds., *Utilitarianism and Beyond* (Cambridge, England: Cambridge University Press, 1982).

56. On the role of ad hoc arguments in practical reason and social science, see, respectively, Joseph Raz, *Practical Reason and Norms* (Princeton, N.J.: Princeton University Press, 1990), pp. 28–35; and Charles E. Lindblom, *Inquiry and Change: The Troubled Attempt to Understand and Shape Society* (New Haven, Conn.: Yale University Press, 1990), pp. 169–170.
57. On classical organization theory, see Gareth Morgan, *Images of Organization* (Newbury Park, Calif.: Sage, 1986), pp. 19–38.
58. For a classic argument that administration is an identifiable domain of governmental activity, see Woodrow Wilson, "The Study of Administration," *Political Science Quarterly* (June 1887): 197–222.
59. National Commission on the Public Service, *Leadership for America: Rebuilding the Public Service* (Washington, D.C., 1989), pp. 173–175.
60. Rosabeth Moss Kanter, *The Change Masters: Innovation and Entrepreneurship in the American Corporation* (New York: Simon and Schuster, 1983), pp. 56–58.
61. National Commission on the Public Service, *Leadership for America: Rebuilding the Public Service*, pp. 21–41.
62. For a discussion of process control, see Robert H. Hayes, Steven C. Wheelwright, and Kim B. Clark, *Dynamic Manufacturing: Creating the Learning Organization* (New York: Free Press, 1988), pp. 185–341; Heskett, Sasser, and Hart, op. cit., pp. 112–158.
63. This empirical claim cannot be substantiated on the basis of social scientific research. It rests on anecdotal evidence derived from extensive contact with public sector managers and from conducting field work for "Denise Fleury and the Minnesota Office of State Claims," John F. Kennedy School of Government case C15–87–744.0.
64. Marshall Bailey of the Defense Logistics Agency argues that process analysis is a way to combat the PHOG (Prophecy, Hearsay, Opinion, and Guesswork) that impairs employee commitment and organizational performance.
65. One interviewee for the Denise Fleury case reported that before engaging in process flow analysis, coworkers viewed one another as job categories; afterward, they viewed one another as people.
66. Some activities in government, such as minting currency and making weapons, are more like manufacturing than like service delivery. Most compliance activities are more similar to services than to manufacturing. *Winning compliance to norms* is an appropriate term for production in a compliance context.
67. The typical accounts of total quality management fail to make the vital distinction between industrial production and service delivery. For a discussion of this distinction, see James L. Heskett, *Managing in the Service Economy* (Boston: Harvard Business School Press, 1986). Indeed, the source domains for total quality management practices are industries and utilities. Viewed at close range, the failure to make the service/industry distinction is a significant handicap of TQM.
68. A background reason was the influence of machine metaphors on organizational thought. See Morgan, op. cit. pp. 19–38.
69. See JoAnne Yates, *Control through Communication: The Rise of System in American Management* (Baltimore, Md.: Johns Hopkins University Press, 1989), pp. 1–20. According to Yates, the notions of control and systems were developed into a management philosophy during the 1890s.
70. For a discussion of frequent mismatches between rules and operational realities, see James Q. Wilson, *Bureaucracy*, 333–345; Steven Kelman, *Procurement and Public Management: The Fear of Discretion and the Quality of Government Performance* (Washington, D.C.: American Enterprise Institute, 1990), pp. 88–90.
71. As mentioned above, the total quality management movement has not focused on compliance processes. If such a focus were to be developed, it might begin by pointing out the similarities between enforcement approaches

to compliance and inspection approaches to quality assurance. In diagnosing problems with the enforcement approach, experience with inspection could serve as a useful source domain. Similarly, as a heuristic device to structure a better approach to compliance, TQM's preferred alternative to inspection should be used as a source domain. From a post-bureaucratic perspective, TQM should not be the only such source domain. Other source domains include the liberal and civic republican strands of American political theory and recent experience with service management.

72. For a discussion of this consequence of an enforcement orientation in the context of social regulation, see Eugene Bardach and Robert A. Kagan, *Going by the Book: The Problem of Regulatory Unreasonableness* (Philadelphia: Temple University Press, 1982), pp. 93–119.
73. See J. Richard Hackman and Greg R. Oldham, *Work Redesign* (Reading, Mass.: Addison-Wesley, 1980).
74. See, generally, Joseph Raz, introduction to *Authority*, ed. Raz (New York: New York University Press, 1990), pp. 1–19.
75. See the discussion of good and bad apples in Bardach and Kagan, op. cit, p. 124.
76. See Jeffrey A. Roth and John T. Scholz, eds., *Taxpayer Compliance: Social Science Perspectives*, vol. 2 (Philadelphia: University of Pennsylvania Press, 1989); Malcolm K. Sparrow, "Informing Enforcement," (Cambridge, Mass.: n.p., December 1991); Mark H. Moore, "On the Office of Taxpayer and the Social Process of Taxpaying," in *Income Tax Compliance*, ed. Philip Sawicki (Reston, Va.: American Bar Association, 1983), pp. 275–292; Manuel Ballbé i Mallol, Catherine Moukheibir, Michael Barzelay, and Thomas D. Herman, "The Criminal Investigation and Prosecution of Tax Fraud in Advanced Societies" (Madrid: Ministry of Economy and Finance, Instituto de Estudios Fiscales, September 1991); State of Minnesota, Department of Revenue, "Strategies for the '90s" (St. Paul, 1990).
77. For the classic statement of the difference between organizations as technical instruments and as committed polities, see Philip Selznick, *Leadership in Administration: A Sociological Interpretation* (New York: Harper and Row, 1957). For a recent argument along similar lines, see Albert O. Hirschman, *Getting Ahead Collectively: Grassroots Experiences in Latin America* (New York: Pergamon, 1984).
78. Robert A. Dahl and Charles E. Lindblom, *Politics, Economics, and Welfare* (New York: Harper Bros., 1953; Charles E. Lindblom, *Politics and Markets* (New York: Basic Books, 1977).
79. Alfred D. Chandler Jr., *Strategy and Structure* (Cambridge, Mass.: MIT Press, 1962).
80. Another valuable concept is strategy, especially as defined in Lax and Sebenius, op. cit., pp. 261–268.
81. This definition is influenced by Mark H. Moore, "What Sort of Ideas Become Public Ideas?" *The Power of Public Ideas*, ed. Robert B. Reich (Cambridge, Mass.: Harvard University Press, 1990), pp. 55–83; and Ronald Jepperson and John W. Meyer, "The Public Order and the Construction of Formal Organizations," in *The New Institutionalism in Organizational Theory*, ed. Walter W. Powell and Paul J. DiMaggio (Chicago: University of Chicago Press, 1991), pp. 183– 203.
82. As mentioned above, services and products in the public sector are often defined metaphorically. The role of structural metaphors in public sector management thought and practice deserves substantial attention. For a beginning, see Michael Barzelay and Linda Kaboolian, "Structural Metaphors and Public Management Education," *Journal of Policy Analysis and Management* (fall 1990): 599–610.
83. See the principles discussed in chapter 7.
84. The bureaucratic paradigm focused attention on functions and non-operational goals rather than producing desired states of affairs. The term *outcome* has a different meaning in this context than in the academic public policy literature, where the concept of outcome generally refers to the ultimate intended consequences of a public policy intervention. As used here, an outcome can be proximate results of an organization's

work. For example, desired outcomes of a plant management operation include clean buildings and satisfied customers.

85. Herbert A. Simon, Donald W. Smithburg, and Victor A. Thompson, *Public Administration* (New York: Knopf, 1950), p. 513.
86. The argument that accountability is a psychological state of affairs that can be influenced by the individual's environment is developed in Hackman and Oldham, op. cit., pp. 71–98. In a similar vein, other social psychologists conclude on the basis of experiments that accountability raises "concerns about social evaluation, so that an individual's interest in appearing thoughtful, logical, and industrious overcomes motivation to loaf." See Elizabeth Weldon and Gina Gargano, "Cognitive Loafing: The Effects of Accountability and Shared Responsibility on Cognitive Effort," *Personality and Social Psychology Bulletin* (1988): 160, cited in Robert E. Lane, *The Market Experience* (Cambridge, England: Cambridge University Press, 1991), p. 49.
87. Robert Nozick, *The Examined Life: Philosophical Meditations* (New York: Simon and Schuster, 1989), p. 174. Nozick also argues, in effect, that being accountable in this sense is necessary for a full, moral life. Drawing on Lockean political theory, Rogers M. Smith makes a similar argument. See *Liberalism and American Constitutional Law* (Cambridge, Mass.: Harvard University Press, 1985), pp. 205–206.
88. Hackman and Oldham, op. cit., pp. 77–81. For a recent summary of the literature on intrinsic and extrinsic motivations at work, see Lane, op. cit., pp. 339–371.
89. Simon, Smithburg, and Thompson, op. cit., pp. 508–509.
90. Allen Schick presents a nuanced statement of this aspect of the bureaucratic paradigm: "Spending agencies usually behave as claimants, but more have procedures to conserve the resources available to them. . . . Similarly, the central budget office has a lead role in conserving resources, but it occasionally serves as a claimant for uses that it favors. It is not uncommon for the budget office to argue that some programs should be given more funds than have been requested." See "An Inquiry into the Possibility of a Budgetary Theory," in *New Directions in Budget Theory*, ed. Irene S. Rubin (Albany: State University of New York Press, 1988), p. 65.
91. See Peter Hutchinson, Babak Armajani, and John James, "Enterprise Management: Designing Public Services as If the Customer Really Matters (Especially Now that Government Is Broke)" (Minneapolis: Center of the American Experiment, 1991); as well as the fiscal 1992–1993 budget instructions for Minnesota state government, reproduced as appendix 3.
92. Many readers will recognize these responsibilities as a subset of the classic POSDCORB role frame. The definitions of planning, organizing, directing, and coordinating are informed by Luther Gulick, "Notes toward a Theory of Organization," in *Papers on the Science of Administration*, ed. L. Gulick and L. Urwick (New York: Institute of Public Administration, 1937), pp. 3–45; Joseph L. Massie, "Management Theory," in *Handbook of Organizations*, ed. James G. March (Chicago: Rand McNally, 1965), pp. 387–401; Simon, op. cit., pp. 123–153.
93. Among the many authors who have formulated, elaborated, restated, and/or popularized such concepts are Mary Parker Follett, Peter Drucker, Herbert Simon, Philip Selznick, Warren Bennis, Donald Schön, J. Richard Hackman, Harold Leavitt, James Q. Wilson, Rosabeth Moss Kanter, James Sebenius, James Heskett, Robert Behn, Philip Crosby, Thomas Peters, and Robert H. Waterman, Jr. These conceptual themes continue to be extended in the public management literature by such writers as Jameson Doig, Steven Kelman, Mark Moore, Ronald Heifetz, Philip Heymann, and Robert Reich.
94. The change process in Minnesota, described in chapters 3–5, accelerated after such arguments—informed by the results of the research leading to this book—were made.

44

Creating Public Value: Strategic Management in Government

Mark H. Moore

Defining Public Value

On the day he was appointed, the sanitation commissioner drove through the city.[1] Everywhere he saw signs of public and private neglect. Trash barrels left too long at the curb were now overflowing. Back alleys hid huge, overflowing bins that had never made it to the curbs. Emptied bins were ringed by trash spilled during the emptying. In the poorer sections of town, rats scurried among the cans.

Perhaps because he was newly appointed, the commissioner felt his public accountability quite keenly. The city spent a great deal of money each year to sustain the organization's activities. Hundreds of employees earned their pay and made their careers in his organization, and scores of trucks were garaged, maintained, and deployed under his supervision. Most important, millions of people relied on his organization to keep the city clean and healthy.

Happily, as he drove through the city, he saw evidence of his organization at work. Huge trucks, painted in distinctive colors, rumbled by, trailed by sanitation workers who tipped garbage pails into their gaping maws. Street-cleaning machines trundled along the gutters in the wake of the tow trucks that removed illegally parked cars from their path. An occasional street sweeper appeared with broom and dustbin, emptying the cans that had been set out to hold the public's litter.

Still, he could not help thinking that his organization could do more. As the newly appointed commissioner, he wanted to make a difference. He wanted his organization to have an impact on the conditions he could see around him. He wanted to create value for the citizens of the city. But how?

The question seemed particularly urgent because the newly elected mayor had asked him to define and set out his management objectives for the Department of Sanitation. As part of that strategic plan, the mayor wanted to know whether it would be advisable to privatize some or all of the operations of the Department of Sanitation.

The Aim of Managerial Work

The sanitation commissioner is a manager at work. The question is: At work on what? What is the point of his efforts?

We know the aim of managerial work in the private sector: to make money for the shareholders of the firm.[2] Moreover, we know the ways in which that goal can be achieved: by producing products (including services) that can be sold to customers at prices that earn revenues above the costs of production.[3] And we know how managerial accomplishments can be gauged: through financial measures of profit and loss and changes in the firm's stock price.[4] If private managers can conceive and make products that earn profits, and if the companies they lead can do this continually over time, then a strong presumption is established that the managers have created value.[5]

In the public sector, the overall aim of managerial work seems less clear; what managers need to do to produce value far more ambiguous; and how to measure whether value has been created far more difficult. Yet, to develop a theory of how public managers should behave, one must resolve these basic issues. Without knowing the point of managerial work, we cannot determine whether any particular managerial action is good or bad. Public management is, after all, a normative as well as technical enterprise.

As a starting point, let me propose a simple idea: the aim of managerial work in the public

---

Source: Reprinted by permission of the publisher from CREATING PUBLIC VALUE: Strategic Management in Government by Mark H. Moore, pp. 27–38, Cambridge, Mass.: Harvard University Press, Copyright © 1995 by the President and Fellows of Harvard College.

sector is to create *public* value just as the aim of managerial work in the private sector is to create *private* value.

This simple idea is often greeted with indignation—even outrage. A liberal society like ours tends to view government as an "unproductive sector." In this view government cannot create value. At best, it is a necessary evil: a kind of referee that sets out the rules within which a civil society and a market economy can operate successfully, or an institution that fills in some of the gaps in free market capitalism. While such activities may be necessary, they can hardly be viewed as value creating. But this view denies a reality that public managers experience daily. From their perspective it is government, acting through its managers, that shields the country from foreign enemies, keeps the streets safe and clean, educates the children, and insulates citizens from many man-made and natural disasters that have impoverished the lives of previous human generations. To them it seems obvious that government creates value for the society. That is the whole point of their work.

Of course, this account is not entirely satisfactory; it looks only at the benefits of governmental activity, not at the costs. In reality public managers cannot produce the desirable results without using resources that have value in alternative uses. To keep the streets clean; to insulate the disadvantaged from the ravages of poverty, ignorance, and joblessness; even to collect the taxes that society has agreed are owed, public managers must have money to purchase equipment, pay their workers, and provide mandated benefits to clients. The money they use is raised through the coercive power of taxation. That money is lost to other uses—principally, private consumption. That loss must be laid against the putative benefits of public enterprises.

Moreover, to achieve their goals, public managers often use a resource other than money: they use the authority of the state to compel individuals to contribute directly to the achievement of public objectives.[6] Litterers are fined to help keep the cities clean; welfare recipients are sometimes obliged to find work; and every citizen is made to feel the weight of the obligation to pay taxes to help the society achieve its collective goals.[7]

In a society that celebrates private consumption more than the achievement of collective goals, values individual liberty greatly, and sees private entrepreneurship as a far more important engine of social and economic development than governmental effort, the resources required by public managers are only grudgingly surrendered. So, it is not enough to say that public managers create results that are valued; they must be able to show that the results obtained are worth the cost of private consumption and unrestrained liberty forgone in producing the desirable results. Only then can we be sure that some public value has been created.

The Political Marketplace: "We Citizens" as a Collective Consumer

But to whom should such a demonstration be made? And how could anyone know whether the demonstration is convincing?

In the private sector these key questions are answered when individual consumers stake their hard-earned cash on the purchase of a product, and when the price paid exceeds the costs of making what is sold. These facts establish the presumptive value of the enterprise. If individuals do not value the products or service enough to pay for them, they will not buy them; and if they do not buy them, the goods will not be produced.[8]

In the public sector, however, the money used to finance value-creating enterprises is not derived from the individual, voluntary choices of consumers. It comes to public enterprises through the coercive power of taxation. It is precisely that fact that creates a problem in valuing the activities of government (at least from one point of view).[9]

The problem (from this point of view) is that the use of the state's coercive power undermines "consumer sovereignty"—the crucial link between the individual judgments of value on the one hand and control over what is to be produced on the other, which provides the normative justification for private sector enterprises.[10] The coercion blots out the opportunity for individuals to express their individual preferences and to have those preferences control what is to be produced. Because individuals do not choose individually to purchase or contribute to discrete governmental activities, we cannot be sure that they want what the government supplies.

And if we cannot be sure that individuals want what the government produces, then, by some reckoning at least, we cannot be sure that the government produces anything of value.

What this account overlooks, however, is that the resources made available to public sector managers *are* made through a process of voluntary choice—namely, the process of representative government. To be sure, *individual*, voluntary choice does not control this system. But the institutions and processes of representative democracy come as close as we now can to creating the conditions under which individuals can voluntarily assemble and decide collectively what they would like to achieve together without sacrificing their individual desires. It is the only way we know how to create a "we" from a collection of free individuals.[11] That "we," in turn, can decide to make common cause, to raise resources, and to organize to achieve its goals—all the activities that go into the policy-making and implementation roles associated with government.

Indeed, it is the explicit recognition of the power of politics to establish normatively compelling collective purposes that makes legislative and political mandates central to traditional conceptions of public administration. Those legislative mandates properly guide public sector production specifically because they define collective aspirations. The collective aspirations, in turn, establish a presumption of public value as strong as the presumption of private value created by market mechanisms—at least if they can be achieved within the terms of the mandate. So, we should evaluate the efforts of public sector managers not in the economic marketplace of individual consumers but in the political marketplace of citizens and the collective decisions of representative democratic institutions.[12]

Precisely to make such demonstrations the sanitation commissioner prepares a plan to present to the newly elected mayor. In doing so, he tries to satisfy representatives of the public that his organization responds to the public's aspirations. Once he presents the plan, he will be accountable for producing measures to show that the goals and objectives of the plan have, in fact, been achieved.[13]

The claim that public managers can presume that public value is created if they meet the test of the political marketplace is also often greeted by derision. We have all become painfully aware of the folly and corruption that can beset the deliberations and choices of representative democratic institutions.[14]

Practicing public managers, however, have no choice but to trust (at least to some degree) in the normative power of the preferences that emerge from the representative processes. Those choices establish the justification for managerial action in the public sector. Because public managers spend public resources in the enterprises they lead, they must act as though a coherent and normatively compelling "we" existed even if they have their doubts. Otherwise, their enterprises are ill-founded.

Different Standards for Reckoning Public Value

Reconciling the tension between the desire to have democratic politics determine what is worth producing in the public sector and the recognition that democratic politics is vulnerable to corruption of various kinds has been the persistent challenge to those who would offer a theory of public management in a democracy.[15] Over time, we have relied on different concepts as standards for defining managerial purposes.

Achieving Mandated Objectives Efficiently and Effectively

For most of our recent history, the predominant conception has been that public managers should work to achieve the legislatively mandated goals and objectives of their organizations as efficiently and effectively as they can.[16] Thus, the sanitation commissioner's job is to clean the streets as efficiently and effectively as possible.

It is quite easy to agree with this conception. Yet, reflection reveals an important feature of this common standard that is often overlooked or taken for granted: namely, this standard establishes the preeminence of *political*—primarily legislative—processes in determining what is valuable for the public sector to produce. To those who value politics as a way of creating a collective will, and who see democratic politics as the best answer we have to the problem of reconciling individual and collective interests, it is hardly surprising that the political process would be allowed to determine what is worth producing with public resources.[17] No other procedure is consistent with the principles of democracy.

But to those who distrust the integrity or utility of political processes, the idea that public value would be defined politically is a little hard to stomach. They have seen too much corruption to trust the determination of public value to political processes. At a minimum these critics want assurances that the political process is a principled one that accepts the proper limits of governmental action or meets some minimal standards of fairness and competence in the deliberations that produce the mandates.[18] Alternatively, they would prefer some more objective ways of ascertaining the value of public sector enterprises and some platform for confronting political processes with this objective information.[19]

Politically Neutral Competence

At the turn of the century Woodrow Wilson offered a solution: separate politics from administration and perfect each activity in its own spheres.[20] Thus, public administrators were to imagine that political mandates came to them in the form of coherent, well-defined policies. As the hard-won products of intense political processes, the policies would have all the moral weight that effective democratic politics could give them.

Given this accomplishment of politics, public administrators could then safely turn their attention to finding the most efficient and effective way to achieve the mandated purposes. To meet these responsibilities, the public administrators were assumed to have knowledge about both the substance of the fields in which they were operating and the arts of administration.[21] By knowing what could be produced and how organizations could be made to produce what was desirable public administrators earned their keep.

However, this traditional conception failed to consider what would happen if the political reality fell short of the ideal. Often, political mandates came loaded down with special interests that were hard to reconcile with the desire to guard the general public interest.[22] Other times, managers received incoherent mandates: they were expected to produce several different things that were inconsistent with one another and were given no useful instructions about which goals and objectives should take precedence over others when conflicts arose.[23] Still other times, political mandates shifted in arbitrary and unpredictable ways, destroying investments and draining momentum that had previously been built up and would be needed again once the political balance was restored to its original position.[24]

Facing this political reality, even Wilsonian public administrators sometimes found it necessary to challenge the wisdom of politically expressed policy mandates. They did so on the basis of their moral obligations to defend the general public interest and preserve the continuity of important public enterprises.[25] In their minds their substantive and administrative expertise gave them the right to stand up to the misguided vagaries of politics. In the pantheon of bureaucratic heroes, the image of a civil servant who challenged badly motivated politicians to defend the long-term public interest stands right alongside the dutiful, responsive servant.

Once revealed, this sort of bureaucratic resistance to political mandates could not stand in a democracy such as ours. Indeed, a favorite target of our populist politics is the bureaucratic mandarin. As a result, much of this bureaucratic resistance went underground. It became a covert but legitimate rationale for bureaucrats of all political stripes to conduct guerrilla warfare against political demands for change on the grounds that the politicians were ill-informed, short-sighted, or badly motivated.

Analytic Techniques for Assessing Public Value

Yet politics, too, is mistrusted in our political culture, and soon a new platform for disciplining and rationalizing democratic politics emerged. This new platform was established on a new kind of expertise. Whereas the traditional theory of public administration acknowledged the substantive and administrative expertise of professionals (developed through professional experience and education), the new formulation held that special analytic techniques, drawn from the fields of economics, statistics, and operations research, could be used objectively to gauge in advance—or to learn after the fact—whether public enterprises were valuable or not.[26] The new techniques included policy analysis, program evaluation, cost-effectiveness analysis, and benefit-cost analysis. Reformers hoped that use of these techniques could infuse policy deliberations with objective facts about the extent to which proposed initiatives could be expected to work and the extent to which the costs of government efforts could be justified by general benefits to society.

There is much to be said about whether these techniques have lived up to their promise—much more than can be said here. From the perspective of someone analyzing their overall impact on policy-making, one can fairly say that the techniques are neither routinely used nor invariably powerful when they are.[27] Still, they have succeeded in changing the political discourse about governmental programs. They have increased the appetite of the political process for fact-based arguments about the extent to which government programs achieve their stated objectives or serve the general interest.[28]

In discussing the utility of these techniques to managers' efforts to define and measure the value of what they are achieving, however, three points seem key. First, for reasons that are not entirely obvious, these techniques seem to be more valuable in estimating the value of particular programs or policies than the overall value of an organization's efforts. One reason, I suspect, is that to deploy these techniques successfully, managers must have narrowly specified objectives and narrowly specified means for achieving the objectives. Specific objectives and specific means are precisely what define governmental policies and programs.

In contrast, an organization is rarely easily conceptualized as a single program or policy. Often, organizations incorporate bundles of programs and policies. The different programs and policies may have been combined to achieve some larger coherent purpose, but the achievement of that larger purpose is often exceedingly difficult to measure and even harder to attribute to the overall operations of any single organization.

It may also be important that, as already mentioned, public organizations have some kind of capital value rooted in their ability to adapt and meet new tasks and challenges. To the extent that they do, an evaluation of their performance in existing tasks and programs would not capture their full benefit to the society. In any case, use of these techniques to evaluate programs and policies has been far more common than their use in assessing the overall value produced by public organizations.

Second, we should distinguish between the use of these techniques to estimate in advance of action whether a particular governmental initiative will prove valuable or not and the use of these techniques after a program has been tried to determine whether it was successful. Policy analysis often focuses on the first, program evaluation on the second. The distinction is particularly important when one uses comparisons with private sector management to offer guidance to public sector managers about how they could better reckon the value of their enterprises.

As noted above, the private sector seems to have a far more reliable way of measuring the value of its production than the public sector. The revenues and profits earned from selling particular products and services—that is, the famed bottom line—provides a direct measure of a private sector enterprise's success. What is interesting about profitability, however, is that it measures what happened in the past. That piece of information is taken very seriously in the private sector, partly because it can be used to hold managers accountable and give them incentives for performance, but also because it gives private sector managers an advantage in thinking about the future. Indeed, many private sector firms have been advised to reduce their reliance on strategic planning efforts designed to produce more accurate predictions about the future and, instead, to rely on their ability to react quickly to the market conditions they encounter through their current operations.

Thus, the lesson from the private sector seems to be that it is extremely valuable to develop accurate information about performance in the past rather than concentrate all one's efforts on guessing about the future. To the extent this is true, it follows that public sector agencies should be focusing more on program evaluation and less on policy analysis. My impression, however, is that they do the opposite. This is unfortunate, for the inconsistent attention given to program evaluation deprives the public sector of the kind of accountability, incentives for action, and capacity to react quickly that the private sector has gained by paying close attention to its bottom line.

Third, we need to look at what sorts of preferences public enterprises are designed to satisfy. Most often, analytic techniques are presented as though they were all useful tools designed to help government learn whether its efforts are valuable or not. Among them, benefit-cost analysis is usually presented as the superior technique, the one that is most general and most reliably linked to value. The only reason not to rely on benefit-cost analyses is that they are more difficult to complete. Thus, program evaluation and cost-effectiveness analysis are presented as poor second cousins to benefit-cost analysis.

Yet I see an important conceptual distinction among the techniques and would argue that for most public purposes, program evaluation and cost-effectiveness analysis are the conceptually as well as practically superior approaches. Benefit-cost analysis, taking guidance from the principles of welfare economics, assumes that public sector activities should be valued by individuals sizing up the (positive or negative) consequences for them as individuals. In contrast, the techniques of program evaluation and cost-effectiveness analysis find their standard of value not in the way that individuals value the consequences of government policy but instead in terms of how well the program or policy achieves particular objectives set by the government itself. Thus, program evaluation measures how well the program achieves its intended purposes, and those purposes are inferred from the language of the statutes or policies that authorized it. Cost-effectiveness analysis measures how well a particular governmental effort scored with respect to a particular set of purposes that had been defined for that particular effort—probably with the help of professionals who could help government policymakers define what constituted a valuable kind of "effectiveness."

In short, both program evaluation and cost-effectiveness analysis define public value in terms of collectively defined objectives that emerge from a process of collective decision-making, whereas benefit-cost analysis defines value in terms of what individuals desire without reference to any collective decision-making process. The reliance of benefit-cost analysis on pure individual preferences is, of course, what makes it a conceptually superior approach to welfare economists. But to those who believe in the capacity of a political process to establish an articulate collective aspiration, and who believe that this is the most appropriate guide to public action, program evaluation and cost-effectiveness analysis seem the better techniques precisely because they look away from individual preferences and toward collectively established purposes.

Focusing on Customer Service and Client Satisfaction

More recently still, public administrators have developed a new conception of how to gauge the value of their enterprises: borrowing from the private sector, they have embraced the goal of customer service, and committed themselves to finding the value of their efforts in the satisfaction of their "customers."[29] This idea has some important virtues. Insofar as it encourages government managers to think about the quality of the interactions that government agencies have with citizens whom they encounter as clients, and to make those encounters more satisfactory, much good will come of adopting this perspective. We have all had our fill of rude bureaucrats and badly designed governmental operations and procedures.

Yet, this idea, too, has flaws. It is by no means clear who the customers of a government agency are. One naturally assumes that they are the *clients* of government organizations—the citizens the organization encounters at its "business end" through individual encounters or transactions.

Insofar as government provides services and benefits to citizens, that model seems to work fairly well. But government is not simply a service provider. Often it is in the business of imposing *obligations*, not providing services.[30] This is true for police departments, environmental protection agencies, commissions against discrimination, and tax collectors among others. These organizations meet individual clients not as service providers but as representatives of the state obliging clients to absorb a loss on behalf of the society at large.

Of course, it may be valuable for regulatory and law enforcement organizations to think of the citizens whom they regulate as customers and to design their "obligation encounters" with as much care as "service encounters" now are.[31] Nevertheless, it is unreasonable to imagine that regulatory and enforcement agencies find their justification in the satisfactions of those whom they compel to contribute to public purposes. More likely, the justification comes from the generally attractive consequences for others of imposing particular obligations on a few. Moreover, there may be many others than those obliged who are interested in the justice or fairness with which the obligations are imposed, the fairness they would wish for themselves if they were similarly obliged.

The point is important because it reminds us that service-providing agencies, too, are judged and evaluated by citizens as well as by those who are clients of the organization. Consider welfare departments, for example. In evaluating the performance of the welfare department, we need to know how clients feel about the services they receive. But we cannot rely on their evaluation as the only or even the most important way of judging the value of the services provided. Citizens and their representatives want to be sure that the total cost of the program remains low, that no one steals from the program (even if it costs more to prevent the stealing than would have been lost if the stealing occurred), and even that the clients experience some degree of stigmatization in enrolling in the welfare program (to mark the distinction between those who can be independent and those who must rely on the state).

In short, it is important to distinguish the evaluation that *citizens* and their representatives give to governmental activities from the evaluation that would be given by *clients*. The arrested offender is not in a particularly good position to judge the value of the police department's operations. And the welfare client might not be either. The ultimate consumer of government operations is not the individuals who are served or obliged in individual encounters (the clients of the enterprise) but citizens and their representatives in government who have more general ideas about how a police department should be organized or welfare support delivered. They decide what is worth producing in the public sector, and their values ultimately matter in judging whether a governmental program is valuable or not.

In the end none of the concepts of "politically neutral competence," "policy analysis" and "program evaluation," or "customer service" can finally banish politics from its preeminent place in defining what is valuable to produce in the public sector. Politics remains the final arbiter of public value just as private consumption decisions remains the final arbiter of private value. Public managers can proceed only by finding a way to improve politics and to make it a firmer guide as to what is publicly valuable. That is why political management must be part of our conception of what public managers should do.[32]

To see how these general considerations might affect the perceptions and calculations of public sector managers, let us return to the problem faced by the sanitation commissioner at the beginning of the chapter. How ought he to think about the question of what value he is creating, for whom, and how?

NOTES

1. This case, like the case of the librarian, is a hypothetical one based on a common story. It comes generally from the experience of public managers but is not the precise history of any particular manager. I use it to illustrate the kinds of problems that managers do face and the ways in which they might think.
2. Richard A. Brealey and Stewart C. Myers, *Principles of Corporate Finance*, 4th ed. (New York: McGraw-Hill, 1991), p. 22.
3. It may not be strictly true that *managers* in the private sector are responsible for *conceiving* products or services. More often, it seems that they are responsible for producing products that have been conceived by others—the chief executive officers of the firm and the marketing people. Yet, if we think of the chief executive officers and marketing people as "managers" as well, then it is true that the managers of a firm are

responsible for conceiving as well as producing products. Moreover, it is increasingly true that private sector firms are structuring themselves to encourage entrepreneurship among midlevel managers. See, for example, Rosabeth Moss Kanter, *The Change Masters: Innovation and Entrepreneurship in the American Corporation* (New York: Simon and Schuster, 1983), pp. 129–179. This also seems to be occurring in the private sector. See United States Department of Agriculture, Forest Service, "The Evolution of Middle Management in the Forest Service," *New Thinking for Managing in Government* (Washington, D.C.: USDA, Forest Service, n.d.).

The fact that we often want to separate the conception of a product (which could be understood as the imagination of something that would be valuable to produce) from the production of that product (which is more often understood as a technical problem), and to associate the conception of products with "leadership" and "entrepreneurship," reflects the discussion in n.9 in Chapter 1. Apparently, we associate leadership and entrepreneurship with the use of imagination to find things that are valuable and management and administration with devising the technical means for achieving what our imaginations suggested would be valuable. For further evidence on the vitality of this distinction, see John Kotter, *A Force for Change: How Leadership Differs from Management* (New York: Free Press; London: Collier Macmillan, 1990), pp. 1–18. For an interesting interpretation of how the distinction between leadership and management is being used in both the theory and practice of management, see James Krantz and Thomas N. Gilmore, "The Splitting of Leadership and Management as a Social Defense," *Human Relations*, vol. 43, no. 2 (February 1990):183–204.

4. These are the criteria Thomas J. Peters and Robert H. Waterman use to identify the firms that embody "excellence"; and it is the creation of organizations that are capable of maintaining profitability over the long run that they take to be the key managerial challenge in the private sector. See Peters and Waterman, *In Search of Excellence: Lessons from America's Best-Run Companies* (New York: Warner, 1982), pp. 121–125.

5. Of course, it is not strictly true that the profitability of a firm in either the short or long run gives certain evidence of the firm's ability to create value. Insofar as the firm uses unowned and unpriced resources valuable to others in its productive activities, such as air or water, or unidentified risks to workers, its financial success may give a distorted view of its overall activity. Still, as a first approximation, the financial success of a firm does create a presumption that some value has been created for consumers and, therefore, for society at large.

6. James W. Fesler and Donald F. Kettl also treat authority as a key resource for public mangers in The *Politics of the Administrative Process* (Chatham, N.J. Chatham House, 1991) p. 9. Terry Moe considers the state's control over the use of public authority one of the things that attract individuals to use the government for their own interests or to impose their idiosyncratic views of the public interest on public policy. See Moe, "Political Institutions: the Neglected Side of the Story", *Journal of Law, Economics, and Organizations*, vol. 6. (1990): 221.

7. For a discussion of how "obligations" to pay taxes might be mobilized, see Mark H Moore, "On the Office of Taxpayer and the Social Process of Taxpaying" in Philip Sawicki, ed. *Income Tax Compliance* (Reston, Va, American Bar Association, 1983), pp. 275–291.

8. Interestingly, the economics profess no longer seems to feel as though it has to defend markets philosophically as an appropriate way to allocate goods in society. Reading through several microeconomics texts in search of a ringing philosophical endorsement of market mechanics, I came up empty. To find the philosophical justification, one must go back to earlier writers who thought they were producing a normative political theory, as well as a technical discussion of how economics functioned. See John Stuart Mill, *Utilitarianism and Other Writings*, ed. Mary Womack (Utica, N.Y. Meridian, 1974) p. 21–30. For more contemporary defenses

of the social value of markets in allocating scarce resources, one has to go to books interpreting economics for others. See Steven E. Rhoads, *The Economist's View of the World, Government, Markets, and Public Policy* (Cambridge: Cambridge University Press, 1985) pp. 62–64.

9. The point of view I am alluding to here is one associated with "welfare economics." For a very good summary of these ideas and how they relate to social decision processes, see Edith Stokey and Richard Zechhauser, *A Primer for Policy Analysis* (New York: Norton, 1978), pp. 257–290, The fundamental idea in welfare economics is that the overall value of a society's activities can be captured by the satisfaction that individuals derive from the activities of that society. In principle, of course, that satisfaction could include the satisfaction that comes from living in a society organized to produce what each individual views as justice and fairness as well as the efficient production of consumer goods. In practice, however, welfare economics generally focuses on the satisfaction that is produced by achieving the efficient production of goods and services that individuals can consume. It devotes less attention to the satisfaction that might come from living in a just society and still less to the satisfactions that might come from participating in political processes that allowed individuals to deliberate with others and then express through the institutions of government a shared idea of a just or virtuous society or what such a society might chose to do in a particular domain of policy. What is particularly alien to welfare economics is any "collectivist" notion that satisfaction could be found anywhere outside an individual's experience. Individuals—their tastes, preferences, and satisfactions—are always the units of analysis; families, groups, or politics never are. In this respect welfare economics departs from Aristotle's understanding of human nature and society and follows John Sturart Mill's. For a discussion of why individuals should not be viewed as existing in isolation from these other mediating structures and how the preferences of individuals expressed within the context of these intermediate structures are the ones the public sector should respond to, see Michael Sandel, "The Political Theory of the Procedural Republic" in Robert Reich, ed. *The Power of Public Ideas* (Cambridge, Mass: Ballinger, 1988) pp. 109–122.

10. Rhoads, *The Economists View of the World*, pp. 62–63.

11. In proposing the existence of a coherent "we" I am departing form a prevailing commitment to "liberal" political and economic philosophies that emphasize the importance of individuals, and the difficulty of impossibility of assembling individuals into coherent wholes that can have preferences, formed within the group through a political process, to develop meaningful collective aspiration. I am entering the realm of "communitarian" philosophies that take a more optimistic view of the possibility (and desirability) of forging aspirations. For some representative examples of works in communitarian philosophies, see Michael Sandel, Liberalism and its Critics (New York: New York University Press, 1984); Amy Gutman "Communitarian Critiques of Liberalism" *Philosophy and Public Affairs* Vol 14, no. 3 (Summer 1985) 308–322; George Will, *Statecraft as Soulcraft: What Government Does* (New York: Simon and Schuster, 1983) and Robert Reich, *The Power of Public Ideas* (Cambridge, Mass: Ballinger, 1988). For a specific argument consistent with the position I am adopting see Sandel, "The Political Theory of the Procedural Republic," pp. 109–122. Such philosophies do not seem all that far from the position that John Rawls also takes in formulating his conception of justice. He asserts: "If men's inclination to self-interest makes their vigilance against one another necessary, their public sense of justice makes their secure association possible. Among individuals with disparate aims and purposes a shared conception of justice establishes the bonds of civic friendship; the general desire for justice limits the pursuit of other ends"; see Rawls, *A Theory of Justice* (Cambridge, Mass Harvard University Press, 1971) p. 5. For an argument that American government can actually approximate some of the ideals of a communitarian political

philosophy, see Steven Kelman, *Making Public Policy: A Hopeful View of American Government* (New York: Basic Books, 1988)

Note that I am adopting a communitarian view of government partly because I prefer it as a philosophical stance. More important, however, public managers must adopt a communitarian stance simply because they cannot make philosophical sense of their lives unless they do. This is the only stance that makes sense when we ask them to deploy public resources for the general benefit of society and instruct them (quite imperfectly) about where public value lies through imperfect political processes.

12. What that marketplace looks like, and what it is trying to purchase, is, as a positive matter, the focus of political science. As a normative matter, it is something that all citizens, elected representatives, and public managers have to be concerned about. For one "hopeful" view of how this market now functions, see Kelman, *Making Public Policy.* For an argument that even that most vilified of institutions, the United States Congress, also aims to produce the public good, see Arthur Maass, *Congress and the Common Good* (New York: Basic Books, 1983), pp. 4–12. And for a view that this is the process that guides the politics of regulation, see James Q. Wilson, "The Politics of Regulation," in James Q. Wilson, ed., *The Politics of Regulation* (New York: Basic Books, 1980), pp. 357–364.
13. William F. Willoughby emphasized the importance of providing accurate information about how plans have been carried out by public administrators in 1918: "The popular will cannot be intelligently formulated nor expressed unless the public has adequate means for knowing currently how governmental affairs have been conducted in the past, what are present conditions, and what program for work in the future is under consideration." Willoughby, *The Movement for Budgetary Reform in the States* (New York: D. Appleton, for the Institute for Government Research, 1918); Jay M. Shafritz and Albert C. Hyde, eds., *Classics in Public Administration*, 2d ed. (Chicago: Dorsey Press, 1987), reprint Willoughby's text. This view is also central to the idea of a proper relationship between "citizen principals" and their agents—legislators and bureaucrats. See John W. Pratt and Richard Zeckhauser, *Principals and Agents: The Structure of Business* (Boston: Harvard Business School Press, 1985), pp. 1–24.
14. Kenneth A. Shepsle, "Positive Theories of Congressional Institutions," occasional paper 92-18, Center for American Political Studies, Harvard University, 1992. For theoretical criticism of political processes, see William Niskanen, *Bureaucracy and Representative Government* (Chicago: Aldine-Atherton, 1971), pp. 138–154. For empirical criticism, see Robert Dahl, *Who Governs: Democracy and Power in an American City* (New Haven, Conn.: Yale University Press, 1961).
15. John Chubb and Paul Peterson make this point succinctly: "The problem of governance in the United States is mainly one of creating institutions or governing arrangements that can pursue policies of sufficient coherence, consistency, foresight and stability that the national welfare is not sacrificed for narrow or temporary gains." See Chubb and Peterson, eds., *Can the Government Govern?* (Washington, D.C.: Brookings Institution, 1989), p. 4. I would agree with this statement even more strongly if I were sure that, first, they included in their idea of "institutions and governing arrangements" an ethic that guides the work of public sector managers and, second, they accepted the idea that the definition of the "national welfare" was importantly influenced by politics and might well change over time as collective aspirations and objective circumstances changed.
16. See Chapter 1, n. 9.
17. For a defense of this position, see Kelman, *Making Public Policy.*
18. Woodrow Wilson, for example, thought that the crucial question politics had to resolve in committing the government to action was to "discover, first, what government can properly and successfully do." Wilson, "The Study of Administration," *Political Science Quarterly*, 2 (June 1887), reprinted in Shafritz

and Hyde, *Classics*, p. 10. Modern economists also prefer that the processes that engage governmental action meet these conditions. See, for example, Stokey and Zeckhauser, *Primer*, pp. 283–285, 292–293, 310–319.

19. Richard Zeckhauser and Derek Leebaert observe: "Our governmental structure requires only that beliefs and values be expressed through the electoral process, whether those beliefs are well- or ill-informed, whether those values are self-serving or public spirited. In practice, our nation has taken minimal steps—most significantly through the support of public education—to encourage a more informed outcome of the political process. Still, the United States has soundly rejected the notion of placing educational requirements on franchise, and has refused to deviate from our representative system of government to achieve more seemingly rational political outcomes. By contrast, it seems to be generally accepted that the policy choices made by government—particularly those of the executive branch—should be based on sound thinking and—where it will make a difference—supported by rational analysis. It is not obvious whence this norm derives. Surely it is not the Constitution. Had our founding fathers foreseen the nature of our modern government, so intricately entwined with so many aspects of its citizens' lives, perhaps they would have laid down rules of procedure for government decision. They left no such instructions, however." Zeckhauser and Leebaert, *What Role for Government: Lessons from Policy Research* (Durham, N.C.: Duke University Press, 1983), pp. 10–11.

20. Woodrow Wilson, "A Study of Administration." For the imagery of perfection in each sphere, see Frank J. Goodnow, *Politics and Administration: A Study in Government* (New York: Russell and Russell, 1900), reprinted in Shafritz and Hyde, *Classics*, pp. 26–29.

21. Edward Banfield makes the distinction between substantive knowledge and administrative knowledge. See Banfield, "The Training of the Executive," *Public Policy: A Yearbook of the Graduate School of Public Administration*, vol. 10 (1960): 20–23.

22. E. Pendleton Herring is most insistent about this fact. See Herring, *Public Administration and the Public Interest* (New York: McGraw-Hill, 1936).

23. This problem continues today and is one of the reasons that public management is so difficult. See Erwin C. Hargrove and John C. Glidewell, eds., *Impossible Jobs in Public Management* (Lawrence: University of Kansas Press, 1990).

24. On the problem of "fickle mandates," see Martha Derthick, *Agency under Stress: The Social Security Administration in American Government* (Washington, D.C.: Brookings Institution, 1990), p. 4. See also Mark H. Moore, "Small Scale Statesmen: A Conception of Public Management," *Politiques et Management Public*, vol. 7, no. 2 (June 1989): 273–287.

25. According to Dwight Waldo, "It can be argued with some persuasiveness that the proper role of a bureaucracy is to act as a stabilizing force in the midst of vertiginous change, and that this is what it is doing when it seems to be unresponsive and stupid. In this view it has a balance wheel or gyroscopic function." It is significant, however, that Waldo goes on to reject this view in favor of increased responsiveness or leadership from public managers. See Waldo, "Public Administration in a Time of Revolution," *Public Administration Review*, 28 (July–August 1968), reprinted in Shafritz and Hyde, *Classics*, p. 367. Rufus Miles worked out a particular set of ideas about the extent to which career civil servants should adapt to the demands of incoming political executives in "Administrative Adaptability to Political Change," *Public Administration Review*, vol. 25, no. 3 (September 1965): 221–225. For a set of cases describing the responses of career civil servants to rather dramatic political change, see "Surviving at the EPA: David Tundermann," KSG Case #C16-84-588.0; "Surviving at the EPA: Mike Walsh," KSG Case #C16-84-589.0; "Surviving at the EPA: Mike Cook," KSG Case #C16-84-590.0; "Surviving at the EPA: Bill Hedeman," KSG Case #C16-84-591.0; "Surviving at the EPA: Gary Dietrich," KSG Case #C16-84-592.0;

"Note on the EPA under Administrator Anne Gorsuch," KSG Case #N16-84-587.0 (all Cambridge, Mass.: Kennedy School of Government Case Program, 1984).

26. There is, now, a large literature that describes the techniques, gives representative examples of their application, assesses their impact on policymaking processes within and outside organizations, and offers critiques of their utility or appropriateness. For examples of early writings setting out the potential of these techniques, see Roland McKean, *Efficiency in Government through Systems Analysis* (New York: John Wiley, 1958); and E. S. Quade, *Analysis for Public Decisions* (New York: American Elsevier, 1975). For more contemporary treatments of the methods, see Stokey and Zeckhauser *Primer;* Peter W. House, *The Art of Public Policy Analysis* (Thousand Oaks, Calif.: Sage, 1982); and David L. Weimar and Aidan R. Vining, *Policy Analysis: Concepts and Practice* (Englewood Cliffs, N.J.: Prentice-Hall, 1989). For doubts about the practical impact of such techniques on governmental decision making, see Laurence E. Lynn, Jr., ed., *Knowledge and Power: The Uncertain Connection* (Washington, D.C.: National Academy of Sciences, 1978); Arnold J. Meltsner, *Policy Analysts in the Bureaucracy* (Berkeley: University of California Press, 1976); Henry Aaron, *Politics and the Professors: The Great Society in Perspective* (Washington, D.C.: Brookings Institution, 1978); and Aaron Wildavsky, *Speaking Truth to Power: The Art and Craft of Policy Analysis* (Boston: Little, Brown, 1979). For a more recent evaluation of the influence of policy analysis, see Laurence E. Lynn's summary of two articles in "Policy Analysis in the Bureaucracy: How New? How Effective?" *Journal of Policy Analysis and Management*, vol. 8, no. 3. (Summer 1989): 375: "Over the long haul, the ideas of policy analysts appear to have counted for something, more or less, in the ordinary exercise of statecraft by ordinary as well as by the occasional extraordinary policymakers." For more radical critiques of policy analysis, see Peter Self, *Econocrats and the Policy Process: The Politics and Philosophy of Cost-Benefit Analysis* (Boulder, Colo.: Westview, 1975); John Forester, *Planning in the Face of Power* (Berkeley: University of California Press, 1989); and Charles E. Lindblom, *Inquiry and Change: The Troubled Attempt to Understand and Shape Society* (New Haven, Conn.: Yale University Press, 1990). For an idea of how policy analysis could support deliberative government, see Giandomenico Majone, "Policy Analysis and Public Deliberation," in Reich, *The Power of Public Ideas*, pp. 157–178.

27. See preceding note, particularly Lynn, Meltsner, Wildavsky, Forester, and Lindblom.

28. The literature on the utility of techniques of policy analysis and program evaluation is more limited than the literature on its successes. It consists mostly of examples of good pieces of policy analysis or program evaluation, not a demonstration that the work had much impact on policy-making processes. For an early example, see John P. Crecine, ed., *Research in Public Policy Analysis and Management* (Greenwich, Conn.: JAI Press, 1981). For a discussion of the sorts of ideas that become important in policy-making, and how techniques of policy analysis would have to be adapted to produce more powerful ideas, see Mark H. Moore, "What Sorts of Ideas Become Public Ideas?" in Reich, *The Power of Public Ideas*, pp. 55–84.

29. See David Osborne and Ted Gaebler, *Reinventing Government: How the Entrepreneurial Spirit Is Transforming the Public Sector from Schoolhouse to Statehouse, City Hall to the Pentagon* (Reading, Mass.: Addison-Wesley, 1992), pp. 166–194; and Michael Barzelay with Babak Armajani, *Breaking through Bureaucracy: A New Vision for Managing in Government* (Berkeley: University of California Press, 1987), pp. 8–9.

30. Malcolm Sparrow, *Imposing Duties: Government's Changing Approach to Compliance* (Westport, Conn.: Praeger, 1994).
31. On the concept of a service encounter in the private sector, see John A. Czepiel, Michael R. Solomon, and Carol F. Surprenant, eds., *The Service Encounter: Managing Employee/Customer Interaction in Service Businesses* (Lexington, Mass.: D. C. Heath, 1985); and James L. Heskett, W. Earl Sasser, and Christopher W. L. Hart, *Service Breakthroughs: Breaking the Rules of the Game* (New York: Free Press, 1990).
32. For a discussion of the function and techniques of political management, see Chapters 4 and 5 of this book.

Part Five

PUBLIC ADMINISTRATION IN THE TWENTY-FIRST CENTURY

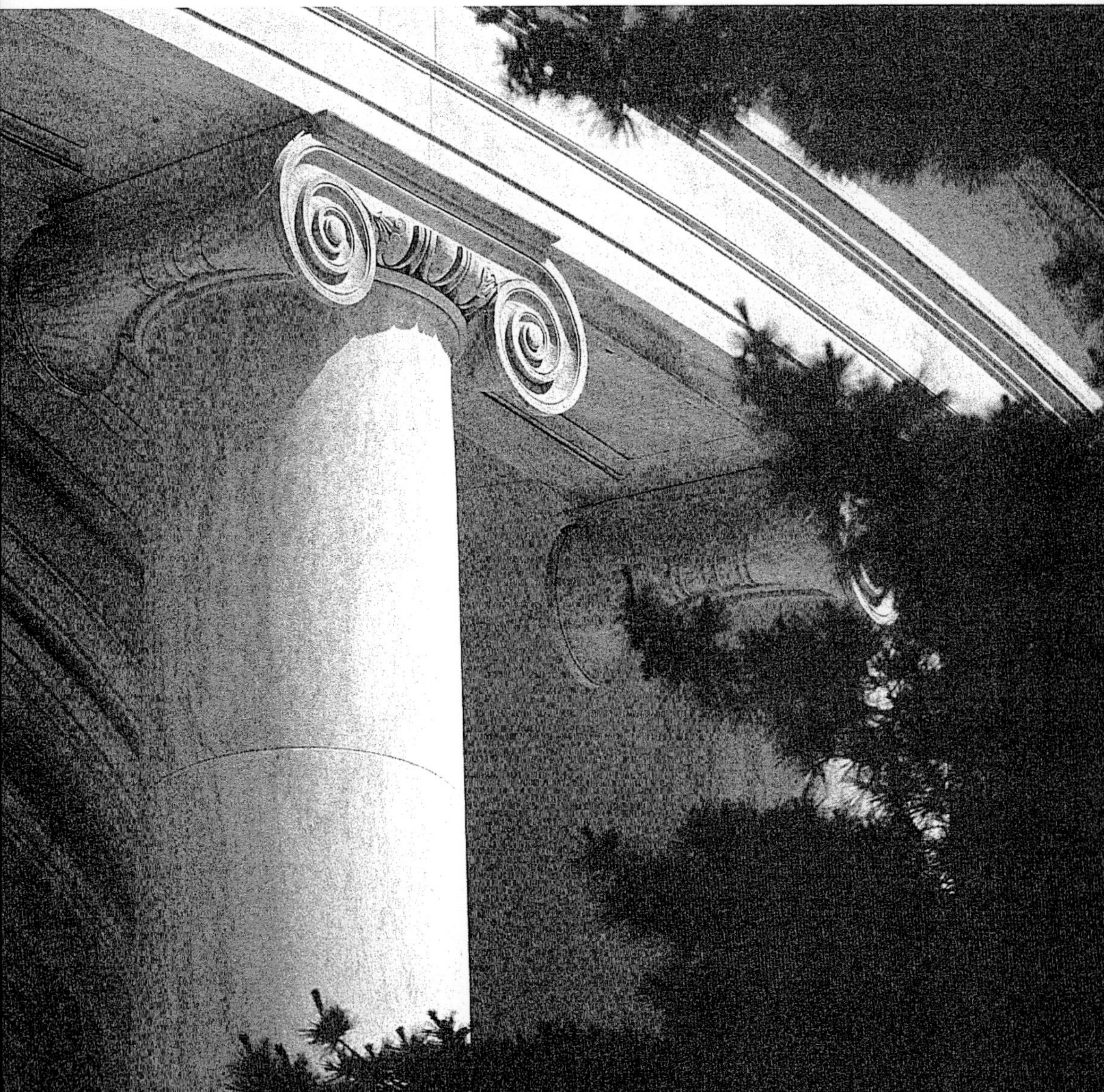

Public administration entered the new century on a dramatic political note following the deadlocked presidential election in 2000, which would be contested up to the Supreme Court. The final election of George W. Bush, only the second president to be elected without a plurality of the actual vote, marked more than the end to the reinventing government movement. It also signaled the recognition that new forces would dominate. Much of the discussion of the driving influences in public administration centered on globalization, marketization, and technology. Although many in government were uncertain of how governments would respond and adapt in the new century, there emerged a clearer understanding that the pace of change would be much more dynamic and far reaching.

This would prove to be true politically as well. Bush's reelection in 2004 (by an uncontested margin this time) after the events of 9/11 and the war in Iraq would be followed in 2006 with the Democrats retaking the Congress and then the election of Barack Obama in 2008 with a strong Democratic majority in Congress. Much of this was fueled by the near collapse of the financial system and the worst recession since the Great Depression of the 1930s.

But the more dramatic change was global. The Cold War was replaced with an international war on terrorism. U.S. military forces were first deployed in Afghanistan and then in Iraq to overthrow Saddam Hussein, but initial military victories were followed by the American forces forestalling a civil war with mounting military and civilian casualties. China and to a lesser extent India and Brazil emerged as new economic superpowers. The United States began a renewed debate on the economic and social impacts of globalization.

Environmental issues, usually relegated to last on the lists of issues voters care about, rose in importance as scientific and political consensus converged over climate change and global warming. Federal inaction and lack of consensus about what to do about the environment did not deter many state and city governments from developing new regulatory standards and environmental safeguards. But perhaps more importantly, within public administration sustainability emerged as a new cornerstone for assessing organizational performance and public stewardship. The terrible loss of life from Hurricane Katrina in 2005 highlighted this further. Federal, state, and local governments' inability to coordinate emergency evacuation and relief efforts resulted in tragic loss of life, but there was also recognition that environmentally unsound land management decisions played a pivotal role in setting up the disaster.

TRANSFORMING PUBLIC ADMINISTRATION—FROM GOVERNMENT TO GOVERNANCE

Governance is hardly a new concept and has been vigorously debated in political sciences circles since the early 1990s. Theorists in political science and public administration created a new dichotomy, what might be called the governance-government dichotomy. Essentially, a new distinction is being made between the "governance," once the noun form of the verb "govern," and "government"—defined as the agency or organization through which a governing body exercises authority. This distinction fits the postmodernist movement in public administration, which has always claimed that relationships between and among government bodies, constituencies, and the environment are what is critical.[1] The governance thesis is that there has been a fundamental shift from big government to the process of political decentralization-diffusion. Joseph Nye in a Harvard University study (reprinted here) on the future of government and governance noted that Daniel Bell's 1999 prediction that the nation-state has "become too small for the big problems of life and too big for the small problems" puts public administration in the dilemma of finding that neither centralization or decentralization works. Nye offers that the answer is "rather a diffusion of governance activities in several directions at the same time."[2]

He also expands on the three driving forces—market, globalization, and technology—or "trends" as he calls them. It is the technology revolution and specifically the Internet that he sees as most significant. Of course, his observations, written in early 2000 before the advent of Web 2.0, Facebook, iPhones, and so on, should be seen as intended—a discussion of the beginning.[3]

Donald Kettl's 2002 work *The Transformation of Governance: Public Administration for the 21st Century* [4] was another early attempt to explain what is different about governance now and what it means for public administration. In Kettl's viewpoint, there is a disconnect between the problems of institutional government (i.e., public administration) and the vision of what the big challenges for models of governance will be. As the environment is dramatically impacted by Nye's forces of globalization, marketization, and the information revolution, governments can no longer keep pace by simply adding more size, restructuring, or shifting resources. Kettl argued that public administration must be different if it is to be relevant for the future. It is just as Woodrow Wilson noted more than 120 years ago, in the first article reprinted in this volume, "The idea of the state and the consequent ideal of its duty are undergoing noteworthy change; and the idea of the state is the conscience of administration."

THE ONGOING DEBATE OVER PUBLIC BUDGETING AND DEFICITS

After the elections of 2000, the political debate over the budget surpluses changed with Republican control of both the Congress and the presidency. The first issue was the Bush administration's tax cuts, which were quickly approved (although the Congress had learned sufficiently from the economic uncertainties of the past at least to make the reductions "non-permanent" and to require reconsideration and repassage in ten years). Of course, the budget surpluses of the late 1990s vanished quickly with the recession of 2001 and the enormous consequences of the September 11 terrorist attacks and the war in Iraq. While budgetary economics have been uncertain, only Republican control of both houses of government (at least until 2006) precluded the type of debates and confrontations of the Reagan-Clinton years.

There would be, however, one more casualty of this budget period. After years of Republican presidents demanding legislation for line-item veto power, a Republican congress passed the line-item veto act for a Democratic president in 1996. Many contend that the line-item veto stands at the heart of the argument over who will control the budget process. (Interestingly, this veto over specific appropriations is generally considered to be an innovation pioneered by the Confederacy during the Civil War.) But the extension of the line-item veto to the federal government would last only two years; it was struck down by the U.S. Supreme Court in 1998.[5] Perhaps anticipating that Republican control of Congress was waning, President Bush asked for a new variation of the line-item veto in his state of the union address in 2006. That legislation failed to get through the Congress. Now, President Obama is asking for similar authorities. In 2010, he signed a new PAYGO statute that reestablished the process of requiring the Congress to ensure that funding is provided to offset the costs for new programs passed into law, which was dominant in the 1990s.

These squabbles between Congress and Presidents for nearly 50 years over how to control and who controls budget decisions have always been a tenet of public budgeting politics. Irene Rubin,[6] one of public budgeting's most prolific scholars, examines these tactics in a *Public Finance & Budgeting* article in 2002 entitled "Perennial Budget Reform Proposals." The article defines the list of budget reforms that have been called for to change budgeting dynamics from balanced budget amendments to lock boxes. Of even greater interest, she explains the source of these reforms in terms of whether they originate from budget staff or elected officials. And while she concludes that most of them have slim prospects for ever being enacted, this is not to say they never will. Indeed, these perennial reforms as the new decade unfolds are very much likely to reappear given the high levels of budget deficits.

Despite the mounting federal deficit, the U.S. economy pushed forward led in part by rising housing values and strong stock market valuations. All of this came to a disastrous end in 2007–2008 in a stunning financial reversal. Subprime mortgages were both fueling a housing bubble and injecting into the financial system highly speculative credit derivatives that would lead to a collapse of several major financial institutions. The stock market tumbled by nearly half, and government intervention on a scale not seen since the Depression was required to prop up the financial system. The financial crises and following recession pushed unemployment rates over 10 percent along with a huge rise in bankruptcies, plunging state and local governments into massive deficit conditions.

Federal intervention involved two major steps. First, in the closing days of the Bush administration, the Troubled Asset Relief Program (TARP) was passed in early October 2008 to the tune of over $780 billion to bail out banks and insurance companies. Even the automakers would get a government bailout. Although the political wisdom of bailing out some of these firms whose speculative behavior led to the crises will be debated for years, the economics look more convincing now that much of the TARP money has been repaid and the country did not fall into a depression. In early 2009, the newly elected Obama administration secured a major stimulus package. The package was priced at over $775 billion (but estimated to be actually more like $850 billion) to prop up state and local governments and create jobs to help keep unemployment from rising further. In the meantime, state and local governments across the country took massive steps in securing spending cuts (tax increases were seldom a viable option) to deal with the requirement to balance their budgets. Public sector budgeting will have much to debate in the years ahead about the outcomes of these responses to financial crises with the very real prospect that new theories of budgeting will emerge that recognize the very different realities governments face in responding to global challenges.[7]

DEVELOPMENTS IN LAW AND ETHICS

By the 1990s, most of the action in equal opportunity had shifted away from the executive branch. The Supreme Court became more conservative even though two of the four newly appointed justices (Souter, Thomas, Breyer, and Ginsburg) were appointed by Clinton. In 1995, the Supreme Court decided a case involving a minority set-aside program overseen by a federal agency. In that decision, *Adarand v. Pena*, the Court did not completely preclude the use of affirmative action measures, but for the first time it required the federal government to meet a higher threshold of justification for establishing such programs.[8] The Clinton administration undertook a review of affirmative action programs at the federal level and declared the administration's commitment "to mend it, not end it." Congressional committees considered proposing legislation to terminate federally supported affirmative action programs, but these bills were eventually withdrawn. Federally, the Court had had the last word.[9]

Meanwhile, the issue was gaining traction at the state and local level. In California, a statewide voters' referendum, Proposition 209, was passed in 1996, eliminating all race-based considerations in hiring, contracting, and selection processes, including university admissions. Other states—Washington and Michigan—would follow, although one proposal to end affirmative action in Houston, Texas, was defeated. The final note in this period was the twin Supreme Court decisions in Michigan (*Gratz* and *Grutter*) in which the undergraduate and law school admissions processes were challenged because they included special consideration for race. The legal rationale for affirmative action was to provide a remedy for past practices of discrimination. But how does one justify the continuation of such remedies when the practices they were designed to remedy were primarily from past generations? This is the question that confronted the Supreme Court in 2003 in the University of Michigan cases.

The Supreme Court, in perhaps affirmative action's last hurrah, upheld the law school policy that considered race among other factors in reviewing the candidate's entire application but disagreed with an undergraduate admissions policy that assigned a fixed number of points based on membership in an underrepresented racial category. In *Grutter v. Bollinger,* the Court agreed that the University of Michigan Law School could continue to give advantages to minority applicants for admission. The justification for such preferences was not to remedy past practices of discrimination, but to further diversify for its own sake. The majority opinion written by now-retired Justice Sandra Day O'Connor held that the Constitution "does not prohibit the law school's narrowly tailored use of race in admissions decisions to further a compelling interest in obtaining the educational benefits that flow from a diverse student body." In this 5-4 decision, the Court asserted that "Effective participation by members of all racial and ethnic groups in the civic life of our nation is essential if the dream of one nation, indivisible, is to be realized." Justice Lewis F. Powell had initially advocated the diversity rationale in the 1978 *Bakke* decision. In this 2003 case, the Court endorsed Justice Powell's "view that student body diversity is a compelling state interest that can justify the use of race in university admissions."[10]

But even in accepting that diversity is a "compelling state interest," the Court has asserted that this interest, no matter how "compelling," must be temporary because such compellance flies in the face of the 14th Amendment's requirement for equal treatment. In an unusually blatant appeal to a future Supreme Court, Justice O'Connor stated that "race-conscious admissions policies must be limited in time. This requirement reflects that racial classifications, however compelling their goals, are potentially so dangerous that they may be employed no more broadly than the interest demands. Enshrining a permanent justification for racial preferences would offend this fundamental equal protection principle." She concluded that "all governmental use of race must have a logical end point." Then she quite literally provides the end point: "We expect that 25 years from now, the use of racial preferences will no longer be necessary to further the interest approved today."

The legal developments that we have just reviewed, while extremely important in their own right, also serve another purpose. They illustrate just how correct Roosevelt Thomas' 1990 *Harvard Business Review* article, "From Affirmative Action to Affirming Diversity" (reprinted in Part IV) was in making essentially the same arguments that in more convoluted language would be repeated in these Supreme Court cases. A classic could hardly be more influential—even if it only reflected the sentiments of the times. As public administration moved into the post 9/11 era, a different type of work appeared that greatly deepened discourse on administrative ethics. Guy Adams and Danny Balfour, both public administration academics with a long interest in the Holocaust, first wrote *Unmasking Administrative Evil* in 1998 with the purpose of helping public administration to see the potential problems inherent in what they called the field's "lack of historical consciousness" and "inability to perceive the reality of administrative evil." Reprinted here is their concluding chapter from the revised edition of their work in 2004, which adds a globalization perspective.

The larger thesis of Adams and Balfour's book is that the techno-rational approach championed by public administration is inadequate for preventing administrative evil. Using the Holocaust as their primary example, they discuss how something totally reprehensible and horrific did in fact occur within bureaucratic organizations following specific rules and procedures and pre-specified public policies. A second extensive case discussion to illustrate how administrative evil can be masked is developed involving the use of the German WWII rocket scientists who, despite their use of slave labor in the Nazi rocket development facilities, became prominent participants in the American space program in the 1950s. Thus it was Nazi war criminals such as Werner von Braun and his associates that gave the American space program its initial boost. Remember that mass slavery, as supervised by von Braun and his ilk, is every bit a war crime as mass murder—if only slightly less odious. Adams and Balfour have continued to pose these difficult questions for public administration in a recent *Public Administration Review* article examining the torture and abuse of Iraqi inmates at Abu Ghraib.[11]

PUBLIC POLICY AND NETWORKS

As public administration moved into the twenty-first century, the study of public policy—from analysis to development to implementation and evaluation—fully emerged as its own discipline. Increasingly, masters of public administration programs would offer concentrations in public policy; some even offer separate degrees in public policy. There are now extensive offerings in public health, social welfare, criminal justice, and environment policy studies. Often there are separate degree programs for each. A vast literature within public policy supports the full development of what can only be described as a separate discipline either inside or outside public affairs.

Deborah Stone, in her book entitled *Policy Paradox and Political Reason* (the first chapter from her 2002 revised edition is reprinted here), illustrates the current understanding of the policy realm. She begins by stating that a paradox is an impossible situation in which two contradictory understandings cannot be simultaneously true. "Political life," says Stone, "is full of them." She explains that we often attempt to rescue policy from such political irrationalities by employing rational, analytical methods. The "rationality project," as she calls it, misses the point. She argues that the political community is, in fact, better equipped to deal with abstract information than with the hard facts of the rational model. Political communities inherently struggle over ideas and exchange meanings that are not mutually exclusive. While the rational model assumes that there are objective facts that can be applied, Stone asserts that "behind every policy issue lurks a contest over conflicting, though equally plausible, conceptions of the same abstract goal or value."

The final selection in this 7th edition of *Classics* deals with governing by networks, raising new questions and thoughts on intergovernmental management. It comes fittingly from a 2006 *Public Administration Review* special issue in 2006 by Robert Agranoff on the importance of collaboration and networks. Here, Agranoff provides direct insight into the operations of public management collaboration and networks. It should be noted that Agranoff, with his earlier books *Managing Within Networks* and *Collaborative Public Management* (the later co-authored with Michael McGuire), has been at the leading edge of network scholarship in the last decade.[12]

Although "collaboration" and "network" have become heavily used terms in the public and non-profit sectors, they are sometimes used without much definitional clarity. Agranoff provides a set of conceptual lessons about what networks are and what they are not. Among his most important observations is that "traditional" organizations are not fading away with the emergence of networks. Governance is more "joined up," but a key challenge of network management is reconciling collaborative activity with the goals and mission of the "home" organization. Agranoff provides managers with insights to aid in this delicate balancing act.

A Closing Note

This section began with the general recognition that the external environment of public administration was undergoing dynamic and systemic change. Government managers in this new century understood that new driving forces—globalization, technology, and marketization—would significantly affect what governments needed to do in terms of roles and responsibilities and also the means of how they would perform new functions and tasks. Concurrently, environmental forces involving accelerating climate change compelled governments to think about sustainability and social responsibility.

Theorists in public administration called for equivalent internal change, arguing that some form of transformation was essential. Transformation in this case meant that governance—the relationships between and among governmental, non-profit, and private enterprises—should be the focus of change, not just reorganizing governments in terms of mission and structure or increasing budgets. Public administration began to grapple with management constructs that were decidedly non-managerial—collaboration, wicked policy problems, and social networks, among others. It is of course too soon to say whether public administration has successfully begun to transform itself. Perhaps the next edition of *Classics* will include readings reflecting this new thinking and much more dynamic approaches to the difficult problems confronting society globally. One thing does seem assured: public administration is recognizing that the future of public administration is no longer administrative.

References

1. Whatever the name, this rising issue area is loosely centered on migrating from hierarchical bureaucratic organizations to more collaborative alliances of public, non-profit, and private organizations. Much of this movement is driven by public policy advocates who have been arguing for decades that government is out, governance is in. One work, Goldsmith and Eggers's *Government By Network* (Washington, DC: Brookings Institution Press, 2004), uses the subtitle *The New Shape of the Public Sector* to describe the significance of what is involved here.
2. There is a larger discussion of the impacts of globalization and technology on governance in *Governance.com* (editors Joseph Nye and Elaine Kamarck (Washington, DC: Brookings Institution Press, 2002). See especially the work of Jane Fountain, "Toward a Theory of Federal Bureaucracy for the 21st Century" and a larger work *Building the Virtual State: Informational Technology and Institutional Change* (Washington, DC: Brookings Institution Press, 2001).
3. See Cass Sunstein, *Infotopia* (New York: Oxford University Press, 2006) or Cass Sunstein, *Republic.com 2.0* (Princeton: Princeton University Press, 2007) for a sense of direction of how Web 2.0 may impact government and public administration in the near future.
4. Donald Kettl, *The Transformation of Governance: Public Administration for 21st Century America* (Baltimore: The Johns Hopkins Press, 2002).
5. For an assessment of what the Line Item Veto Act of 1996 proposed, see Phil Joyce and former Congressional Budget Director Robert D. Reischauer's article, "The Federal Line-Item Veto: What Is It and What Will It Do?" *Public Administration Review* 57 (1997): 95–104. A superb overview of the line-item veto and its increasing complexity by Robert Lee, "State Item-Veto Legal Issues in the 1990s," *Public Budgeting & Finance* (Summer 2000): 49–73 aptly sums up what states have learned.
6. Irene Rubin's contributions to budgeting theory are numerous, but her work *The Politics of Public Budgeting: Getting and Spending, Borrowing and Balancing* (Washington, D.C.: CQ Press, 2010) is consider an essential reading.
7. A useful guidebook to future discussion of what public budgeting needs to encompass to recapture the larger economic dimension can be found in Inge Kaul and Pedro Conceiocao, *The New Public Finance: Responding to Global Challenges* (New York: Oxford University Press, 2006).
8. The case citations for the court decisions discussed in this section are *Adarand Constructors Inc. v. Federico Pena* 515 US 200 (1995), *Regents of the University of California v. Bakke* 438 US 265 (1978), *Grutter v. Bollinger* No 02-241 (2003), and *Gratz v. Bollinger* No 02-516 (2003).
9. A superb assessment of court decisions following the passage of the 1991 Civil Rights Act can be found in J. Edward Kellough, *Understanding Affirmative Action* (Washington, DC: Georgetown University Press, 2007). See especially Chapter 6, "Cases from 1995 to 2003: Challenges, Uncertainty and the Survival of Affirmative Action."
10. For a policy and institutional perspective, see Katherine C. Naff, "From Bakke to Grutter and Gratz: The Supreme Court as a Policy Institution," *Review of Policy Research* (May 2004): 405–428.
11. The 2006 September/October issue of *Public Administration Review* has articles by Carol Lewis, "In Pursuit of Public Interest" (694–701), and Guy Adams and Danny Balfour (joined by George E. Reed), "Abu Ghraib, Administrative Evil, and Moral Inversion: The Value of Putting Cruelty First," (680–693) as part of a short series of essays on practical ethics. Lewis has recently added to the burdens of complexity for ethical responsibility, arguing in her recent *PAR* essay that public managers must also factor in responsibilities for future generations, ensuring that current decisions effectively weigh long-term as well as short-term outcomes.
12. See Robert Agranoff and Michael McGuire, *Collaborative Public Management: New Strategies for Local Governments* (Washington: Georgetown University Press, 2003) and *Managing within Networks: Adding Value to Public Organizations* (Washington: Georgetown University Press, 2007).

Information Technology and Democratic Governance

Joseph S. Nye Jr.

Public confidence in government has declined over the past few decades in a large number of democratic countries.[1] The causes are complex. Some see the decline, at least in the United States, as a return to a deeply ingrained American suspicion of concentrated power after expectations about government rose to unrealistic heights in the aftermath of success in World War II.[2] Others see it as a result of a long-term shift toward postindustrial values that emphasize the individual over the community and diminish respect for authority and institutions.[3] Still others see it as a reaction against the centralization of government in the twentieth century that saw the federal budget grow from 3 percent of gross national product in 1929 to 20 percent in the past two decades. Some analysts argue that centralized government, unlike private enterprise, has not yet adapted to the changes being wrought by the "third industrial revolution."[4]

Historical Analogies

In the first industrial revolution around the turn of the nineteenth century, the application of steam to mills and transportation had a powerful effect on the economy, society, and eventually government. Patterns of production, work, living conditions, social class, and political power were transformed. Public education arose, as literate trained workers were needed for increasingly complex and potentially dangerous factories. Police forces such as London's "bobbies" were created to deal with urbanization. Subsidies were provided for the necessary infrastructure of canals and railroads.[5] In what is sometimes called the second industrial revolution, around the turn of the twentieth century, electricity, synthetics, and the internal combustion engine brought similar economic and social changes. The United States, for example, went from being a predominantly agrarian to a primarily industrial and urban nation. In the 1890s most Americans still worked on farms or as servants. A few decades later, the majority lived in cities and worked in factories.[6] Social class and political cleavages were altered. Once again, with lags, the role of government changed. The bipartisan Progressive movement ushered in antitrust legislation, early consumer protection regulation by the forerunner of the Food and Drug Administration, and economic stabilization by the Federal Reserve Board.[7] In what some have called the third industrial revolution, at the turn of the twenty-first century, the impact of computers and communications technology on the economy and society should eventually produce analogous major changes in the functions of government.

A number of criticisms of such grand analogies can be raised. At a semantic level, the term *industrial revolution* is not totally appropriate for what is sometimes called a postindustrial phenomenon. Daniel Bell, for example, argues that the term mistakenly conflates the introduction of steam power as a form of energy and the creation of factories, which are social organizations. He prefers to refer to three great technological revolutions, with the current one marked by electronics, miniaturization by transistors, digitalization, and software.[8] In addition, "revolution," defined as a disjunction of power, is often difficult to discern except in retrospect. Moreover, historians differ on the dating and duration of earlier industrial revolutions. The term was not coined until 1886, a century after the first industrial era began.[9] Although there may have been discontinuities in technological progress, with new leading sectors in each era, it has been difficult to prove the existence of long waves or cycles of economic growth Efforts to specify exact timing of Eric Kondratieff's or Joseph Schumpeter's cycles of technological change have not been successful.[10] Finally, one

Source: Joseph S. Nye, Jr. Information Technology and Democratic Governance from Governance.com: Democracy, pp. 1–16. (Washington, D.C.: The Brookings Institution).

must be wary of technological determinism.[11] Technology affects society and government, but the causal arrows work in both directions. Technological change creates new challenges and opportunities for social and political organization, but the response to those challenges depends on history, culture, institutions, and paths already taken or forgone.

Nonetheless, with appropriate caveats and caution, the historical analogies can help suggest hypotheses and avenues for exploration. Abrupt changes often occur after a long buildup, and punctuation points can often be found. Analysts need not fall into the fallacy of technological determinism to see that technology is one of the significant causes of social and political change. As Bell argues,

> Since the techno-economic changes pose 'control' problems for the political order, we find that the older social structures are cracking because political scales of sovereignty and authority do not match the economic scale. In many areas we have more and more economic integration and political fragmentation. . . . If there is a single overriding sociological problem in post-industrial society—particularly in the management of transition—it is the management of scale.[12]

Centralization or Diffusion?

Six decades ago, the eminent sociologist William Ogburn cited technology as one factor in his prediction of greater political centralization; In 1937 he argued that "government in the United States will probably tend toward greater centralization because of the airplane, the bus, the truck, the Diesel engine, the radio, the telephone, and the various uses to which the wire and wireless may be placed. The same inventions operate to influence industries to spread across state lines. . . . The centralizing tendency of government seems to be world-wide, wherever modern transportation and communication exist."[13]

By and large, Ogburn was right about his next half century, but will this continue to be true in the twenty-first century? President Bill Clinton and other politicians proclaimed that the era of big government is over, but they have said little about what will take its place. Is the basic premise correct—and if so, is it correct for all dimensions of democratic government? If this is the case, what are the causes and how reversible are they?

Questions of appropriate degrees of centralization of government are not new. As Charles Kindleberger points out, "How the line should be altered at a given time—toward or away from the center—can stay unresolved for long periods, typically fraught with tension."[14] If Bell and others are correct that the nation-state has "become too small for the big problems of life and too big for the small problems,"[15] we may find not centralization or decentralization but rather a diffusion of governance activities in several directions at the same time. Some functions may migrate to a supragovernmental or transnational level, and some may devolve to local units. Other aspects of governance may migrate to the private sector. The matrix presented in figure 1-1 lays out the possible diffusion of activities away from central governments, vertically to other levels of government and horizontally to market and private nonmarket actors—the so-called third sector. The matrix is simply a map of the possible dimensions of the locus of collective activities. It can be combined with a hypothesis that the twentieth century saw a predominance of centripetal forces and that the next period may see a greater role of centrifugal forces.

There is some evidence of diffusion. For example, between 1962 and 1995, federal civilian employment in the United States saw a net growth of 15 percent, while state and local employment grew by 150 percent.[16] As a share of gross national product, federal expenditures (excluding transfers) have fallen, while state and local expenditures have increased.[17] In the past two decades, privatization has transferred a number of functions out of the public sector in a large number of countries.[18] Nonprofit organizations are playing an increasingly large role in the United States, where after two decades of proliferation they represent almost 7 percent of all paid employment.[19] International nongovernmental organizations have multiplied tenfold over the past two decades and have increased their influence on a number of issues.[20] Transgovernmental networks of bureaucrats and judicial officials have expanded in autonomy and number, with the effect of disaggregating the state for certain policy issues.[21] The transnational domains of international production set

FIGURE 1

THE DIFFUSION OF GOVERNANCE IN THE TWENTY-FIRST CENTURY

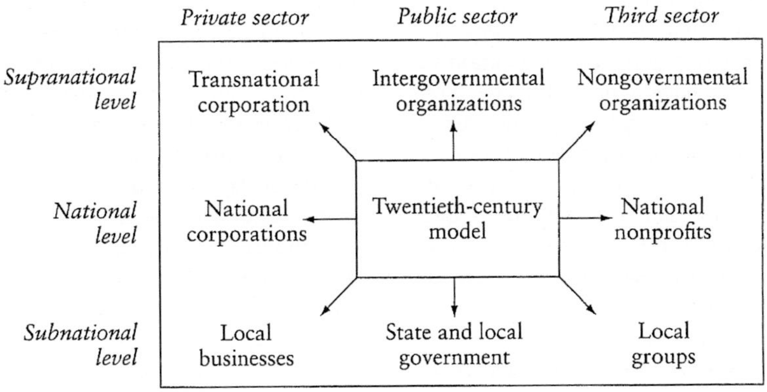

limits on national welfare measures, and many functions such as credit ratings and arbitration of disputes are handled largely in the private transnational sector.[22] International security, the ultimate function of the state, now involves defense against transnational actors as a primary threat.

On the other hand, the overall trends are far from clear. Some issues show centralization, some decentralization, and some show both at the same time. For example, in the area of personal security, there has been an enormous increase in privatization of security forces. In 1970 there were one-and-a-half times as many private as public security personnel; by 1996 that factor had doubled.[23] Nonetheless, the early 1990s witnessed a demand for federalization at the same time, suggesting a rise in the demand for several types of governance in response to a perception of rising crime. Even after the privatizations of state-owned enterprises in the 1980s, the share of national income spent by the state in the wealthy democratic countries averaged 46 percent.[24] Moreover, countries vary: In contrast with Europe, total government spending has held steady in the United States and Japan, at around a third of the economy, and has declined in New Zealand.[25] Some states are weaker than the private forces within them; others are not. Panama, Sierra Leone, and Haiti are different from Brazil, South Africa, and Singapore. The trends from external forces feel stronger for European states than they do for the American superpower. In short, the jury is still out, and it is not clear how strong the trends toward decentralization will be in an information age. More work needs to be done in refining the dependent variable and understanding the implications for democratic governance, as well as analyzing the strength of the causes that could be leading to diffusion.

Three Trends

Three independent but interrelated current trends give credence to the prospect that the new century may see a shift in the locus of collective activities away from central governments. These are globalization, marketization, and the information revolution.

Globalization refers to the increase in the scale and speed of flows of goods, people, and ideas across borders, with the effect of decreasing the effects of distance. It is not new.[26] Globalization increased rapidly in the nineteenth century and during the first decades of the twentieth but was curtailed, at least in its economic dimensions, from the early 1930s through the end of World War II. Globalization preceded the information revolution but has been greatly enhanced by it. In its recent incarnation, globalization can, in part, be traced back to American strategy after World War II and the desire to create an open international economy to forestall another depression and to balance Soviet power and contain communism. The institutional framework and political pressures for opening markets were a product of American power and policy, but they were reinforced by developments in the technology of transportation and communications, which made it increasingly costly for states to turn away from global market forces. Raymond Vernon argues that nearly half of all industrial output is produced by multinational enterprises whose strategic decisions on the location of production now have a powerful effect on domestic economies and wage structures, even in the absence of international trade.[27] At the same time, as Dani Rodrik points out, globalization still has a long way to go, and its post—World War II progress in democratic countries has been concomitant with the development of the welfare state in what John Ruggie calls "embedded liberalism."[28] A failure of that social contract in the democracies or a financial crisis turning into a world depression might revive protectionism, but predictions to that effect have proved wrong for the past three decades. Meanwhile, globalization constrains states' ability to levy taxes and maintain lavish benefits, and it opens opportunities for private transnational actors to establish standards and strategies that strongly affect public policies that were once the domain of central governments.

Marketization is part of globalization and, like it, has been enhanced by the information revolution, but it also has an independent domestic aspect and independent origins. Susan Strange argues that the balance between states and markets has shifted since the 1970s in a way that makes the state just one source of authority among several and that leaves "a yawning hole of non-authority or ungovernance."[29] She argues that power has diffused from governments to markets in such critical functions as maintaining the value of the currency, choosing the form of the economy, taxation, and providing infrastructure, countercyclical policy, and protection from crime. This can be debated, as we have seen, by citing the fact that government spending as a percentage of gross national product remains above 40 percent in a number of major European countries. Even such states as Sweden and France, however, not to mention eastern Europe and the less economically developed countries, have seen significant privatizations and expansion of market forces in the past two decades. The causes of marketization are complex. They include the failure of planned economies to adapt to the information revolution, the inflation that followed the oil crises of the 1970s, the early success of the East Asian economies, and changes in political and ideological coalitions inside wealthy democracies. The net effect, however, is to accelerate the diffusion of power away from governments to private actors.

Information revolution refers to the dramatic decrease in the costs of computers and communications and the effects that has on the economy and society. According to Jeremy Greenwood, the price of a new computer has dropped by 19 percent a year since 1954, and information technologies have risen from 7 percent to about 50 percent of new investment.[30] Information technology has been responsible for a quarter of U.S. growth over the past five boom years and makes up 8 percent of gross domestic product.[31] Microprocessors have doubled computing power every eighteen to twenty-four months, and computing power now costs less than 1 percent of what it did in 1970.[32] As late as 1980, phone calls over copper wire could carry information at the rate of one page a second; today a thin strand of optical fiber can transmit ninety thousand volumes in a second.[33] The growth in Internet use has been extraordinary, with traffic increasing by 100 percent every year, versus less than 10 percent for the voice network.[34] The effect has been the virtual erasing of costs of communicating over distance.

As with steam in the late eighteenth century and electricity in the late nineteenth, there have been lags in productivity growth as society learns to fully use the new technologies.[35] Social organization changes more slowly than technology. For example, the electric motor was invented in 1881, but it was nearly four decades before Henry Ford pioneered the reorganization of factories to take full advantage of electric power. Computers today account for 2 percent of America's total capital stock, but "add in all the equipment used for gathering, processing, and transmitting information, and the total accounts for 12% of America's capital stock, exactly the same as the railways at the peak of their development in the late 19th century. . . . Three-quarters of all computers are used in the service sector such as finance and health, where output is notoriously hard to measure."[36] Whether in reorganization or measurement, it is generally agreed that we are still in the *early* stages in the current information revolution.

Political Effects of the Information Revolution

Critics correctly point out that the current period is not the first to be strongly affected by changes in the technology and flows of information. Johannes Gutenberg's invention of movable type, which allowed printing of the Bible and its accessibility to large portions of the European population, is often credited with playing a major role in the onset of the Reformation. The advent of truly mass communications and broadcasting a century ago, which was facilitated by newly cheap electricity, might be considered a second information revolution. It ushered in the age of mass popular culture.[37] The effects of mass communication and broadcasting, though not the telephone; tended to have a number of centralizing political effects. Although information, was more widespread, it was also more centrally influenced, even in democratic, countries, than in the age of the local press. Franklin D. Roosevelt's use of radio in the 1930s is a case in point. These effects were particularly pronounced in countries with totalitarian governments, which were able to suppress competing sources of information. Indeed, some theorists believe that totalitarianism could not have been possible without the mass communications that accompanied the second industrial revolution.[38] On the other hand, as films, cassettes, and faxes proliferated, the later technologies of the second information revolution helped to undermine governmental efforts at information autarky. The overall effects were not always democratizing. In some cases, such as Iran, the technologies of the second information revolution merely changed the nature of the autocracy.

At one stage, it was believed that the computers and communications technology of the third information revolution would also have the effect of further enhancing central governmental control. George Orwell's vision of 1984 was widely feared. Mainframe computers seemed set to enhance central planning and increase the surveillance powers of those at the top of a pyramid of control. State-controlled television would dominate information flows. Even today, through central databases and by removing the gray areas of noncompliance, computers can enhance some central government functions, and privacy issues remain an important concern. Some aspects of surveillance have become cheaper and easier. Nonetheless, on balance the prevalent current view is closer to Ithiel de Sola Pool's description of "technologies of freedom."[39]

As computing power has decreased in cost and computers have shrunk in size and become more widely distributed, their decentralizing effects have outweighed their centralizing effects. Moreover, the marriage of computers and communications technology that has evolved into the Internet creates a system with few central nodal points and with a robust capacity in case of a central failure. Power over information is much more widely shared. Central surveillance is possible, but governments that aspire to control information flows through control of the Internet face high costs and ultimate frustration. Rather than reinforcing centralization and bureaucracy, the new information technologies have tended to foster network organizations, new types of community, and demands for different roles for government. By changing how we work, they change our social attitudes and political behavior.

Morley Winograd and Dudley Buffa argue that the extensive corporate work pyramid dominated by centralized commands divided management and the working class, white-collar and unionized blue-collar workers.[40] This pyramid dominated the political process and strongly influenced the evolution of government in the second industrial revolution that shaped the twentieth century. Now, they argue, new information technologies are again reorganizing work. Speed, agility, and customization are the best ways to produce value in the consumer marketplace. Large bureaucratic pyramids turn out to be a less effective way to organize such work than are networks within and between firms. The knowledge workers who staff network organizations see themselves neither as labor nor as capital. To earn the loyalty of their employees, both companies and governments must appeal to them in new ways. They want government to have the convenience and flexibility of the marketplace. The result may be a transformation of politics and, more slowly, of government.

Information technology may affect politics and collective action in a number of other ways. First, information technology reinforces global production strategies and markets with the constraining effects on governmental action already noted. Second, it decreases the relative importance of commodities and territory, which makes geographic distance less important. This in turn has an effect on the communities that underlie political action. Third, the Internet makes borders more porous and jurisdiction less important. Fourth, information technology is changing the nature of banks; and money in a way that will make both taxation and central control of monetary policy more difficult. The exponential rates of technological change and the shortening of product cycles make it difficult for governmental institutions and regulations to keep up. More information and shorter news cycles mean less time for deliberation before response. Fifth, e virtual communities may develop interests and power independent of geography. In some countries the Internet may enhance both local and transnational communities more than national community. Sixth, the demise of broadcasting and the rise of narrowcasting may fragment the sense of community and legitimacy that underpins central governments. Seventh, educational patterns will change, and the greater agility of younger generations with the new technologies may further erode deference to age, authority, and existing institutions.

Obviously, these hypotheses about the information revolution are not the only possible sources of change in the locus and quality of governance activities in the twenty-first century. We have already shown that globalization and marketization, though closely related to and enhanced by the information revolution, have autonomous causes. Moreover, there are strong cultural institutional and political forces that are particular to each country. Race for example, has had a strong effect in American history: decentralizing before 1865; centralizing during Reconstruction; decentralizing before World War II; centralizing shortly after the war; perhaps decentralizing since the defection of the South from the Democratic coalition after 1970. Immigration and ethnic diversity may have a decentralizing effect, though that has been a recurrent and sometimes exaggerated concern in American history. The current demographic trends toward older populations with their entitlements may have a centralizing effect. Although there may be changes at the margin, the entitlement philosophy of the welfare state remains strong. A variety of forces tug the locus of collective activity in different directions, and in different ways on different issues and in different countries. Nonetheless, it seems plausible to look closely at the hypothesis that the three new interrelated trends, and particularly the information revolution (or whatever other label), will have a stronger net effect of diffusion.

Although there is evidence to support the effects of these three trends, it would be a mistake to believe that such effects are irreversible. Technology is only one factor in a complex set of social causes. We should also ask what conditions these trends depend upon and what it would take to slow, derail, or reverse them. For example, would a strong and prolonged economic downturn lead to demands for government response that would alter marketization and globalization? Will "grand terrorism" on the scale of the World Trade Center attacks lead to a demand for intrusive government even at the cost of civil liberties?[41] Would the increasing power of states such as China, India, or a revived Russia—particularly if accompanied by an expansionist ideology—transform the international system so that the defense functions of government would return to the cold-war model? Could ecological trends such as global warming become so clear and alarming that the public would demand much stronger governmental action? Such scenarios are worth exploring both as contingencies and counterfactual thought experiments to check our reasoning about the strength of the new causes. On the other hand, barring such low-probability but high-impact events, a trend toward diffusion of governance activities seems plausible.

The effects on central governments of the third information revolution are still in their early stages. The dispersal of information means that power is more distributed and networks tend to undercut the monopoly of traditional bureaucracy. The speed or instantaneity of Internet time means that all governments, whether central or local, have less control of their agendas. This may make all government more difficult, as there will be fewer degrees of freedom for political leaders to enjoy before they must respond to events. Changes in the nature of money, the disintermediation of banks, and the diminished ability to identify and collect taxes may particularly reduce central governmental capacity. More privatization and public-private partnerships may be a response. Horizontal shifts on the matrix outlined earlier in this chapter may outweigh vertical changes. All government bureaucracy may become flatter and more service oriented. Moreover, though government may become flatter, governance may nonetheless become more complex. At this stage, however, all of the foregoing is speculation.

Similar changes may occur in the political processes of democracy—what might be considered the input rather than the output side of government. One can imagine both a better and a worse political world resulting from the impact of the third information revolution. In a bleak vision of the future, one can imagine a thin democracy in which deliberation has greatly diminished. Citizens will use the set-top boxes on their Internet televisions to engage in frequent plebiscites that will be poorly understood and easily manipulated behind the scenes. The growth of thin direct democracy will lead to a further weakening of institutions. In addition, political community will be fragmented by the replacement of broadcasting by narrowcasting. Broadcasting may have often produced a lowest common denominator, but at least something was common. In the new world, each community will "know" only its own perspective. The prospects for deliberative democracy as outlined in the Federalist Papers will look dim.

Alternatively, one can envisage a better political process in the future. New virtual communities will cross-cut geographic communities, both supplementing and reinforcing local community. In Madisonian terms the extensive republic of balancing factions will be enhanced. Access to information will be plentiful and cheap for all citizens. Political participation, including voting, can be made easier. The low costs of contact and contract will reduce the costs of participation. The Internet may end the hegemony of broadcast television that has undercut political parties and made the process of politics extremely costly in terms of the funds that must be raised. Just as television came to dominate campaigns some four decades ago, the Internet may come to dominate the political process in the decades to come. Access to the political process will be easier and cheaper. Again, both of these futures are highly speculative at this point. Technology alone will not produce one or the other outcome. Much will depend on other political choices.

Political Choices

"This is the second age of democracy," argues British prime minister Tony Blair. "The first was the vote, getting the basic decent standard delivered and pensions, housing, and all the rest of it, but people want choice today, and people want freedom to do things differently at [the] local level, to have better and more innovative ways of deciding their own priorities."[42] Information technology has the capacity to make such a world possible, but it will not happen automatically. As collective activities diffuse across the space described by the matrix outlined in this chapter, there will be important implications for democratic governance. The European Union extols the principle of "subsidiarity" or deciding issues at the lowest possible level as a means of bringing government closer to the people. In the American federal system, public opinion polls show that local and state governments enjoy somewhat higher levels of public trust than does the central government.[43]

In principle, devolution and subsidiarity seem to enhance democratic governance, but as James Madison pointed out two centuries ago, local communities with dominant factions are more likely to suffer from a tyranny of the majority. In American history, for example, central government interventions in the states were essential for the democratic enfranchisement of African American citizens. Moreover, as some actors become more mobile across state and national jurisdictions, local government tax bases erode and burdens are shifted onto the shoulder of those who are relatively immobile, which often means those who are poor.[44] The unstructured development of information technology may increase inequality and accentuate gaps between the haves and the have-nots. Information technology may enhance life choices for some people while diminishing it for others.

A strong libertarian tendency among many enthusiasts of information technology assumes that the growing perfection of markets through the Internet will solve the problems of democratic governance. They believe that as more and more activities shift horizontally on the matrix in this chapter, the role of government will diminish. Microcontracting will allow people to make their own choices on an ever increasing range of issues. It is true that markets enhance choice, but they provide more choices for those who can enter the game with a large pile of chips than for those who cannot.

Aside from the question of inequality of opportunity, there is also a question of public spaces and public goods.[45] Public goods are nonexclusive and nonrivalrous. Once produced, no one can be excluded from their consumption, and one person's consumption does not diminish that of others. Lighthouses have been a classic example used in economics textbooks. Today's technology, however, makes it possible to construct a lighthouse (or a navigational satellite) whose signal can be made available to some users and not to others. This ability to exclude lays the basis for a private market relationship and diminishes one of government's traditional roles, the provision of public goods. Highways, including the information highway, can be turned into toll roads. Indeed, one can imagine a situation in which information technology produces automated pricing systems that privatize all public spaces such as roads and parks. Alternatively, one can imagine deliberate government actions to preserve public spaces and to widen the access to information technology across social and organizational barriers. Such policies could encourage the use of the Internet as an adjunct rather than a substitute for face-to-face relations in reinforcing civic involvement. Similarly, one can imagine alternative choices in the governance of cyberspace. As Lawrence Lessig argues, software and hardware codes and architecture constitute cyberspace. They imbed political values that have constitutional importance. Yet "they are private and therefore outside the scope of constitutional review."[46]

In short, we are only in the early stages of this latest information revolution. As in earlier periods of industrial revolution, public responses to technology are lagging behind private ones. Some aspects of that lag are fortuitous, but some are not. The future of democratic governance depends upon improving our ability to make the relevant distinctions.

REFERENCES

1. Joseph Nye, "The Decline of Confidence in Government," introduction to Joseph S. Nye Jr., Philip D. Zelikow, and David G. King, eds., *Why People Don't Trust Government* (Harvard University Press, 1997), pp. 1–2; Pippa Norris, ed., *Critical Citizens: Global Support for Democratic Government* (Oxford University Press, 1999).
2. See, for example, Robert Samuelson, *The Good Life and Its Discontents: The American Dream in the Age of Entitlement, 1945–1995* (Vintage, 1995).
3. Ronald Inglehart, "Postmaterialist Values and the Erosion of Institutional Authority," in Nye, Zelikow, and King, *Why People Don't Trust Government*, pp. 217–36.
4. See, for example, Peter Drucker, "The Next Information Revolution," *Forbes*, August 24, 1998, pp. 46–58; Alvin Toffler and Heidi Toffler, *The Politics of the Third Wave* (Kansas City, Mo.: Andrews and McMeel, 1995); Morley Winograd and Dudley Buffa, *Taking Control: Politics in the Information Age* (Henry Holt, 1996); Don Tapscott, *The Digital Economy: Promise and Peril in the Age of Networked Intelligence* (McGraw-Hill, 1996).
5. David S. Ländes, *The Unbound Prometheus: Technological Change and Industrial Development in Western Europe from 1750 to the Present* (Cambridge University Press, 1969), chaps. 2–3; David Thomson, *England in the Nineteenth Century 1815–1914* (Viking Penguin, 1978), pp. 63–68; Alfred Chandler Jr., *The Visible Hand: The Managerial Revolution*

in American Business (Harvard University Press, Belknap Press 1977) pp 90–91.

6. Zane L. Miller, *The Urbanization of Modern America: A Brief History*, 2d ed. (San Diego: Harcourt Brace Jovanovitch, 1987), passim.
7. Stuart W. Bruchey, *Growth of the Modern American Economy* (New York: Dodd Meade, 1975); Thomas McCraw, *Prophets of Regulation: Charles Francis Adams, Louis D Brandeis, James M. Landis, Alfred E Kahn.* (Harvard University Press, Belknap Press 1984) chaps. 1–5.
8. Daniel Bell, foreword to *The Coming of Post-Industrial Society: A Venture in Social Forecasting* (Basic Books, 1999), p. 8.
9. Ibid., p. 5.
10. Nathan Rosenberg, *Exploring the Black Box: Technology, Economics, and History* (Cambridge University Press, 1994), chap. 4.
11. See Anthony G. Oettinger, "Information Technologies, Governance, and Government: Some Insights from History," paper presented at the 1998 Visions in Governance Conference at Bretton Woods, sponsored by the Kennedy School of Government, Harvard University, July 19–22, 1998 (www.ksg.edu/visions/conferences/bretton-woods3/ettinger95.ppt [October 15, 2001]).
12. Bell, *The Coming of Post-Industrial Society*, pp. 94, 97.
13. William Fielding Ogburn, "The Influence of Inventions on American Social Institutions in the Future," *American Journal of Sociology*, vol. 43 (November 1937), p. 370.
14. Charles P. Kindleberger, *Centralization versus Pluralism* (Copenhagen: Copenhagen Business School Press, 1996), p. 13.
15. Bell, *The Coming of Post-Industrial Society*, p. 94.
16. John D. Donahue, *Disunited States* (Basic Books, 1997), p. 11.
17. Ibid., pp. 9–11.
18. Daniel Yergin and Joseph Stanislaw, *The Commanding Heights: The Battle between Government and the Marketplace That Is Remaking the Modern World* (Simon and Schuster, 1998); Susan Strange, *States and Markets*, 2d ed. (New York: Pinter, 1994), pp. 14, 73.
19. *Nonprofit Almanac, 1996–97* (San Francisco: Jossey-Bass, 1996), p. 29.
20. Jessica T. Mathews, "Power Shift," *Foreign Affairs*, vol. 76, no. 1 (1997), pp. 50–66; Marc Lindenberg, "Declining State Capacity, Voluntarism, and the Globalization of the Not-for-Profit Sector," *Nonprofit and Voluntary Sector Quarterly*, vol. 28, no. 4 (1999), supplement, pp. 147–68.
21. Anne-Marie Slaughter, "The Real New World Order," *Foreign Affairs*, vol. 76, no. 5 (1997), pp. 183–97; see also Robert Keohane and Joseph S. Nye Jr., "Transgovernmental Relations and World Politics," *World Politics*, vol. 27 (October 1974), pp. 39–62.
22. Deborah Spar and Jeffrey J. Bussgang, "Ruling the Net," *Harvard Business Review* (May-June 1996), pp. 125–33; Saskia Sassen, *Globalization and Its Discontents* (New York: New Press, 1998), p. 16.
23. "Policing for Profit: Welcome to the New World of Private Security," *Economist*, April 19, 1997, pp. 21–24.
24. "The Visible Hand," *Economist*, September 20, 1997, pp. 17–18.
25. Organization for Economic Cooperation and Development, "General Government Total Outlays," *OECD Economic Outlook*, vol. 68 (December 2000), statistical annex, table 28, p. 236.
26. David Held and Anthony McGrew, eds., *The Global Tranformations Reader: An Introduction to the Globalization Debate* (Cambridge: Polity Press, 2000).
27. Raymond Vernon, *In the Hurricane's Eye: The Troubled Prospects of Multinational Enterprises* (Harvard University Press, 1998), chaps. 1–2.
28. Dani Rodrik, *Has Globalization Gone too Far?* (Washington: Institute for International Economics, 1997), p. 65; John Ruggie, "At Home Abroad, Abroad at Home: International Liberalization and Domestic Stability in the New "World Economy," *Millennium: Journal of International Studies*, vol. 24, no. 3 (1995), pp. 507–26, p. 508.
29. Susan Strange, *The Retreat of the State* (Cambridge University Press, 1996), p. 14.
30. Jeremy Greenwood, *The Third Industrial Revolution: Technology, Productivity, and*

Income Inequality (Washington: American Enterprise Institute Press, 1997), pp. 20–23.

31. "Electronic Commerce Helps to Fuel U.S. Growth," *Financial Times* (London), April 16, 1998, p. 5.
32. Intel cofounder Gordon Moore formulated his now-famous "Moore's law" of microprocessing power and cost in 1965. As Intel's website essay on Moore's law notes, "The average price of a transistor has fallen by six orders of magnitude due to microprocessor development. This is unprecedented in world history; no other manufactured item has decreased in cost so far, so fast" (developet.intel.com/update/archive/issue2/focus.htm#ONE [October 15, 2001]).
33. U.S. Department of Commerce, *The Emerging Digital Economy,* chap. 1, "The Digital Revolution" (www.doc.gov/ecommerce/dancl.htm [October 15, 2001]).
34. K. G. Coffman and Andrew Odlyzko, "The Size and Growth of the Internet," *First Monday: Peer-Reviewed Journal on the Internet,* vol. 3 (October 1998) (www.firstmonday.dk/issues/issue3_10/coffman/index.html [October 15, 2001]).
35. Douglass North, *Structure and Change in Economic History* (W. W Norton), pp. 163–64.
36. "Productivity: Lost in Cyberspace," *Economist,* September 13, 1997, p. 72.
37. See, for example, Drucker, "The Next Information Revolution"; Neal M. Rosendorf, "El Caudillo and American Pop Culture: How Postwar Franco Spain Attempted to Use Hollywood, U.S. Tourism, and Madison Avenue for Its Own Political and Economic Ends," Ph.D. diss., Harvard University, 2001, chap. 1.
38. Carl E Friedrich and Zbigniew Brzezinski, *Totalitarian Dictatorship and Autocracy,* 2d ed. (Harvard University Press, 1965).
39. Ithiel de Sola Pool, *Technologies of Freedom* (Harvard University Press, Belknap Press, 1983).
40. Winograd and Buffa, *Taking Control: Politics. in the Information Age.*
41. Ashton Carter, John Deutch, and Philip Zelikow, "Catastrophic Terrorism: Tackling the New Danger," *Foreign Affairs,* vol. 77, no. 6 (1998), pp. 80–94.
42. Quoted in "Undivided Loyalties: FT Interview with Tony Blair," *Financial Times* (London), January 14, 1999.
43. Nye, "The Decline of Confidence in Government," passim; David W. Moore, "Public Trust in Federal Government Remains High," Gallup News Service, January 8, 1999 (www.gallup.com/poll/releases/pr990108.asp [October 18, 2001]).
44. Donahue, *Disunited States.*
45. Deborah L. Spar, "The Public Face of Cyberspace: The Internet as a Public Good," in Inge Kaul, Isabelle Grunberg, and Marc A. Stern, eds., *Global Public Goods: International Cooperation in the Twenty-first Century*" (Oxford University Press, 1999).
46. Lawrence Lessig, "Cyber-Governance," *CPSR Newsletter,* vol. 16 (Fall 1998), p. 4.

Policy Paradox: The Art of Political Decision Making

Deborah Stone

Paradoxes are nothing but trouble. They violate the most elementary principle of logic: Something cannot be two different things at once. Two contradictory interpretations cannot both be true. A paradox is just such an impossible situation, and political life is full of them. Consider some examples.

Losing Is Winning

When the Republicans gained control of the House of Representatives after the 1994 midterm elections, passing a balanced-budget amendment to the U.S. Constitution was tops on their legislative agenda. Republicans had long criticized Democrats for profligate government spending and high deficits. Getting a constitutional amendment to require a balanced budget would be a powerful legal weapon they could use to cut government programs drastically. Early in 1995, it looked like both houses of Congress would pass the budget amendment easily. As time got closer to a Senate vote in March, however, the Republicans didn't seem to have the 67 votes necessary to pass a constitutional amendment. Senator Bob Dole, the Republican majority leader, kept postponing the vote, hoping to pick up more support, but eventually he brought the bill to a vote without having 67 votes lined up. Why would he bring the matter to a vote, knowing that the Republicans would fail to pass it? On the eve of the vote, he explained: "We really win if we win, but we may also win if we lose."[1]

After the vote, the headlines were unanimous: "Senate Rejects Amendment on Balancing the Budget; Close Vote is Blow to GOP," went the *New York Times*' verdict. "GOP is Loser on Budget Amendment," echoed the *Boston Globe*.[2] What did Dole mean by claiming that a loss could be a victory?

Politicians always have at least two goals. First is a policy goal—whatever program or proposal they would like to see accomplished or defeated, whatever problem they would like to see solved. Perhaps even more important, though, is a political goal. Politicians always want to preserve their power, or gain enough power, to be able to accomplish their policy goals. Even though a defeat of the balanced budget amendment was a loss for Republicans' policy goal, Dole thought it might be a gain for Republicans' political strength. (So, apparently, did the *New York Time*, whose sub-headline read "Risk to Democrats.") Republican leaders acknowledged that they had lost a constitutional device that would have helped them immensely in redeeming their campaign pledge to enact the "Contract with America." But they also saw some important political gains. Senator Orrin Hatch, the chief sponsor of the amendment, called the vote "a clear delineation between the parties." A Republican pollster explained how the vote might help Republican candidates in the next Congressional election: "It lays out the differences as sharply as we could want them: We want to cut spending, and they don't."[3] Dole, already campaigning for the Presidency, used the occasion to lambaste President Clinton for "abdicating his responsibility" to control federal deficits, while Republicans in both houses talked about making Democrats pay at the polls in the next election. "As far as I'm concerned," Newt Gingrich crowed, "it's like a fork in chess. They can give us a victory today; they can give us a victory in November'96."[4]

Parades: Recreation or Speech?

An Irish gay and lesbian group wanted to march in Boston's annual Saint Patrick's Day parade. The organizers of the parade wanted to stop them. The gay and lesbian group said a parade is a public recreational event, and therefore, civil rights law protected them against discrimination in public accommodations. The parade organizers claimed a parade is an expression of beliefs, really an act of speech. Their right to say what they wanted—by excluding from the parade those with a different message—should be protected by the First Amendment. Is a parade a public recreational event or an act of self-expression? Might it be both? What would you do if you were a justice on the Supreme Court and had to decide one way or the other?[5]

For or against Welfare?

When asked about public spending on welfare, 48 percent of Americans say it should be cut. But when asked about spending on programs for poor children, 47 percent say it should be increased, and only 9 percent want cuts.[6]

Do Americans want to enlarge or curtail welfare spending? It all depends on how the question is framed.

Enemies or Allies?

The Food and Drug Administration (FDA) regulates the testing and marketing of new pharmaceutical drugs. For decades, drug manufacturers have complained that the regulations make developing new drugs excessively costly and painfully slow. Thanks to the FDA, they have argued, the pharmaceutical industry is hardly profitable anymore, and the United States has lost its lead as the world's innovator of medical miracles. Drug companies have consistently wanted the FDA off their backs. When, however, the Republican party finally took control of the House in 1995 and prepared to privatize most of the functions of the FDA, the pharmaceutical manufacturers were the first to rush to the FDA's defense.

Why the sudden turnabout? At one level, an industry and its regulatory agency are adversaries. One is a watchdog for the other, a guardian of the public interest against exploitation by those with more narrow self-interests. At another level, though, regulators and the regulated always have a symbiotic relationship. They depend on each other. Without an industry to regulate, the regulatory agency would be out of business. And, in the case of drug manufacturing, without the seal of government approval for its drugs, the industry would lose the "world's confidence in the superiority of American drugs," and the American public's confidence in the safety and efficacy of drugs. "We are for a strong F.D.A.," said the head of the Health Industry Manufacturers' Association. "They are our credibility."[7]

In politics, as in life, many relationships are simultaneously adversarial and symbiotic.

Which Came First—The Problem or the Solution?

In the 1950s, a federal program for mass transit was proposed as a solution to urban congestion. Subways and buses were presented as a more efficient means of transportation than private cars. In the late 1960s, environmental protection was the word of the day, and mass transit advocates peddled subways and buses as a way to reduce automobile pollution. Then with the OPEC oil embargo of 1972, Washington's attention was riveted by the energy crisis, and mass transit was sold as an energy-saving alternative to private automobiles. Was this a case of three problems for which mass transit just happened to be a solution, or a constant solution adapting to a changing problem?[8]

Babies: Product or Service?

New reproductive technologies have fundamentally changed the way people can have babies and create families. "Baby M" was born in 1986 as the result of a contract between William Stern and Marybeth Whitehead, both married, though not to each other. The contract provided for Mrs. Whitehead to be artificially inseminated with Mr. Stern's sperm, to bring the baby to term in her womb, and then to give the baby to Mr. and Mrs. Stern to raise as their child. In return, Mr. Stern would pay Mrs. Whitehead $10,000, plus expenses.

After the birth, Mrs. Whitehead decided she wanted to keep the baby, who was, after all, her biological daughter. The case went to court. Although the immediate issue was who would win the right to raise "Baby M," the policy question on everybody's mind was whether the courts should recognize and enforce surrogate motherhood contracts. Most states prohibit the sale of babies in their adoption laws. So the question of paramount importance was whether a surrogate motherhood contract is a contract for the sale of a baby or for a socially useful service.

On the one hand, Mrs. Whitehead could be seen as renting her womb. Like any professional service provider, she agreed to observe high standards of practice—in this case, prenatal care. According to the contract, she would not drink, smoke, or take drugs, and she would follow medical advice. Like any physical laborer, she was selling the use of her body for a productive purpose. By her own and the Sterns' account, she was altruistically helping to create a child for a couple who could not have their own.

On the other hand, Mrs. Whitehead could be seen as producing and selling a baby. She underwent artificial insemination in anticipation of a fee—no fee, no baby. She agreed to have amniocentesis and to have an abortion if the test showed any defects not acceptable to Mr. Stern. She agreed to accept a lower fee if the baby were born with any mental or physical handicaps—low-value baby, low price.

Is a surrogate motherhood contract for a service or for a baby?

How can we make sense of a world where such paradoxes occur? In an age of science, of human mastery over the innermost and outermost realms, how are we to deal with situations that will not observe the elementary rules of scientific decorum? Can we make public policy behave?

The fields of political science, public administration, law, and policy analysis have a common mission of rescuing public policy from the irrationalities and indignities of politics, hoping to make policy instead with rational, analytical, and scientific methods. I call this endeavor "the rationality project," and it has been at the core of American political culture since the beginning. The project began with James Madison's effort to "cure the mischiefs of faction" with proper constitutional design, thereby assuring that government policy would be protected from the self-interested motives of tyrannous majorities.[9] In the 1870s, Christopher Columbus Langdell, dean of the Harvard Law School, undertook to take the politics out of law by reforming legal training. Law was a science, he proclaimed, to be studied by examining appellate court decisions and distilling their common essence into a system of principles. There was no need to gain practical experience.

At the turn of the twentieth century, the rationality project was taken up in spades by the Progressive reformers, who removed policymaking authority from elected bodies and gave it to expert regulatory commissions and professional city managers, in an effort to render policy making more scientific and less political. The quest for an apolitical science of government continues in the twentieth century with Herbert Simon's search for a "science of administration," Harold Lasswell's dream of a "science of policy forming and execution," and the current effort of universities, foundations, and government to foster a profession of policy scientists. At the turn of the twenty-first century, the rationality project was in full bloom in the discipline of political science, under the banner of "rational choice," and in law, under the banner of "law and economics."

This book has two aims. First, I argue that the rationality project misses the point of politics. Moreover, it is an impossible dream. From inside the rationality project, politics looks messy, foolish, erratic, and inexplicable. Events, actions, and ideas in the political world seem to leap outside the categories that logic and rationality offer. In the rationality project, the categories of analysis are somehow above politics or outside it. Rationality purports to offer a correct vantage point, from which we can judge the goodness of the real world.

I argue, instead, that the very categories of thought underlying rational analysis are themselves a kind of paradox, defined in political struggle. They do not exist before or without politics, and because they are necessarily abstract (they are categories of *thought,* after all), they can have multiple meanings. Thus, analysis is itself a creature of politics; it is strategically crafted argument, designed to create ambiguities and paradoxes and to resolve them in a particular direction. (This much is certainly awfully abstract for now, but each of the subsequent chapters is designed to show very concretely how one analytic category of politics and policy is a constantly evolving political creation.)

Beyond demonstrating this central misconception of the rationality project, my second aim is to derive a kind of political analysis that makes sense of policy paradoxes such as the ones depicted above. I seek to create a framework in which such phenomena, the ordinary situations of politics, do not have to be explained away as extraordinary, written off as irrational, dismissed as folly, or disparaged as "pure politics." Unfortunately, much of the literature about public policy proceeds from the idea that policy making in practice deviates from some hypothetical standards of good policy making, and that there is thus something fundamentally wrong with politics. In creating an alternative mode of political analysis, I start from the belief that politics is a creative and valuable feature of social existence.

The project of making public policy rational rests on three pillars: a model of reasoning, a model of society, and a model of policy making. The *model of reasoning* is rational decision making. In this model, decisions are or should be made in a series of well-defined steps:

1. Identify objectives.
2. Identify alternative courses of action for achieving objectives.
3. Predict the possible consequences of each alternative.
4. Evaluate the possible consequences of each alternative.
5. Select the alternative that maximizes the attainment of objectives.

This model of rational behavior is so pervasive it is a staple of checkout-counter magazines and self-help books. For all of its intuitive appeal, however, the rational decision-making model utterly fails to explain Bob Dole's thinking or behavior at the time of the balanced budget amendment vote. Did he attain his objective or didn't he? Did he win or lose? Worse, the model could not help formulate political advice for Dole beforehand, for if we accept his reasoning that he wins either way, then it doesn't matter which way the vote goes and he should just sit back and enjoy the play. Of course, Dole was not only reasoning when he claimed that losing was winning. He was also trying to manipulate how the outcome of the vote would be perceived and how it would influence future political contests between the Republicans and the Democrats. In fact, all the Republican credit-claiming and victory speeches upon losing the vote suggest that politicians have a great deal of control over interpretations of events, and that the political analyst who wants to choose a wise course of action should focus less on assessing the objective consequences of actions and more on how the interpretations will go. If politicians can attain their objectives by portraying themselves as having attained them, then they should be studying portraiture, not cost-benefit analysis.

A model of political reason ought to account for the possibilities of changing one's objectives, of pursuing contradictory objectives simultaneously, of winning by appearing to lose and turning loss into an appearance of victory, and most unusual, of attaining objectives by portraying oneself as having attained them. Throughout this book, I develop a model of political reasoning quite different from the model of rational decision making. Political reasoning is reasoning by metaphor and analogy. It is trying to get others to see a situation as one thing rather than another. For example, parades can be seen as public recreational events, or as collective marches to express an idea. Each vision constructs a different political contest, and invokes a different set of rules for resolving the conflict. Babies created under surrogate motherhood contracts are a phenomenon quite unlike anything we already know. The situation is not exactly like professional service, not exactly like wage labor, not exactly like a contract for pork bellies, not exactly like a custody dispute between divorced parents, and not exactly like an adoption contract. Legislatures and courts deal with the issue by asking, "Of the things that surrogate motherhood isn't, which is it most like?"

Political reasoning is metaphor-making and category-making, but not just for beauty's sake or for insight's sake. It is strategic portrayal for persuasion's sake, and ultimately for policy's sake. This concept of political reason is developed and illustrated throughout the book, and I take up the idea directly again in the last chapter.

The *model of society* underlying the contemporary rationality project is the market. Society is viewed as a collection of autonomous, rational decision makers who have no community life. Their interactions consist entirely of trading with one another to maximize their individual well-being. They each have objectives or preferences, they each compare alternative ways of attaining their objectives, and they each choose the way that yields the most satisfaction. They maximize their self-interest through rational calculation. The market model and the rational decision-making model are thus very closely related.

The market model is not restricted to things we usually consider markets, that is, to systems where goods and services are bought and sold. Electoral voting, the behavior of legislators, political leadership, the size of the welfare rolls, and even marriage have all been explained in terms of the maximization of self-interest through rational calculation. The market model posits that individuals have relatively fixed, independent preferences for goods, services, and policies. In real societies, where people are psychologically and materially dependent, where they are connected through emotional bonds, traditions, and social groups, their preferences are based on loyalties and comparisons of images. How people define their preferences depends to a large extent on how choices are presented to them and by whom. They want greater welfare spending when it is called helping poor children, but not when it is called welfare. Sometimes, as in the case of "Baby M," they are not quite sure what they are buying and selling, or whether they have engaged in a sale at all.

In place of the model of society as a market, I construct a model of society as a political community (Part I). Chapter 1, "The Market and the Polis," sets forth the fundamental elements of human behavior and social life that I take to be axiomatic, and contrasts them with the axioms of the market model. I start with a model of political community, or "polis," because I began my own intellectual odyssey in this territory with a simple reflection: Both policy and thinking about policy are produced in political communities.

The observation may be trite, but it has radical consequences for a field of inquiry that has been dominated by a conception of society as a market. To take just one example, the market model of society envisions societal welfare as the aggregate of individuals' situations. All behavior is explained as people striving to maximize their own self-interest. The market model therefore gives us no way to talk about how people fight over visions of the public interest or the nature of the community—the truly significant political questions underlying policy choices.

The *model of policy making* in the rationality project is a production model, where policy is created in a fairly orderly sequence of stages, almost as if on an assembly line. Many political scientists, in fact, speak of "assembling the elements" of policy. An issue is "placed on the agenda," and a problem gets defined. It moves through the legislative and executive branches of government, where alternative solutions are proposed, analyzed, legitimized, selected, and refined. A solution is implemented by the executive agencies and constantly challenged and revised by interested actors, perhaps using the judicial branch. And finally, if the policy-making process is managerially sophisticated, it provides a means of evaluating and revising implemented solutions.

So conceived, the policy-making process parallels the cognitive steps of the rational model of decision making. Government becomes a rational decision maker writ large—albeit not a very proficient one. Much of the political science literature in this genre is devoted to understanding where and how good policy gets derailed in the process of production. This model of policy making as rational problem solving cannot explain why sometimes policy solutions go looking for problems. It cannot tell us why solutions, such as privatizing the FDA's drug evaluation, turn into problems. It only tells us things are working "backward" or poorly.

The production model fails to capture what I see as the essence of policy making in political communities: the struggle over ideas. Ideas are a medium of exchange and a mode of influence even more powerful than money and votes and guns. Shared meanings motivate people to action and meld individual striving into collective action. Ideas are at the center of all political conflict. Policy making, in turn, is a constant struggle over the criteria for classification, the boundaries of categories, and the definition of ideals that guide the way people behave.

Chapters 2 through 15 examine the constituent ideas of policy and policy analysis in light of their construction in a political community. Each idea is an argument, or more accurately, a collection of arguments in favor of different ways of seeing the world. Every chapter is devoted to showing how there are multiple understandings of what appears to be a single concept, how these understandings are created, and how they are manipulated as part of political strategy. Revealing the hidden arguments embedded in each concept illuminates, and may help resolve, the surface conflicts.

The reader would certainly be justified in asking why I chose the particular set of ideas included here. The broad architecture of the book takes its shape from the notion of a policy issue implied in the rationality project: We have a goal; we have a problem, which is a discrepancy between the goal and reality; and we seek a solution to erase the discrepancy. Parts II, III, and IV correspond to the three parts of this framework: goals, problems, and solutions.

As I demonstrate throughout the book, the political careers of most policy issues are not nearly so simple as this three-part formula would suggest. For example, people do not always perceive a goal first and then look for disparities between the goal and the status quo. Often, they see a problem first, which triggers a search for solutions and a statement of goals. Or, they see a solution first, then formulate a problem that requires their solution (and their services). Nevertheless, I use this framework because it expresses a logic of problem solving that is widespread in the policy analysis literature and because it parallels the models of rational decision making and the policy-making process.

Part II is about goals—not the specific goals of particular policy issues, such as expanding health insurance coverage or lowering health care costs, but the enduring values of community life that give rise to controversy over particular policies: equity, efficiency, security, and liberty. These values are "motherhood issues": everyone is for them when they are stated abstractly, but the fight begins as soon as we ask what people mean by them. These values not only express goals, but also serve as the standards we use to evaluate existing situations and policy proposals.

One tenet of the rationality project is that there are objective and neutral standards of evaluation that can be applied to politics, but that come from a vantage point outside politics, untainted by the interests of political players. The theme of Part II is that behind every policy issue lurks a contest over conflicting, though equally plausible, conceptions of the same abstract goal or value. The abstractions are aspirations for a community, into which people read contradictory interpretations. It may not be possible to get everyone to agree on the same interpretation, but the first task of the political analyst is to reveal and clarify the underlying value disputes so that people can see where they differ and move toward some reconciliation.

There might well have been other ideas in the section on goals. Justice, privacy, social obligation, and democracy come to mind. Equity, efficiency, security, and liberty begged more insistently for political analysis only because, sadly, they are invoked more often as criteria in policy analysis. Once having read this book, the reader will have no trouble seeing some of the paradoxes in other criteria.

Part III is about problems and about how we know there is a disparity between social goals and the current state of affairs. There are many modes of defining problems in policy discourse, and each mode is like a language within which people offer and defend conflicting interpretations. "Symbols" and "Numbers" are about verbal and numerical languages, respectively, and both examine devices of symbolic representation within those languages. We also define problems in terms of what causes them ("Causes"), who is lined up on each side ("Interests"), or what kind of choice they pose ("Decisions"). Here, too, I might have chosen other categories; for example, one could examine problem formulation according to different disciplines, such as economics, law, political science, or ethics. I did not choose that framework because it would only perpetuate the somewhat artificial divisions of academia, and the categories I did choose seem to me a better representation of modes of discourse in political life.

Part IV is about solutions, or more accurately, about the temporary resolutions of conflict. These chapters start from the assumption that all policies involve deliberate attempts to change people's behavior, and each chapter in this section deals with a mechanism for bringing about such change—creating incentives and penalties ("Inducements"), mandating rules ("Rules"), informing and persuading ("Facts"), stipulating rights and duties ("Rights"), and reorganizing authority ("Powers").

The common theme of this part is that policy instruments are not just tools, each with its own function and its own appropriateness for certain kinds of jobs. In the standard political science model of the policy-making process, policy solutions are decided upon and then implemented, though things usually go awry at the implementation stage. The task of the analyst is to figure out which is the right or best tool to use, and then to fix mistakes when things don't go as planned. I argue, instead, that each type of policy instrument is a kind of sports arena, each with its peculiar ground rules, within which political conflicts are continued. Each mode of social regulation draws lines around what people may and may not do and how they may or may not treat each other. But these boundaries are constantly contested, either because they are ambiguous and do not settle conflicts, or because they allocate benefits and burdens to the people on either side, or both. Boundaries become real and acquire their meaning in political struggles. The job of the analyst, in this view, is to understand the rules of the game well enough to know the standard moves and have a repertoire of effective countermoves.

If deep down inside, you are a rationalist, you might want to know whether the topics covered by the chapters are "exhaustive" and "mutually exclusive." They are most assuredly not. Our categories of thought and modes of argument are intertwined and not easily delineated. That is one reason, I shall argue, why we have and always will have politics. Then, too, I remind you that I am trying to demonstrate precisely that essential political concepts are paradoxes. They have contradictory meanings that by formal logic ought to be mutually exclusive but by political logic are not. I do hope, however, that my categories at least provide a useful way to divide up an intellectual territory for exploration, and at best provide a new way of seeing it.

As for whether my categories are exhaustive, I can only plead the quintessential political defense: I had to draw the line somewhere.

Notes

1. Quoted in Jill Zuckman, "No Voting, More Anger on Budget," *Boston Globe*, March 2, 1995, p. 1.
2. Both headlines on front page, *New York Times*, March 3, 1995; *Boston Globe*, March 2, 1995.
3. Quotations in "GOP Is Loser on Budget Amendment," *Boston Globe*, March 5, 1995, p. 1.
4. Quotation from "Senate Rejects Amendment on Balanced Budget," *New York Times*, March 3, 1995, p. A1.
5. Linda Greenhouse, "High Court Lets Parade in Boston Bar Homosexuals," *New York Times*, June 20, 1995, p. Al.
6. Jason DeParle, "Despising Welfare, Pitying Its Young," *New York Times*, December 18, 1994, p. E5.
7. Philip J. Hilts, "FDA Becomes Target of Empowered Groups," *New York Times*, Feb. 12, 1995, p. 24.
8. John Kingdon, *Agendas, Alternatives and Public Policies* (Boston: Little Brown, 1984), p. 181.
9. This was the argument of his *Federalist Paper No. 10,* about which more is said in Chapters 10 and 15.

47

Unmasking Administrative Evil

Guy B. Adams and Danny L. Balfour

In The Face of Administrative Evil

Searching for a Basis for Public Ethics

> If history is a nightmare, it is because there is so much cruelty in it. In peace as in war members of our species are cruel to one another, and human progress seems to consist not so much in diminishing that cruelty as in finding more impersonal and efficient ways of crushing and grinding one another.
>
> —*Philip Hallie, 1969 (xv)*

Administrative evil poses a fundamental challenge to the ethical foundations of public life. Our reluctance to recognize the importance of administrative evil as part of the identity and practice of public policy and administration reinforces its continuing influence and increases the possibility of future acts of dehumanization and destruction, even in the name of the public interest. The Holocaust and other eruptions of administrative evil show that the assumptions and standards for ethical behavior in modern, technical-rational systems are ultimately incapable of preventing or mitigating evil in either its subtle or its more obvious forms. With this final chapter, we consider the nature of and prospects for ethics in public life, living as we do in the shadow of administrative evil.

Source: From Guy B. Adams and Danny L. Balfour, UNMASKING ADMINISTRATIVE EVIL, 3d ed. (Armonk, NY: M.E. Sharpe, 2009): 161–170.

Necessary but Not Sufficient: The Technical-Rational Approach to Public Service Ethics

Ethics is the branch of philosophy concerned with systematic thought about character, morals, and "right action." In the modern age, until recently, two main versions of ethics have dominated Anglo-American philosophical thinking, namely *teleological* (or consequentialist) ethics and *deontological* ethics (Frankena, 1973). Both share an interest in determining the rules that should govern—and therefore be used to judge—individual behavior as good or bad, right or wrong. Teleological ethics, based on utilitarianism and tracing its lineage to Bentham (1989, orig. 1789) and others, offers the overarching principle of the greatest good for the greatest number. Oriented toward the results or consequences of actions, teleological ethics tends to elevate the ends over the means used to achieve those ends. Deontological ethics, founded in the thought of Kant (1959, orig. 1786) and his support of duty and order, reverses this emphasis, holding that the lower-order rules governing means are essential for the higher-order rules that concern the ends to be achieved. For our purposes, the important point is that both of these traditions have focused on the individual as the relevant unit of analysis.

Ethics in the technical-rational tradition draws upon both versions of ethics and focuses on the individual's decision-making process in the modern, bureaucratic organization and as a member of a profession. In the public sphere, deontological ethics are meant to safeguard the integrity of the organization by helping individuals conform to professional norms, avoid mistakes and misdeeds that violate the public trust (corruption, nepotism, and so forth), and assure that public officials in a constitutional republic are accountable to the people through their elected representatives. At the same time, public servants are encouraged to pursue the greater good by using discretion in the application of rules and regulations and creativity in the face of changing conditions (utilitarianism). The "good" public servant should avoid both the extremes of rule-bound behavior and undermining the rule of law with individual judgments and interests.

It is fairly self-evident that public (and private) organizations depend on at least this level of ethical judgment in order to function efficiently and effectively, and to maintain public confidence in government (and business). At the same time, it has to be recognized that these ethical standards of an organization or profession are only safeguards, not failsafes, against unethical behavior. Nor do they necessarily help individuals to resolve tough moral dilemmas that are often characterized by ambiguity and paradox. Indeed, these problems provide the grist for the discourse among ethical theorists in the rational tradition. The Friedrich–Finer debate on public service ethics is still a useful way of describing the ethical terrain in public life. Finer (1941) argued for a version of ethics that emphasized external standards and controls, laws, rules, regulations, and codes. By contrast, Friedrich (1940) maintained that ethics was of necessity a matter of the individual's internal standards of conduct—a moral compass that guides the public servant through the morass of ethical dilemmas.

The Finer position of external controls is most compatible with a view of the public servant as a neutral functionary who carries out, in Max Weber's phrase, *sine ira ac studio* (without bias or scorn), policy decisions made in the political sphere or by those in higher echelons of the organizational hierarchy. One author has gone so far as to argue that both an ethic of neutrality (decisions from politics) and an ethic of structure (decisions from higher up) preclude public service ethics altogether because they deny the legitimacy of administrative and professional discretion (Thompson, 1985; see also, Ladd, 1970). Today, arguments in the literature are primarily over just which ethical grounds might justify such discretion. Prominent among the arguments for administrative and professional discretion are: (1) justice-based claims, usually following Rawls (Hart, 1984); (2) citizenship (Cooper, 1991); (3) American regime values (Rohr, 1978); (4) stewardship (Kass, 1990); (5) phronesis (Morgan, 1990); (6) conservation (Terry, 2002); and (7) countervailing responsibility (Harmon, 1995), among others.

In both public and private organizations, it has become almost an article of faith that professionalism imbues its practitioners with a public service ideal and a code of ethics—that is, internalized standards (after Friedrich) that provide the ethical compass for administrative discretion. To this way of thinking, professionalism becomes the basis for a version of virtue or character ethics (Stewart, 1985; see also Cooper, 1987, and MacIntyre, 1984). On the other hand, professionalism can also offer grounding for the external version of ethics (after Finer). Professions have codes of ethics, and they also often have some method of peer control in which ethics and standards are enforced, and in the extreme, in which the serious transgressor can be drummed out of the profession (Kemaghan, 1980). At the same time, most of the activity in the world of public service has been directed at external controls.

The Challenge of Administrative Evil

Despite the extensive literature on public service ethics, there is little recognition of the most fundamental ethical challenge to the professional within a technical-rational culture: that is, one can be a "good" or responsible administrator or professional and at the same time commit or contribute to acts of administrative evil. As Harmon (1995) has argued, technical-rational ethics has difficulty dealing with what Milgram (1974) termed the "agentic shift," where the professional or administrator acts responsibly toward the hierarchy of authority, public policy, and the requirements of the job or profession, while abdicating any personal, much less social, responsibility for the content or effects of decisions or actions. There is little in the way of coherent justification for the notion of a stable and predictable distinction between the individual's personal conscience guided by higher values that might resist the agentic shift, and the socialized professional or administrator who internalizes agency values and obedience to legitimate authority. In the technical-rational conception of public service ethics, the personal conscience is always subordinate to the structures of authority. The former is "subjective" and "personal," while the latter is characterized as "objective" and "public."

The specter of the agentic shift and the tightly controlled but soulless functionary, and the need for administrative discretion, helps explain why much of the recent literature in public service ethics has leaned toward Friedrich's emphasis on internal control and personal conscience as the center of ethical behavior and standards. But some see this trend as leading to the usurping of democratic controls over public policy and a slippery slope toward government by bureaucracy (see Lowi, 1993).

This paradox is starkly illustrated in the Third Reich and the Holocaust. Many of the administrators directly responsible for the Holocaust were, from the technical-rational perspective, effective and responsible administrators who used administrative discretion to both influence and carry out the will of their superiors. Professionals and administrators such as Eichmann, Speer, and Arthur Rudolph obeyed orders, followed proper protocol and procedures, and were often innovative and creative while carrying out their assigned tasks in an efficient and effective manner (Keeley, 1983; Hilberg, 1989; Harmon, 1995; Lozowick, 2000). Ironically, the SS was very concerned about corruption in its ranks and with strict conformance to the professional norms of its order (Sofsky, 1997).

As Rubenstein (1975) points out, no laws against genocide or dehumanization were broken by those who perpetrated the Holocaust. Everything was legally sanctioned and administratively approved by a legitimated authority, while at the same time, a number of key programs and innovations were initiated from within the bureaucracy (Browning, 1989; Sofsky, 1997). Even within the morally inverted universe created by the Nazis, professionals and administrators carried out their duties within a framework of ethics and responsibility that was consistent with the norms of technical rationality (Lifton, 1986). Hilberg (1989) points out that the professions were "everywhere" in the Holocaust. Lawyers, physicians, engineers, planners, military professionals, accountants, and more all contributed to the destruction of the Jews and other "undesirables." Scientific methods were used in ways that dehumanized and murdered innocent human beings, showing clearly how the model of professionalism consistent with modernity empties out moral reasoning. The moral vacuity of professional ethics is clearly revealed by the fact that the vast majority of those who participated in the Holocaust were never punished, and many were placed in responsible positions in post-war West German government or industry, as well as our own NASA and other public and private organizations in the United States. The need for "good" managers to rebuild the German economy and to develop our own rocket program outweighed any consideration of the reprehensible activities in which they were complicit.

The historical record is such that we must conclude that the power of the individual's conscience is very weak relative to that of legitimated authority in modern organizations and social structures more generally, and that current ethical standards do too little to limit the potential for evil in modern organizations. Even if the individual finds the moral strength to resist administrative evil, the technical-rational perspective provides little in the way of guidance for how to act effectively against evil. As public service ethics is now construed, one cannot be a "civil servant" and be in public disagreement with legally constituted political authorities (Trow, 1997). A public servant can voice disagreement with a public policy privately, but if this does not result in a change of policy, the only acceptable courses of action that remain are exit or loyalty (Hirschman, 1970; Harmon, 1995). One can resign and seek to change policy from the outside (leaving only silent loyalists in the organization), or remain and carry out the current policy. This was the choice faced by German civil servants in the early 1930s, as observed by Brecht (1944). If legitimate authority leads in the direction of administrative evil, it will certainly not provide legitimate outlets for resistance. In a situation of moral inversion, when duly constituted authority leads in the direction of evil, public service ethics is of very little help.

Why, one might ask, does professional ethics focus so much on the decision processes of individual administrators at the expense of collective outcomes? Why is the individual conscience primarily responsible for ethical behavior, when it is political and managerial authority that are responsible for public policy and organizations? Because, operationally (theory-in-use), the central value is the primacy of legitimated authority. This is buttressed by the focus on the utility-maximizing individual as the locus of ethical decision making. In short, the ethical problem is construed as one of individual conformance to legitimate authority as a function of self-interest. The fact–value distinction (Simon, 1976) further separates the individual administrator from substantive judgments by limiting the field of ethical behavior to questions of efficiency and proper or innovative implementation of policy as determined by those who deal in the realm of values (policy makers). In effect, the ethical purview validated by technical rationality relieves, and even prohibits, individual administrators from making substantive value judgments.

Within the technical-rational tradition, there seems to be little or no room for allowing or encouraging public servants to publicly disagree with policies that threaten the well-being of members of the polity, particularly policies that may produce or exploit surplus populations. Rather than expecting the individual public servant to exit voluntarily when in serious disagreement with such public policies, public disagreement might press those in authority either to dismiss the offending administrator or to engage in a public debate over the policy. In either case, the policy makers would have to take responsibility for their policies, rather than place that responsibility on the shoulders of functionaries. One can only imagine whether things might have been different in Germany had the civil service spoken out against Nazi policies in the early days of the regime. True, individual civil servants would have done so at great personal risk, but, at the same time, the newly constituted government could not have sustained itself without their collective support. The fact that the vast majority of the German civil service willingly carried out their duties once the legal basis for the new regime was established (Brecht, 1944), and that U.S. government scientists continued the Tuskegee experiments long after a cure for syphilis had been developed, along with numerous other examples, reveals how the ethical framework within a culture of technical rationality leaves little room for moral choice or for resistance to administrative evil that is promoted by legitimate authority.

If the Holocaust teaches us anything, it is that individual administrators and professionals, far from resisting administrative evil, are most likely to be either helpless victims or willing accomplices. The ethical framework within a technical-rational system posits the primacy of an abstract, utility-maximizing individual while binding professionals to organizations in ways that make them into reliable conduits for the dictates of legitimate authority, which is no less legitimate when it happens to be pursuing an evil policy. An ethical system that allows an individual to be a good administrator or professional while committing acts of evil is necessarily devoid of moral content, or perhaps better, morally perverse. When administrative evil can be unmasked, no public servant should be able to rest easy with the notion that ethical behavior is defined by doing things the right way. Norms of legality, efficiency, and effectiveness—however "professional" they may be—do not necessarily promote or protect the well-being of individuals, especially that of society's most vulnerable members, whose numbers are growing in the turbulent years of the early twenty-first century.

Globalization, the Corrosion of Character, and Surplus Populations

Since the fall of the Berlin Wall in 1989, a new, global world order has emerged (for discussions, see Friedman, 1999; Farazmand, 1999; Bauman, 1999; Sassen, 1998; Huntington, 1996; Fukuyama, 1992). The relatively stable and predictable system of the Cold War, at least for most industrialized nations, has given way to a new global system that is much more complex and unpredictable (Balfour and Grubbs, 2000), a process that was accelerated by the events of September 11, 2001. Where once two great nation-states defined the parameters of the world's political and economic systems, we now find instead a constantly shifting balance of powers in the relationships between nation-states, between these states and super-markets (such as NAFTA and the European Union), and between states, super-markets, and super-empowered individuals (Friedman, 1999). Old boundaries no longer restrict movement as the world moves toward greater integration of markets, nation-states, and technology. These developments have created phenomenal opportunities to create wealth and prosperity, but have also opened the doors to new conflicts and to deepening poverty among those who lack access to these new opportunities.

A key consequence of this new world order is that individuals are less and less tied to the traditional moorings of organization, community, and nation that once nurtured and protected them, although these moorings had already loosened considerably in the last century. For some, this represents a great opportunity to explore new horizons and possibilities. Many others, however, have found themselves adrift in a world that offers no haven, no safe port in which to land and settle into a stable life. At the extreme end of this spectrum are millions of refugees—surplus populations. The dimensions of this problem are such that no nation or community remains untouched by it (Fritz, 1999, 5):

> An estimated 50 million people were either driven from their countries or uprooted within them by the mid-1990s, roughly one out of every hundred people on earth. Counting those who emigrated for what were viewed as dire economic reasons, the figure more than doubles. The impact of this great migration has been enormous. It has compelled U.S.-led armies to intervene in faraway wars. It has led to a reactionary wave of restrictive immigration laws around the world. And it has planted the seeds of countless future conflicts.

Each new refugee crisis challenges already overstressed nation-states and nongovernmental organizations to find ways to absorb and care for these people with limited resources within an increasingly unsupportive political and social environment.

On another level, millions more individuals feel threatened by the new world order, fearful that they too will be uprooted and left hanging without a safety net. The underlying anxiety of the Cold War era was the fear that the conflict between the two superpowers would escalate into a nuclear holocaust. While that concern has diminished since the upheavals of the early 1990s, new anxieties have emerged. People feel threatened by terrorism and by the rapid changes and painful dislocations caused by unseen and poorly understood global forces. They fear that their jobs, communities, or workplace could be changed or even taken away at any moment by anonymous and turbulent economic, political, and technological forces. A new technology can transform an industry in a matter of months, making an individual's skills obsolete, or one's organization can disappear overnight in a new wave of mergers. The mass of refugees throughout the world serves as a constant reminder of how anyone can be overtaken and made superfluous by the dynamics of the new global system.

In his book *The Corrosion of Character: The Personal Consequences of Work in the New Capitalism,* Richard Sennett (1998) discusses how organizations are changing in the new global system and looks at some of the effects of these changes on the individual worker. He encapsulates many of these developments in his conversations with Rico, a "successful" businessman in the electronics industry whose wife is also a working professional. While in many ways they exemplify success in the contemporary economy, they also suffer from deep anxieties about the future and the quality of their lives—anxieties that have turned all too real for many thousands of people like them in the wake of the "Tech Bust."

Rico struggles to maintain a sense of identity and ethical integrity in an atmosphere of continual change and low levels of commitment to anything other than short-term gains (Sennett, 1998, 20–21):

> He feared that the actions he needs to take and the way he has to live in order to survive in the

> modern economy have set his emotional, inner life adrift... his deepest worry is that he cannot offer the substance of his work life as an example to his children of how they should conduct themselves ethically. The qualities of good work are not the qualities of good character.

One result of the focus on the short-term is low levels of trust and commitment. The pace of change in contemporary organizations means that for most there is "no long term." Rico both values the independence he has found in the new economy, but also feels adrift, with no strong bonds of commitment or trust (Sennett, 1998, 25). "'No long term' means keep moving, don't commit yourself, and don't sacrifice." For managers and policy makers, this means that individual employees are all expendable. Any notion that organizations should care for their employees, or make long-term commitments to them, is seen as an anachronism, an impossible luxury. Translated to the individual level, the short-term orientation of the new global economy tends to undermine character, especially those qualities that bind people to each other and furnish the individual with a stable sense of self.

Under these conditions, the requirements for success in organizations make moral inversions and administrative evil all the more likely. Where once bureaucracy and stable lines of authority and routine were valued, today the emphasis is on flexibility and autonomous action. Corporations and governments want employees who can think on their feet and adroitly adjust to rapid change, but also want to retain the right (in the name of adaptability) to let these employees go at any time for the good of the organization. It would be a mistake to conclude, therefore, that more flexibility means more freedom for employees (as the song has it: Freedom's just another word for nothing left to lose). Instead, the move away from bureaucratic structure to more flexible forms of organization has replaced one structure of power and control with other, less visible forms of control and compliance (Barker, 1993). The threat of expendability and fear of social breakdown make people all the more prone to protect their self-interest rather than consider the implications of their actions for the well-being of others. The context these developments provide for ethics in public life is a difficult one.

The Prospects for Reconstructing Public Ethics

As the twenty-first century dawns, two trends seem clear. First, interdependence is greater than it has ever been—people's fates are deeply intertwined—and this is less recognized than ever; and second, social groups are more and more fractionated and fractious—socially centripetal forces are as powerful as they have ever been, with more surplus populations appearing, and being created, at the fringes of American society. We live in a time in the United States when politics has become more sharply partisan, when public discussion in many forums has degenerated well below hard-edged debate, when hyperpluralism underlines our differences perhaps beyond repair, and when the relentless pressure to entertain in the media has made even the somewhat thoughtful sound bite seem deliberative by comparison with the serial-monologue-by-interruption so common on television. Without the cohesion provided by a much greater sense of community, it is hard to see how American society can be kept from literally flying apart, except through coercive power and even public policies of elimination, the most perversely tempting technical-rational solution to social and political disorder (Rubenstein, 1975, 1983). As a response to serious social fragmentation and economic dislocation, an authoritarian America now seems to be in the realm of the possible, one in which the barriers to "final solutions" can all too easily fail. Many political, economic, and social responses to these conditions have been suggested from a wide variety of perspectives. However, any viable response must be plausible within the American political system of liberal democracy.

Liberal Democracy

Liberalism and democracy came together in the American founding period. A clear account of the marriage between the two appears in C.B. Macpherson's *The Life and Times of Liberal Democracy* (1977). The core values of classical liberalism are: individualism, the notion of rights (particularly to property), the sanctity of contracts, and the rule of law. Classical liberalism sets the philosophical foundation for American society, which allows for and encourages differential achievement by individuals. Democracy's chief value—equality—is often outweighed within this framework. Americans of the founding period lived, as we twenty-first century Americans do, in an order fraught with the tension between the liberal and the democratic traditions.

Democratic principles were a driving force in the American Revolution (Countryman, 1985). While political beliefs were widely divergent, there was widespread popular support for the democratic aims of the revolution; there had to be for the armies to be manned, and for the struggle to be successfully pressed against the British. What lingers decisively, however, is not a polity based on the revolutionary rhetoric, but the state that was built following the war during a time that has been appropriately called counterrevolutionary. The constitutional framework that was laid down during the founding period was formed far more from the principles of liberalism than those of democracy. The core value of the more democratic, revolutionary period—equality—was given a severe reduction in rank by the founding fathers. And the value of liberty—and its repository in the individual—was elevated and buttressed by law, by contract, and by right. The American liberal democracy is thus predominantly procedural—civil liberties, voting, fair procedures in decision making, and technical-rational policy making (Adams et al., 1990). Within the context of American liberal democracy, there appear to be two divergent scenarios in which public ethics will either flourish or wither.

Putting Cruelty First

"Putting cruelty first," our first scenario, is more apparent in American public life at the national level; it gives precedence to liberty within the pantheon of American political values, and offers a public ethics which at best provides a scant defense against administrative evil. This version of liberalism is perhaps best articulated by Judith Shklar in *Ordinary Vices* (1984), in which she advances a "liberalism of fear" predicated on the rather dismal track record of human beings, particularly in the twentieth century. Among the pantheon of human vices, including treachery, disloyalty, tyranny, dishonesty, and cruelty, Shklar argues for "putting cruelty first" (1984, 7–44). If our first consideration in public life is the cruelty that human beings all too often inflict on one another, our normal response is a healthy fear of cruelty, leading us to a liberalism of fear; one whose first and foremost mission is to avoid the worst excesses of state power run amok (Shklar, 1984, 5):

> Tolerance consistently applied is more difficult and morally more demanding than repression. Moreover, the liberalism of fear, which makes cruelty the first vice, quite rightly recognizes that fear reduces us to mere reactive units of sensation. . . . The alternative . . .; is . . .; between cruel military and moral repression and violence, and a self-restraining tolerance that fences in the powerful to protect the freedom and safety of every citizen, old or young, male or female, black or white.

A polity based on the liberalism of fear is focused on avoiding our worst proclivities. At the same time, it paradoxically makes strenuous ethical demands on citizens: "liberalism imposes extraordinary ethical difficulties on us: to live with contradictions, unresolvable conflicts, and balancing between public and private imperatives which are neither opposed to nor at one with each other" (Shklar, 1984, 249). In a liberalism of fear, into which we are prompted by our "ordinary vices" and by the forces of globalization, we are left utterly dependent on the development of the character of our citizens—too many bad characters and we lapse into the excesses of evil. Too much of an organized, systematic program by government or by religious or social institutions to reform character on a large, social scale, and we risk falling into evil through arrogance (Shklar, 1984, 39), "Nothing but cruelty comes from those who seek perfection and forget the little good that lies directly within their powers." It is just as easy to overreach as to underreach for character development within a liberalism of fear, leading to those cruel consequences which surely warrant our fear.

In this first scenario, one is left with a minimalist public ethics. Transparency becomes the chief principle, under the assumption that when people can see the worst excesses, they will respond to correct them. A system of laws and regulations that make public deliberations and decisions *visible* to the public becomes the pillar of public ethics. Along with a system of transparency, public ethics under a liberalism of fear would include a program of laws and regulations that set minimum floors below which we would not want to allow people's behavior to sink (in full knowledge and expectation that at least from time to time it will).

This is not a version of public ethics that inspires much optimism about future instances of administrative evil. The assumptions about human nature under a liberalism of fear are essentially misanthropic, anticipating the worst from human beings, having been given so little encouragement from the events of the twentieth century. Indeed, the difficulties of getting liberalism right, along with the corrosion of character exacerbated by globalization, suggest that administrative evil may well increase, perhaps even dramatically.

Deliberative Democracy

The second scenario for public ethics focuses on the democratic aspect of our political heritage—in particular, deliberative democracy—and has been more visible at the local level of our polity (Box, 1998; Chaskin, Brown, Venkatesh, and Vidal, 2001). In its most basic sense, deliberation is careful thought and discussion about issues and decisions. Deliberative processes comprise discussion and consideration by a group of persons of the reasons for and against a measure, or, put another way, consulting with others in a process of reaching a decision (Fishkin, 1991). According to Dryzek (2000), deliberation is a process of social inquiry in which participants seek to gain understanding of themselves and others, to learn and to persuade. Thus, one of the cornerstones of deliberative processes is the nature of the communication involved: participants strive to rise above win-lose exchange; over time, they may aspire to dialogue, and even to become a learning community (Yankelovich, 1999).

Participants in deliberative processes are expected to be open to change in their attitudes, ideas, and/or positions, although such change is not a required outcome of deliberation. It is a process that can, over time, grow citizens, fostering growth both in the capacity for practical judgment and in the art of living together in a context of disagreement—hence, a public ethics. As in a liberalism of fear, tolerance is elevated to a central virtue in public life.

Deliberative democracy insists on a meaningful role for citizens in public decisions, although sorting out which citizens and what decisions are appropriate for deliberation represent ongoing problems. There is a considerable theoretical literature on both deliberative democracy (Gutmann and Thompson, 1996; Dryzek, 1990) and deliberative governance (Forester, 1999; Hajer and Wagenaar, 2003; Fischer, 2000; deLeon, 1997). Deliberative processes have seen use at all levels of government (although mostly at the local level), and share in common involving citizens in public discussion and decision making (Dryzek and Torgerson, 1993). Insistence on "full" deliberation sets a very high standard that has been met only rarely, and then, only after multiple iterations.

A public ethics appropriate for deliberative democracy offers a possible alternative to the technical-rational approach to administrative ethics, and the associated complex of problems associated with administrative evil. Alasdair MacIntyre (1984) provided the groundbreaking work within this literature (also known as neo-Aristotelian, character, or virtue ethics). This tradition does not locate ethics in the autonomous individual, but within the community. That is, ethics emerges from the relational context within which people act—within the public square.

The process of building a community, in this case, an inclusive, democratic community, develops public life and public ethics at the same time. As detailed by Deborah Stone, a political community has the following characteristics (1988, 25):

It is a community;
It has a public interest, if only an idea about which people will fight;
Most of its policy problems are common problems;
Influence is pervasive, and the boundary between influence and coercion is always contested;
Cooperation is as important as competition;
Loyalty is the norm;
Groups and organizations are the building blocks;
Information is interpretive, incomplete, and strategic;
It is governed by the laws of passion as well as of matter; and
Power, derivative of all those elements, coor dinates individual intentions and actions into collective purposes and results.

Publicness is a key aspect in this development as Ventriss (1993, 201) notes: "A public, therefore, is a community of citizens who attempt to understand the substantive interdependency of social and political issues on the community, and who maintain a critical perspective on the ethical implications of governmental policy making." In this view, it would be unethical for public servants *not* to speak publicly to policy issues. As citizen professionals and administrators in a democratic community, they would have a special responsibility to guard against policies and practices that might engender eruptions of administrative evil.

This critical and active citizenship is a key aspect of building a viable deliberative democracy. Camilla Stivers (1993, 441) has articulated the following characteristics of democratic citizenship:

The exercise of authoritative power, using sound judgment and relying on practical knowledge of the situation at hand;
The exercise of virtue, or concern for the public interest, defined substantively in particular contexts through reasoned discourse;
The development of personal capacities for governance through their exercise in practical activity;
The constitution of community through deliberation about issues of public concern;
In summary, then, active citizenship means participation in governance; the exercise of decisive judgment in the public interest, an experience that develops the political and moral capacities of individuals and solidifies the communal ties among them.

Deliberative democracy clearly makes demands on individuals, and on individuals acting together in the public interest. It views exclusion and nonparticipation in public life as major problems in and of themselves. Public policies based on exclusion and exploitation are entirely inimical to a deliberative democracy because they "weaken the community by undermining the civic bonds that unify it, while eroding the political process by converting what should be a dialogue between fellow citizens into a repressive hierarchy" (Farber, 1994, 929). This of course is precisely what occurred in Nazi Germany. Under the rhetoric of a unified community, the Nazis' racist and exclusionary policies created a polity held together not by civic bonds but by the terror of the concentration camps (Gellately, 2001; Sofsky, 1997).

A public ethics within a deliberative democracy would require that professionals and administrators be attentive to social and economic outcomes of public policy, as well as to their proper and faithful implementation. Public servants could not ethically implement a policy that was overtly detrimental to the well-being of any segment of the population. It would be unethical, for example, to cooperate with cutting off disability benefits to legal immigrants, many of whom are elderly and are likely to wind up malnourished and/or homeless. Such a policy amounts to defining this group as a surplus population, and an ethical public service cannot be complicit in that sort of public policy.

Cruelty, Deliberation, and Administrative Evil

Within our liberal democratic polity, at least these two versions of public ethics can be imagined. The first, based on a liberalism of fear, stems from an essentially misanthropic view of human nature: We have repeatedly seen the worst from human beings, and we should expect no better. In this scenario, we should understand that only a minimalist public ethics can be expected to be workable, but even more importantly, we must beware the arrogance of a public ethics based on grand designs about human perfectability—for such designs are the well-traveled avenues to those horrific eruptions of evil that we have seen throughout human history, and especially in the last century.

The second version, based on deliberative democracy, while not blind to human vices, including cruelty, does assume that we humans can—with hard work and great vigilance—do better. In this scenario, we can strengthen our public life and our public ethics through the rigor and tribulations of deliberative processes. This is not an easy road; not only does it risk arrogance and a concomitant descent into evil, but it assumes more—perhaps far more—than we have yet achieved. Yet it does have the considerable attraction of imagining a future that can hope for fewer lapses into administrative evil.

Regardless of which assumptions about human nature one holds—and which version of public ethics one thus finds persuasive—no human communities, even deliberative and democratic ones, offer any guarantees against administrative evil. And they certainly offer no escape from evil itself, which remains a part of the human condition. Still, one might hope—perhaps without lapsing into fantasy—that administrative evil may not be so easily masked in deliberative democratic communities. And public servants might not so easily wear the mask of administrative evil when their role entails a critically reflexive sense of the context of public affairs, and a duty to educate and build an inclusive and active citizenry. Our argument in this book thus offers no easy or sentimental solutions; offers no promise of making anything better; but only offers an inevitably small and fragile bulwark against things going really wrong—those genuinely horrific eruptions of evil that modernity has exacerbated very nearly beyond our willingness to comprehend.

> Do not despair. You need not worry so much about the future of civilization, for mankind has not yet risen so far, that he has so very far to fall.
>
> —*Sigmund Freud, Vienna, the 1920s (personal recollection of Raul Hilberg)*

References

Adams, G. B. et al. (1990). "Joining purpose to practice." In H. D. Kass & B. L. Catron, *Images and identities in public administration* (pp. 219–240). Newbury Park, CA: Sage.

Balfour, D. L., & J. W. Grubbs. (2000). "Character, corrosion, and the civil servant: The human consequences of globalization and the new public management." *Administrative Theory and Praxis*, 22, 570–584.

Barker, J. R. (1993). "Tightening the iron cage: Coercive control in self-managing." *Administrative Science Quarterly*, 38, 408–437.

Bauman, Z. (1999). *In search of politics*. Stanford, CA: Stanford University Press.

Bentham, J. (1989). *Vice and virtue in everyday life*. New York: Harcourt, Brace, Jovanovich (original work published 1789).

Box, R. C. (1998). *Citizen governance: Leading American cities in the 21st century*. Thousand Oaks, Ca: Sage.

Brecht, A. (1944). *Prelude to Silence*. New York: Oxford University Press.

Browning, C. (1989). "The Decision Concerning the Final Solution." In F. Furet (Ed.), *Unanswered Questions: Nazi Germany and the Genocide of the Jews* (pp. 96–118). New York: Schocken.

Chaskin R. L. et al. (2001). *Building community capacity*. New York: Aldine.

Cooper, T. L. (1991). *An ethic of citizenship for public administration*. Englewood Cliffs, NJ: Prentice Hall.

Countryman, E. (1985). *The American revolution*. New York: Hill and Wang.

Dryzek, J. (1990). *Discursive democracy: Politics, policy, and political science*. Cambridge: Cambridge University Press.

Dryzek, K., & D. Torgerson. (1993). "Democracy and the policy sciences: A progress report." *Policy Sciences*, 26, 127–149.

Farber, D. A. (1994). "The outmoded debate over affirmative action." *California Law Review, 82*, 893–934.

Finer, H. (1941). "Administrative responsibility in democratic government." *Public Administration Review, 1*, 335–350.

Fishkin, J. S. (1991). *Democracy and deliberation*. New Haven, CT: Yale University Press.

Frankena, W. (1973). *Ethics* (2nd ed.). Englewood Cliffs, NJ: Prentice Hall.

Friedman, T. (1999). *The lexus and the olive tree*. New York: Farrar, Strauss and Giroux.

Friedrich, C. J. (1940). "Public policy and the nature of administrative responsibility." In C. J. Friedrich & E. S. Mason (Eds.), *Public Policy* (pp. 221–245). Cambridge, MA: Harvard University Press.

Fritz, M. (1999). *Lost on earth: Nomads of the new world*. Boston: Little Brown.

Fukuyama, F. (1992). *The end of history and the last man*. New York: Free Press.

Gellately, R. (2001). *Backing Hitler: Consent and coercion in Nazi Germany*. New York: Oxford University Press.

Gutman, A., & D. F. Thompson. (1996). *Democracy and disagreement*. Cambridge, MA: Harvard University Press.

Haile, P. (1969). *Cruelty*. Middletown, CT: Wesleyan University Press.

Harmon, M. M. (1995). *Responsibility as paradox: A critique of rational discourse on government*. Thousand Oaks, CA: Sage.

Hart, D. K. (1984). "The virtuous citizen, the honorable bureaucrat and public administration." *Public Administration Review, 44*, 111–120.

Hilberg, R. (1989). "The bureaucracy of annihilation." In Furet (Ed.), *Unanswered questions: Nazi Germany and the genocide of the Jews*. (pp. 119–133). New York: Schocken.

Hirschman, A. (1970). *Exit, voice, and loyalty*. Cambridge, MA: Harvard University Press.

Huntington, S. (1996). *The clash of civilizations and the remaking of the world order*. New York: Touchstone.

Kant, I. (1959). *Metaphysical foundations of morals*. Indianapolis, IN: Bobbs-Merrill.

Kass, H. D. (1990). "Stewardship as a fundamental element in images of public administration." In H. D. Kass & B. L. Catron (Eds.), *Image and identity in public administration*. Newbury Park, CA: Sage.

Keeley, M. (1983). Values in organizational theory and management education." *Academy of Management Review 8*(3): 376–386.

Ladd, J. (1970). "Morality and the ideal of rationality in organizations." *The Monist, 54*, 488–516.

Lifton, R. J. (1986). *The Nazi doctors: medical killing and the psychology of genocide*. New York: Basic Books.

Lowi, T. J. (1993). "Legitimizing public administration: a disturbed dissent." *Public Administration Review*, 53, 261–264.

Lozowick, Y. (2000). *Hitler's bureaucrats: The Nazi security police and the banality of evil* New York: Continuum.

MacIntyre, A. (1984). *After virtue* (2nd ed.). Notre Dame, IN: University of Notre Dame Press.

Macpherson, C. B. (1977). *The life and times of liberal democracy*. New York: Oxford University Press.

Milgram, S. (1974). *Obedience to authority*. New York: Harper and Row.

Morgan, D. G. (1990). "Administrative phronesis: Discretion and the problem of administration legitimacy in our constitutional system." In H. D. Kass & B. L. Catron (Eds.), *Image and identity in public administration*. Newbury Park, CA: Sage.

Rohr, J. A. (1978). E*thics for bureaucrats*. New York: Marcel Dekker.

Robenstein, R. L. (1975). *The cunning of history: The Holocaust and the American future*. New York: Harper and Row.

Sassen, S. (1998). *Globalization and its discontents*. New York: Free Press.

Sennett, R. (1998). *The corrosion of character; the personal consequences of work in the new capitalism*. New York: W.W. Norton.

Shkal, J. N. *Ordinary vices*. Cambridge, MA: Harvard University Press.

Simon, H. A. (1976). *Administrative behavior*. New York: Free Press.

Sofsky, W. (1997). *The order of terror: The concentration camp*. Princeton, NJ: Princeton University Press.

Stivers, C. (1993). "Citizenship ethics in public administration." In T. L. Cooper (Ed.), *Handbook of administrative ethics* (pp. 435–455). New York: Marcel Dekker.

Stone, D. A. (1988). *Policy paradox and political reason*. New York: Harper Collins.

Terry, L. D. (1995). *Leadership of public bureaucracies: The administrator as conservator*. Thousand Oaks, CA: Sage.

Thompson, D. F. (1985). "The possibility of administrative ethics." *Public Administration Review, 45*, 555–561.

Trow, M. (1997, May 16). "The chiefs of public universities should be civil servants, not political actors." *Chronicle of Higher Education*, p. A48.

Yankelovich, D. (1999). *The magic of dialogue: Transforming conflict into cooperation*. NewYork: Simon and Schuster.

48

Inside Collaborative Networks: Ten Lessons for Public Managers

Robert Agranoff

It is time to go beyond heralding the importance of networks as a form of collaborative public management and look inside their operations. At this point in the development of the field, it is well known (1) that "the age of the network" has arrived (Lipnack and Stamps 1994), (2) that hierarchy and markets are being supplemented by networks (Powell 1990), (3) that public managers are enmeshed in a series of collaborative horizontal and vertical networks (Agranoff and McGuire 2003), and (4) that networks need to be treated seriously in public administration (O'Toole 1997). If this form of organizing is so important to public managers, why not study it in the same sense that hierarchical organization or human resources or the budget process is examined? That is what this article addresses, taking a deeper look into how public networks are organized and how they are managed. It offers some empirically based experiences, addressing 10 important features of collaborative management.

The issues raised here are based on a study of the operations of 14 public management networks in the central states, comprising federal, state, regional, and local government officials and nongovernmental managers—that is, officers from nonprofits, for-profits, universities, and other organizations (Agranoff, forthcoming). Such networks can be chartered (organized by some formal mechanism as an intergovernmental agreement or by statutory action) or nonchartered (informal in legal status but equally permanent, organized, and mission oriented). These networks are interorganizational (Alter and Hage 1998) and should be distinguished from social networks, which involve "studied nodes linked by social relationships" (Laumann, Galaskiewicz, and Marsden 1978) or recurring relationships (Nohria 1992), both within and outside organizations, for which there is an already developed rich tradition (Burt 1992; Granovetter 1973; White 1992). Public management networks are, in every sense, collaborative connections like social networks, although they not only comprise representatives of disparate organizations but also go beyond analytical modes. They are real-world public entities.

The frequently used term *network* (broadcast, supply service, professional, friendship) needs to be further defined. A term is required that fits the activity of cooperation or mutual action without being so broad that it encompasses every human connection. *Cooperation* refers to the act of working jointly with others, usually to resolve a problem or find a corner of activity. It can be occasional or regular, and it can occur within, between, or outside formal organizations. Here the interest is focused on the activities of individuals who represent organizations working across their boundaries. Agranoff and McGuire define such collaborative management processes as "the process of facilitating and operating in multi organizational arrangements to solve problems that cannot be solved, or solved easily, by single organizations" (2003, 4). In other words, the focus of public management networks goes beyond studies of informal and intraorganizational networking among individuals to include interorganizational—in this case, intergovernmental—entities that emerge from interactions among formal organizations. These bodies, according to the literature, tackle the most nettlesome of public problems (O'Toole 1997) and "connect public policies with their strategic and institutionalized context" (Kickert, Klijn and Koppenjan 1997, 1).

Ten practical suggestions emanating from a larger study of public management networks are offered here. Readers who wish to gain deeper insights into the workings of such networks will have to go beyond the limited pages of this overview. The issues are empirically derived from

---

Source: Reprinted with permission from Public Administration Review.

a grounded theory methodology (Strauss and Corbin 1998). In other words, it is an inductive study in which the theoretical findings emanate from field-based data. Thus, the methodology places heavy emphasis on the responses of the public managers themselves. Extended discussions were undertaken in the field on two separate occasions with more than 150 public officials, in addition to field observation and examination of network documentation. In essence, the managerial lessons that follow come from the managers themselves. Hopefully, these insights will not only contribute to the collaborative management literature but also will be of use to those who practice this form of management.

Lesson 1: The network is not the only vehicle of collaborative management. Networking is a buzzword around public organizations these days that signifies social networking, within-organization lateral relationships, and a host of other collaborative endeavors. When it comes to cross-organization contacts, the managers in the study related that work within the network represents just one of several collaborative contacts.

Foremost among these contacts are informal bilateral linkages with representatives of other organizations. These used to be face-to-face and telephone contacts, but now e-mail allows for nonsimultaneous contact. Managers continue to spend a lot of effort on one-on-one relationships with those in other organizations. In addition, one must remember that many local governments, nonprofits, and for-profits are bilaterally linked with state and federal agencies through grants, contracts, or cooperative agreements. In some cases, these collaborative efforts are multilateral, involving three or more entities. There are also interagency agreements among organizations within the same government. These can be either bilateral or multilateral. At the interlocal level, there are a host of mutual service, compact, assumption of service, and other arrangements that will be familiar to those who study local governments (Walker 2000).

This is not to say that networks are unimportant vehicles of collaboration. They bring many organizations to the table. They are, as we will see, important vehicles for resource pooling, mutual exploration, and knowledge creation. Most importantly, networks open up new possibilities that would be hard for one, two, or even three organizations working together to achieve. But they are not the be-all and end-all of collaborative management. They share a place—in many cases, a small place—alongside literally thousands of interagency agreements, grants, contracts, and even informal contacts that involve issues such as seeking information or some form of program adjustment (Agranoff and McGuire 2003).

Lesson 2: Managers continue to do the bulk of their work within the hierarchy. A familiar refrain is that networks are replacing hierarchies (Castells 1996; Koppenjan and Klijn 2004). Although it is certainly true that mutual dependency is leading to an increasing number of horizontal relationships crossing many boundaries, lateral connections seem to overlay the hierarchy rather than act as a replacement for them. According to the managers in the study, there is a premium on the ability to understand and function across boundaries, but this skill has not necessarily replaced the need for internal skills.

When asked, most managers said that they spent most of their time working within the hierarchy. There seemed to be a sort of consensus that only 15 percent to 20 percent of their total work time was consumed by all forms of collaborative activity, including their participation in networks. The typical public management network meets as a body monthly or quarterly, and focused project or workgroup efforts usually involve no more than five to seven hours per month. The managers reported that the rest of their time was filled with various nonnetwork (e.g., bilateral) collaboration. "Most of my work is still in planning, budgeting and human resources, like my other counterparts in _____," said one agency head. Another said, "In my agency I am the orchestra leader, dealing with all of the tasks of a public agency. In _____, I am just one player, and a part-time one at that."

This does not include the growing number of boundary spanners or program specialists who are involved in networks and thus spend somewhat more time on collaboration. Program specialists frequently (and more naturally) work across agency boundaries. Their work is technical or based on specialized knowledge, and it is geared to solving problems, belonging to epistemic communities, and acting on shared beliefs. For example, developmental disabilities professionals inside and outside government in one public management network reported spending considerably more time solving overlapping problems with clients, services, and funding. "We have worked together so long and so much that now we finish one another's sentences," explained one longtime advocacy association specialist. Professionals working on problems seem to form these epistemic communities naturally and reach across boundaries for routine as well as program interagency accommodation (Thomas 2003), and thus they spend more time in collaboration.

The same held true for the few administrators in the study who were full-time boundary spanners. For example, one administrator in the Nebraska State Game and Fish Commission related that his entire job involved acting as a liaison with environmental agencies and bodies, along with those dealing with rural development. Another federal official with the Economic Development Administration was the sole staff person for two midwestern states. He spent most of his time in the field working with local governments or economic development groups, along with collaborative efforts with other federal and state agencies.

For the line administrator, however, it is largely business as usual most of the time, dealing with internal POSDCORB matters, along with increasing collaborative pressures. Of course, as external connections increase, there will be more internal work related to outside-agency contacts.

Lesson 3: Network involvement brings several advantages that keep busy administrators involved. One clear observation is that sustained collaborative activity, such as that of ongoing networks, must demonstrate worth or busy managers will not waste their time on participation. The networks in this study were not all without stability threats, but all had been ongoing for a considerable period of time. The oldest, an Ohio-based public management network that assisted small communities with their water-supply and wastewater problems, dated back to the late 1980s. This was no easy accomplishment, inasmuch as this network was nonchartered. Why do bodies such as these persist? Because they deliver different forms of public value to their multiple participants.

Performance counts in collaborative activity. But the type of result is not completely tied to making the type of policy adjustments mentioned at the beginning of this article. Actually, networks can perform a great many public service purposes. They not only bring many parties to the table but also have the potential to expand the resource base. The most important element of the resource base is the potential for knowledge expansion, a function that administrators said was indispensable. From knowledge comes the possibility of new solutions derived by, owned, and implemented by several parties. Finally, many managers related that a great deal of one-to-one networking went on in and around network activities, "reducing telephone and e-mail tag," as the saying goes.

The key to sustained network involvement is performance, and the key to performance is adding public value (Moore 1995) by working together rather than separately (Bardach 1998, 8). In the 14 public management networks studied, four types of public value were queried, and managers found substantial benefits in each dimension. The first benefit is the value added to the manager or professional, such as learning new ways to collaborate, intergovernmental skills, and how to network, along with enhanced technical and information and communications technology skills. Second are the benefits accruing to the home agency, such as access to other agencies' information, programs and resources; access to information and communications technology; cross-training of agency staff; and most important, enhanced external input into the internal knowledge base. Third are the collective process skills that accrue from working together over a sustained period of time—for example, developing interagency planning, piloting an adaptation of a new technology, developing a mutual interagency culture that leads to subsequent problem solving, and experimenting with electronic group decision technology. Fourth are the concrete results accrued, such as an action plan, a capability building conference, new interagency strategies, and multiagency policy and program changes. These types of value-adding performance results sustain administrators' efforts in collaborative undertakings.

Lesson 4: Networks are different from organizations but not completely different. When managers become involved in these emergent collectives, they find an interesting mixture of old and new practices. Yes, networks are different in the sense that they are non-hierarchical, players at the table begin largely equal as organizational representatives, most actions are discussed and decided by consensus, resources are multi-sourced, and there are relatively few sanctions for withdrawal. But networks are not different in the sense that they require some form of organization, operating rules, routines, and so on. Most have stated missions, goals, and objectives to frame their type of organization, which, in many ways, look more like the structures of nonprofit organizations than those of large bureaucracies.

Virtually all of the 14 networks studied operated with some form of council or board, elected by the entire body of agency representatives, very much like the board of directors of a nonprofit organization. Normally, the various sectors (federal, state, nonprofit, for-profit) or identified interests (universities, regional agencies) have a seat at the table, but these bodies rarely do the work beyond strategic planning and final approval of projects and efforts. The real work in all of the networks studied was done in either standing committees (e.g., finance, technology transfer, tele-medicine, educational applications, transportation technical review) or focused and usually shorter-term workgroups (e.g., ortho-infrared mapping, bicycle and pedestrian, broadband usage, community visitation, water and wastewater treatment). Such bodies, of course, resemble the standing committees and task forces of nonprofits in that their participation is voluntary, they reach out to expertise inside and outside the network wherever it can be found, and they generally try to reach agreement on technical merits and possibilities without hierarchical involvement.

There is thus much less difference between organizations and networks than initially appears, particularly when one accounts for the fact that hierarchical organizations themselves are changing. It is an accepted fact that bureaucratic structures have become more flexible and permeable over the past century (Clegg 1990, 181). Today's organizations are becoming more *conductive*—that is, they are continuously generating and renewing capabilities, bearing in mind the alignment between internal forces and external demands, including the importance of creating partnerships through internal–external interaction, building alliances and coalitions, forming and reforming teams across functions and organization boundaries, and collaborating to actively manage interdependencies (Saint-Onge and Armstrong 2004, 191). In this sense, perhaps bureaucracies and standing networks appear a good deal alike because both need to be concerned with managing complex partnerships, with blurring boundaries. The difference is that one structures and creates rules and strategies under the umbrella of one organization, whereas the other must interorganizationally and collectively create structures, rules, and strategies that fit their multiorganizarional needs.

Lesson 5: Not all networks make the types of policy and program adjustments ascribed to them in the literature. There are many public value benefits of collaboration, and not all of them fall neatly into the "solving nettlesome interagency problems" domain. When asked how they were able to forge agreement and arrive at a mutually beneficial course of action, managers from a number of networks related that they did not really engage in that type of activity. Subsequent investigation revealed that actually there were four different types of networks among the 14.

Three networks proved to be *informational*, wherein partners came together almost exclusively to exchange agency policies and programs, technologies, and potential solutions. Any changes or actions were voluntarily taken up by the agencies themselves. Another four networks were *developmental*, wherein partner information and technical exchange were combined with education and member services that increased the members' capacities to implement solutions within their home agencies and organizations. Another three networks were identified as *outreach,* wherein the activities of the developmental network were engaged; in addition, however, they also blueprinted strategies for program and policy change that led to an exchange or coordination of resources, although decision making and implementation were ultimately left to the agencies and programs themselves. Finally, four networks were *action* networks, wherein partners came together to make interagency adjustments, formally adopt collaborative courses of action, and deliver services, along with information exchanges and enhanced technology capability.

The fact that informational and developmental networks do hot become directly involved in program and policy adjustments does not make them any less public management networks. The study of collaborative management is relatively recent, and no public sector interagency body should be bound by preconceived or deductive research frameworks or definitions. They are every bit collaborative, public-serving bodies. Moreover, their actions often indirectly lead to subsequent strategies, adjustments, programs and policies. Indeed, there may well be more types of networks and collaborative structures—equally successful—waiting to be discovered. Like other aspects of collaboration, the typology suggests that networks must be analyzed with an open mind.

Lesson 6: Collaborative decisions or agreements are the products of a particular type of mutual learning and adjustment. Despite a form of organization that resembles a nonprofit organization, networks rarely follow parliamentary procedure. First, because all networks do not really make decisions, it is preferable to refer to many of their deliberative processes as "reaching agreements" rather than "decisions," as the latter normally connotes the action of implementation. In collaborative bodies, decisions and agreements are necessarily based on consensus, inasmuch as participating administrators and professionals are partners, not superior–subordinates. As such, they are co-conveners, co-strategists, co–action formulators, co-programmers, and so on. It is also true that public agency administrators possess neither ultimate legal authority (except of course, within one's home agency domain) nor control over all technical information. Authority in the network is shared with the many stakeholders at the table: other administrators, program specialists, research scientists, policy researchers, and interest group and advocacy association officials. Among the partners, it is unlikely that any single agency or representative at the table will have the legal authority or financial resources to completely approach a problem. Finally, the all-important potential for agency-based implementation for most collaborative solutions lies not in the network itself or in any one agency or program but among the many.

Collaborative decision making and agreement are no doubt similar to the functions of knowledge-seeking workgroups within single organizations (Newell et al. 2002). Consensus prevails over motions and voting. For example, one study participant related, "We have Robert's rules in our by-laws, but only use them after we have reached agreement." Another network chair said, "Parliamentary procedure rules won't work—as a last resort when we are near consensus we may resort to informal Robert's rules to move things along." The learning process is clearly and directly a parallel component of network decisions. "Once we agree that a problem is an issue we care to look into, we study it and discuss the results before any action is taken," reported one participant. "We try to get on the same technical page if we possibly can. That means someone or a work group has to study a problem, then we discuss it," said another. "Our Technology Transfer Committee is charged with finding feasible small town water solutions used elsewhere; they then become the basis of Steering Committee discussions." Finally, one manager interviewed commented, "The Transportation Technical Committee is charged not only with looking at the feasibility of projects, but to advance state-of-the-art [transportation] programming to the Policy Committee agenda." These comments from the discussants highlight the centrality of making the network a learning entity in the sense of Senge's (1990) learning organization. One can then characterize the typical network decision-making process as involving joint learning that leads to brokered consensus.

Most importantly, this process is oriented toward creating a collective power of new possibilities. In a confusing, complicated world in which institutional arrangements are loosely arranged, "The issue is to bring about enough cooperation among disparate community elements to get things done" (Stone et al. 1999, 354). In order to open up new possibilities, the networks studied used six distinct predecision or agreement learning strategies. They prepared for brokered consensus through (1) group discussion or exchange of ideas; (2) political negotiation of sensitive concerns and intensely felt needs; (3) direct application of technology or preestablished decision rules or formats; (4) application of preestablished, formulaic procedures (e.g., those related to regulations, grants, or loans); (5) data-driven decisions or agreements (e.g., market studies, usage patterns, traffic or accident counts); and (6) predecision simulation or electronic base groupware or other decision techniques. The informational and developmental networks tended to be involved in the first two categories exclusively—discussion and exchange and political negotiation—whereas the outreach and action networks engaged many of the six. In all, public management networks probably do not make decisions all that differently from the internal processes of learning organizations, but organizational boundaries must be acknowledged through what one could characterize as partner respect or nonhierarchical behavior.

Lesson 7: The most distinctive collaborative activity of all of the networks proved to be their work in public sector knowledge management. In our contemporary information-based society, work is increasingly knowledge based, but substantial gaps in knowledge led each public management network to seek more and, in the process, somehow manage this commodity. "Knowledge is a fluid mix of framed experience, values, contextual information, and expert insight that provides a framework for evaluating and incorporating new experiences and information" (Davenport and Prusak 2000, 5). Whereas data refer to discrete, objective facts, and information is a message in the form of a document or an audible or visual communication, knowledge is more action oriented, both in process and in outcome. Knowledge management has two dimensions: explicit knowledge, which can be codified and communicated easily in words, numbers, charts, or drawings, and tacit knowledge, which is embedded in the senses, individual perceptions, physical experiences, intuition, and rules of thumb (Saint-Onge and Armstrong 2004). Knowledge management is the process of bringing together explicit and tacit knowledge and displaying and manifesting it, "as it involves skilled performance, i.e., KM [knowledge management] praxis is 'punctuated through social interaction'" (Tsoukas 2005, 158–59).

In the networks studied, the process of knowledge management in many ways defined the major focus of their standing committees and working groups. First, essentially all of them began by surveying the universe of data and information that their partners had developed or could access, plus external databases of use to them. Second, this information then used to develop their "own source" explicit knowledge using resources such as libraries, map inventories, strategic plans, fact sheets and policy guides, focused studies, surveys, conferences and workshops, electronic bulletin boards, process reviews, long-range plans, models and simulations, and market studies. Third, tacit knowledge was rarely formally codified, but it was regularly approached through stakeholder consultations, best practices booklets, workgroups as "communities of practice," study project report panels, expert presentations, specialized workshops, SWOT workshops, hands-on technical assistance, community leadership development sessions, forums on "what works," direct agency outreach, help desks, and public hearings. Fourth, the networks tried to organize the explicit/tacit interface not through codification but through informal feedback on the myriad of knowledge management activities in which they engaged, usually through some informal post-project assessment or at its board or steering committee meetings. Fifth, most of the networks directly served some of the knowledge management needs of their partner agencies by producing formal reports, responding to data requests, supplying modeling and planning data, circulating policy reports, sponsoring in-agency forums and report sessions, providing technical expert linkages between the network and specific agencies, and in some cases, providing agency-requested studies.

All of these knowledge management activities are now supported by the use of information and communications technology, such as e-mail, teleconferencing, Web-based geographic information systems, decision-support software, and the like. These are essential for partners that are situated in disparate organizational locations, although they are no substitute for face-to-face communication, the normal mode of detailed knowledge management work. In the same way that organizations seek structured predictability, networks try to use their open-ended processes of coordinating purposeful individuals who can apply their unique skills and experiences to the local problem confronting the collaborative undertaking (Tsoukas 2005, 111). They are part of the distributed knowledge systems that are created across boundaries, possessing somewhat fewer constraints or rule-bound actions and approaching those problems beyond the scope of any one agency.

Lesson 8: Despite the cooperative spirit and aura of accommodation in collaborative efforts, networks are not without conflicts and power issues. These concerns became quite evident when the networks' agreements and actions were broken down. Collaborative management, with its joint learning, consensus, and mutual accommodation orientation, may be assumed to be all hugs and kisses as the group sits in the "hot tub" of small groups, contemplates, becomes mellow, and somehow agrees. In fact, a number of the networks participants studied reported that many of their challenges related to conflicts among partners.

For example, the Darby Partnership, an informational watershed network in central Ohio, almost fell apart when some of its members supported a congressional bill to make the Darby Creek a national wildlife refuge. The wildlife refuge was so divisive that it impeded the partnerships efforts to exchange ideas about the environmental status and remediation efforts in the watershed. Likewise, the Iowa Geographic Information Council struggled for more than two years with the state of Iowa's chief information officer. The officer was unwilling to support the council's efforts to recruit a field technical officer to help local governments access the geographic information system. The Kentucky-Indiana Planning and Development Agency had to deal with major conflict over the siting of a second bridge over the Ohio River into the city of Louisville. After years of conflict, two bridges were proposed (city/suburban), displacing many other local transportation improvements.

These "mega-conflicts," so to speak, illustrate the point that all is not harmony in collaboration. Numerous mini-conflicts occur over agency turf, the contribution of resources, staff time devoted to the network, the location of meetings and conferences, and most importantly, threats of withdrawal because of frustration over the time and effort expended to achieve results. These are the more or less hidden aspects or the other side of collaboration,

Also hidden is the issue of power within networks. Some look at policy networks as coequal, interdependent, patterned relationships (Klijn 1996). On the other hand, it appears that different actors can occupy different role positions and carry different weights, creating unequal opportunity contexts and filling "structural holes" (Burt 1992, 67), whereas others may be less willing or able players. Indeed, Clegg and Hardy conclude that "[We] cannot ignore the façade of 'trust' and the rhetoric of 'collaboration' used to promote vested interests through the manipulation and capitulation by weaker partners" (1996, 679). It is also possible that this type of "power over" exists alongside the "power to," depicted earlier as the power of possibility. In fact, both are at work in networks and other collaborative enterprises. Indeed, both types proved to be the case in the 14 public management networks studied.

In fact, the two dimensions of power were manifest in a complex power structure found in each network. Beyond the formal structure of the governing body and working committees and groups were four elements of power. First, virtually every network had a *champion* (and in two cases, two champions)—a visible, powerful, and prestigious public agency head or nonprofit chief executive officer who organizes or sustains the network. The presence of the champion in the network signaled to others in the field to "stay in" and "cooperate." Second, there was a *political core*, normally comprising the primary participating department heads or federal government state directors and chief executive officers of the nongovernmental organizations. These managers tended to be part of the governance structure, they sent a message to other participants that the network was important to be involved with, and they were the people who were most likely to be involved in high-level interagency negotiations and resource accommodations. Third, there was a *technical core*, primarily workgroup or committee activists who knew the most about a particular topic (e.g., watershed management, planning, geographic information systems, finance, regulation, information and communications technology, and so on). Because a great deal of the work was bound up investigating problems, creating knowledge, and looking for feasible solutions, their work was at the core of network activity, and the most knowledgeable of these individuals held considerable operating power. Finally, there were paid staff who held the network together through their support efforts, which in the 14 networks ranged from one or two persons who devoted to the network full time to 18 full- or part-time participants in one action network. Because staff orchestrated all of the work—arrangements, negotiations, technical—they had a foot in every phase of the operations and, in their own way, hold considerable sway over network's work. This power structure is deep, and the four dimensions overlap in practice—it is every bit as real as those in the organizations from which representatives are drawn.

Lesson 9: Networks have their collaborative costs, as well as their benefits. If managers give up or add to the job of internal operations to engage in cooperation, they obviously do this at some cost. To most managers, the most primary costs are related to giving up agency authority or turf and giving up agency resources (Bardach 1998). Many line managers are said to be protective of agency autonomy for one of four reasons: (1) the agency manager knows best, and therefore should carry out its mission and programs; (2) loss of autonomy is associated with the loss of control and guidance of the agency; (3) people place a greater value on losses than on gains; and (4) autonomy reduces uncertainty (Thomas 2003, 33–34). In the study, these turf questions existed, but they were not foremost because most managers thought they had sufficient control over their own organizations and that the collaborative work of the network rarely cut into their core missions. Most managers felt they had ultimate policy control. Resource contributions were somewhat different. For the informational and developmental networks, the only resources contributed involved staff time and information, which normally come at a low or marginal cost. The other networks did have to yield resources for the cause, but when the partners could see their contribution to the larger issue or cause, they felt they could make such contributions. The only problematic issue occurred when resources were withheld.

There were, however, other real costs associated with network participation that the managers and professionals articulated. Six general cost categories were indicated: (1) time and opportunity costs lost to the home agency as a result of network involvement; (2) time and energy costs resulting from the protracted decision-making process, based on nonhierarchical, multiorganizational, multicultural human relations processes; (3) agreements not reached because of the exertion of organizational power or the withholding of power; (4) network gravitation toward consensus-based, risk-aversive decision agendas; (5) resource "hoarding," or agencies' failure or unwillingness to contribute needed resources; and (6) public policy barriers embedded in legislation, coupled with legislators' or other policy makers' unwillingness to make needed changes, which, in turn, frustrated collaborative decisions. All of these appear to thwart progress within networks.

In the literature, there has been less emphasis on the costs than on the benefits of collaborative efforts. Because the seven costs identified here (turf plus the six drawn from the study) do not nearly exhaust the list, more emphasis must be placed on this dimension. For public managers, they are as real as the benefits.

Lesson 10: Networks alter the boundaries of the state only in the most marginal ways; they do not appear to be replacing public bureaucracies in any way. Just as some assert that networks are replacing hierarchies, there are those who believe that collaborative structures such as networks are pushing out the traditional role of government to include a host of nongovernmental decision makers. Have the boundaries of government changed? Rhodes (1997) refers to the multiple influences of complex networks, among other forces, as differentiating the British polity. Loughlin's (2000) analysis of European regionalism suggests that the transformation from a welfare state to a liberal state to a communitarian state has transformed government into an enabling state in which decentralized public—private partnerships, among other forces, are diminishing governments' hold. Frederickson (1999) points to the increasing disarticulation of the state, where there is an increasing gap between jurisdiction and program management.

Most of the managers and other partners studied felt this to be true, but only to a limited extent. To a degree, the deliberations of the network and the involvement of nongovernmental organizations clearly influenced the courses of action taken by government, and in some cases, new programs and strategies emanated from network deliberations. But the partners were quick to point out three large caveats. First when it comes to policy decisions, it is almost always the public institutions that make the ultimate call, and in the case of implementation, it is the agency. Second, in virtually every public management network, it is government administrators at federal, state, and local levels who are the core or among the core actors in the network. They are able to inject legislative, regulatory, and financial considerations right into the network mix, which hardly marginalizes them.

Third, many collaborative efforts outside the network form are more tightly controlled by the government, in the form of grant expectations, contract provisions, or loan conditions, tying the nongovernmental organization to the public agency in a tighter way. One might also add that for informational and developmental networks, there is hardly any governmental scope at issue, at least in any direct form. In fact, in most cases, even the outreach and action strategic networks worked on a rather narrow scope of issues—federal transportation funding, educational broadcast policies, rates for use of the state Web portal—or strategies that did not compel but assumed voluntary compliance, such as a small-town water upgrade or a value-added agricultural initiative. In all, networks have some impact on traditional government agency powers, but it is far too early to discuss closing them down.

Hirst (2000) cautions us that government retains essential powers over decision making and traditional normative and services domains. As Sharpe (1986) once suggested, government is not just another organization in the mix of interorganizational actors. The important issue appears to be taking the next research-oriented step to examine just how and how much network-generated complexity affects what we have traditionally known as *government*. Do complexes of networks extend public management processes outward to nongovernmental organizations? In the interim, the research reported here suggests that it is far too early for practicing managers to look for other work. Their "day jobs" appear safe.

Conclusion

These lessons represent a start in understanding how collaborative bodies such as networks work on the inside. Theoretically, the broader study is able to make several arguments that add fuel to the debate regarding networks. As suggested here, however much the "era of the network" is present, hierarchies persist to fulfill the legal and policy functions of government. It also demonstrates that not all public networks are alike; they are differentiated by what they do—or more precisely, by what powers they have. Many have few or no powers. An internal look at networks indicates that although they are largely self-organizing, they require structuring that reflects their knowledge-seeking orientation. They need to be managed like organizations but in collaborative, nonhierarchical ways. Indeed, the data–information–knowledge function of networks is so paramount that their collaborative communities of practice across agencies distinguish them from more bureaucratically oriented hierarchies. Although most public management networks lack formal power to make policy and program adjustments, they do make a difference in other ways. In particular, they add value through their knowledge-enhancement functions, which, in the long run, bring beneficial outcomes to the participating managers and professionals, the partner agencies, the collaborative process, and to short- and long-term policy and program solutions. Finally, networks do change the way in which public managers work, inasmuch as their actions and behaviors are influenced by collaboration, but there are other means of collaborative management and real legal and regulatory limits to the amount of flexibility that most managers have within networks. In this sense, networks threaten or hollow the boundaries of the state in only the most subtle ways.

A research tradition on network operation is beginning to fill in some of the theoretical blanks—for example, the work of Provan and Milward (1991, 1995) on governance structure and outcomes, Mandell (1999) on management styles and instruments, Agranoff and McGuire (2003) on collaborative instruments, Bardach (1998) on theories of collaborative leadership, Koppenjan and Klijn (2004) on management knowledge to deal with uncertainty, McGuire on management styles, and O'Toole and Meier on managerial strategies and behaviors. In addition, Agranoff and McGuire (2001) have pulled together a number of core concepts in collaborative network management into a post-POSDCORB paradigm.

The lessons related here suggest that in some areas of study, there is more than meets the eye, but in many more, there is substantially less. In regard to the latter, networks are far from the only form of collaborative management, and they may be much less important than contractual or interagency and other cooperative agreements. Managers do spend more time in collaboration, at some cost, but less than one would think. Today's wicked policy problems, dispersed knowledge and resources, first- and second-order effects, and intergovernmental overlays guarantee that managers must engage other governments and nongovernmental organizations (Agranoff and McGuire 2003; O'Toole 1997). The payoff is that public management networks have a lasting collaborative effect, as they build collective capacity for subsequent collaborative solutions and teach managers the essential skill of collaboration.

As observed earlier, it may be impossible to precisely weigh the benefits of networks against the costs, but the advantages must be there—busy administrators and program specialist partners would not engage in collaboration solely for social purposes or for the intrinsic merit of cooperation. There has to be something more in terms of holding participants in. It is hoped that these 10 lessons will be of use to managers who are engaging in or contemplating network collaborative public management.

References

Agranoff, Robert. Forthcoming. *Managing Within Networks: Adding Value to Public Organizations.* Washington, DC: Georgetown University Press.

Agranoff, Robert, and Michael McGuire. 2001. Big Questions in Public Network Management Research. *Journal of Public Administration Research and Theory* 11(3): 295–326.

_____. 2003. *Collaborative Public Management: New Strategies for Local Governments.* Washington, DC: Georgetown University Press.

Alter, Catherine, and Jerald Hage. 1993. *Organizations Working Together.* Newbury Park, CA: Sage Publications.

Bardach, Eugene. 1998. *Getting Agencies to Work Together: The Practice and Theory of Managerial Craftsmanship.* Washington, DC: Brookings Institution Press.

Burt, Ronald. 1992. *Structural Holes: The Social Structure of Competition.* Cambridge, MA: Harvard University Press.

Castells, Manuel. 1996. *The Rise of the Network Society.* Maiden, MA: Blackwell.

Clegg, Stewart R. 1990. *Modern Organizations: Organization Studies in the Postmodern World.* London: Sage Publications.

Clegg, Stewart R., and Cynthia Hardy. 1996. Conclusions: Representation. In *Handbook of Organization Studies,* edited by Stewart R. Clegg, Cynthia Hardy, and Walter R. Nord, 676–708. London: Sage Publications.

Davenport, Thomas H., and Laurence Prusak. 2000. *Working Knowledge: How Organizations Manage What They Know.* Boston: Harvard Business School Press.

Frederickson, H. George. 1999. The Repositioning of American Public Administration. *PS: Political Science and Politics* 32(4): 701–11.

Granovetter, Mark S. 1973. The Strength of Weak Ties. *American Journal of Sociology* 78(6): 1360–80.

Hirst, Paul. 2000. Democracy and Governance. In *Debating Governance: Authority, Steering, and Democracy,* edited by Jon Pierre, 13–35. Oxford: Oxford University Press.

Kickert, Walter J. M., Erik-Hans Klijn, and Joop F. M. Koppenjan. 1997. Introduction: A Management Perspective on Policy Networks. In *Managing Complex Networks,* edited by Walter J. M. Kickert, Erik-Hans Klijn, and Joop F. M. Koppenjan, 1–13. London: Sage Publications.

Klijn, Erik-Hans. 1996. Analyzing and Managing Policy Processes in Complex Networks. *Administration & Society* 28(1): 90–119.

Koppenjan, Joop, and Erik-Hans Klijn. 2004, *Managing Uncertainties in Networks.* London: Routledge.

Laumann, Edward O, L.. Galaskiewicz, and P. V. Marsden. 1978. Community Structure as Interorganizarional Linkages. *Annual Review of Sociology* 4: 455–84.

Lipnack, Jessica, and Jeffrey Stamps. 1994. *The Age of the Network.* New York: Wiley.

Loughlin, John. 2000. Regional Autonomy and State Paradigm Shifts. *Regional and Federal Studies* 10(2): 10–34.

Mandell, Myrna P 1999. Community Collaborations: Working through Network Structures, *Policy Studies Review* 16(1): 42–64.

McGuire, Michael. 2000. Collaborative Policy Making and Administration: The Operational Demands of Local Economic Development. *Economic Development Quarterly* 14(3): 276–91.

Moore, Mark H. 1995. *Creating Public Value: Strategic Management in Government.* Cambridge, MA: Harvard University Press.

Newell, Sue, Maxine Robertson, Harry Scarbrough, and Jacky Swan. 2002. *Managing Knowledge Work.* New York: Palgrave.

Nohria, Nitin. 1992. Information and Search in the Creation of New Business Ventures: The Case of the 128 Venture Group. In *Networks and Organizations: Structure, Form, and Action,* edited by Nitin Nohria and Robert Eccles, 240–61. Boston: Harvard Business School Press.

O'Toole, Laurence J., Jr. 1997. Treating Networks Seriously: Practical and Research-Based Agendas in Public Administration. *Public Administration Review* 57(1): 45–52.

O'Toole, Laurence J., Jr., and Kenneth J. Meier. 2001. Managerial Strategies and Behavior in Networks. *Journal of Public Administration Research and Theory* 11(3): 271–94.

Powell, Walter W. 1990. Neither Market nor Hierarchy: Network Forms of Organization. In *Research in Organizational Behavior,* vol. 12, edited by Barry M. Staww and Larry L. Cummings, 295–336. Greenwich, CT: JAI Press.

Provan, Keith G., and H. Brinton Milward. 1991. Institutional-Level Norms and Organizational Involvement in a Service-Implementation Network. *Journal of Public Administration Research and Theory* 1 (4): 391–417.

______. 1995. A Preliminary Theory of Interorganizational Effectiveness: A Comparative Study of Four Community Mental Health Systems. *Administrative Science Quarterly* 40(1): 1–33.

Rhodes, R. A. W. 1997. *Understanding Governance: Policy Networks, Governance, Reflexivity and Accountability.* Buckingham, UK: Open University Press.

Saint-Onge, Hubert, and Charles Armstrong. 2004. *The Conductive Organization.* Amsterdam: Elsevier.

Senge, Peter M. 2006. *The Fifth Discipline: The Art and Practice of the Learning Organization.* Rev. ed. New York: Doubleday.

Sharpe, Laurence J. 1986. Intergovernmental Policy-Making: The Limits of Subnational Autonomy.

In *Guidance, Control and Evaluation in the Public Sector: The Bielefeld Interdisciplinary Project,* edited by Franz-Xaver Kaufmann, Giandomenico Majone, and Vincent Ostrom, 159–81. Berlin: Walter de Gruyter.

Stone, Clarence, Kathryn Doherty, Cheryl Jones, and Timothy Ross. 1999. Schools and Disadvantaged Neighborhoods: The Community Development Challenge. In *Urban Problems and Community Development,* edited by Ronald F. Ferguson and William T. Dickens, 339–69. Washington, DC: Brookings Institution Press.

Strauss, Anselm, and Juliet Corbin. 1998. *Basics of Qualitative Research: Techniques and Procedures for Developing Grounded Theory.* Thousand Oaks, CA: Sage Publications.

Thomas, Craig W. 2003. *Bureaucratic Landscapes: Interagency Cooperation and the Preservation of Biodiversity.* Cambridge, MA: MIT Press.

Tsoukas, Haridimos. 2005. *Complex Knowledge.* Oxford: Oxford University Press.

Walker, David B. 2000. *The Rebirth of Federalism: Slouching toward Washington.* 2nd ed. New York: Chatham House.

White, Harrison C. 1992. *Identity and Control: A Structural Theory of Social Action.* Princeton, NJ: Princeton University Press.

A Chronology of U.S. Public Administration

1776 to the Present

1776 Declaration of Independence is signed.

Adam Smith in *The Wealth of Nations* advocates the ability-to-pay principle of taxation and discusses the optimal organization of a pin factory—the most famous and influential statement on the economic rationale of the factory system and the division of labor.

1787 Northwest Ordinance provides for (1) future states to enter the union and (2) federal aid to local public schools.

Constitutional Convention convenes in Philadelphia.

1789 U.S. Constitution is adopted.

Congress establishes the first federal administrative agencies (the Departments of State, War, Treasury, and the Office of Attorney General). The Federal Judiciary Act creates the Supreme Court; it is organized in 1790 with John Jay as the first chief justice.

New York City becomes the first capital of the United States.

1790 First national census sets population at 4 million; Philadelphia is the largest city with 42,000 people.

U.S. capital moved from New York to Philadelphia.

1791 Ratification of the Bill of Rights (the first ten amendments) to the Constitution is completed.

Congress passes the first internal revenue law, a tax on distilled spirits.

Alexander Hamilton's *Report on Manufactures* advocates government intervention in the economy.

1800 U.S. capital is moved from Philadelphia to Washington, D.C.

1803 The Supreme Court first asserts the right of judicial review in the case of *Marbury* v. *Madison.*

1806 In the case of *Commonwealth* v. *Pullis,* unions are judged to be criminal conspiracies at the Philadelphia trial of striking cordwainers (shoemakers).

1813 Robert Owen in his "Address to the Superintendents of Manufactories" puts forth the revolutionary idea that managers should pay as much attention to their "vital machines" (employees) as to the "inanimate machines."

1814 A president of the United States (James Madison) for the last time took to the field as commander in chief of the armed forces at the Battle of Bladenburg (Maryland); the British soundly defeated the Americans and then marched on to burn the White House.

1819 The Supreme Court case of *McCulloch* v. *Maryland* establishes the doctrine of implied constitutional powers and the immunity of the federal government from state taxation.

1823 Jeremy Bentham philosophizes that the role of government is to strive to do the greatest good for the greatest numbers.

1829 President Andrew Jackson in his first annual message to Congress provides justification for the spoils system that followed when he asserts that "the duties of public officers are, or at least admit of being made, so plain and simple that men of intelligence may readily qualify themselves for their performance."

1832 Senator William L. Marcy gives title to the spoils system when he asserts in a Senate debate that politicians "see nothing wrong in the rule, that to the victor belongs the spoils of the enemy."

1833 Charles Babbage's "analytical engine" is the first mechanical device to contain the basic elements of the modern computer.

1836 Alexis de Tocqueville publishes *Democracy in America,* his classic study of U.S. political institutions and political culture.

1840 President Martin Van Buren establishes the 10-hour day for most federal employees.

1842 In *Commonwealth* v. *Hunt* the Supreme Judicial Court of Massachusetts issues the first ruling establishing the legality of the right of workers to strike for higher wages.

1844 The New York City Police Department is established by the Municipal Police Act; the mayor is empowered to select two hundred officers to patrol the streets 24 hours a day.

1849 The U.S. Department of the Interior is created.

1851 Massachusetts enacts the first law permitting towns to use tax revenues to support free libraries.

1862 The Morill Land Grant Act endows state colleges of agriculture and industry.

1863 First military draft enacted during the Civil War; one could avoid conscription by paying for a substitute.

1865 New York City establishes the first fire department with full-time paid firefighters.

The Thirteenth Amendment is ratified, abolishing slavery.

1868 Judge John F. Dillon first puts forth his rule that local governments may exercise only those powers unambiguously granted to them by their states.

The Fourteenth Amendment providing that no state shall "deprive any person of life, liberty, or property without due process of law" is ratified.

President Andrew Johnson is impeached by the House of Representatives; he is tried and acquitted by the Senate.

Congress mandates an eight-hour day for federally employed laborers and mechanics.

1871 A rider to an unrelated appropriations bill allows President U. S. Grant to create the shortlived (1872–1873) first federal Civil Service Commission.

The exposure of corruption by New York's Tammany Hall would eventually send William "Boss" Tweed to prison.

I. Early Voices and the First Quarter Century

1880 Donman B. Eaton advocates the adoption of the merit system in America.

1881 President James Garfield is assassinated by a deranged office-seeker.

1883 The Pendleton Act creates the U.S. Civil Service Commission.

1885 Captain Henry Metcalfe, the manager of an army arsenal, publishes *The Cost of Manufactures and the Administration of Workshops, Public and Private,* which asserts that there is a "science of administration" that is based upon principles discoverable by diligent observation.

1886 Henry R. Towne's paper "The Engineer as an Economist," read to the American Society of Mechanical Engineers, encourages the scientific management movement.

American Federation of Labor is formed, with Samuel Gompers as its president.

1887 Congress creates the Interstate Commerce Commission, the first federal regulator)' commission.

Woodrow Wilson's "The Study of Administration" is published in the *Political Science Quarterly.*

1888 Lord James Bryce's analysis of the U.S. political system, *The American Commonwealth,* finds the government of U.S. cities to be a "conspicuous failure."

1894 National Municipal League founded to fight local government corruption.

The Dockery Act creates (1) the first federal fiscal accounting practices and (2) the Office of the Comptroller of the Treasury.

1899 National Municipal League issues the first Model City Charter.

Hollerith cards, punched cards used by computers, were first developed by Herman Hollerith for the U.S. Bureau of the Census.

1900 Frank J. Goodnow's *Politics and Administration* provides the first definition of the politics-administration dichotomy.

1901 Galveston, Texas, devastated by a hurricane in the previous year, is the first city to install the commission form of government.

1902 Vilfredo Pareto becomes the "father" of the concept of social systems; his societal notions would later be applied by Elton Mayo and the human relationists in an organizational context.

Oregon becomes the first state to adopt the initiative and referendum.

1903 Frederick W. Taylor publishes *Shop Management.*

Congress provides for a general staff for the U.S. Army.

The American Political Science Association is founded.

U.S. Department of Commerce and Labor is established.

The Boston police are the first to use an automobile, a Stanley Steamer, for regular patrol.

1904 Lincoln Steffens's muckraking *Shame of the Cities,* which finds Philadelphia to be "corrupt and contended," arouses sentiment for municipal reform.

Frank B. and Lillian M. Gilbreth marry; they then proceed to produce many of the pioneering works on motion study, scientific management, applied psychology, and 12 children.

Ukiah, California, establishes the first chief executive officer post to manage municipal affairs.

Jane Addams explores the roles of government, administrators, and citizens in *The Problem with Municipal Administration.*

1905 New York City starts the first police motorcycle patrol.

1906 The Bureau of Municipal Research is founded in New York City to further the management movement in government.

The Pure Food and Drug Act is passed.

1908 Staunton, Virginia, appoints the first city manager (unless one considers Ukiah's chief executive officer to be the first city manager).

Arthur F. Bentley's *The Process of Government argues* that political analysis has to shift its focus from the forms of government to the actions of individuals in the context of groups.

1910 Louis D. Brandeis, an associate of Frederick W. Taylor (and later a Supreme Court justice) coins and popularizes the term *scientific management* in his *Eastern Rate* case testimony before the Interstate Commerce Commission by arguing that railroad rate increases should be denied because the railroads could save "a million dollars a day" by applying scientific management methods.

Ohio is the first state to empower its governor to prepare and submit a budget to the legislature.

Los Angeles hires the first policewoman, Mrs. Alice Stebbins Wells, a former social worker.

1911 Frederick W. Taylor publishes *The Principles of Scientific Management.*

1912 The Commission on Economy and Efficiency, the Taft Commission, headed by President William Howard Taft, calls for a national executive budget.

The first position-classification program is adopted at the municipal level in the city of Chicago.

Sumter, South Carolina, is first to install the council-manager form of city government.

The Lloyd-LaFollette Act guarantees the right of federal civilian employees to petition Congress, either individually or through their organizations, and provides the first statutory procedural safeguards for federal employees facing removal.

Congress approves the eight-hour day for all federal employees.

1913 The sixteenth Amendment to the US Constitution creates the first permanent federal income tax.

The Federal Reserve Act creates a central bank responsible for national monetary policy.

The U.S. Department of Commerce and Labor is divided into two separate cabinet departments.

1914 The City Manager's Association is formed (in 1924 it changes its name to the International City Manager's Association; in 1969 "Manager's" is changed to "Management").

The University of Michigan creates the first master's program in municipal administration.

Dayton, Ohio, is the first major city to have a city manager.

Robert Michels in his analysis of the workings of political parties and labor unions, *Political Parties,* formulates his iron law of oligarchy: "who says organization, says oligarchy."

1916 In France, Henri Fayol publishes his *General and Industrial Management,* the first complete theory of management.

The Institute for Government Research is established in Washington, D.C., by Robert Brookings (in 1927 it becomes the Brookings Institution with William F. Willoughby as its first director).

1917 Robert M. Yerkes, president of the American Psychological Association, creates the first modern personnel research unit in the federal government by developing mental ability tests for the U.S. Army.

1918 William F. Willoughby in *The Movement for Budgetary Reform in the States* outlines developments that were leading to the creation of modern budget systems.

1919 The failure of the Boston police strike sets back municipal unionization and makes Calvin Coolidge, the governor of Massachusetts, a national hero.

The Eighteenth Amendment, Prohibition, is ratified; the Volstead Act is passed to enforce it.

1920 The Retirement Act creates the first federal service pension system.

The Nineteenth Amendment is ratified, giving women the right to vote.

1921 The Budget and Accounting Act establishes the Bureau of the Budget in the Department of the Treasury and the General Accounting Office as an agency of the Congress.

The Port of New York Authority is created by the states of New York and New Jersey.

1922 Max Weber's structural definition of bureaucracy is published posthumously; it uses an "ideal type" approach to extrapolate from the real world the central core of features that characterizes the most fully developed form of bureaucratic organization.

1923 The Classification Act brings position classification to Washington-based federal employees and establishes the principle of equal pay for equal work.

The Teapot Dome scandals reveal widespread corruption in the Harding administration.

1924 The Maxwell School of Citizenship and Public Affairs is established at Syracuse University to offer graduate work in the social sciences and public administration.

Hawthorne studies begin at the Hawthorne Works of the Western Electric Company in Chicago; they will last until 1932 and lead to new thinking about the relationship of the work environment to productivity.

The Rogers Act creates a merit-based career system for the Department of State.

1926 Leonard D. White's *Introduction to the Study of Public Administration* is the first text in public administration.

The first factor-comparison position-classification system is installed by Eugene J. Benge at the Philadelphia Transit Company (the federal government will adopt this kind of system in 1975).

Mary Parker Follett, in calling for "power with" as opposed to "power over," anticipates the movement toward more participatory management styles.

1927 The Brookings Institution is formed.

1929 The University of Southern California establishes the first independent professional school of public administration.

II. The New Deal to Mid-Century

1930 Durham County, South Carolina, is first to install the county manager form of county government.

1931 James D. Mooney and Alan C. Reiley in *Onward Industry* (republished in 1939 as *The Principles of Organization*) show how the newly discovered "principles of organization" have really been known since ancient times.

Congress designates "The Star Spangled Banner" as the national anthem.

1932 Wisconsin passes the nation's first unemployment insurance law.

1933 President Franklin D. Roosevelt's New Deal begins.

1936 J. Donald Kingsley and William E. Mosher's *Public Personnel Administration* becomes the first text in this field.

John Maynard Keynes publishes his *General Theory of Employment, Interest and Money,* which calls for using a government's fiscal and monetary policies to positively influence a capitalistic economy.

The President's Committee on Administrative Management is established; known as the Brownlow Committee after its chairman, Louis Brownlow (the other two members are Charles Merriam and Luther Gulick), it will examine the organization of the executive branch.

E. Pendleton Herring in *Public Administration and the Public Interest* asserts that bureaucrats, by default, must often be the arbiters of the public interest.

1937 The Brownlow Committee's report says that the "president needs help" and calls for the reorganization of the executive branch.

Luther Gulick and Lyndall Urwick edit the *Papers on the Science of Administration*, an attempt to summarize the state of the art of organizational theory that is now considered to be the high-water mark of public administration's "period of orthodoxy"; Gulick's "Notes on the Theory of Organization," which calls attention to the various functional elements of work of an executive with his mnemonic device POSDCORB, is first published in this collection.

1938 The Fair Labor Standards Act provides minimum wages, overtime pay, and limits on child labor.

Chester Barnard's *The Functions of the Executive*, his sociological analysis of organizations, encourages and foreshadows the postwar revolution in thinking about organizational behavior.

1939 The American Society for Public Administration is founded.

The Reorganization Act enables the creation of the Executive Office of the President and the transfer of the Bureau of the Budget from the Treasury to the White House.

Lewis Meriam's *Reorganization of the National Government* offers arguments against the expansion of executive powers at the expense of the Congress.

The Hatch Act is passed to prohibit political activities by federal employees (the next year it is amended to also prohibit political activities by state and local government employees who are paid with federal funds).

F. J. Roethlisberger and William J. Dickson publish *Management and the Worker*, the definitive account of the Hawthorne studies.

The federal government first requires the states to have merit systems for employees in programs aided by federal funds.

1940 Robert K. Merton's article "Bureaucratic Structure and Personality" proclaims that Max Weber's "ideal-type" bureaucracy had inhibiting dysfunctions leading to inefficiency and worse.

Carl J. Friedrich in "The Nature of Administrative Responsibility" asserts that accountability and responsibility are best assured internally through professionalism and professional standards.

The *Public Administration Review* is first published; Leonard D. White is its first editor.

V. O. Key, Jr., bemoans "The Lack of a Budgetary Theory" in the *American Political Science Review*.

1941 James Burnham in *The Managerial Revolution* asserts that as the control of large organizations passes from the hands of the owners into the hands of professional administrators, the society's new governing class will be the possessors not of wealth but of technical expertise.

Herman Finer in "Administra-tive Responsibility in Democratic Government" argues that accountability and responsibility can be maintained externally only through legislative or popular controls.

The Japanese sneak attack on Pearl Harbor brings the United States into World War II.

1943 Abraham Maslow's "needs hierarchy" first appears in his article "A Theory of Human Motivation" in *Psychological Review.*

Withholding for federal income tax begins as a temporary wartime measure.

1944 J. Donald Kingsley's *Representative Bureaucracy* develops the concept that all social groups have a right to participate in their governing institutions in proportion to their numbers in the population.

David E. Lilienthal in *TVA: Democracy on the March* writes that the planning process of government is a blatantly political enterprise, a situation that is both healthy and beneficial for a democratic society.

1945 Paul Appleby leads the postwar attack on the politics-administration dichotomy by insisting in *Big Democracy* that apolitical governmental processes contradict the American experience.

With the dropping of the atomic bomb and the end of World War II, the suddenly public Manhattan Project marks the federal government's first major involvement with science in a policymaking role.

1946 The Employment Act creates the Council of Economic Advisors and asserts that it is the policy of the federal government to maintain full employment.

The Administrative Procedure Act standardizes many federal government administrative practices across agencies.

1947 The National Training Laboratory for Group Development (now called the NTL Institute for Applied Behavioral Science) is established to do research on group dynamics and later sensitivity training.

The first Hoover Commission (1947–1949) recommends increased managerial capacity in the Executive Office of the President.

The National Security Act creates the Department of Defense.

Robert A. Dahl in "The Science of Public Administration" argues that public administration needs to deal with its normative aspects, that the study of it has become too parochial, and that workers can no longer be viewed in the scientific management tradition as human interchangeable parts in a bureaucratic machine.

Herbert A. Simon's *Administrative Behavior* urges that a true scientific method should be used in the study of administrative phenomena, that the perspective of logical positivism should be used in dealing with questions of policy making, and that decision making is really the true heart of administration.

President Harry S. Truman's Executive Order 9835 launches the federal government's loyalty program designed to root out subversives in the bureaucracy.

1948 Dwight Waldo publishes *The Administrative State,* which attacks the "gospel of efficiency" that dominated administrative thinking prior to World War II.

The Inter-University Case Program is started to encourage the development and dissemination of case studies in public administration.

Wallace S. Sayre in *Public Administration Review* attacks public personnel administration as the "triumph of techniques over purpose."

President Harry S. Truman orders the integration of the armed forces.

1949 Philip Selznick in *TVA and the Grass Roots* discovers "cooptation" when he examines how the Tennessee Valley Authority subsumed new elements into its policy-making process in order to prevent those elements from being a threat to the organization.

In his *Public Administration Review* article, "Power and Administration," Norton E. Long finds that the lifeblood of administration is power and that managers have to do more than just apply the scientific method to problems—they have to attain, maintain, and increase their power or risk failing in their mission.

1951 David Truman's *The Governmental Process* calls for viewing interest groups as the real determinant of the focal point of study on public policy.

Kurt Lewin proposes a general model of change consisting of three phases, "unfreezing, change, refreezing," in his *Field Theory in Social Science*; this model becomes the conceptual frame for organizational development.

Ludwig von Bertalanffy's article, "General Systems Theory: A New Approach to the Unity of Science" is published in *Human Biology;* his concepts will become the intellectual basis for the systems approach to organizational thinking.

1952 Harold Stein edits the first major casebook, *Public Administration and Policy Development.*

Verne B. Lewis's "Toward a Theory of Budgeting" presents a theory of alternative budgeting that will be an important link to the planning programming budgeting systems of the 1960s and the zero-based budgeting systems of the 1970s.

1953 The second Hoover Commission (1953–1955) recommends the curtailment and abolition of federal government activities that are competitive with private enterprise.

The Department of Health, Education, and Welfare (HEW) is created.

1954 Peter Drucker's book, *The Practice of Management,* popularizes the concept of management by objectives.

The Supreme Court in *Brown* v. *Board of Education Topeka, Kansas* holds that racially separate educational facilities are inherently unequal and therefore violate the equal protection clause of the Fourteenth Amendment.

Senator Joseph McCarthy (and in effect McCarthyism) is censured by the U.S. Senate.

Lakewood, California, pioneers the service contract whereby a small jurisdiction (such as Lakewood) buys government services such as police and fire protection from a neighboring large jurisdiction (such as Los Angeles).

Alvin Gouldner's *Patterns of Industrial Bureaucracy* describes three possible responses to a formal bureaucratic structure: "mock" where the formal rules are ignored by both management and labor, "punishment centered" where management seeks to enforce rules that workers resist, and "representative" where rules are both enforced and obeyed.

1955 The Kestenbaum Commission on Intergovernmental Relations recommends the establishment of a "permanent center for overall attention to the problems of inter-level relationships."

The AFL-CIO is formed by the merger of the American Federation of Labor and the Congress of Industrial Organizations.

Marver Bernstein in *Regulating Business by Independent Commission* develops a life-cycle theory of regulatory commissions with these stages: gestation, youth, maturity, and decline.

Catheryn Seclder-Hudson takes a technical approach to the development of "Basic Concepts in the Study of Public Management."

Dwight Waldo's *The Study of Public Administration* seeks a fusion of the longstanding art of public administration with the newly emerging science of public administration.

1956 William H. Whyte, Jr., first profiles *The Organization Man* as an individual within an organization who accepts its values and finds harmony in conforming to its policies.

1957 C. Northcote Parkinson proffers his law that "work expands so as to fill the time available for its completion."

Chris Argyris asserts in his first major book, *Personality and Organization,* that an inherent conflict exists between the personality of a mature adult and the needs of modern organizations.

Douglas M. McGregor's article, "The Human Side of Enterprise," distills the contending traditional (authoritarian) and humanistic managerial philosophies into Theory X and Theory Y.

Program Evaluation and Review Technique (PERT) is developed by the United States Navy during planning for the Polaris ballistic missile system.

Anthony Downs's *An Economic Theory of Democracy* establishes the intellectual framework for "public choice" economics.

Philip Selznick in *Leadership in Administration* anticipates many of the 1980s notions of "transformational leadership" when he asserts that the function of an institutional leader is to help shape the environment in which the institution operates and to define new institutional directions through recruitment, training, and bargaining.

1958 James G. March and Herbert A. Simon in *Organizations* seek to inventory all that is worth knowing about the behavioral revolution in organization theory.

Wallace S. Sayre in "Premises of Public Administration: Past and Emerging" predicts that a "new orthodoxy" in public administration will evolve to replace the "old orthodoxy."

The Government Employees Training Act allows federal agencies for the first time to spend significant funds for employee training and development.

1959 New York City is the first major city to allow for collective bargaining with its employee unions.

Wisconsin is the first state to enact a comprehensive law governing public-sector labor relations.

The Advisory Commission on Intergovernmental Relations is established.

Charles A. Lindblom's "The Science of 'Muddling Through'" rejects the rational model of decision making in favor of incrementalism.

Fredrick Herzberg, Bernard Mausner, and Barbara Snyderman's *The Motivation to Work* puts forth the motivation-hygiene theory.

III. From JFK to Civil Service Reform

1960 Richard Neustadt's *Presidential Power* asserts that the president's (or any executive's) essential power is that of persuasion.

Herbert Kaufman's *The Forest Ranger* shows how organizational and professional socialization can develop in employees the will and capacity to conform.

1961 Victor A. Thompson's *Modern Organization* finds that there is "an imbalance between ability and authority" causing widespread bureaucratic dysfunctions.

Who Governs? is published; Robert A. Dahl's description of community power in New Haven, Connecticut, would become one of the most famous descriptions of U.S. pluralism at the local level.

Tom Burns and G. M. Stalker's *The Management of Innovation* articulates the need for different types of management systems (organic or mechanistic) under differing circumstances.

Rensis Likert's *New Patterns of Management* offers an empirically based defense of participatory management and organizational development techniques.

President Dwight D. Eisenhower in his farewell address warns the nation that "in the councils of government we must guard against the acquisition of unwarranted influence, whether sought or unsought, by the military industrial complex."

President John F. Kennedys Executive Order 10925 for the first time requires that "affirmative action" be used to implement the policy of nondiscrimination in employment by the federal government and its contractors.

The Peace Corps is established.

Alan B. Shepard becomes the first U.S. astronaut to fly in space. President Kennedy calls for the landing of U.S. astronauts on the moon by the end of the decade.

David Novick and the Rand Corporation help the Department of Defense install PPBS.

1962 President John F. Kennedy issues Executive Order 10988, which authorizes the unionization of federal workers.

Robert Presthus's *The Organizational Society* presents his threefold classification of patterns of organizational accommodation: "upward mobiles" who identify and accept the values of the organization, "indifferents" who reject such values and find personal satisfaction off the job, and "ambivalents" who want the rewards of organizational life but can't cope with the demands.

1963 The "March on Washington" for civil rights takes place on August 28; Martin Luther King, Jr., delivers his "I have a dream" speech.

President John E Kennedy is assassinated on November 22 in Dallas, Texas; Vice President Lyndon B. Johnson becomes president.

1964 The Civil Rights Act prohibits discrimination on the basis of race, color, religion, sex, or national origin in most private sector employment; creates the Equal Employment Opportunity Commission for enforcement.

Aaron Wildavsky publishes *The Politics of the Budgetary Process,* which becomes the definitive analysis of the tactics public managers use to get budgets passed.

The Economic Opportunity Act becomes the anchor of President Lyndon B. Johnson's "war on poverty" and other major initiatives in his Great Society domestic programs.

Robert R. Blake and Jane S. Mouton's *The Managerial Grid* explains how a graphic gridiron can facilitate an organizational development program.

Michel Crozier in *The Bureaucratic Phenomenon* defines a bureaucracy as "an organization which cannot correct its behavior by learning from its errors."

1965 PPBS is made mandatory for all federal agencies by the Johnson administration.

Don K. Price publishes *The Scientific Estate* in which he posits that decisional authority inexorably flows from the executive suite to the technical office.

Robert L. Kahn's *Organizational Stress* is the first major study of the mental health consequences of organizational role conflict and ambiguity.

James G. March edits the huge *Handbook of Organizations* that tries to summarize all existing knowledge on organizational theory and behavior.

The Department of Housing and Urban Development is established.

Medicare is created through amendments to the Social Security Act.

1966 The Freedom of Information Act allows greater access to federal agency files.

Morton Grodzins claims in *The American System* that the federal system is a marble cake, instead of a layer cake, because "no important activity of government in the United States is the exclusive province of one of the levels."

Daniel Katz and Robert L. Kahn in *The Social Psychology of Organizations* seek to develop an open systems theory to unify the findings of behavioral science on organizational behavior.

Warren Bennis in *Changing Organizations* sounds the death knell for bureaucratic institutions because they are inadequate for a future that will demand rapid organizational change, participatory management, and the growth of a more professionalized workforce.

1967 The Age Discrimination in Employment Act is passed; it will be amended to raise to 70 the minimum mandatory retirement age for all employees except federal employees, who have no mandatory retirement age.

The National Academy of Public Administration is organized; its first members will be all of the living past presidents of the American Society for Public Administration.

Edward A. Suchman's *Evaluation Research* puts forth the concept that evaluation is a generic field of study and that evaluative research and practice can and must be studied in a general context outside of evaluation applications in the various specialty fields.

The National Advisory Commission on Civil Disorders, the Kerner Commission, established to study the causes of urban riots, reports that the "nation is rapidly moving toward two increasingly separate Americas," one black and one white.

James D. Thompson's *Organizations in Action* seeks to close the gap between open and closed systems theory by suggesting that organizations deal with the uncertainty of their environments by creating specific elements designed to cope with the outside world while other elements are able to focus on the rational nature of technical operations.

Terry Sanford in *Storm Over the States* develops the concept of "picket-fence federalism," which holds that bureaucratic specialists at the various governmental levels exercise considerable power over the nature of intergovernmental programs.

Anthony Downs's *Inside Bureaucracy seeks* to develop laws and propositions that would aid in predicting the behavior of bureaus and bureaucrats.

Yehezkel Dror in his *Public Administration Review* article, "Policy Analysts," identifies an old function but new occupational speciality, that of policy analyst.

Anthony Jay in *Management and Machiavelli* applies Machiavelli's political principles (from *The Prince)* to modern organizational management.

1968 "Younger" public-administration scholars meeting at Syracuse University's Minnowbrook conference site call for a "new public administration" that would emphasize social equity concerns.

Harold Wilensky's *Organizational Intelligence* presents the pioneering study of the flow and perception of information in organizations.

The Federal Executive Institute in Charlottesville, Virginia, is established as an in-residence training facility for executive development.

Frederick C. Mosher's *Democracy and the Public Service* traces the evolution of the U.S. civil service and confronts the problem of professionalism.

Martin Luther King, Jr., is assassinated.

Robert E Kennedy is assassinated.

Richard M. Nixon is elected president.

Dwight Waldo asserts that public administration is in a time of revolution.

1969 The "rape of the merit system" is encouraged by the *Federal Political Personnel Manual,* popularly known as the Malek Manual after Fred Malek, chief of the Nixon administration's White House personnel office.

Aaron Wildavsky explains in "Rescuing Policy Analysis from PPBS" how the planning and analytical functions of PPBS are contradictory to the essential nature of budgeting.

Herbert Kaufman addresses the administrative implications of the 1960s cry of "power to the people" in "Administrative Decentralization and Political Power."

Theodore Lowi's *The End of Liberalism* attacks interest-group pluralism for paralyzing the policy-making process.

President Richard M. Nixon's Executive Order 11491 expands the scope of collective bargaining for federal employees.

Neil Armstrong, a U.S. astronaut, becomes the first person to walk on the moon.

Martin Landau argues that public organizations might find that redundancy is something to be sought, not avoided.

1970 The National Civil Service League revises its Model Public Personnel Administration Law to call for the replacement of traditional civil service commissions with (1) personnel directors directly responsible to an elected political executive, and (2) a labor relations board.

The Intergovernmental Personnel Act allows for the temporary exchange of staff between the federal government and state, local, and nonprofit organizations.

The Bureau of the Budget is given responsibility for managerial oversight and reorganized as the Office of Management and Budget.

The Postal Reorganization Act creates the U.S. Postal Service as a public corporation within the executive branch and allows for collective bargaining over wages by postal employee unions.

David T. Stanley in "What Are Unions Doing to Merit Systems?" correctly predicts structural changes in both public sector personnel systems and public sector unions.

Hawaii becomes the first state to allow state and local government employees the right to strike.

The Occupational Safety and Health Act creates the Occupational Safety and Health Administration (OSHA).

The Environmental Protection Agency (EPA) is established.

1971 The Supreme Court attacks restrictive credentialism when in *Griggs* v. *Duke Power Company* it rules that Title VII of the Civil Rights Act of 1964 "proscribes not only overt discrimination but also practices that are discriminatory in operation"; thus, if an employment practice operating to exclude minorities "cannot be shown to be related to job performance, the practice is prohibited."

PPBS is formally abandoned in the federal government by the Nixon administration.

Graham T. Allison's *Essence of Decision* demonstrates the inadequacies of the view that the decisions of a government are made by a "single calculating decision-maker" who has control over the organizations and officials within government.

1972 The Equal Employment Opportunity Act amends Title VII of the Civil Rights Act to include prohibitions on discrimination by public sector employers.

The Watergate scandal erupts when men associated with the Committee to Reelect the President are caught breaking into the campaign headquarters of the Democratic opposition located in the Watergate hotel-office-apartment complex.

The wildcat strike at General Motors' Lordstown, Ohio, automobile assembly plant calls national attention to the dysfunctions of dehumanized and monotonous work.

The Equal Rights Amendment is passed by Congress; it does not become law because too few states ratify it.

The Technology Assessment Act creates the Office of Technology Assessment to help Congress anticipate and plan for the consequences of the uses of technology.

Harlan Cleveland in *The Future Executive* asserts that decision making in the future will call for "continuous improvisation on a general sense of direction."

Charles Perrow's *Complex Organizations* is a major defense of bureaucratic forms of organization and an attack on those writers who think that bureaucracy can be easily, fairly, or inexpensively replaced.

H. George Frederickson's paper "Toward a New Public Administration" makes him the leading voice in the call for a more responsive, more prescriptive, and more normative public administration.

Frederick C. Mosher in "The Public Service in the Temporary Society" accepts Warren Bennis's premise of a "temporary society" and assesses its implications for public administration.

Revenue sharing is introduced with the passage of the State and Local Fiscal Assistance Act.

1973 Vice President Spiro Agnew resigns after pleading "no contest" to a charge of tax evasion stemming from illegal payments made to him by contractors when he was governor of Maryland; Gerald R. Ford becomes vice president.

The Comprehensive Employment and Training Act creates a program of financial assistance to state and local governments to provide job training and employment opportunities for the economically disadvantaged, unemployed, and underemployed.

Jeffrey Pressman and Aaron Wildavsky publish *Implementation* and create a new subfield of public administration and policy analysis.

1974 The Congressional Budget and Impoundment Control Act revises the congressional budget process and timetable and creates the Congressional Budget Office.

The Supreme Court in *United States* v. *Nixon* denies President Nixon's claim of an absolute and unreviewable executive privilege, and Nixon is forced to resign in the face of certain impeachment because of Watergate.

Gerald R. Ford becomes president and grants former president Nixon a full pardon for all possible crimes.

At the request of Congress, a panel from the National Academy of Public Administration headed by Frederick C Mosher examines the administrative abuses of Watergate: in their report, *Watergate: Implication for Responsible Government,* they urge educational institutions to "focus more attention on public service ethics."

Samuel Krislov's *Representative Bureaucracy* builds upon Kingsley's concepts and denies that the goal of government employment is efficiency; rather it is to minimize social conflict and gain the acquiescence of the governed.

An amendment to the Social Security Act provides for automatic cost-of-living adjustments in social security payments.

1975 The federal government adopts the factor-evaluation system of position classification for nonsupervisory positions.

The Municipal Assistance Corporation (Big MAC) is created to lend money to New York City so that the city can avoid default.

1976 The Sharon Report finds extensive corruption in the U.S. Civil Service Commission.

Uniform Guidelines on Employee Selection Procedures are issued by the four federal compliance agencies.

Colorado is the first state to enact "sunset laws" as a method of program review and evaluation.

1977 Zero-based budgeting is required of all federal agencies by the Carter administration; Peter A. Phyrr becomes the guru of the zero-based approach to government budgeting.

Hugh Heclo's *A Government of Strangers* becomes the leading analysis of the relationships between political and career executives in the federal bureaucracy.

The Presidential Management Intern Program is established as a special means of bringing public administration masters' graduates into the federal bureaucracy.

The Government in the Sunshine Act requires all multiheaded federal agencies to have their business sessions open to the public.

Herbert Kaufman's *Red Tape* finds that "one person's red tape may be another's treasured procedural safeguard."

The Department of Energy is created.

1978 The Civil Service Reform Act abolishes the U.S. Civil Service Commission and replaces it with (1) the Office of Personnel Management, (2) the Merit Systems Protection Board, and (3) the Federal Labor Relations Authority.

The Ethics in Government Act seeks to deal with possible conflicts of interest by former federal employees by imposing post-employment restrictions on their activities.

Proposition 13 requiring reduction in local property taxes is voted into law in California.

The Supreme Court in *Regents of the University of California* v. *Bakke* rules that a white male applicant denied admission to medical school in favor of minorities with lesser objective credentials had been discriminated against and had to be admitted; but at the same time the Court holds that race is a factor that can be taken into account in admissions decisions.

The Supreme Court in *City of Los Angeles, Department of Water and Power* v. *Manhart* rules that Title VII of the Civil Rights Act requires that male and female employees contribute equally to pension plans even though females as a group live longer.

The Pregnancy Discrimination Act amends Title VII of the Civil Rights Act to include prohibitions on discrimination on the basis of pregnancy, childbirth, or related medical conditions.

Charles H. Levine, in a *Public Administration Review* symposium, uses "cutback management" to describe the decline of public organizations in times of fiscal stress.

1979 The Department of Health, Education, and Welfare is divided into (1) the Department of Education and (2) the Department of Health and Human Services.

IV. From Reagan to Reinvention

1980 The Equal Employment Opportunity Commission issues legally binding guidelines holding that sexual harassment is sex discrimination prohibited by Title of the Civil Rights Act and drat employers have a responsibility to provide a place of work that is free of sexual harassment or intimidation.

The Supreme Court in *Branti* v. *Finkel* rules that the dismissal of nonpolicy-making, nonconfidential public employees for their partisan affiliation violates the First and/or the Fourteenth Amendments.

The Supreme Court in *Fullilove* v. *Klutznick* rules that Congress has the authority to use racial quotas to remedy past discrimination.

Graham T. Allison seeks to answer Wallace S. Sayre's question of whether public and private management are "fundamentally alike in all unimportant respects."

1981 President Carter's zero-based budgeting requirements are rescinded by President Reagan.

David Stockman, director of the Office of Management and Budget, tells the *Atlantic Monthly* that "none of us really understand what's going on with all these numbers."

Professional Air Traffic Controllers (PATCO) strike, and President Reagan fires 11,500 of them for striking in violation of federal law.

1982 The Grace Commission, the President's Private-Sector Survey on Cost Control, finds widespread inefficiencies in the federal government.

The Comprehensive Employment and Training Act is superseded by the Job Training Partnership Act.

1983 The birthday of Martin Luther King, Jr., is made a national holiday.

The Supreme Court questions the constitutionality of the legislative veto in the case of *Immigration and Naturalization Service* v. *Chadha.*

1984 The American Society for Public Administration adopts a code of ethics.

The Supreme Court in *Fire Fighters Local Union No. 1784* v. *Stotts* rules that courts may not interfere with seniority systems to protect newly hired minority employees from layoffs.

1985 The Gramm-Rudman-Hollings Act is signed into law; it seeks to balance the federal budget by mandating across-the-board cuts over a period of years.

The Department of Commerce announces that the United States has become the world's largest debtor nation; for the first time since 1914 the United States owed foreigners more than they owed the United States.

1986 The Tax Reform Act revises the federal income tax.

The Supreme Court in *Meritor Savings Bank* v. *Vinson* finds that sexual harassment is prohibited by the Civil Rights Act of 1964.

The national debt passes $2 trillion.

The space shuttle *Challenger* explodes on takeoff, killing seven astronauts.

The Iran-Contra scandal begins to unfold.

1988 George Bush is elected president.

The United States and Canada reach a free-trade agreement.

The Civil Rights Restoration Act is passed over President Reagan's veto.

1989 *The New York Times* in an editorial declares that the "cold war . . . is over."

The Supreme Court in *Wards Cove Packing* v. *Antonio* puts the burden of proof upon the plaintiff in equal employment opportunity cases.

The Financial Institutions, Reform, Recovery, and Enforcement Act is passed to help clean up the $500 billion savings and loan scandal.

The National Commission on the Public Service, the Volcker Commission, calls for a revitalization of the public service.

1990 The Budget Enforcement Act amends the Gramrn-Rudman-Hollings Act to require that new spending be balanced by new taxes or spending reductions.

The Credit Reform Act (in response to the savings and loan scandal) tightens requirements on federal lending and loan guarantees.

The Chief Financial Officers Act requires federal agencies to create a chief financial officer position to oversee agency finances.

1991 Soviet Union dissolves. The cold war is over.

Civil Rights Act of 1991 overturns a series of Supreme Court decisions (most notably the 1989 *Wards Cove* v. *Antonio* ruling) that made it more difficult for employees to sue employers for job discrimination.

1992 Bill Clinton is elected president.

David Osborne and Ted Gaebler publish *Reinventing Government.*

1993 The Government Performance Results Act requires agencies to justify their budget requests on the basis of the results or outcomes to be achieved.

The Supreme Court in *Harris* v. *Forklift Systems* rules that a person complaining about sexual harassment did not need to have a "nervous breakdown" or prove the offensive conduct to be "psychologically injurious."

The Clinton administration announces that a National Performance Review will be undertaken to "reinvent government." The *Gore Report* is the result.

Omnibus Budget Reduction Act reduces defense spending and raises taxes on upper-income citizens.

1994 Republicans gain control of both houses of Congress for the first time in 40 years.

1995 State of California dismantles many of its affirmative action programs.

Over a third of the federal government shuts down for two several-week periods (the second extending into 1996) when Congress and the president fail to agree on the budget for fiscal year 1996.

In reaffirming his administration's support for affirmative action, President Bill Clinton asserts that "affirmative action should not go on forever."

1996 The Clinton administration announces that it is suspending all federal programs that reserve some contracts exclusively for minority and women-owned companies.

Congress approves the line-item veto for the president (beginning in 1997).

V. Public Administration in the Twenty-First Century

2000 George W. Bush is elected president.

2001 Terrorists attack the World Trade Center and Pentagon.

2003 Congress creates the Department of Homeland Security.

The Supreme Court in two landmark education cases concerning the University of Michigan upheld the law school policy that considered race among other factors in reviewing the candidate's entire application but denied the undergraduate program practice that assigned a fixed number of points based on membership in an underrepresented racial category.

2004 George W. Bush is reelected president.

2005 The storm surge from Hurricane Katrina causes levee breaches flooding most of New Orleans, resulting in one of the worst engineering disasters and failures in government emergency response in modern U.S. history. Over 1000 deaths were attributed to the disaster.

2006 The Democratic Party wins the control of both houses of Congress.

2008 A global financial crises—caused in part by high risk financial speculation and unsecured subprime loans leads to a global recession, bankruptcies, and huge declines in housing prices and the stock indexes. The federal government creates the Troubled Asset Relief Program (TARP) and provides funding to banks to preclude a financial meltdown.

Barack Obama is elected president and the Democrats add to their majorities in Congress

---

2009 A fiscal stimulus package totaling over 750 billion dollars is passed to stem the recession, which many fear will lead to a depression.

2010 The Democratic congress passes and President Obama signs the first comprehensive health care bill in more than 40 years that extends health care coverage to 30 million people over the next 5 years.
